Bulletproof Unix®

Timothy T. Gottleber

North Lake College
Irving, Texas

Prentice Hall

Pearson Education, Inc.
Upper Saddle River, New Jersey 07458

Library of Congress Cataloging-in-Publication Data
CIP DATA AVAILABLE.

Vice President and Editorial Director, ECS: *Marcia Horton*
Executive Editor: *Petra Recter*
Editorial Assistant: *Renee Makras*
Vice President and Director of Production and Manufacturing, ESM: *David W. Riccardi*
Executive Managing Editor: *Vince O'Brien*
Assistant Managing Editor: *Camille Trentacoste*
Production Editor: *Irwin Zucker*
Manufacturing Manager: *Trudy Pisciotti*
Manufacturing Buyer: *Lisa McDowell*
Director of Creative Services: *Paul Belfanti*
Creative Director: *Carole Anson*
Art Director: *Jayne Conte*
Cover Designer: KIWI Design
Cover Art: *Photograph "Bullet Holes of Terror," Bruce Heinemann, Getty Images, Inc. / PhotoDisc, Inc.*
Executive Marketing Manager: *Pamela Shaffer*
Marketing Assistant: *Barrie Reinhold*

© 2003 Pearson Education, Inc.
Pearson Education, Inc.
Upper Saddle River, New Jersey 07458

The author and publisher of this book have used their best efforts in preparing this book. These efforts include the development, research, and testing of the theories and programs to determine their effectiveness. The author and publisher make no warranty of any kind, expressed or implied, with regard to these programs or the documentation contained in this book. The author and publisher shall not be liable in any event for incidental or consequential damages in connection with, or arising out of, the furnishing, performance, or use of these programs.

TRADEMARK INFORMATION
Unix is a registered trademark of The Open Group.
Solaris, SunOS, and StarOffice are trademarks of Sun Microsystems, Inc.
Linux is a registered trademark of Linus Torvalds.
WordPerfect is a registered trademark of Corel Corporation.
Word is a registered trademark of Microsoft Corporation.

Printed in the United States of America

10 9 8 7 6 5 4 3 2 1

ISBN 0-13-093028-8

Pearson Education Ltd., *London*
Pearson Education Australia Pty. Limited, *Sydney*
Pearson Education Singapore Pte. Ltd.
Pearson Education North Asia Ltd. *Hong Kong*
Pearson Education Canada Inc., *Toronto*
Pearson Educación de Mexico, S.A. de C.V.
Pearson Education—Japan, Inc., *Tokyo*
Pearson Education—Malaysia Pte. Ltd.
Pearson Education Inc., *Upper Saddle River, New Jersey*

Contents

Preface

I wrote this book for you, and to you. I spent over a dozen years helping students learn Unix in both a training environment and in academia. I watched them struggle with concepts and found ways to help them learn. Now, through the medium of this book, I hope to help you as well.

This isn't a traditional textbook. I don't use the editorial "we." When I talk to you ... well, I'm talking to you. I will show you things that work, and sometimes things that don't, so you don't have to make the same mistakes I've made. I've used a lot of examples in the text, so you can play along and see how the commands work firsthand. Playing is an important part of learning Unix. You can't learn Unix just by reading about it any more than you can learn to ride a bicycle just by reading about it. To get the most out of the book, you need to have a Unix system available to you and try the things I show you. Then you need to do the exercises at the end of each chapter to better learn the commands and concepts.

This isn't a reference book. There are a plethora of reference books out there, and you'll need to acquire a few of them, for reference. This is a textbook. The order in which I present the concepts in this book is sometimes very important. For example, first I teach you about grep, next I teach you about sed, and then I teach you about awk, which is based on grep and sed. That may not be the order you wish to use for reference, which is why this isn't a reference book.

This isn't a "complete" Unix book either, it's a beginning Unix book. Together we will acquire the skills you need to be a Unix "power user." We're not going to dabble with Unix system administration—that's a whole different ballgame. The skills you learn in this book are the groundwork you need before you begin Unix system administration. We also don't get heavily into shell scripting, for that, too, is a different skill set.

What you hold in your hands is the better part of a year of my life. It's based on how Unix is used in industry, how industry trains Unix folks, and on watching students work at learning Unix. I hope you enjoy learning about Unix and working with Unix as much as I do. If you're new to Unix you're about to begin a wonderful adventure. If you're already familiar with Unix you're holding a tool that can help you become much more proficient. Either way, we will have some work ahead of us and, hopefully, as well, some fun!

If you have just a little faith in me, together we will build a solid beginning for your journey into the wild, wonderful, and sometimes wacky world of Unix. Enjoy!

To the Instructor

Teaching a subject like Unix is an awesome task. Just deciding *what* parts of the vast universe of Unix to teach can be intimidating. I built a book to help you help your students learn about Unix. Together I'm sure we can wean your students away from substandard operating systems and help them learn the One True Operating System.

The chapters are ordered in a way that I have found helps students learn. For example, teaching them the ed editor first makes learning both vi and sed easier. Besides, if you teach them ed first, when you finally let them use vi they'll thank you for it. I found that when I taught vi first, students bemoaned the fact that it didn't have the features of a word processor. But when I taught them the ed editor first, they were delighted with vi.

Another example: Both grep and sed are presented before awk, since the design of awk was based on sed and grep.

Following are some tools that will be helpful in conjunction with this book:

1. The companion Web site for the book contains all of the data files I used in the examples and all of the sample scripts I show in the book. The URL is

   `http://www.prenhall.com/gottleber`

2. There are also some self-test questions on the Web site so your students can check their understanding.

3. TeraTerm Pro is the telnet software used for most of the screen captures. It can be downloaded from

   `http://hp.vector.co.jp/authors/VA002416/teraterm.html`

   Using that software your students can telnet into your server from their Windows machines at home provided they have a Web connection.

4. You can, at least at the time I am writing this book, download a free copy of secure shell from SSH Communications Security for personal use. Their Web site is

   `http://www.ssh.com`

   and they have both a telnet and FTP tool. If you're worried about secure communications, use these tools.

5. Mandrake Linux offers an easy-to-install version of the Linux operating system as a free download from

   `http://www.linux-mandrake.com/en/`

   So your students have a choice. They can install a real operating system on their home machine as well. Any version of Linux that your students use will work with this text; the examples are generic-Unix except where noted. In addition, if your students are using Mac OSX, the examples should work as well, since OSX is BSD Unix.

6. There's a test bank available for instructors with, multiple-choice and short-answer questions on the Instructor CD.

7. I've created a PowerPoint presentation to go along with the book as well, also available on the companion Web site.

8. Finally, and I believe most importantly, I would like to invite you to join the CRISP (College Resource and Instructor Support Program), an online community of Unix faculty and devotes. At the CRISP you can find syllabi, PowerPoint

presentations, learning resources, and the community of devoted Unix folk who can help you develop a Unix program or add to your existing program. We are nondenominational, so we support all flavors of Unix. The URL of the CRISP is http://snap.nlc.dcccd.edu. We urge you to visit and to join. Our primary mission at the CRISP is to help you do a better job teaching *your* Unix classes.

The most important goal of any text, I believe, should be to handle the groundwork so you can focus on teaching your students the things you believe they need to know. I hope I have in some small way achieved that goal for you with this text. Enjoy your students, enjoy their beginnings with this, the greatest of all operating systems, and most of all, have fun.

Acknowledgements

The days when an author sat down and penned a book alone in a Paris garret are long past. There is a whole collection of folks that are necessary to bring a book from the author's concept to something useful and readable. All those involved in this production know who they are, and to all of you I give my sincerest thanks. I want to recognize some special folks who went above and beyond to make this happen. First, I wish to thank my wife and son, who did without a full-time husband/father for all those nights and weekends when I was home, but was away in my writing. Without your support I couldn't have made this happen.

All of us in the Unix community must thank Dennis Ritchie and Ken Thompson. Without their work there would have been no need for this book. Along that same line, thanks go to Linus Torvalds, who built another, parallel kernel, GNU/Linux, and was very helpful answering my questions. I am most grateful to Dennis Ritchie, Ken Thompson, Bill Joy, Al Aho, Brian Kernighan, Mark Horton, and Doug McIlroy, who answered all of my many questions about the hows and whys of the creation of Unix and its many parts.

I wish to thank Don Loe, a wonderfully patient Unix shaman who started me on my quest to learn how to teach Unix.

I also wish to thank my long-suffering students, who have used parts of this book, given me feedback, and listened with real or pretended interest to my lectures.

There are a number of professionals who helped make this book possible. Petra Recter managed the whole process and had the faith necessary to make this book a reality. Byron Black is "the real artist" referred to in the text. He took my scratchings and made them understandable. Maggie Jarpey, way up there in the cold North, took my words and, as she has before, made them flow in some kind of grammatical order so as not to offend the reader's ear.

Buddy Mondlock graciously allowed me to use the words of one of his songs, and listening to his music helped keep me focused. In addition, Mannheim Steamroller, Bach, and LVB all provided background accompaniment to my musings.

Thanks to Louis Taber, out West at Pima College, who read the whole manuscript and gave me pointers, background, and a wonderful sanity check. Bob Nelson at North Lake College also read major portions of this book and shared his insights and real-world examples. Randy Harwood, out west, gave me valuable feedback.

Thanks to the Vintage Computer Festival for permission to reproduce the photo of the ADM-3A terminal in Chapter 7 (Figure 7.1).

Last but not least, I must thank Wendy the Pooh, who did her level best to remind me that playing tug and chase-the-laser or wrestling with the puppy were *much* more fun and, at times, a *far* better use of my time than sitting in the study working away at the computer.

Introduction to Unix

CHAPTER OBJECTIVES
After reading this chapter, you should be able to:

- Understand the purpose of an operating system.
- Explain the nine tenets of the Unix Philosophy.
- Describe the Unix "onion".
- List four common Unix shells.
- Successfully log into a Unix system.
- Create a correctly formed password.
- Log out of a Unix system.

Welcome to what is most likely the first in-depth look most of you have taken at an operating system. You have chosen very well. For Unix is not just *an* operating system; for those of us who know and love it, it is *the* operating system. It's more stable, reliable, and powerful than any other commercial operating system. To call Unix *an* operating system is like calling a Lamborghini a car. A Volkswagen Beetle is a car; a Lamborghini is a *car!* Okay, now that we know that Unix is *the* operating system, we need to determine just exactly what an operating system is.

⊕ What Is an Operating System?

Computer programs can generally be divided into three classes, or categories. **Applications programs** allow users to perform some sort of work, like writing a book or building a spreadsheet. **Utility programs** let the user perform maintenance-type tasks on their computer, like backing up their hard drive or recovering deleted files. The **operating system**, usually written in the machine language of a particular processor, is designed to manipulate the hardware environment so utilities and applications can run. The operating system takes care of all those little details like spinning up the hard drive, moving the read/write head, arranging communications between the keyboard and the applications program, and all the other tasks that would be so time-consuming for you to perform yourself.

On most computers the operating system is written in the assembly or machine language of that particular processor. For example, on a DEC (now Compaq) VAX computer the operating system is written in Macro, DECs assembly language, while the operating system for an IBM mainframe may well be written in 390 Assembler, IBM's proprietary assembly language. (An *assembly language* is just a more easily programmable form of machine language, with each assembly instruction translating directly into one machine instruction.) Hardware-specific assembly languages are used because they are the most efficient languages in which to write programs for a particular processor. Normally, operating systems are written for a specific family of machines.

One of the unique things about Unix, especially at the time when it was created, was that Thompson and Ritchie had the foresight to write it in a high-level language. They did so in order to make it easier to convert Unix to different computers. As you will see when we talk about the history of Unix, Dennis Ritchie wrote the high-level programming language C for the purpose of having a high-level language in which to rewrite Unix. Consequently, if a computer has a C compiler, it can create its own version of Unix. That is why we find versions of Unix running on IBM, HP, DEC, Sun, Sparc, Intel, Apple, handheld computers, and even BlueTooth watches.

In summary, an operating system is a set of computer code that, running on a particular processor, handles the nanosecond-to-nanosecond details of maintaining an environment that allows utility and applications programs to function.

A Brief History of Unix

To understand the importance and versatility of Unix, as well as some of its idiosyncrasies, you must know a little about its history. This brief synopsis hardly does justice to this wonderful operating system, and there are more detailed histories on the Net. Please, at your leisure, take the time to search the Net and invest some time in exploring the history of Unix so that you'll better understand the evolution of this marvelous operating system.

It all began back in 1964 when AT&T Bell Labs, General Electric, and MIT (Massachusetts Institute of Technology), embarked upon a project to create a multitasking, multi-user operating system. The concept was a new one. Back then a computer would devote all of its resources to running a single program. Each program was run sequentially and had the computer's full attention. Running one program after another sequentially is called **single threading**. This new operating system was to be called Multics, which stood for (MULTiplexed Information and Computing Service.) The Multics project was intended to produce a general-purpose, multi-user, time-sharing system running on new hardware, supporting a new file system and employing a new user interface. These were lofty goals, and the Multics system never realized them sufficiently to be a commercial success, although some folks used, and still use, it. After four years of development, the Multics project was able to support only three or four concurrent users, and Bell Labs decided to withdraw from the project.

Bell Labs' withdrawal was very unfortunate for the members of Multics team who worked there, for they had become used to the cooperative and collaborative environment that a multi-user, multitasking operating system needed. In the old, single-thread machine model, a programmer would go to the machine room to submit a program to the computer. Then the programmer would have to wait minutes, hours, or even days to get the output back. With the output in hand, the programmer would return to his or her office or cubicle. When the Multics group was working on a program, they could collaborate one with another because they all spent time in the same terminal room. This sharing, social environment became one of the integral parts of the Unix phenomenon.

When the Multics project was scrapped, Ken Thompson also lost his game machine. He had developed an elegant space-travel simulation that allowed the player to fly a spaceship through the solar system. The game played nicely on the Multics system, but on the mainframes at Bell Labs it was very slow and difficult to play. On top of that, playing the game cost $75.00 per hour. Thompson went looking for another computer and found an old PDP-7 that had been used as a graphics terminal. He ported Space Travel to that machine.

The old Multics group began developing code to run on this little PDP. (Please understand that the term "little" refers to the processor and memory; this machine was approximately twelve feet long, six and a half feet wide, and eight feet tall.) This was the embryo of the Unix operating system. Actually, the first implementation of Unix is one of the more amazing programming efforts ever documented. Over the course of one month, in the summer of 1969, Ken Thompson built the core of what has become Unix. He allocated one week to the operating system, one week to the editor, one week for the assembler, and one week to develop the user interface, or shell.

Brian Kernighan is credited with naming the new operating system, UNICS (UNiplexed Information and Computing Service), which Dennis Ritchie calls a "somewhat treacherous pun on Multics." The name was later shortened to Unix. No one knows who substituted the "x" for the "cs;" it is one of the great mysteries in the history of Unix.

At about this time, Bell Labs' management caught the team playing with their new toy, and asked what they were doing. Thompson explained that they were building a text-processing system. Remember that in 1969 there were no word processors. A text-processing system is a program designed to produce "fancy" output on a line printer. This is similar to the way HTML is used to produce marked-up copy on screen. Management was very excited about this idea and gave the team a bigger computer. (This is why we find some interesting text-processing commands built into Unix.)

The first version of Unix was written in PDP-7 assembler language. When they were going to make the transition to the new machine, Thompson and Ritchie considered rewriting Unix in the B language, a condensed version of the BCPL language. However, when they tested a couple of utilities written in B, they found them too slow. B was an **interpreted language** meaning one in which every instruction is translated *each time* before it is executed. (By contrast, in a **compiled language** all the instructions are translated into machine language at one time by a separate program called a *compiler*.) Since the B language was too slow, Ritchie decided to write a new high-level language that could be used to rewrite Unix. He named this new language C.

As mentioned before, it was very fortunate that Ritchie chose a high-level language, for that has allowed Unix to be ported to many different hardware platforms. The term **hardware platform** refers to a particular vendor's CPU, memory, and peripheral devices. Back in the late 1960s and early 1970s, a very fast I/O device transmitted data at about 10 cps (characters per second). This is why many Unix commands are just a few characters long. That made them faster to type on a very slow terminal. In addition, many of the error messages are very short, so they would be faster to display on a very slow terminal. In the 1970s Bell Labs was prohibited from selling software, so when people outside the labs would ask for copies of Unix, Thompson and Ritchie simply gave it away. What they distributed was, of course, the source code. The sharing of source code has continued throughout most versions of Unix, including the most recent alternative, Linux.

Documentation proved to be another headache for the Unix development team. Each time they created another distribution, they had to write extensive documentation to go with it. At one point, Thompson complained that he was spending more time writing documentation than code, and Ritchie suggested they include the documentation with the code. This was the beginning of the **man** pages, online documentation about each command in Unix system *contained within the operating system itself*.

From this brief history you can see that many of the "features" of the Unix operating system were reactions to the environment in which the team found themselves. We will see how these historic elements keep cropping up over and over throughout our study of Unix.

⊕ The Unix Philosophy

Among the books written about the philosophy inherent in the Unix operating system, one of the best is *The Unix Philosophy* by Mike Garantz, published by Digital Press in 1995. It would be well worth your time to read this text. Following are its nine major tenets. This brief list does not do justice to Mike's elegant discussion, so you should read his book.

- **Small is beautiful**—Small programs load quickly, consume few resources, and are generally easy to understand.
- **Make each program do one thing well**—Small, well-designed programs should perform one task, efficiently and elegantly. If many things need to be done, it is best to combine several small programs.
- **Build a prototype as soon as possible**—Spending weeks, months, or years on the design benefits no one but the bean counters. Get something to work, then add to and enhance it.
- **Choose portability over efficiency**—It's better to have a single script that runs on all your machines than to have many different, albeit more efficient, scripts for each of your different machines.
- **Store numerical data in flat ASCII files**—I will expand on Mike's tenet here. Actually, I strongly recommend using flat ASCII files for all types of data. ASCII is

the common interface for all properly constructed Unix scripts and programs. If your data are in ASCII files, you can use all the Unix tools to process them.

- **Use software leverage to your advantage**—Ken Thompson probably said this best in his famous quote, "Good programmers write good programs; great programmers steal great programs." By this he meant that it makes little sense to reinvent the wheel. Rather than recreating programs that do the same thing as existing code, utilize that code and build upon it.

- **Use shell scripts to increase leverage and portability**—If you write your tools in a high-level language, like C or Java, they may well not work on someone's machine that has a different version of the language. However, if you write a Bourne shell script, it will most likely work on *any* Unix machine.

- **Avoid captive-user interfaces**—This one doesn't apply so much to an introductory Unix class. You should always allow your user the maximum possible flexibility. In addition, always allow your user access to the command line.

- **Make every program a filter**—In Unix parlance, a **filter** is a program that reads from standard input and writes to standard output. If you create each program as a filter, you can then use those programs successfully in pipes. (We will discuss this in detail later.)

⊕ Myths (and Realities) about Unix

Many students come to class having heard a mixture of myths and truths about Unix. We will dispel some of the myths and confirm the realities. Then we can get down to the business of learning about The One True Operating System that all the other operating systems wish they were. First, a few truths.

Unix is a very powerful operating system. It is the most complete operating system developed to date. Within the actual operating system are a full suite of file management tools, three or four editors, a couple of text processors, the best graphical user interface around, and at least one programming language. All are self-contained, with no extras to buy, beg, borrow, steal, or load. In addition, with some of the more modern versions of Unix, like Linux, you get a Web server, ftp server, telnet client, domain name server (DNS), and some other networking tools as well. Pretty good value!

Another important aspect of Unix is its stability. With some operating systems, it is common, almost expected, to have to reboot the machine once every day or two. But not with Unix! For example, the sun.com database server was up for over 400 days without rebooting. One of the advertising slogans for the Sun Microsystems Solaris operating systems was Zero Reboot Solaris! Believe it or not, computers don't need to be rebooted daily. Normally my Unix machines get rebooted only when one of the following four conditions happens:

1. I have a significant hardware failure, such as a disk drive crashing.
2. I have built a new kernel and need to install it.
3. There is a power failure. (As good as Unix machines are, they just can't seem to run without electricity.)
4. I have bought some new hardware, like a zip drive, and want to install it.

Unix is Spelled Funny

By the way, some of you have seen the word UNIX spelled in all capital letters. That has some historical precedence; however, many modern writers have taken to spelling Unix with just a capital U. In this book, I use the mixed-case spelling. I think it is less grandiose. Since Unix is without doubt a major player in the OS market, we can afford to be a bit understated. Now for the myths!

Unix is Hard to Learn

The first question must be, "Compared to what?" Compared to learning nuclear physics, Unix is relatively simple. On the other hand, learning Unix is more difficult than learning how to operate an FM radio. You must also realize that to some extent "you get what you pay for." Perhaps it's time for a demonstration. Take out a clean, blank sheet of paper. Turn to the exercises at the end of this chapter and do Exercise 1.1. When you have finished Exercise 1.1, come back here and continue with your reading. Yes, I mean it, go do Exercise 1.1 now.

Having finished Exercise 1.1, you now have your very own personal paper airplane. Now I have a question for you, which is more difficult to learn to fly: your paper airplane or a Boeing 747? Obviously, it's more difficult to learn to fly the 747. But let's add a level of complexity: suppose your task is to get a bag of mail from San Francisco to Boston. Which would you rather use, the easy-to-fly paper airplane or the more-difficult-to-learn 747?

The point being, while it is more difficult to learn Unix than to learn some other operating systems, you can also do far more with Unix than with many of those other operating systems. The time you spend learning Unix will be paid back many times over because of the efficiency and power that Unix gives you. Much like the 747, it's a far better way to "carry the mail."

Unix Commands are Terse and Difficult to Understand

Hmmm. Another way to put this might be, "Unix commands are very efficient." It is true that Unix commands are not verbose. In many cases the commands are only a couple of characters long. The reason for this command structure is historical. Back in the late 1960s, the most common way to input an instruction to a computer was to use punched cards. Interactive I/O devices were in their infancy, and one of the most advanced was a Teletype terminal. Now, you have to understand that a Teletype terminal sends and receives information at a rate of about 10 characters per second, not exactly blazing speed. Short commands were faster to type than long commands. In other words, short commands were (and are) more efficient than long commands. In addition, short commands provide less opportunity for "fat-finger errors." So yes, Unix commands are short, even terse, but as you learn them you'll find they are not difficult to understand, and they are more efficient.

Unix is Only for "Geeks"

This may have been true back in the very early days of Unix, but it is certainly no longer true. Many people find that X-Windows, one of the Unix **GUIs** (graphical user interfaces), is as friendly as any other windowing environment. There are many users who never leave the GUI. On the other hand, people who really want to utilize the power of Unix generally spend their time at the command line using a GUI to open several windows with command lines. We will explore these two ways of interfacing with Unix in a bit. Unix has become both common enough and "friendly" enough to be considered a mainstream operating system. It's not just for geeks; it's for anyone who wants to use a powerful, reliable, functional operating system.

There are Too Many Versions of Unix

Indeed, there are a number of flavors of Unix, and all have their own little idiosyncrasies. The important thing to focus on is the similarities, not the differences. From the user's perspective Unix is Unix, Linux is Unix, Solaris is Unix, AIX is Unix, Xenix is Unix, etc. The important thing is that *all of them are Unix*. (Technically, Linux is a kernel that is associated with the GNU collection of software. However, for our purposes, all of the *nixes listed look and feel like Unix.) There may be slight differences among the various options on different commands, but for the most part all of the commands you learn will work the same way on any version of Unix. There will be some instances where one version of Unix may have a command that another version doesn't, but those situations are fairly rare, and we will discuss them when they happen.

Now, it's true that from the system-administration point of view, there are significant differences across the various "flavors" of Unix. Fortunately, we won't need to address those in this book. From the user's point of view, even from the scripting or programming point of view, Unix is Unix. It's a great deal of fun. It's powerful, stable, and generally a joy to work with.

Linux, a free variant of the Unix kernel, is a very useful tool both for learning Unix in an educational environment and for use as a production system in a commercial environment. It doesn't matter if you learn Unix using a Linux system, a Sun system, an AIX system, or a Xenix system, the majority of the Unix commands you learn will apply to the other Unix variants.

Unix is Not Friendly

This statement is patently false. Unix is *very* friendly; however, it is a bit picky about whom it chooses to be its friends! Another way to say it is, "Unix is expert-friendly." Don't worry, you will soon be an expert, too!

⊕ A Few Thoughts about Unix

Learning Unix is unlike learning any other modern operating system. You don't need a GUI in Unix. However, the X-Windows system is the GUI that all other windows systems wish they were. We will spend our time working at the command line, not wasting time moving mice, pulling down menus, and playing with pointers. In addition, you are joining a very special group of people. Unix folks are unlike any other group of computer professionals you'll have the opportunity to work with. Unix people believe in sharing rather than hoarding their discoveries. Unix professionals gladly help each other and help others learn Unix. You are joining an extraordinary group of computer professionals—people who believe that an operating system doesn't have to be rebooted everyday to keep it functional, a group who shares a common knowledge base.

This feeling of community has been a part of Unix since the very beginning. Doug McIlroy described the personal environment of Bell Labs during the developmental phase of the Unix product:

> As I recorded this summary, I recalled vivid individual moments when new ideas or startling combinations of old ideas flashed through the lab, when programming met theory and *vice versa*, and when advances on many simultaneous fronts built upon and reinforced one another. I was forcibly reminded over just how wide a spectrum of activities and interests each member of the group has ranged and how freely and without fanfare collegial help has flowed among them. The primary dividends to the participants have been the fun of doing, the joy of accomplishment and the satisfaction of seeing one's handiwork used. Intellectual proprietorship and physical ownership count for little; there's more than enough of both for everyone.[1]

Whether your particular flavor is Solaris, Linux, BSD, AIX, or any of the other variants of Unix, you will be joining a loosely gathered enclave of really cool people. As Unix professionals we are all continually expanding our knowledge of the operating system, and many of us know that there is no finer operating system. Welcome to our guild!

⊕ An Overview of Unix

There are a number of interesting, useful, and powerful features of Unix. Some of these features have been mentioned before; others may be new to you. The majority of these features were very rare at the time they were first implemented in Unix.

Multi-user

As you may remember from our discussion of history, the Multics project, and subsequently the Unix project, were very early multi-user operating systems. A **multi-user** operating system is one that can share its resources among several users. These systems usually give each user the impression that they have the machine all to themselves. When you log into your Unix machine, you will probably be sharing that machine with many of your fellow students, and yet it will seem as if the machine is giving you its undivided attention. The collection of processes that enable this to happen are both fascinating and complex, and are beyond the scope of this book. Suffice it to say that depending on the speed of the processor(s), the speed of the network, and the amount of memory available, one Unix machine can serve from one to thousands of users.

Multitasking

Multitasking allows Unix to support multiple pseudo-simultaneous users, who are seemingly doing more than one thing, at the same time. We will look at this in more depth when we discuss the multiple processes running on your Unix system. Fact: a computer with a single processor, or CPU, can execute only one instruction at a time.

---

[1]M. H. McIlroy, Computing Science Technical Report No. 139, AT&T Bell Labs, Murry Hill, New Jersey 1987.

Therefore, if a single processor machine has to perform two separate, pseudo-simultaneous, tasks it must switch from one task to the other very quickly.

The CPU does this by giving each task a **quantum**, or allotted time interval, switching its attention from task to task as each task's quantum expires. If there are only two processes, then multitasking is somewhat simple. The processor only has to switch between two tasks. However, normally a single Unix machine has dozens or even hundreds of processes in various states of execution at the same time. To add to the wonder, a separate program must run to move one process out of execution and another into execution. As you can see, this very quickly becomes marvelously complicated. The software to perform this type of process switching is a great example of the complexity of the operating system.

The Unix Onion

We need to discuss the structure of the Unix operating system and how it relates to the hardware. Understanding the relationship of the hardware to the operating system and to the user interface is essential. It's this relationship that makes Unix look nearly identical regardless of the platform you're working on.

When we talked about the history of Unix, I mentioned that the operating system was cross–platform transportable. This is true from the users' point of view. However, the central part of Unix is unique to each hardware platform.

Most operating systems are written in the machine language or assembly language of a particular computer. This means that an operating system written in IBM's mainframe assembly language can be used only on an IBM mainframe. Unix is a delightful exception. Since it's written in C, a high-level language, any machine that has a C compiler can build the machine-dependent part of Unix. The structure of Unix is something like an onion or a golf ball. (Please, don't chop up golf balls to see their structure. Many of the new golf balls have a high-pressure core that could hurt you if you cut into it. Feel free, however, to dissect onions.) Look at Figure 1.1, and notice the onionlike structure.

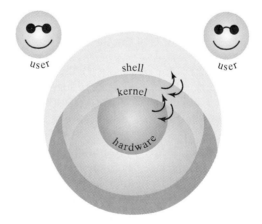

FIGURE 1.1
The structure of Unix, the Unix onion.

Hardware

The innermost core of the onion is the **hardware platform**, a term that, in this instance, describes a particular configuration of equipment. This equipment includes the memory, processor, and all other devices on the system, like graphics cards or CD-ROM players.

Kernel

Surrounding the hardware and communicating with it directly is the **kernel** of the Unix operating system. The kernel is hardware-dependent. That means that a kernel compiled on a Sun computer won't run on an Intel processor, and the kernel built for an Intel processor won't run on a Mac. The kernel code is mostly written in C and then compiled for a particular hardware platform. To add features to Unix, like support for a particular device, you must recompile the kernel. For example, when I added a ZIP drive to my Linux computer I had to build a new kernel, adding software to use the ZIP drive. While it may sound complex, usually recompiling the kernel is a straightforward task. In many flavors of Unix, there are even tools to help you build a new kernel.

Shell

The **shell** is the user interface. The shell surrounds and interacts with the kernel, providing a consistent environment for the users. As you can see from Figure 1.1, the user interacts with the shell, the shell talks to the kernel, and the kernel actually drives the hardware. The shell provides two different functions for the user. First, it reads and processes commands as they are typed on the command line (from the keyboard). Second, the shell functions as a program language interpreter, parsing and executing commands stored in shell scripts, or programs.

Although the hardware interface, or the kernel, must be specific for a particular machine; the user interface, or shell, is pretty much consistent across the various flavors of Unix. A Bourne shell on an AIX machine and a Bourne shell on a Solaris machine appear nearly identical to the user. The consistency of the user interface is why it is so easy to move from Unix on one machine to Unix on another. It is also why Unix is said to be cross–platform compatible, because from the user's point of view the command interface is the same regardless of the flavor of Unix used.

Some Common Shells

A number of different shells are available on most Unix installations. Here are the five most commonly used shells:

sh   The *Bourne shell (sh)* is the great-grandfather of all the modern Unix shells. Steve Bourne at AT&T wrote it very early in the history of Unix. It was the first shell, and it is the only shell guaranteed to be on every Unix system you might ever use. It is the shell-scripting language of choice for most system administrators. This is also one of the fastest shells, primarily because it has few fancy features. For these reasons, it is one of the two shells we will focus on in this book. (The *bash shell* is a GNU descendant of the Bourne shell, and the standard shell on Linux machines. Anything you write in the Bourne shell language is understood by the bash (*Bourne-again*) shell.)

csh   The *C shell (csh)* was written by Bill Joy while he was at Berkeley. It was the first interactive shell that had user-friendly features like command history. Joy wanted to have a shell that employed C programming like syntax. The downside of the C shell is that it has relatively poor I/O and is not suitable for writing complex scripts. Joy subsequently improved on the C shell, adding command-line editing and some other features. This enhanced version is the Tcsh shell, discussed next. Since the C shell is available on nearly every distribution of Unix, and it's a reasonably friendly user interface, it will be the first shell we use.

tcsh   The *T shell (tcsh)* is a better user interface than the C shell, but it is not uniformly available across all platforms, so it isn't included in this book. It is the default shell of the Mac OS X operating system.

ksh   David Korn successfully blended the functionality of the C shell with the scripting strength of the Bourne shell when he wrote the *Korn shell (ksh)*. Although the Korn shell is a very useful tool, it is not yet as common as the Bourne and C shells, so we won't be learning it, either.

bash   The Bourne-Again *(bash)* shell, obviously a pun on the Bourne shell, was created for the GNU project by Brian Fox in 1988. It was designed to be the standard shell for the GNU operating system and is the default shell for Linux. Chet Ramey has been the official maintainer of the bash shell since 1993. Since the bash shell is backward-compatible with the Bourne shell, everything we learn about in the Bourne shell will also work in the bash shell. If you're using Linux with this book, you'll find that many of the features that make the C shell user-friendly, like command-line history and command-line editing, are also available in the bash shell. However, like the Tcsh and the Korn shells, the bash shell is not standard across all distributions of Unix and so will not be discussed in detail here.

There are two distinct families of shells with backward compatibility from the new shell to the parent shell. The Bourne shell gave rise to both the Korn shell and the bash shell; therefore, both of those newer shells will successfully run Bourne-shell scripts. The C shell gave rise to the Tcsh, so if you must write C-shell scripts, they will also run in the Tcsh. Our focus will be on the Bourne shell and the C shell, since they are still the most common shells available across all of the different variants of Unix.

Files

Most operating systems have many different file types and formats. They may have index files, indexed-sequential files, random access files, and other specially formatted files. As was mentioned in the history section, Thompson and Ritchie were incredibly smart, or really lucky, when they decided to use plain ASCII text as the universal interface for all Unix commands. This meant that a file could be handled just the same way as a device, like the keyboard or the screen. Each device wrote or read a stream of bytes.

That brings us to our first *refrigerator rule*. This small collection of very important rules will be referred to as refrigerator rules because I expect you to write each rule on a three-by-five index card and stick it on your refrigerator door. Then each time you go to the refrigerator you can review these rules. By the end of the book, you will have a nice collection of these rules and a wonderful decoration for your refrigerator.

Refrigerator Rule No. 1:

A file is a stream of bytes.

Remember, write this rule on a card and put it on your refrigerator. It will soon have company. Yes, I really mean it: put it on your refrigerator.

As you will see later when we talk about multiprocessing and redirecting input and output, the ramifications of this concept are profound. Besides, it makes writing a device driver for Unix relatively easy.

Editors

Ah, and now we stumble into our first "**holy war**," by which we mean an ongoing, probably never-ending discussion or argument that is taking place among the members of a community about an essentially meaningless issue. There have been many holy wars in the history of computing. There was the *Mac vs. PC* holy war. There was the *keypunch vs. terminal* holy war. And while the participants in any holy war are terribly serious, the historical ramifications are usually quite silly. Besides, there are only two sides in any holy war; either you agree with me or you're wrong, right?

In this particular holy war there are basically three camps. The first camp, sometimes called the Young Turks, favors the complex and powerful **emacs** editor. These folks look with scorn upon the users of "lesser" editors and often laugh up their sleeves watching users wrestle with the older editors.

The second camp could be called the KISS (Keep It Short and Sweet) supporters. They really like the **pico** editor because it's simple, easy to use, and fairly intuitive. These folks think that **emacs** is far too difficult to learn and represents an example of overkill. The third group, probably best characterized as the Classics, feels that the original Unix editors, available on every machine, are the editors of choice. This group staunchly supports **ed**, **ex**, and **vi**, the original Unix editors. Your author falls into this last group, so this text spends the most time with **ed**, **ex**, and **vi.** We will look at **pico** when we discuss the **pine** mail program, because **pico** is the default editor for **pine**. And, lest we leave anyone out, Appendix G is a treatise on the **emacs** editor.

Case Sensitivity

It's refreshing to use an operating system as intelligent as Unix. For many older programmers, using an operating system that knows the difference between "*A*file" and "*a*file" is wonderful. Unix is **case sensitive**. That means that Unix is sensitive to, or aware of, the case (upper or lower) of commands and options. Case sensitivity is especially important when you enter commands into the Unix operating system. Commands, many options, and most arguments will be entered in lowercase. There were two primary reasons why the designers of Unix chose to use lowercase. Lowercase is easier to read, because it has more visual cues like descenders and ascenders (the things that hang down from letters, like g, or stick up, like the lines on b or d.), and it doesn't require using the SHIFT key. You are free to choose to use a mixture of uppercase and lowercase letters when you create filenames or variable names in Unix, but you'll quickly find that lowercase names are easier to use.

The exception to this rule is if you see an uppercase login prompt and must type your login ID in all uppercase characters. In that event Unix will believe that you are using a terminal that can display only uppercase characters, and everything you see—both prompts and commands—will be displayed in uppercase only. (Usually this means you have your CAPS LOCK key pressed. The best thing to do is log out, turn off CAPS LOCK, and log in again.)

How Unix Looks at You

Unlike the operating systems you may be accustomed to, Unix considers you a cognizant, careful, thoughtful adult who knows exactly what you want to do. That can be good, but it can cause some "interesting" problems. It is wonderful to have an operating system respect your wishes, and do exactly what you tell it to do, unquestioningly. However, when you tell it, for example, to remove every file on the hard drive, then unquestioning obedience may not always be such a good thing. What you must remember is that Unix expects you to know what you are doing.

This fact leads us to an important rule of the Unix Wizards: Don't ever do something you can't undo. Keep this rule in mind, and you may not end up spending the night trying undo something you told Unix to do. This is the second rule in our collection of refrigerator rules. Remember, write this rule on a three-by-five card, and put it on your refrigerator door, right under Refrigerator Rule No. 1.

Refrigerator Rule No. 2:

Don't do anything you can't undo.

Using Unix with a GUI

Many folks coming to Unix from less functional operating systems seem to be infatuated with using a GUI and may start out feeling a little uncomfortable working on a naked command line. System administrators, Unix programmers, and most Unix Power

Users spend nearly all of their time at the command line. If you want to play games, a GUI environment is wonderful, but most real work is done at the command line. As the GUI environments evolve, and more tools like Star Office become available, the GUI will become more popular for the regular, desktop user. However, power users will still work at the command line. The only real use many Unix Wizards have for a GUI is to open multiple command-line windows. Remember that we Unix users don't want to be WIMPs (Windows Icon Mouse Pointer).

Using Unix at the Command Line

True Unix Wizards know that the most efficient way to use Unix is from the command line. While the GUI can be great fun, the real work of Unix is done at the command line. Currently, your humble author has 12 windows open on his Linux box, 10 of them being command lines, one a browser, and one running Star Office. That way I can work on several command lines at the same time.

Before we start working at the command line, we need to learn the general format for a Unix **command**. Like any other operating system, Unix has a particular **syntax**, or set of rules, that you must follow to construct correctly formed commands.

The shell uses spaces or tabs to separate the parts of the command, just as you use them to separate the parts of a sentence. In the Unix world we use the term **white space** to mean one or more spaces or tabs. So, to rephrase, the Unix shell uses white space as the delimiter when parsing or dividing the parts of a command. When you type commands, you need to separate the parts of the command by one or more spaces or one or more tabs, the shell doesn't care which. When you touch the ENTER or RETURN key, the shell **parses**, or divides, the command you've entered into its parts. The first part is the command itself, the second part is optional, and consists of one or more command *options*. The third part of the command, sometimes optional and sometimes required, consists of one or more *arguments*. Both options and arguments will be discussed here in detail. Here is the generic form of the Unix command:

```
command  [-option(s)] [argument(s)]
```

When part of a command description is enclosed in square brackets, [ ], that tells you that whatever is enclosed within the brackets is optional. This is a pretty universal way of indicating optional parts of a command sequence. In Unix almost all options are preceded by hyphens. The presence of the hyphen is how Unix distinguishes between options and arguments.

Consider, for example, this command:

```
ls -l goober*
```

The **ls** is the command, the **-l** is the option, and the **goober*** is the argument. Some books call the argument the *command-line argument*, because it occurs, of all places, on the command line.

Options
Command options, or *command-line options*, are used to *modify* the way the command works. Some commands, like **cd,** have no options. Even in commands that recognize them, options are never required to make the command work. In other words, **options**

are optional (which is why they're called options, I guess.) Command-line options are almost always preceded by a hyphen.

It is important to understand that there is no absolute consistency among the options for Unix commands. Remember our discussion of Unix history in which we noted that Unix was developed by lots of people, over a long time. This is why there is no necessary consistency across the universe of Unix commands. Neverthess, in almost all cases command options are preceded by a hyphen. Most Unix commands have many options. In some cases the options will work in concert; in other cases the options are exclusionary. Let's look at an example.

I'm going to use the `ls` or, list, command as an example to illustrate the use of command options. Don't worry, at this point, about just exactly what the `ls` command does. You will learn all about it in Chapter 3. For now let's just look at how a couple of the command-line options change the way the `ls` command works. Figure 1.2 shows the output of the plain vanilla `ls` command. Notice that all it shows are the file names and that there are no command-line options, or arguments. The first line of the figure shows a prompt,

```
[ttg@tux stuff]$
```

What this prompt tells us is that I am user **ttg**, on a system named **tux**, in the **stuff** directory. The dollar sign is the standard prompt that tells us we are in the Bourne, or bash, shell. Depending upon how your system administrator has set up prompting, your prompt will probably look significantly different than mine. Don't worry about the way the prompt looks. About the only semi-standard for prompts is that those in the shells descended from the Bourne shell usually terminate in a dollar sign, those in shells descended from the C shell usually end in a percent sign, and shell prompts that end in an octothorp (also called hash mark, pound sign, number sign, sharp sign, or even tic-tac-toe symbol), "#," usually indicate that the user is *root* (explained later).

Following the prompt is `ls`, the list command. The next line shows the names of the five files that are stored, or reside, in the **stuff** directory. Notice that the plain vanilla version of `ls` shows us only the file names. The shell prompt following the five file names tells us that tux is ready for us to enter another command.

Now let's add an option to the `ls` command. Suppose we want to see more information about the files stored the directory. The `-l` (hyphen ell) option specifies a long file listing. Figure 1.3 shows the output of the `ls` command with the `-l` option. Again, don't worry about everything you see here. When we study the `ls` command you will

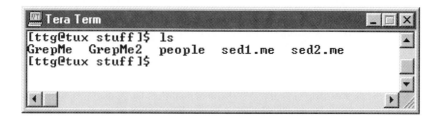

FIGURE 1.2

The plain vanilla `ls` command.

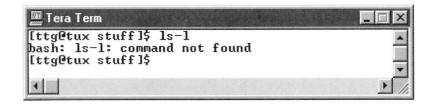

FIGURE 1.3

The ls command with the -1 option.

learn all about this option. What is important now is to notice that by simply adding a
-1 (hyphen ell), I've modified what the command sends to the screen. Notice as well
the space between the "s" of ls and the hyphen; remember that Unix shells use white
space to parse the commands. The white space between the command and the option is
required. If I forget to include that white space, the shell will be confused, as shown in
Figure 1.4.

```
 Tera Term                                      _ □ ×
[ttg@tux stuff]$ ls-1
bash: ls-1: command not found
[ttg@tux stuff]$
```

FIGURE 1.4

The ls-1 command with missing white space.

With no white space to help him to parse the command, the shell tries to find a command called ls-1. Alas, there is no such command. By the same token, since the shell is
just looking for white space, I could insert more than one space, as shown in Figure 1.5.
Unlike the missing white space in Figure 1.4, extra white space in Figure 1.5 doesn't
bother the shell at all. One space, two spaces, twenty spaces, three tabs, the shell doesn't
care as long as there is some white space he can use to parse the command.

There are a number of options to the ls command. Most Unix commands allow
you to group multiple options after a single hyphen (-). Many Unix commands also
allow you to list a series of options, each preceded by its own hyphen. Figure 1.6 shows
the ls command with two options: -1 for the long version and **-a** to show all the files,
even hidden ones. Notice that both options are coded after a single hyphen.

In the early days of Unix some commands were created that required a hyphen
before each option. Figure 1.7 shows how the ls command would look if we coded
both options prepending a hyphen to each one. As you can see, the output is exactly the
same whether the two options are coded together or as distinct options, each preceded
by a hyphen.

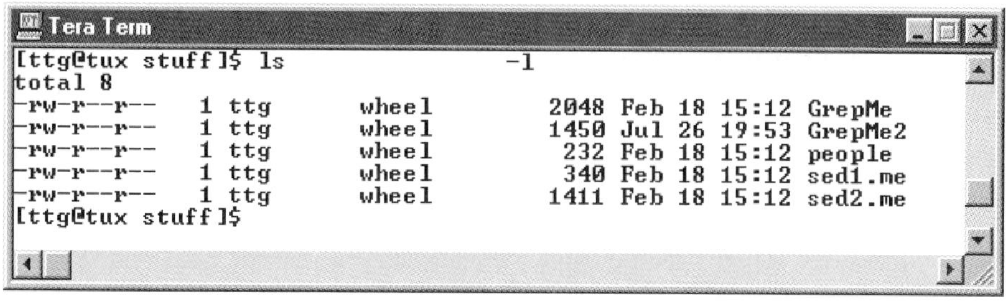

```
Tera Term                                                    _ □ ×
[ttg@tux stuff]$ ls                -l
total 8
-rw-r--r--    1 ttg        wheel        2048 Feb 18 15:12 GrepMe
-rw-r--r--    1 ttg        wheel        1450 Jul 26 19:53 GrepMe2
-rw-r--r--    1 ttg        wheel         232 Feb 18 15:12 people
-rw-r--r--    1 ttg        wheel         340 Feb 18 15:12 sed1.me
-rw-r--r--    1 ttg        wheel        1411 Feb 18 15:12 sed2.me
[ttg@tux stuff]$
```

FIGURE 1.5

The ls -l command with extra white space.

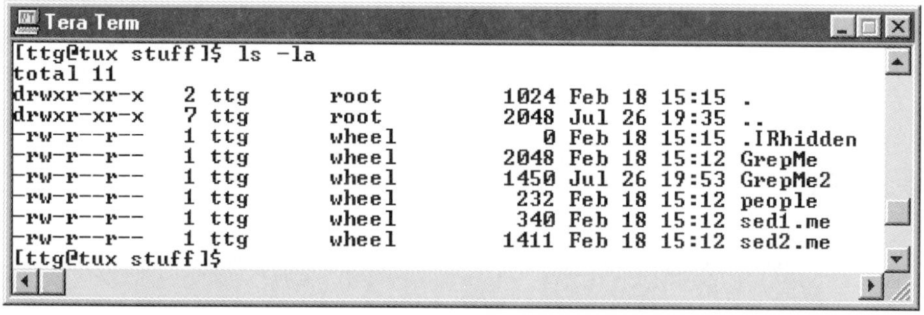

```
Tera Term                                                    _ □ ×
[ttg@tux stuff]$ ls -la
total 11
drwxr-xr-x    2 ttg        root         1024 Feb 18 15:15 .
drwxr-xr-x    7 ttg        root         2048 Jul 26 19:35 ..
-rw-r--r--    1 ttg        wheel           0 Feb 18 15:15 .IRhidden
-rw-r--r--    1 ttg        wheel        2048 Feb 18 15:12 GrepMe
-rw-r--r--    1 ttg        wheel        1450 Jul 26 19:53 GrepMe2
-rw-r--r--    1 ttg        wheel         232 Feb 18 15:12 people
-rw-r--r--    1 ttg        wheel         340 Feb 18 15:12 sed1.me
-rw-r--r--    1 ttg        wheel        1411 Feb 18 15:12 sed2.me
[ttg@tux stuff]$
```

FIGURE 1.6

The ls command showing two options.

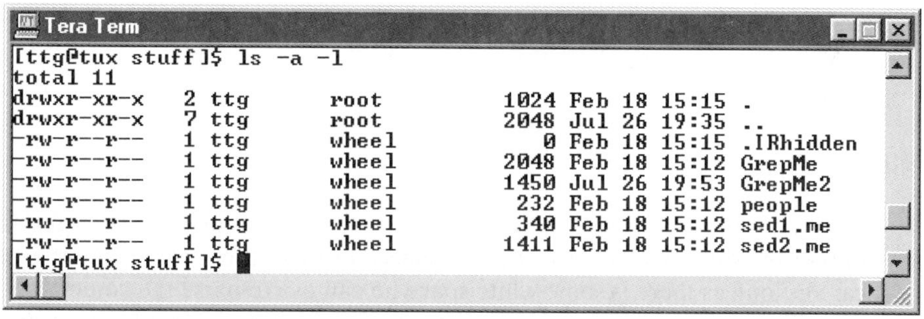

```
Tera Term                                                    _ □ ×
[ttg@tux stuff]$ ls -a -l
total 11
drwxr-xr-x    2 ttg        root         1024 Feb 18 15:15 .
drwxr-xr-x    7 ttg        root         2048 Jul 26 19:35 ..
-rw-r--r--    1 ttg        wheel           0 Feb 18 15:15 .IRhidden
-rw-r--r--    1 ttg        wheel        2048 Feb 18 15:12 GrepMe
-rw-r--r--    1 ttg        wheel        1450 Jul 26 19:53 GrepMe2
-rw-r--r--    1 ttg        wheel         232 Feb 18 15:12 people
-rw-r--r--    1 ttg        wheel         340 Feb 18 15:12 sed1.me
-rw-r--r--    1 ttg        wheel        1411 Feb 18 15:12 sed2.me
[ttg@tux stuff]$
```

FIGURE 1.7

The ls command with two distinct options.

Arguments

Command-line **arguments** are used to tell the command what to work with or upon. A command-line argument is often a filename. However, command-line arguments can also provide input to the command. In the case of the ls command, the command-line argument tells the command which filename(s) to display.

Figure 1.8 shows a request for the ls command to display only files with names that begin with a capital G. Again, don't worry about the actual syntax of the command, or of the argument; we will cover those in exquisite detail shortly. For now, just look at the way the command is formed. Notice that there are no options. However, using a command-line argument does not exclude the use of options. Figure 1.9 shows how the ls command performs if the -l option and the **G*** argument are both supplied. As expected, the -l option causes ls to show the file data in the long format, and the argument **G*** tells ls to show only files with names that begin with an uppercase G.

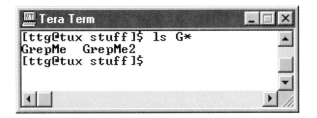

FIGURE 1.8

The ls command with an argument.

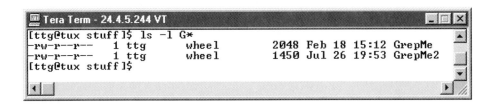

FIGURE 1.9

The ls command with an option and an argument.

⊕ Some Useful Keys

There are handful of keyboard keys that you'll find useful. The actual position of these keys is keyboard-dependent. For example, on most new Intel keyboards the Control (Ctrl) key is located in the lower left-hand corner. On one version of Sun Microsystems's keyboard, known as a Unix keyboard, the Control key is located partway up the left-hand side. You will need to look at your keyboard to determine exactly where these keys are located—but remember not to look at it when you type; touch typing is a very important skill!

Most of these keys are actually combinations of two concurrent key presses. For example, **control-C** means that you hold down the Ctrl key while you touch the C key. Even though the C character is shown in uppercase, the common standard, you don't need to hold the SHIFT key down. Simply holding down the control key and touching C sends the correct key combination. The control keys are often represented as caret key, for example, **^C**.

Control-C (^C), or interrupt, will usually terminate a running program. You can easily remember this by remembering that **Control-C** stands for "Kill." You will also use this key combination to abandon a partially completed command on the command line. On some systems the DELETE key functions like **Control-C**.

Control-D (^D) is the end-of-file marker (I am **D**one with sending input.) Use **Control-D** to tell programs that read from the keyboard that you're finished. For example, you many be writing a mail message, and want to tell mail you're finished with input. If you type **Control-D** on a line by itself, mail will interpret that as end-of-file and process your message.

Control-Z (^Z) puts processes to sleep (ZZZZZZZ) or suspends them. When we study process control you'll learn how to use **Control-Z** to stop an executing process. Misuse of **Control-Z** results in incorrectly stopped jobs. If you get the message "There are stopped jobs" when you attempt to logout, you most likely have used **Control-Z** incorrectly.

Enter (the ENTER key) sends a new line character to the currently running process. On some keyboards **Enter** is the RETURN key, and on some Unix-specific keyboards it is actually labeled NEWLINE. Regardless of its name, this is one of the most commonly used keys on the keyboard.

Backspace (the BACKSPACE key) erases the character immediately in front of the cursor. On some systems the DELETE key is used to erase characters. Frequently, the BACKSPACE key is not correctly set when you log into a Unix system using **telnet**. You may have to use **Control-H (^H)** to backspace. In Chapter 2 we will learn how to set particular key combinations, and especially how to correctly set the backspace key.

⊕ Logging in

Enough of this dry, boring stuff! Let's get you logged on to a Unix computer so you can start playing with the Greatest Operating System in the Known Universe. Before you can login, though, the Unix computer must know who you are. Your instructor or system administrator will need to provide you with a login ID for your computer. If you're working on your own computer, make sure you have created a regular user account, not a root account.

Root is the ultimate user on a Unix system. There are no controls strong enough to hinder root. No file protection will stop root from doing what root wants to do. That is why wise Unix users, even system administrators, regularly log in with a normal user account, and use their root login only to perform special tasks that require the power of root.

The first step in connecting to a Unix computer is to establish **connectivity** between your terminal and the Unix server. (This assumes you're not working on a Unix system on your own PC. In that case, all you have to do is sit down at the console and you are connected.)

The usual way to establish connectivity is to use some sort of telnet package running on your local machine to connect to a Unix machine. Figure 1.10 shows how a Windows box can be used as a dumb terminal to connect to a Unix server. In this case the server is our friend tux, and the telnet software is the freeware package Tera Term

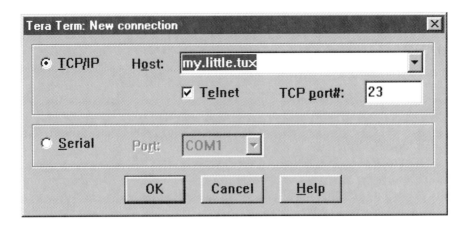

FIGURE 1.10

The initial Tera Term Pro screen used to connect to a Unix computer.

Pro. This package was written by Takashi Teranishi, who distributes it free of charge. If you have a different telnet package, feel free to use it. How you get to the Unix machine isn't important—what matters is that you get there.

When you start Tera Term Pro you can select "New connection," and it will bring up the screen shown in Figure 1.10. Here we are connecting to a computer called my.little.tux. To make the connection click the OK button. If your communications software is configured correctly, Tera Term Pro will reach across the Internet and open a session with the computer of choice, in this case tux.

Figure 1.11 shows the initial login screen on tux. The Unix computer we have connected to tells us a little bit about itself—in this case, that it is running Red Hat Linux version 6.0, the 2.2.5-15 version of the kernel, on an Intel 686 processor. Tux then displays the **login:** prompt requesting a valid login ID. That would be ttg for this user.

In addition to a known login ID, most Unix systems are set up to require the user to have a password. If you're working on a large Unix system the system administrator

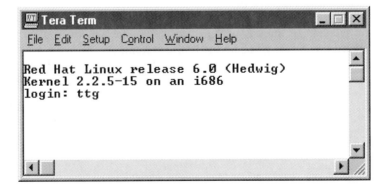

FIGURE 1.11

The initial login screen on a Unix computer.

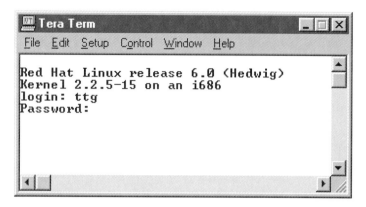

FIGURE 1.12

The password prompt.

may have given you a default password. In some rare cases, you'll be given an account without any initial password. If you have no password assigned to your account, the Unix system will simply log you in when you touch ENTER after typing your login ID.

In the normal case, however, the system administrator will have given you a password, and the Unix system will prompt you for that password. Figure 1.12 shows that the system administrator on tux has given ttg a password, so tux asks ttg for his password. When you type a password, the Unix system does not echo what you type, so you can't see what you've typed. By the same token no one else can look over your shoulder and steal your password.

After you have typed your password and touched the ENTER key, Unix goes through a very interesting password-validation process. Passwords on a Unix system are stored in an encrypted mode. The algorithm used to encrypt a password is called a *one-way encryption algorithm*. That means that even knowing the algorithm, you can't run it backward to determine the password. It's something like an egg: once you scramble an egg you just can't unscramble it. When the user types her password at the prompt, Unix takes the password as typed and runs it through the encryption algorithm using the password as the key. It then compares the encrypted password to the stored version of the password. If the newly encrypted password matches the stored password the user is given access to the system.

Figure 1.13 shows that ttg provided the correct password, and tux logged him in. In this case, once tux recognizes the user, he tells ttg when he last logged in and then gives him the familiar command-line prompt. The system administrator can set up any number of events that are tied to a user's login. We'll see one of the more common ones shortly.

The "Last login" information (Figure 1.13) is very important. Always note the last login day and time. If you see a login date or time that you suspect to be incorrect, *immediately* notify your system administrator or your instructor. Extra logins could mean that someone, perhaps a cracker, is using your account. Remember that you are often the first line of defense against unauthorized use. I can assure you that a system administrator would much rather research 20 "mistakes" than have one user not report a possible break-in.

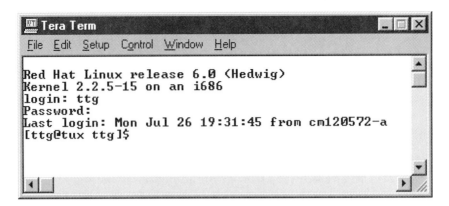

FIGURE 1.13

The login screen on tux.

passwd

```
passwd
```

The first time you log into a Unix system you should set a new password for yourself. To set a password or to change your password, use the **passwd** command. This command has no options or arguments. (Okay, the truth is that there is an argument, but you can use it only if you are root. As root, you can specify the user ID of another user and change her password. Since this isn't a textbook on system administration, we don't need to discuss that further.)

Figure 1.14 shows ttg changing his password. First he typed passwd at the command line. Tux asks him for his old password, to make sure that the user at the keyboard is actually ttg. (Without this verification step another user could come up to ttg's terminal while he was away from it and change his password. That would be a Bad

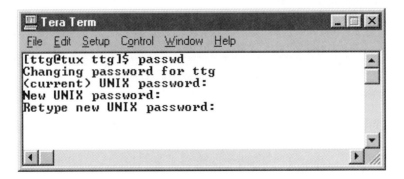

FIGURE 1.14

Changing the user's password, the passwd command.

Thing.) If the password entered is ttg's, then tux asks ttg to enter a new password. Since the password does not show on the screen, tux asks ttg to type it a second time, the theory being that if users type the same password twice, they're typing it correctly.

Different Unix systems respond differently to the passwd command. When changing the password on a Sun OS system, for example, the user enters the new password twice, and the system simply responds with the standard system prompt. On the other hand, on a Linux or Solaris system, the shell tells the user that the password was accepted. Figure 1.15 shows how the passwd command works on a Linux box (top) and on a Solaris computer (bottom). Notice how the prompt for the original password is slightly different—that is an example of the small differences among the various flavors of Unix. We will see other flavor differences as we study these two variants of Unix.

Creating Good Passwords

Let's talk for a minute about passwords. On most Unix systems your password is the only thing that keeps a nefarious cracker from stealing your login; reading, modifying, or even deleting your files; sending mail in your name; or wreaking other havoc that you could be blamed for. The password you select is very important. Here are some rules for forming passwords:

1. Don't use a word that appears in any dictionary in any language as your password. Crackers have programs that try dictionary words as passwords, attempting to break into accounts.

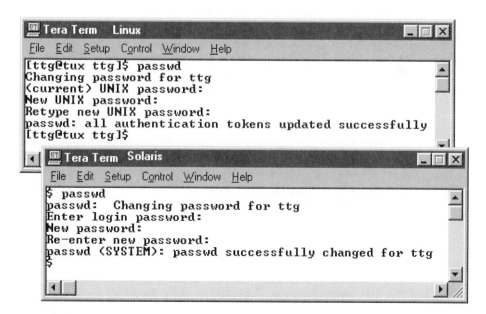

FIGURE 1.15

Successful password changes on a Linux system (top), and on Solaris (bottom).

2. Make sure your password is at least six characters long. Longer passwords are harder to guess. By the same token, most Unix systems look at only the first eight characters of the password, so having a 30-character password is just making more work for yourself.

3. Don't include any information about yourself in your password. Some easily guessed passwords are your name, parts of your name, the name of your pet, the name of your significant other, the name of your child, or your date of birth.

4. Don't use any names—not your name, not your friend's name, *no* names.

5. Don't try simple substitutions. For example if you wanted your password to be hello, you might try substituting the number 1 for the letter "l" and zero for the letter "o." That would give you a password that looked like **he110** (h e one one zero). Unfortunately, the password-guessing software out there also knows that trick. (I know that hello is too short to be good password as per Rule 2; I used it because of the "l"s and "o"s.)

6. Use a mixed-case password, that is, one containing both uppercase and lowercase letters. These are much more difficult to guess than those that are either all uppercase or all lowercase.

7. Include special characters. Passwords that contain special characters like commas, periods, asterisks, ampersands, slashes, percent signs, and octothorps are much more difficult to guess.

8. Make your password one you can remember. If you forget your password, no one can remember it for you. Your password needs to be something you can remember.

9. *Don't write your password down*, anywhere, ever! This means you! Yes, you!

Some Unix systems limit passwords to eight characters, so creating a long, complex password may not make your account any more secure than a well-designed eight-character password. Check with your instructor or system administrator. Many system administrators have software programs that try to break users' passwords. They run these programs against the password file regularly. Follow the password-creation rules, and you will not suffer the embarrassment of having an administrator guess or break your password. That means that a cracker trying to break into the Unix system won't be able to guess your password, either.

To increase the security of their site many system administrators will also activate a password-aging function. If password aging is enabled, your password will expire after a certain length of time, and you'll be required to pick a new password. Some administrators also prevent the users from changing their password until a specified length of time has passed. This prevents users from changing their password to a new password and then changing it back to the old password immediately, thereby thwarting the password-aging function.

⊕ Secure Shell

Some system administrators are incorporating tools within their systems to increase the security of network transmissions. One of the problems with telnet is that the data are sent in the clear, exactly as they are typed. Crackers can use tools like "sniffers" to see all of the data passed over a network. If you are using plain old telnet, a sniffer can see both your login name and your password. That can be a problem.

To combat sniffers, some system administrators are asking their users to use secure-transmission tools like *secure shell (ssh)*. Ssh software encrypts everything sent over the network, so crackers may be able to sniff the data, but since it is encrypted, it does them no good. If your system administrator asks that you use secure communications, please respect that request. A safer Net is better for all of us.

exit

```
exit [number]
```

Okay, you've logged into a Unix system and changed or given yourself a password. Now it's time to learn how to logout. Different systems use different commands to log a user off. However, almost every Unix system recognizes the **exit** command.

Notice that exit has an optional numeric argument. If you include a number with `exit`, that number will be reported as the "return status." Most Unix commands provide a return status to indicate whether they were successfully completed. A return status of zero indicates success, and any other number indicates some problem. When you're using `exit` to log off from Unix machine, you won't have a return status. Later, when you **write** shell scripts, you may find supplying a return status is useful.

Figure 1.16 shows ttg logging off from tux. As soon as he touches the ENTER key, tux will process the exit command, close the login session, and disconnect. The Terra Term Pro window will close when the connection is lost.

Many Unix systems also accept the **logout** command to close a session. Some system administrators have implemented other commands that invoke the `exit` command, like **bye**, **caio**, and even **adios** in Texas.

Now that you know a little bit about Unix and Unix commands, it's time for you to play a little. For the following exercises you will need to talk to either your instructor or your system administrator to obtain your user ID and password.

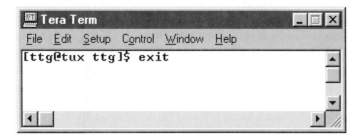

FIGURE 1.16
Exiting from a Unix system.

KEY TERMS

application program
argument
case sensitive
command
compiled language
connectivity
filter
GUI
hardware platform
holy war
interpreted language
kernel
multitasking
multi-user
operating system
option
parse
quantum
root
shell
single-thread
syntax
utility program
white space

NEW COMMANDS

```
exit
passwd
```

REVIEW QUESTIONS

1.1 Explain why Unix is such a powerful operating system.
1.2 List three of the important contributors to the development of Unix.
1.3 List and explain two of the myths or realities about Unix.
1.4 Explain the significance of the Multics project in the development of Unix.
1.5 Describe the similarities, if any, between Linux and Unix.
1.6 List, describe, and differentiate among the three parts of the Unix command.
1.7 Explain the term *white space*.
1.8 List at least four rules for creating a good password.
1.9 Discuss whether or not a user can determine another user's password by seeing the encrypted version.
1.10 List and describe the three layers of the Unix "onion."

EXERCISES

    1.1 Follow the instructions in Figure 1.17 to build a paper flying machine.

    1.2 Obtain your user ID and password from your instructor or system administrator. (If you are functioning as a system administrator, create a *user-level* account for yourself. Do not, under any circumstances, use a privileged account to do the labs in this course.)

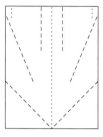
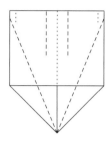
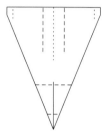

1. Fold along centerline, fold 7, and reopen.   *2. Fold along lines 1 and 2.*   *3. Fold along lines 3 and 4.*

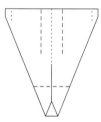

4. Fold nose up on line 5.   *5. Fold nose up on line 6 and tuck under flap.*   *6. Rotate plane and fold in half along its centerline, fold 7.*

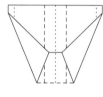

7. Fold wing along line 8.   *8. Flip plane over.*   *9. Fold wing down along line 9.*

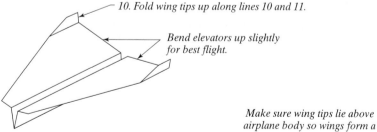

10. Fold wing tips up along lines 10 and 11.

Bend elevators up slightly for best flight.

Make sure wing tips lie above airplane body so wings form a slight "Y" shape with body.

FIGURE 1.17
Building a complex flying machine.

1.3 Unless directed otherwise, use the `passwd` command to create a good Unix password.

1.4 Log out of the Unix system, then log back in using your new password.

2

Getting Started

CHAPTER OBJECTIVES

After reading this chapter, you should be able to:

- Explain the Unix process model.
- Research Unix commands using the `man` command.
- Determine information about people on the system using `who`, `w`, and `finger`.
- Communicate with other users via `talk`, `write`, `mail`, and `pine`.
- Know better than to use the `wall` command except in emergencies.
- Determine the system date and format it.
- Use the `cal` command to display calendar information.
- Carefully modify some terminal parameters with `stty`.

Now that you're an old hand at logging in and logging out, it's time to learn a few more commands that are infinitely more fun. However, before we get into the wild, woolly world of Unix commands, we need to discuss one very important concept: the process.

⊕ The Process

Every command in Unix is a program. Thus, each time you type in a command, you're actually running a program. To understand how these programs work, we need to consider how the operating system handles them. Have faith—this will take just a few moments to explain.

Whenever a program is executed, or run, the operating system must create an environment for the program to run in. This means the operating system must allocate resources for the program to use. For example, a program needs to have a place in memory to store its instructions and data, and it must be allowed some time when it can use the CPU. In addition, most programs require access to files or devices from which they can read *input* data and to which they can write *output* data. In Unix a **process** is the name we give to that collection of resources, access to files/devices, and the rest of the environment necessary to run a particular program.

As we will discuss in detail later, a process can be in one of several different states of execution. For example, a process can be running, it can be asleep, it can be waiting for input, or it can even be a zombie. Another way of defining a process would be "a program and its associated resources, in any execution state."

At process-creation time, each process is usually given access to three files, rather than just the two (input and output) files mentioned earlier. The first file is **standard input**, from which the process takes its input. It is usually associated with the keyboard. The second file, **standard output**, is where the process sends normal and expected output. It is usually connected to the screen. The third file, **standard error**, is where the process sends any error messages. It, too, is normally connected to the screen. Standard input, standard output, and standard error are also called **data streams**, a term that describes a flow of data, just as a water stream is a flow of water.

Having a file just for error messages, like standard error, is very unusual among operating systems. The reason the creators of Unix divided the normal output data stream (standard output) from the error stream (standard error) goes back to one of the fundamental tenets of the Unix philosophy: "Proper processes don't create extraneous data." In other words, a process should not create superfluous data in the normal output stream. In most other operating systems, if the process encounters an error, it adds the error message to the regular output data stream. That action creates a potential problem, as the normal output for the process will be intermixed with the error messages. Consequently, the user might have difficulty determining which messages are normal data and which are error messages. In the Unix environment output is directed to one file and error messages to another, so there can be no confusion.

The need for standard input is self-explanatory. The process needs to take input from someplace, and that place is designated as "standard input."

To review, then: An executing program and its supporting environment constitute a process. Most processes have three files associated with them; standard input, standard output, and standard error. Now that we know what a process is, let's look at some.

man

```
man [options] [subject(s)]
```

Before we discuss other Unix commands, we need to examine a valuable and unique feature of Unix called the **man** command. When Ken Thompson was sending out Unix tapes in the very early days of Unix, he included a printed version of the operations manual with each tape. He complained to Dennis Ritchie that he was spending more time writing documentation than he was writing code, because each version of Unix was slightly different. In the discussion that ensued, they decided to prepare an *online* manual that could be included as part of the distribution tape instead of creating a new hard-copy manual to accompany each tape. This documentation became known as the *manual* (*man* for short) *pages*. They have been an integral part of each Unix system ever since.

So what does that mean to you? Well, for one thing, it means that any time you are logged into a Unix system you have a complete set of documentation for that system available. Not only is this a complete set of documentation, but it is the best documentation for your particular system. As I mentioned earlier, there are subtle differences among the different versions of Unix. The local man pages will reflect the particular flavor of Unix running on the machine you are logged into. To use these pages, simply type the command man followed by the name of the command you wish to learn about.

Figure 2.1 shows the first page of output produced when ttg asked about the command man on tux. This online manual is for the most part quite extensive. It often tells you far more than you really wanted to know. Nonetheless, it is an excellent source of information about the commands on your particular system.

One important option is the -s, or *section*, option. The manual pages are divided into nine sections based upon their content. For example, Section 1 is about commands and command formats, and it is the default section. Section 4 is about file formats. Section 5 is the collection of miscellaneous "stuff" that doesn't fit elsewhere. Section 6 documents games. If the item you are seeking is in another man section, you need to use the

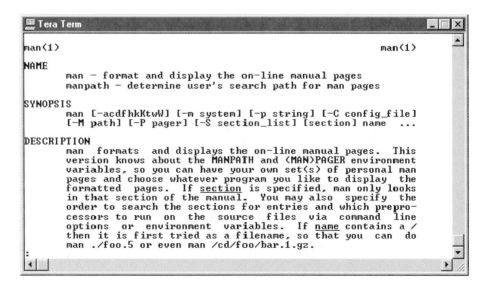

FIGURE 2.1

Sample man page.

-s option followed by the section number to retrieve it. To see the difference, first enter this command to bring up the man command discussion:

```
man man
```

Now enter this command to bring up the "other" discussion of the man system:

```
man -s 5 man
```

In the man pages, a number in parentheses following the item name designates the section. For example, "see man(5)" tells you to look in Section 5 of the man pages. This brings us to another feature of Unix. Because of the slight flavor differences, there is by necessity an **order of precedence** of truth about any given command. The order of precedence is the sequence of priority of the various elements of a list. An example you may be familiar with is the order in which arithmetic operations are performed in an equation.

Listed below is the order of precedence of the sources of truth, that is, true information. The most accurate information about any given command on any given system is obtained by executing the command and *seeing what it does*. That is, if you will, *absolute truth*. The next most accurate information about a command is what is listed in the man pages. The third best source of information about any given command is what you read in a book—yes, even this book. And the least accurate information about a command would come from what another person tells you.

To summarize: Information about a command, in order of most credible to least credible, is as follows:

1. What the command actually does.
2. What the man page says the command does.
3. What a book says the command does.
4. What someone else says the command does.

You will find the man pages are an extremely handy reference as you learn about Unix.

who

```
who [options]
who am I
whoami
```

In Chapter 1 we discussed the notion that Unix commands are terse, difficult to understand, and generally make no sense by themselves. The **who** command is a perfect example to prove this point. This command is used to determine *who* is currently on the system. Who is on the system ... who ... no, there is no logical relationship—it is far too cryptic! So terse, so difficult to understand ... hmmm, right.

```
Tera Term                                                        _ □ ×
[ttg@tux /etc]$ who
root        tty1      Jul 10 12:34
ttg         ttyp0     Jul 10 19:08  (ftwrth1.tx.home.com)
kpace       ttyp1     Jul 10 19:21  (tron.dcccd.edu)
nattired    ttyp2     Jul 10 19:22  (de.dcccd.edu)
gwire       ttyp3     Jul 10 19:24  (awk.dcccd.edu)
rbanks      ttyp4     Jul 10 19:27  (red.dcccd.edu)
dtomes      ttyp5     Jul 10 19:28  (tux.home.com)
tlunch      ttyp6     Jul 10 19:30  (bo.dcccd.edu)
rtyde       ttyp7     Jul 10 19:33  (de.dcccd.edu)
sbeach      ttyp8     Jul 10 20:54  (tron.dcccd.edu)
nweigh      ttyp9     Jul 10 20:56  (awk.dcccd.edu)
[ttg@tux /etc]$
```

FIGURE 2.2

Output of the plain vanilla who command.

The who command has a slightly different flavor on different versions of Unix. However, as mentioned earlier, this flavor difference is far less important than the way the command actually performs. Used with no options, the who command lists the login IDs of users that are currently logged into the system, the terminal or port they are logged into, when they logged in, and where they logged in from.

Figure 2.2 shows the standard output from the who command. As you can see, there are several users on tux, and they have logged in from several different locations. It is very handy to use the who command this way, to see who is currently logged into the system. Because Unix users form a type of community, it's nice to know who else is around.

There is an alternate form of the who command that gives us some insight into the mind of the Unix programmer. This alternate form has two variants. Both variants are shown in Figure 2.3. The first, whoami, shows only the user's login ID. The second, who am i, shows the standard who information about the user: her login ID, terminal line, when she logged in, and where she logged in from.

Initially, it may give one pause to think that Unix users need a command to tell them who they are. However, there are times when a Unix user may be logged in more than once, using different IDs. For example, the system administrator may be logged in as root, and also logged in with her own user ID. Some commands she performs as root

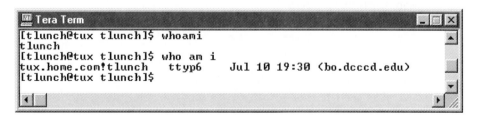

FIGURE 2.3

Output of who am i and whoami commands.

will not work under her normal user ID because she doesn't have the privilege to run them. By the same token, there are some commands she may run under her user ID that she would not want to run as root. Of course, it's also true that after an all-night session playing with a Unix box, it is sometimes nice, or even necessary, to be able to ask whoami .

So the who command can tell you who's logged on, but sometimes it's also nice to know what people are doing. In just a bit we will learn about a couple of commands that will let us establish a dialog with another user. Before we attempt a dialog, though, we need to know if the user is busy. After all, we wouldn't want to interrupt a user who is working on a project and wouldn't appreciate being bothered.

w

---

w [options] [login id]

The w command tells us a lot of things. Figure 2.4 shows the output from this command. The first line of output gives us some system information. Specifically, it tells us the current time on the system, how long the system has been up, how many users are on the system, and the average system load for the past one, five, and fifteen minutes. The heading line in the default output sets columns for the following information: login ID, name of the terminal port in use, where the users logged in from, when they logged in, how long they've been idle, the total CPU usage for this session, the CPU usage for the current command, and the command they're currently running. While this information may all be fascinating, the only data that are important to us at this point are the login ID, how long the users have been idle, and what they're doing.

This would be a time when we could use the -s (short form) option of the w command. Figure 2.5 shows the output of the w -s command. In this instance we can see that several users—gwire, rbanks, and nweigh—are editing files. Root, tlunch, and sbeach are at the command-line prompt in the bash shell. The user named nattired is

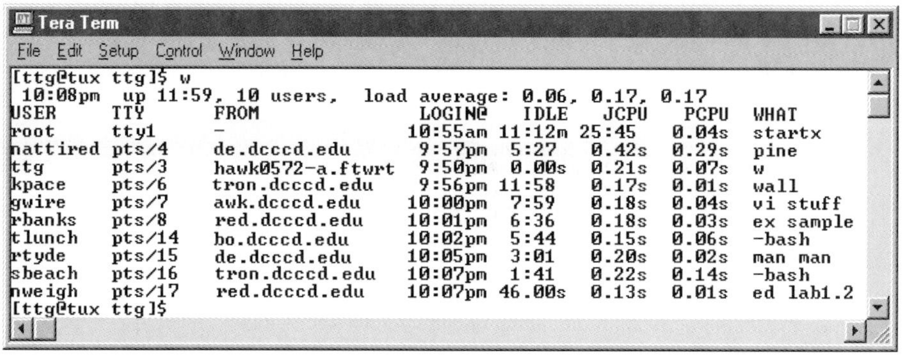

```
[ttg@tux ttg]$ w
 10:08pm  up 11:59, 10 users,  load average: 0.06, 0.17, 0.17
USER     TTY      FROM           LOGIN@   IDLE   JCPU   PCPU  WHAT
root     tty1     -              10:55am 11:12m 25:45  0.04s  startx
nattired pts/4    de.dcccd.edu    9:57pm  5:27  0.42s  0.29s  pine
ttg      pts/3    hawk0572-a.ftwrt 9:50pm 0.00s  0.21s  0.07s  w
kpace    pts/6    tron.dcccd.edu  9:56pm 11:58  0.17s  0.01s  wall
gwire    pts/7    awk.dcccd.edu  10:00pm  7:59  0.18s  0.04s  vi stuff
rbanks   pts/8    red.dcccd.edu  10:01pm  6:36  0.18s  0.03s  ex sample
tlunch   pts/14   bo.dcccd.edu   10:02pm  5:44  0.15s  0.06s  -bash
rtyde    pts/15   de.dcccd.edu   10:05pm  3:01  0.20s  0.02s  man man
sbeach   pts/16   tron.dcccd.edu 10:07pm  1:41  0.22s  0.14s  -bash
nweigh   pts/17   red.dcccd.edu  10:07pm 46.00s 0.13s  0.01s  ed lab1.2
[ttg@tux ttg]$
```

FIGURE 2.4

Output of the w command.

```
 Tera Term                                                        _ □ ✕
 File  Edit  Setup  Control  Window  Help
[ttg@tux ttg]$ w -s                                                  ▲
 10:30pm  up 12:21, 10 users,  load average: 0.49, 0.49, 0.38
USER      TTY      FROM              IDLE   WHAT
root      tty1     -                 11:35m startx
nattired  pts/4    de.dcccd.edu      27:42  pine
ttg       pts/3    hawk0572-a.ftwrt  0.00s  w -s
kpace     pts/6    tron.dcccd.edu    34:13  wall
gwire     pts/7    awk.dcccd.edu     30:14  vi stuff
rbanks    pts/8    red.dcccd.edu     28:51  ex sample
tlunch    pts/14   bo.dcccd.edu      27:59  -bash
rtyde     pts/15   de.dcccd.edu      25:16  man man
sbeach    pts/16   tron.dcccd.edu    14.00s -bash
nweigh    pts/17   red.dcccd.edu     25.00s ed lab1.2
[ttg@tux ttg]$                                                       ▼
 ◄                                                                ► //
```

FIGURE 2.5

Output of the w -s command.

using the pine mail program (discussed later in this chapter) rtyde is investigating the man command, kpace is writing a message to all the users, and ttg is running the w command. All the users except for ttg have been idle for either minutes or hours. For example, root has been idle for nine hours and nineteen minutes. A close look at the output enables us to determine if the idle times are in minutes and seconds or in hours and minutes. If the idle time has an "s" appended to it, then the idle time is in seconds. If the idle time has no letter appended to it, it shows minutes and seconds. If the idle time has an "m" appended to it, it represents hours and minutes.

There are several options for the w command. Two that are of interest to us are the -h, which suppresses headers, and -s, which gives us the short form (shown in Figure 2.5) without the login time, JCPU or PCPU times. The w command also takes as an argument the login ID of a single user for which you would like to collect information. Figure 2.6 shows the output of the w command using both these options and an argument of tlunch. As we can see from the output, tlunch is busy working in **vi** (an editor). We know he's busy, because he's been idle for only 12 seconds. Using the man pages, or looking in your reference book, you'll notice that there are other options for the w command. Feel free to explore those other options, though they are not as commonly used as -s and -h.

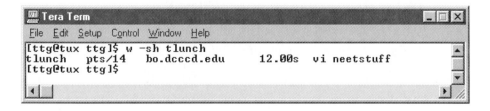

```
 Tera Term                                                        _ □ ✕
 File  Edit  Setup  Control  Window  Help
[ttg@tux ttg]$ w -sh tlunch                                          ▲
tlunch    pts/14   bo.dcccd.edu      12.00s  vi neetstuff
[ttg@tux ttg]$                                                       ▼
 ◄                                                                ► //
```

FIGURE 2.6

Output of the w command with options and an argument.

talk

```
talk login-id[@hostname] [device]
```

Sometimes it is nice to be able to communicate with other Unix users on the system. There are three different tools available to enable user to user communication: `talk`, `write`, and `mail`.

The **talk** command establishes an interactive communications session between you and *one* other user. Obviously, if you are going to have an interactive dialog, the other user must also be logged onto the system You also must be using a terminal type that allows Unix to control your screen. For example, you could be emulating a VT-100 or other recognized terminal type.

The format of the `talk` command is `talk` followed by the login ID of the person to whom you wish to talk. Figure 2.7 shows the interchange initiated by this command. The top screen shows what user sbeach sees after she types the command `talk dtomes` and touches ENTER. The bottom screen shows what dtomes sees on his screen after sbeach tries to initiate a talk session.

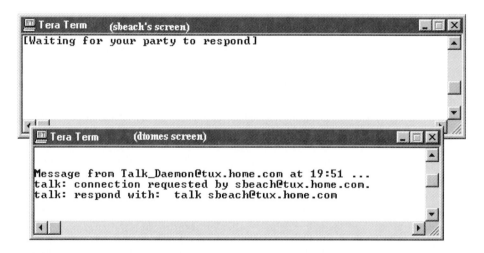

FIGURE 2.7

Messages shown when user asks to initiate a `talk` session.

Figure 2.8 shows a sample of sbeach's screen after she types a message to dtomes and he replies. When using `talk`, your words always appear in the top half of the screen, and the words of the person you're talking with appear in the lower half of the screen. (Notice that you can `talk` to a user on a different machine if you append the "at" sign (@) and the machine name to the user name. If you are trying to `talk` to a user on your own machine, you need only use the login ID of the person. In this case, all dtomes would need to do is type `talk sbeach`.)

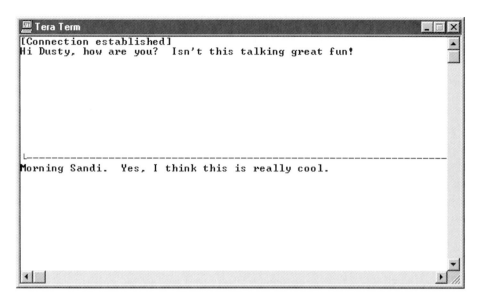

FIGURE 2.8

Two users during a talk session.

There are only a few of drawbacks to using the talk command:

1. Both users have to be logged on the system.
2. Both users have to be using a terminal type that Unix can control—normally a VT-100 type terminal.
3. Neither user should be involved in something that precludes giving control of the screen to the talk command.

We can use the who command to determine whether the user with whom we wish to talk is logged on. In almost all cases, on a modern Unix system, we can assume that users are using a VT-100, or other compatible type of terminal, so that's usually not a problem. We can use the w command to find out what the users are doing so that we won't interrupt them with the talk command when they're trying to do something of a serious nature.

The talk command is a valuable tool, allowing you to ask questions of other users and communicate with them in general, which facilitates the sharing of information, always a good thing. But certain rules of etiquette should be observed:

1. Remember that the person with whom you are talking sees each character as you type it. That means that good spelling and good grammar are important. However, avoid the neophyte's error of backspacing across most of a line to correct an obvious typing mistake early in the line. That could drive your reader crazy, especially on a somewhat slow system. If you spell *and* as *adn* or *the* as *teh*, don't worry about it; your reader can probably figure it out.

2. Generally it's best to take turns when "talking" to another user, much as you do in everyday speech. Since you don't have body language to tell when it's your turn,

you can use the standard convention of touching the ENTER key *twice* to indicate "I'm done, your turn," kind of like the old radio operators' use of "Over." This simple convention will save you lots of time answering questions that weren't asked or providing information that wasn't requested.

3. When you're finished talking, tell your talk partner that you're finished. Don't just end the talk, leaving the other person hanging. In other words, follow the example of the "Over and out" message in radio communications.

After politely telling your talk partner that you need to get back to work, you can end the talk session by pressing the Ctrl (Control) key and the c key at the same time. These two keys together (^C) are sometimes called the interrupt key, because they interrupt the current process, causing it to terminate and exit. Even though two keys are actually pressed, we will refer to the combination of them as the Ctrl-c key, or the interrupt key, for convenience sake. Usually, you can stop any process and return to the command-line prompt by pressing these keys.

finger

finger [options] [users]

In addition to knowing the login IDs of the users on the system and what they're doing, there's one other piece of information that is helpful for conversing with other users. When initiating a talk session, it would be very nice to be able to call our partner by his real name. We can use the **finger** command to find out some information about a particular user, a collection of users, or everyone on the system. The example of the talk command shown in Figure 2.8 shows dtomes talking to sbeach. It would seem that sbeach must have used the command finger dtomes to find out dtomes real name. (Actually, she may well have been in his class and known it from there as well, but we can pretend she used the finger command as shown in Figure 2.9.)

The default finger command tells us a lot of things. It tells us login name, real name, home directory, default shell, when the user logged on and from where, how long

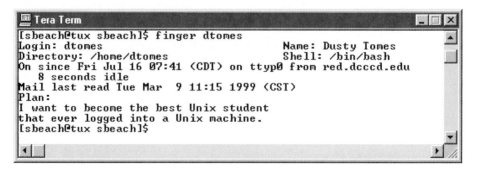

FIGURE 2.9

Output of the finger command.

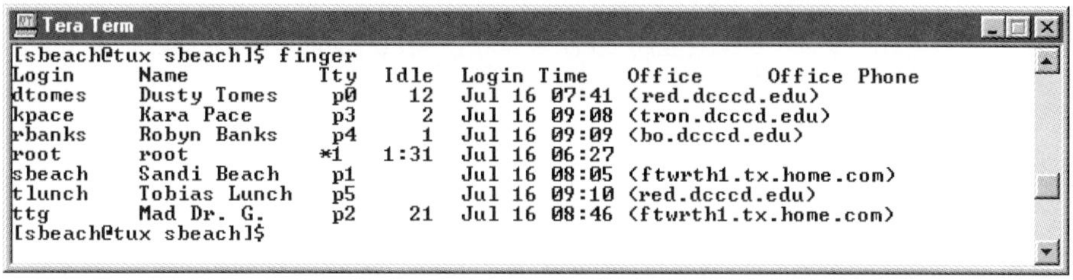

```
Tera Term                                                          _ □ ×
[sbeach@tux sbeach]$ finger
Login      Name          Tty  Idle  Login Time    Office      Office Phone
dtomes     Dusty Tomes   p0     12  Jul 16 07:41  <red.dcccd.edu>
kpace      Kara Pace     p3      2  Jul 16 09:08  <tron.dcccd.edu>
rbanks     Robyn Banks   p4      1  Jul 16 09:09  <bo.dcccd.edu>
root       root          *1   1:31  Jul 16 06:27
sbeach     Sandi Beach   p1         Jul 16 08:05  <ftwrth1.tx.home.com>
tlunch     Tobias Lunch  p5         Jul 16 09:10  <red.dcccd.edu>
ttg        Mad Dr. G.    p2     21  Jul 16 08:46  <ftwrth1.tx.home.com>
[sbeach@tux sbeach]$
```

FIGURE 2.10

Output of finger with no argument.

she's been idle, when she last read her mail, and even her plan. For our purposes right now, the significant data are the user's real name and how long she's been idle. Using the default form of the finger command and supplying a login ID is one of the more common practices. Another way to use the finger command is to type the finger command with no argument. Figure 2.10 shows what happens when sbeach does this. As you can see, finger tells sbeach about everyone who is logged onto the system, where they logged in from, and how long they've been idle.

It's even possible to run the finger command across the network. If the target system allows it, a user could type

    finger @tux.somewhere.com

That command would list all of the users currently logged on to the system of tux.somewhere.com. If the curious user knows the login ID of the person he wishes to finger on the remote system—for example, rbanks—he could type.

    finger rbanks@tux.somewhere.com

In this case, the finger command would return information about rbanks on the tux system.

Please be advised, however, that the remote finger command is seen as a security concern by many system administrators. Therefore, on many systems remote finger is disabled. If the target system does not allow remote finger, you will get a message indicating that the connection was refused.

A number of options are available for the finger command, but it is usually used in the plain vanilla form, so we will leave the exploration of the options up to you.

write

    write user [tty]

Sometimes, we may not want to engage in dialogue with another user, but simply send that user a short message. In this case, the **write** command is the tool of choice. This command has no options and normally only takes the user's login ID as an argument.

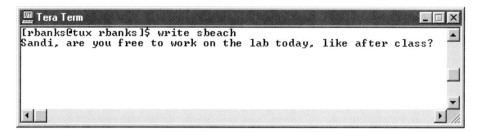

FIGURE 2.11

Output of the `write` command.

Figure 2.11 shows rbanks writing to sbeach. Notice that all rbanks needs to do is type the `write` command and the login ID of the user to whom she wishes to send a message. The system then drops to the next line, allowing her to type her message. When she finishes typing her message, rbanks touches ENTER to go to the next line and then presses **Ctrl-D**, which is the combination of the Ctrl key plus the D key to produce the **EOF (end-of-file)** message that tells the `write` command that she has no more input.

You will see this pattern repeated over and over again. Most times, when you need to indicate to a Unix command that you have finished supplying input, you use **Ctrl-D** to indicate EOF. In this case, the file you are ending is standard input. This is one of the standards across the flavors of Unix: Ctrl-D is the EOF mark.

The message that appears on sbeach's screen is shown in Figure 2.12. Sbeach sees who sent the message, the terminal from which it was sent, and at what time it was sent. All of these data are important if sbeach wants to reply to rbanks. The terminal number is important only if the user is logged in more than once. In that case you should specify the terminal ID along with the user's name.

It is possible to create a dialogue using the `write` command. Two users could take turns, much as you learned to do with the `talk` command. Since there's no onscreen formatting, using the `write` command to create a dialogue is less convenient than using `talk`. However, if one or both of the users are at terminals that do not support full-screen addressability, the `talk` command is not an option, whereas the `write` command will still work.

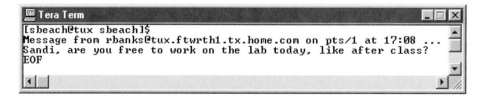

FIGURE 2.12

Receipt of a message from `write`.

wall

```
wall
```

The **wall** command is a particular form of the write command that stands for "write to all" and has the effect of broadcasting the message to every user currently logged onto the system. Because this command is easily abused, some instructors—and even more system administrators—cringe at the thought of teaching garden-variety users this command. I have faith that you will not abuse the wall command. Normally it should be reserved for a situation that affects all of the users. Issuing spurious wall commands will irritate your fellow users.

This command takes no options and reads its input from standard input. As with the write command, you will use an EOF to end the message. (EOF? Oh yes, that was the Ctrl-D key, wasn't it?) Use wall judiciously.

mesg

```
mesg [y/n]
```

Sometimes you will not wish to be interrupted by people talking or writing to you—for example, while you are deeply engrossed in solving a problem. You can disable your process's ability to receive messages from other users by setting the **mesg** command argument to n, "no." Since the y or n is an argument, you won't *prepend* (add in front) a hyphen to the command. If you enter the command mesg n, you will prevent other users writing or talking to you. To keep things fair, you can neither talk nor write to others while you have forbidden others from talking or writing to you. This prevents the mischievous user from turning off his ability to receive messages while he writes messages to another user.

When you want to receive messages again, enter the command mesg y, which means, "Yes, I will receive messages." When you can receive messages, you'll be able to write and talk to other users again.

It's considered poor form to turn off messages unless you are *really* busy. Since the Unix community is based on sharing, turning off your ability to answer questions and help other users is not the way we usually behave.

You may wonder whether setting mesg n will stop *all* messages from reaching your terminal. Nope, it won't. There is one user who can always send you messages. That user is, of course, root. If you think about it, you wouldn't want to stop root from sending you messages. There are times when root *must* get a message to you. If you missed a message like "System shutting down. You have 10 seconds. Save your files" or "Print queues have been disabled. DO NOT PRINT!" it could be a Bad Thing. Therefore, the system administrator, or root, can send you messages whether or not you elect to receive messages from other users.

Wouldn't it be nice to know which users have messages enabled and which are the unsociable creeps—err, really busy people—who don't want to talk? Well, like almost

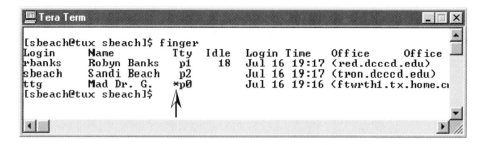

FIGURE 2.13

Output of `finger`, showing which users can receive messages.

anything else in Unix, where there is a need, there is a way. Figure 2.13 shows another example of the output of the `finger` command. Notice the asterisk (*) in front of the designation of the *tty (terminal ID)* associated with ttg. That asterisk shows you that ttg has turned messages off and so cannot receive them. He has also prevented anyone from talking to him. Only root, or the operator, can send him messages. He must be very busy working on an important task, like writing a book or something!

mail

---

mail [options] [user(s)]

Up until now we have learned ways to communicate with users who are currently logged into the system. Sometimes it's handy to be able to leave a message for someone to retrieve later. Electronic mail (email) provides that ability. This is our third communications tool.

Several different email tools are available to the Unix user. In proper Unix parlance, each of the mail tools is most correctly called a *Mail User Agent*. The original mail program is called **mail**. According to the man page, "Mail is an intelligent mail-processing system, which has a command system reminiscent of ed." Now, that doesn't help a lot, since you don't know ed (nice guy, ed, you'll meet him later). Even though you don't know ed, let's look at `mail` briefly.

As the first electronic mail tool, the mail command follows the early Unix pattern of using short commands. Looking in your reference book, you can see that there are a number of options for this command. Some Unix users really like using the `mail` tool, while others prefer more intuitive mail user agents. Figure 2.14 shows dtomes logging on. Notice that during the login process, the system tells him he has new mail.

In Figure 2.15 we see that Dusty (dtomes), being a conscientious member of the Unix community, has started the mail tool by simply typing `mail` at the command line and then touching ENTER. Mail tells Dusty that he has two messages. If he wants to read the first message, all he needs to do is touch the ENTER key. In Figure 2.16 we see that he has chosen to read the second message first. He indicates that by simply typing a 2 and then touching ENTER. By the way, the & (ampersand) is the default mail prompt.

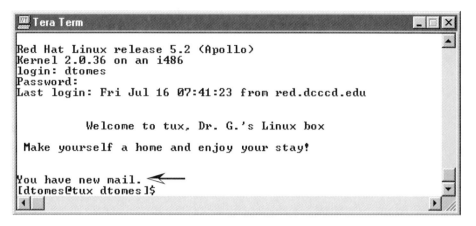

FIGURE 2.14

Login showing new mail message.

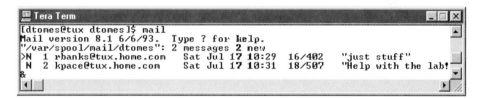

FIGURE 2.15

Starting a mail session.

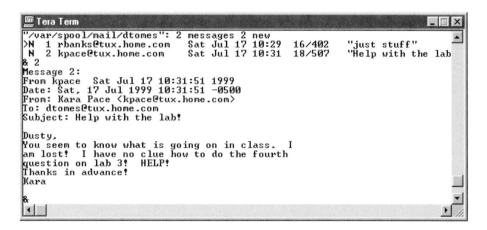

FIGURE 2.16

Reading a mail message.

The mail package tells Dusty who sent him the message, when that person sent it, and the subject of the message. (Every message should have an appropriate subject so the sender knows what the message is about.) The (-0600) after the time is the difference between the time the message was sent and Greenwich Mean Time. In this case, Dusty is in the Central Daylight time zone, which is six hours later than the time in Greenwich, England. Finally, mail also shows Dusty the message from someone by the name of kpace (Kara).

Figure 2.17 shows Dusty replying to Kara's message. To reply to the current message, you simply type an R (for reply) at the command prompt. Dusty does this, and mail fills in both the To: and the Subject: for him. He types his response to Kara and then types a period (.) on a line by itself to tell mail that he has finished his input. (Using a period on a line by itself to indicate end of input is one of those ed things you will learn later.) Finally, mail asks Dusty if he wants to send a carbon copy (Cc:) to anyone. He just touches the ENTER key to say "No, thank you," and mail prompts him for his next instruction.

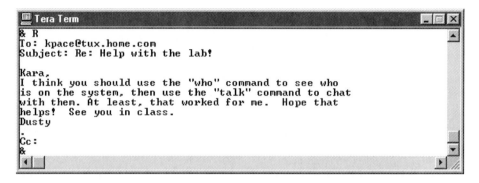

FIGURE 2.17

Replying to a mail message.

The last thing Dusty needs to do is remove the message from his mailbox. It's always a good idea to clean up old mail messages. If you don't, they can quickly consume lots of disk space, and that doesn't make system administrators happy. When you finish with a mail message, either file it for later reference, if it's really important, or delete it to save disk space. To delete the current email message, simply type a d at the mail command prompt. The message will be removed from your in-box.

Quite a few options and arguments are available for the mail utility. We have examined only a few of them—enough to give you minimal functionality. If you have no other option for sending email, you can use the mail utility, which will become easier to use the more you try it. However, mail, while powerful, is a bit awkward for the novice to use, and even for some not-so-novice users. Next we will discuss a much more intuitive email program.

Table 2.1 shows the commonly used commands for the mail program. In each case, the annotation message(s) refers to the message number. If you omit the message number, the command will apply to the current message. For example, if you want to respond

TABLE 2.1 Common Mail Utility Commands

If you want to do this:	Use this command:
Invoke a Unix shell command	**! command.**
Delete the current or specific message	**d [message(s)]**
Undelete current or specific message	**u [message(s)]**
Save current or specific message.	**s [message(s)]**
Reply to sender of current or specific message	**r [message(s)]**
Reply to sender *and all recipients* of current or specific message	**R [message(s)]**
Read the current message	**<return>**
Read a message other than the current one	**p [message(s)]**
See the top (default five lines) of a message	**top [message(s)]**
Show the next (or previous) page of message headers	**z [-]**
Edit the current or specific message with the vi editor	**v [message(s)]**
Look at the next message in the mailbox	**n**
Save the current or specific message	**S [message] filename**

to the message you are currently reading, you should use the r command. If you want to respond to message number 23, you should enter the command r23.

pine

```
pine [options] [user(s)]
```

As we mentioned before, a number of mail utilities, or mail user agents, have evolved over time. Dave Taylor wrote a somewhat user-friendly system he called **elm**. Elm stands for Electronic Mail. There are many **elm** fanciers in the Unix community, but **elm** is not for everyone. You may have **elm** on your system; if so, feel free to experiment with it.

Long long ago (actually 1989), on a campus far, far away (specifically, the University of Washington in Seattle), a group of people came together to build a better electronic messaging tool. They designed a tool that would handle electronic mail and also usenet news. They called their tool **pine**, which stands for Program for Internet News & Email. Now, some people say that **pine** stands for Pine Is Not Elm, but your humble author couldn't find any conclusive documentation to support that. Although it is true that the developers started with **elm**, as that source code was freely distributed, no trace of **elm** code remains in the current versions of **pine**. After all, **pine** is not **elm**.

Pine is a very powerful tool, but for purposes of this text we will examine only those features necessary to send and receive email. A very substantial Help facility is built into pine, and you may find out more hints about its use at the pine project's Web site at http://www.washington.edu/pine/.

Even though the pine mail tool is not part of the standard Unix distribution, many system administrators put it on their systems to make life easier for the users. If you don't have pine installed, skip this discussion; it won't be of use to you.

To invoke the pine mail utility, simply enter the command pine on the command line, and touch ENTER. The very first time you start pine, it will create a set of directories in which it will keep its messages and do some other initialization. Be patient; it may take a few seconds.

What happens next depends on the version of pine installed on the system you are using. Some versions of pine ask if you want to have the manual downloaded to your directory. Since the manual is rather large, it's probably not a good idea to have it downloaded. Besides, the internal Help is really quite good. So if pine asks you if you want the manual, please say no. Newer versions of pine ask you to touch the RETURN key to send a message back to the pine group, so they can count how many people are using this mail agent. I would encourage you to send this message to help and support the pine development team.

Figure 2.18 shows the main menu screen Kara sees when she starts pine. The first thing pine shows us is the main menu. The most important thing to remember about pine is that *you need to read the screen*—especially the last two lines on the screen. They will give you hints to the commands you need to perform the different tasks to handle your email.

When Kara starts pine, it tells her that she has a new message in her inbox. To access her inbox Kara could touch the L key to list the folders she has available and then select I to open her in-box. Figure 2.19 shows the screen Kara sees after she touches the L key.

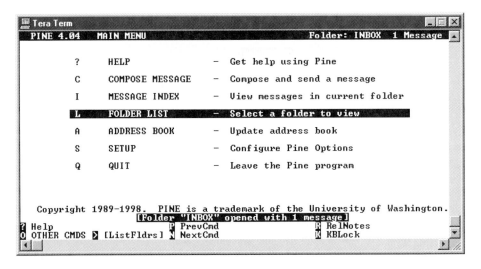

FIGURE 2.18

Main menu page for pine.

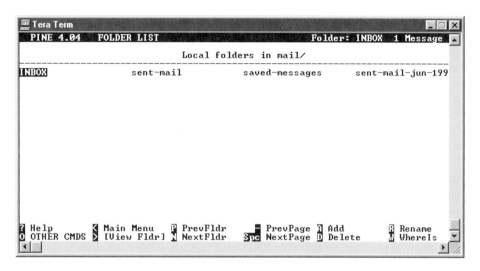

FIGURE 2.19

Folder List page for pine.

On the Folder List screen Kara sees the folders she currently has available. Pine built these folders for her. She can add or delete folders to better compartmentalize her mail. Right now, however, she's interested in seeing the new message in her inbox. To open her inbox, she touches the I key. Figure 2.20 shows Kara's inbox. Again, note the commands along the bottom of the screen; some of them are new. It's important to always read the bottom of the screen in pine. Most of the time the commands you need will be displayed there. As you learn pine, you will learn about shortcuts. For example,

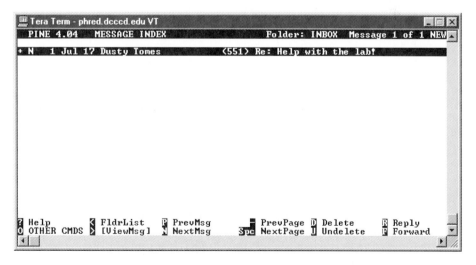

FIGURE 2.20

Contents of inbox.

Kara could simply have touched the I key on the main menu, since Folder List is automatically selected by pine when the main menu is opened for the first time.

In this example Kara has only one message. Obviously, this is a contrived example because nobody has just *one* email message. Since this message is highlighted, Kara can simply touch the ENTER key to read it. If there were several messages here, she could touch ENTER to read the first message, or use the arrow keys on her keyboard to move the highlighted line to the message she wants to read first, and then touch ENTER. Once again, notice the commands along the bottom of the screen, they list the things the user would most likely want to do. (Okay, I am repeating myself, again, but this is one of the things students have the most trouble with. They get confused about which command to use, or what commands are available. While the ? is always there to give help, just reading the bottom of the screen usually answers the student's questions. Tell you what, I won't mention it again if you promise to remember it. Deal? Great!)

Figure 2.21 shows the email message that Kara is reading. As with the mail command, pine tells us when the message was written, who wrote it, and the subject of the message. If the message is longer than a single page, touching the space bar will display the next page of the message. Touching the D key will mark the message for deletion, touching the R key will initiate a reply, and touching the F key will forward the message.

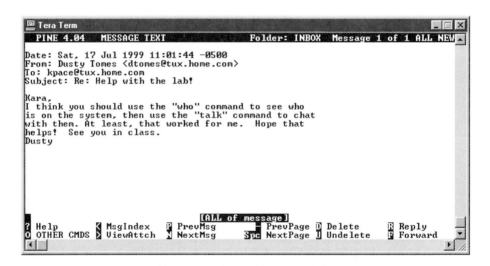

FIGURE 2.21

Reading a mail message in pine.

Figure 2.22 shows the next screen Kara sees after having touched the R key to send a reply to Dusty. Notice the highlighted line at the bottom of the screen. The first question pine asks when generating a reply is if it should include the original message in the reply. Whether or not to include all or part of the original message is a very important consideration. Generally it is best to include at least part of a long message or all

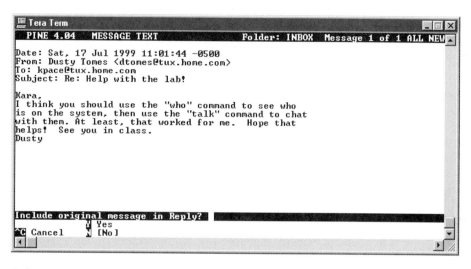

FIGURE 2.22

The first part of the Reply process.

of a short message so the recipient knows what you're talking about. For example, if Dusty got dozens of email messages every day, and Kara replied, "What do you mean talk?" Dusty might be confused. However, if Kara includes Dusty's message in her reply, he will know what she is talking about.

Figure 2.23 shows that Kara chose to include Dusty's message in her reply. When Kara finishes typing her response to Dusty, using the *pico editor* (discussed shortly), she looks at the bottom of the screen (smart student!) and sees that Ctrl-x (^X stands for

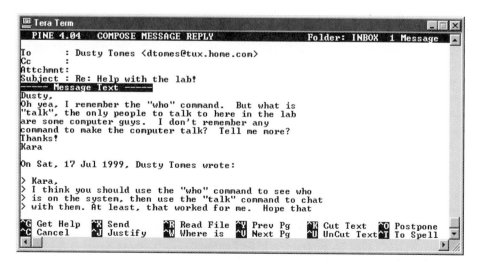

FIGURE 2.23

Generating a reply, including the previous message.

Ctrl-x) will send her message. **Ctrl-x** is the combination for the send command. After she touches Ctrl-x, pine will confirm that she wishes to send a message.

Notice that each line of the included message has a > prepended to it. In addition, pine generated the line that indicated when the included message was written and by whom.

It's always wise to review your message and verify that you do indeed wish to send it to the person listed in the To: field. Remember that once you tell pine to send the message, it's gone, and you can't take it back. There are few feelings worse than sending an email and realizing just after you touch the Y key that you really didn't want that email sent to that person. Pine gives you one last chance to think about it before the message is sent.

After Kara confirms that she does indeed want to send this message to Dusty, pine gives her a status message as the email is sent. Then it returns her to the message she had been reading.

After sending her message to Dusty, Kara decides to delete Dusty's message to her. She touches the D key to mark the message for deletion. Note: At this point the message is still in the inbox, and it will not be deleted until Kara exits from pine. Figure 2.24 shows the screen Kara sees when she presses Q to quit the pine mail utility. It first asks her to confirm that she wishes to quit. Next, pine asks if she wants the message she had marked for deletion to be **expunged** from her in-box. Now that is a great word! According to *The Illustrated Oxford Dictionary*, 1998, to expunge is to erase or remove (especially a passage from a book or a name from a list). An ideal word for what pine is doing. This is another example of the wonderful character of the Unix community. The folks up at the University of Washington could have used a boring word like delete or remove, but no, they chose a truly wonderful word, expunge, instead.

Pine is very conservative, so it asks the user to confirm any irrevocable action before it performs the action. If Kara touches the N key, pine will not remove the message

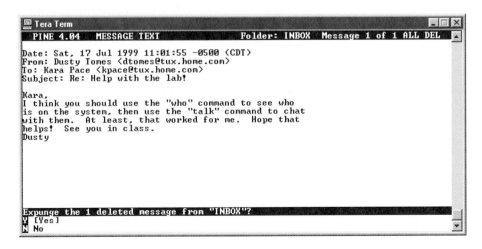

FIGURE 2.24

Leaving pine after pressing Q and confirming quitting.

marked for deletion from her in-box. The message will remain there, marked for deletion, but will not be removed until she confirms that it should be expunged.

As you can see from the preceding figures, pine is a very easy-to-use email program. It is also very powerful. You should spend some time exploring the many features of pine. For example, one of the great time-saving features of pine is its address book. Plan to check out that particular feature soon. In addition, if you investigate usenet, you can use pine to read those messages as well. Have fun exploring pine!

pico

---

    pico [options] [file]

When you use the pine mail user agent, you are also using an editor developed especially for pine, **pico**. Pico stands for ***Pi***ne ***Co***mposition. When you edit email messages in pine, you're using pico. This editor is a very simple, easy-to-use tool, one that novice Unix users find useful. We will learn about more sophisticated editors in a few chapters, but if you need some editing done right now, you can use pico. According to the pico documentation:

> Pico is a simple, display-oriented text editor based on the Pine message system composer. As with Pine, commands are displayed at the bottom of the screen, and context-sensitive help is provided. As characters are typed they are immediately inserted in the text.

To differentiate between regular text and instructions, pico uses Ctrl key combinations for commands.

In Figure 2.25 we see the screen that the user sees when starting pico with an existing file. Here ttg is starting the pico editor and editing a file called story0. This is by far the most common way of starting the editor, however, a number of options are available that will cause pico to act differently. For example, if ttg had given pico the options of -r40 -n90, the editor would have used 40 as its right margin and would check for mail every 90 seconds. To learn all about the command-line options for the pico editor on your system, use the man command.

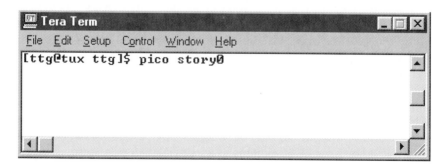

FIGURE 2.25
Starting the pico editor using an existing file.

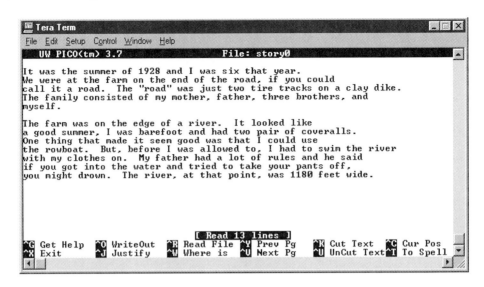

FIGURE 2.26

The pico editor screen display.

The pico screen display, shown in Figure 2.26, has a very specific format. The first line is always shown in **reverse video**—white letters on a black background—and gives the version of pico (in this example 3.7) and the name of the file being edited (story0). The second line of the display is never used. On lines 3 through 21, pico displays, and you edit, the text of the file. Line 22 is used to display information or to prompt for instructions; these messages and prompts are always in reverse video. In the figure, pico told us that it read 13 lines from the file. The last two lines of the screen, lines 23 and 24, display many of the pico commands. (Since pico is the pine editor, it isn't too suprising that the screen looks like the message-composition screen in pine, is it?)

The text entry always happens at the current cursor position. What is typed on the keyboard appears in the text window. You can move the cursor around the file using the arrow keys on your keypad, or you can use the control characters shown in Table 2.2 to move the cursor. If you wish only to move a few characters in any direction, the arrow keys will probably suffice. However, if you are performing significant edits to a file, the arrow keys quickly become cumbersome.

Probably the most important command we can discuss is the Ctrl + x (^X) or exit, command mentioned earlier. This command actually serves two functions. If you have modified the file you're editing, pico will ask if you want to save the file before you exit. If you press Y, pico will save your changes or updates to the disk file and then exit. If you haven't modified the file you're looking at, the **^X** command will terminate pico and send you back to the command line. A number of additional commands that you may find useful are listed in Table 2.3.

TABLE 2.2 Cursor Movement Commands for `pico`

Command	Associated Cursor Movement
Ctrl + **B** (^B)	Moves the cursor *back* one character (left)
Ctrl + **F** (^F)	Moves the cursor *forward* one character (right)
Ctrl + **P** (^P)	Moves the cursor to the *previous* line (up)
Ctrl + **N** (^N)	Moves the cursor to the *next* line (down)
Ctrl + **V** (^V)	Moves the cursor to the *next screen* (varoom)
Ctrl + **Y** (^Y)	Moves the cursor *back one sc*reen

TABLE 2.3 Some Common `pico` Commands

Command	What the Command Does
Ctrl + **C** (^C)	Shows the current position of the cursor on line 22
Ctrl + **D** (^D)	Deletes one character to the left of the cursor
Ctrl + **E** (^E)	Moves the cursor to the end of the current line
Ctrl + **I** (^I)	Insert a tab character
Ctrl + **J** (^J)	Justify the paragraph, (set off by blank lines)
Ctrl + **K** (^K)	Delete the entire line that contains the cursor
Ctrl + **L** (^L)	Redraw the screen, to eliminate system or other messages
Ctrl + **M** (^M)	Insert a carriage return, (new line)
Ctrl + **O** (^O)	Save the current file, or save the file under a different name
Ctrl + **T** (^T)	Start the spell checker
Ctrl + **U** (^U)	Undo (uncut), the most recently deleted line
Ctrl + **W** (^W)	Search the text for a specified character string

Using the cursor-movement commands that are shown in Table 2.2, the editing commands from Table 2.3, and just a little practice, you should be able to perform simple edits in your files. In subsequent chapters you will learn how to use much more powerful and versatile editors, but for now `pico` is a great tool. Have fun with it!

Date

```
date [options] [+format]
date [options] string (privileged users only)
```

Several tools in Unix give you information either about the system or about what the system knows. One of these tools is the **date** utility. This is a very powerful and flexible tool. Its simplest form just reports the system date and time. Figure 2.27 shows that output. In this default mode date tells us the day of the week, the month, the day of the month, and time to the second. In addition, it shows us the time zone and the year. Remember, these data are for the *host system*, so if you're connected to a machine in California while sitting at a terminal in Maine, the time you see on your screen will be California time. That's why the date command includes the time zone in its output.

Much of the time the standard output from date is all we need. However, date includes a very rich set of formatting options. In your reference book you can see that most of the date formatting options begin with the percent sign (%) and are only two characters long. Unlike the other commands we have seen, the formatting options for the date command have a plus sign (+) prepended to them rather than a hyphen. Figure 2.28 shows

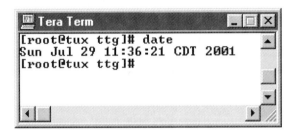

FIGURE 2.27

Output of the date command.

FIGURE 2.28

Examples of fancy formatted output of date.

three examples of different formatting using the date command. Notice that the formatting string is enclosed in quotation marks (" ") and that it is possible to embed nonformatting characters within the formatting string.

Each format in Figure 2.28 has some additional text characters embedded in it. In the first example I simply inserted a comma after the day of the week. The second example includes the words "It is now" and "on" within the data provided by date. The third example includes some additional line-formatting commands, specifically tab (%t) and the newline character (%n). Actually, I added a newline character to the end of each example to separate the example from the command prompt following it.

Later, as you begin developing **shell scripts**, which are collections of shell commands that can be run like programs, you'll find the date command is very useful. Using it will allow you to write time-sensitive scripts. For example, you could write a script that would greet the user differently depending on the time of day. This can cause some slight confusion, however, with users located across the globe, because date reports only the time at the server. That would mean a user in Greenwich, England, running a Unix machine like tux in Texas could have a local time, or **wall time**, of three o'clock in the afternoon and yet get a "Good Morning" message from tux because it's still morning where tux lives.

As you progress in your Unix wizardhood, you'll find that the date command is a very useful tool. It is also possible to use date to *set* the system date and time. However, you need to be the system administrator to do that, so we won't discuss it any further here.

cal

```
cal [options] [[month] year]
```

Another interesting, time-related, tool is the calendar function, **cal**. In its default mode the cal utility prints out a calendar of the current month. An example of the default output of cal is shown in Figure 2.29.

FIGURE 2.29

Output of the plain vanilla cal command.

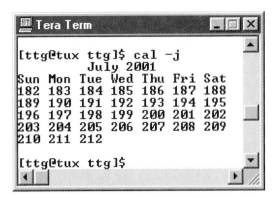

FIGURE 2.30

Output showing Julian form (-j) of the cal command.

There are two options to the cal command. The first, -j, presents the days of the month in what Unix calls the *Julian format*. Actually, this isn't a true Julian format. Julian dates are counted consecutively from noon, January 1, 4713 BC. Joseph Justus Scaliger (1540–1609), an Italian-French philologist and historian, invented the system in 1582, possibly naming it after his father, Julius Caesar Scaliger. The reason 4713 BC is important is because it is a time when the three major dating systems of his time all coincided. (Those three systems were the solar, or 28-year, system, the Metonic system, and the Roman system, as decreed by Emperor Constantine.) Julian dates are still used by astronomers because they make calculating the time between any two events easy; you simply subtract one Julian date from another.

Since Unix provides a count of the number of days since January 1st of the current year, it is not a true Julian date. However, it is very handy to calculate the number of days until or since a particular date in the current year. Figure 2.30 shows the output of the cal command with the -j option.

The second option, -y, presents the calendar for the year, not just for the current month. Figure 2.31 shows the output from the cal -y command. This screen capture shows only the calendar for the year 2001. I did have to stretch the screen display of the Tera Term screen to fit it all in.

There are also two different command-line arguments you can specify with the cal command. You can enter a month, by number, and cal will show you a calendar for that month of the current year. You can specify a year, by number, and cal will show you a calendar for that year. You can combine those two options and specify a month and year, and cal will show you a calendar for that month from that year. This can be useful, for example, if you want to determine the day of the week you were born. All you need to do is ask cal for a calendar of the month and year of your birth, and you can see which day of the week you were born.

It is important to remember that cal will create a calendar for any year from year 1 through year 9999. It's easy to get an incorrect calendar by trying to shorten the year to two digits (a.k.a. the Y2K bug!). Figure 2.32 shows how ttg asked cal for the calendar for

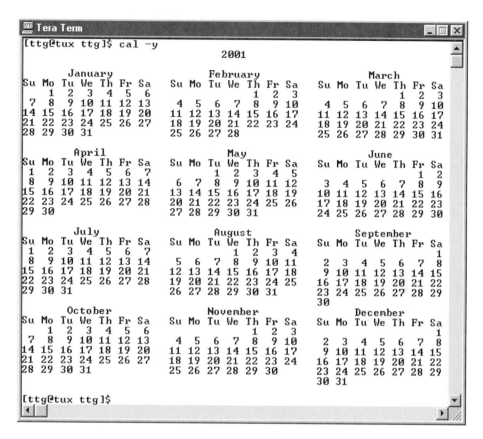

FIGURE 2.31

Output of cal with –y option.

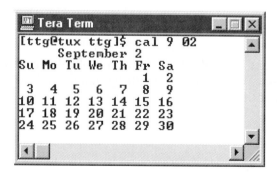

FIGURE 2.32

Output of cal with both month and year specified.

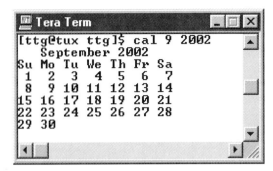

FIGURE 2.33
Correct output of `cal`.

September of 2002 but got the calendar for September of the year 2! Figure 2.33 shows the actual calendar ttg was looking for, with the correct options. You won't use `cal` all that often, but it is handy to have this kind of utility available when you need it.

We will see this time and time again as we study Unix: you will learn commands that won't be used every day but that are extremely useful when you need them. Unix users who had a need for a particular feature developed tools like `cal`. They built the tool they needed and then gave that tool to the Unix community. Therefore, that tool is available when you need it.

stty

```
stty [options] [modes] < device
```

The last command we will address in this chapter is **stty**, an extremely powerful and potentially dangerous utility that is used to set the input and output options for your terminal. The majority of the options and modes for `stty` are set when you log in. Beware: playing with the different modes and values in `stty` is a very good way to render your terminal temporarily inoperable. That's why it's a potentially dangerous command. If you step on, or damage, your `stty` file, you can cause your terminal to render its output in very strange characters, or even refuse to talk to you any more. Normally, when you log out and log back in, the system will reset your terminal. If you make a mistake and step on your `stty` file, you can usually recover simply by logging out and back in.

The main use you will have for the `stty` command is to change the way your terminal responds to certain keys. **Key mapping** is the term we use to describe the relationship between a particular key and the function associated with that key. Frequently, your terminal (or the PC you are using) won't have certain keys, such as BACKSPACE, mapped the way Unix expects. You can use `stty` to alter the key mapping for such keys.

Here is an example of flavor differences among the various versions of Unix. In Linux, at least in the 2.0 kernel, you can change the key assigned to erase, but the BACKSPACE key still works! So, for example, on tux you can type

```
stty erase .
```

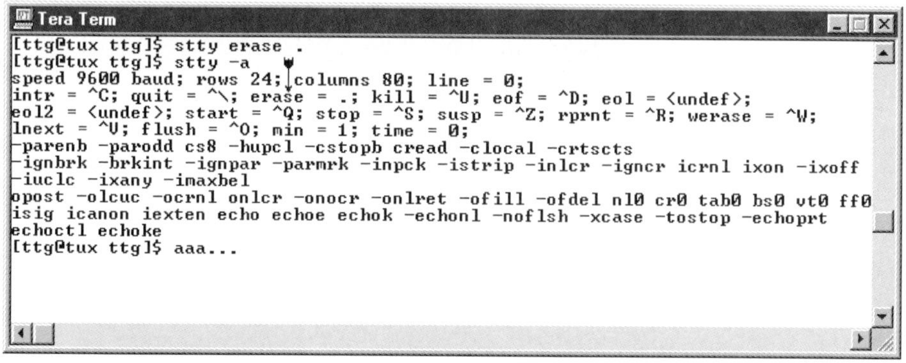

```
Tera Term                                                        _ □ ×
[ttg@tux ttg]$ stty erase .
[ttg@tux ttg]$ stty -a
speed 9600 baud; rows 24; columns 80; line = 0;
intr = ^C; quit = ^\; erase = .; kill = ^U; eof = ^D; eol = <undef>;
eol2 = <undef>; start = ^Q; stop = ^S; susp = ^Z; rprnt = ^R; werase = ^W;
lnext = ^V; flush = ^O; min = 1; time = 0;
-parenb -parodd cs8 -hupcl -cstopb cread -clocal -crtscts
-ignbrk -brkint -ignpar -parmrk -inpck -istrip -inlcr -igncr icrnl ixon -ixoff
-iuclc -ixany -imaxbel
opost -olcuc -ocrnl onlcr -onocr -onlret -ofill -ofdel nl0 cr0 tab0 bs0 vt0 ff0
isig icanon iexten echo echoe echok -echonl -noflsh -xcase -tostop -echoprt
echoctl echoke
[ttg@tux ttg]$ aaa...
```

FIGURE 2.34

A conundrum involving the stty command.

and then look at the key mapping using the -a option on stty, and it will dutifully tell you that the period key (.) has been mapped to erase. However, when you type the period key, you will see a period, not a backspace or an erase. If you perform the same operation on a machine running the Solaris, the period key becomes a backspace key as you expect.

After encountering this seemingly odd behavior, I looked to all the standard places that I could expect to find the answer. The man pages didn't tell me, and none of my reference books told me, so I did what Unix folks do: I asked the Unix community. In less than an hour, Rob Funk from Ohio State University explained it to me. It seems that this is a feature of the shell, not the version of Unix. Some modern shells, (bash and tcsh in this instance), accept either Ctrl-? or Ctrl-H as the backspace key and basically ignore the stty mapping. On the other hand, commands that use the stty values will, indeed, use the key we set. (Thanks, Rob!) This feature is consistent across both RedHat and Mandrake Linux.

Figure 2.34 shows the three steps in the process of setting and testing the erase key. First I set the erase key to period. Then I used stty to display all of the mapped values. Finally I typed three lowercase "a"s and then the period key three times. What I expected was that typing the period key would cause the "a"s to disappear. As you can see from the last line in Figure 2.34, that's not exactly what happened.

The shell (bash in this case, simply considers the period as a period, period. It knows that in the vast majority of cases, the keyboard will send either ^H (Ctrl-H), or ^? (Ctrl-?) as the erase key and so accepts only those values.

Solaris will happily make the period key the erase key, as shown in Figure 2.35. You can't see it from the figure, but I typed my "aaa" test at the command line following the stty. Since you can't see any "a"s there, it proves that the period became the erase character. Well, it may not prove it, I guess; you just have to trust me.

The most common way you will use the stty command is to change the map of the backspace key in your login session to match the character the BACKSPACE key on

FIGURE 2.35

Using the `stty` command on Solaris system.

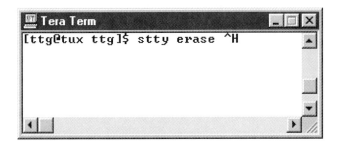

FIGURE 2.36

Using `stty` to map BACKSPACE key to the erase function.

your keyboard sends to the shell. Figure 2.36 shows ttg setting the backspace key to Ctrl-H the coding his computer sends to Unix when he touches the BACKSPACE key. This is a common use for `stty`. You will find that many times when you log into a new computer system, the BACKSPACE key on your keyboard is not mapped correctly to the erase function. The process to set it is a very valuable little nugget of knowledge to tuck away. Later we will learn how to have Unix automatically set features like this when you log in, or when a shell starts.

That's enough for this chapter. It's time for you to have a chance to play with Unix for a while.

KEY TERMS

argument
Ctrl-c
Ctrl-d
data stream
EOF (end-of-file)
expunged
interrupt key
key mapping
order of precedence
process

reverse video
shell script
standard error
standard input
standard output
wall time

NEW COMMANDS

```
cal
date
finger
man
mail
mesg
pine
stty
talk
w
wall
who
write
```

REVIEW QUESTIONS

2.1 Define each of the key terms listed for this chapter.

2.2 List three ways to send a message to one of your fellow students while he or she is logged into the same computer you are logged into.

2.3 Describe a situation where you would use the `write` command to chat with a fellow user rather than the `talk` command.

2.4 How would you use the `cal` command to find out the day of the week for your birthday in the year 2025?

2.5 Look in your reference book. Which directives would cause the date command to display the day of the week for today—just the day of the week?

2.6 Explain three different ways to determine who is on the system right now.

2.7 Describe the difference between the output of `who` and `w`.

2.8 How can you prevent other users from writing messages to you, and from interrupting you with requests to talk?

2.9 Would it be good if you could prevent root from sending you messages?

2.10 Can you prevent root from sending you messages?

EXERCISES

2.1 Send a message to one of your peers who is currently logged into the system.

2.2 Find out the real-life name of a user on the system other than yourself!

2.3 Engage in a dialog with another user on the system. (It would be best if you already knew who that user was!)

2.4 Set your session so that no users can send you messages or talk with you. (Verify that you have set this correctly by asking another user to send you a message or try to talk with you.) Once you have verified your success, allow others access to you again.

2.5 Determine the day of the week on which you were born.

2.6 Use the man command to determine the date-formatting options for the next question.

2.7 Have the date command display the current day of the week, the month, and the year in a four-digit format.

2.8 Explore the parameters of your terminal session. What is your baud rate? What key combination erases text?

2.9 Send yourself an email message using the mail process. Read the email message you sent to yourself, and reply. (Yes, this can become an endless cycle; you can stop after reading the reply unless you really get into mail.)

2.10 See if the pine mail utility is installed on your system. If it is, perform the same tasks that you did in Exercise 2.9 but using pine.

2.11 Use stty to set your BACKSPACE key correctly. If it is already set correctly, thank your system administrator, set it incorrectly, and then set it back.

3

File Handling in Unix

CHAPTER OBJECTIVES

After reading this chapter, you should be able to:

- Describe the meaning of the term *file* in the Unix parlance.
- Display your current working directory.
- Effectively use the common file handling commands: `mkdir`, `cd`, `cp`, `mv`, `more`, `less`, `rm`, and `rmdir`.
- Create well formed Unix filenames.
- Dissect the permissions mask for a file or directory.
- Explain the structure of `/etc/passwd`.

All operating systems use files. Files are where data are kept, and the programs themselves are usually files, so all in all, dealing with files is one of the most significant tasks for the OS.

⊕ What Is a file?

When Ken Thompson designed the file system for Unix he made a brilliant decision that has simplified life for everyone who followed in his footsteps. He designed the whole file system and the I/O system around the concept that the best interface was a stream of simple ASCII characters. What that means to us is that a file is nothing more than a **stream of bytes**. So from now on, when you see the word *file*, you think "stream-o-bytes." (But you knew that, didn't you, because you have Refrigerator Rule No. 1

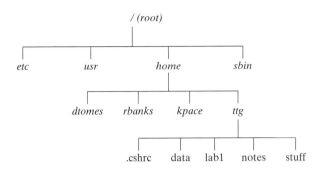

FIGURE 3.1

Sample directory structure, showing the inverted tree.

posted on your refrigerator!) Since an ASCII character stream is the standard interface, the keyboard produces a simple stream-o-bytes, and the monitor sees a nice, clean
stream-o-bytes. That means that it would be very easy to replace the keyboard with a
file, or send the output to a file rather than to the screen. Using a stream-o-bytes as the
standard interface makes our job much easier.

Okay, it's your turn now. What is a file? That's right! It's a stream-o-bytes! You
did say it out loud, didn't you? Don't be shy; go ahead and say aloud, "Stream-o-bytes."
There, that wasn't so bad, was it?

Remember Refrigerator Rule No. 1? Now you can see how important that rule
really is.

Before we look at creating or moving files, we need to talk about the **directory
structure**. Ken Thompson is credited with implementing the inverted **tree structure** in
Unix. It has since become the standard for many operating systems. Figure 3.1 shows a
sample of the inverted tree directory structure. It is called an inverted tree because it
looks as if the branches of the tree are down and the root, or trunk, is uppermost.

Obviously, the figure does not show the full tree. It shows only four of the directories under "home" and only a partial set of files in the user directories. What you can
see from the figure is that if all the files were shown they would indeed create the look
of a tree standing on its head. Hence the term "inverted tree."

pwd

pwd

Probably the first question you might ask is, "Gee, just where am I in this directory
structure?" The **pwd** command stands for *P*rint the path to the current *W*orking
*D*irectory, or "Tell me where I am." There are no options or attributes to this command;
it's used simply to tell you where you are in the directory structure. At times this information is very important. For example, if you have gone to a public directory to read a

file and then attempt to write a new file, you may well get a "Permission denied" error message when you try to save the new file. The first thing you should do when you see this message is use the pwd command to figure out exactly where you are. You might then notice that you are not in a directory you own, and you can remedy the situation straight away. So, pwd is a handy, albeit infrequently used, command.

mkdir

---

    mkdir [options] directory

Now that we can determine where we are in a file structure, let's add some complexity to it. The **mkdir** command allows us to create an additional directory, or even a directory structure. Figure 3.2 shows ttg creating a labs directory with the mkdir command, and then displaying all of the files in his directory. This is the most common use for mkdir—creating a new directory within an existing directory structure. Normally, you will be creating a new directory structure within an existing directory.

   Point of clarification: Some people speak of a directory within a directory as a *subdirectory*. Following this logic, a directory created within a subdirectory would then

```
[ttg@tux ttg]$ ls -l
total 13
drwxr-xr-x   3 ttg      wheel        1024 Mar 27 16:36 area51
-rw-------   1 ttg      wheel         288 Jul 17 08:58 dead.lette
-rw-r--r--   1 ttg      wheel          13 Mar 27 10:07 filea
-rw-r--r--   1 ttg      wheel          13 Mar 27 10:25 fileb
-rw-r--r--   1 ttg      wheel          28 Jul  2 09:44 junk
drwx------   2 ttg      wheel        1024 Mar  1 20:26 mail
-rw-r--r--   1 ttg      wheel         105 Feb 18 20:28 sigfile
drwxr-xr-x   2 ttg      root         1024 Jul 30 10:49 stuff
drwxr-xr-x   2 ttg      wheel        1024 Mar 26 13:58 tech
-rw-r--r--   1 ttg      wheel        3110 Mar 20 13:32 touch.man
-rw-r--r--   1 ttg      wheel           0 Mar 20 13:24 wowsers
[ttg@tux ttg]$ mkdir labs
[ttg@tux ttg]$ ls -l
total 14
drwxr-xr-x   3 ttg      wheel        1024 Mar 27 16:36 area51
-rw-------   1 ttg      wheel         288 Jul 17 08:58 dead.lette
-rw-r--r--   1 ttg      wheel          13 Mar 27 10:07 filea
-rw-r--r--   1 ttg      wheel          13 Mar 27 10:25 fileb
-rw-r--r--   1 ttg      wheel          28 Jul  2 09:44 junk
drwxr-xr-x   2 ttg      wheel        1024 Jul 30 10:51 labs
drwx------   2 ttg      wheel        1024 Mar  1 20:26 mail
-rw-r--r--   1 ttg      wheel         105 Feb 18 20:28 sigfile
drwxr-xr-x   2 ttg      root         1024 Jul 30 10:49 stuff
drwxr-xr-x   2 ttg      wheel        1024 Mar 26 13:58 tech
-rw-r--r--   1 ttg      wheel        3110 Mar 20 13:32 touch.man
-rw-r--r--   1 ttg      wheel           0 Mar 20 13:24 wowsers
[ttg@tux ttg]$
```

FIGURE 3.2

Using mkdir command to create a directory.

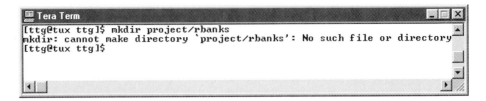

FIGURE 3.3

A failed attempt to create directory structure in one pass.

be a *sub-subdirectory*. I think you can see where this is leading. For this reason, I will speak simply of *directories*, and perhaps directories within directories. After all, Unix looks at all directories the same way. The only special directory we need to consider is the root directory, which is the parent for all other directories within a directory structure.

Suppose, for example, ttg wanted to create a project directory, and within that the directory for rbanks. Figure 3.3 shows his first attempt. As you can see, the error message is a little bit cryptic. What it's actually saying is that since the project directory doesn't exist, mkdir can't create the rbanks directory. To remedy this we use the -p, or path, option to create the intermediate, or parent, directories for the target directory. In this case the project directory is the parent directory to the rbanks directory.

Figure 3.4 shows ttg's second attempt to create the directory structure, this time using the -p option. The ls -R command shows not only the files but also descends down directories to show the files within each directory. This is a useful example of *recursion*. In this example ttg asked ls to list the contents of a specific directory, but when it encountered a directory within that directory it also did an ls of the other directory.

FIGURE 3.4

Successful creation of directory structure with one command.

Should it encounter a further directory in that directory, it will do another ls, and so on. Recursion is a powerful property of Unix.

Don't worry about the ls command right now; you will learn all about it in a bit. Just notice that the rbanks directory is located in the project directory.

Creating directories is an important step in the process of organizing your files. Crafting a workable, manageable directory structure is an essential skill for the wise Unix wizard. Organization will help you work more efficiently and find the things you need more quickly. In general, good organization will make your tasks much easier to perform.

Now that we know how to create directories, let's see how to traverse the directory tree we have created.

cd

```
cd [directory path]
```

In the preceding section we discussed moving about in the directory tree. The **c**hange **d**irectory, **cd**, command allows you to move about in the directory tree. This command has no options, and the normal parameter is the path to the directory to which you wish to go. The term *path* may be confusing. The **path** is the actual route that the computer needs to take to arrive at the directory you have specified, or the route the computer needs to take to find the file you are looking for.

There are two different ways to specify a target directory for this command. Figure 3.5 shows a little more detail of the directory structure that we saw in Figure 3.1. Looking at this expanded directory structure, notice the "You are here." that indicates

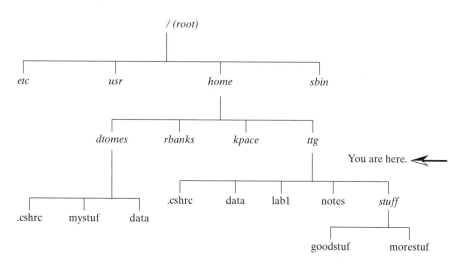

FIGURE 3.5

Expanded directory tree with current location shown.

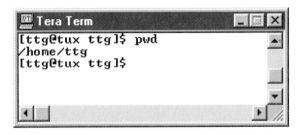

FIGURE 3.6
Output of the pwd command.

your current position in the directory structure. Figure 3.6 shows the output from the pwd command at the "You are here." as indicated in Figure 3.5.

There are two ways to specify the address of the directory we want as our current directory: as a **relative address** based on the current address or as an **absolute address**, the full, complete path to the directory.

Relative Address

The relative address is one specified relative to the current address; that is, it uses the current address as a starting place. For example, if you wanted to change your current directory to the stuff directory and you were in the ttg directory (see Figure 3.5), you could simply type the command

```
cd stuff
```

That would change your current directory to stuff. Being able to specify directory names as relative addresses is very handy. It will be the most common way you specify addresses in your day-to-day work. When you use relative addressing, the shell will add your current location to the directory or filename you specified. In this case, assuming you were at /home/ttg, the shell would actually execute the command

```
cd /home/ttg/stuff
```

prepending the current location to the directory specified.

Two shortcuts can help us with relative addressing. The first is the dot dot (. .), which stands for "go up one level," or "go to the directory that contains this directory," or "go to the parent directory of this directory," each time it is used. When you are speaking this, you will say "dot dot" to refer to the double dot. Using the dot-dot short-cut with the cd command enables us to back up one level in the directory structure. So if ttg were to type cd . . he would change from /home/ttg, up to the directory /home. If he were at /home/ttg and typed cd ../.. he would go to the directory /, or the root.

Let's see. Figure 3.7 shows the results of this action. Notice that user ttg first displayed the current directory, backed up one level, and then displayed the current working directory again, using the pwd command. The dot-dot shortcut is very handy not only for moving up one level in the directory hierarchy, but also for moving across and down a directory hierarchy. Obviously, you aren't really moving across or down; you are moving from place to place on the hard disk. However, to have a frame of

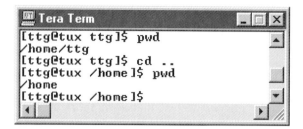

FIGURE 3.7

Demonstration of the dot-dot (. .) shortcut.

reference, we will pretend that we are actually traversing the directory tree shown in Figure 3.5, moving up, which is closer to root, and over, or across the same directory, and then down into a directory farther away from the root.

For example, suppose user ttg wants to change from his directory to the directory owned by dtomes. From ttg's directory, shown by the "You are here." in Figure 3.5, all he would have to type is cd ../dtomes, which would change the directory up one, over, and down into the dtomes directory. Figure 3.8 shows how that would work. (Note: we are assuming that ttg starts in his home directory, not where we left him in Figure 3.7.)

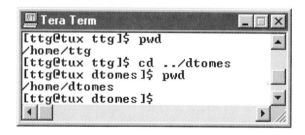

FIGURE 3.8

Demonstration showing movement up, across, and down.

In Figure 3.8 ttg also uses the pwd command to show where he started and where the cd command took him. All in all, the dot-dot shortcut is very handy. It makes it easy to use relative addressing to move about in the same directory tree.

Do be aware of one real common mistake that new Unix Wizards seem to make. They forget the white space between the command and the shortcut. As you know, if you forget the white space, the shell can get confused. The command cd.. isn't really a command! You need to add white space after cd.

The other shortcut is the single dot (.), which stands for "here." Copying files from somewhere else to your current directory is the most common use for this short-cut. For example, if ttg is in his home directory and wants to copy the file neat.stuff from rbanks (assuming he has permission), he should type the following:

```
cp ../rbanks/neat.stuff .
```

I realize you don't know the cp, or copy, command yet—we'll get to that shortly. What the shell sees is the following command: "copy from a directory that is up one level, called rbanks, the file called neat.stuff to the current directory." To show you how much typing the two shortcuts saved us, here is the way ttg would have to type it without shortcuts:

    cp /home/rbanks/neat.stuff /home/ttg

As I count on my fingers it seems that using shortcuts saved about 12 keystrokes. Not too shabby!

Absolute Address

In our most recent example, which was the "long" version, the addresses were both absolute rather than relative addresses. An absolute address always starts with a forward, or right, slash, indicating that the path described starts at the root of the file structure. The absolute address always describes the *complete* path to the file or directory in question. Although the relative address is usually shorter than the absolute address, there are times when using the relative address is actually longer. For example, if ttg wanted to change from his current directory to the /usr file structure, he could type cd /usr, providing the absolute address, rather than typing cd ../../usr. In this example, using the absolute address saves five keystrokes.

As you begin to learn more and more about Unix you should start to look at efficiency as an important consideration. Using the most efficient command will make your time spent with Unix more enjoyable as well as more productive. Make efficiency one of the criteria when you choose commands.

Speaking of efficiency, there is another special use of cd that will help you always get home regardless of where you roam through the directory structures on your system. If you type cd by itself on the command line, it will always take you to your home directory. Your home directory is the one you are placed in when you log in. This is a real time-saver!

touch

---

    touch [options] filename(s)

The **touch** command performs a number of useful functions that involve the different **timestamp** data, data that describe the last time the file was modified or accessed. These data are stored as part of the file description. There are several options for this command, and all of them are listed in your reference guide for your later perusal, but we will consider here only the two that are most commonly used, the -c and -t options.

One interesting use for touch is to create new, empty files. This can be useful for testing purposes or to create a set of target files for later use. The format of the touch command is simply

    touch filename

In this form, touch will change the last accessed and last modified date information in the file description to reflect the current date and time. Figure 3.9 shows how touch

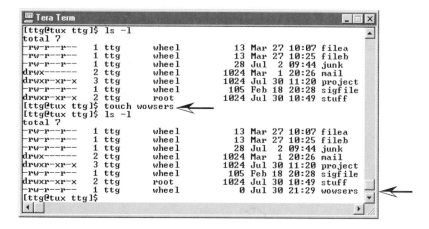

FIGURE 3.9

Using the touch command to create an empty file.

can be used to create a new, empty file, or to change the date last modified field of an existing file. Don't worry about the ls command in Figure 3.9—we'll learn about that in a moment. For now concentrate on the date and time stored with the files.

In Figure 3.9 ttg first lists the current files in the directory, then uses touch to create the new file called wowsers, and finally lists the files again, showing that the file called **wowsers** has been created. Notice that this new file was created at 21:29. The second-to-last column of the ls output lists in hour-and-minute format the time that the file was created or last accessed.

Figure 3.10 shows how touch can be used to update the file's last accessed time. In this example, I first issued the ls command to show the date and time last modified for each file. Next I touched the wowsers file, then did another ls to show that the time last modified on wowsers had changed (from 21:29 to 21:34). Using touch in this way is sometimes useful.

One of the interesting options for the touch command is the -c option, which tells touch *not* to create a file. It is sometimes useful to prevent touch from creating a new file if that file does not exist. However this is not the normal state of affairs. This option is used only to update the date last modified.

The touch command has as an argument the name of the file or files to be touched.

The other interesting option for the touch command is the -t, or timestamp, option. If you don't specify a time, touch will use the current system time. Using the -t option, you can specify the timestamp you want touch to use instead of the current date/time. For example, Figure 3.11 shows how ttg set the date on the wowsers file to Christmas Day, 2010. The format of the date here might look a little odd. It is of the form

YYYYMMDDHHMM.SS

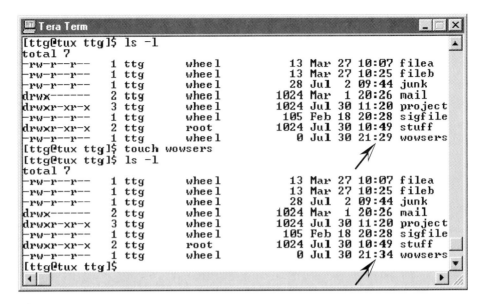

FIGURE 3.10

Using the touch command to change date last accessed/modified.

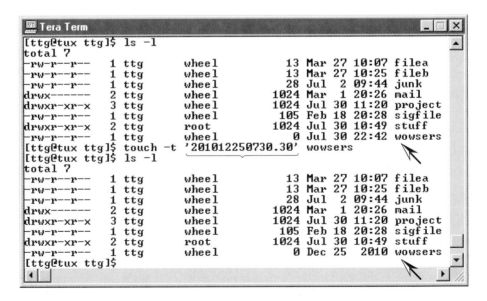

FIGURE 3.11

Using the touch command to set timestamp to specific time.

Thus, YYYY = year, MM = month, DD = day, HH = hour, MM = minute, and SS = second. Since this isn't 2010, we don't see the minutes and seconds displayed, only the month, day, and year.

ls

ls [options] [file(s)]

As promised, we will now, finally, discuss the **ls** command. The ls command directs the shell to list the contents of the current directory. If no options or attributes are supplied, ls simply lists the names of each file in the current directory. Among the plethora of options to the ls command, we will examine only those that are commonly used, and you should consult the reference guide for the others. Figure 3.12 shows the output of the plain vanilla ls command.

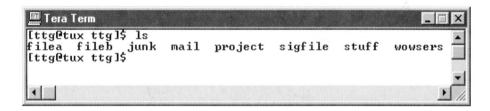

FIGURE 3.12

Output of the plain vanilla ls command.

In its simplest state, all ls does is list the filenames in alphabetic order; it presents no additional information.

Figure 3.13 shows one of the more common options for the ls command, -l, (hyphen ell), which stands for "long" listing.

```
Tera Term                                                    _ □ ×
[ttg@tux ttg]$ ls -l
total 7
-rw-r--r--    1 ttg     wheel         13 Mar 27 10:07 filea
-rw-r--r--    1 ttg     wheel         13 Mar 27 10:25 fileb
-rw-r--r--    1 ttg     wheel         28 Jul  2 09:44 junk
drwx------    2 ttg     wheel       1024 Mar  1 20:26 mail
drwxr-xr-x    3 ttg     wheel       1024 Jul 30 11:20 project
-rw-r--r--    1 ttg     wheel        105 Feb 18 20:28 sigfile
drwxr-xr-x    2 ttg     root        1024 Jul 30 10:49 stuff
-rw-r--r--    1 ttg     wheel          0 Dec 25    2010 wowsers
[ttg@tux ttg]$
```

FIGURE 3.13

Output of the ls command with the -l (long) option.

We've actually seen this figure before, when we were talking about touch, but now we will examine it more closely and dissect the various fields. There are eight data elements shown in each line of the ls -l command. The exception is the first, or total, line that shows the total number of files in the current directory. The actual data presented to us by ls -l are important, so let's look at each of the eight different data elements individually. Figure 3.14 diagrams those eight chunks-o-data. Please look at it closely for a minute, and then we will discuss each part.

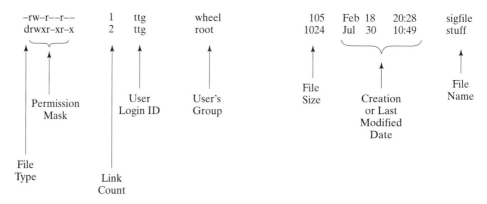

FIGURE 3.14

Examination of output of ls -l.

We will start our discussion of Figure 3.14 looking at the leftmost byte, or character. This is the File Type indicator; it tells us what type of file is described on that line. The two most common file types are d, indicating the file is a directory file, and -, hyphen, indicating the file is a regular, good old-fashioned file. In Figure 3.14 the file sigfile is a regular file, and the file stuff is a directory file.

Permission Mask

The next 9 bytes describe the different permissions that are set for the file. These 9 bytes are called the **permission mask**, and they play a very important role in how you, and others, deal with a file. Figure 3.15 shows a breakdown of this permission mask. It is divided into three areas of 3 bytes containing three permissions each called **levels of permission**. The leftmost group of three permissions are those that apply to the user, the individual who owns the file. (We refer to this individual as the *user* rather than the *owner* because the third field, *other*, starts with the letter "o," and we don't want to get confused later when we learn how to change the permissions.) The user identification number, assigned when the file is created, determines ownership. Don't worry about the user identification number at this point; we'll discuss it when we look at how your user record is created and stored in the /etc/passwd file.

The second set of three permissions are those assigned to all the individuals who share the same *group* identification number as the user. We will discuss groups when we take a closer look at the /etc/passwd file, too.

```
rw--r--r--
rwxr-xr-x
 U G  O
```

U = User permissions
G = Group permissions
O = Other permissions

r = read
w = write
x = execute
– = no permission

FIGURE 3.15

Closer look at permission mask.

The third triad of permissions are those assigned to the *other* users. Anyone who has a valid login ID on the system but is not the user of the file, nor in the user's group, is considered "other."

To restate: The 9-byte permission mask is divided into three 3-byte permission submasks, one for *user*, one for *group*, and one for everyone else, *other*. Each permission submask, or level of permission, is divided into three different permissions. The leftmost permission, r, allows the file to be read. The center permission, w, allows the file to be written. The rightmost permission, x, allows the file to be executed.

The *write* and *execute* permissions have slightly different meanings depending on whether the file is a regular file or a directory. Write permisson simply means that the contents of the file can be modified. Executing a regular file means that the command-line interpreter (the shell) will attempt to run the text contained within the file as if it were shell commands. In the case of a directory file, write permission allows the contents of the directory to be changed, that is, files added or deleted. Execute permission on a directory file allows searching within the directory. If you think about it, writing is actually the same for a directory or regular file, because both are simply files, and as our first Refrigerator Rule tells us, a file is simply a stream-o-bytes.

Rest of ls -l Command

To prevent your having to page back and forth, I've duplicated Figure 3.14 in Figure 3.16 to continue our examination of the output of the ls command. Moving to the right of Permission Mask, you see that the next field is Link Count. We will examine links in greater detail shortly, but for now simply consider a link to be a name for, or pointer to, a file. The link count is the count of the names associated with a single file. (Yes, that does imply that one file can have multiple names, and you will have to wait until we discuss the ln, link, command before you find out how that works. Isn't anticipation a wonderful thing?)

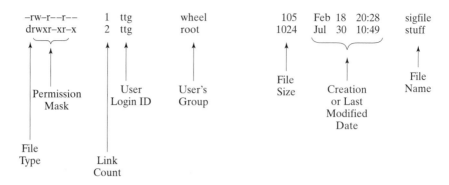

FIGURE 3.16

Output of the ls -l command (copy of Figure 3.14).

The next field, User login ID, shows the login ID of the person who owns the file. (The user permissions mask applies to this ID.)

Following the user field is User's Group, indicating the group to which the user who created the file belongs. In our example the first file was created by an individual in the group named wheel. The second file was created by a user in the group named root. (Not all systems show the group field.)

Following the group field is File Size, which tells us the size of the file. The way this field is displayed differs across the various flavors of Unix. In Figure 3.16, showing the output from Linux, the size of the file is shown in bytes. Solaris also shows the file size in bytes, but some variants of Unix show the file size in blocks rather than bytes. Block size also varies across Unix systems, with block sizes of 512 or 1024 bytes the most common sizes.

Following the File Size field is Creation or Last Modified Date, the date and time the file was created or last modified. Actually, the command tells us the date and time only if the file was created or modified within the last year (or last six months on some systems). If the last change to the file occurred more than a year ago, the command will report only the *day and year* the file was last modified. Therefore, if you see a time in addition to a date, you know the file is relatively recent.

The last field in this display is File Name. Unix is very flexible in its file-naming conventions. If you're used to the restrictions imposed by other operating systems you will undoubtedly find Unix's file-naming conventions a delight. With all of this power and flexibility, though, comes the responsibility to create meaningful, useful filenames.

⊕ Filenames

A filename in Unix can be composed of any character on the keyboard except the forward slash, /, which is used to divide the parts of the path. On a few older Unix file systems, the length of a filename is limited to 14 characters, but newer Unixes allow up to 255 characters. The other restriction on filename length is the length of the total path, which on most Unix machines is somewhere between 255 and 4096 bytes.

Now let's talk about making *good* filenames! A good filename is meaningful and useful. Meaningful means that the filename tells us about the file, what's in it or how it's used. A useful filename is one that's reasonable to use; it's neither too long, nor does it contain difficult-to-type characters. While it is possible to use any character except forward slash in a filename, some of the special characters (***[]-?><)(}{";&!**) can cause problems because the command interpreter will try to use them as metacharacters. We will learn all about metacharacters in Chapter 4.

A good rule of thumb is to always start your filenames with an alphabetical character or digit. In addition, it's generally a good idea to limit your filenames to alphabetical characters, digits, the dot, and the underscore (_). Although it is possible, with a little effort, to include spaces in filenames, spaces can cause problems if a filename is used in a command. Rather than using spaces in a filename, use the underscore to mark a space. Likewise, it is possible to start a filename with the hyphen (-), but that is a Very Bad Idea. It is bad because if a file starting with the hyphen is the first file in a list (and it usually will be), the command that reads the filename may try to interpret the filename as an option. This happens because the shell will first expand any file-matching metacharacters, and then pass the expanded filenames to the shell. If, for example, the first file in your directory is –l(hyphen ell), and you type the ls command, the first thing the ls command will see is the –l filename. Since options start with a hyphen, how will the poor ls command know that the –l is a file and not an option?

The last bit of advice pertains to those of you who will be creating a set of files that have very similar names—for example, saving the logs from a particular process. You could name the files daily_log_01012003, daily_log_01022003, daily_log_01032003, and so on, for each of the first three days in January of 2003. However, as you shall learn in Chapter 9, there is a really nice way to have the shell complete your filenames for you that is more efficient if the names differ in their *first* few characters rather than the *last* few characters. So, with that in mind, it would be better to name your log files 01012003_daily_log_file, 01022003_daily_log_file, 01032003_daily_log_file, and so on. That way, you would need to type in only the first four characters of the filename and could let the shell complete the name for you. (Yes, you may look ahead to Chapter 9 if you feel compelled to do so. Filename completion is a really neat feature. I will wait for you here.)

As I mentioned earlier, it is possible to include special characters like **[,], *, ?**, or even a space within a filename. Although it's not a good idea to do so, and it cause confusion for both the system and other users, there may be times when you are forced into this alternative. To include special characters within a filename, you need to precede them with the backslash (\) character. Preceding each special character with the backslash will "protect" the following character from interpretation by the shell, so the shell will treat that character like any other character and include it in the filename. For example, if you want to create a filename like my[weird]file, you need to enter the following command:

```
touch my\[weird\]file
```

Remember, however, that each time you want to access this file you will need to protect those special characters. Should you forget to protect them, the shell will interpret the [and] as special characters and become confused. In all but the most extreme case the niftiness of a filename that contains special characters isn't worth the additional work required.

There is another way to protect the special characters from interpretation by the shell. You can enclose the special characters, or the whole filename, within apostrophes ('), or tick marks. Either of the two following `touch` commands will also create the `weird` filename:

```
touch 'my[weird]file'
```

```
touch my'['weird']'file
```

Although I strongly recommend against it, you can use the same procedure to include a space within a filename. Some substandard operating systems allow you to easily use spaces in filenames. Remember that all of the shells use white space to parse the command line. If you include a space within a filename and don't protect it, the shell will use that space when it parses the command line. I promise you won't like the results.

The bottom line is, you *can* use special characters, and even spaces and nonprinting characters, within filenames, but it's a *very poor practice*. I urge you to use such characters only if you have no possible alternative.

Dots in Filenames

One other character deserves special recognition when we talk about filenames. Now, I must warn you, if you are used to other operating systems, you may find the following a little strange, so take a deep breath and hang on—everything will be okay. As far as Unix is concerned, the dot is *just another character* that can be placed in filenames. Unix does not require any sort of artificial filename.extension format. Actually, you can have as many dots in the filename as you wish. For example, the filename `I.have.lots.of.dots` is a perfectly valid filename in Unix. There are, however, two filenames you must not use, dot (.) and dot dot (..), because, as you have already learned, Unix has a special use for those two filenames.

Frequently you will see files named by wise Unix users that have a format like `fixname.sh`, `initialcap.sed`, or `lab1.3.awk`, which look something like files named in other operating systems. Filenames like this reflect the contents or use of the files, which make the names more useful to people. It is important that you understand that although this naming convention is handy, it is not required by Unix. The only special formatting in Unix is that imposed by the C compiler, which wants all C source files to end in `.c`. There is one special use for the dot, as follows.

Dotted Files

The only time the dot has a special meaning in Unix is if it is the *first* character of a filename. Files that have a name that begins with a dot are referred to as *dotted files, protected files*, or *hidden files*. They're called hidden files because if you use the `ls` command without the `-a` or `-A` option, you won't see them. In Chapter 4 we will learn about file-matching metacharacters. You cannot use file-matching metacharacters to match dotted files under normal circumstances.

FIGURE 3.17

Output of two ls commands, showing dotted files.

Figure 3.17 shows the output of the ls command followed by the output of an ls -a command. The first ls command shows only five files, while the second shows that there are really 24 files in the directory! Look at all those dotted files. In most cases dotted files are created by the system or are used by utilities.

Figure 3.17 also shows another commonly used option for the ls command, the -a option, which says "Show me *all* the files." Another, sometimes interesting, option is -i, which asks the ls command to list the index node number associated with the file. Figure 3.18 shows the output of the ls -i command.

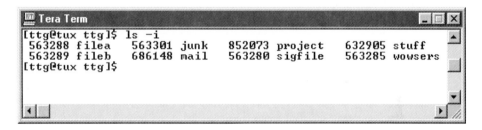

FIGURE 3.18

Output of the ls -i command.

The file's index node identifier number, or inode, precedes each filename in the listing. This option for the ls command will be useful to us as we discuss links in Chapter 4.

As was mentioned when we started talking about the ls command, there are many options that have specialized purposes. For example, there are several ways to sort the output: -t sorts and displays the files in time order rather than by alphabetical name order, -s sorts the files by size largest to smallest, -u sorts the output according to the access time with the most recently accessed files shown first, and -r reverses the order of the sorted output for either the time or name sorts. Should you want to see a list of the contents of all subdirectories within the current directory, you can add the -R option to the ls command. Obviously, some of these options are mutually exclusive. You can't, for example, tell ls to sort the filenames by both size and date. As you

TABLE 3.1 Some Commonly Used **ls** Options

Option	Action Performed
-a	Show all files, even hidden ones.
-d	List directory names only, not contents.
-i	Display inode number.
-r	Reverse order of sorted files.
-R	Recursively display all files in all directories under current directory.
-s	Sort files by size, largest to smallest.
-t	Sort files by time rather than name.
-u	Sort files by access time.
-x	Create multicolumn output.
-1	Print each entry on its own line.

experiment with the ls command you'll find that some of the options are more useful to you than others; it is indeed a fascinating command. Table 3.1 shows some of its commonly used options.

cp

```
cp [options] source target
or
cp [options] source files target-directory
```

It's often necessary to copy some data in a file from one place to another. We copy files to back them up (so we can obey Refrigerator Rule No. 2); we copy files to take them with us or to give them to someone else; and we copy them to make variations on them. Indeed, copying files is an everyday occurrence. In the Unix environment we use the **cp** command to copy files. It has two forms:

```
cp source target
```

which makes a copy of a *single* file, and

```
cp files directory
```

which copies a collection of files to a directory.

The copy command is an example of Unix considering the user to be a cognizant adult. Figure 3.19 shows the danger in that. In this instance there are two files, filea and fileb. I first list the contents of each file, then copy the first to the second, and then list the contents a second time. (We'll examine the cat command in just a bit, for now we will just use it to show us the contents of a file.)

Notice in Figure 3.19 that the contents of filea *replaced* the contents of fileb! In this instance, the shell said, "You want to overwrite the contents of fileb; consider it done."

```
Tera Term                                    _ □ ✕
[ttg@tux ttg]$ cat filea                          ▲
I am file A.
[ttg@tux ttg]$ cat fileb
I am file B.
[ttg@tux ttg]$ cp filea fileb  ←———
[ttg@tux ttg]$ cat filea
I am file A.
[ttg@tux ttg]$ cat fileb
I am file A. ←———
[ttg@tux ttg]$
                                                  ▼
◄ ▯                                          ► ▯
```

FIGURE 3.19

Series of commands showing how cp will overwrite existing file.

There was no warning; the file was simply overwritten. Since the shell considers the user to be aware of what he is doing, it just does what is asked of it. Unfortunately for me, there is no Undo command in Unix. If I don't have a backup of fileb, I will have to spend however long it takes to retype the contents of that extensive file. While this aspect of Unix can be viewed as dangerous, it's also refreshing to have an operating system that does what you tell it to without question. And as you will notice from looking at your reference guide, there's a healthy collection of options for the cp command, even one that can alleviate the danger. Some of the more useful will be discussed here.

Probably the most commonly used option for the cp command is -i, which stands for either "inquire" or "interactive" and directs cp to ask before it overwrites an existing file. Figure 3.20 shows how this option would have saved me from making the mistake I made in Figure 3.19. Notice that in this instance copy asks for confirmation before overwriting fileb.

There is a way to make copy use the -i option automatically, and it is possible that your system administrator has yours set up this way to make using Unix just a little safer for you while you are learning. I realize that having the command check to see

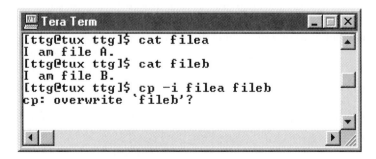

```
Tera Term                                    _ □ ✕
[ttg@tux ttg]$ cat filea                          ▲
I am file A.
[ttg@tux ttg]$ cat fileb
I am file B.
[ttg@tux ttg]$ cp -i filea fileb
cp: overwrite `fileb'?
                                                  ▼
◄ ▯                                          ► ▯
```

FIGURE 3.20

Using the -i option on cp command.

if you really want a file destroyed is not really Unix-like. But is another example of the power of Unix. This OS will allow us to set our level of comfort with commands. Most neophyte Unix users go through a phase where they don't think they need the baby options on commands, like the -i on cp. They like to live fast and loose, on the edge of disaster. Then, once they have accidentally destroyed all or part of a file system, they learn why the designers of Unix allow for such safety options. You can use it and be safe, or not use it and live dangerously. It all depends on how much time you have to recreate files you have damaged.

We will learn how to cause commands to automagically execute with particular options by creating command aliases in Chapter 10.

The second form of the cp command, sometimes called the *mass copy*, can save you a great deal of time when copying a collection of files. Suppose, for example, you wanted to copy all of the files necessary to work on a particular project to a new user in your group. Well, you could copy each file one at a time using the form of the cp command you currently know, but that could take a while. Figure 3.21 shows rbanks copying

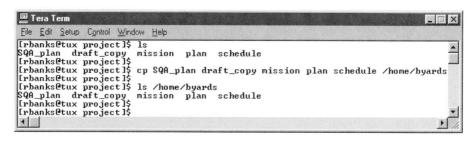

FIGURE 3.21

Copying multiple files to a directory.

five files from her project directory to the directory of byards. (Of course, rbanks must have permission to write to that directory before doing so)

The copy command is quite intelligent. Notice that in this case, since there were more than two files listed, cp checked to make sure that the last entry was a directory and that all the other entries were files to be copied into that directory. This feature of that command makes copying a collection of files somewhat faster. We will learn in Chapter 4 that there are file-matching metacharacters that would have speeded up the process still more.

Moreover, had rbanks used another option of the cp command, she could have both created a project directory in the directory of byards and copied all of the files into it with one command. Figure 3.22 shows how this could have been accomplished using the -r (recursive) option for the cp command. Notice how much shorter the copy command is here. The directory and its contents were copied to the byards directory. Had the rbanks project directory contained additional directories, those directories, and their contents, would also have been copied.

The cp command is a relatively quiet command. Like most other Unix commands, copy doesn't normally provide an extensive explanation of what it's doing. It simply copies the files and then returns you to the command-line prompt. If you really

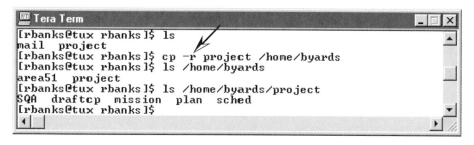

FIGURE 3.22

Using -r option on the cp command.

want to see what copy is doing, you can use the -v option, which asks copy to be verbose, or tell you what it is doing. Figure 3.23 shows how this works. The **-v**, or verbose, option shows each filename as it is copied from the source to the target.

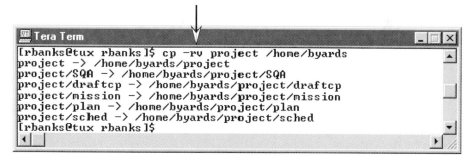

FIGURE 3.23

Copying with both -r and -v options.

While this is an interesting option, it's not commonly used, because most Unix wizards trust cp. One word of warning: had the byards directory already contained a project directory, the project directory of rbanks would not have been copied, but instead its files would have been put into the existing project directory of byards.

Another file-naming shortcut that's handy when copying files from one user's directory to another's is shown in Figure 3.24.

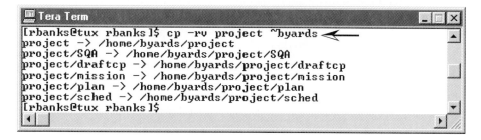

FIGURE 3.24

Shortcut of cp to target directory.

Look closely at that figure, and check out the way the target directory is specified. Notice that there is no absolute path to the byards directory. Some shells allow us to use a shortened form of the path when we are trying to address a user's home directory. In Figure 3.24, rather than typing /home/byards all rbanks had to type was ~byards. The use of the tilde (~) is a very handy shortcut to reference a user's home directory.

The copy command on some versions of Unix may not have all of the options shown in your reference manual. For example Solaris Version 7 doesn't support the verbose option.

Now we come to a warning that is so important it has become a Refrigerator Rule:

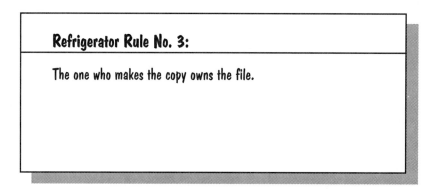

Refrigerator Rule No. 3:

The one who makes the copy owns the file.

What this means is that, unless you use the -p (preserve the ownership) option, if you copy my file, then you are the owner of the new copy of the file. However, if I copy the file to your directory, then I own the new copy of the file! In the preceding example, Robyn copied the files to Bill, so Robyn is still the owner of the files. Let's see; look at Figure 3.25. Notice in the owner field that rbanks owns all of the files. Look just above the 1s line, and notice that the path is byards. Since rbanks did the copy command back

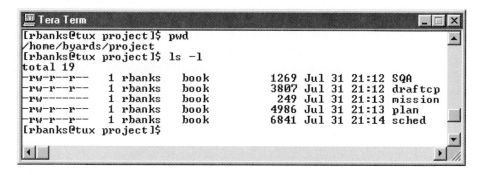

FIGURE 3.25

Showing that the one who made the copy owns the file.

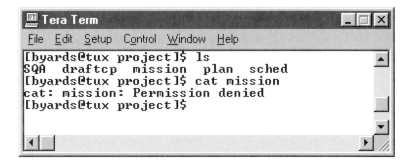

FIGURE 3.26

Showing what happens when byards tries to read his own file.

in Figure 3.24, she owns the files even though they are in the byards directory. This can cause problems if, for example, Bill wants to read the mission statement. Examine the permission mask for the mission file. Notice that *only the owner can read it*, and rbanks is the owner! Bill can't read a file in his own directory. Now look at Figure 3.26 to see what happens. Because the permission mask specifies that only the user can read the file, and because byards doesn't own the file, he can't read it. Since he can't read it, he can't copy it. Suppose Bill works for Robyn, and she copied the file to his directory so he could work on it while she was on vacation. Bill would be in trouble, wouldn't he? In this case, Robyn didn't remember Refrigerator Rule No. 3, 'The one who makes the copy owns the file'.

mv

---

mv [options] source(s) target

Sometimes it's necessary to move a file from one place to another rather than copying it. After you copy a file, it exists in two places, but after you move a file, it exists in only one place. Copying creates two instances of the file; moving leaves you with only one instance—the original. The **mv** command is used to move a file from one place to another in the directory structure. Actually, the move is equivalent to copying and then deleting the original file and so saves us the time those two procedures would take.

Like the cp command, mv can inadvertently destroy existing files if you move a file onto a target that already exists. The -i, "inquire" or "interactive" option, works just like it does on the cp command, preventing mv from stepping on, or overwriting, an existing file without your approval.

The move command can also be thought of as a *rename* command. Take your pick: If it makes more sense to you to think about moving a file from one place to another, then think about mv as the move command. On the other hand, if it makes more sense to you to think that this command is simply renaming the file, then think of it as the rename command. I can assure you that mv doesn't really care which way you think

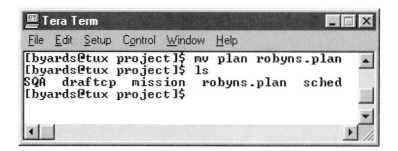

FIGURE 3.27

Using mv to rename a file.

of it as long as you think of it kindly and often. Just like cp, mv can be used to move a single file, a collection of files, or a directory.

Figure 3.27 shows byards using the mv command to rename one of the files rbanks sent to him. Bill renamed (or moved) the plan file to identify the source for the plan in his directory. Who knows? He may even have other plans.

Another useful function of the mv command is to transfer a collection of files from one place to another within a directory structure. For example, suppose that byards wants to compartmentalize his files. He could create a directory for the project and then move all of the project files into a project directory under the new directory. Let's assume he has already used the mkdir command to create the rbanks directory. He could move the project directory to that directory, and then move the files into that directory structure. The mv command can simplify the task for him. Look at the example in Figure 3.28.

These are the steps shown in Figure 3.28:

1. Bill runs the ls process to list the files/directories in his home directory.
2. He moves the project directory to the rbanks directory.

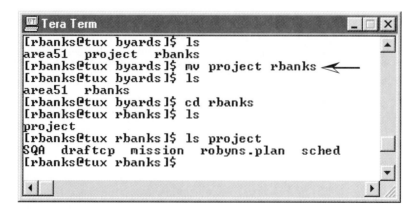

FIGURE 3.28

Moving the whole directory structure.

3. He then does another ls to show that the project directory is no longer there.
4. Next he changes the directory to the rbanks directory.
5. The ls in that directory shows where the project directory was moved.
6. He then changes to the project directory.
7. He then does an ls to show that not only was the directory moved, but so were all the files under that directory.

This is a very powerful command, enabling you to leap tall buildings—er, move whole directories—with a single command. Remember, however, that just like with the copy command, you need to be careful with mv, as you can overwrite files unless you use the -i option. One note: unlike the cp command, the mv command preserves the ownership of the file, so Refrigerator Rule No. 3 does not apply to moving.

cat

---

cat [options] [files]

As promised earlier in the chapter, it's time to learn **cat**. This command has two separate and distinct uses. We saw cat being used to display the contents of file, its first use, when we were discussing the cp command. The cat command is often used to send the contents of a file, or files, to standard output for display on the screen.

Figure 3.29 shows how we can use cat to display a short file. This works well for files less than about 24 lines in length. The reason we normally use cat only to display short files is that it will display *all* of the lines of the file without stopping. That makes it difficult to read a long file, unless you happen to be a very fast speed-reader or you have a teletype or other hard-copy terminal.

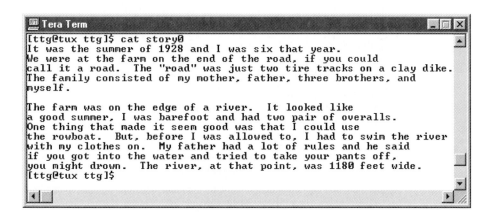

FIGURE 3.29

Using cat to display a short file.

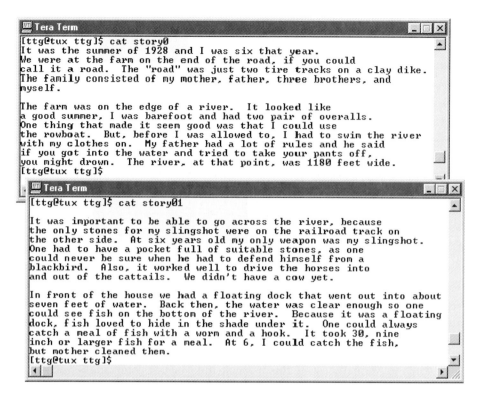

FIGURE 3.30

Screen captures of two files.

The second use of cat (which is short for concatenate) is to combine two or more files into a third file, or to append one or more files to an existing file. (The following code will make more sense to you after Chapter 9, when you know about redirection.) Figure 3.30 shows that user ttg has found two files that make up the beginning of a story. These two files, story0 and story01, need to be joined into one complete story. Figure 3.31 shows how the cat command is used to do just that. Looking closely at the figure, you can see that cat is actually used twice! First it is used to combine, or concatenate, the two story files into a new file, story_A, and then it is used to display the contents of the newly created story file. Pretty neat command, huh! Useful too. Don't worry about the strange syntax > following the cat; that is redirection, used to send standard output to a file rather than to the screen. We will explore all sorts of redirection in Chapter 9. Let's wait until then to worry about just how it works.

Actually, there is another way to use the second form of cat. Suppose you want to create a small file but don't want to bother to invoke one of the editors to do so. The cat command comes to the rescue! Figure 3.32 shows how ttg used cat to create a file that contained a short note. There are a couple of interesting things in this figure. First, we can see that the cat command is sending the output to a file. But where is the input file? There isn't one. In this instance, cat takes its input from standard input, which is connected to the keyboard. (You do remember that standard input is normally connected

```
Tera Term                                                        _ □ ×
[ttg@tux ttg]$ cat story0 story01 > story_A ←
[ttg@tux ttg]$ cat story_A ←
It was the summer of 1928 and I was six that year.
We were at the farm on the end of the road, if you could
call it a road.  The "road" was just two tire tracks on a clay dike.
The family consisted of my mother, father, three brothers, and
myself.

The farm was on the edge of a river.  It looked like
a good summer, I was barefoot and had two pair of coveralls.
One thing that made it seem good was that I could use
the rowboat.  But, before I was allowed to, I had to swim the river
with my clothes on.  My father had a lot of rules and he said
if you got into the water and tried to take your pants off,
you might drown.  The river, at that point, was 1180 feet wide.

It was important to be able to go across the river, because
the only stones for my slingshot were on the railroad track on
the other side.  At six years old my only weapon was my slingshot.
One had to have a pocket full of suitable stones, as one
could never be sure when he had to defend himself from a
blackbird.  Also, it worked well to drive the horses into
and out of the cattails.  We didn't have a cow yet.

In front of the house we had a floating dock that went out into about
seven feet of water.  Back then, the water was clear enough so one
could see fish on the bottom of the river.  Because it was a floating
dock, fish loved to hide in the shade under it.  One could always
catch a meal of fish with a worm and a hook.  It took 30, nine
inch or larger fish for a meal.  At 6, I could catch the fish,
but mother cleaned them.
[ttg@tux ttg]$
```

FIGURE 3.31

Using cat to combine two files into one new file.

to the keyboard? Yes, I thought you did.) When a program is designed to take input from standard in, and send output to standard out, it is referred to as a **filter**. The cat command is an example of a filter. When ttg wanted to end his file, he entered a Ctrl-D (^D) as the only input on a line. As I am sure you remember, Ctrl-D is called an EOF, or end-of-file character. You will use Ctrl-D any time you want to end the input of a filter that is reading from standard input (when standard input is associated with the keyboard).

So, as we have seen, the cat command is very versatile. This versatility of commands is a phenomenon we will see over and over again as we explore Unix. Obviously,

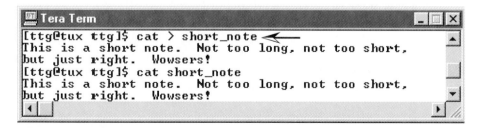

```
Tera Term                                                        _ □ ×
[ttg@tux ttg]$ cat > short_note ←
This is a short note.  Not too long, not too short,
but just right.  Wowsers!
[ttg@tux ttg]$ cat short_note
This is a short note.  Not too long, not too short,
but just right.  Wowsers!
```

FIGURE 3.32

Using cat to create new file.

the cat command was designed to concatenate, or combine, files. However, over time that use has been augmented as creative people looked for ways to solve problems using the existing tools in different and exciting ways.

more

```
more [options] [files]
```

The next command we will consider was designed to address the problem we found with cat when we tried to examine a file that was longer than 24 lines. Since cat displays the whole file, a file that is too long will simply scroll off the top of the screen. (I have a confession to make. In Figure 3.31 I cheated in order to show you the whole file. I stretched the size of the Tera Term window so I could capture the whole file rather than having to explain, then, that cat would lose part of the file.) Figure 3.33 shows the real output from a cat of story_A. Notice that the story, in Figure 3.33, seems to start with the second paragraph. This is an example of how cat can cause a problem when displaying longer files. The more command was designed to overcome this limitation.

Figure 3.34 shows **more** used to display the contents of the story file. A couple of things immediately catch our eye. First, only the first three paragraphs of the story are shown on the screen. Second, there is a new line at the bottom of the screen that says –More–(71%). That line tells us we are using the more utility to view the file. The percentage, in this case 71%, tells us how much of the file we have seen. There are two ways to ask more to show us more of the file. The first is to touch the ENTER key. That will direct more to show us the next *line* of the file. This is the best choice when we want

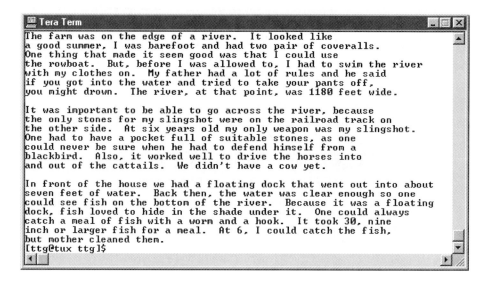

FIGURE 3.33

Correct screen capture for cat.

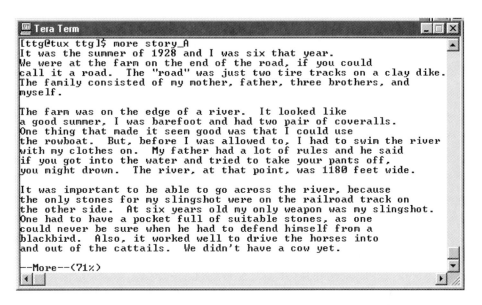

FIGURE 3.34

Using the more command.

to step slowly through a file. The other way is to touch the space bar. That tells more to show us the next *page* of the file. A page is the number of lines your display can present, usually 23 lines of data and one line for the more information. Figure 3.35 shows the result of touching the space bar; it is a continuation of the information in Figure 3.34.

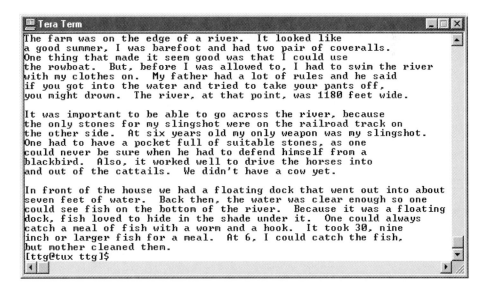

FIGURE 3.35

Result of touching the space bar with the more command.

In the example shown in Figure 3.35, since the file is only another paragraph long, when I touched the space bar, the rest of the file was displayed—and since more is finished, I see the command-line prompt.

Okay, time for a quick test. Where have you seen, and used, the more command already? Yes, you have used it, and no, it wasn't just in examples in the text. Think back. That's right! You were actually using more when you used the man command. Part of the processing man does is to use more to display the information one screen at a time. See, more is already an old friend. (You have been invoking the man command on each new command as you read about it, haven't you???)

The more command has a number of interesting options, but most people use the command in its plain vanilla form. Perhaps this is because they just don't know how handy more can be when used with certain options and commands. One of the somewhat esoteric options is -c, which asks more to clear the screen rather than scrolling the screen as it advances from page to page. It is sometimes faster to do this when you are using a slow connection speed.

New users may find it helpful to include the -d option, which displays the prompt [press space to continue, 'q' to quit.] at the bottom of each screen of text on the Linux system. Here again we have a small flavor difference. On the Solaris system the prompt reads [Hit space to continue, Del to abort]. This prompt may be a bit confusing at first. It isn't really telling you to touch the DELETE key but rather to use the delete key combination of Ctrl-C to stop more.

These two prompts tell us a little more about the complexity of more, which recognizes a number of commands. Some of the more interesting are shown in Table 3.2.

TABLE 3.2 Some interesting more commands

Command	Action Performed
< space >	Display next screen full of text.
< return >	Display next line of text.
d or ctrl-D	Scroll 11 lines forward.
q or Q or < interrupt >	Exit from more. (Remember, interrupt is Ctrl-c.)
f	Skip forward one full screen of text.
b or ctrl-B	Skip backwards one full screen of text.
=	Display current line number.
/ < pattern >	Search for the pattern in the file.
v	Start up vi at current line (This will be *very* handy after you learn vi. Remember it!).
h	Display the Help message.
ctrl-L	Redraw screen (for times when somebody sends you a message or wants to talk).
:f	Display current filename and line number.
.	Repeat previous command.

Many of the commands shown in Table 3.2 can have a number prepended to them to alter the way they work. For example, you could enter the command 3f and move forward three screens in the file rather than the default one screen. This gives you a lot of control as you move around in the file. Notice the forward slash, /, or *search* command. It will be very useful to you if you need to search through the file for a particular word or string. In Chapter 11 we will learn about regular expressions, and you'll find that the search command in more also uses regular expressions as patterns. This will make the search command within more even more powerful.

As useful as more is, some people want to be able to do other things like use the arrow keys to scroll back and forward within a file. More doesn't have that particular feature, so the developers of Unix created another tool that does.

less

```
less [options] file[s]
```

The less command is more powerful than the more command. Unfortunately, it is not yet a standard across all the flavors of Unix. (This is the second of the two tools I have included in the text that aren't standard across all distributions of Unix. The first was pine.)

Linux has **less**, but Solaris doesn't. Less is available for most flavors of Unix from the Free Software Foundation, and some system administrators will have already downloaded and installed it for you.

This may be a good time to discuss the GNU project. GNU stands for *GNUs Not Unix*, a bit of a play on words as it is a recursive definition. Inherent within the name is a second play on words, since the GNU animal name is pronounced "wildebeest," er, "new." The mission of the GNU project is to create a collection of 'free' software, that is, software given to the community of computer users to use, copy, distribute, and modify, but not to sell. I would urge you to visit the GNU site at http://www.gnu.org and explore their site in detail. There are thousands of programs you may find valuable, all free to downloading use. I would also encourage you to consider writing software using the Free Software Foundation license and then sharing your expertise with the rest of the community. Free software can make a real difference in our world of computing, and the Unix community has always been one of sharing.

But back to less: since it's not universally available yet, you will need to see if it's on your particular system. To do that, type less file-name on the command line. Figure 3.36 shows how this works on both a Linux machine and a Solaris machine. Please note that for purposes of illustration I have chosen a very short file to display. Obviously, since Solaris doesn't know what less is, we get the "not found" message. The file edtext.3 is only nine lines long, so less doesn't have much room to play. I encourage you to explore less if you have it on your system, as you'll find it is a powerful tool for examining files. Check out the man page on less and you'll see that it has an amazing number of options. Figure 3.37 shows the first screen of the man page on a Linux computer.

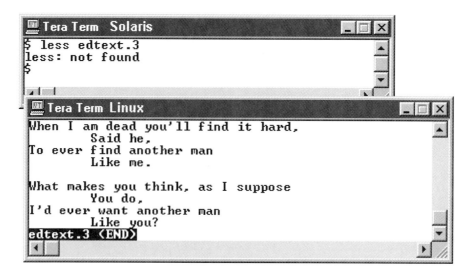

FIGURE 3.36

Solaris (top) and Linux (bottom) responses to the less command.

For most users, the advantage of less is that it recognizes the arrow keys and uses them to move forward or backward in the file rather than using keyboard keys like F or B. However, as is obvious from Figure 3.37, less is a very powerful command, and I encourage you to explore it if it is on your system.

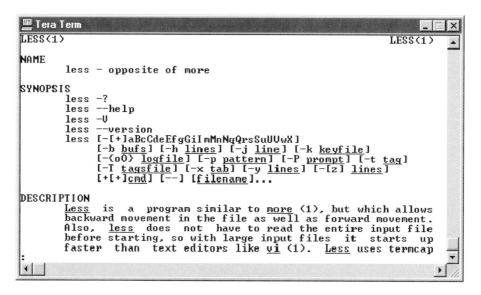

FIGURE 3.37

Opening the man page for less.

So why did the developers call it less? As you have undoubtedly heard many times, "Less is more." Even though the man page says that less is the opposite of more, we all know that indeed, less is more than more.

rm

---

rm [options] file[s]

The **rm**, or *remove*, command is one of the more dangerous ones out there. This command is used to delete files. Wait a minute—that isn't actually, completely true. The truth is that the rm command actually removes a *link* to a file. But I haven't talked about links yet; I will do that in Chapter 4. So for now you can just consider that the rm command removes a file. The danger here is that there is no "un-remove" command in Unix. Once a file is deleted, it's gone, forever and always.

To remove a file from a directory you must have write permission for that directory. As we discussed earlier in this chapter, the second digit in each permission submask determines whether user, group, or other has write access to that file. In the case of directories, write access allows additions and deletions from the directory. If you don't have write access to a directory, you simply cannot delete files from that directory.

As we saw with the copy command, one of the most important options for the remove command is −i, which stands for either interactive or inquire depending on the book you choose to read. In any event, the −i option causes rm to ask you before it removes a file. Generally speaking, the wise Unix user will set this option. It takes only one instance where you accidentally delete critical files before you learn that while it may be slower to confirm each deletion, it's much faster than recreating a collection of files that have been inadvertently deleted.

Figure 3.38 shows how the rm command is used to remove a collection of files.

The ? (question mark) in Figure 3.38 is called a **file-matching metacharacter**. A metacharacter, in the Unix environment, is a symbol used to stand for one or more characters. We will discuss metacharacters in detail in the next chapter. For now, it is

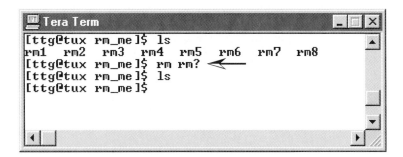

FIGURE 3.38

Using rm to remove a collection of files.

```
Tera Term                                    _ □ ✕
[ttg@tux rm_me]$ ls
rm1    rm2    rm3    rm4    rm5    rm6    rm7    rm8
[ttg@tux rm_me]$ rm -i rm?  ←
rm: remove `rm1'? y
rm: remove `rm2'? y
rm: remove `rm3'? y
rm: remove `rm4'? y
rm: remove `rm5'? y
rm: remove `rm6'? y
rm: remove `rm7'? y
rm: remove `rm8'? y
[ttg@tux rm_me]$ ls
[ttg@tux rm_me]$
```

FIGURE 3.39

Using rm with -i option.

sufficient for you to understand that the rm? in this example represents all of the file-names within this directory. (It matches all files called rm that are followed by one character.)

Notice that rm didn't tell us what it did, but rather simply did as it was told and deleted all the files. Figure 3.39 shows how this command would have worked had we wisely used the -i option. Using the inquire option causes rm to ask us to confirm each deletion. Answering with anything but y for yes tells rm not to delete the file. Many wise, kind system administrators will set up the rm command to automatically incorporate the -i option for you, however, this may not necessarily be the case, so you must be very careful with this command.

Figure 3.40 shows a seeming contradiction to what we've seen before. Look carefully: we entered the remove command that should have simply removed all the files.

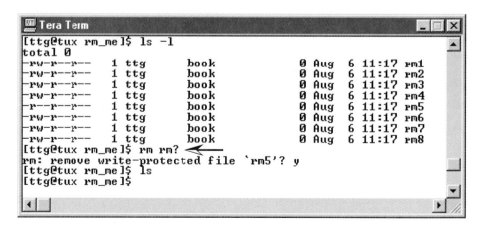

```
Tera Term                                                    _ □ ✕
[ttg@tux rm_me]$ ls -l
total 0
-rw-r--r--    1 ttg        book         0 Aug  6 11:17 rm1
-rw-r--r--    1 ttg        book         0 Aug  6 11:17 rm2
-rw-r--r--    1 ttg        book         0 Aug  6 11:17 rm3
-rw-r--r--    1 ttg        book         0 Aug  6 11:17 rm4
-r--r--r--    1 ttg        book         0 Aug  6 11:17 rm5
-rw-r--r--    1 ttg        book         0 Aug  6 11:17 rm6
-rw-r--r--    1 ttg        book         0 Aug  6 11:17 rm7
-rw-r--r--    1 ttg        book         0 Aug  6 11:17 rm8
[ttg@tux rm_me]$ rm rm?  ←
rm: remove write-protected file `rm5'? y
[ttg@tux rm_me]$ ls
[ttg@tux rm_me]$
```

FIGURE 3.40

Interesting results from the rm command.

Yet it asked us before removing the file rm5. What makes rm5 different from the other files in the directory? The output from the ls -l command gives us the answer. The file rm5 does not give write permission to the user. In this special case, rm will prompt before deleting files for which the user does not have write access. You can disable this feature with the -f option.

The next option we need to discuss is the - - (hyphen-hyphen) option. Look at Figure 3.41 to see why and where we would use this option.

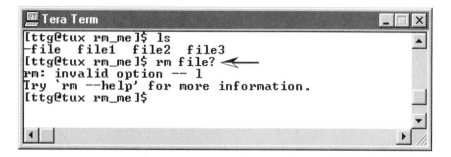

FIGURE 3.41

A small problem with the rm command.

From the response to rm shown there, it would seem that somehow remove has become terribly confused. There is no option coded, so why does remove tell me that there's an invalid option? Notice that the first filename listed, -file, starts with a hyphen. Since the shell expands the metacharacter before passing control to rm, what rm sees is

```
rm -file file1 file2 file3
```

Thus the first thing following the command starts with a hyphen, and rm assumes it is supposed to be an option. It doesn't know about any -file option, so it generates an error message. I followed rm's advice and read the man page. Now look at Figure 3.42, and notice the slightly different syntax in rm command.

The difference between the two rm commands is that I used the hyphen-hyphen option the second time. That option tells rm that anything following that

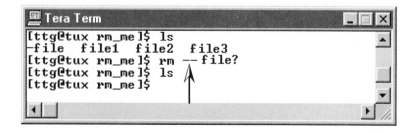

FIGURE 3.42

Resolving the small problem with the rm command.

option is an argument, not an option, regardless of whether it starts with a hyphen. Seldom will you use this option, but it's very handy in certain cases, so you will want to remember it.

The last option for the rm command is undoubtedly the most dangerous. Misuse of the -r, or recursive, option is probably responsible for more lost files than any other single command. I'm sure there are system administrators out there who cringe at the very thought that I've included this option in the book because it is so dangerous. Nevertheless, I believe that if you know what this command can do, you won't accidentally invoke it and cause a catastrophe for yourself. What this option says is, simply, remove this file, or directory, *and all of the files and/or directories contained within it!* Major house cleaning.

Look at Figure 3.43. It shows a small sample directory structure. (I know all the files are empty; this is just used for an illustration.) You can see in this directory structure that there are three directories and 12 files. Now look at Figure 3.44. It shows the recursive remove. In one command we have removed all of the directories and files shown in Figure 3.43. On one hand, this is a most valuable tool; on the other, it can spell trouble. Remember: *there is no undelete command in Unix*, so all of those files are completely gone.

You need to be very careful with recursive remove, obviously, and that's why I think it's important that you learn it now, before you make a mistake.

```
[ttg@tux ttg]$ ls -lR rm_me
rm_me:
total 2
drwxr-xr-x   2 ttg        book        1024 Aug  6 13:37 dir1
drwxr-xr-x   3 ttg        book        1024 Aug  6 13:38 dir2
-rw-r--r--   1 ttg        book           0 Aug  6 13:36 file1
-rw-r--r--   1 ttg        book           0 Aug  6 13:36 file2
-rw-r--r--   1 ttg        book           0 Aug  6 13:36 file3

rm_me/dir1:
total 0
-rw-r--r--   1 ttg        book           0 Aug  6 13:36 filea
-rw-r--r--   1 ttg        book           0 Aug  6 13:37 fileb
-rw-r--r--   1 ttg        book           0 Aug  6 13:37 filec

rm_me/dir2:
total 1
drwxr-xr-x   2 ttg        book        1024 Aug  6 13:38 dirdir3
-rw-r--r--   1 ttg        book           0 Aug  6 13:36 filew
-rw-r--r--   1 ttg        book           0 Aug  6 13:38 filex
-rw-r--r--   1 ttg        book           0 Aug  6 13:38 filey

rm_me/dir2/dirdir3:
total 0
-rw-r--r--   1 ttg        book           0 Aug  6 13:37 fileA
-rw-r--r--   1 ttg        book           0 Aug  6 13:38 fileB
-rw-r--r--   1 ttg        book           0 Aug  6 13:38 fileC
[ttg@tux ttg]$
```

FIGURE 3.43

A set of directories and files.

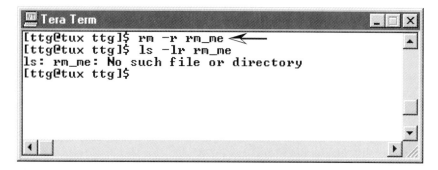

FIGURE 3.44

The recursive rm in action.

rmdir

```
rmdir [options] directory [directory]
```

Although you can use the recursive option on the remove command to remove a directory, there is actually a Unix command designed specifically to remove directories. The **rmdir,** or remove directory, command is designed to remove one or more *empty* directories. Figure 3.45 shows a set of directories and files.

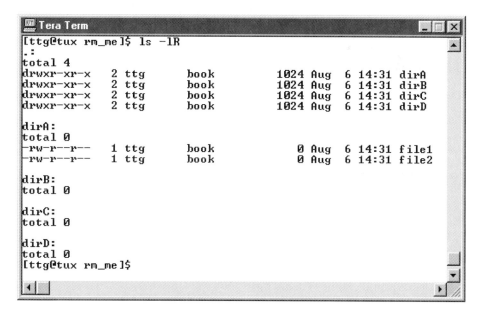

FIGURE 3.45

Collection of directories and files.

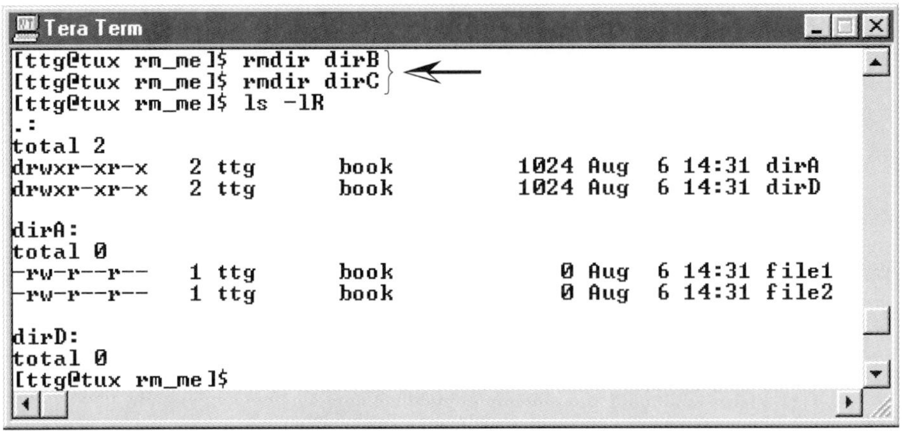

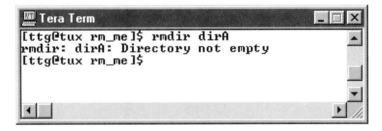

FIGURE 3.46

Using the rmdir command.

Figure 3.46 shows how the rmdir command is used. Two examples of this command are shown. First we removed the dirB directory and then the dirC directory. The ls shows us that the directories were indeed removed. Notice as well that the dirA directory contains two files.

Look at what happens, in Figure 3.47, when we try to remove that directory.

FIGURE 3.47

Using the rmdir command to remove a directory that is not empty.

As I hope you expected, the rmdir command failed when we tried to remove the dirA, because that directory contains files, and rmdir removes only empty directories. If you really want to remove a directory that contains files you have two choices, you can first remove the files within the directory using the rm command and then remove the directory using the rmdir command. Or, as you just learned, you can use the more dangerous recursive rm and remove the directory and all of its contents in one command. As we have already seen, and will see many times in the future, there are multiple ways to perform the same task in Unix.

⊕ /etc/passwd

The last topic we will discuss in the chapter on files is a particularly important file called **/etc/passwd**. This is the repository of almost all the information the system has

```
Tera Term                                                    _ □ ×
tlunch:x:102:1000:Tobias Lunch:/home/tlunch:/bin/bash
dtomes:x:103:1000:Dusty Tomes:/home/dtomes:/bin/bash
rbanks:x:104:1000:Robyn Banks:/home/rbanks:/bin/bash
sbeach:x:105:1000:Sandi Beach:/home/sbeach:/bin/bash
nweigh:x:106:1000:Noah Weigh:/home/nweigh:/bin/bash
kpace:x:107:1000:Kara Pace:/home/kpace:/bin/bash
byards:x:110:1000:Bill Yards:/home/byards/:/bin/bash
nattired:x:111:1000:Natalie Attired:/home/nattired:/bin/bash
gwire:x:112:1000:Guy Wire:/home/gwire:/bin/bash
sfourth:x:113:1000:Sally Fourth:/home/sfourth:/bin/bash
rtyde:x:114:1000:Rip Tyde:/home/rtyde:/bin/bash
newbie:x:999:1000:Newbie User:/home/newbie:/bin/bash
ttg:x:200:1000:Mad Dr. G.:/home/ttg:/bin/bash
[ttg@tux ttg]$
```

FIGURE 3.48

Part of /etc/passwd file.

about any individual user. Figure 3.48 shows an example of part of the /etc/passwd
file on a Linux computer. As you can see, there is a great deal of information stored in
/etc/passwd. The file is a **colon-delimited** file, which means that the various fields are
separated from each other with colons. There are seven primary fields in the
/etc/passwd file shown in this example. It's important that you know and remember
the different fields in this file. Figure 3.49 shows you the contents of each of the seven
fields. Study that figure carefully. You will need to know what each field of the
/etc/passwd file contains.

The data shown in Figure 3.49 are representative for most Unix systems. The first
field, starting from left, is the Login ID for the user. This field should be unique for

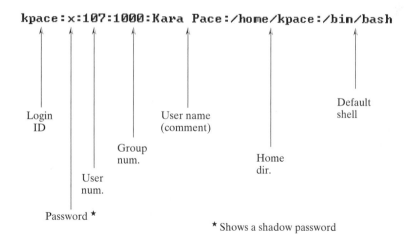

FIGURE 3.49

Fields in /etc/passwd.

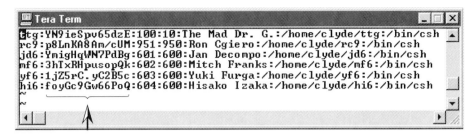

FIGURE 3.50

Sample from `passwd` file on a system that does not support shadowed passwords.

each individual user. The second field is Password. One difference among Unixes is how the password is stored. In this example, the password field is simply an x. This indicates that the system is using a *shadow password* file. Some variants of Unix don't support a shadow password file. On those systems, the second field will contain the encrypted password rather than the x. This is shown in Figure 3.50. One advantage of a shadowed password file is that a more secure encryption method can be used. Both the newer versions of Linux and Solaris support shadowed password files. Figure 3.50 shows a small segment of the password file from a Sun OS system that does not support shadowed passwords.

Back in Chapter 1 you learned about passwords and how to build good ones. Now you know where those encrypted passwords are stored.

The third field is User num., the numeric user ID. In theory this ID should also be unique for each user. Sometimes, though, more than one user can share the same user ID even though it is a Very Bad Thing to do and will be rectified by the system administrator as soon as possible. The user ID is also what the system uses to determine the "owner" of a file or directory.

The fourth field, Group num., contains the numeric group for that user. This group number is used to determine access via the group permissions on a file or directory. Many users are normally assigned to the same group, and these groups are often created around particular tasks. For example, all of the salespeople may be in one group, the accounting people in another group, and programmers working on a particular project will often have the same group number. (Note: one user can be a member of several groups.)

The content of the fifth field, User name, varies greatly across operating systems. In most cases it contains, as a minimum, the actual name of the user. On some systems it can also contain information like office number, phone number, and other such data.

The sixth field, Home dir., contains the path to the user's home directory. The system uses this information when the user logs in.

The last field, Default shell, contains the path to the user's default shell. In Figure 3.48 all the users were assigned the bash shell (/bin/bash), as their default. In Figure 3.50, the users are all assigned the C shell (/bin/csh).

It will be very important both later in this text and in your career as a Unix specialist that you are able to recall the contents of each of the seven fields in `/etc/passwd`.

TABLE 3.3 The contents of /etc/passwd

Field	Contents
1	Login ID.
2	Password, either the encrypted password or an x if a shadowed password file is used.
3	Numeric user ID.
4	Numeric group ID.
5	Name in real life.
6	Path to the user's home directory.
7	The user's default or login shell.

Go back and review Figure 3.49 and study Table 3.3, until you are confident that you can recite the contents of each field from memory.

Now it's time to put some of this fascinating information to work.

KEY TERMS

absolute address
colon delimited
directory structure
file-matching metacharacter
filter
levels of permission
path
permissions mask
relative address
stream of bytes
timestamp
tree structure

NEW COMMANDS

```
cat
cd
cp
less
ls
mkdir
more
mv
pwd
rm
rmdir
touch
```

REVIEW QUESTIONS

3.1 Define all of the key terms for this chapter.

3.2 List the contents of the seven fields in /etc/passwd in reverse order, without looking at your notes or the text.

3.3 Describe two ways to remove a directory from your home directory.

3.4 Explain Refrigerator Rule No. 3.

3.5 Explain the difference between mv and cp.

3.6 Which option on the mv, rm, and cp commands will protect you from accidentally destroying a file?

3.7 Would the cat or more command be a better choice to view a 200-line file? Why?

3.8 Which option on the ls command allows you to see both hidden and regular files?

3.9 How do you create a hidden file in your directory structure?

3.10 Is it possible to include special characters, like the open square bracket ([), within a filename? If so, how?

3.11 Suppose you are currently in the directory /var/spool/locks. How can you get back to your home directory by typing only two characters and touching <enter>?

EXERCISES

3.1 Ensure you are in your home directory by first changing to your home directory and then verifying that you are in the correct directory.

3.2 Create a new directory within your home directory called play.files.

3.3 Display the long directory listing of your new directory and record the permissions mask for your newly created directory.

3.4 Change your current directory to the play.files directory using absolute addressing.

3.5 Move back up one directory level using only five keystrokes (counting the <enter>).

3.6 Change your current directory to the play.files directory again, this time using relative addressing.

3.7 Verify that you are in the play.files directory.

3.8 With one command, create the following empty files:

    zot   zot1   zot2   zot3   zot.   zot.dot   zots   zotty   zot[

(Yes, there is a zot followed by a period, and a zot followed by an open square bracket.)

3.9 Now create a dotted file, .zot, that is also empty.

3.10 Show the files in this directory using the plain vanilla ls command. Notice that one of the 10 files you created does not show.

3.11 Now show all the files in this directory. There should be 12 files showing.

3.12 Copy the file /etc/passwd to your current directory (play.files).

3.13 Change the name of your copy of the passwd file to mypasswd.

3.14 Use the cat command to examine the contents of mypasswd, looking for your entry.

3.15 Okay, that went pretty fast, didn't it? Now look at mypasswd using the more command, again looking for your entry. Exit from more after you have found your entry.

3.16 Look at mypasswd using the less command. (This assumes that less has been installed on your system. If not, I guess you can skip this question.)

3.17 Look closely at each field in your entry in `mypasswd`. Notice that the file is colon-delimited. Does your system use shadow passwords? Review the order and contents of each of the fields.

3.18 Remove all of the `zot` files in this directory, one at a time.

3.19 Now move up one level, to your home directory. Remove the directory `play.files`.

3.20 Oops, didn't work, did it? Why not? Find a way to remove the play.files directory and its contents from your home directory with one command.

CHAPTER

4

File-Matching Metacharacters, Commands, and History

CHAPTER OBJECTIVES

After reading this chapter, you should be able to:

- Use the file-matching characters on the command line.
- Effectively utilize the C-shell history command.
- Explain the purpose for inodes.
- Use the `head` and `tail` commands to display parts of files.
- Create both hard and soft links.
- Count the lines, characters, and words in a file.
- Describe the purpose and use of the `quota` command.

⊕ File-Matching Metacharacters

Before we can discuss file-matching metacharacters, we need to define the term **metacharacter**. A metacharacter is a character that takes the place of, or can be used to represent, more than just itself. Some folks may call file-matching metacharacters *wild cards*, but I prefer that you call them file-matching metacharacters. *Wild card* is a general term that may confuse you later when we start talking about regular expressions.

A file-matching metacharacter, then, is a character the shell understands can be used to represent one or more characters. In essence, it is a handy type of shorthand to represent several filenames with just one, or a few, characters.

The shell uses a specific set of rules to expand file-matching metacharacters. The process of applying these rules to a metacharacter so that it is replaced or expanded into all the filenames that match the pattern supplied is called **globbing**. The term *glob* is derived from the early Unix program /etc/glob. In the beginning the shell did not expand metacharacters; rather, the shell passed the metacharacters to the /etc/glob program, which returned the matching filenames. According to Dennis Ritchie, *glob* is a contraction, most likely for the word "global," much like *grep* is a contraction of "global regular expression print."

The three standard file-matching metacharacters currently supported by all the shells are the asterisk, question mark, and square brackets.

Asterisk

The asterisk (*) can be used to represent *zero or more instances of any character*. Look at the list of files shown in Figure 4.1.

```
Tera Term
File  Edit  Setup  Control  Window  Help
[ttg@tux files]$ ls
f          file.one     file2   fun01   fun07   fun12   fun24   fun42   old4
fi         file.seven   file3   fun02   fun08   fun13   fun31   fun43   old5
fil        file.six     file4   fun03   fun09   fun14   fun32   fun44
file       file.three   file5   fun04   fun10   fun21   fun33   old1
file.five  file.two     file6   fun05   fun101  fun22   fun34   old2
file.four  file1        file7   fun06   fun11   fun23   fun41   old3
[ttg@tux files]$
```

FIGURE 4.1
A list of files.

As you can see from the figure, ttg has quite a few files. Suppose he wants to copy all of the fun files to another directory. He could use the tedious method of copying each file, one at a time, from this directory to another. Part of that laborious process is shown in Figure 4.2.

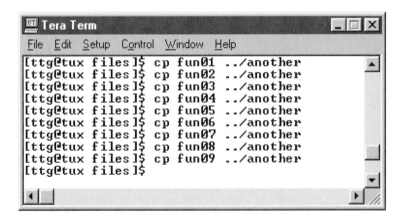

```
Tera Term
File  Edit  Setup  Control  Window  Help
[ttg@tux files]$ cp fun01 ../another
[ttg@tux files]$ cp fun02 ../another
[ttg@tux files]$ cp fun03 ../another
[ttg@tux files]$ cp fun04 ../another
[ttg@tux files]$ cp fun05 ../another
[ttg@tux files]$ cp fun06 ../another
[ttg@tux files]$ cp fun07 ../another
[ttg@tux files]$ cp fun08 ../another
[ttg@tux files]$ cp fun09 ../another
[ttg@tux files]$
```

FIGURE 4.2
Copying files the hard way.

There are a couple of problems with this one-file-at-a-time method of copying. First, since there are over 25 of these fun files, the process will take a while. Second, all that typing leaves lots of opportunities for "fat finger" errors, which would increase the copying time. Using file-matching metacharacters will streamline this process.

Figure 4.3 shows how *all* the fun files can be transferred using a single copy command and a file-matching metacharacter.

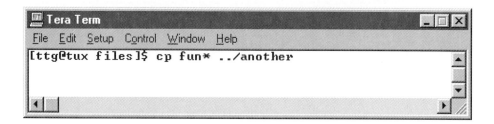

FIGURE 4.3

Using the * file-matching metacharacter.

The shell expands, or globs, the pattern fun* into all the filenames that start with the character string fun followed by *zero or more instances of any character*. This means that typing fun* would be the same as typing fun01, fun02, fun03, fun04, fun05, fun06, fun07, fun08, fun09, fun10, fun101, fun11, fun12, fun13, fun14, and so on. I'm sure you get the idea.

This is one of the many efficient features of Unix. You should strive to take advantage of all such features. Efficiency is one telling characteristic of a true Unix wizard.

Using the file listing in Figure 4.1, make a list of the filenames that would match the following pattern: file* Yes, go back and look. Since the * matches *zero or more instances of any character*, the pattern file* will match the following filenames from Figure 4.1:

```
file         file.five   file.four   file.seven   file.one   file.six
file.three   file.two    file1       file2        file3
file4        file5       file6       file7
```

Does your list agree with mine? The filename file matches because it has zero characters after the string file, and the file-matching metacharacter of the asterisk (*) matches *zero* or more instances of any character.

I hope you didn't fall into the "dot trap"! Remember that the dot is treated like any other character in a filename unless it's the first character. Therefore, file.four is one of the matching globbed filenames because it contains the string file followed by zero or more of any other character.

The asterisk is the most powerful file-matching metacharacter, so it's the one that can get you into the most trouble. Before you use it in a destructive command, like rm, be sure to test it using something safe, like ls.

Question Mark

The question mark ? file-matching metacharacter matches *exactly one character*. Using again the set of files in Figure 4.1, let's explore this new metacharacter. Figure 4.4 shows how it can be used. There are 15 files in ttg's directory with filenames that start with the string `file`, but only seven of them are selected in Figure 4.4. That's because only seven of the filenames consist of the string `file` followed by *exactly one character*.

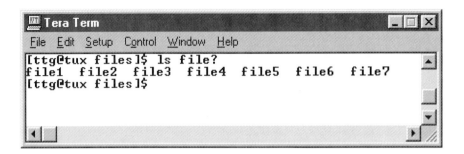

FIGURE 4.4

Using the ? file-matching metacharacter.

The question mark file-matching metacharacter is used less often than the asterisk. In certain situations, though, it is essential, as we shall see.

Now take a look at Figure 4.5.

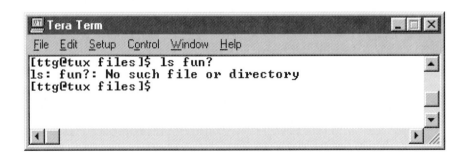

FIGURE 4.5

Another example of using the (?) file-matching metacharacter.

Why did the `ls` command fail in this instance? It failed because there are no files in ttg's directory that contain the string `fun` followed by one, and only one, character. Which file-matching metacharacters would you use if you wanted to find all of the filenames in ttg's directory that contain the string `file` followed by one or more characters? Figure 4.6 shows you my proposed answer to the question.

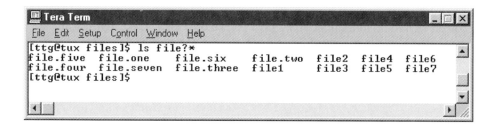

FIGURE 4.6

Using the ? and (*) file-matching metacharacters.

Look carefully at the file-matching metacharacters in the ls command. I ask the shell to find all files with names that start with the character string file followed by exactly one character (?), followed by zero or more instances of any character (*). You begin to see the real power of file-matching metacharacters when we begin combining them in this way.

Square Brackets

The asterisk usually provides the most matches, but the square brackets, [ ], allow you to be precise. They allow you to select *one from a collection* of characters. This works something like the menu in a restaurant: you can select one entree from the dinner menu. Suppose I wanted to choose the odd-numbered files from the range of file1 through file9. In other words, I want to select files that start with the character string file followed by one of the digits 1, 3, 5, 7, or 9. (Okay, I know there's no file9, but if there were …) If I were to specify the pattern file?, I would match all of the file-names that started with the string file and ended with any single character. That's not what I want. I need a way to select only particular files from the whole collection. Look at the example in Figure 4.7; it shows the use of the square brackets file-matching metacharacter to do this.

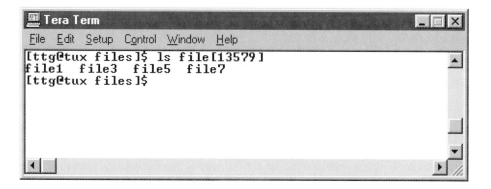

FIGURE 4.7

Using the [] file-matching metacharacter.

You can see from Figure 4.7 that only filenames consisting of the string `file` followed by one of the odd integers (enclosed in the brackets) matched our pattern. Filenames with two digits after the string `file` did not match, nor did filenames in which an even digit followed the string.

The use of the square brackets gives you unambiguous control. Suppose you wanted to select only filenames starting with the character string `fun` followed by either a 1 or a 2, which was followed by an even integer. Names like `fun12` or `fun24` are examples of the filenames sought. That sounds pretty easy, but the solution is more complex than you might think. Figure 4.8 shows two attempts at solving this problem.

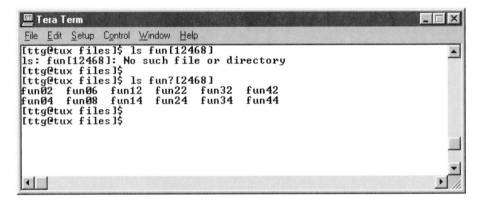

FIGURE 4.8

Two unsuccessful attempts to match a range of filenames.

As you can see, these attempts are not successful. In the first instance I was looking for filenames that started with the string `fun` followed by a 1, 2, 4, 6, or 8, thinking that names like fun12 or fun24 would match. Alas, instead they generated an error message, because there were no files with names like `fun1` or `fun6`.

In my second attempt I tried to use two different file-matching metacharacters. I was looking for filenames that started with the string `fun` followed by a single character that was in turn followed by an even integer. That pattern did find the filenames `fun12`, `fun14`, `fun22`, and `fun24`. However, the pattern also found filenames that were outside the intended scope of my search.

I was on the right track by using two metacharacters, I simply chose the wrong ones. Look at Figure 4.9, my third attempt. Combining two range-selection file-matching metacharacters enabled me to target exactly the files I was seeking. What I told the shell was to list files with names that started with the character string `fun` followed by either the digit 1 or 2, followed in turn by one of the even integers. You can build very precise patterns using multiple pairs of square brackets this way.

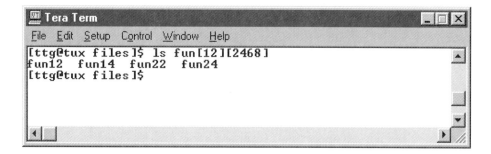

FIGURE 4.9

Success!

Another way to use square brackets to select particular filenames is shown in Figure 4.10.

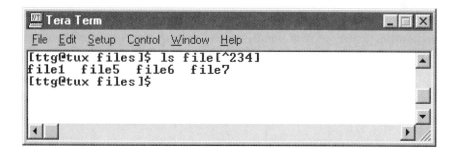

FIGURE 4.10

Selection by specifying what you don't want.

This is an example of a **not logic** construct because you are specifying the filenames you *do not want* rather than those you want. Notice the first character inside the square brackets. The caret, ^, *when used as the first element inside a pair of square brackets*, instructs the shell to match any filenames that *don't* contain one of the characters shown in the collection. This is exactly the opposite of the way square brackets are normally used. I asked the shell to match filenames that start with the character string `file` and are followed by any single character except the digits 2, 3, or 4. Notice that the way the shell interprets this particular directive. It shows us only filenames that start with the character string `file` and are followed by one additional character. The square bracket still specifies the selection of only a single character.

Now let's consider the situation where we want to find filenames that start with a certain word followed by any character except a 0 or a 2 and then by an even digit. Figure 4.11 shows an example of this pattern. Here I instruct the shell to show me

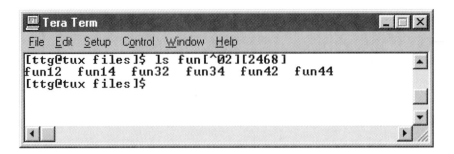

FIGURE 4.11

Using the "not" (^) to match a set of files.

filenames that start with the character string fun followed by any character that's not a 0 or 2, this being followed by an even digit. This more sophisticated use of the file-matching metacharacters serves to further illustrate their power.

Ranges

If you are using a continuous range of letters or numbers, you can abbreviate that range by specifying the first and last elements of the range separated by a hyphen. Figure 4.12 shows how to use this feature.

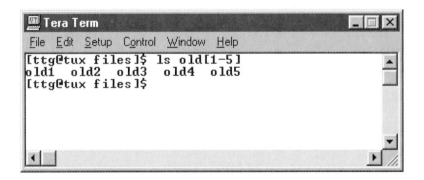

FIGURE 4.12

Using a range within the [] file-matching metacharacter.

Notice that I specified only two numbers (1 and 5), yet the shell matched each of the numbers in the range (1, 2, 3, 4, and 5). This is a handy shortcut when you are trying to match a series of filenames.

You must be careful, however, if you try to use alphabetic ranges. If you ask the shell to match a range like file[a-z], it will understand perfectly. But should you ask the shell to match a range like file[a-Z], you may get some unexpected results—as shown in Figure 4.13. The shell is confused because I gave it a strange range to work with. Please turn to the ASCII character representation chart in Appendix C. Notice that uppercase Z is represented by decimal number 90, and lowercase a is represented

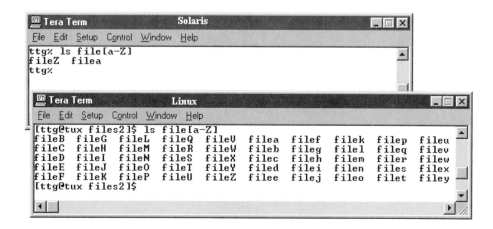

FIGURE 4.13

Specifying a backward range.

by decimal number 97. By specifying all the range of [a-Z], I specified a backward range from 97 to 90. The Solaris C shell decided that since I was specifying what looked like a backward range, I actually was looking for files that started with the string `file` followed by one of the three characters, lowercase a, hyphen, or uppercase Z. The Linux bash shell made a different assumption and showed me all the filenames with alphabetic suffixes except `filea` and `fileZ`.

Don't use backward ranges. If you do, you may well find yourself subject to those immortal words from the old IBM mainframe programming manuals: "The results will be unpredictable." And that, dear reader, is A Bad Thing.

Command History

history

Almost every shell can remember your commands and allow you to reuse them. The only commonly used shell that doesn't support command history is the Bourne shell. That's one reason why the Bourne shell runs faster—it doesn't have to remember things. I could work a lot faster if I didn't have to remember things, too! We are focusing on the C and Bourne shells, and command history is available only in the C shell.

Your system administrator may have already turned on history recording for you. At the command line, type the command **history** to see your history buffer. You should see something similar to the history buffer list shown in Figure 4.14.

The history buffer is a place in memory where the shell records the most recent set of the commands you have typed on the command line. Exactly how many are stored is determined by running the `history` command. The format of this output is a sequential command number followed by the actual command. The last command number in the history buffer in Figure 4.14 is 1016; ttg has been a busy boy!

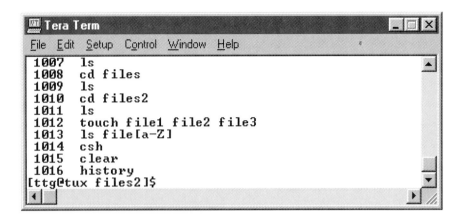

FIGURE 4.14

Output of the history command.

If you don't see any commands listed, as in Figure 4.15, then either history hasn't been enabled for your account or your haven't done anything. (Actually, even typing the history command enters that command into the history buffer, so you know that if you type history, and see nothing, history has not been enabled.) If you have history enabled, you see a list of commands when you type in the history command, and you can skip the next section. If you see what ttg saw in Figure 4.15, then you need to read about how to turn on history, as follows.

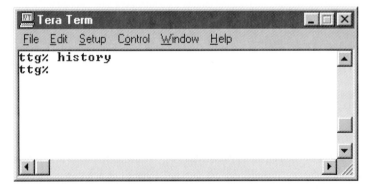

FIGURE 4.15

An account that doesn't have history enabled.

Enabling History

To enable history, you need to use the set command. In the C shell set is used to modify many of the shell's characteristics. Figure 4.16 shows you how to enable history and set a history-buffer size of 40 commands. Forty commands are enough for most users.

The second line in Figure 4.16 shows how to enable history saving.

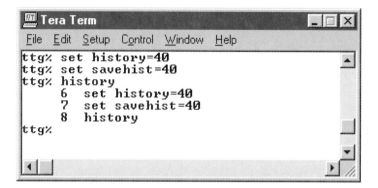

FIGURE 4.16

Setting history and saving history values.

If you set the **savehist** shell parameter, the number of commands you specify will be saved for you, on disk, when you log out. Then, when you log in the next time, those commands will be read from the disk and preloaded into your history buffer.

Notice that after setting history and savehist, I was able to see the last three commands I had entered.

Before you set savehist, please check with your instructor or system administrator. They may have guidelines as to how large to make your history buffer, or even whether to set it. On some systems, with few resources, the system administrator may not want you to save your history.

Now that we all have history enabled, let's see how to use it.

Using History

In the C shell we evoke history with a bang (!)—that is, an exclamation point. There are two ways to reexecute a command: by the numbers or by the letters.

History by the Numbers

Figure 4.17 shows how to reuse a command by number.

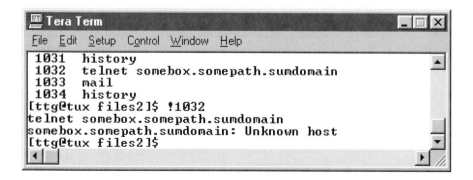

FIGURE 4.17

Recalling a command by number.

Here ttg tried to **telnet** to a computer, then he read his mail, and then he decided to execute the telnet command again. Rather than typing in that great, long, complex command, he used the history command to see the *command number* of the telnet command. All he had to do then was type the bang (!) and the number. Typing five characters is much faster and more efficient than typing 33 characters.

History by the Letters
In some instances, using the letter or letters of commands to access history can be even more efficient than using the numbers. Consider Figure 4.18.

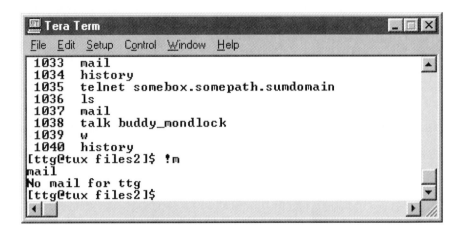

FIGURE 4.18

Invoking a previous command by letter.

In this example ttg performed some common activities and then wanted to check his mail again. Rather than using the history buffer number, in this case 1037, he simply typed bang (!) and the letter m. Bang invoked history, and then the history process searched *backward*, starting at the most recent command for the most recent command that began with the letter m. The first command encountered was mail, so it reexecuted that command. This is an even more efficient way to use history. Rather than typing five characters, ttg typed only two.

The downside of this particular methodology is that you must remember what commands were executed, in what order. If ttg had wanted to reexecute the telnet command, and typed !t, he would have reissued the talk command instead. To redo the telnet command, he would have had to type !te, in which case history would have looked backward for the most recent command that started with the characters te. Reexecuting previously typed commands speeds up your work and reduces potential typing errors.

Modifying Commands
In addition to simply reexecuting previous commands exactly as they were entered, the C shell also allows the user to modify the last command that was executed (the command most recently entered into the history buffer). I must admit that the C shell's implementation of this particular feature is a little clumsy. Some of the newer shells

provide more editing power and grace. This is not to say that the C shell's editing features are archaic, though. They will get the job done, either by simple substitution, global substitution, or reusing parts of a command.

Simple Substitution.   Figure 4.19 shows an example where I made a typographic error, a "fat finger" mistake, and then used history to correct it using simple substitution. The filename that I was trying to copy was a.really.long.file.name, but I made a mistake, leaving out the first dot. Rather than retyping the command, I used history and corrected the error. To correct a mistake in *the most recent command*, type a caret (^), the character or characters you wish to change, another caret, the character or characters you wish to substitute for the mistake, and a closing caret. History will then find the *first occurrence* of the character or characters you wish to change and make the substitution. Then it will reexecute the command. You can modify only the most recent command in the history buffer using the caret.

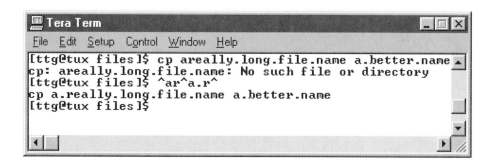

FIGURE 4.19

Correcting a command using history.

But what if I want to use the caret method to modify and reexecute a command that isn't the most recent command in the history buffer? Since the caret works only on the most recent command, the first thing I have to do is make the command that I wish to modify the most recent command. Figure 4.20 shows this process. As you can see, the last command in the history buffer was history. I wanted to modify the talk command. To do so I invoked history, with a bang, and asked it to find the most recent command the started with ta (since I knew that was the talk command). This use of history is a little different than the previous examples. There is a :p appended to the command. The :p asks history to print the command *without executing it*, and make it the most recent command in history buffer. History dutifully prints or displays the command, making it simple to edit.

Sometimes it's useful to recall a command using something other than the first few characters of the command. For example, in Figure 4.21 you can see that I have performed a series of copy commands. If I want to recall one particular copy command without using the command number, I can ask history to recall a command using a unique character string that occurred in the command.

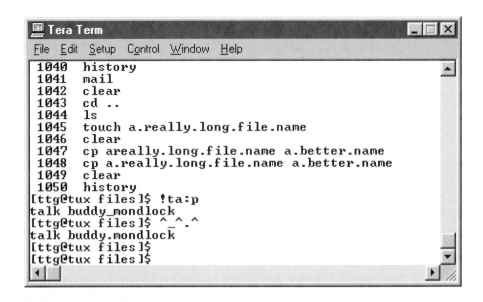

FIGURE 4.20

Recovering an older command and then editing it.

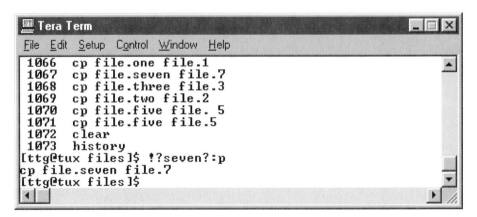

FIGURE 4.21

Searching for a particular string in the history buffer.

In this case I wanted to recall the copy command that had copied file.seven. Rather than using the history command number (1067), I asked history to search backward through the history buffer to find and print the first command that contained the string seven. The question mark, ?, meaning "search backwards," is also an editor command, as you will learn later.

Global Substitution

Another useful editor command is global substitution. You know how to do a simple, quick substitution for the first occurrence of a particular character string using the caret. Now let's do something more complex. First, look at Figure 4.22, which illustrates a common, important procedure—a backup operation, copying a file to make a duplicate with a slightly different name. Suppose I wanted to perform the same operation for the rest of the files in the directory without having to retype the commands. Wouldn't it be handy if history would substitute both occurrences of the integer 1 at the same time? Look at Figure 4.23. Using global substitution, history will do exactly that.

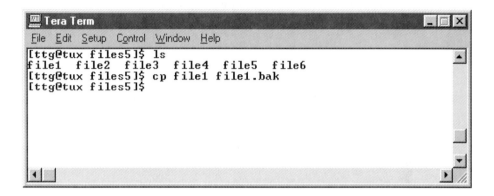

FIGURE 4.22

A common copying job.

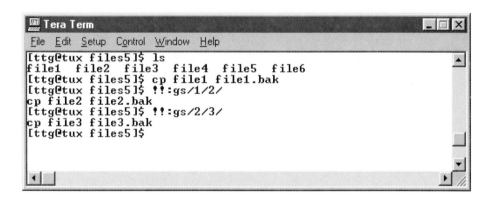

FIGURE 4.23

Using global substitution with history.

Using bang (!) twice tells history to recall the previous command, in this case copy. The :gs tells history to globally substitute (substitute all occurrences) of 2 for 1 in the command. This makes it very efficient to back up a whole collection of files that have similar names—an extremely handy use of history!

Reusing Parts of Commands

In addition to being able to globally substitute, there are times when it's useful to be able to reuse part of the previous command. For example, suppose I wanted to perform

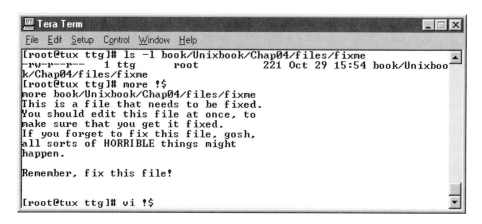

FIGURE 4.24

Using part of the previous command to reduce typing.

a series of actions on the same file. Let's say I wanted to do an ls on the file, then a cat of the file, and finally edit the file. Figure 4.24 shows this process using the !$ history command. First I did an ls on the file called book/Unixbook/Chap04/files/fixme. Having determined that the file was indeed in that directory, I wanted to see its contents to make sure it was the correct file to edit. Rather than retyping the whole path, I used the !$ history command, along with the more command. The bang currency symbol asks history to recover the *last* portion of the preceding command, in this case the path and filename. In the last command shown in Figure 4.24, I am about to invoke the vi editor, again asking history to supply the path and filename. Talk about saving my poor, tired fingers! The path and filename in each command are 32 characters long. Using history required only two characters. In those two commands alone, history saved me from typing more than 60 characters! This command is especially useful when you are reusing the same path and filename.

As you continue to explore command history in the C shell, you will find other nice shortcuts. The ones I've shown in this chapter are the most commonly used, and they will save you the most typing. For example, using !0 will recall the previous command without the arguments. There are more ways to reuse parts of the previous command, but I will leave them for you to discover.

⊕ i-nodes

The Unix file system is based around the concept of an i-node (the file system index node). Unix files don't really have names but rather numbers. At least, that's how Unix looks at them. The names that people use are nothing more than *links* to a file's i-node number. The i-node is the repository of all the information about the file. It contains

- The permissions mask.
- Pointers to the actual data on disk.
- The I.D. of the individual who owns the file.

- The owner's group number.
- Three time stamps (creation date and time, last access time, and date last modified).
- A count of the number of names associated with that particular i-node number (link count).

There is exactly one i-node for each file and exactly one file for each i-node. However, Unix allows any particular i-node to have several names, called **links**. The link count actually determines when a file is removed from the system and the space reclaimed. Remember when I told you about the rm command? I told you that the rm command removes the file, but that wasn't exactly true. What the rm command does is remove a link to an i-node. When the link count in the i-node is reduced to zero, then the file system reclaims the space on disk and frees the i-node. Once the i-node is freed, there is *no way* to recover the file. Like I told you in Chapter 3, when a file is gone, it is *gone*. Forever. Totally, absolutely, and irrecoverably lost. The key to this whole issue is the link count. Remember, the file is not actually deleted until the link count reaches zero.

ln

```
ln [options] current_file_name new_file_name
```

The link, or **ln**, command is used to create names associated with i-node numbers. Unix allows multiple names to be associated with any i-node number. That can be confusing for users who come from restrictive operating systems that allow you only one name for each file. Remember that if a file has two names, it's still the same file with the same permissions in the same content. For example, my friends call me "Tim." I know whom they are referring to. And when my mother calls me "Timothy!" I also know to whom she's referring, and that I am probably in deep trouble. That's an example of two different names for the same person. Suppose I have a file called richard, and I want to give it a second name like rich. Figure 4.25 shows this process. Examine the figure carefully; there are several steps shown.

Analyzing Figure 4.25, we notice the following:

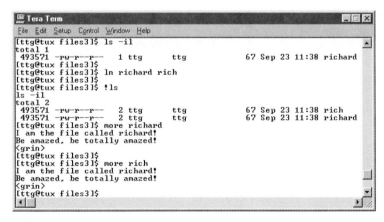

FIGURE 4.25
Using the ln command.

1. The first line of the figure shows a seldom used option of the `ls` command, `-i`, which tells `ls` to shown the i-node number associated with each filename.

2. The file named `richard` has an i-node number of 493571.

3. The next command links the file named `richard` with the filename of `rich`.

4. Next I used history to reexecute the `ls` command, and we see that both `rich` and `richard` have the same i-node number, proving they are exactly the same file. Also, notice that the link count, the third field in the listing, changed from 1 to 2 when I created a second link.

5. Finally, I ran the `more` command on both files, showing that the content was also identical.

Now I'm going to show you a little trick that can save you from accidentally deleting an important file. Look at Figure 4.26. Let's examine the problem presented there. It seems ttg has a bunch of junk files and one `VeryImportantFile` in this directory. Because his `VeryImportantFile` is, well, very important, he had the foresight to make a link to a dotted filename. After working on his file all day, and in a rush to leave, he

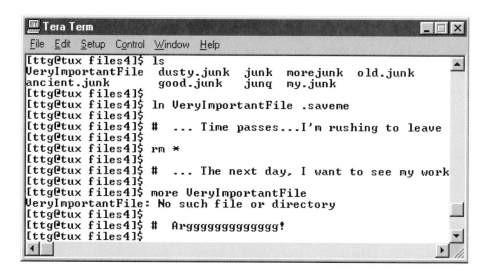

FIGURE 4.26

Hasty deletes can create a problem!

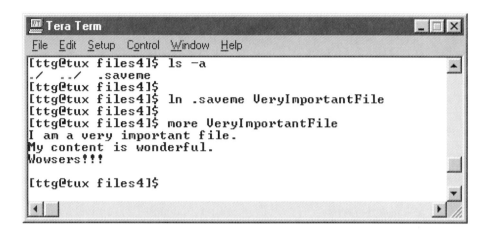

FIGURE 4.27

Recovering a "lost" file using ln.

decides to get rid of all his junk files by doing a rm*. Not a good choice! The next day he comes in, tries to read his file, and realizes he's removed all his files. It looks hopeless. He knows there is no undelete in Unix. But wait, perhaps all is not lost. Remember that link he did, and remember how dotted files are exempt from file-matching metacharacter expansion? Now look at Figure 4.27. Remembering that he had linked a dotted file to his VeryImportantFile, ttg looked at all his files, saw the dotted file, linked the dotted file back to his important file, and saved the day. You'll find other times when it's useful to use ln to create more than one name for a particular i-node.

Hard versus Soft Links

In the Unix world there are two different types of links. The links we just described are called **hard links** because the two names apply, or point to, the same i-node number. Since each file structure has its own i-node table, a hard link cannot point across file systems. For example, suppose the /home file structure contains a file called myfile, linked to i-node number 12397 in the /home i-node table. That file could be linked to file name myfile2 in the same file structure. Now suppose there is also a file named myfile in the /etc file structure that is linked to i-node number 98445 in the /etc i-node table. There is no way to create a filename within one file structure that directly points to an i-node entry in another file structure, since each set of names is tied directly to its associated i-node table. Hard links can work only within a single file system.

 Symbolic links, also known as **soft links**, are a special type of file in which the link filename actually refers to a different file, by name. This type of linking started at Berkeley. Note: Not all kernels support symbolic links. For example, release 3 of System V lacks support for symbolic links, as do most older flavors of Unix.

 When the shell gets a symbolic link in place of a filename, it usually translates the symbolic link name into the actual i-node of the file it's linked to, a process called **dereferencing**. In some special cases, though, the shell uses the symbolic name itself.

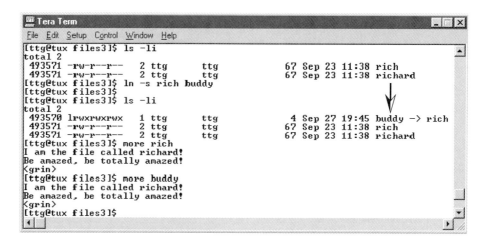

FIGURE 4.28

Using symbolic, or soft, link.

For example, when you remove a symbolic link name, that particular symbolic link is removed rather than the link to the i-node.

Figure 4.28 shows an example of a soft link. The first `ls -li` shows our two linked files, `rich` and `richard`. Now we create a soft link using the `-s` option on the `ln` command. The next `ls -li` shows our new soft link, buddy, pointing to the filename of `rich`. Notice that buddy is a new file type, it has an `l` as the first character, indicating that it is a symbolic link. Also notice that the link count on rich did not increase.

The final bit of proof is the i-node number. Both **rich** and **richard** have an i-node number of **493571**; **buddy**'s i-node number is **493570**. Remember that i-nodes are reused; it just so happens that on this system, on this day, the i-node number 493570 was available, but usually the i-nodes wouldn't be that close together. The different i-node numbers prove that the two files, **buddy** and **rich**, are in fact two different entities. Another clue is that the link count on rich did not increase after I created a symbolic link.

Because soft links associate two different filenames, it is possible to symbolically link files in two different file structures together. This is not considered a good thing to do at the user level. If you must try it, just experiment with it, and then remove all the symbolic links you create.

Suppose the file you've symbolically linked to is removed and then the symbolic link is used? In that case, the shell will fail to dereference the pointer. Usually it will report that the target file doesn't exist. Were I to remove both rich and richard and then do a `more` on buddy, the shell would tell me that there is no such file or directory. If I tried to remove buddy, the shell would process the command as usual because the remove command does not require dereferencing. For now, hard links will meet most of your linking needs, but when you become a system administrator, you will see the value of soft links.

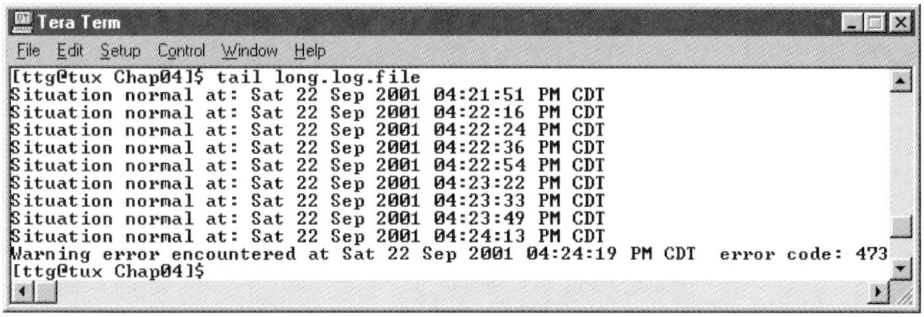

```
 Tera Term                                                    _ □ ×
File  Edit  Setup  Control  Window  Help
[ttg@tux Chap04]$ tail long.log.file                              ▲
Situation normal at: Sat 22 Sep 2001 04:21:51 PM CDT
Situation normal at: Sat 22 Sep 2001 04:22:16 PM CDT
Situation normal at: Sat 22 Sep 2001 04:22:24 PM CDT
Situation normal at: Sat 22 Sep 2001 04:22:36 PM CDT
Situation normal at: Sat 22 Sep 2001 04:22:54 PM CDT
Situation normal at: Sat 22 Sep 2001 04:23:22 PM CDT
Situation normal at: Sat 22 Sep 2001 04:23:33 PM CDT
Situation normal at: Sat 22 Sep 2001 04:23:49 PM CDT
Situation normal at: Sat 22 Sep 2001 04:24:13 PM CDT
Warning error encountered at Sat 22 Sep 2001 04:24:19 PM CDT   error code: 473
[ttg@tux Chap04]$                                                 ▼
◄ │                                                             ► //
```

FIGURE 4.29

Using the tail command.

tail

```
tail [options] file
```

Sometimes it's useful to be able to see just the last few lines of a particular file. Suppose you have a job that produces messages about its status as it runs. An example of this type of log file is the long.log.file contained on the web site and shown, in part, in Figure 4.29. This particular file is 502 lines long. If you just wanted to see what the last few lines of the file looked like, you could, of course, cat the file and just look at the last few lines. This approach is far from efficient, because you would need to watch all of those lines stream past. The **tail** command provides a better way.

Figure 4.29 shows the tail command run against the long log file. By default, the tail command shows the last 10 lines of the target file. You can specify the number of lines displayed with a command line option, -n, in which n is the number of lines you want to see.

Generally, tail is used to see the end of the file. If, you want to see lines at the beginning of the file instead, you can use the +n option. For example, with the -n option,

```
tail −4 way.big.file
```

would show me the last four lines of the file, counting from the end of the file, because I used the hyphen. On the other hand,

```
tail +4 way.big.file
```

would show me the end of the file, starting with the fourth line of the file.

Suppose the file is 20 lines long. The first tail, **−4,** will show me four lines: line 17, line 18, line 19, and line 20. The second tail, **+4,** will show me 17 lines: line 4 through line 20. Having these two options gives you quite a bit of flexibility in viewing the contents of a file.

The -f option is also helpful in certain cases. It causes tail to begin executing an endless loop in which it (1) returns the most recent line or lines from the file you specified, (2) sleeps for one second, and then (3) reads the file again. This option is a good way to keep track of the growth of a file as it is being written by another process. It will seem as though you are seeing the file being created line by line, as it is built.

head

```
head [options] file
```

As you know, the development of Unix was not a planned event. Rather, the operating system grew and developed over time. We will see evidence of this many times as we explore new commands. One such command is **head**. Sometime after the `tail` command was incorporated into Unix, a wise programmer thought, "Gee, I can see the *last* few lines of a file using `tail`; wouldn't it be spiffy to see the *first* few lines?" That thought led to the development of the `head` command, which, by default, will show you the *first* 10 lines of a file but lets you specify, as a command-line option, the exact number of lines you wish to see—just as you can do with `tail`.

Whereas the `tail` command is most often used with files like a log file, the `head` command is often used to see what a particular file is used for. Figure 4.30 shows how to see the first 12 lines of a file using `head`. Here we find out about the file called `add_user.sh`. The first 12 lines tell what the program does, who wrote it, who fixed it, and when it was last modified. (Note: Putting this kind of information at the beginning of your scripts and programs is very useful.) Opening the file with `head` is more efficient than using `more`, or `cat`, because you don't need to exit from the process; it simply displays the lines you want to see. You'll find head very convenient for taking a quick peek at the first few lines of a file.

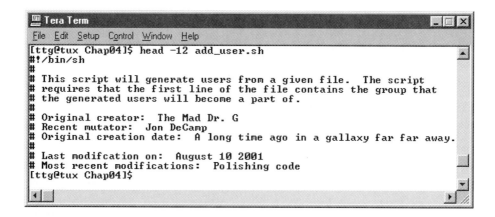

FIGURE 4.30

Using the head command.

clear

```
clear
```

The **clear** command, unless you have some strange terminal configuration, simply clears your screen, placing the cursor in the top left corner. There are no options for this command. It just clears your screen. I could show you an example, but all you would see is an empty screen, and that isn't at all exciting. I will trust that you can use your imagination to visualize an empty screen.

wc

```
wc [options] file
```

When Thompson and Ritchie were caught working on the infant Unix, they claimed it was a "text-processing" language. Interestingly enough, the first version of Unix was used primarily to process and print contracts for the legal department at AT&T Bell Labs—text processing, indeed! From time to time we will run into Unix commands that reflect these text-processing roots. The **wc**, word count, command is one of the leftovers. Initially wc was designed to count the number of characters, words, and lines in a file.

Figure 4.31 shows how wc can be used in this way.

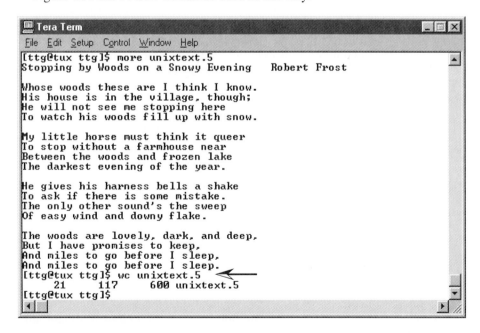

FIGURE 4.31

Using wc to discover information about a file.

I first used more to see the contents of the file (and read the poem) and then issued the wc command to obtain information about the file. The word count process tells me that there are 21 lines, 117 words, and 600 characters in the file unixtext.5. Boy, is that fascinating! It may seem that this command is of little use unless you're writing a paper for English class that has to be 600 words long. But, there are some creative ways to use this tool. It is, actually, a general counting tool. For example, Figure 4.32 shows how wc can be used to tell us the number of files in a directory.

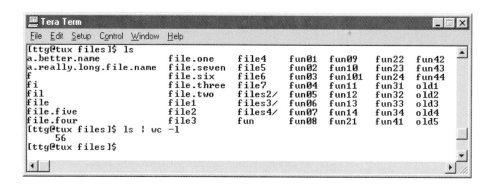

FIGURE 4.32

Using wc to count files in a directory.

By looking at the output from the ls command I can tell that I have a lot of files in the files directory. But just how many? I can use wc to tell me. *Piping* the output of the ls command into wc and using the -l (just count lines) option tells me that I have 56 files in this directory. Piping allows you to send the output of one command into a subsequent command. Chapter 9 covers piping in detail. For now we can see that the wc command can be useful if we want to count things. It will be used more later for other counting operations. (You may wonder why the wc command found 56 lines when Figure 4.32 shows only 8 lines of file names. It so happens that when ls notices that it is sending its output down a pipe, it sends the list of files one per line.)

quota

```
quota [-v]
```

Quotas are limits. In the Unix environment **quota** is used to limit the amount of disk space any individual user can consume. The system administrator can impose quotas on all or just a subset of the users of the system. And although today's large hard drives make disk space a relatively inexpensive commodity, some organizations, especially schools, still find disk space to be a precious resource.

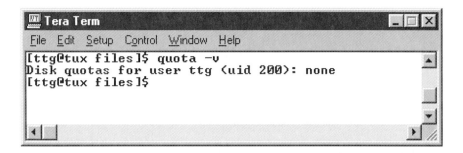

FIGURE 4.33

No quotas are set on this machine.

A system administrator can control the consumption of disk space in two different ways. First, the administrator can limit the number of *bytes* a particular user can store on the file system. Second, the system administrator can specify the maximum number of *i-nodes* a particular user can own. Limiting the number of bytes any given user can control allows the system to accommodate a large number of users. Limiting the number of i-nodes any given user can possess ensures that all of the users in a particular file system will be able to create files. The number of i-nodes available in any file system is a finite number, and each file created in a file system must have an i-node associated with it.

To see whether you have a quota, you can type quota -v at the shell prompt, and see what the system says. Figure 4.33 shows the system response if you do not have a quota set. As you can see, no quotas are set for ttg on this Linux machine. However, Figure 4.34 shows a different situation. Here, on wilbur, a Solaris box, ttg is limited both in the number of bytes he can consume, and the number of i-nodes he is allowed to own. In this case ttg's **soft limits** are 1000 1-Kilobyte blocks of disk space, and 60 i-nodes. His absolute or **hard limits** are 1500 1-Kilobyte blocks of disk and 100 i-nodes.

The difference between the soft limit (quota) and the hard limit (limit) is that you may temporarily exceed your quota but you can never exceed your hard limit. The system administrator sets three different quota values for each user:

1. Quota, the amount of disk space you are supposed to use.
2. Limit, the absolute maximum amount of disk space you can temporarily use.

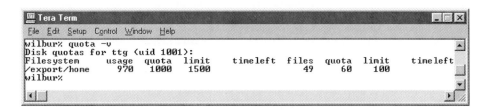

FIGURE 4.34

Here ttg has both types of quotas on his account.

3. Time left, the number of days you have to reduce your disk consumption to less than your quota.

The *quota* is the amount of disk space you are supposed to use. However, knowing that there may be occasional times when you briefly need more space, the system administrator will also set a second, higher value called the *limit*. If you exceed your quota, but are still using less space or less i-nodes than your limit, you will see a warning message something like that shown in Figure 4.35.

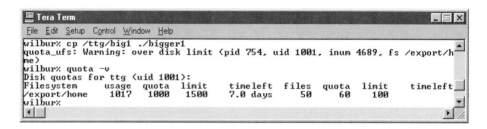

FIGURE 4.35

Exceeding the quota but not the limit in a directory.

When ttg copied the `big1` file, he consumed more than his allocated number of bytes. To find out how much he was exceeding the quota, he used to `quota -v` command. Quota tells him that he is 17 blocks over quota, and that he has seven days to correct this situation. The `timeleft` value is very important. If ttg fails to reduce his usage below his quota within the allotted seven days his `limit` will change to 1017 blocks! The process happens automatically; the system administrator has nothing to do with that particular change. (Note: although the vast majority of systems use the default seven-day time limit, I have encountered systems that have a `timeleft` value of only *three* days.) If quotas are implemented for your account, you need to check them daily.

Figure 4.36 shows what happens when a user exceeds his **limit** rather than his **quota**.

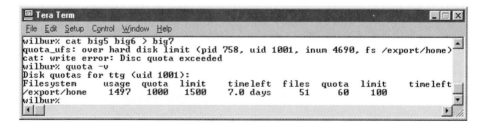

FIGURE 4.36

Exceeding the `limit` rather than just the `quota`.

When this user tried to cat the two files and store them as a third, he exceeded his **limit**. From now on when he tries to create a file in his directory structure—whether that file is a mail message and download from the net or even a file created with an editor—he will be prevented from storing the new file. This can be an extremely serious situation because critical data could be lost. If you ever see a message like the one shown in Figure 4.36, be sure to remove files to reduce your disk utilization *immediately*.

Fewer and fewer companies impose disk quotas upon their employees, yet they are still common in environments where large numbers of people are competing for relatively scarce disk resources, like colleges.

One interesting feature of the quota process is that files owned by the user *before* quota is imposed are exempt from the quota calculations. This "grandfather" feature can be very confusing if quotas are enabled for existing users.

As soon as you log on to your Unix account, you can determine if quotas apply to that account with the quota -v command. If you are living under a quota system, you will need to check your quota every day. Make that a regular habit, just like checking your email.

Now it's time for you to have some fun with the exercises!

KEY TERMS

dereference
globbing
hard link
hard limit
link
metacharacter
not logic
quota
soft link
soft limit

NEW COMMANDS

```
clear
head
history
ln
quota
set
tail
wc
```

REVIEW QUESTIONS

4.1 Define each of the key terms for this chapter.

4.2 Explain what a metacharacter is, and how it is used in file matching.

4.3 List and explain how each of the three file-matching characters works.

4.4 What, if anything, is wrong with the file-matching metacharacter range [A-z] if I intend to match all the letters, both uppercase and lowercase?

4.5 Explain how to use the argument of the last command in the current command.

4.6 Define and describe an i-node.

4.7 Differentiate between hard and soft links.

4.8 What does the head command do?

4.9 What does the tail command do?

4.10 If a file has 100 lines, which lines would be displayed if I typed tail −20?

4.11 Which command from this chapter shows that the roots of the Unix operating system may have included text-processing functions?

4.12 Explain the importance of and relationship between a quota and a limit.

EXERCISES

4.1 First things first: let's make it easier to correct errors (not that I expect you to make any errors, but sometimes strange things happen). Set your backspace key to a backspace rather than putting out those weird characters. (If your backspace key already works, thank your instructor. Then change it to something like ctrl-!, and then change it back to the correct key.)

4.2 Determine if history is turned on for your shell. If not, and your shell supports history, turn on history recording. If you are using a shell that doesn't support history, skip this question.

4.3 Re-create the directory play.files in your home directory, and then create the following files within it:
zot zot1 zot2 zot3 zot4 zot] zot* zot. zot.dot
(Yes, this is a review from last chapter, but now we can have more fun with the files!)

4.4 Issue the following command from within the play.files directory, then see which files were removed. (First predict which files will be left after the command executes; then do it and see if you were correct. *Make SURE you are in the play.files directory before you execute the command!*)
rm *.*
Now restore the files that were removed. (Hint: Would the history command help here?)

4.5 Get a long directory listing for those files that end in an even number.

4.6 Get a long directory listing for all the files that contain the string zot followed by exactly one character.

4.7 Add the following files to the play.files directory:
zot11 zot21 zot22 zot23 zot31 zot42 zot51 zot52 zot102

4.8 Get a long directory listing for all the files that have two digits after the filename, where the last digit is an even number. For example, zot42 and zot22.

4.9 Get a long directory listing for all the files that contain the string zot, followed by zero or more characters.

4.10 If you have history enabled, use it to reexecute the command that listed all the files with an even last digit in the name. (You should see a few more files now.)

4.11 If you have history enabled, use it to reexecute the command in Exercise 8, but change the command to display files that end in odd digits, not even ones.

4.12 Display the long file listing, showing the i-node number for each of the files you have created.

4.13 Copy the /etc/passwd file to your directory. Rename it important.

4.14 Create a link from the important file to .zot.

4.15 Display the long file listing, showing i-nodes, and prove that both important and .zot point to exactly the same file.

4.16 Display the first 10 lines of important.

4.17 Display the last 15 lines of important.

4.18 Display the number of lines, and only the number of lines, in the file important.
Make SURE you are in the play.files directory before you do the next exercise.

4.19 Issue this Command:
rm *
Now that all the files are gone, restore the important file without doing a copy! (Yes, if you have followed each step in this set of exercises, you *can* do it easily, with one short, two-letter command!)

4.20 Determine if you have a quota set for your account. If so, remember to check it every day.

CHAPTER

5

Editing 101: Meet ed

CHAPTER OBJECTIVES
After reading this chapter, you should be able to:

- Explain the importance of the ed editor.
- Use the ed editor to create and modify files, including:
- Starting the editor with a different command prompt.
- Adding, deleting, and changing lines in the file.
- Using ed to save, copy, move, and replace lines of text.
- Modify the contents of a line of text using substitution.
- Save changes made to a file in either the original file or another file.
- Use shell commands from within the editor.

⊕ Text Editors

Editing is the process of adding, changing, or deleting text within a file. As you remember, a file is nothing more than a "stream-o-bytes." Actually, in Unix a file is nothing more than a stream of ASCII bytes. *ASCII* stands for *American Standard Code for Information Interchange* and is one of the worldwide standards. The ASCII code was the first 7-bit standard code that let characters—that is, letters, numbers, punctuation, and other symbols—be represented by the same 7-bit patterns on many different kinds of computers. It is limited to the alphabet popular at the time in the United States but has been used internationally.

An **ASCII editor**, also called a *text editor*, produces an ASCII file, one that consists entirely of ASCII characters. Unix editors are ASCII editors. In this chapter you will meet **ed**, the first widely used Unix editor. Like all Unix editors, it differs from word processors in three ways:

- It is a simple text editor.
- It is a line editor rather than a page editor.
- It works in two modes, command and text-entry.

The first way that Unix editors differ from word processors like StarOffice Writer, WordPerfect, or Word is that they produce a file that is pure, simple text. (This has nothing to do with how sophisticated the editors are; they are very complex, but they produce files with a simple format.) The WYSIWYG word processors that you're probably used to add an amazing amount of data to the actual text you enter. For example, if I create a file using Microsoft Word that only contains the two words *Unix Rules*, with no special formatting, no special fonts, that word processor creates a file that contains 19,456 bytes! If I create the same file using ed, on tux, the file size is 11 bytes. (The words *Unix Rules* are 9 bytes, the space between is 1 byte, and the end-of-line byte is 1 byte.) Quite a difference!

The reason for the huge discrepancy is that Word has to keep track of all kinds of ancillary information besides the actual text. For example, it must record the font type, the font size, paragraph-formatting information, page-number information, and so on. The ed editor keeps track of only 11 little bytes, 10 for the characters and 1 for the end-of-file mark. Now, to be fair, Word can do all kinds of things that ed can't, but in the Unix world we don't want most of those things done for or to us anyhow.

If size weren't enough of a problem, another conundrum shows itself when we try to display the contents of the file. Figure 5.1 shows the output of the more command for a file called unixrules, which was created on tux.

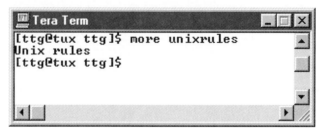

FIGURE 5.1

Contents of unixrules, a file produced with the ed editor.

In contrast, Figure 5.2 shows the contents of Unixrules.doc, which was copied to tux so I could use the more command to show it as well.

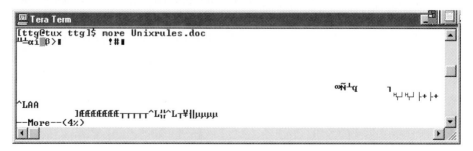

FIGURE 5.2

Contents of Unixrules.doc, a file produced with Microsoft Word.

Notice that Figure 5.2 shows only part of the contents of the file. The rest of the file contains more of the same, with a few understandable characters scattered throughout.

Needless to say, it is very difficult to try to read the file shown in Figure 5.2. Perhaps it's written in Ferengi, a strange dialect of Romulan, or even ancient Aramaic, but I sure can't read it! Therein lies the rub: neither the shell nor any other Unix command can read it, either. Therefore, using a word processor to create files that we are going to use in a Unix system makes little sense, because nothing except the word processor that created them can read them anyway. Oh, sure, I know we could use the word processor and then save the files in ASCII. But that just means we have to go through extra steps, and going through extra steps is not efficient.

Since we would like to create readable, reasonably sized ASCII files, using an ASCII editor makes good sense. You're already familiar with the pico editor; now it's time to learn how to use the first of the true Unix editors, ed.

⊕ Meet ed

The early versions of the ed editor, which is today known as the *standard Unix editor*, were written by Ken Thompson. They descended from the **QED editor**, which might be called the parent of ed. It was written by Butler Lampson and Peter Deutsch at Berkeley in the middle 1960s. Before he wrote ed, Thompson wrote a version of QED for the Multics project. Dennis Ritchie also worked on that early, Bell Labs version of QED. However, QED grew to be complex, and Thompson wanted a simpler editor, so he built the first version of ed. In its evolution, many other people have worked on ed, and it has become a more complex and more powerful editor. Nonetheless, ed has retained much of the original flavor and functionality given it by Thompson in the early 1970s.

⊕ Line Editors

The standard Unix editors (ed and ex/vi) are **line editors** rather than page or document editors. This feature sometimes takes a little getting used to, as most of us are more familiar with the modern, full-document word processors. To understand ed we need to consider when ed was developed and what technology was available at the time.

Remember that ed was developed back in the early 1970s, when the state-of-the-art input device was the Teletype, actually the **ASR-33**, which first saw the light of day in the early 1960s. This absolutely classic all-around I/O device was able to print a screaming (for its time) 10 characters per second (uppercase and symbols only). It generated input at the same speed from its keyboard. The expensive, full-featured versions had a built-in punched paper tape reader, and could punch paper tape for output and off-line storage. Some models of this unit could even start and stop the paper tape reader or the paper tape punch on command from a host computer, which is the reason for the ASR (Automatic Send & Receive) designation.

With a very slow, noisy I/O device, long, involved command names are inefficient. That is why the ed commands are only one character long. In addition to being slow, the Teletype, or ASR-33, was a hard-copy device. Therefore, the users could look back on the paper and see everything they had typed, unlike the case of a computer monitor, where you can see only 24 lines at a time. So there was no need to "refresh the screen"; that would simply print a lot of lines, pushing the paper up at 10 characters per second, chewing up a lot of time. The ed editor was designed to work on *a single line* of the input file at a time. Hence the appellation *line editor*.

As ed grew and developed over time, he acquired the ability to perform edits on a number of lines, sequentially, with one command. He also acquired new, additional, features that made him more powerful and more useful, but he has remained true to his roots, and is still an excellent example of a simple, powerful ASCII editor.

⊕ Editing Modes

The third interesting feature of ed is that he operates in two different modes: command mode, and text-entry mode. When ed is in **command mode**, he will attempt to interpret each character you type as a command. When he is in **text-entry mode**, he will enter each character you type into the file you are creating. Switching between the two modes, and remembering which mode you are in, is one of the more difficult operations in using ed. We will address this task soon, but first, we need to look at the space ed works in—his workshop, as it were.

⊕ Buffers

The first thing ed does when he starts an editing session is to reserve an area within the computer's memory where he will do his work. This chunk-o-memory is referred to as a **buffer**. If you ask ed to edit an existing file, he copies the contents of that file from the disk to the buffer. Working completely in memory means that ed can perform updates very quickly. It also means that everything ed does, any changes he makes, only modify the contents of a *copy* of the file in memory. If you want to save the work you've done, you will need to tell ed to write those changes out to disk. Should you forget to save your changes, all your hard work will be lost. This can be both a blessing and curse. It can be a blessing if you make some sort of horrible mistake in your editing, and want to forget the whole mess. In that case, all you need to do is exit from ed, and none of your changes will be written to the disk. On the other hand, if you're in a hurry and exit from ed without saving your work, everything you've done will be lost. Remember, Unix considers you to be a cognizant adult, so if you exit from ed without saving your work, ed believes that's what you wanted to do.

It's important to remember this concept of buffering. Whereas ed uses a single buffer to hold the input file, the *ex/vi editor* can work in multiple buffers while it modifies a file. The use of buffers makes the editing process faster at the expense of automatically saving your work. There is no "automatic save after *n* seconds" option in ed. So, remember, to save your work, you must move the contents of the editing buffer to a file on the disk. It's not really as bad as it sounds, because given the chance, ed will politely remind you that you have not saved your work should you try to quit without saving.

⊕ Why Learn ed?

Before we go any further we need to consider why there is any value in learning ed. Undoubtedly, you're wondering why you should bother to learn an ancient editor that only edits lines. I mean, after all, you probably weren't even born when this silly, old editor was invented! That's a fair question. There are several good reasons to learn ed:

1. Much of what you learn to do in ed will apply to the other editors you'll use.
2. The syntax of the commands you learn in ed will be used in other Unix commands. Learning this syntax now will make learning other commands easier.
3. Learning ed will make it much easier to learn the sed editor, discussed later in Chapter 12.
4. If you're working from a hard-copy terminal, or if your stty settings become corrupted, you can still use a line editor like ed to edit your files.
5. If you need to make a one-line change, there is no more efficient way to do that than to use ed.
6. Last but far from least, it is much easier, in almost all cases, to talk someone through an ed editing session than it is to use one of the other editors. This is especially true if you are dealing with a neophyte Unix user. You will undoubtedly be put in the situation, at some time in your Unix career, of having to talk someone through editing a file over the phone. You'll find that using ed makes it much easier for both of you.

Now that you have such compelling reasons to learn ed, and now that you know a little bit about how ed works, let's jump in and learn how to edit!

⊕ General Command Format

As a rule, ed commands have the following format:

```
[address[,address]] command [parameters]
```

What this means is that the ed command can be preceded by one address or a range of addresses specifying the line or lines to which the command applies. An address can be the line numbers of the lines you wish to modify, or you can specify a pattern that the line must contain if it is to be modified. Some metacharacters, called *regular expressions,* allow you greater flexibility in this pattern matching. Figure 5.3 shows these three different types of addressing, all used with the print command. In the first example, 1p, we instruct ed to print the first line, line number one. Notice that in this instance there is no need to type anything but the line number followed by a p at the command prompt. In the second example, we ask ed to print a range of lines starting with line 3 and ending with line 6. Whenever we use a range as an address, ed includes both the beginning line and the ending line that we specify.

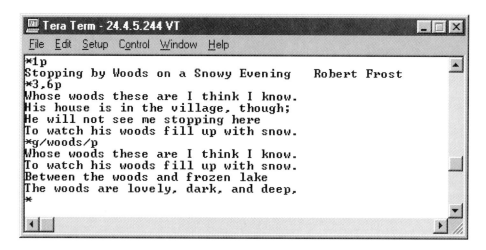

FIGURE 5.3

Three different types of addressing in ed.

The third example in Figure 5.3 is slightly more complex. The g, or global identifier tells ed to search the entire file looking for lines—now, you're going to have to work with me a little bit here on the concept of *address*—selected because they contain the word woods. Okay, the example is a little rough, but the address of those lines is actually specified by their contents. Instead of an address, you could think of this as an identifier.

While we're talking about addressing, let's consider some special symbols, or metacharacters, we can also use to address lines. Following is a partial list:

1. Period (.). The period is used to represent the current line being edited in the buffer.

2. Dollar sign ($). The dollar sign represents the last line in the buffer, or the end-of-file mark.

3. Lowercase *n*. The *n* represents any number and indicates the line number you wish to become the current line, the line you wish to go to, or the line to which you wish to apply the change.

4. Caret (^) or hyphen (-). The caret or the hyphen addresses the previous line, that is, the line before the current line in the buffer. This is equivalent to −1. In addition, you can type −n or ^n, where *n* is the number of lines you wish to back up in the buffer.

5. Plus sign (+). The plus sign is the opposite of the hyphen. By itself it specifies the next line in the buffer. Followed by some number, *n*, it specifies the number of lines you wish to move down or forward in the buffer.

Ed recognizes a handy shortcut here: white space followed by a number is the same as the plus sign followed by a number. So the ed command in Figure 5.4 would move four lines forward in the buffer. (The asterisk is ed's command-mode prompt.)

Note Space

FIGURE 5.4
Using a space rather than a plus sign to move forward in the buffer.

As you begin to use ed, the subtle difference between *4, which makes line number four from the buffer the current line, and * white space 4, which would make the line four lines farther into the buffer the current line, can be a little confusing. However, like most other things in Unix, with a little practice you will come to view it as natural.

6. Comma (,) or percent sign (%). The comma or the percent sign is a very handy shortcut. It is the same as 1, $, which addresses *all* the lines in the file. Warning: the % shortcut is not available on all versions of ed, although the comma is.

7. Semicolon (;). The semicolon is another really handy shortcut. It can be used to replace the address ., $ which specifies all lines from the current line to the end of the buffer.

8. Pattern (/pattern/ or ?pattern?). You saw an example of pattern back in Figure 5.3 where we ask ed to print all the lines containing the word woods in the file. A pattern can be either the exact string of characters you want ed to match, or it can be a combination of characters and some special characters called *regular expressions*. We will discuss regular expressions in great detail when we learn about the grep sisters in Chapter 11. For now just think of them as patterns to match. The regular expressions ed understands are listed in Appendix D. Using right or forward slashes asks ed to search forward or downward in the file. Using question marks tells ed to search backward or upward in the file. In either case, ed will continue to search through the buffer as if the top of the buffer were attached to the bottom. Imagine that the editing buffer is like a piece of paper wrapped around a cylinder. If you were reading down the paper, and came to the bottom, the next line you would see would be the first line of the paper. This concept is called a **circular buffer**; it is a feature of both standard Unix editors, ed and ex/vi.

9. Lowercase g. Using g as a *prefix* to a search expression tells ed to globally search through the file and find all the the lines that contain the pattern. Without the g prepended to the search, ed will find the closest line that has an instance of the pattern either forward or backward depending on how you code the search, slash or question mark.

10. Lowercase v. The v is the opposite of the g prefix. Where g asks ed to find all the lines that matched the pattern, v asks ed to find all the lines that *don't match* the pattern. This is a great option for people who don't know what they want but do know

what they don't want! It may sound a little strange, but you will find that there are times like this—when you know exactly what you don't want and that is a more efficient way to have ed search.

11. Apostrophe (') plus a lowercase character. The apostrophe, or tick mark, will make a previously marked line the current line. We will discuss marking lines later. The string 1c stands for any lowercase letter that was previously used with a mark, k command, which will be discussed in a bit.

It may seem that there are a lot of different, and confusing ways to address lines in ed. However, as you practice with them and use them, they will really begin to make sense. Each has its time and place when using it will make you much more efficient. Trust me.

Starting ed

```
ed [options] [file]
```

The command used to start the ed editor is another example of a Unix command that is both terse and confusing. As you have seen time and time again, Unix is just filled with commands that make no logical sense. This is another example, sigh. To start ed you need to type the ed command. Figure 5.5 shows how to do this. Looking at that figure, the first thing we notice about starting ed is that he doesn't even clear the screen! (Remember, when ed was created, the fast terminals were hard-copy ones—how do you clear a hard-copy terminal? I guess by tearing off the paper!) Anyway, whatever we did before, it is still on the screen. This can sometimes prove to be quite confusing, so our first rule about starting ed is that we should always clear the screen before we invoke the editor. Figure 5.6 shows ed starting on an empty screen; obviously the user cleared the screen before starting ed.

The second thing to notice about starting ed, is the rich expansiveness of messages he provides. All I get is a blinking cursor. No prompt, no messages, just a cursor

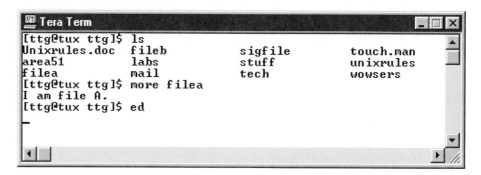

FIGURE 5.5
Starting ed.

FIGURE 5.6

Starting ed after having first cleared the screen.

indicating that ed is both ready and willing to do my bidding. Notice I did not specify a filename when I started ed. That means there is no file currently associated with the buffer ed created. I will need to specify a filename before I can save my work. However, we won't worry about that right now.

While we're talking about starting ed, let's look at how to invoke the editor to modify an existing file. Figure 5.7 shows how to start ed and load the unixrules file.

The only differences between Figure 5.6 and Figure 5.7 are that in Figure 5.7 I have included a filename, and ed has told me how many bytes of data he read from that file. In this case, the file is 11 bytes long.

There is one very interesting option for ed. The -p prompt string allows the user to specify a prompt string other than the default asterisk (*). This is sometimes useful for beginning ed users as they can have ed display a prompt that is more meaningful, or even more fun, then the plain, vanilla *. For example:

```
ed -p "What's up Doc? "
```

This code would cause ed to display the string "What's up Doc? " when the user turns on command-mode prompting, which we will discuss next.

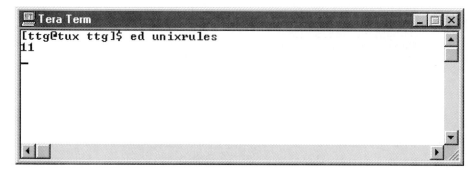

FIGURE 5.7

Invoking ed to edit an existing file.

FIGURE 5.8

The P command and the resulting prompt.

Command-Mode Prompt

When ed starts he is always in command mode. There is no default indicator to tell you which mode ed is in; you just have to know. The first ed command we will learn asks ed to tell us which mode he's working in. The **P** command is the *prompt* command—it asks ed to give you a prompt when he is in command mode. Figure 5.8 shows how this works. In this case, ed displays the asterisk to indicate that he is in command mode. When he is in one of the text-entry modes, there will be no prompt. Each time you start ed, you'll need to enter the P command to ask ed to display the command-mode prompt.

⊕ Error Messages

Sometimes ed can get confused and not understand what it is you're asking him to do. At such times he indicates his confusion with an error message. Figure 5.9 shows how ed responds when I type a lowercase p rather than an uppercase P, asking him to prompt me when he is in command mode. Look carefully at the figure, or you may just

FIGURE 5.9

An error message in ed.

miss the error message. The question mark (?) is the only indication that ed doesn't understand what I meant by the lowercase p. (Actually, the lowercase p command asks ed to output one or more lines, it's the *print* command.) In this context, since ed doesn't understand what I mean by the p command, he outputs a question mark. When I see a question mark like this, I can almost hear old ed saying, "Huh?" I can ask ed to explain his confusion and give us a little better idea of what he doesn't understand by using the lowercase h command. Figure 5.10 shows the output of this *help* command.

FIGURE 5.10

Using the h command to ask ed to help explain the error.

Now, admittedly, Invalid address isn't all that much help, but it does give us some idea of the problem ed is having. In this case I've entered a print command and not told ed which lines to print, so the address of the lines to print is invalid.

Fortunately, ed isn't all that difficult to use and you will very quickly learn to understand his somewhat terse error messages. Most of the time it is of value to have ed tell you exactly what confused him. To do this, you can turn on the *verbose help* option by using the capital **H** command. Figure 5.11 shows how this works. The first thing I did was turn on verbose help, then when I entered the incorrect lowercase p command, ed provided me with an explanation of his confusion.

Notice the line that says /usr/share/locale in Figure 5.11. You may or may not see this when you turn on verbose help. This is actually a system level error message.

FIGURE 5.11

Turning on verbose help first.

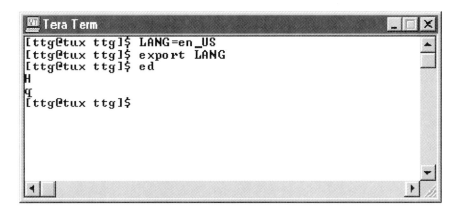

FIGURE 5.12

Setting the language using the LANG shell variable.

Linux, through ed, is asking us what language we are speaking. If you get this message, you can ignore it. However, if it really bothers you, you can set a shell variable, LANG, and ed won't have this problem again. Figure 5.12 shows how to set the shell variable and export it so that other processes can use it. We will discuss shell variables in great detail in Chapter 9. If your ed displays this message, and if you want to fix it, you can follow the example in Figure 5.12.

Notice that after setting the language and exporting that shell variable, I no longer see the error message when I turn on verbose help. Solaris doesn't use the same structures, so it doesn't provide this message. It simply turns on verbose help. It's just one of those little flavor differences we have seen from time to time.

Now, since I entered the H command, each time I confuse ed during this session he will explain his confusion. This gives us a second command you should always use when you start ed.

So, to summarize, when you start ed, you will

1. Clear the screen.
2. Issue the P, prompt command, so ed will tell you when he is using command mode.
3. Issue the H, verbose help command, asking ed to explain to you how you have confused him.

Now that we know how to get into ed, with or without a file, let's find out how to leave.

⊕ Bidding ed Adieu

There are two ways to leave the ed editor. I strongly recommend that you always use the first method, q, shown in Figure 5.13.

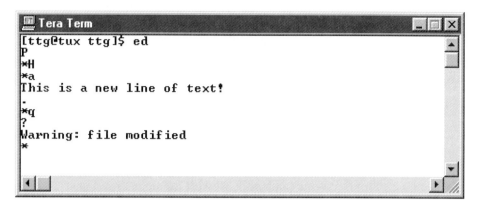

FIGURE 5.13

Trying to quit ed without having saved the changes.

Quitting ed

Figure 5.13 also shows a way to start text-entry mode. Don't worry about that for now; we will get into how to do that after the next section. Remember our discussion of buffers, when I told you that, given the chance, ed would politely remind you if you forgot to save your work? Figure 5.13 shows that polite reminder, "Warning: file modified." At this point ed allows you to make a decision. If you type in another q command, telling ed to quit, he will, and your work will *not* be saved. Figure 5.14 shows that process.

The first time I tried to quit ed, he gave me warning that I had not saved my work. When I told him to quit again, he did, and my work was lost. Had I not turned on verbose help, all I would have seen after the first q command was a question mark. That would not have been as good a warning as the actual warning text. That's why I recommend you always turn on the verbose-help command.

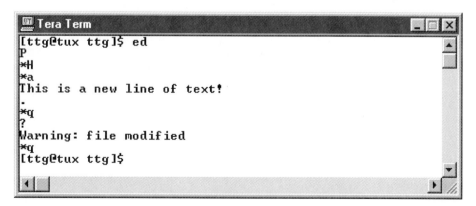

FIGURE 5.14

Leaving ed without saving the changes.

Absolute Exit, Danger Danger!

Now I'm going to teach you something I hope you use only in extreme cases. Actually, I hope you *never* use this command. Okay, so why am I teaching you about it? Remember when we talked about the remove command? I told you about the recursive remove because I didn't want you to accidentally delete a substantial collection of your files. This is the same kind of situation. The Q command will *absolutely* quit the ed editor. You will not be prompted if you have not saved your work; ed will simply quit.

Some novice Unix users fall into the habit of using the **Q** command after they have written the editing buffer to disk. This is a Very Dangerous Habit! The problem seems to manifest itself when the user is in a hurry. Say, for example, you have been working all morning on a complex file. It's lunchtime, you're hungry, and someone walks by your office and says, "We're on our way to lunch. Let's go!" If you are a novice Unix user, you might, as per the Very Dangerous Habit of many novices, simply type Q and walk out the door. I don't even want to talk about what happens when you come back from lunch and realize that your whole morning's work is gone.

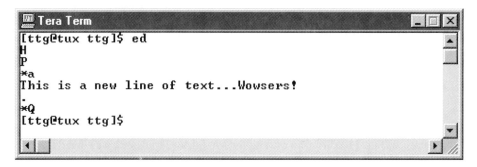

FIGURE 5.15
Leaving ed using the Very Dangerous method.

Figure 5.15 shows how this command is used—err, misused, or even, perhaps, abused. Notice in the figure that there is no warning—ed simply quits. All the work was lost. Now, it is true that if you really want to bail out, you can use the Very Dangerous command and your work will not be saved. However, two successive quit, q, commands will achieve the same end and not put you at risk for developing a Very Dangerous Habit. Okay, you may think that this long discussion is overkill, that you would never do something so silly, but I have seen it happen to my students, to my fellow Unix professionals, and yes <blush> I have even done it. Consider yourself warned.

⊕ Saving Your Work

I realize you haven't got anything to save yet, but I want to share with you how to save your work, because you will usually save your work before you exit and now you know how to exit from ed. One of the problems you are faced with, while using the ed editor, is the confusing number of options you have available to save your work. These commands, in alphabetical order, are the w command, or the W command. Decisions, decisions, decisions.

The **w**, *write*, command tells ed to write the contents of the buffer to the disk file currently associated with that buffer. It is important to note that the lower case w command will cause the current contents of the buffer to *replace* the contents of the file. Whatever you have done to the file while it was in memory will be written to the disk. This is the normal way you will save your work. Actually, it would be a good habit to develop a practice of doing a write, w, every few minutes as you are editing the file. That way you can keep saving your most recent changes to disk.

The uppercase W command asks ed to *append* the contents of the buffer to the end of the specified file. In most cases that would result in a file that had the original contents followed by the second copy of those contents with the changes you had made. This option is very seldom used.

"But wait," you say. "I haven't a file to write to!" Not to worry. There are a couple of different ways to tell ed which file he is to associate with the text currently in the buffer. The first way, and generally the most common way, to associate a file with the current buffer is to specify the filename following the w command. Figure 5.16 shows how this is accomplished. Here I saved my file by simply adding the filename after the write command.

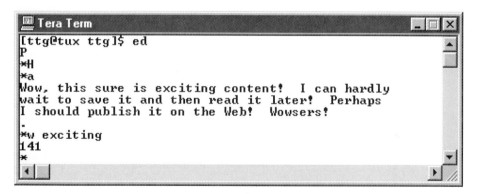

FIGURE 5.16

Saving the buffer contents by specifying a filename.

When ed writes the contents of the buffer to the file, he dutifully reports how many bytes of data he wrote. In this case he wrote 141 bytes to the file named exciting. If you are one of those people who just has to count things, you'll notice that there are only 138 characters in the message. (There are two spaces after each punctuation mark.) So where do the other 3 bytes come from? There are two new lines, and an end-of-file (**EOF**) mark.

Once ed has a filename to associate with the buffer, you don't need to tell him again. From now on, in this editing session, each time you instruct ed to write the contents of the buffer to disk, he will write to the file named exciting. If you asked ed to

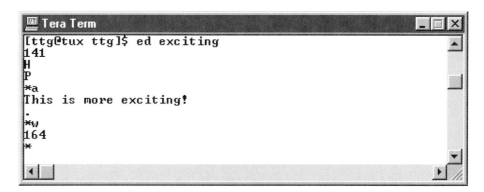

FIGURE 5.17

Starting to edit an existing file.

use an existing file, as in the session shown in Figure 5.17, then each time you issue a write command, ed will write to the file he initially opened and read from.

In Figure 5.17 I asked ed to open the exciting file when I started him, and he told me how many bytes of information he read from the file into the memory buffer. Then I added another line to the file. When finished with my arduous editing task, I simply told ed to write the contents of the buffer to disk. He dutifully told me he wrote 164 bytes.

⊕ Finding or Changing Associated Filename

There is another ed command that allows me to see, and change, the file associated with the editing buffer. Figure 5.18 shows how the **f**, or *file*, command, when used alone, shows the filename currently associated with the buffer. As you can see, I'm currently editing the file called exciting. Okay, you're right, I'm actually editing the contents of the buffer associated with the file named exciting. Good for you!

FIGURE 5.18

Output of the f command.

You can also use the f command to specify an association or to change the file associated with the buffer. Figure 5.19 shows how the f command can be used to ask ed

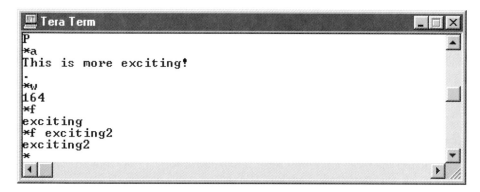

FIGURE 5.19

Using the f command to associate a different filename with the editing buffer.

to associate a different file with the buffer. Notice that when I use the f (file) command to associate a different file with the editing buffer, ed again reports this change by listing the new filename. From now on, in this editing session, each time I write the contents of the buffer to disk, ed will write to the file named exciting2 rather than to the file named exciting. As you can see from the ls listing, the size of the files shown in Figure 5.20, exciting is 164 bytes in length, and exciting2 is longer (207 bytes), and newer (created at 20:09 rather than 20:08).

Let's examine Figure 5.20 closely. First we see where I saved the contents of the buffer to the file exciting. Next, I changed the file associated with the buffer to exciting2. I then added an additional content to the buffer and wrote the contents to the file currently associated with the buffer, in this case, exciting2. In the last step in this example, I exited from the editor, then asked for a listing of all filenames in the current directory that started with the letter e. That listing showed me two files, exciting, which is 164 bytes long and was last modified at 20:08, and exciting2, which is 207 bytes long and was last modified at 20:09.

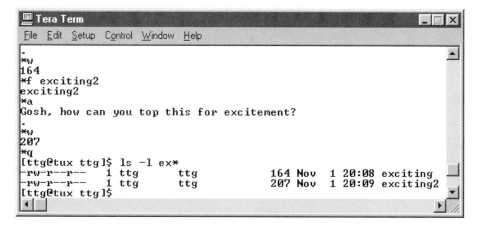

FIGURE 5.20

Results of changing the file associated with the buffer.

Using the f command is a handy way to create a new version of an existing file so that you can follow the rule, "Never do something you can't undo." However, the downside of creating multiple versions of a file is that you can consume lots of disk space in a hurry. My general rule of thumb is to create a copy of the file before I begin to edit it, and then use the file command within ed if I'm going to make a series of questionable changes. Generally, though, people use the f command to simply remind themselves of the name of the file they are currently editing.

Examining the Contents of the Editing Buffer

One of the more common uses for any editor is to simply look at the contents of a file. You know about more, less, and cat. Those are all fine if you simply want look at the contents of the file in some sort of sequential order. Using an editor to examine a file allows you to use the search tools that are built into that editor. In addition, all of the Unix editors will also provide you with line numbers when they show you the contents of a file. These are very convenient options.

When you enter the line number of the line you wish to see, ed will show you its contents. Figure 5.21 shows how ed will display the contents of various lines when those line numbers are entered. For this example I have selected a file that contains a few lines of text.

Looking at Figure 5.21 you can see that ed opened the file called edtext.1, which contains 834 characters. By typing individual line numbers, I make each of those lines the current line—that is, the line ed will edit for me. As part of preparing to edit, ed displays the line he's ready to work on. By entering a numeral, 1, at the command prompt, I tell ed we are going to work on the first line of the file. He then displays the first line. That file contains the poem "Sea Fever" by John Masefield.

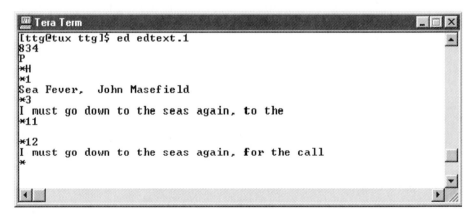

FIGURE 5.21

Looking at individual lines in ed.

By typing the numbers of the successive lines, 3, 11, 12, I make each of those, in turn, the active line, and ed displays each of them for me. Notice that line 11 is blank. Now if I wanted to, I could type each successive line number one after the other and look at each line in the file, but that would be terribly inefficient, and we know that efficiency is one of our goals. So Thompson, and the unnamed programmers who followed him and added to ed, gave us several different ways to see all, or part, of a file.

l (list)

To see the contents of the file, you can use the l (ell), or *list*, command. This will display the current line, or a set of lines, if you provide an address or range of lines to list. Figure 5.22 shows how the list command can be used to show the current line, a range of four lines, and the first line after line 9 that contains the word "sea".

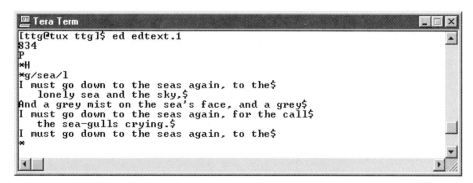

```
Tera Term
[ttg@tux ttg]$ ed edtext.1
834
H
P
*1
Sea Fever,   John Masefield
*1
Sea Fever,   John Masefield   $
*5,8l ◀─────────── This is 5,8 ell
And all I ask is a tall ship and a star to steer$
    her by;$
And the wheel's kick and the wind's song and$
    the white sail's shaking,$
*/sea/l
And a grey mist on the sea's face, and a grey$
*
```

FIGURE 5.22

Using the l, or list, command.

One of the things that stands out in the output from the list command is the dollar sign ($) at the end of the line. List is supposed to display the line or lines addressed "unambiguously," which is why there is a dollar sign to unambiguously mark the position of the end of line character. The list command will also show tabs with the /t designation.

As you remember from our discussion of addressing early in the chapter, using search patterns is an easy way to find lines with particular content. You may also remember that the g, prepended to the search string, asked ed to search every line in the file reporting all the lines that matched the regular expression. Figure 5.23 shows how we can ask ed to list all the lines that contain the word "sea".

```
Tera Term
[ttg@tux ttg]$ ed edtext.1
834
P
*H
*g/sea/l
I must go down to the seas again, to the$
    lonely sea and the sky,$
And a grey mist on the sea's face, and a grey$
I must go down to the seas again, for the call$
    the sea-gulls crying.$
I must go down to the seas again, to the$
*
```

FIGURE 5.23

Asking ed to show all lines in the buffer that contain word "sea".

Looking at the first line that ed returned, we see the word seas, not the word sea. Actually, I misspoke myself earlier when I said I wanted ed to list all lines to contain the ***word*** sea. To be precise, what I should have said was that I wanted ed to display all the lines that contain the ***string*** sea, not the word sea. Since the word seas contains the string sea, it meets our criteria as well. This is an important distinction. When we speak of a **word**, we are generally speaking of a character string that is delimited by either white space or some other recognized punctuation. On the other hand, when we speak of a **string**, we're speaking simply of a series of characters, usually letters, punctuation, and white space. I will try to use this distinction from here on in the text.

n (number and list)

The **n**, or *number*, command is very useful if you write programs, HTML files, or other types of files in which lines can be referenced by their numbers. For example, if I were writing a C program and made a mistake in my code, when I passed it to the compiler I might be told that I had an error in line number 36. Of course, I could open the program in ed, and type in 36 to see the 36th line. But the error might actually be in line 34, and the C compiler might not become completely confused until line 36 and so report that line to me. It would be much more efficient to simply have ed number all lines and show them to me.

Figure 5.24 shows our poem, with each of the lines numbered. We used the " , " as a shorthand address to specify all the lines, and then used the n command to list and number them. (We will discuss all the addressing options in just a bit.)

This recent version of ed, included in RedHat Linux 7.0, has a very nice feature. It acts something like the more command in that it asks us to touch the RETURN key to see the next screenful of lines from the file. It seems to recognize that our screen size is 24 lines, so it doesn't scroll the beginning of the file off the screen. Quite helpful! Other versions of ed simply list and number all of the lines in the file, showing only the last 23 lines of the file on the screen.

Figure 5.25 shows how a different version of ed works in Solaris. This version shows the last 23 lines in the file. It isn't always as helpful as the RedHat version of ed, but you can learn to use either one.

p (print)

The third way to display the contents of file in ed is to use the p, or *print*, command. Figure 5.26 shows an example of printing the first 10 lines from the "Sea Fever" file. This is the "plain vanilla" way of displaying the contents of the buffer. It doesn't show the end of line bytes the way the list (1) command does, and it doesn't put numbers on the lines the way the number and list (n), command does. All ed does here is show the contents of the file. Unless I am working with a program or HTML file, print is the most common display tool I use.

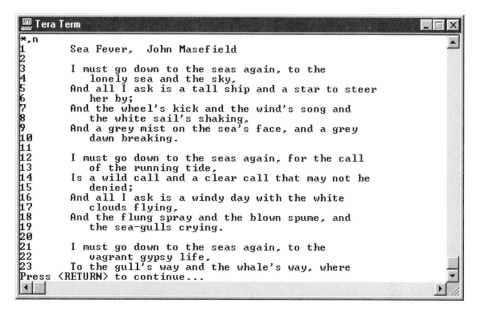

FIGURE 5.24

A numbered listing of a file.

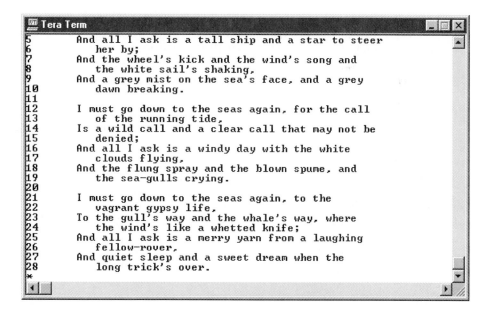

FIGURE 5.25

Asking an older version of ed to number the lines.

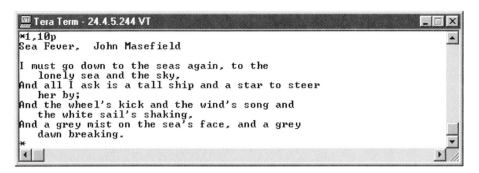

FIGURE 5.26

Having ed print 10 lines in Linux.

⊕ Adding Text to a File

There are three ed commands that are commonly used to enter new text into a file: a (append), i (insert), and c (change). Each of these three commands will start *text-entry mode*.

a (append)

The first command of the three, **a**, or *append*, will insert text *after* the current line or after the line specified in the address. This is the command we must use to enter text into a brand-new file. Figure 5.27 shows how this command works. In this case I will be entering the poem "High Flight," written by John Gillespie Magee, Jr., who joined the Royal Canadian Air Force in October 1940 at age 18. He went to England and began flying Spitfires. He was flying a Spitfire on a test flight at 30,000 feet when he got the inspiration for this poem. McGee was killed in action in a dogfight on the 11th of December 1941. He was only 19 years old.

   In Figure 5.27, notice that there is no prompt telling me I am in text-entry mode. The only way I know I'm not in command mode is the absence of the * prompt. Everything I type is added to the file. (I know there are a couple of typos in the file; we will fix them later.) Each time I touch ENTER I get a new line in the file. I can continue entering new lines of text in this manner until I reach the end of the document or until I get tired of typing. To get out of append mode and back into command mode I need to enter a period (.) as the *first and only* character on the line. Think back to our discussion of pico and pine. This procedure should be familiar from our discussion of those editing tools. Figure 5.28 shows how it works. After I type the period and touch ENTER ed takes me out of append mode and puts me back in command mode, as shown by the asterisk prompt.

i (insert)

Append is used to add text to the end of the file or after a given line. If you want to *insert* text *before* a particular line, you use the i, or *insert*, command. Remember that relationship: append adds *after*, insert adds *before*. We will see this again.

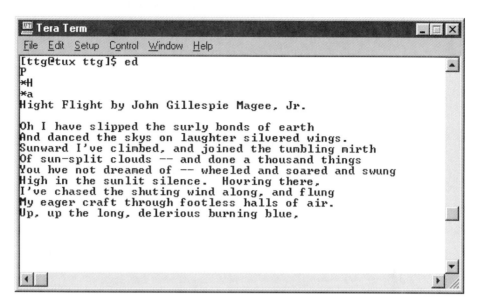

FIGURE 5.27

Using the a (append) command.

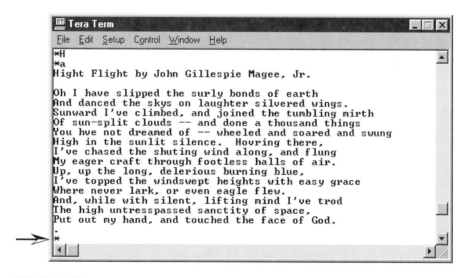

FIGURE 5.28

Leaving append mode and coming back to command mode.

Suppose I want to insert a line before the title of the poem. Figure 5.29 shows how to do this. Since I wanted to insert the line before the first line of the file, I made the first line of the file active by typing a 1 (digit one), then touched i, for insert. I could have also simply entered the command 1i to start insert mode before line 1. As with append, to end the text-entry mode and get back to command mode, type a period as the first and only character on a line.

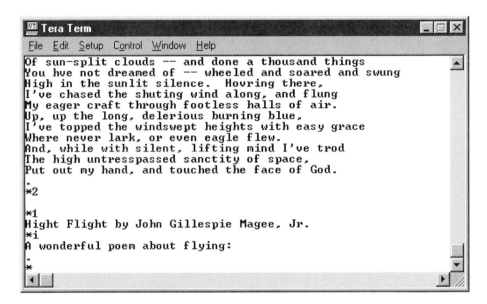

FIGURE 5.29

Using the i (insert) command.

c (change)

The third way to enter text is slightly more complex—at least it makes ed do a little more work. When you use the **c**, *change*, command, ed first deletes the line or lines you specified to change, then puts you into text-entry mode so you can enter new text.

Figure 5.30 shows how this process is used to change the first three lines of the file. In this example, after I entered a new line of text, I asked ed to change lines 1, 2, and 3. At that time ed erased the contents of those lines. Next, ed put me into text-entry mode so I could retype whatever I wanted to replace the content of those lines. Note: I could have replaced the three lines I asked ed to change with any number of lines; I just happened to pick a 3 for three replacements, in this instance. As with append and insert, when I wanted to leave text-entry mode I typed a period all by itself. To show what I had accomplished, I then listed the first four lines of the file.

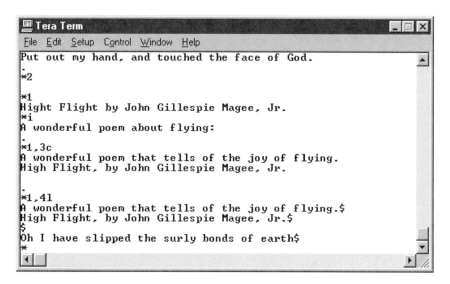

FIGURE 5.30

Using change to alter the contents of a file.

Deleting Text from a File

Now that we can add and change lines in the buffer, it might be nice to be able to re-move text from the buffer. The **d**, or *delete*, command allows us to remove one or more lines from the buffer. Figure 5.31 shows the process of deleting text from a file.

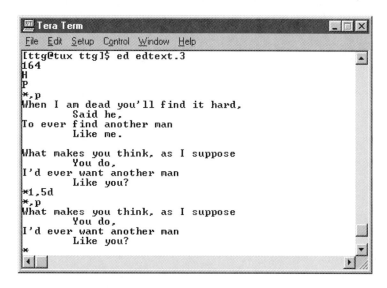

FIGURE 5.31

Deleting text from a file.

The following are the steps of this process.

1. Start ed with the file `edtext.3`: `ed edtext.3`
2. Do the normal startup stuff: `H` for verbose help, and `P` for command prompt.
3. Display the contents of the entire file: `p`
4. Delete lines 1 through 5: `1,5d`
5. Redisplay the entire contents of the file, showing the deleted lines. (`,p`)

(Actually I can't show the deleted lines because, well, they're gone. However, you can see where they should've been, and so they are conspicuous by their absence.) Just typing a d at the command prompt will delete whichever line is currently the active line. That can be quite dangerous, so I recommend you always provide delete with one or more line numbers you wish to delete.

One other feature of the delete command that you'll quickly come to appreciate is that delete always deletes an entire line. After all this is a "line editor," so we expect most of the commands to operate on lines, not characters or words. We will learn how to remove portions of a line when we get to the substitute command.

⊕ Combining Two Lines

It is sometimes useful to be able to combine two or more lines from a file into a single line. Take for example, the customer data shown in Figure 5.32. This is a pretty standard data file, in which each customer record takes up three lines. However, for some types of processing it may be useful to have all the customer data on a single line, and ed has the **j**, or *join*, command for just this purpose. Figure 5.33 shows how to join three lines in a single ed command.

The form of the join command is

```
address1,address2j
```

where address 1 and address 2 define a ***contiguous*** range of lines, meaning a range in which the lines are in sequential order skipping none. If you don't correctly specify a range of lines to be joined, ed will simply ignore the command—not giving you an error message, but just not doing anything.

Again look at Figure 5.33, for it shows another little problem with the join command in ed. Join removes the new line characters from all but the last line in the range. If the person who entered the data did not put one or more spaces at the end of each line before touching the ENTER key, but rather just touched the ENTER key at the end of the data, joining the lines will cause the problem shown in this figure. We will learn how to fix this problem when we get to substitution.

⊕ Copying Lines

Sometimes it's useful to copy one or more lines from one place to another in file. The **t**, *transcribe* or *transfer*, command accomplishes that particular task. (Okay, I know that

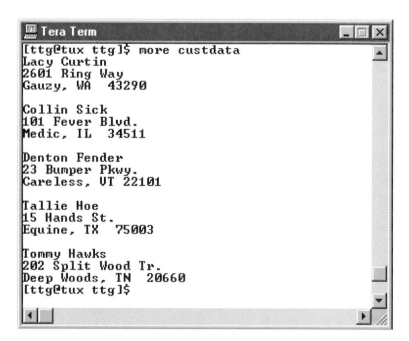

FIGURE 5.32

A Customer data file.

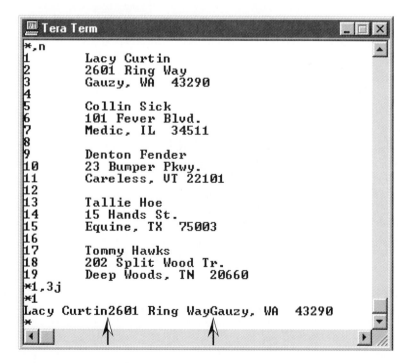

FIGURE 5.33

Joining three lines.

neither transcribe nor transfer really are good synonyms for *copy*. I have no earthly idea why the creators of the ed chose t to stand for copy. They had already used c for change, so that letter was taken, and if you look at the list of letters they used, there weren't many left. If you can come up with a better "t" word for copy, please let me know.)

Figure 5.34 shows an early version of the customer data file. Obviously our data entry person was trying to be efficient, and created a small, albeit difficult-to-read, file. The only blank line in the file is line 16. We can copy that blank line using the t command.

Figure 5.35 shows the copy command in use. If you take a close look at the figure, you can see that I created a little problem. The first copy command, 16t3, worked just as expected, duplicating the 16th line *after* the target line. But when I did the same thing to insert a blank line after Collin's record, I corrupted the data file! This is a very common error. What happened was that when I inserted the new line, the blank line number, 4, and all the lines from there on down increased their line numbers by 1. So 16 became line number 17, and line 6 became line 7. Since I didn't take that into account, I copied the Deep Woods line (the new line 16) after the line beginning with 101 Fever (the new line 6). This is an example of how each increase or decrease in lines in the file will change the numbering of the remaining lines. You need to be aware of that fact.

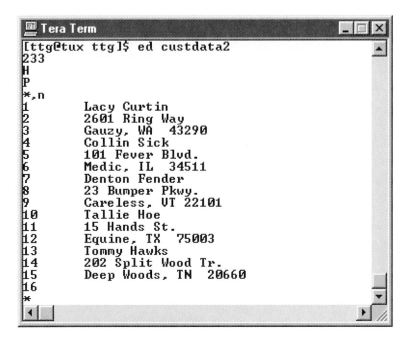

FIGURE 5.34

First version of the customer data without separations.

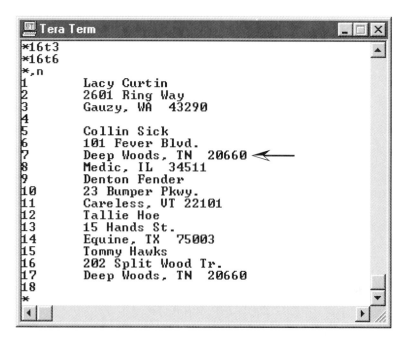

FIGURE 5.35

Using the t (copy) command to duplicate lines.

Of course, you can also copy a range of lines from one place to the other in the file. What you can't do is copy *to* more than one location at a time. Figure 5.36 shows how I repaired my mistake by using the **u**, or *undo*, command and then copied the blank line where it should be for readability.

The first thing to look at in Figure 5.36 is the u command. This is a very handy command to know, because it will allow you to undo *the most recent change* to the buffer. It works only on the most recent change; if you type it a second time, you will undo what you just undid. Type it three times in a row and you will undo the undoing of what you undid. Err … I think that's enough of that. You get the picture.

After I undid my mistake, I copied the blank line, now line 17, after line 7. Then I copied the blank line, now number 18, after the new line 11. Finally, I copied the blank line, now number19, after line 15. Copy (t) is a very useful tool.

⊕ Moving lines

While it is useful to be able to copy or join lines, sometimes you'll also need to move them. Figure 5.37 shows a file that needs to be rearranged. We can see here that there are a couple of lines out of place. First, line 2 should come after line 3. Second, line 6 should come before line 1. Figure 5.38 shows the **m**, *move*, commands necessary to implement both of those changes, and the outcome.

The m command acts very much like c copy, in that it moves the source line, or lines, to the line *after* the target line. So the first move, 2m3, moved line 2 after line 3, in

FIGURE 5.36

Undoing, and then correctly copying lines.

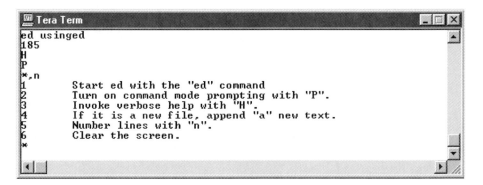

FIGURE 5.37

The initial file.

effect switching the two lines. The second move is a little less obvious. We want line 6 to be the first line of the file. To do that we must specify a line number before the first line of the existing file. Hence, we use line number 0. It is sometimes nice to be able to move lines, however, you probably won't use this command as often as some others.

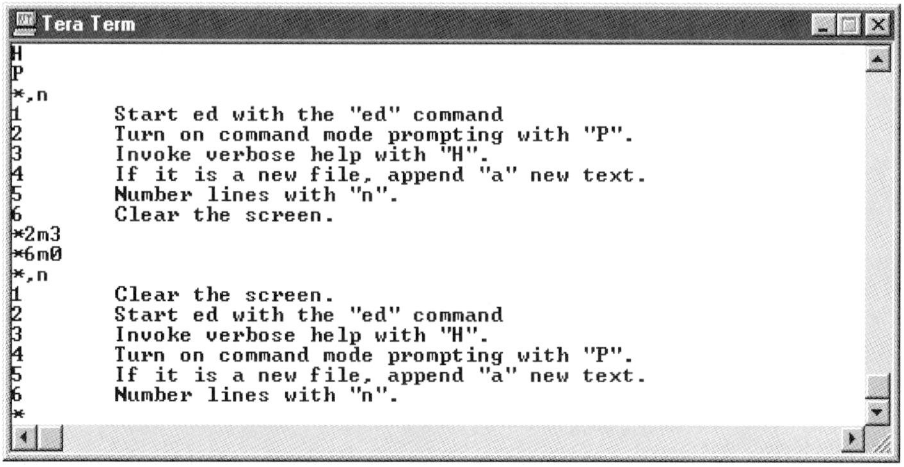

```
[[]] Tera Term                                              _ □ ✕
H
P
*,n
1              Start ed with the "ed" command
2              Turn on command mode prompting with "P".
3              Invoke verbose help with "H".
4              If it is a new file, append "a" new text.
5              Number lines with "n".
6              Clear the screen.
*2m3
*6m0
*,n
1              Clear the screen.
2              Start ed with the "ed" command
3              Invoke verbose help with "H".
4              Turn on command mode prompting with "P".
5              If it is a new file, append "a" new text.
6              Number lines with "n".
*
```

FIGURE 5.38

Moving lines about in the file.

⊕ Substitution, Your Best Friend

All the changes we've learned to make to our file so far have involved changes to whole lines. Any change you wish to make *within a line* will entail using the **s**, or *substitute*, command. Actually, about 70 percent of the work I do in ed is done with the substitute command.

The form of the substitute command is slightly more complex than that of the other commands we've seen so far. This is how the substitute command is coded:

```
[address1,address2]s/oldtext/newtext/n
```

As with many other commands, the addresses are optional. The **s** command will replace (substitute) the first occurrence of oldtext with the newtext unless a value is specified for the n modifier. The default value for n is 1. If you specify another value, you are asking substitute to replace the nth occurrence of oldtext with newtext.

Fixing Existing Text

Remember when we were appending and inserting text, and I had a few typos in the "High Flight" poem, and I told you not to worry about them because we would correct them later? Well, now is later. Figure 5.39 shows how I can use substitute to correct one of those errors. I told ed to replace the character string hve with the character string have in line 9. This is not the most efficient way to do this substitution. Instead, I should have coded it:

```
9s/h/ha/
```

That code would save me typing the ve twice, a savings of four characters. "Whoopee!" you exclaim. "Four whole characters, wowsers!" Okay, I realize it may not be much of a savings in this instance, but if you make it a habit to be as succinct and efficient as possible whenever you use substitute, you end up with a fair chunk of time.

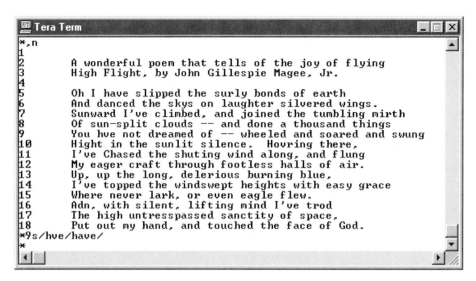

FIGURE 5.39

Using s (substitute) to correct an error.

On the other hand, you can be too terse. Look at the example in Figure 5.40. In this instance, I was trying to fix the word shuting in line 11. I wanted to insert an "o" after the "h" to make it shouting. By trying to be overly efficient I ended up introducing another error. Since substitute replaces the first occurrence of the old text, it found the first h in the line and replaced it with ho, creating the new word Choased. Figure 5.41 shows what I should've done to correct that error, as well as the substitutes to fix the rest of the file. I saved this version of the file as edtext.2a so that you can see edtext.2 as it looked in the beginning of this chapter.

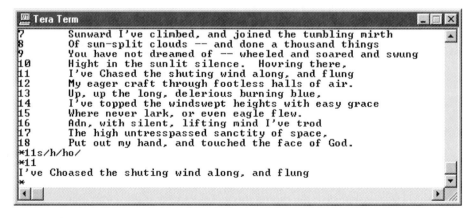

FIGURE 5.40

Trying to be too efficient with s.

```
Tera Term                                                    _ □ X
9      You have not dreamed of -- wheeled and soared and swung  ▲
10      Hight in the sunlit silence.  Hovring there,
11      I've Chased the shuting wind along, and flung
12      My eager craft through footless halls of air.
13      Up, up the long, delerious burning blue,
14      I've topped the windswept heights with easy grace
15      Where never lark, or even eagle flew.
16      Adn, with silent, lifting mind I've trod
17      The high untresspassed sanctity of space,
18      Put out my hand, and touched the face of God.
*11s/hu/hou/
*10s/v/v'/
*13s/le/li/
*16s/dn/nd/
*11s/C/c/
*10s/t//                                                       ▼
◄ │                                                          ► │
```

FIGURE 5.41

Using s to correct "High Flight".

Entering New Text

Substitute is not only used to correct existing words but also to enter new text within a line and to delete a word or words from within a line. Figure 5.42 shows the customer data file that we first saw when we talked about joining lines. Here all the lines for each customer have been joined.

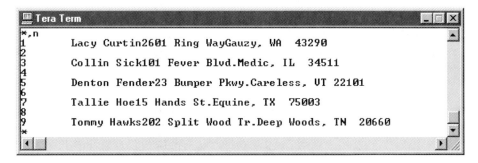

FIGURE 5.42

The customer data file, once again.

To fix the customer database, which was saved as custdata2, we need to insert blanks where the new lines were in the original file. Figure 5.43 shows those edits for the first couple of records. Notice that I used the most efficient method of locating the string for each substitution. This shows how to insert characters using substitute.

Deleting text

Besides adding text, you can use substitute to delete parts of a line. For example, Tommy really lives in Woods, not Deep Woods, TN. Figure 5.44 shows how to use substitute to

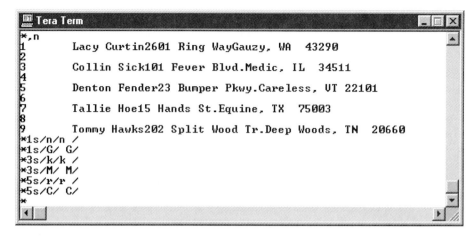

FIGURE 5.43

Adding spaces using the s command.

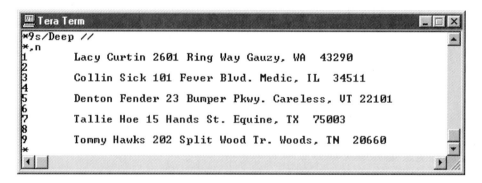

FIGURE 5.44

Using substitute to remove a word.

remove the word "Deep" from the record. To use substitute to delete a set of characters you simply replace those characters with nothing. In this case "nothing" is actually nothing—there is nothing between the two slashes. If you put a space between the two slashes, then you would substitute a space for the word Deep rather than simply removing the word from the line.

Speaking of spaces, look carefully at the substitution in Figure 5.44, I included the space following the word Deep in the old-text string. I did that so that there wouldn't be an extra space between the period following Tr. and the word Woods after I deleted Deep.

⊕ Picking a Pattern

By default, ed selects the first occurrence of the pattern within the line to edit. However, by using the numeric suffix after the new text string, you can tell ed which occurrence of a particular pattern you wish to modify. Figure 5.45 shows how the numeric suffix can be used in three different substitutions. The first substitution,

    s/jam/jelly/

replaces the first occurrence of the word jam in line 2 with the word jelly, because replacing the first occurrence is the default. The second substitute,

    s/jam/marmalade/2

exchanges the word marmalade for the *second* instance of the word jam in line 2, because the 2 suffix has been appended to the substitution. In the third substitution,

    s/jam/preserves/g

we see a special-instance indicator, the g, which directs ed to replace all the occurrences of the word jam on line 2 with the word preserves. (Notice that I undid each change.)

The use of the **g**, or *global instance indicator*, is very handy. Placed at the end of the substitute command, it will replace all the instances of the string on the current line. (When you learned about addressing, you learned the other use for the global address, at the beginning of the command, where it tells ed to search globally through the file for all occurrences of the pattern.)

As you continue to use ed I think you'll find that you use substitute far more often than any other command. So it only makes sense to become as efficient as possible with substitute, considering how often you will use it.

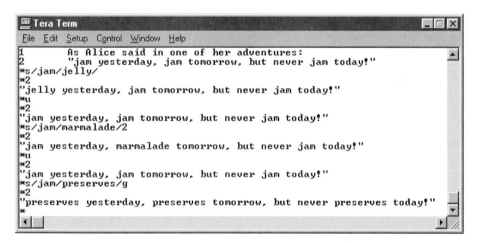

FIGURE 5.45
Using the suffix on the s command.

⊕ Using Shell Commands

It is sometimes useful to be able to issue a shell command from within ed. For example, suppose you want to check the contents of the directory while you are in an editing session. Or perhaps you would like to write a short message to someone who is online without leaving the editor. A third possibility is that you might wish to respond to a talk session without leaving the safety and security of ed. In any of those cases—indeed, anytime you want to issue a shell command from within ed—all you need do is enter a bang (!) at the command prompt and follow it, on the same line, with the command. You will *not* be able to capture the output of the command directly into the editing buffer. However, as you will learn in Chapter 9, you can redirect the output of the command into a file. Then you can read that file into the editing buffer (you'll learn how to do that in a couple of pages). This is sort of a roundabout way of accomplishing the task, but, as you will come to learn, there is probably a way to do almost *anything* in Unix. Figure 5.46 shows you an example of my issuing an ls command while I was in ed to see what files were in the current directory.

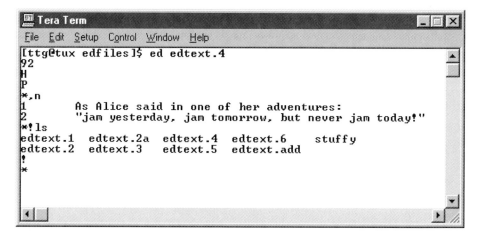

FIGURE 5.46

Using a shell command from within ed.

One important feature of this option is that ed puts another bang (!) that marks the end of the output from the command. This marking is very important if the output of the command looks similar to the contents of the file that you are editing. It is a good habit to always look for that closing bang to make sure you know where the output of the command ends. Of course, you are not limited to a single command; you can issue a pipe following the bang and see the output of that as well.

⊕ Other Interesting Commands

Some interesting commands that are used infrequently but are nonetheless valuable when you need them are discussed next.

Marking Your Place

The **k**, *mark*, command is usually used only with large files, or when you wish to keep track of particular positions within a file so that you can go back to them. It functions something like putting bookmarks at some pages in a long document so that you can return to those pages easily. This command assigns a single lowercase letter as the marker for the current line. For example, the command ka would set the letter "a" as the marker for the current line in the file. Then, after paging a few thousand lines down through the file, if I wanted to return to the marked line, all I need do is type an apostrophe, or tick mark, followed by the mark letter. Thus, 'a asks ed to make the line marked with an "a" the current line.

Figure 5.47 shows how this command can make moving to specific places in a file very simple. Notice here that the first command you can see (down there beneath line 20) sets a marker, a, at line 3. The next command makes line 60 the active line (line 60 happens to be blank). The third command uses the marker labeled a to reset the active line to line 3. This is of great benefit if you need to move around in a large file, cutting blocks of text from one location and moving them to another, or even if you just need to refer back to a particular part of a large file on a regular basis. Do remember, however, that the markers you set will be valid only during the editing session in which you set them. If you close the ed editor and then come back at some later date, none of your marks will have been saved.

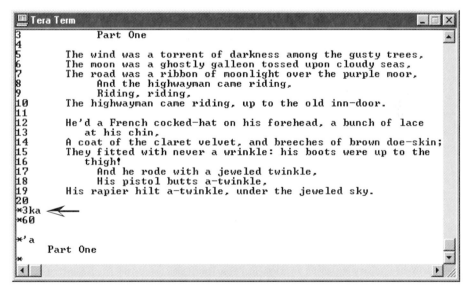

FIGURE 5.47

Setting and using line markers.

Reading Other Files

Not only can I instruct ed to write the changes made to the buffer to disk, but I can also ask him to read another file into the current buffer. Using the **r**, *read*, command I can

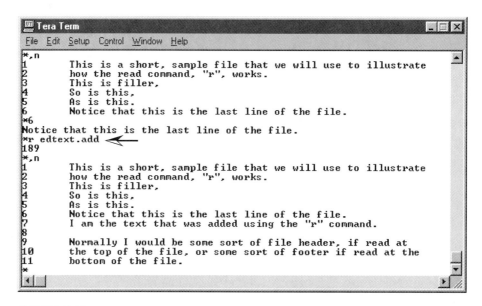

FIGURE 5.48

Reading a second file into the buffer with the r (read) command.

have ed *add* the contents of a second file to the buffer at the location of my choice. Figure 5.48 shows this process. Lines 7 through 11 are the contents of the file edtext.add, which we read in after line 6. Using the read command in this way, we can add to the buffer. But we cannot use read to replace lines. Were we to give read a range of lines, such as

    3,5r edtext.add

ed would insert the contents of edtext.add *after* line 5, rather than replacing lines three to five with the contents of the file. The read command is just what you want when you need to enter a block of boilerplate into your files. Be aware, however, that this command can create some unexpected results if you don't give it a file from which to read. If you simply enter the read command, ed will read from the current file, that is, the file you are currently editing! If you don't put a line-number prefix on the read, ed will read another copy of the original file from the disk into the buffer at the end of the current file. If you prepend a line number on the read and do not specify a file to read from, read will take a copy of the current file from disk and insert it after the line number specified in the command. Figure 5.49 shows an example of this.

Notice that line 1 in Figure 5.49 appears twice. That is because the file being edited was read in and inserted after line 1 as per the r command shown. As we have seen several times before, Unix considers us to be cognizant adults who know what we're doing, and so ed does what we tell him to, whether it makes sense or not.

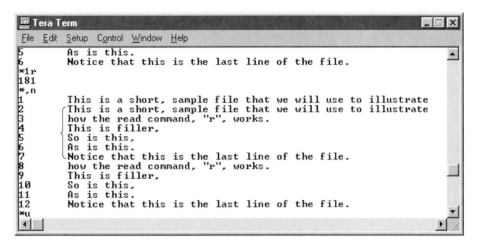

FIGURE 5.49

Without a target file, the r command reads from the input file.

Reloading the Buffer from the File

On rare occasions you may create a situation with ed in which you have totally trashed the contents of the buffer. You can, of course, exit from ed without saving the changes and restart ed. However, there is a simpler way. The e command, perhaps standing for *eradicate,* will read the contents of the file associated with the buffer into the buffer, *overwriting the current contents of the buffer!* You won't need this one very often, but it can save you a little time.

In addition to the commands we have discussed here, there are a handful of other ed commands you may find useful later. We haven't looked at every possible ed command, because some are rarely used and others require knowledge you haven't gained yet. In addition, different flavors of ed, on different platforms, have some additional commands available, because, believe it or not, ed continues to evolve. Now go work with ed and have fun!

KEY TERMS

ASCII editor
ASR-33
buffer
circular buffer
command mode
EOF
line editor
QED editor
string
text-entry mode
word

NEW COMMANDS

ed
' - apostrophe (go to mark)
! - bang (execute shell command)
, - comma (shortcut for 1, $)
. - period (current line)
; - semi-colon (shortcut for . , $)
$ - currency sign (shortcut for last line in the buffer)
a - (append)
c - (change)
d - (delete)
e - (reload the buffer)
f - (file associated with the buffer)
g - (global)
H - (turn on verbose help)
h - (help)
i - (insert)
j - (join)
k - (mark position)
l - (list the file)
m - (move)
n - (number)
P - (turn on command-mode prompting)
p - (print)
Q - (*dangerous* absolute quit)
q - (quit)
r - (read a file)
s - (substitute)
t - (copy)
u - (undo)
W - (append the buffer to file)
w - (write)

REVIEW QUESTIONS

5.1 Define each of the key terms for this chapter.
5.2 Explain the difference between a line editor and a word processor. Why do we want line editors and not word processors to build files in Unix?
5.3 Explain the two editing modes in ed.
5.4 List three reasons to learn an ancient editor like ed. (Now, believe those reasons!)
5.5 Describe the general form of the ed command.
5.6 List three options for the ed command.
5.7 What steps did I recommend you take each time you start ed?
5.8 Explain the two ways to exit from ed. Why is one recommended over the other?
5.9 List three ways to view the contents of the editing buffer, and explain the features of each method.

5.10 Describe the different search processes in ed.

5.11 Explain how appending information differs from inserting it.

5.12 What command would you use to delete a line or lines from the buffer?

5.13 How do you move lines in the buffer? If the target of a move is line 15, where would the moved line appear?

5.14 What command would you use to copy line 34 to line 46?

5.15 Explain how to use substitute to

a. change the string snorble to the string snowball.

b. Add the words Oh what fun after the word Unix in a line.

c. Remove the words after all from the line I like ed after all.

5.16 Differentiate between a word and a string.

5.17 How can you use shell commands in ed?

5.18 Describe a situation where it would be useful to be able to mark several places in the buffer, and list the command you would use to do it.

5.19 List the command to read the contents of the file Idontexist.ed into the current editing buffer after line 23.

5.20 How can you reload the current version of the file into the editing buffer?

EXERCISES

5.1 Start the ed editor without an associated file.

5.2 Turn on prompting and verbose help if you didn't do that in step 1.

5.3 Enter this text: Sweet Sally sells shiny sea shells down by the slick, silvery sea shore.

5.4 Exit from the editor without saving your work, and without using the Very Dangerous Command.

5.5 Redo steps 1 through 3. Now save your work to the file sally.ed.

5.6 Change the associated file name from sally.ed to sally2.ed.

5.7 Duplicate the line in the file five times. You should end up with six identical lines in the file.

5.8 Place a number before each line in the file. (No, don't use the n command to do this, actually enter the numbers into the file.) Your file should now look like this:

```
1Sweet Sally sells shiny sea shells down by the slick, silvery sea shore.
2Sweet Sally sells shiny sea shells down by the slick, silvery sea shore.
3Sweet Sally sells shiny sea shells down by the slick, silvery sea shore.
4Sweet Sally sells shiny sea shells down by the slick, silvery sea shore.
5Sweet Sally sells shiny sea shells down by the slick, silvery sea shore.
6Sweet Sally sells shiny sea shells down by the slick, silvery sea shore.
```

5.9 Display the contents of the file using each of the three buffer display commands.

5.10 Make the following changes to the file:

a. In line 2 change Sally to Sheila.

b. In line 4 change sea shells to rock lobster tails.

c. In line 6 change the word silvery to sublime.

d. Duplicate lines 3 through 6 after line 6.

e. Change the numbers on the new lines 7 through 10 to 7, 8, 9, and 0, respectively.

5.11 Make line 1 your current line and then find the first occurrence of the word `sublime`.

5.12 Duplicate line 8 after line 10.

5.13 Delete line 10.

5.14 Correct the number on line 10, changing it from 8 to 0.

5.15 Insert a line between lines 9 and 10 that says `Sultry`.

5.16 Delete the word `Sweet` from line 11.

5.17 Join lines 10 and 11.

5.18 Move line 10 to line 1.

5.19 While in ed, determine the number of files in your current directory, or write a message to one of your peers.

5.20 Read the contents of `/etc/passwd` into your buffer after line 4.

5.21 Mark the line that is your entry from the password file.

5.22 Go to line 1.

5.23 Return to the line that was your entry in the password file.

5.24 Delete all the lines you added except your entry.

5.25 Save the contents of this buffer as the file `Ilike.ed`.

6

Editing 102: ed's Younger Brother, ex

CHAPTER OBJECTIVES
After reading this chapter, you should be able to:

- Use the **ex** editor to create and modify files, including:
- Start the editor with different command-line options.
- Add, delete, and change lines in the file.
- Use multiple buffers to save, copy, move, and replace lines of text.
- Modify the contents of a line of text using substitution.
- Save changes made to a file in either the original file or another file.
- Set and understand various **ex** editor options.
- Use shell commands from within the editor.

Now that you're familiar with the ed editor, it's time to meet his younger brother, **ex**. Like ed, ex is a line editor that has two distinct modes and is addressed from the command line. If you skipped over the chapter on ed, please go back and at least read the first four sections, which describe Unix editors in general. You will find the present chapter easier to understand if you study ed first.

⊕ Origins of ex

In 1976 Bill Joy and Chuck Haley were working on a Pascal interpreter at Berkeley when Ken Thompson brought Unix there from Bell Labs during a one-year sabbatical.

Joy and Haley were frustrated with the ed editor, and therefore switched to using an editor called **em**, written by George Colouris from Queen Mary College in London. The name em stood for "editor for mortals," which Joy and Haley used because "only immortals could use ed to do anything." Of em, Joy commented, "It at least had error messages—might have even have had Undo." Using em as a basis, Joy wrote **en**, referred to as the "new editor" for Unix until, after a few iterations, it evolved into ex.

About that time the computer lab at Berkeley got video terminals, specifically Lear Siegler ADM-3s and ADM-3As. These were state-of-the-art, albeit dumb, video terminals, and Joy had one at home, hooked to a 300-baud modem. What the acronym ADM stands for is in question. Some say it stands for "Analog Digital Monitor"; others, not so kind, say it stands for "A Demonic Monster." According to the Vintage Computer Festival, it stands for "American Dream Machine." Pretty amazing, isn't it?

To utilize this new technology, Joy started working on a full-screen, or visual, interface for ex that he called **vi**. We will meet vi in the next chapter.

How ex Is Like ed

Both ed and ex are line editors, and both copy the target file into a buffer and make all of the changes in that buffer. Since ex is loosely based on ed—that is, the creator of ex (Joy) knew how ed worked—the command structure is similar for the two editors. The commands you learned in ed will work in ex, because they are simply the most logical commands to use. All in all, your study of ed will facilitate your learning to use the ex editor.

How ex Is Not Like ed

Since "only immortals could use ed to do anything," Bill Joy added a number of features to ex to make it more "user-friendly" and, some may say, more intuitive. One of the big differences is the number of commands available. Nearly all of the ed commands are available in ex. However, since he wasn't limited by the slow I/O devices of ed, Joy used full words for his command names. To make typing quicker, the commands can be abbreviated to one or two characters, but the whole word can also be used.

Another significant difference is the way ex uses buffers. In ed there are only two buffers: the editing buffer, where ed modifies the file, and an Undo buffer, where ed holds an image of the file as it existed before the most recent change. This allows ed to undo the most recent change. In contrast, ex supports a number of buffers. In addition to the editing buffer, the Undo buffer, and an unnamed holding buffer, ex has 26 additional buffers, named a through z. These additional buffers allow you to store text that can be retrieved or inserted in multiple locations throughout the document. In most versions of ex these buffers are also available when you begin editing in the command mode, using the edit, e, command.

You don't have to turn on command-mode prompting with ex the way you do with ed, because ex tells you when it's in command mode by displaying the command-mode prompt, :, from the very beginning. You can't change the command prompt in ex; it is always a colon. Help or verbose-help error messages are automatically enabled and are somewhat more helpful than ed's. This doesn't mean that ex holds your hand when you make a mistake, or print a *War and Peace*-length dissertation when you do something that confuses him. But Joy did try to make the error messages more meaningful, and for the most part he was successful.

Another difference you'll notice with ex is that he seems to be much more forgiving or at least more understanding. For example, if you're starting a new file, ex will allow you to either *insert* or *append* text whereas ed, you will remember, allows you only to append text into a new file.

In addition, you'll see that ex has many more command-line options than ed. The only significant command-line option in ed is changing the command-mode prompt. Although you can't do that in ex, several additional options are available when you start ex.

Another useful feature of ex is that you can give some commands as full words rather than just single characters. When Joy built ex he was not constrained to terribly slow I/O devices, so the commands are permitted to be more verbose.

The most significant new feature of ex is his visual, or full-screen, mode, which lets you see many of the lines in the buffer you are modifying at the same time—something like the pico editor but much more powerful. The ex command set is always available when you are using the vi mode. In the next chapter you will learn how to flip-flop between ex and vi. Now, let's start playing with ex!

Starting ex

```
ex [options] [file]
```

While there are over a dozen options available for the ex command, some of them are very specialized and others take us far beyond the initial introduction to ex. Let's look at the most important ones.

-c [command]

Start ex by executing the command specified—that is, use **-c** to start it, followed by whatever specific command you want executed. Normally this command is either a search command or positioning command. There is an obsolete version of this option that uses a plus sign instead of a hyphen in front of the c. This option requires that you enter a command.

-l

The lowercase letter ell, **-l**, directs ex to edit in Lisp mode. Lisp is the original language of artificial intelligence, and it has a very strange format, using parentheses to direct the flow of control. You probably won't find this option very handy unless you happen to be a Lisper.

-r [file]

The lowercase **r**, or *recover*, option is very useful if your connection fails or for some reason your processes terminates while you're working in the ex editor. This command tells ex to try to recover the contents of the editing buffer if he's been interrupted. You can also save a particular version of the editing buffer by executing the `preserve` command. Please note that if ex is terminated abnormally instead of going through his normal shutdown process, the number of changes that are recovered vary depending upon the exact situation. However, recovering some of your work is always better than not recovering any of it. In almost all cases, after an abnormal termination, ex will send you an email message telling you how to recover your file.

If you don't specify a filename to recover, ex may be able to give you a list of recoverable files. Then, after reading the email that ex sent you, you can specify the filename in the command. Figures 6.1 through 6.3 show some of the steps in this process. (Please note that it is most unusual for the ex editor to crash; I had to use system-administrator privileges to kill the editing processes so that I could illustrate the recovery procedure.) Since there are some differences between Linux and Solaris, the same process is shown on both machines (on Linux in Figure 6.1 and on Solaris in Figure 6.2).

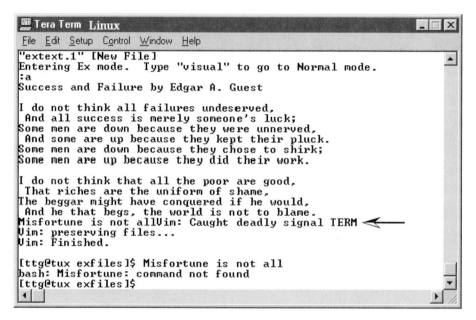

FIGURE 6.1

Starting ex, on Linux, after which ex crashes.

In Figure 6.1 you can see where I started ex with the file `extext.1`. Since this is a Linux box, and vi is considered the "Normal" text editor, vi tells me that it's going into ex mode and then gives me the expected ex command-mode prompt, a colon. I entered the a, append, command and began entering text. Then I logged in as the system administrator in another window and killed the ex process. You can see the process messages as the vi (called *Vim* in some implementations of Linux) intercepted the "deadly signal," preserved the contents of the editing buffer as well as it could, and then exited.

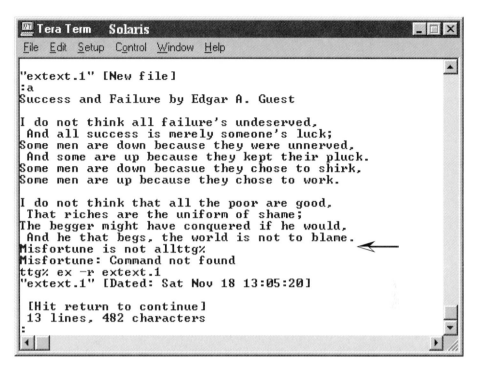

FIGURE 6.2

Starting ex, after which ex crashes and is recovered.

Figure 6.2 shows the same situation on a Solaris box. Here I started ex, added some text, then killed the edit session. Notice the difference between the Solaris version and the Linux version in Figure 6.1. In the Solaris version I got no messages, I just saw the command-line prompt. When I touched ENTER, the command-line interpreter tried to execute the command Misfortune is not all because that was still in the input buffer. Obviously there is no Misfortune command, so the shell gave me an error message.

I then ran the ex command with the -r option, giving it the name of the file I hoped it had preserved for me. As you can see from the message, it found 482 characters in 13 lines that had been preserved. After ex loaded them into the editing buffer, he gave me the expected command-mode prompt. In an effort to be helpful, he also sent me an email (Figure 6.3) containing instructions on how to recover the file. As you can see, ex suspects I was using the visual mode of the editor and so details the vi recovery process. It seems Bill Joy did a very good job of creating a friendly editor, one that even recovers our work for us if there's a catastrophic failure.

Okay, that is enough talking about software crashes, as crashes are rare on a Unix system anyway. More common is the case where your login session is killed because somebody picks up the extension while you are remotely logged in, or your online session dies for some other reason.

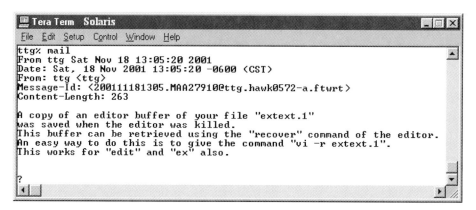

FIGURE 6.3

Email from ex telling me how to recover my work.

-R

The **-R** option starts the ex editor in the read-only mode, where you can use all the ex search tools and perform any text manipulation you'd like but cannot save those changes and thus inadvertently damage the disk version of the file. This mode is the one you want if you wish to use the tools in ex editor without changing the file you're working with. Should you decide that you want to save your changes, you can use the ! suffix on the write command to override the read-only mode (w!).

-s or —

The **-s** or – option tells ex to suppress writing prompts or other normal messages to standard output. Error messages are still written to standard error. It directs ex to ignore the value of the TERM and EXINIT environment variables, as preparation to run ex within a shell script, often called *running in batch mode*, instead of interactively on the command line. This option is not frequently used, because most people use sed, the stream editor, to perform edits when they write scripts.

-t tag

The **-t** *tag*, option is the most esoteric of the options for the ex command. It is primarily designed for programmers who are working with a series of C, C++, Pascal, or FORTRAN programs and want to be able to switch among them easily. To use this option you must first run the ctags program to create the tags file that contains a series of specific tags and the files that contain those tags. If you're going to edit a large number of programs, it may be worth your time to pursue the study of this option. However, when you are just learning ex you probably don't need this particular option. If you use the -t option you must specify a tag.

-v

The **-v** option asks ex to start in the visual mode. It is the same as typing vi on the command line.

-w window size in lines

The importance of the –w, window-size, option dates back to the days when we had slow modems, or slow devices. In the visual mode, ex displays a screenful of lines. Using the window-size option allows you to set a number of lines in the working window down so you don't have to wait for, say, 22 lines to display. Most of us won't find this option useful.

-x or -C

In these days of privacy concerns and worries about crackers breaking into a system and retrieving valuable data, or even if you're a worried about the system administrator reading your files, you might want to use the **-x** (or **-C**) option to have ex encrypt the file you are working on.

    When you invoke encryption, ex will use the **crypt** tool and the keyword you supply. When the ex editor is given the –x option, it will make its best determination as to whether or not the file you pass to it has already been encrypted. If it thinks the data are in plain text, it will encrypt them using the key. And if you ask ex to use a file it thinks is encrypted, it will do its best to decrypt it using the key you provide.

    The major difference between the –x option and the –C option is that whereas they both encrypt the data, –C is much more simplistic and always assumes the data it reads are encrypted. This can make a real mess of a file if you ask ex to work on a file that is not currently encrypted. I recommend that if you are encrypting your files, you use the –x option rather than the –C. Figure 6.4 shows how to use the –x option. The first thing I did here was start the ex with the –x option, asking him to encrypt the text I was going to add to extext.2. The ex editor skipped to the bottom of the current screen and prompted me for the key to use in the encryption process. (I have taken the liberty of removing the majority of the blank lines to make the figure more readable.)

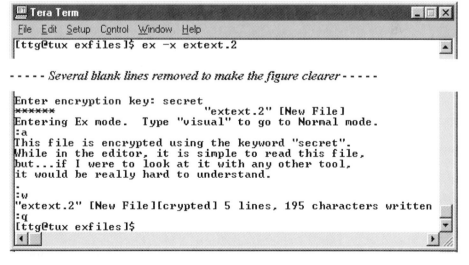

FIGURE 6.4

Using the -x option to encrypt files.

I typed in my very secret encryption key, and ex started in normal fashion, telling me that my file was a new file. Next, I entered the append mode and typed in some lines of text. I left text-entry mode and asked ex to write the contents of the editing buffer out to the file. Finally, I exited from the editor.

Figure 6.5 shows what happened when I tried to see the contents of the file without using the encryption tool in ex. You can see that I first tried to use the more command to view the contents of the file. Obviously that didn't work! Then I tried to use the ex editor to see the contents. Well, it did show me the contents, but not in the way I expected. A word of warning here: when I tried to use more on the encrypted file on my Linux box, I locked up the screen. Sometimes when you use more, or cat, to view a file that's not an ASCII text file, it can put your terminal in an unstable state, either locking up your terminal or making your screen unreadable.

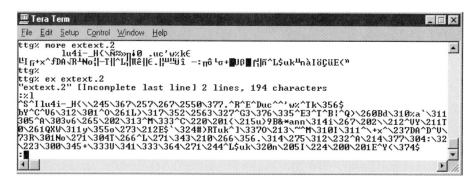

FIGURE 6.5

Trying to read an encrypted file without using the -w option on ex.

It's important to remember that once a file has been encrypted, you have to know the key to read it. The downside of encryption, as far as I can tell, is that when you encrypt a file, it is encrypted forever. I haven't found a way to have ex save a decrypted version. You can, however, use the crypt tool to create a decrypted version of the file. I don't usually teach crypt in an introductory class, but it might be valuable for you to know how to decrypt a file you create with a -x option. Figure 6.6 shows how I decrypted extext.2. Notice that the input file must be redirected into the command, and you must redirect output to another filename if you wish to save the decrypted version.

As you can see from Figure 6.6 I used the crypt command to decrypt the encrypted file. I still had to know the key, and crypt turned off the display when it asked me to type in the key. Since I wanted to save the decrypted version, I redirected standard out to a file.

Obviously ex has many more options than ed. Now let's see how to start using this editor.

The only command-line argument that ex recognizes is the name of the target file to edit. If you don't supply a filename when you start ex, you will need to supply one

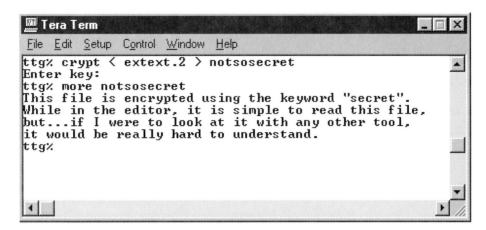

FIGURE 6.6

Decrypting an encrypted file and saving the decrypted version.

when you write the contents of the buffer disk, providing, of course, that you wish to save your work.

General Command Format

Commands in ex have the following general form:

    [address1[,address2]] command [argument(s)] [option(s)]

This format looks something like the ed command format you're familiar with, and has some additional features. The first thing we should consider is how we address lines in ex. Much of this is directly descended from ed, but ex has some new wrinkles.

Addressing

Commands that accept addresses will all take zero, one, or two addresses in the address field. If you provide a single address to an ex command, ex will make changes on a single *line*. If you provide a pair of addresses, ex will consider that the two addresses form the *range* over which the command will execute. The two addresses in a range must be separated by either a comma (,) or a semicolon (;). If you choose to use a semicolon, ex will first make the first address the current line before he evaluates the second address. While the difference is subtle, it can be important for things like searches.

There are two constraints you must adhere to when creating numeric addresses:

1. The first address of a range must be less than or equal to the second address in the range, and it must be greater than or equal to the first line of the editing buffer.
2. The second address in a range must be greater than or equal to the first address, and it must be less than or equal to the last line of the editing buffer.

I realize these rules are probably just common sense, but ex is a little bit fussy about them. You cannot use addresses with some commands, like the preserve command. If you try to use an address with one of those commands, ex will complain at you.

There are 10 different ways to provide an address to an ex command:

1. The period (.) refers to the *current line*. This is usually the default address.

2. The dollar sign ($) is the address of the *last line* in the editing buffer.

3. The decimal, integer number *n*, refers to the nth line in the editing buffer. For example, 26p would print the 26th line of the file. (Remember that this can also be a range of line numbers (n,m) or (n;m).

4. A tick mark (apostrophe) followed by any lowercase alphabetic character—for example, tick c ('c)—would address the line previously marked with the ma or k commands. We will examine this particular addressing style when we look at the mark command.

5. A numeric address followed by a plus sign (+) or a hyphen (-) will point to either one line above or one below the line specified. This represents an offset value from the numeric address specified. One of the interesting features of this particular addressing mode is that it is cumulative. For example, an address of 586+++ would address line 589, three lines beyond or below line 586. If you do not specify the numeric address, ex uses the current line as default. Therefore, an address of --- would specify a line up three lines from the current line.

6. You may also specify a relative address from the current line. For example, if you want to print a line seven lines above the current line you're editing, you can simply enter -7p, and ex will print the line seven lines above your current line. By default, ex supplies the . (current line) address for you when you start your addressing with a plus or minus. Therefore, -7p is really .-7p.

7. Another way to specify a relative address is to provide a numeric address and append either a plus sign (+) or hyphen (-) followed by the decimal integer number indicating the number of lines offset from the address specified. As an example, 243-6 would address line 243 less six, or line 237.

8. Any pattern, either a regular expression or a fixed pattern, surrounded by slashes (/) causes ex to search forward or downward in the file until he encounters the first line that matches the pattern you have specified between the slashes. This is like the forward search we learned about in ed. The buffer is circular.

9. Any pattern, either a regular expression or fixed pattern, surrounded by question marks (?) causes ex to search backward or upward in the file until he encounters the first line that matches the pattern you have specified between the question marks. This is like the backward search we learned about in ed.

10. Last, but far from least, the percent sign (%) is an extremely handy address in that it specifies the address range 1, $, or *all the lines in the file*. This is one of the handiest addressing shortcuts available in ex, and it is probably the one most frequently used.

Figure 6.7 shows a series of these addressing modes in use. Please study it carefully. In an effort to make the figure more readable I turned on the line-numbering option in ex before I began demonstrating addressing modes. We will explore many of the ex options shortly. The first addressing option I used was the %, which, when coupled with the print command (p), printed every line in the file. Next I used the numeric line-addressing mode to print lines 1 through 5. This left line 5 as my current line, so the

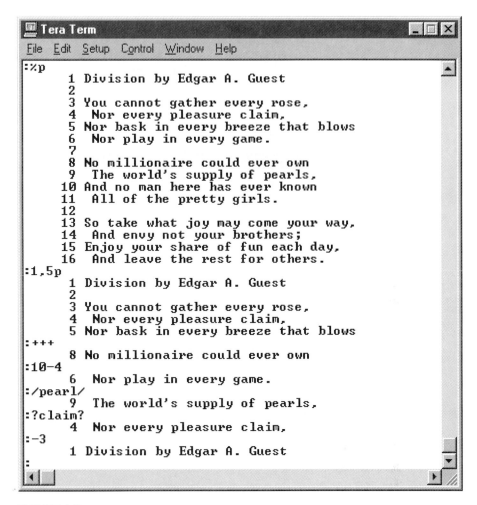

```
:%p
     1 Division by Edgar A. Guest
     2
     3 You cannot gather every rose,
     4  Nor every pleasure claim,
     5 Nor bask in every breeze that blows
     6  Nor play in every game.
     7
     8 No millionaire could ever own
     9  The world's supply of pearls,
    10 And no man here has ever known
    11  All of the pretty girls.
    12
    13 So take what joy may come your way,
    14  And envy not your brothers;
    15 Enjoy your share of fun each day,
    16  And leave the rest for others.
:1,5p
     1 Division by Edgar A. Guest
     2
     3 You cannot gather every rose,
     4  Nor every pleasure claim,
     5 Nor bask in every breeze that blows
:+++
     8 No millionaire could ever own
:10-4
     6  Nor play in every game.
:/pearl/
     9  The world's supply of pearls,
:?claim?
     4  Nor every pleasure claim,
:-3
     1 Division by Edgar A. Guest
:
```

FIGURE 6.7

Using several addressing modes to move about in one file.

next command, +++, addressed the current line plus three, or line 8. In the second addressing example I told ex to go to line 10-4, and he dutifully showed me line 6. Then I told him to go to the next, or closest downward line in the file that contains the character string pearl. He made line 9 the current line and displayed it. Having searched downward in the file, I asked ex to search upward, or backward, for the closest line that contained the character string plain. He found and displayed line 4. The last example of addressing shows how you can move upward from the current line, in this case line 4, by simply giving ex the minus-digit command. Here I told him to move upward three lines.

The ex editor gives you a great deal of control in how you move around the editing buffer. Now let's look at what happens when ex gets confused.

⊕ Error Messages

One of the goals Bill Joy set for himself when he decided to modify the em editor and make it better than the ed editor was to have more helpful and meaningful error messages. Figure 6.8 shows how I deliberately confused ex several times to cause him to display error messages. Remember that, unlike ed, ex always has verbose error messages turned on.

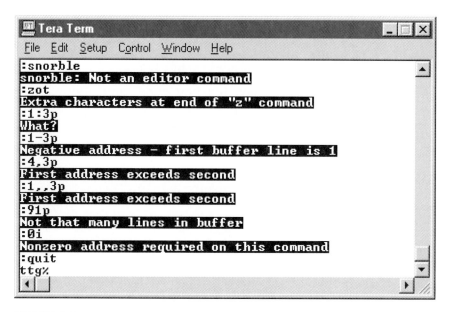

FIGURE 6.8

Some ex error messages.

I must admit that it wasn't all that easy to bewilder ex. He's pretty good at explaining what he doesn't understand, but once, in the third example in Figure 6.8, I really confused him. First I gave him a nonsense command, and he told me it wasn't a command. Next I gave him an actual command with extra characters after it. He recognized that z was a command but didn't understand what the ot was all about.

Since addressing errors are the most common errors, the next several commands in the figure all illustrate different types of addressing errors. To really confuse ex, I used colon instead of a semicolon in the address range. Next I tried to specify a range using a dash to separate the two addresses. He dutifully tried to subtract 3 from 1, and came up with address of −2. Since the first line of the buffer is line 1, and since a numeric address must be equal to or greater than the address of the first line of the buffer, ex told me about it.

I asked ex to show me lines 4 through 3, a backward range, which is also illegal. I'm not sure exactly how he interpreted the double comma in the next example, but he told me that the first address was larger than the second address. Then I asked him simply to show me line 91. The only problem with that request was that the file had only

15 lines. The last mistake I made was to direct ex to insert a line before line 0. Insert requires a nonzero address, and ex politely informed me of that.

The error messages in ex are much clearer and more exact than the error messages we saw from ed. They make it easier for you to correct the occasional mistake.

⊕ Bidding ex Adieu

There are a number of ways to leave the ex editor, one being better than the others. Let's look at it first.

q[uit]

---

q[uit] [!]

The usual way to exit from ex is to use the **quit** command, abbreviated **q**. As mentioned earlier, ex was designed when there were faster terminals than existed at the time ed was designed, so many of the ex commands are complete words. Nevertheless, most Unix wizards use the abbreviated form because it's faster and minimizes fat-finger errors.

Because ex was designed to be "friendlier" than ed, it usually won't let you exit until you save your work. However, you can force ex to exit without saving your work by using the **quit!** command. Typing **q!** or **quit!** directs ex to terminate without saving the contents of the buffer to disk. It won't ask you about saving your work; it will simply bail out and drop you back to the command line. Figure 6.9 shows how this works.

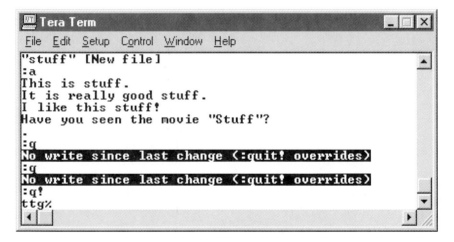

FIGURE 6.9

Using the q! (quit) command to exit from ex after failing to exit with q (no exclamation mark).

As you can see from the figure, I started a new editing session, appended some text to the new file, stopped text-entry mode, and tried to exit with q. Realizing that I had not saved the contents of the buffer to disk, ex gave me an error message and the quit attempt failed. I tried to quit again, and again ex refused to comply. Then I used the q! to override ex's protective nature.

There are a number of commands that use the bang (!) to either override normal protections or direct ex to function in a special manner. If you think back to the ed command, you'll remember that the ultimate quit was the capital **Q**. In ex we will use the Q command to move from the visual mode to the line mode, or from vi to ex. We'll also use Q to return from open mode. What we won't do is use Q to exit from the editor. We have q! to serve as the bailout command.

sus[pend]
st[op]

```
sus[pend] [!]
st[op] [!]
```

There's another way to *temporarily* leave the ex editor, but it's somewhat drastic. You can stop or suspend the execution of the ex editor, dropping out to the command line by using either the **stop** or **suspend** command. Both commands do precisely the same thing. This is exactly equivalent to stopping the ex editor process using process-control commands like ^Z. It may be handy to suspend the execution of the editor to reply to a talk request, or to perform some other command-line function. As you will learn when we discuss process control, you can use the fg, or foreground, command, at the command prompt to restart the editor and resume your session.

The other way to exit from ex is to use the xit command. Since that command also saves the contents of the editing buffer to a file, we'll explore it in the next section.

⊕ Saving Your Work

Since it seems to be so important to ex that we save our work, let's look at the ways we write the contents of the buffer to disk. Three different commands will do this.

w[rite]

```
[range]w[rite][!] [>>] [file]
```

The most straightforward way to save the contents of the editing buffer to a file is to use the **write** command. Most of the time you'll use this command to update the disk file associated with the editing buffer. Develop the habit of issuing a w command at regular intervals throughout your editing session. That way, if ex fails to completely recover your file, in the event of a catastrophic failure, you won't lose your work. But the `write` command can do much more than just save the contents of the editing buffer to the associated file.

A quick note on terminology here. When I speak of a filename, or file, you can substitute either the relative or absolute path to the file. So, for example, I could specify the filename `stuff` in the write command. By the same token I could specify `/home/ttg/stuff` as the target of the write. For purposes of convenience, I will just refer to a file and expect you to understand that it could be either a relative or an absolute path. This will be true for the rest of the book.

Although `write` is most often used to save the contents of the whole editing buffer, the line-range option allows you to specify some subset of the buffer that will be written to the file. You'll appreciate this if you find a chunk of code in a file and want to capture just that code in another file. All you need to do is specify the range of lines you wish to `write` and a new filename. Be careful to specify a filename. Without a filename `ex` will think he's supposed to `write` that subset of lines to the file associated with the editing buffer. That would replace the existing file with just the lines you specified. If you really want to replace the existing file, you can use the bang (!) to force `ex` to perform the `write`.

Any time you want to create a new file, you can provide `write` with a new filename and it will dutifully save the contents of the editing buffer to that new file. If the file you specify already exists, `write` will not destroy the contents of that file by overwriting it *unless you force the write* by appending a bang (!) to the command. Here's another example of Unix considering you to be a cognizant adult, allowing you to destroy the contents of a file if you decide to. This was the same override mechanism we saw with `quit`, where we could force the command by appending a bang (!) to it.

Another instance where `write` may initially refuse to write is if you have changed the associated file with the `file` command, and that file exists. Again, you can override this protection by using the bang. Joy made the `write` command pretty careful; it won't overwrite files unless you specifically tell it to.

Using output redirection, `write` also allows you to append the contents of the editing buffer to another file. You do that by using the append redirection operator (>>) and specifying the name of the file to which the contents of the buffer should be appended. To append to a file, `write` expects that file to exist, so if you specify the name of a nonexistent file, `write` will fail and `ex` will tell you that the file doesn't exist. Of course, as you must expect by now, you can force `write` to create the new file by using the bang override.

Writing the contents of the buffer to the associated file is frequently the last thing you do in an editing session. In response to that, a combined command evolved that first writes the contents of the buffer to the associated file and then exits.

wq

`[range]wq[!] [>>] [file]`

The *write, then quit* command, **wq**, combines the last two commands we learned. It first writes the contents of the editing buffer to the file associated with the editing buffer, or to the file specified, and then exits from the ex editor. It has the same options as the write command, and the same constraints. Since the command first writes and then exits, if there's a problem with the write, *it will not exit.* If there is no file associated with the editing buffer, and if you do not supply a filename to this command, the command will also fail. This is one of the most common ways people exit from the editor, yet an even more concise command has evolved: x.

x[it]

[range]x[it][!] [file]

The **x** command seems to serve the same purpose as the plain vanilla wq command, and saves you one keystroke. However, it is actually more efficient than wq, because it will only write to the file *if the buffer has been changed* since the last write. It seems that x is a recent addition to the ex command set; Bill Joy doesn't remember including it as part of the original ex. Mark Horton took over the development of ex when, as he puts it, "Bill grew tired of vi when it exceeded 64 K., the limit on PDP-11" in about 1979. Horton had proposed xit to Joy, but Joy built wq instead. So when Horton took over, he added the more efficient **xit** command.

If you don't specify a filename, x will write the contents of the editing buffer to the file associated with that editing session and then exit from the ex editor. All the same rules apply when it comes to overwriting files.

On a Solaris system, if you try to use x to overwrite an existing file, ex will tell you to use the w! to override the write. That seems to indicate that although the user enters the x command, ex is seeing the wq anyway. Or maybe x is sharing error messages with write.

⊕ Finding or Changing Associated Filename

As you can see from the preceding discussion of the various ways to write the contents of the editing buffer to a file, it's very important to know what file is associated with the editing buffer. Let's deal with that subject next.

f[ile]

f[ile] [file]

In almost all cases, when you start the ex editor you'll specify a filename that ex will associate with the editing buffer. Sometimes, though, you might want to start ex and associate a file later, or change the file that ex associates with the editing buffer. On rare occasions you might also wish to see the file ex is associating with the editing buffer. The **file** command will accomplish all of these goals.

Figure 6.10 shows how the `file` command is used first to determine the current file associated with the buffer and then to change the file associated with the editing buffer. In this case, I was working along entering text when I wondered what file was associated with the editing buffer. I entered the `file` command, and `ex` told me I was currently editing the buffer associated with `extext.3`. It also told me I had modified the file, which means I had made alterations but had not written the changed buffer to disk.

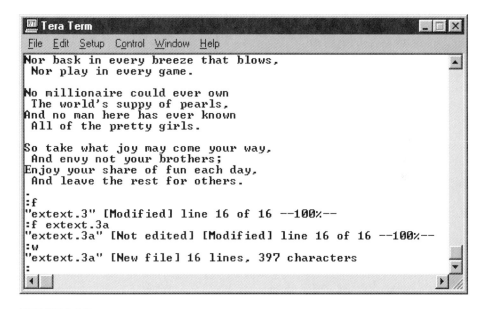

FIGURE 6.10

Using the `file` command to view and then alter associated file.

Next I used the `file` command to associate the editing buffer with a different filename, in this case `extext.3a`. When I issued the `write` command without specifying a filename, I wrote to the most recently associated file. Remember, if you use the `file` command to associate the editing buffer with an *existing file* and then try to `write` new content to that file, your `write` will fail unless you override `ex`'s protection.

The `file` command is not one you use every day, but it is worthwhile knowing about. One very useful way to use it is to create generations of a file. In this case, had `extext.3` existed, it would have been unchanged, and all of my edits would have been stored in `extext.3a`. Consequently, had I wanted to undo the changes I had made, I could have used the earlier generation of the file. This is a common practice in many professional programming shops. Saving two or more generations of a file is a good way to preserve the process of program evolution. The downside of that technique is that it does consume disk space.

⊕ Displaying Contents of File

It seems that Bill Joy felt the display tools available in the ed editor, with slight modifications, were quite sufficient. The three ed display verbs, `list`, `number`, and `print`, are the three display verbs available in ex.

l[ist]

```
[range]l[ist][count][flags]
```

The `list` command is useful because it displays the normally nonprinting characters, like tabs and new lines, in your file. Also, it reveals any other unusual characters embedded in your file. Figure 6.11 shows the `list` display of a small text file. You need to look closely at this figure to notice the tab character. In this version of ex its marked by ^I. The newline character is $. Notice that in the second verse, second line, I used spaces instead of a tab. This method of viewing the file makes that sort of difference very obvious.

You can specify a range of lines to be displayed by preceding the command with either line numbers or, as in Figure 6.11, an addressing character. The other way you can specify a set of lines is to use the **count** option. That option overrides the range of lines, if you chose to provide one, and takes the last number of the range as the beginning line. Ex then displays the number of lines you specified.

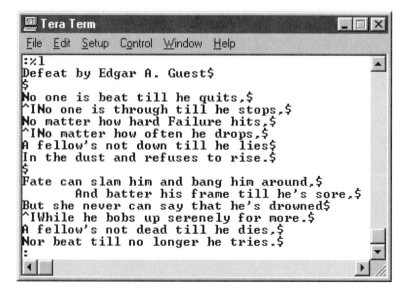

FIGURE 6.11
Displaying file with `list`.

The flags option is generally used to tell ex how to display output. The three flags indicate list, print, or numbered forms. In this case, since we are already telling ex to display the output in list fashion, the only flag that makes sense is the octothorp (#) that would ask ex to add line numbers to the lines he displayed.

When ex finishes displaying the lines, the current line indicator will be set to the last line displayed. Since we're talking about line numbers, let's see how to ask ex to display line numbers with the contents of the file.

nu[mber]

```
[range]nu[mber] [count] [flags]
```

It's advantageous, especially in a programming environment, to have the editor show us line numbers. Most of the time error messages direct us to problems with a particular line. The number command asks ex to display the contents of the file, prepending the line number to each line. Usually there's no special formatting, and the text looks very much like it did when we entered it.

Figure 6.12 shows the same poem we saw in Figure 6.11, this time with line numbers. You can see how handy numbered lines can be by looking at this figure. Now, instead of directing you to the second line of the second verse, where I use spaces instead of tabs to indent the text, I can simply ask you to look at line number 11, and we can notice that I was one space short. Numbering is very important in many applications. Later, when we discuss the set command, you'll learn how to turn numbering on for the whole editing session. Notice that the command abbreviation is nu, not n as it was in ed.

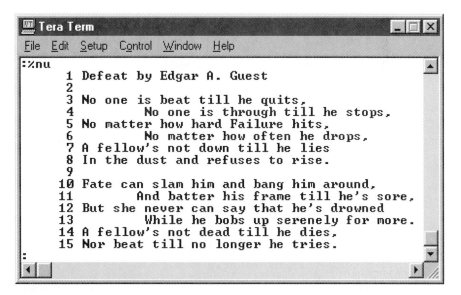

FIGURE 6.12

Displaying a file with line numbers.

As with the list command, you can specify a range of lines to display with the address range, or you can use the **count** option to specify the number of lines to display. The count option will override the range of lines you specify, taking the last line in the range as the beginning line to display.

The only **flags** option that seems to make sense with the number command is the list (l) flag, which would direct ex to display nonprinting characters. The print (p) flag would direct ex to turn off line numbers, so that wouldn't make sense, and the number (#) flag would tell ex to number the lines, but he's doing that already. Remember, not all versions of ex support flags.

p[rint]

```
[range]p[rint] [count] [flags]
```

The last of our output options is the one most frequently used outside a programming environment. The **print** command simply directs ex to output the lines pretty much as we entered them, with no numbers and no special character representations. Figure 6.13 shows the print command used to output our poem.

Most of the time you'll display the contents of the editing buffer using the print command. In some flavors of ex, print is the default output if you simply specify a range of lines or an address. As with list, the number you can specify with print can be either a range of lines or a count of lines. On systems that support flags, like Solaris, you can specify either or both the list and number flags.

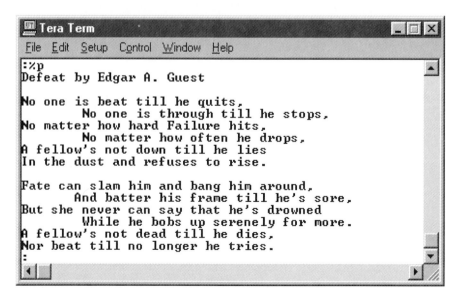

FIGURE 6.13
Displaying a file with print.

⊕ **Adding Text to File**

As you undoubtedly remember from your extensive study of the ed editor, there are three ways to start text-entry mode and begin to enter new text. They are, append, insert, and change. The ex editor follows this same pattern.

a[ppend]

[line]a[ppend][!]

The **append** command behaves very much like the a command you learned in the ed editor. It starts text-entry mode and turns off the prompt. The absence of the prompt tells you that you're in text-entry mode. Append adds lines *after the line* specified by the address, or after the current line if you don't specify an address. To exit from append mode—or, for that matter, any ex text-entry mode—type a period (.) as the only character on a line, just as in ed.

According to the documentation, you can put a bang (!) after the append command to toggle Auto Indent on or off. This seems to be a flavor difference. On my Solaris machine Auto Indent works as expected, but on my Linux machine, ex seems to ignore the bang. Figure 6.14 shows examples of both systems. As you can see, once I

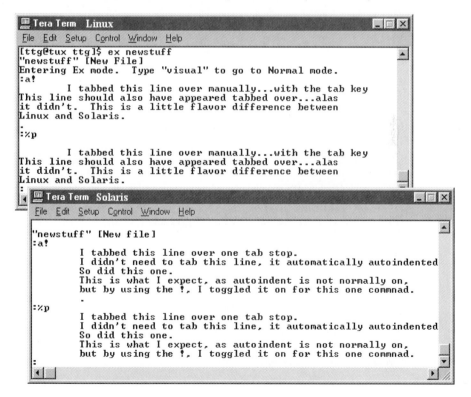

FIGURE 6.14

Using append with both Linux (top) and Solaris (bottom).

tabbed over for the first line, all the other lines on the Solaris machine (bottom of figure) automatically maintained that tab setting. However, on the Linux machine (top of figure) Auto Indent failed to work. This is a small difference, but it may be important to you. Experiment on your machine to see whether the bang will or will not toggle Auto Indent in your version of ex.

i[nsert]

```
[line]i[nsert][!]
```

The **insert** command, (**i**), works as expected, starting text-entry mode and inserting lines *before the line* specified, or the current line if you don't specify a line address. You leave text-entry mode by typing a period (.) on a line by itself.

According to the documentation, you can toggle Auto Indent by appending a bang to the insert command just as you can with append. However, if you look at Figure 6.15, you'll see that the two different versions of ex behave differently. As we saw with append, the Linux version (top of figure) of ex ignores the bang, while the Solaris version (bottom of figure) performs as documented. Figure 6.15 shows another

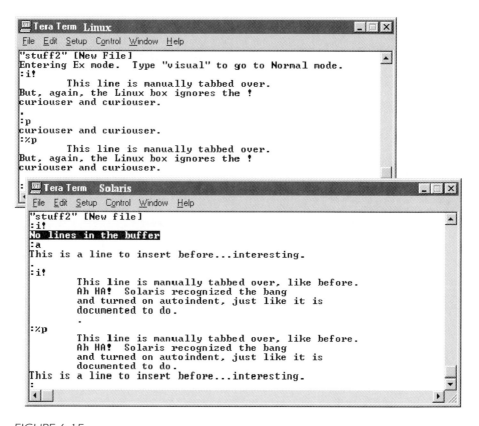

FIGURE 6.15

Using insert with Linux (top) and Solaris (bottom).

difference, too. Notice that on the Linux box, even though there were no initial lines, it accepted the `insert` command and started text-entry mode. In essence, it began inserting before line 0! The Solaris version of `ex`, on the other hand, considered it an error when I tried to insert a line before line 0. I had to use the `append` command to put one line into the file before I could insert a line *before* that line.

The small flavor differences we have just seen with `append` and `insert` serve to reinforce the precedents of truth we learned earlier. You may read in the documentation that a particular command works in a particular way. You may hear someone talk about how a particular command behaves. But the absolute truth about the way a command works is how it actually behaves on *your* system. Your version of `ex` may both understand the bang and allow you to insert before line 0, or it may do neither. Only through experimentation can you know. Remember, the truth is what the command really does, not what someone says it does.

c[hange]

```
[range]c[hange][!][count]
```

The **change** command is normally used to replace a block of text. In most cases you will specify a range of lines that need to be replaced, and `ex` will delete the line(s) you identified and put you in text-entry mode. If you enter fewer lines than the number of lines you specified in the range, the file will be shorter. If you enter more lines than the number of lines you specified, the file will be longer. The `change` command does not require a line for line replacement.

As you can see in Figure 6.16, in either flavor of `ex` you can `change` multiple lines into one line, or one line into multiple lines.

As I hope you expected, both Solaris and Linux are consistent with the way they handled the bang from command to command. Solaris turned on Auto Indent, and Linux didn't. The `count` option on the `change` command allows you to specify the number of lines to be replaced, starting with the address specified, or the current line if no address is specified. Using the `count` option causes `change` to ignore the range you specified. Instead it takes the *last address* of the range as the first line it is to replace, and replaces count lines from there down. Look at Figure 6.17 to see exactly how this works.

Here I told `ex` to change lines 3 through 6, and I added a `count` of 6 as an option on the `change` command. I then typed in a single line of text and stopped text-entry mode. Looking at the contents of the file you can see that all lines, starting with line 6, were changed. Since `count` overrides the range (no, that's not a cowboy joke), lines 3 through 5 are untouched. The `count` option of the `change` command can be useful, especially if you're trying to replace a large section of text and you don't particularly want to specify the range.

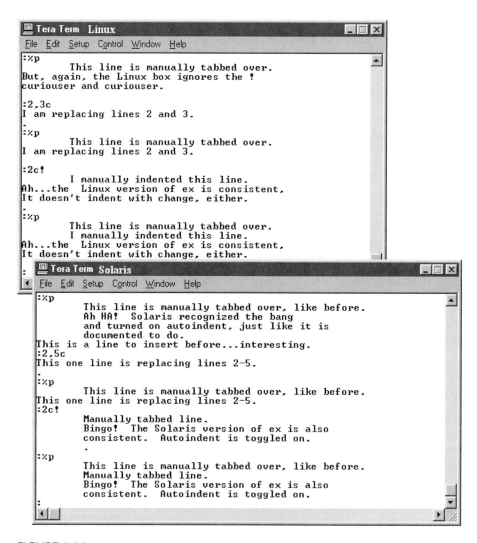

FIGURE 6.16

Using change with both Linux (top) and Solaris (bottom).

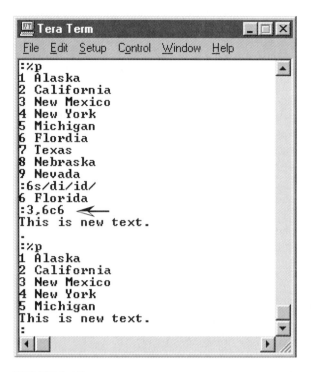

FIGURE 6.17

Using change with the count option.

⊕ Deleting One or More Lines from File

Just removing lines from a file with ex is very similar to removing lines using the ed editor. However, ex gives us a couple of different and more powerful features.

d[elete]

```
[range]d[elete][buffer][count][flag(s)]
```

If we just want to make a particular range of lines disappear, we can specify the line range followed by the **delete** command, which works pretty much like the delete command in ed. There are a couple of differences, though. One difference is where the deleted text goes. And that brings us to the subject of buffers.

Buffers

The ex editor has 26 special storage locations, or **buffers**, where text being processed is held. Each is named with one of the lowercase letters (a–z) of the alphabet. If you specify a named buffer as an option to the delete command, the text that you remove will be stored in that buffer. It will remain there for the duration of the editing session unless you replace it with other text. If you don't specify one of these *named buffers*, ex will place your deleted line or lines in the unnamed, or **anonymous**, **buffer**, where it will remain only until something else is put there with either a delete or yank command. You can recall text from any of the buffers with the put command, discussed later.

Figure 6.18 shows how you can delete text and save it in a named buffer. The figure shows the following process: I displayed the nine lines currently in the editing buffer. Next I deleted lines 1 through 3, and stored them in a named buffer, v. Notice that after deleting the first three lines, ex shows me the current line, which happens to be line 4, with the state name New York. I then displayed the contents of the editing buffer again to show that the first three lines had disappeared. That makes line number 6, which contains the digit 9 and the state name Texas, the current line. After ex shows that there are only six lines left, I use the put command (which, as promised, we'll discuss later) to put the contents of named buffer v back into the editing buffer. Again ex shows me the current line, which happens to be line 9, containing the number 3 and the state name New Mexico. Finally I display the whole contents of the editing buffer to show that lines containing the numbers 1 through 3 have been appended to the end of the file.

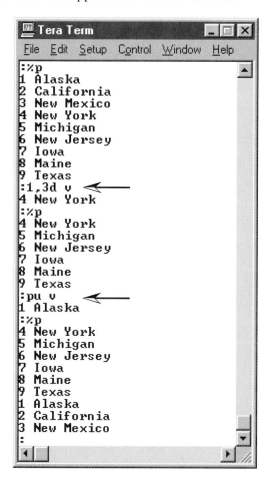

FIGURE 6.18

Deleting text and saving it into a named buffer.

The count option works just as it does with change, specifying the number of lines to delete starting with the address of the current line or of a specified line. Just like with change, count overrides the range of addresses and takes the last address in the range as the starting address for the delete.

In addition to the count option, the delete command supports two or three flags, or special directives. These flags tell ex the format in which to display a line following the last deleted line after it performs the delete. The three possible flags are p, #, and l. The third flag is the letter ell, not the number 1. The first flag (p) tells ex to print the current line—just like the p command. This seems to be the default in the Solaris world. Similarly, the octothorp (#) tells ex to show the line number as well as the current line and the ell (l) asks ex to display both printing and nonprinting characters.

Figure 6.19 shows examples of the delete that include examples of the flags. As you can see, I performed three deletes, saving the deleted lines in named buffer v. I used a named buffer to avoid confusing ex. If I had typed 1,3d p, ex would have had to decide whether I wanted to use the p as the name of a buffer or as the flag. Given this choice, ex would have decided that I was naming a buffer, stored the three lines in named buffer p, and then displayed the line. It would have displayed the line because that's its default action, displaying the current line.

In the other two examples in Figure 6.19, I directed ex to display the line number as well as the contents of the line with the # and to display the line including nonprinting characters with the l. The example in the figure is taken from a Solaris computer; the version of ex on my Linux machine does not support flags.

You can, of course, also use the change command to delete lines. All you have to do is change the range of lines to nothing. An example of that is shown in Figure 6.20.

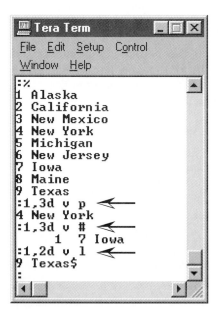

FIGURE 6.19
Deleting text and using flags.

FIGURE 6.20

Deleting text using the change command.

As you have probably come to expect, the first thing I'm showing you here are the nine lines in the file. Next I told ex that I wanted to change the contents of lines 1 through 5. I immediately stopped text-entry mode, in essence entering nothing. Displaying the complete contents of the editing buffer shows that lines 1 through 5 have been effectively deleted. Obviously, this procedure isn't as fast as using the delete command, but it does give you another option. Another important consideration if you're going to use change to delete lines is that change *does not save those lines anywhere*. The lines to be changed are deleted from the editing buffer but not preserved in any of the other buffers. When change deletes lines, they're gone for good.

Putting Lines Back

Sometimes you need to put back lines you've deleted or stored in one of the named buffers at a particular place in the editing buffer. Remember that the delete command places the lines we've deleted in either the anonymous buffer or, if we specified one, a named buffer. The ex editor offers a way to get these lines back.

pu[t]

    [line]pu[t] [buffer]

The **put** command takes the contents of either the anonymous buffer or a named buffer and puts those contents into the editing buffer *after the line* specified.

Figure 6.21 shows two examples of deleting a line from the file and putting it somewhere else. There are a couple of things I would like you to notice about the figure. In the first example, deleting line 8, I used the anonymous buffer because I didn't specify a buffer name. When I put line 8 back, notice that I specified line 0 as the target line. Since I wanted to make the inserted line the first line of the file, and since put inserts lines *after* the target line, I needed to specify line 0. In the second example I deleted lines 5 and 6 and stored them in named buffer z. I then went to the last line of the file using the $ address, and put the contents of named buffer z after the current line.

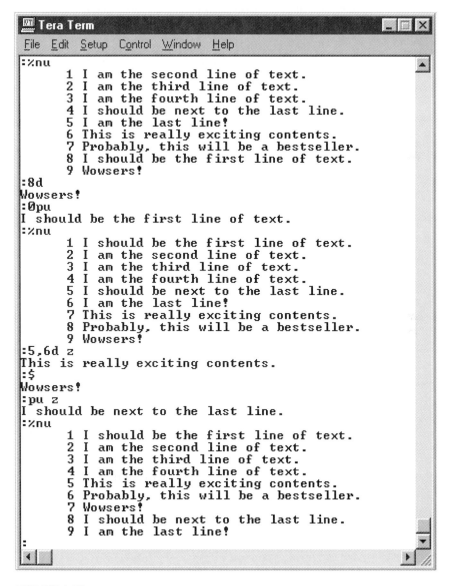

FIGURE 6.21

Putting deleted text back into the buffer.

Deleting lines and then putting them back into the edit buffer is functionally the same as the cut-and-paste operation in a word processor. But unless you're going to put the lines back in several places, it's often more efficient to use the move command.

⊕ Copying Lines

Instead of deleting lines, you might want to copy them to somewhere else in the editing buffer. There are two ways to do this. The first is to make a single copy of the selected line or lines somewhere else in the editing buffer. The second is to use a buffer to hold the line or lines and then copy them to multiple places in the buffer.

co[py]

```
[range]co[py] target line [flag(s)]
[range]t target line [flag(s)]
```

The **copy** command duplicates one or more lines as specified by the range *after the line* designated as the target line. Two different commands copy lines, the copy command and the **t** command. The t command seems to be included for backward compatibility with ed.

Figure 6.22 shows how the copy command is used. In this example, I identified lines 1 and 2 and copied them after line 3. Copy is a pretty straightforward command. As with put, if you wish to copy lines to the very beginning of the buffer you would copy them after line 0.

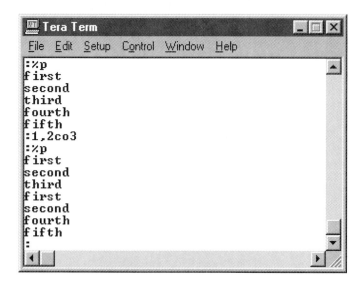

FIGURE 6.22
Copying text with copy.

The copy command will accept the three different flags arguments, but they are of little value most of the time. They will, of course, change the way ex displays the current line after the copy command, if it displays the current line.

y[ank]

[range]y[ank] [buffer] [count]

There's another way to make duplicate copies of one or more lines using either the anonymous buffer or a named buffer. The **yank** command copies either (1) a range of one or more lines or (2) the number of lines specified by count, starting with the last line in the specified range, to either a named buffer or the anonymous buffer. Unlike the delete command, yank leaves the lines right where they are and *copies* are stored in the buffer. This is a very useful command if you want to duplicate a set of lines in several different locations in the editing buffer.

Figure 6.23 shows how you can get in trouble very quickly with yank if you don't pay attention to line numbers. You can see here that I had a paragraph of text that was

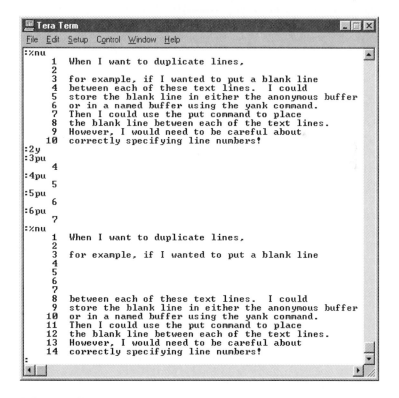

FIGURE 6.23

Using yank to duplicate a line several times.

mostly single-spaced. I wanted to double-space the paragraph without having to insert a bunch of lines using the insert or append commands. Since I know the yank command, I thought it would be easy to simply yank the blank line into the anonymous buffer and then put it between each line. Good thought, bad execution. What I forgot was that each time I put a line, I increased the number of lines in the file and pushed all lines below the inserted line down. Obviously, had I started at the bottom, I wouldn't have had this problem. If I had first put the blank line after line 13, then put the blank line after line 12, and so on, I wouldn't have had to worry about the line numbers.

Either using yank and then put, or using the copy command, perform the same activity as the word-processing copy-and-paste operation. The original lines are left unchanged and duplicates of those lines are inserted back into the editing buffer.

Moving Lines

While I can use the delete command to remove lines and then use the put command to put them somewhere else in the file, it's much less cumbersome to simply use the move command to move a range of lines.

m[ove]

```
[range]m[ove] [line]
```

Like the copy command, the **move** command is very straightforward and easy to use. Simply specify one or more lines that you wish to relocate, then tell move the *line after which* you wish to place those lines. Move will delete the lines from their original location in the editing buffer and append them after the line you specified. The current line will be set to the *first line* of the collection of lines that was moved. Since move doesn't use either the anonymous or named buffers, you can move a particular range of lines only once. After the move, the lines you moved no longer exist at the original location; they've been moved to a new address in the buffer.

Combining Lines

Suppose you want to combine two or more lines into a single line. You can do it!

j[oin]

```
[range]j[oin] [!][count][flag(s)]
```

The **join** command is quite sophisticated. You can specify a range of lines to be joined, or you can specify a number of lines, count, to be joined, starting with the last line in the range or the current line if no range is specified.

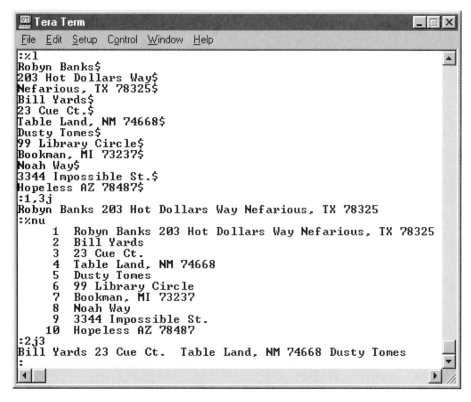

```
:%l
Robyn Banks$
203 Hot Dollars Way$
Nefarious, TX 78325$
Bill Yards$
23 Cue Ct.$
Table Land, NM 74668$
Dusty Tomes$
99 Library Circle$
Bookman, MI 73237$
Noah Way$
3344 Impossible St.$
Hopeless AZ 78487$
:1,3j
Robyn Banks 203 Hot Dollars Way Nefarious, TX 78325
:%nu
     1   Robyn Banks 203 Hot Dollars Way Nefarious, TX 78325
     2   Bill Yards
     3   23 Cue Ct.
     4   Table Land, NM 74668
     5   Dusty Tomes
     6   99 Library Circle
     7   Bookman, MI 73237
     8   Noah Way
     9   3344 Impossible St.
    10   Hopeless AZ 78487
:2j3
Bill Yards 23 Cue Ct.  Table Land, NM 74668 Dusty Tomes
:
```

FIGURE 6.24

Using join to combine lines in simple database.

Figure 6.24 shows an example of using the join command to combine lines in a database. First I've displayed the 12 lines in the current database. Since I wanted to combine each individual's data into one line, I used the join command. In the first example of the join, I combined lines 1 through 3 using the range method. Look closely at the second example. I wanted to combine Bill's data into one line, but the way the count method works, it started with line 2 and then joined the next three lines after line 2. Not exactly what I expected!

The join command actually *modified the data* for me as it joined the lines. The first time I displayed the contents of the file, I used the list command so you could see the actual contents of each line. Look closely: there is no space at the end of each of the lines, nor is there space at the beginning of each line. Yet, when join combined the lines it put a single space between the contents of each of the lines. That sure makes my life easier.

Along that same line, and flying in the face of current publishing convention, if one of the joined lines ends in a period, join will insert *two spaces* after the period. If the last character of the joined line is a single space, or if it's a closing parenthesis, join won't put any spaces in front of it. If you don't want join to add spaces, you can turn off this feature by appending a bang to the join command.

Join also recognizes the three flags that modify the display of the joined lines. Since you're old hands at using those flags, I won't discuss them again.

⊕ Substitution, Your Best Friend

Up until now, we've looked only at commands that modify whole lines. The **substitute** command gives you the ability to go inside the line and modify its contents. Just as it is in ed, substitute in ex is a very powerful and useful command.

s[ubstitute]

```
[range]s[ubstitute][/pattern/replacement/ [options][count][flags]]
```

As an interesting note, the version of ex in Solaris that I am using recognizes only the abbreviation s and does not recognize the fully spelled-out word substitute. Just another example of the small flavor differences between different Unixes. I mean, really, who wants to spell out the word "substitute" anyway?

Most of the time you will use substitute to modify the contents of one or more lines in a file. Figure 6.25 shows several different examples of substitutions. Notice the use of the options confirm (c) and global (g). The first example in this figure shows how I corrected the misspelled word spulling in line 2. Next I told substitute to find all the lines that contained the string SU and replace the *first occurrence* of that string with the string su. Substitute always changes the first occurrence unless directed otherwise. The substitution on line 7 is an example of "otherwise." On line 7, by using the global (g) option, I directed substitute to find *all* the capital-F characters in

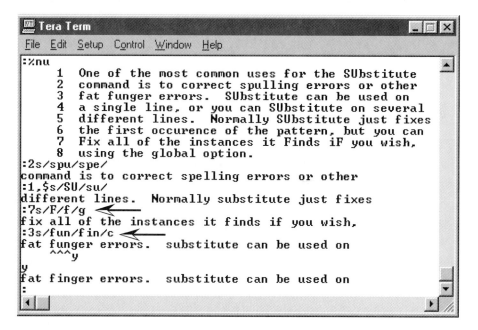

FIGURE 6.25

Several different examples of substitute.

the line and replace them with lowercase-f characters. The global (g) option on this command tells substitute to find *all occurrences in the line.*

Finally, the substitution of fin for fun shows the use of the confirm (c) option. When you include this option, substitute will show you exactly what it's going to change by putting caret symbols (^) under each letter in the pattern it proposes to change. You must confirm each substitution, usually using a y for "yes." If you do not confirm the substitution, it will not be made. If you interrupt the substitution, usually with a Ctrl-C, the substitution will stop, all substitutions completed before the interrupt will remain, and ex will return to command mode.

The confirm option is very useful if you need to change a particular string in a large number of lines but not all the lines that contain the string. You won't use **confirm** often, but it's awfully nice to know about. If you don't supply a pattern-and-replacement pair, substitute will use the previous substitute's pattern-replacement pair. That can be helpful in cases where you're making the same substitution in several places in a file.

As you learned with ed, you can use substitute to delete words by replacing them with nothing, and you can use substitute to add words if you substitute multiple words for one. Probably two-thirds of the editing you do to a file will be done using substitute.

As with many of the other ex commands you have already learned, you can give substitute a count of lines over which to work, starting with the line number specified, or the last line of the range. Substitute also recognizes the three flags, list, print, and number. A shorthand method to execute a substitute command over a different range of lines follows:

```
[range] & [options][count][flags]
```

This command will execute the same pattern-replacement pair as the previous substitute, over the range of lines specified. (If you don't give substitute a pattern-replacement pair, it will use the previous pattern-replacement pair. This is just another way to efficiently invoke substitute.)

There is a tilde (~) form of resubstitution as well. The difference between the ampersand (&) form and tilde form is in the choice of pattern. In the ampersand form, substitute will use the previous *substitute's* pattern-replacement pair. In the tilde form, it will use the most recent pattern in the pattern-replacement pair regardless of which command supplied the pattern.

For example, suppose I enter the following four commands:

```
:1,50s/big/little
```

```
:/humongous
```

```
:60,70&
```

```
:80,90~
```

In the first 50 lines, the word little would be substituted for the word big. Then I would search for the first occurrence of a line contain the word humongous. In lines 60 through 70 I would repeat the initial substitution of the word little for the word big. However, in lines 80 through 90, I would substitute the word little for the word humongous. This alternate form of substitute will prove valuable as your ability with ex increases. It is a wonderful shortcut but can be confusing until you play with it.

Another, very handy use for the ampersand is to represent the search string in the replacement string. For example, in Figure 6.26 I wanted to shift the case of the first instance of each lowercase blank to uppercase. The two shifting tools are \U to shift letters to uppercase and \L to shift to lowercase. If you need to shift only one or two characters, it is faster to use a plain substitute. However, if you are shifting more than two characters, using one of these shifting tools is more efficient. Remember that you must protect the tools with the backslash. If you forget that, you will substitute a U or L for the string.

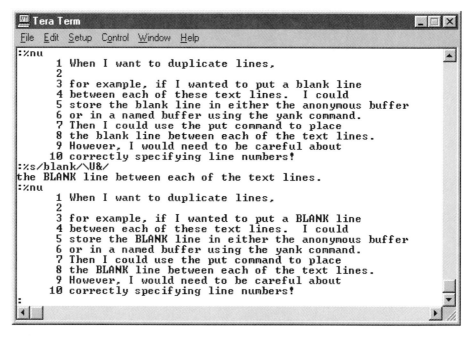

FIGURE 6.26

Yet another example of the use of the ampersand.

global

When is a command still a command even if it doesn't act like a command?

g[lobal]

```
[range]g[lobal] /pattern/ [command(s)]
[range]v /pattern/ [command(s)]
```

Although global is a command, it acts rather like a super range designator. When you use **global** (**g**) as your only address, you are directing ex to apply the command(s) that follow the g to all the lines in the buffer.

Don't confuse this g *command* with the global (g) *option* on substitute. The g-option directs substitute to apply the change specified to all occurrences of the pattern *in the current line*.

You can also consider the global command as a super search tool. Since global really is a command, you can preface it with the line range and it will work only within that range of lines. For example, if you were to enter 20,60 global. . . the command would work only from line 20 to line 60. The line range is inclusive, which means that both lines 20 and 60 are *included* in it.

The way global works is to search, top to bottom, either the whole file or the range specified and apply the command or commands you provided to each line that matches the pattern. There's a lot of flexibility in the way you define your patterns. You can use many different characters to mark the beginning and ending of the pattern. With the global command you are not limited just to the forward slash. For example, all three of these patterns would match the word guzzle:

    global /guzzle/

    global +guzzle+

    global [guzzle[

Be careful using characters like the open square bracket ([ ), because you must use exactly the same character on both ends of the pattern. It's a common error to use the open square bracket ([ ) at the beginning of the pattern and the close square bracket ( ]) at the end of the pattern. Since the two characters are not the same, global gets confused.

Don't use the bang (!) character to mark your patterns, because in some versions of ex, the bang is used as a *logical not*, directing global to apply the command to any line that does *not* match the pattern. If your version of ex supports the bang, it must be appended directly to the end of the global command with no intervening space.

In all versions of ex, the v version of global is used to select all the lines that *do not* match the pattern. This is a very important option, because there are many instances where you'll know what you *don't want* from a file rather than what you do want. Suppose you had a file that contained 23,612 lines, and all but 16 of them said Normal completion. You could use the v form of the global command to select all the lines that did not match the pattern /Normal completion/, correctly selecting just the 16 lines you wanted to see. (Remember the v command; we will see something very similar when we learn grep.)

While it is possible to specify multiple commands to be executed when global finds a line that matches the pattern, at this point in your exploration of ex that probably isn't a real good idea. If you do wish to specify multiple commands you need to separate them with the vertical stroke (|) operator. However, I would strongly urge that you use global with a single command for now.

⊕ Using Shell Commands

You can execute a shell command from within the ex editor by preceding the command with the bang (!).

!

```
! command
[range]! command
```

In some flavors of ex the output of the command will be followed by the bang character (!); in other versions you'll simply see the ex prompt (:). It just so happens that my version of ex running under Linux doesn't show the second bang, while the version I use under Solaris does. Figure 6.27 shows both flavors. On the Linux side of the house ex echoes my command, executes the shell command, and then simply gives me the command-mode prompt. The version of ex that runs under Solaris, version 8, performs as documented: it executes the shell command, giving me a bang (!) to mark the end of the output from the command. If you wish to repeat the most recently executed shell command, you can do so just by specifying bang bang (! !), which will repeat the last shell command you used.

It is possible to capture the output from a shell command directly into the editing buffer. This can be a real nifty feature, as long as you're careful where you put that captured output. Figure 6.28 shows how to make this work. First I've showed you the contents of a short file. Next I used the bang to execute the ls shell command. However, unlike the example in Figure 6.27, in Figure 6.28 I prepended a line number before the bang. That directed ex to replace the range of lines (in this case the range is one line) with the output of the command. There will be instances when you will really appreciate knowing this trick. You can use it to import the contents of another file into the editing buffer by specifying a line number and then issuing a cat command. If there's any content at the line number you specify, that content will be replaced by the contents of file you specify. Yet, there's an even better way to import another file's contents: the read command.

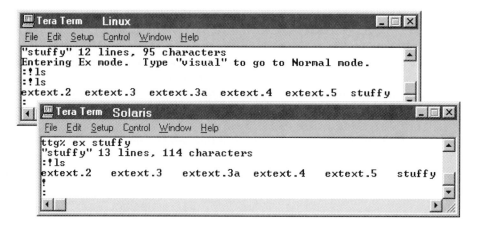

FIGURE 6.27

Issuing a shell command in both flavors of ex, Linux and Solaris.

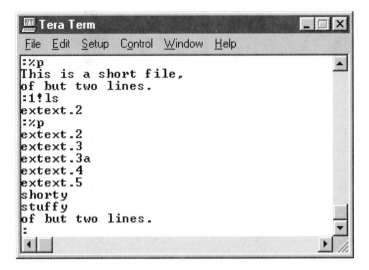

FIGURE 6.28

Capturing the output of a shell command directly into the editing buffer.

Reading Other Files

Sometimes it's extremely useful to be able to read the contents of another file directly into the editing buffer, in essence combining two files together.

r[ead]

```
[line]r[ead][!] [file]
```

The **read**, **r**, command will place a copy of the contents of the file specified *after* the line specified in the editing buffer. However, there are a couple of caveats when using this command. First, if there is no file specified, then the current file, the file that has already been read into the editing buffer, is used. That means if you just issue a read command, it will reread and add the contents of the current file into the buffer. If there is no current file, then the file you specify in the read command will *become* the current file. Both of these situations can have strange and unhappy ramifications. For example, look at Figure 6.29. Notice what happened here when I accidentally typed the read command while transcribing a poem by Edgar Allan Poe. Suddenly, with that one keystroke, I had two copies of all the text in the file I was working from. Not exactly what I had in mind.

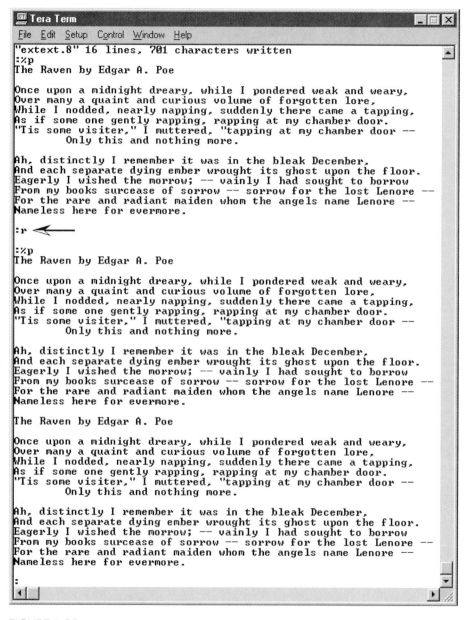

FIGURE 6.29

What happens if you read without specifying a file.

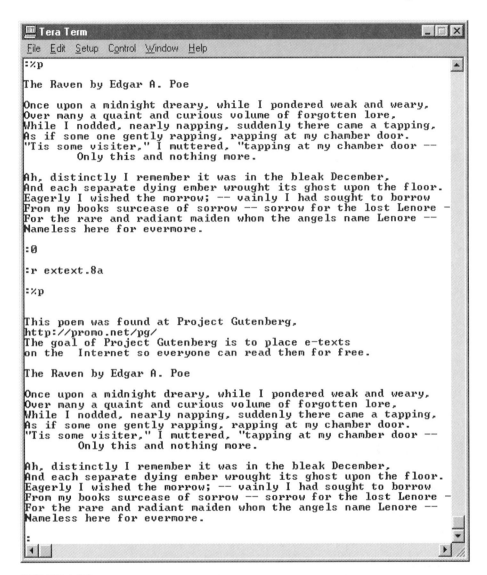

FIGURE 6.30

Using the read to insert standardized text into the editing buffer.

The read command makes it easy to include a block of standard text in several files. Figure 6.30 shows how I used it to insert text from a different file into the editing buffer. (Note: I did correct the duplication first.) As you can see in this figure, I first showed you the contents of the file and then set my current line to line 0, which asked read to put the new text at the beginning of the file. Then I displayed the file extext.8a again—and behold! It contains the new information about Project Gutenberg.

You'll be glad you know of the read command when you have a particular block of text in one file that you want to duplicate in the current editing buffer. Do remember, however, that if you forget to specify a filename, the read command will read from the current file and duplicate it into the editing buffer as you saw in Figure 6.29.

⊕ Editing Other Files

There are two ways to load a file other than the one currently being edited into the editing buffer, without leaving ex: next and edit.

n[ext]

```
n[ext][!] [file]
```

The **next** command will read the next (not surprisingly) file from the argument list, either the next file on the command line or in the list of files specified. If the editing buffer has been modified and those changes have not been written to the file associated with the editing buffer, ex will issue a warning message and refuse to overwrite the changes. You can force ex to overwrite the editing buffer by appending a bang (!) to the command.

Figure 6.31 shows how the next command can be used to read a subsequent file from the list of files on the command line. Notice that ex gave me a different message when he started, because I told him that there are two files to edit, not just one. After showing you the contents of the first file, I made a change and attempted

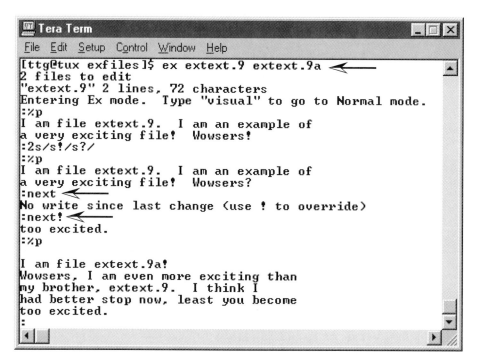

```
[ttg@tux exfiles]$ ex extext.9 extext.9a  ⟵
2 files to edit
"extext.9" 2 lines, 72 characters
Entering Ex mode.  Type "visual" to go to Normal mode.
:%p
I am file extext.9.  I am an example of
a very exciting file!  Wowsers!
:2s/s!/s?/
:%p
I am file extext.9.  I am an example of
a very exciting file!  Wowsers?
:next  ⟵
No write since last change (use ! to override)
:next!  ⟵
too excited.
:%p

I am file extext.9a!
Wowsers, I am even more exciting than
my brother, extext.9.  I think I
had better stop now, least you become
too excited.
:
```

FIGURE 6.31
Using next.

to load the next file into the editing buffer using the **next** command. Since I hadn't written the change out to the file, ex refused to destroy the contents of the buffer. I then forced ex to overwrite the contents of the buffer by appending a bang to **next**. As you can see from the final ex command, the second file replaced the contents of the buffer.

e[dit]

```
e[dit][!] +line] [file]
```

If you're specifying a single filename, the **edit** command works very much like the next command. If the contents of the editing buffer have been changed and not saved to disk, the edit command will fail. As with next, you can override this protection by appending a bang to the end of edit. If you specify a line number with the +line option, edit will make that line number the current line. Otherwise, the last line of the new file will be the current line. It's interesting to note that the +line option can be either a /pattern or a ?pattern. In the first case ex will begin searching starting with the *first line* of file and stop when it finds the pattern. In the second case ex will begin searching starting with the *last line* of file, searching upward into the file, and stop when it encounters the first instance of the pattern. In either case the line where ex found the pattern will be set as the current line.

The next command is handiest if you have a series of files you know you must modify, and want to list them all on the command line and then change them one by one. The edit command is handiest if you have one more file you wish to modify, and you don't want to leave the editor and restart.

⊕ Oops

There will be times when you do something to the editing buffer that you really wish you hadn't done. It is for precisely that reason that the undo command was created.

u[ndo]

```
u[ndo]
```

As documented, the **undo** command "reverses the changes made by the previous editing command, a command that changes the contents of the buffer." As you experiment with undo, you will again encounter a flavor difference. It seems that the undo in ex on my Linux machine is much more pervasive than the undo in ex on my Solaris machine. Figure 6.32 shows how both of them handled an undo.

I performed the same edits on both machines. Well, actually I didn't misspell silken on the Solaris machine, but for all practical purposes I performed the same operations on both boxes. When I issued the undo command on the Linux box it undid *all*

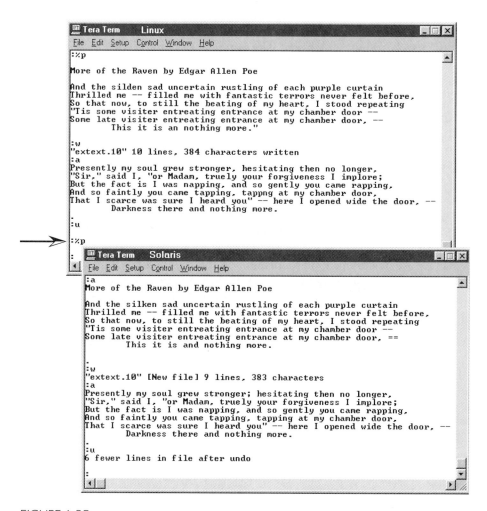

FIGURE 6.32

Undoing a change in both Linux and Solaris.

the changes I had made to the buffer, even those I made *before the write* (there are no lines left in the buffer.) That is one way to interpret the definition. On the Solaris box the undo command undid all the changes I had made *since the write*. That is what I expected the undo command to do, or to undo—the other wasn't. You will need to experiment with your flavor of ex to find out exactly how your undo works. You can undo what you just undid by issuing another undo. And, of course, you can undo what you undid by undoing what you did by issuing another undo command. Hmmm, I think this is a good place to stop talking about this.

⊕ Marking and Returning to Places in File

If you're working in a large file or if you need to frequently return to a particular place in a file, it's useful to be able to place a mark at a particular location in the file.

ma[rk]

```
[line]ma[rk] c
```

The **mark** command is used to set the specified mark, one of the lowercase letters, a–z, at a particular line in the file. You can have up to 26 marks. They will be available only for the current editing session. Let's say you mark line 9 with the letter g, and subsequently mark line 43 with the letter g. In this case, ex will dutifully change the marked line from line 9 to line 43. It's up to you to keep track of which letter corresponds to which line. Figure 6.33 shows how to mark a couple of different lines in a file.

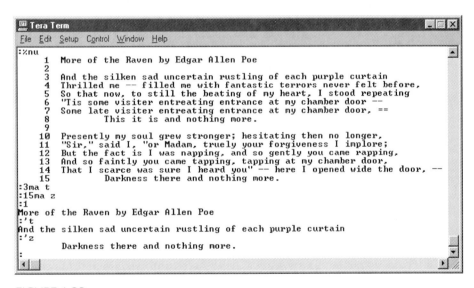

FIGURE 6.33

Marking lines and transferring control to marked lines.

Being able to mark particular lines is a wonderful thing—as long as you can transfer control to those marked lines at will.

```
' c
```

The apostrophe ('), or tick mark, followed by one of the letters set as a mark in the file, will transfer control to that marked line. If you attempt to transfer control to a letter you have not set as a mark, ex will give you an error message and the transfer will fail.

Refer again to Figure 6.33—it shows how to transfer control to a marked line. I set the letter t to mark line 3 and the letter z to mark line 15. I then used the tick mark to transfer control first to the line marked with the letter t and then to the line marked with the letter z. Obviously, in this example I don't need to set marks, but I didn't think you needed to see me mark an 8000-line file, no matter how fascinating its contents. It's especially useful to know how to mark lines in a file if you're dealing with a very large file or a file that has certain places to which you frequently return.

⊕ Setting Options for ex

You can set a number of options to specify the way ex will work for you. Many of these will be more important when we start talking about the visual mode of the ex editor, but some are useful in the command-line mode as well.

se[t]

```
se[t][option[=[value]]. . .] [nooption. . .] [option?. . .] [all]
```

Table 6.1 shows you a whole series of options you can set using, of course, the **set**, command. Please understand that since flavors of ex differ, the options available to you may differ from those in the table. Some of these options have values and so are called **name-value pairs**. An example of a name-value pair is tabstop=4, which sets the number of spaces that the TAB key moves to the right to four characters instead of the default of eight. Other options, called **switches** or **toggles**, are either on or off. Toggles are also called Boolean variables because they have a value of either 1 (on) or 0 (off), but you must set them using the name of the option.

An example of a toggle is the **terse** option. The default for terse is off (set noterse), but if you set the terse option (set terse), some of the error messages you receive may not be so verbose. Table 6.1 shows the default values and a very short description of the common ex options. If the description of the options contains the words (visual mode), that means that the action applies only to the visual mode of ex. While many of the options are more useful in the visual mode, some, like tabstop, number, and autoindent, are very useful to programmers using either mode of ex/vi. As your experience with ex grows, you will find more of the options helpful.

TABLE 6.1 Options available in ex

Option (abb.)	Default	Purpose
autoindent (ai)	Off noautoindent (noai)	Match the indent of the previous line. ^D moves left one tab stop.
autoprint (ap)	On autoprint	Write the current line after each change in the buffer.
autowrite (aw)	Off noautowrite (noaw)	Automatically write the buffer to the file if next, rewind, tag, edit, suspend, stop, or ! commands are executed.
beautify (bf)	Off nobeautify (nobf)	Discard all nonprinting characters except tab, newline, and form-feed from files read into the buffer.
directory (dir)	None	Specify the directory where the edit buffer is to be placed.
edcompatible (ed)	Off noedcompatible (noed)	Remember the g and c suffixes on substitute commands.
errorbells (eb)	Off noerrorbells (noeb)	Don't beep the terminal on errors, instead flash the screen or otherwise silently indicate an error.
exrc	Off noexrc	Read and follow any .exrc file in the current directory.
ignorecase (ic)	Off noignorecase (noic)	Ignore the case of patterns in searches.
lisp	Off nolisp	Autoindent on and (,), {,}, [[,]] are set for Lisp coding (visual mode).
list	Off nolist	When showing the content, use the list format (nonprinting characters are visible).
magic	On magic	Interpret regular expressions and substitution strings.
mesg	On mesg	Allow others to talk or write to you while in visual mode.
number (nu)	Off nonumber (nonu)	When showing content, number the lines. (Handy for programmers!)
paragraphs (para)	None	Define additional paragraph boundaries for the {and} commands in visual mode.
prompt	On prompt	Show the command-mode prompt (:). If unset, you will have no prompt.
readonly	Variable	Prohibit writing buffer changes to the file. Can be overridden with !. Normally off unless user doesn't have permission to write.
redraw	Off noredraw	Simulate an intelligent terminal on a dumb terminal—not usually used anymore.
remap	On remap	Allow multilevel macro definition.
report	5	Set the number of lines that can be changed by a command before a reporting message is generated.
scroll	Default window	Number of lines scrolled on an EOF command in visual mode.
sections	Variable	Define additional section boundaries for [[and]] in visual mode.
shell (sh)	Variable	The path to the shell to be executed when ! is used.

TABLE 6.1 (continued)

Option (abb.)	Default	Purpose
shiftwidth (sw)	8 shiftwidth = 8 (sw = 8)	Indentation level used with autoindent and shift commands.
showmatch (sm)	Off noshowmatch (nosm)	Show matching (or } when) or } typed in visual mode.
showmode	Off noshowmode	Write current mode to last line of screen in visual mode.
showopen	Off noshowopen	Prevent screen updates during text entry in visual mode. (this improves performance on slow terminals)
tabstop (ts)	8 tabstop = 8 (ts = 8)	Define how many spaces a TAB key expands to.
tags	Variable	Specify a list of space-separated path names used with the tag command.
term	Variable	Tell ex what kind of terminal you are using. Defaults to the value set in the shell variable and TERM.
terse	Off noterse	Give shorter error messages, sometimes. Many messages don't change, but the output from showmode may.
warn	On warn	Issue a warning message if the editing buffer has not been saved before a ! command executes.
window	Variable	Number of lines in a screenful, used by the z command.
wrapscan (ws)	On wrapscan (ws)	Consider the buffer circular when searching with / or ?.
wrapmargin (wm)	0 wrapmargin = 0 (wm = 0)	If greater than, insert a newline to end lines at least the number of spaces before the right margin of the screen.
writeany (wa)	Off nowriteany (nowa)	Ignore file-overwriting checks before write and xit commands.

⊕ Other ex Commands

There are a collection of additional ex commands that either have very specialized uses or are considered somewhat more advanced commands. I have grouped them here so that you will know of their existence and can experiment with them later. I won't discuss them in as much depth as I did the previous set of commands, because you probably don't need them right now. I want you to focus first on the commands you need to know to be functional in ex, then later you can experiment with these other commands. By that time, you'll be so comfortable with ex that you won't need detailed explanations.

chd[ir]

```
chd[ir][!] [directory]
cd[!] [directory]
```

The **change directory**, **chd** or **cd**, command is used to do exactly what its name implies, change the current working directory to the directory supplied. If there is no directory argument, ex will look in the *HOME* environment variable, and set that directory as the current working directory. If the *HOME* environment variable is empty, the command will most likely fail.

map

```
map[!] [char set-of-commands]
```

The **map** command will be of no real value to you until the next chapter, because it is designed to work in the *visual mode*. However, since it is part of the ex command set, I chose to include it in this chapter.

You can use this command to associate a particular character with some command stream. Then typing the character will be the same as typing that command stream. In other words, the map command can create macros. A **macro** is a single command, often just a single character, that is used to invoke a series of commands. If you append a bang (!) to the map command, you create a command stream that is active during text-entry mode. If you use the map command without a bang, the command stream is active during command mode.

unm[ap]

```
unm[ap][!] char
```

If you wish to remove the macro definition of a particular character, you can remove the mapping to the definition with the **unmap**, **unm**, command.

preserve

```
pre[serve]
```

The **preserve**, **pre**, command will perform the same actions that the editor goes through in the event that an ex editing session is interrupted. It saves a copy of the editing buffer in a form that can be restored using the recover command (discussed next). It also sends a mail message to the user telling her that the file was preserved and how to recover it. I must admit I have never used the preserve command, but it's nice to know that it's there.

rec[over]

```
rec[over] file
```

You would use the **recover**, **rec**, command to restore a file that was preserved with the preserve command or, far more likely, was preserved when the editor was interrupted.

I hope you'll never need to use this command, but if for some reason your editing session is interrupted, you will use this command to restore the buffer to nearly the state it was when the editor terminated. You can accomplish the same task is using the -r option on the ex command line.

rew[ind]

```
rew[ind][!]
```

The **rewind**, **rew**, command is seldom used. It allows you to reset the argument list on the command line to the first file in the argument list. That is like issuing the next command with the current argument list as the option. If the current buffer has been modified since the last write, ex will issue a warning and will fail unless you override this safety feature by using a bang.

shift right and left

```
[range] > [count][flags]
[range] < [count][flags]
```

The shift, > or <, command will shift the text left (<) or right (>) over the range specified or, starting with the last line in the range, for the number of lines specified by count for a specific number of blank characters. The exact number of blanks to shift the line is specified by the shiftwidth option. The default shiftwidth on both of my versions of ex is 8 bytes. That means that when I tell ex to shift right, it inserts eight blank characters in front of the first character, putting the first character in position 9.

If I direct ex to shift one or more lines left, it will remove **shiftwidth** *blank* characters from the beginning of each line in the range or, starting with the last line in the range, it will shift the number of lines specified by count. The shift-left command will remove only non-blank characters; it will not destroy data.

Figure 6.34 shows how the left shift works. Notice that I created a set of lines with one, two, three, etc., spaces preceding a number. Then I shifted the first 10 lines left using the shift-left (<) command. This command shifted each of the first eight lines to the left margin by removing, respectively, one through eight spaces from the beginning of each of the specified lines. Lines 9 and 10 have leading spaces left because the shift-left command removes a maximum of eight spaces.

The flags option works as expected, telling ex how you'd like the output formatted. You can use multiples of the shift commands to shift the text multiple shiftwidths either left or right. For example, the command 1,5 >>> would shift the text in the first five lines 24 spaces to the right (assuming the default shiftwidth of eight blanks.)

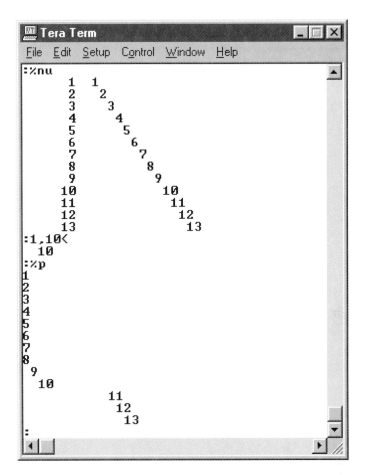

FIGURE 6.34

Using < to shift several lines of text left.

sh[ell]

sh[ell]

When you issue the **shell** command, ex will tell you whether you have unsaved changes in the buffer and then drop you out to the command line. When you finish doing whatever it was you wanted to do at the command line *and type exit,* you will resume the edit session exactly where you left off. This is a wonderful option! Suppose someone tries to talk to you while you are editing a file. All you need to do is issue the shell command, then talk to your friend, and when you finish talking, enter the exit command and return to editing your file just where you left it.

so[urce]

---

so[urce] file

You can create a file that contains a series of ex commands, and then perform those commands on the current editing buffer by sourcing—using the **source**, **so**, command on—the file containing those commands. This process allows you to store a collection of commands that you use often so that you can retrieve and execute those commands without having to retype them. Usually, you would use the sed editor to accomplish this task, but you can do the same sort of thing using the source command in ex.

If you don't want to create a file of ex commands, you can store a collection of commands in a named buffer and then execute them directly out of that buffer. For example, suppose I want to (1) find lines with a particular pattern and (2) delete that line and the three lines following. In addition, let's pretend that I have to perform that action 73 times in a given file. Now look at Figures 6.35, 6.36, and 6.37. Figure 6.35 shows

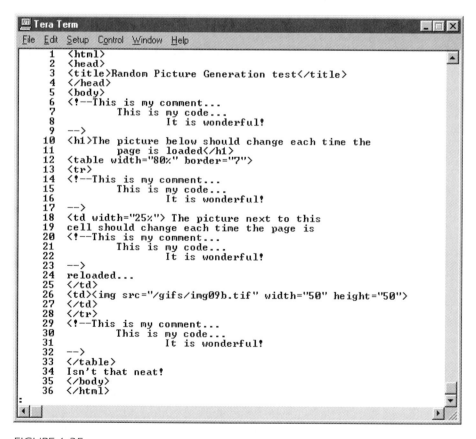

```
 1  <html>
 2  <head>
 3  <title>Random Picture Generation test</title>
 4  </head>
 5  <body>
 6  <!--This is my comment...
 7          This is my code...
 8              It is wonderful!
 9  -->
10  <h1>The picture below should change each time the
11          page is loaded</h1>
12  <table width="80%" border="7">
13  <tr>
14  <!--This is my comment...
15          This is my code...
16              It is wonderful!
17  -->
18  <td width="25%"> The picture next to this
19  cell should change each time the page is
20  <!--This is my comment...
21          This is my code...
22              It is wonderful!
23  -->
24  reloaded...
25  </td>
26  <td><img src="/gifs/img09b.tif" width="50" height="50">
27  </td>
28  </tr>
29  <!--This is my comment...
30          This is my code...
31              It is wonderful!
32  -->
33  </table>
34  Isn't that neat!
35  </body>
36  </html>
```

FIGURE 6.35

An HTML file with annoying comments that need to be removed.

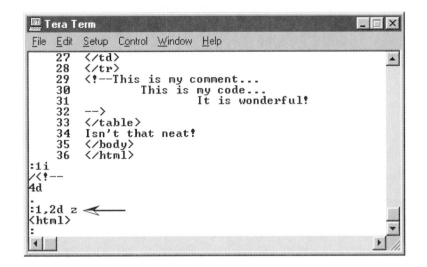

FIGURE 6.36

Storing commands in a buffer.

FIGURE 6.37

Using commands stored in a buffer to simplify fixing the HTML file.

an HTML file that needs to be repaired, Figure 6.36 shows how to store commands in a buffer, and Figure 6.37 shows how stored commands could make that repair a little easier. As you can see in Figure 6.35, the author of this HTML page likes to use comments. Unfortunately, those comments are worthless and should be removed. While I could search through the file and manually remove those lines of comments, there is an easier way. Look at the code in Figure 6.36. In this step I inserted two lines before line 1 and then deleted those lines storing them in a buffer named z. What those two lines will do is search for a pattern, then delete the four lines starting with the line containing that pattern. Let's see how I use the buffered commands.

In Figure 6.37 you can see where I deleted the two lines of commands from the front of the file. Then I executed the contents of buffer z four times, once for each comment in the file using the @ shortcut to the source command. Finally, I printed out the editing buffer again, just to be sure I had successfully cleaned it up. Notice that each time I executed the commands in the buffer, ex first echoed the line he matched, then echoed the current line, the line following the deleted lines. This is a pretty quick way to perform a series of repetitive tasks.

ta[g]

```
ta[g][!] tagstring
```

The **tag**, **tg**, command is an advanced ex command. You probably won't use it until you find yourself in an environment where you are regularly editing a large collection of files. To use tag, you first must create a file that contains a collection of tag strings and their associated filenames. Then, when you issue the tag command and one of the tag strings, ex will load the file associated with the tag string into the editing buffer. As you would expect, if the current buffer has been modified since the last write, ex will issue a warning message and abort the command. You can override this safety feature with the bang (!) character.

This is a very sophisticated command. You will need to do some research on your system before you begin using it. As a start you should look at the ctags utility.

o[pen]

```
[line] o[pen] [/pattern/] [flags]
```

There are two commands that will take you out of the line mode of the ex editor and put you into the visual mode. The first of these is the **open**, **o**, command. This command will put you in the equivalent of the visual mode *for a single line*. It will allow you to use all the vi commands on that single line. To return to line mode, enter the Q command. Some types of terminals, called *block-mode terminals*, may not support this command.

vi[sual]

```
[line] vi[sual] [type] [count] [flags]
```

Used by itself, the **visual**, **vi**, command will switch you from ex mode to visual mode. (The Q vi command will put you back into line mode.) Most of the time you will use the visual command to flip-flop between line mode and visual mode. The type option, which seems to be supported only on my Solaris version of ex, can include any of the following:

Use - to place the line specified at the bottom of the screen.

Use + to place the line specified at the top of the screen.

Use . to place the line specified in the middle of the screen.

Use ∧ to write out count lines starting count lines before the line specified.

The count and flags options work as we have discussed for many other commands.

Adjust the Window

```
[line]z [type] [count] [flags]
```

The **z** command allows you to display the contents of the editing buffer starting at a particular line. It uses the same type options as the visual command, and the count and flags options work as we have discussed before.

Now that you are an expert with two editors, why don't you do a little practice on your own. Then you can read the next chapter and learn about the visual mode of the ex editor. That is a whole new world of commands.

KEY TERMS

buffer
macro
switch
toggle

NEW COMMANDS

ex
'
!
ab[brev]

```
a[ppend]
c[hange]
chd[ir]
co[py]
d[elete]
e[dit]
f[ile]
g[lobal]
i[nsert]
j[oin]
l[ist]
map
ma[rk]
m[ove]
n[ext]
nu[mber]
o[pen]
pre[serve]
p[rint]
pu[t]
q[uit]
r[ead]
rec[over]
rew[ind]
se[t]
sh[ell]
shift right and left
so[urce]
st[op]
s[ubstitution]
sus[pend]
ta[g]
una[bbrev]
u[ndo]
unm[ap]
vi[sual]
w[rite]
wq
x[it]
y[ank]
z
```

REVIEW QUESTIONS

6.1 Define each of the key terms for this chapter.

6.2 Briefly explain the history of the ex editor. Who wrote it, and why?

6.3 List two ways ex is like the ed editor.

6.4 List three significant differences between ed and ex.

6.5 Explain how to recover a file if your ex session is interrupted.

6.6 Describe the general format of an ex command.

6.7 List six of the ten ways to provide an address to a command.

6.8 Describe the difference between the error messages in ex and those in ed.

6.9 List three ways to view the contents of the editing buffer, and explain the features of each method.

6.10 Describe the different search processes in ex.

6.11 Describe how the undo command works.

6.12 Explain the differences among the three ways to stop ex.

6.13 Explain the difference between the wq command and the x command.

6.14 Explain the use of named buffers.

6.15 How does copy differ from yank?

6.16 Describe how to use substitute to

    a. Change the string snorble to the string snowball.

    b. Add the words Oh what fun after the word Unix in a line.

    c. Remove the words after all from the line I like ed after all.

6.17 Explain the difference between a word and a string.

6.18 Describe can you use shell commands in ex.

6.19 Describe a situation where it would be useful to be able to mark several places in the buffer, and list the command you would use to do it.

6.20 List the commands to read the contents of the file iamnew.ex into the current editing buffer after line 23? Assume you are starting with the cursor on line 4. List *both* ways.

6.21 How can you reload the current version of the file into the editing buffer?

6.22 Describe a situation when the recover command would be useful.

EXERCISES

(Okay, I know some of these look like the ed exercises but now you get to do them with a different editor!)

6.1 Start the ex editor without an associated file.

6.2 Turn on prompting and verbose help if you didn't do that in Exercise 1.

6.3 Enter this text:
```
Peter Piper picks pints, pounds, and pecks of purple pickled peppers.
```

6.4 Exit from the editor without saving your work.

6.5 Redo Exercises 1 through 3. Now save your work to the file peppers.ex.

6.6 Change the associated filename from peppers.ex to peter.ex.

6.7 Duplicate the line in the file five times. You should end up with six identical lines in the file.

6.8 Place a number before each line in the file. (No, don't use the nu command to do this, actually enter the numbers into the file.) Your file should now look like this:
```
1Peter Piper picks pints, pounds and pecks of purple pickled peppers.
2Peter Piper picks pints, pounds and pecks of purple pickled peppers.
3Peter Piper picks pints, pounds and pecks of purple pickled peppers.
4Peter Piper picks pints, pounds and pecks of purple pickled peppers.
5Peter Piper picks pints, pounds and pecks of purple pickled peppers.
6Peter Piper picks pints, pounds and pecks of purple pickled peppers.
```

6.9   Display the contents of the file using each of the three buffer display commands.

6.10   Make the following changes to the file:

   a.   In line 2 change `Peter` to `Paul`.
   b.   In line 4 change `purple pickled peppers` to `profound pink peonies`.
   c.   In line 6 change the `picks` to `procures`.
   d.   Duplicate lines 3 through 6 after line 6.
   e.   Change the numbers on the new lines 7 through 10 to 7, 8, 9, and 0, respectively.

6.11   Make line 1 your current line, and then find the first occurrence of the word `peonies`.

6.12   Duplicate line 8 after line 10.

6.13   Delete line 10.

6.14   Correct the number on line 10, changing it from 8 to 0.

6.15   Insert a line between lines 9 and 10 that says `Preposterous`.

6.16   Delete the `pints, pounds,` and from line 11.

6.17   Restore line 11 to its original beauty and fullness.

6.18   Copy line 4 into buffer p.

6.19   Delete line 4.

6.20   Replace line 4 from the named buffer.

6.21   Join lines 10 and 11.

6.22   Move line 10 to line 1.

6.23   Display the contents of the file using all three display tools. Note the differences.

6.24   While in ex, determine the number of files in your current directory, or write a message to one of your peers.

6.25   Read the contents of `/etc/passwd` into your buffer after line 4.

6.26   Mark the line that is your entry from the password file.

6.27   Go to line 1.

6.28   Return to the line that was your entry in the password file.

6.29   Delete all the lines you added *except your entry*.

6.30   Save the contents of this buffer as the file `ireallylike.ex`.

6.31   Preserve your editing session, then ask your instructor, system administrator, or other privileged user to kill your editing session. Recover it.

6.32   Shift lines 4 through 8 two stops right.

6.33   Experiment with any command we haven't played with as yet that piques your interest.

Let's Get Visual!

CHAPTER OBJECTIVES

After reading this chapter, you should be able to use the vi editor to:

- Create and modify files.
- Start the editor with different command-line options.
- Add, delete, and change lines in the file.
- Use multiple buffers to save, copy, move, and replace lines of text.
- Use numeric buffers to retrieve deleted text.
- Modify the contents of a line of text using substitution.
- Save changes made to a file in either the original file or another file.
- Set and understand various ex editor options as they apply to visual mode.
- Use shell commands from within the editor.

The **vi** editor is a visual interface to the ex editor, or more simply put, the ex editor is the vi editor. If you wish to confuse the naive about it, you could also say that the vi editor is the visual mode of the ex editor or the ex editor is the command-line mode of the vi editor. However you want to say it, please remember that all of the commands you learned in the previous chapter will work with the vi editor because, well, it is the ex editor, too.

Before we dive into studying the vi editor, it is important that you know how to correctly pronounce it. You pronounce the letters of the name, so it's the "vee eye" editor. It's not the "vie" editor, nor is it the "six" editor. This is one of those small bits of knowledge that separates the true Unix aficionado from the Unix wannabe.

There are a number of vi clones. One is called **vim** (vi improved), another is called **vile**, and there's even a variant of vi known as **Elvis**. We will be studying good old-fashioned vi on the Solaris system and vim, which is the default flavor of the vi editor, on many Linux implementations.

Another thing you need to realize is that to some of us vi is more than just an editor. The choice of editors is one of the "holy wars" that rage from time to time within the Unix community. There are those that prefer the Emacs editor, and those that prefer other, here unnamed, editors. I have chosen to teach you vi because I know it is the most universally used and most often available visual editor found across all the denominations of Unix. On top of that, it's almost magical! When you become proficient with vi, you will be able to perform complex editing tasks with just a few, well-chosen strokes. Besides that, *I like it.*

Initially you may view vi with alarm, worry, confusion, perhaps even frustration. But if you will trust me and give vi a chance, you will come to love using it. True, vi requires a little different mindset than the other full-screen editor you may be used to. Programs like StarOffice, Word, or WordPerfect are not editors, they are word processors. As I'm sure you remember from Chapter 5, we use an ASCII editor to produce cleanly usable text without the superfluous formatting data that are added by word processors.

⊕ Origins of vi

As you remember from our discussion of the ex editor, Bill Joy first created ex, which was command-line based, because the terminals people had to work with at the time were hard-copy terminals. (A hard-copy terminal gives you access to only one line.) While Joy was still working on ex, Berkeley got its first video terminals, AMD-3As. An ADM-3A is shown in Figure 7.1. Notice how much it looks like an Apple iMac. These were state-of-the-art machines, which, being video terminals, allowed the cursor to move around the screen. All at once Joy had a machine that would allow him to display a full page of text to be edited rather than a single line. It was also significant when the new read-only memory for the ADMs came in, because for the first time Joy & Co. had terminals that would display *both upper and lower case.*

It's important to understand this history, because it explains why the vi command set is so terse. In an article from the November 1999 issue of *Linux* magazine entitled "The Joy of Unix," Bill Joy explains how he developed vi: "I had terminal at home and a 300 baud modem so the cursor could move around and I just stayed up all night for a few months and wrote vi." When asked about the rumor that he wrote vi in a weekend, Joy said,

> No. It took a long time. It was really hard to do because you've got to remember that I was trying to make it usable over a 300 baud modem. That's also the reason you have all these funny commands. It just barely worked to use a screen editor over a modem, it was just barely fast enough. A 1200 baud modem was an upgrade. 1200 baud now is pretty slow. 9600 baud is faster than you can read. 1200 baud is way slower. So the editor was optimized so that you could edit and feel productive when it was painting slower than you could think. Today computers are so much faster than you can think, nobody understands this anymore.
> http://www.linux-mag.com/1999-11/joy_04.html

FIGURE 7.1

ADM-3A terminal. Photo courtesy of The Vintage Computer Festival.

Please keep this historical information in mind as you begin to learn vi; it will help you understand the command structure and give you some insight into why vi is so efficient.

How vi Differs from ex

Even though all of the ex commands are available in vi, using the vi command set is very different from entering commands in ex in two ways. First, none of the vi commands are *echoed to the screen*. That means you can't see the command you just typed; you see only the result of that command. This feature of vi can be somewhat intimidating to the new user, but don't let it bother you. You will become used to it very quickly. Second, while you had a choice of using the full version or the abbreviated version of the ex command set, the vi command set is composed of single characters. (There will be times when you type several characters, but they will be modifiers to the command itself.) Since you are now expert with both ed and ex, working with an editor that has a command mode and a text-entry mode is old hat to you.

⊕ Editing Modes

In the most general terms, `vi` has two editing modes: text-entry and command. However, some flavors of `vi` further subdivide text-entry mode into the following specific modes:

- Insert—adding text *before* the current cursor position.
- Append—adding text *after* the current cursor position.
- Open—adding text before or after the current *line*.
- Replace—*overwriting* all or part of a line.
- Replace one character—overwriting a *single* character.

You can enter text in any of these modes—in fact, everything you type at the keyboard will be assumed to be text. (Actually, that's not entirely true. In some versions of the `vim` editor, the arrow keys are interpreted as cursor-movement keys even when you are in text-entry mode. That is not true in all versions of `vi`.)

You return to command mode from any of these text-entry modes by pressing the escape, ESC, key. In fact, one of the marks of a veteran `vi` user is that she will tap the ESC key several times before doing anything else. (Some folks say that `vi` users pound on the ESC key, but they just don't understand deliberate and enthusiastic *tapping*.) By pounding . . . er, tapping . . . the ESC key, `vi` users make sure that they are in command mode. You too will acquire this habit.

⊕ Format of `vi` Commands

All `vi` commands are composed of a single character, either a letter or special character, entered at the keyboard when in command mode. In many instances a single letter can represent three different commands, depending on whether you use the lowercase version of the letter, the uppercase version of the letter (also called the *shifted version*), or the control version of the letter. For example, lowercase e moves the cursor to the end of the current word, uppercase E moves to the end the word but ignores punctuation marks, and control Ctrl-E (^E) shows one more line at the bottom of the current screen. Of course you know that the caret (^) indicates the Ctrl key, so Ctrl-E is represented as ^E. And as you no doubt remember, the control character does not need to be capitalized, but it is the convention to show it that way.

In addition to having three different forms of the same letter do three different things, Bill Joy also added two other conventions to `vi` commands: a repeat count and a span of control. We'll look at the *repeat count* first.

The general form of a `vi` command is

```
[rep-count]command[span of control]
```

Let's decipher this command format. Most, but not all, `vi` commands can be preceded by a **repeat count** (**rep-count**), telling `vi` to repeat the command the number of times you specify. The first time this command will be of value to you is when we start learning about moving the cursor around on the screen. For example, if you want to move five characters to the left, you can type 1 (ell) five times (11111) or you can type 5l (five ell). Both would have exactly the same effect, but the second version would save you three keystrokes.

Some vi commands also allow you to specify their **span of control**. As an example, the delete command (**d**) can be modified as to its span of control. The command **de** will delete to the end the current word, while the command **db** will delete forward to the beginning of the current word. The command **d$** will delete from the cursor to the end of the line. (However, the command D (note case) will also do that and is a tad more efficient.) The command **dG** will delete the current line and all the lines to the end of the buffer.

To recap, then, many vi commands can be automatically executed multiple times by using the repeat count before the command. They can also have their span of control altered by including some special character or characters after the command. I know, this sounds a little confusing right now, but trust me, it will quickly become second nature to you.

Starting vi

---

vi [options] [file]

As with the editors that you've already learned, you can either associate a file with the editing buffer or start the vi editor without an associated file. In either case vi will take control of your screen and either display the beginning of the file or give you a screenful of tildes.

A critical assumption is involved here. If vi is going to control your screen, it must know and recognize the type of terminal you're using or the type of terminal your telnet or secure-shell session is emulating. If you are logging directly into a Unix computer, this isn't usually a problem. However, if you are telnetting or secure-shelling in from, let's say a PC, you must ensure that your telnet program is emulating a known terminal type, and that the shell understands what terminal type your program is emulating. Although both shells and vi understand a fairly wide range of terminal types, let's stick with a really standard terminal type, the VT-100.

Since there are dozens of different telnet programs available, and I don't know which one you have chosen to use, I will discuss the program Tera Term Pro. Figure 7.2 shows a sample Tera Term session, where I have chosen to set up the terminal type. The first thing I did here was click the Setup option and then highlight and clicked on "terminal." Figure 7.3 shows the terminal setup screen that Tera Term provides.

The field we are concerned with in Figure 7.3 is the one labeled Terminal ID: this field identifies the terminal type that Tera Term will emulate. I can't be sure, because I've used Tera term for years, but I think the default terminal type is VT-100. Which ever telnet program you choose to use, you will need to ensure that it is emulating a known terminal type. I recommend that you choose VT-100 emulation simply because it is very common. DEC, the Digital Equipment Corp., produced millions of VT-100 (Video Terminal model 100) terminals, and its keyboard layout and communications

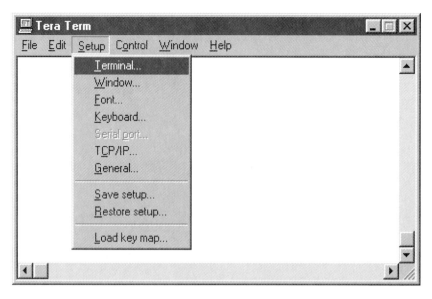

FIGURE 7.2

Setting terminal type in Tera Term Pro.

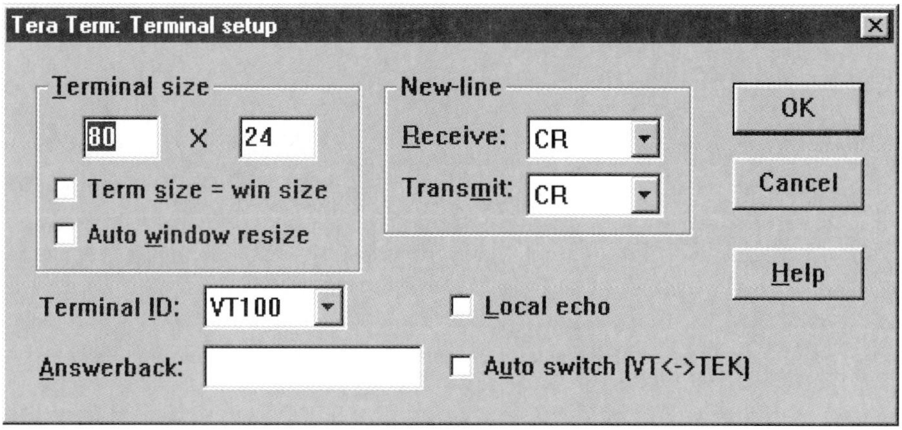

FIGURE 7.3

Setting terminal type to VT-100.

protocols have become the standard for computer-to-computer communications. That takes care of one side of the connection. Now let's look at the other.

In addition to having your telnet program emulating a usable terminal type, you need to make sure that the shell, and vi, understand which terminal type your telnet program is emulating. To do that, you need to tell the shell your terminal type. Figure 7.4 shows how to set your terminal type in both the C shell and the bash shell.

When we discuss the different shells in detail, we'll talk about setting shell variables. For now, notice that we used the set command in the C shell, and the variable

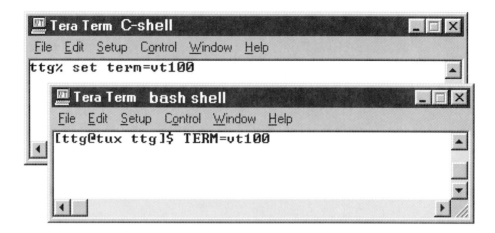

FIGURE 7.4

Setting the terminal type in the C shell (top) and the bash shell (bottom).

name is lowercase. In the Bourne and bash shells we don't use the set command, and the variable name is all uppercase. Remember: Unix is case-sensitive.

"Suppose," you ask, "that I am using a secure shell program that doesn't support any terminal type that vi knows?" Well, that's exactly why we learned the line editors first. There will be times when you encounter a data transfer program that does not correctly emulate a known terminal type. In those cases you will use a line editor.

Now that we have the terminal emulator talking to the shell, let's look at the ways we can start the vi editor. Since vi is ex, it supports all the command-line options you learned with ex. In addition, you can use the -w option to set the number of lines in the editing window. This option is useful for slow connections when you don't want a full-screen repaint each time you make a change.

view

```
view [options] [file]
```

Using the **view** command is a special way to start the vi editor in read-only mode. That's just like using the -R option in vi or ex. When vi is in view mode you can't change the contents of the file you have opened; you can only read it. (Of course, you can override this protection by appending a ! to the write command.)

When you start the vi editor without specifying a file to associate with the editing buffer, vi will give you a screenful of tildes. The tildes indicate unfilled lines. You will always be in command mode when you start the editor, just as you were with ex (surprise, surprise).

Figure 7.5 shows what a screen full of tildes looks like. The black block in the upper left corner is the cursor. When you're using the editor the cursor will usually blink, but it's hard to make an image blink in a textbook. Probably the most frustrating thing for brand-new vi users is that they can't immediately start typing text. That's

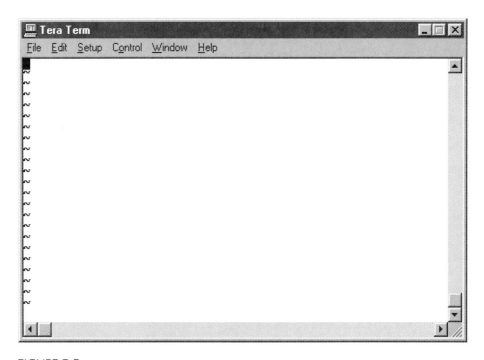

FIGURE 7.5

Starting vi without associating a file with the editing buffer (or a screen full of tildes—how exciting!).

because vi always starts in command mode, and to enter text you need to be in one of the text-entry modes. Before we start discussing how to add text, let's look at how to leave vi.

⊕ Say Good-bye to vi

There are a number of ways to exit from the vi editor, and it seems that everyone has his own particular favorite. You're already familiar with the two ways to exit from ex, and since ex is vi, you can use them. There's one little peculiarity you have to take into account when you want to use ex commands from within the vi editor. You must first tell the vi editor you wish to use an ex command.

Colon (:)

Bill Joy's choice for the ex mode command was pretty intuitive if you remember that the prompt for the ex editor is the colon. All you have to do to use an **ex** command is type a colon (from command mode.) The editor will put a colon as the first character of line 24 and also put the cursor there. Figure 7.6 shows how this looks. The numbers along the left-hand margin of the figure are not part of the normal vi screen; I added them for reference.

Figure 7.6 shows you the format of the vi screen. The first 23 lines are used to display the actual text in the file. The last line, line 24, is an informational line, sometimes

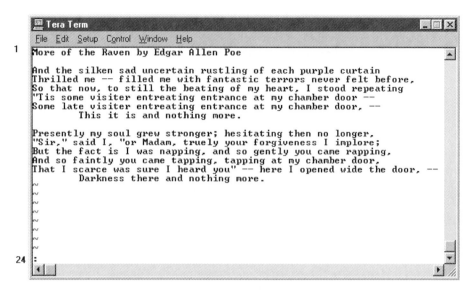

FIGURE 7.6

The ex command prompt, shown on line 24.

called the *status line*. That last line is also where ex commands and other special commands like search commands are displayed. In this figure I have entered the colon command to tell vi that I'm going to use an ex command, but I have not yet entered the command. Figure 7.7 shows how I would write and then quit the vi editor using ex

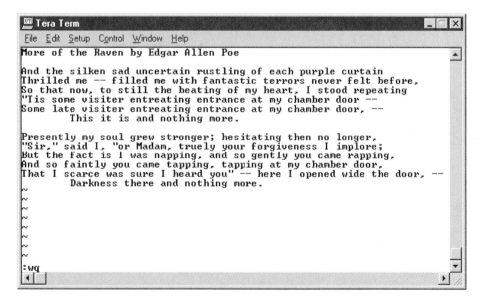

FIGURE 7.7

Using ex commands to save buffer changes, then quit.

commands. Remember that if you want to save your work, you should either issue a write (w) command and then a quit, (q), or combine them by using the **write**-and-**quit** command, **wq**. As the figure shows, I can issue an ex command just as I could in the ex editor. In this case, I wrote the contents of the buffer to the file and then exited from the vi editor.

ZZ

For some reason, perhaps because of their familiarity with the ex editor, many of my students choose the **write**-and-**quit** (wq) option shown in Figure 7.7. But the **ZZ** command is a more efficient way to achieve the same results. This command performs exactly the same operations, as wq, first writing the contents of the buffer to the file, then exiting from the editor. I think it's much more efficient to simply type two uppercase Zs, than to type :wq and touch ENTER.

How you choose to exit from the editor is up to you, but at least consider the double-Z command, I think you will appreciate its speed. I know I do. Of course, if you wish to leave the editor without saving your changes, you would use the ex command of a quit with a bang, q!. Remember, vi is ex, so all the ex commands work with it.

⊕ Error Messages

There are very few error messages in vi. If you try to use a command vi doesn't understand, it will either blink the screen or ring the terminal bell, indicating it's confused. By default, it sounds the bell, but you can use the set command to make it flash the screen instead. Just enter this command:

```
:set noerrorbells
```

I find the flashing distracting, but when I am teaching, the beeps are sometimes distracting to the students, so I set flashing or beeps based on my environment. (Remember, this is an ex command, so you must first type the colon to tell vi you are entering an ex command.)

⊕ Adding Text to File

Okay, enough of this boring stuff—let's start typing! But wait—before we jump into typing we need to address one of the most common complaints about the vi editor: "How do I know what mode I am in?" In most flavors of vi, there is no difference in the appearance of the screen whether you are in text-entry mode or in command mode. The problem with that feature of vi is that most versions will enter *every keystroke* into the file when you're in text-entry mode even when you use the arrow keys. Look at Figure 7.8. Notice the odd collection of "As" in the middle of the page. Those are how **vi** interprets the codes for the up-arrow key. There is nothing on the screen to tell me

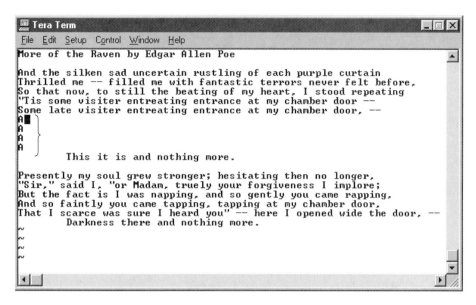

FIGURE 7.8

Oops—using the arrow keys when in text-entry mode gets ugly.

that I am in text entry mode. Let's change that. In the ex chapter, you learned how to use the set command to specify particular settings for the editor. You will find the set command very handy in vi as well since, you guessed it, vi is ex! The command

> :set showmode

turns on the option **showmode**, which asks vi to tell—err, show—us, what mode we are currently operating in down on line 24. It's interesting to note that this option works exactly opposite from the other editors. In ex and ed we were given a prompt when we were in *command* mode; in vi we are told when we are in *text-entry* mode. Exactly what vi tells us differs among the various versions of vi. Some, like the Solaris version, tell us explicitly each mode (insert, append, replace, open, change, etc.). Others, like the Linux version, tell us only that we are in an insert mode.

Figure 7.9 shows the same situation in both editors after I have told vi to turn on showmode. For both the screen captures I first turned on showmode (you can still see the command in the Solaris version) and then moved my cursor to the h in the word This and entered append mode. Solaris told me I was in APPEND mode, while Linux simply told me I was in INSERT mode. It doesn't really matter exactly what the message is—what's important is that now I know that vi is expecting to enter every keystroke into the file—well, every keystroke except escape, ESC, which ends text-entry mode and drops me back into command mode.

FIGURE 7.9

Messages from vi when showmode is enabled.

⊕ Text-Entry Modes of vi

You could probably get by just knowing one way to enter text-entry mode, as you saw on the "vi cheat sheet" if you looked ahead. However, using vi is all about being efficient. The ability to efficiently edit a file is one of the things that separates a true Unix master from a novice. As you spend time with Unix folk, you will soon realize that some people have an almost magical ability to perform edits to files. With deceptively few keystrokes they make wonderful things happen to the files they are editing. These people have spent the time it takes to learn how to effectively use the vi editor. I urge you to make this promise to yourself: "I will learn one new feature of the vi editor each time I use it." It will take time, but your ability to use vi will increase, and you will one day become a wizard.

The first way to become more productive with vi is to choose the correct text-entry mode. This choice may seem relatively unimportant—after all, what do a few extra keystrokes mean in the big picture? Let's consider that question for a moment. Suppose, just by using the most effective text-entry mode, you can save a mere three keystrokes each time you want to enter text. And let's say, conservatively, that you use text-entry mode 50 times each day. And let's say that you work five days a week and 45 weeks a year. Just by using the correct text-entry mode you can save yourself 33,750 keystrokes in a single year! That's almost twice as many characters as I have typed in this chapter so far. (In the initial draft, there were 18,956 characters, including spaces, up to and including the exclamation point following the word "year.") I think that's a substantial saving of both time and effort. So, what are these different text-entry modes?

append

---

a

The lowercase **a**, standing for *append*, begins text-entry mode at the character position *following the cursor*. (The case of the command is very important, as you'll see in a moment. The uppercase A is a different append command.) You will use the lowercase a to begin entering text after the current cursor location. Remember to go back to command mode, press the ESC key.

Append

A

The uppercase **A**, another form of the *append* command, begins text entry *at the end of the current line*. This is a very significant command, because it can save you a great deal of time and keystrokes. Suppose, for example, the cursor is currently on the second word of the second line of the file shown in Figure 7.10. Suppose Joe User wants to begin entering text at the end of that line. Let's look at the number of keystrokes the A could save him. The most efficient way to just go to the end of the line is to use the $ command. Without using the A to begin text entry at the end of the line, Joe would need to type a $ followed by an a. However, it's unlikely that Joe would use the most efficient way to go to the end of the line if he didn't know the most efficient way to go into text-entry mode. Therefore, we'll assume that Joe uses the "move right to the end of the word" (**e**) command to move to the end of the line and then begins to append text. It will take nine keystrokes to get to the end of the line and one to enter the a command. But if Joe is really inefficient and uses the right-arrow key, it will take him 54 keystrokes just to get to the end of the line, and then he will still have to type the append command to begin text entry. The savings of A are obvious.

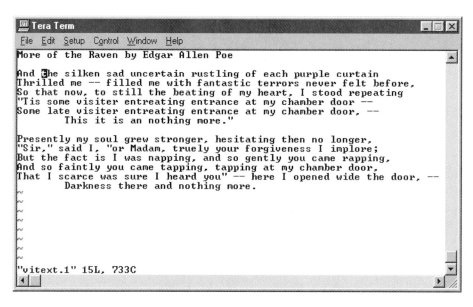

FIGURE 7.10

Selecting the more efficient append command.

insert

i

The lowercase **i**, or *insert*, command begins text entry *at the current cursor position*. This has the effect of entering text *before* the character at the cursor. As you can see, the difference between the lowercase a and the lowercase i is simply where, relative to the cursor, they'll begin text entry. As with append, to go back to command mode you press the ESC key.

Insert

I

In general terms, the append command adds text *after*, and the insert command adds text *before*. In the case of the uppercase **I**, text entry starts *at the beginning of the current line*. As with the uppercase A, this is a much quicker way to begin text entry at the beginning of the line. It's another one of those handy vi commands that can save you a great deal of time.

open

o

Insert and append are fine if you want to enter text on an existing line, but if you want to enter text on a brand-new line *after or below* the current line, you can use the lower-case **o**, (**open**). Figure 7.11 shows how I used the lowercase o command to begin entering text on a brand-new line. I realize that I could have used the A command to go to the end the line, and then touched the ENTER key to begin text entry on a new line. However, the o command is more efficient. When you finish entering text and want to go back to command mode, press the ESC key.

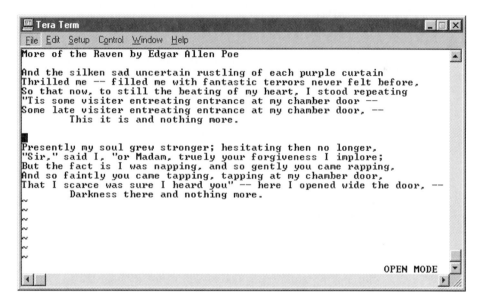

FIGURE 7.11
Using lowercase (open) mode.

As you can see from Figure 7.11, the cursor is at the beginning of a new line, and vi is telling me I am in OPEN MODE. Okay, time for a little test: which vi am I using in Figure 7.11—the Solaris or the Linux version?

Open

O

The uppercase **O** mode works just like the lowercase o (*open*) mode except that the line will be opened *above* the current line rather than *below* it. We will see this pattern again when we talk about the put command, uppercase above lowercase below. Figure 7.12 shows exactly the same operation as in Figure 7.11, except that I issued the uppercase O instead of the lowercase. Notice the position of the cursor in the figure. This is the only obvious difference between Figure 7.11 and Figure 7.12. In both cases the Solaris version of vi tells us that we are in OPEN MODE—oops, I gave away the answer. In the Linux version we would be told only that we were in INSERT MODE. As with insert and append, to get back to command mode you simply touch the ESC key.

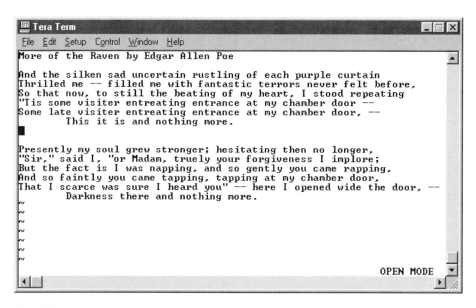

FIGURE 7.12

Using uppercase O (open) command.

You can begin entering new text six different ways in the vi editor. Which one you choose depends on exactly what you're trying to do. To begin with, simply using the append command will probably suffice. However, you should try to use the most appropriate vi command each time you choose one. That way you'll become more efficient and proficient very quickly.

⊕ Moving about in vi

Probably the most common activity you'll perform in vi is moving around in an existing file. There are more ways to move around in vi than there are to perform any other activity. I have broken the movement commands into four general categories, starting with moving the cursor from character to character and working our way upward to moving throughout the file.

Before we begin discussing the actual cursor movement commands, I need to touch again on a feature of many of the vi commands. Although the commands themselves are usually a single character, you can prepend a number to the beginning of the command. That number, called the ***repeat count*** (which we discussed earlier under "Format of vi Command") directs vi to perform a specified command a specified number of times. This repeat count is a very efficient way to perform certain activities. For example, rather than pressing the right-arrow key 20 times to move 20 spaces across the line, you could enter the number 20 and then touch the right-arrow key. Those two procedures would yield exactly the same result.

Cursor Control (letters vs. arrows)

There are two different ways to move the cursor from character to character within the screen. I will address the preferred way (letter keys) first, and then we'll look at the other way (arrow keys).

h, j, k, l

```
[rep-count]h
[rep-count]j
[rep-count]k
[rep-count]l
```

If you are fortunate enough to have at your disposal an ADM-3A, you will notice that there's no difference between using the letters (**h**, **j**, **k**, **l**) and the arrow keys, because arrows are embossed upon those four keys. For those of us less fortunate, the four lowercase alphabetic keys immediately available to your right hand provide one-space cursor movement. Table 7.1 describes those four movements.

Using the four letter keys to move the cursor has a couple of distinct advantages. First, you don't have to move your hands off the keyboard and reach way over there to the arrow keys to move the cursor. Second, when you play the game Rogue or Hack on your Unix system you will already know how to move the character right, left, up, and down because that game also uses this key combination in addition to the repeat-count option. (Don't have Rogue or Hack on your computer? Speak to your instructor and see if you can have it installed. It's a great way to practice your cursor-movement key strokes! Rogue was either the first, or at least one of the very first, graphical computer games. Michael Toy and Glenn Wichman wrote it back in 1980. The greatest feature of Rogue was that it generated a new dungeon each time you started a new game, so you couldn't learn a standard dungeon and have an advantage. It was first distributed widely when it was included in the 4.2 distribution of BSD Unix, and it became the most

TABLE 7.1 Cursor Movement Keys

Letter	Cursor Movement
h	Left one character
j	Down one character
k	Up one character
l	Right one character

popular game on college campuses. It is now available on many platforms, from Unix servers to Palm® devices.)

On the other hand, if you're using one of the newer versions of Linux, the `vim` editor (the default `vi` editor in Linux) treats the arrow keys in a special way. If you're in text-entry mode, you can use the arrow keys to move around the line or move up, down, right, and left on the screen without leaving text-entry mode.

The choice of whether to use the arrow keys or the letter keys is, obviously, up to you, but you won't find true Unix wizards using the arrow keys very often. I suggest you become comfortable using the letter keys; you will be more efficient. This is one of the major advantages of the `vi` editor—touch typists don't need to move their hands from the keyboard except to use the ESC key.

Space Bar

```
[rep-count]<space bar>
```

When you're in command mode you can also use the space bar to move across the line. It will operate just like the right-arrow or the lowercase `l` (ell). You can prepend a repeat count to the command and move to the right across the line the number of characters specified by the repeat count.

⊕ Moving within Line

A number of different commands will move your cursor across the single line within the `vi` editor. Obviously, you can use the `h` and `l` and space bar to move one character left or right, so let's talk about larger movements.

w

```
[rep-count]w
```

Suppose you want to move to the next word on the line. You can use the **w** (word) command to move, one word at a time, across the line to the right. Figure 7.13 is a composite I created combining six different screen captures. It shows the cursor moving to the right, one word at a time, in response to my typing six separate w commands. (This figure was the best I could do for a static medium like a book. Please try the procedure out on your computer to see what I mean. The file is called `vitext.2` and is on the companion Web site for the book. If possible, log on to a Unix system and open the file in the **vi** editor while we discuss these commands. You won't see the commands I type—all you will see are the results of the commands. If I do a series of screen captures, I can show you the cumulative results, as in Figure 7.13.)

Each time I typed a lowercase w, I moved to the *beginning* of the next word or to the next punctuation mark. Notice that the sixth w took me to the comma, following the word `peering`. Of course, if I had known that the comma was the sixth "word" across

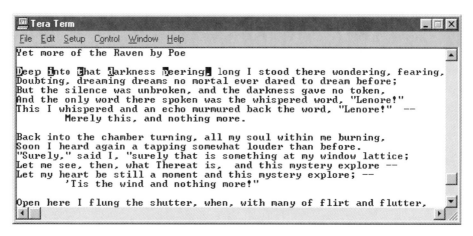

FIGURE 7.13

Moving across a line, one word at a time.

the line, I could have issued a 6w using the repeat count. But suppose I don't want to stop at all the punctuation marks?

W

```
[rep-count]W
```

The uppercase W command moves me one word at a time across the line to the right *without stopping for punctuation marks.* That's the only difference between the lower-case w command and the uppercase W. Figure 7.14 is a composite of two screen

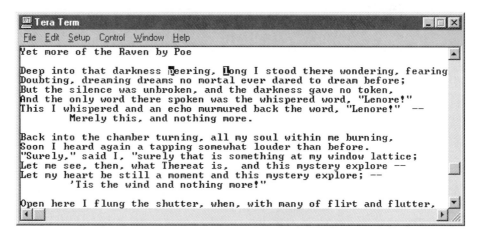

FIGURE 7.14

Moving across the line one word at a time, skipping punctuation.

captures. My cursor started out on the p of the word peering. I typed one uppercase W, and the cursor moved to the l of long. But suppose I want to move to the left, not to the right, across the screen.

b

```
[rep-count]b
```

The lowercase **b** command moves the cursor backward, or to the left, one word at a time across the line. Like the w command, it moves the cursor to the *first* character of each word. Also like the lowercase w command, it stops for punctuation.

B

```
[rep-count]B
```

Ahhh, consistency! The uppercase **B** command is consistent with the uppercase W command. It moves the cursor across the line, right to left, from beginning of word to beginning of word, *skipping punctuation*. It's nice to see some consistency among Unix commands, even though the commands are within the same editor, written by the same person. Relish consistency—it's not all that common.

Enough for beginnings; what about ends of words?

e

```
[rep-count]e
```

The lowercase **e** command moves the cursor across the line, left to right, stopping at the *end* of each word. Like the lowercase b and w commands, the lowercase e command recognizes, and stops for, punctuation marks. You can include a repeat count, so that, for example, if you want to move to the end of the word six words to the right, you can type 7e or type the e command seven times. Seven times? Yes. I want to move the cursor to the end of the word six words to the right. Look at Figure 7.15, and count the number of cursors you see. I started with the cursor at the beginning of the word Some and wanted to end the series with the cursor at the end of the word my. As you can see, the cursor started on the S of Some and then moved across seven ends of words to the right, finally resting on the y of my.

The most common use I have for the e command is to simply move to the end of the current word. Depending on the length of the word, of course, it is certainly more efficient than using the arrow keys or even the l (ell) command.

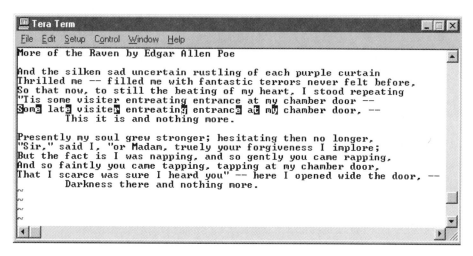

FIGURE 7.15

Moving across the line from end of word to end of word.

E

[rep-count]E

Good grief! Consistency across three whole commands! As I hope you would expect, the uppercase **E** command moves the cursor across the line from left to right, stopping at the end of each word, skipping punctuation.

^

---

^

The ^ (caret) command moves the cursor to the first *nonblank* position in the line. Don't confuse this command with the next command, (0) zero. The caret command is extremely useful. Since you can go to the first nonblank character of the line just once, this command supports neither a repetition count nor span of control. In addition, we will see the same concept repeated when we discuss regular expressions. Obviously, Bill Joy was familiar with regular expressions when he built the editor and used that knowledge.

0

0

The **0** (zero) command moves the cursor to the first position, or leftmost position, on the line, whether it is blank or not. If it helps you to remember how to use this command, you can think of it as going to the "zeroeth" position of the line or to position zero. As with the ^ command, you can't do this more than once, so there is no repeat count nor is there a span of control.

$

$

The **$** (dollar sign) command moves the cursor to the last character, or rightmost character, of the line. Another way to say this is that the $ positions the cursor immediately before the newline character. Like the ^ command, the $ command has its origins in regular expressions. Also like the ^, this command accepts neither repeat count nor span of control.

Four other commands will move the cursor within the current line, but these are very specialized and not often employed by novice vi users. I have included them here for completeness, and because you may find them to be of value in particular situations you may encounter.

f

```
[rep-count]fz
```

The lowercase **f** command moves the cursor forward, across the line to the right, to the next occurrence of the letter that follows it—in this case z—on the line. This command is handy if you want to move to a particular character partway across the line. It's more efficient than typing a series of ws, es, right-arrow keys, or even 1s.

F

```
[rep-count]Fz
```

Now, what do you suppose the uppercase **F** command does? Did you guess that it moves the cursor across the line, skipping punctuation? Sorry. So much for consistency. The uppercase F command moves the cursor *backward*, to the left, across the line to the closest occurrence of the character that follows the command. In this case it would move the cursor left to the first z on the line.

"Suppose," you say, "there is no z on the line—what happens then?" Good question! If you tell vi to move the cursor to a character that doesn't exist in the line, it will either beep or blink the screen depending on how you have instructed it to inform you of errors. It will not go to another line that contains a character.

t

[rep-count]tz

There's a subtle difference between the **t** command and the f command. The t command will move the cursor forword, across the line to the right, and position it *just before* the character specified after the command. In this case, it would put the cursor just before the closest occurrence, to the right, of the "z" character. In contrast, the f command would move the cursor *to* the letter specified. Learning this small but important difference between f and t will enhance your efficiency.

T

[rep-count]Tz

Initially the uppercase **T** command seems to behave like the uppercase F command, moving the cursor backward across the line. Again, though, we have a subtle difference. The T command moves the cursor to the position *just after*, or just behind, the character specified, whereas the F moves it *to* the character. Notice that the T command both moves in the opposite direction and positions the cursor on the opposite side of the target character.

Now that we can use these commands wherever we wish within the line, let's start talking about moving within the screen.

⊕ Moving within the Screen

Three commands let you jump the cursor around the current screen. Figure 7.16 is a composite screen capture showing the cursor position after each of these three commands. First let's describe the commands, and then we'll look again at the figure.

H

H

The **H** command moves the cursor to the *head* position on the screen, meaning the top left corner of the screen—position zero (or 1 if you want to start counting with 1) of line 1. This command is very useful to go to the top of the screen. Remember that this is a screen command, not a buffer command, so you'll move about only in the 23 lines that vi displays for you. Since this command moves the cursor to a particular location, neither a repeat count nor a modifier is available to you.

M

M

The M command moves the cursor to the leftmost position of the middle line on the screen. The middle line is the 12th line on the screen, since there are 23 available lines. Just like the H command, the M command is an absolute cursor-positioning command and thus has neither a repeat count nor an action modifier.

L

L

I'll bet you can guess where the L command places the cursor! Right you are! It puts the cursor on the leftmost byte of the last (23rd) line of the screen. Take a look at Figure 7.16. It shows the three different cursor positions after I typed the following (but remember that this is a composite figure):

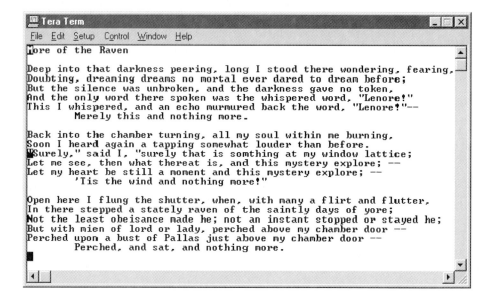

FIGURE 7.16

Using absolute cursor-positioning commands.

H—which put the cursor on the M of the first line.

M—which put the cursor on the quotation mark before the word Surely.

L—which put the cursor on the first byte of the 23rd line.

Although these three commands allow us to move the cursor around the current screen, it's often more useful to be able to move about in the buffer.

⊕ Moving within the Buffer

Usually the files you edit will contain more than 23 lines. To make it simple to move around in the editing buffer, Bill Joy added buffer-movement commands to vi. These commands can be divided into two general categories: transfering to a specific line or scrolling through the buffer. First we will look at transfering, or moving, the cursor to a particular line in the buffer.

G

```
[line number]G
```

The **G**, or *go to*, command moves the cursor to either (1) the last line of the file, if you don't specify line number or (2) the specific line number specified before the command. This command is frequently used to go to either the first line of the file (1G) or to the last line of the file (G). The other common use for the go-to command is to transfer control to a specific line, usually to correct a problem with that line.

Suppose you're compiling a C program and the compiler complains about an error in line 2341. It is easy to transfer control to that line using this command (2431G). Note that this command allows no range modifier.

There are several ways to move around in the buffer other than using the cursor-movement keys or the arrow keys. Generally, these commands enable you to read through the file stored in the buffer. The next commands we will learn represent a whole new class of vi commands. So far all the commands we've seen are either uppercase or lowercase letters standing by themselves. This next group adds the caret symbol (^), which stands for the control (Ctrl on most keyboards) key to a letter. As you remember from our earlier discussion, many of the alphabetic keys have three different meanings depending on whether you use them uppercase, lowercase, or in combination with the Ctrl key. The following commands, for scrolling through the buffer use the Ctrl key.

^B

```
^B
```

The **^B** command scrolls one screenful backward, or upward, through the buffer. It is useful for reading backward through the contents of the buffer one screenful at a time.

^F

---

^F

If you wish to move quickly through the buffer, you can use the **^F** command to move forward, or downward, one complete screen at a time. This command allows you to step through the buffer very quickly, either reading the contents or scanning for a particular character string.

^D

---

^D

If you want to go forward, or downward, in the file, you can use the **^D** command to move *one-half screen* at a time toward the end of the file. This helps you keep the context of your reading in mind, because you can see the preceding line each time you move downward through the file.

^U

---

^U

It's all well and good to be able to work downward, or forward, into the file one-half screen at a time, but suppose you want to move backward, or upward, in the file instead? If ^D stands for downward, it only makes sense that **^U** stands for upward. The ^U command will allow you to move upward one-half screen at a time. Moving backward in the file one-half screen at a time makes it easy to remember the context of what you are reading.

^E

---

^E

The **^E** command, and the command discussed next, ^Y, serve as excellent illustrations of the precise control you have with the vi editor. The ^E command shifts the display up *one line*, showing one more line at the bottom of the screen. This is useful in those instances when you want to see "just one more line" at the bottom of the screen but do not want to jump to the bottom of the screen and scroll down. It's also important to note that the cursor doesn't move when you use the ^E command.

^Y

---

^Y

The ^Y command is the opposite of the ^E command. The ^Y command will shift the display down one line, showing one more line at the top of the screen.

Other Cursor-Movement Commands

Some additional cursor-movement commands that you can research follow:

)—move right or forward to next *sentence*.
(—move left or backward one *sentence*.
}—move right or forward to next *paragraph*.
{—move left or backward one *paragraph*.

Since this is an introductory textbook, and since my students don't seem to use these additional commands, I have not included a detailed discussion of them. These commands are more useful with text files than programs or scripts, and the focus of this book is on using the editor to write scripts. You can, of course, use a repeat count to move forward or backward multiple sentences or paragraphs with these text-oriented commands.

Searching in Buffer

I hope it comes as no surprise to you that the two commands you use to search for a particular character or character string in vi are the same ones you learned when we discussed ex. Also, as you learned when we discussed ex, the buffer you are searching is circular. You can search off the bottom, and continue right back at the top.

/

```
/[search string] (Both flavors)
[rep-count]/[search string] (Linux)
```

The forward slash (/) command tells us the vi editor to search forward, rightward, or downward into the buffer for the string specified. When you enter the slash command the cursor will drop to the 24th line of the screen, and vi will display a slash indicating that it is in search mode. You can then type character, a character string, a word, or even several words, and vi will move the cursor to the next occurrence of that particular search string. Since you're down to the 24th line, you will need to touch the ENTER key after you type in your search string.

If you type a slash without entering a search string and then touch ENTER, vi will search forward for the most recent search string you entered. This is true for both the forward and backward searches. The slash is an efficient way to search through the buffer for a particular character string.

I have included both a repeat-count version and a non-repeat-count version of the search command, because the vi editor I have running under Linux differs from the vi editor running under Solaris. In the Linux version I can supply repeat count and have vi search forward to the *n*th occurrence of the search string. This is just another one of those little flavor differences. (Okay, I know, I should get a life and not spend my time figuring out subtle little differences like this, but you must admit it is interesting.)

Figure 7.17 shows a search into the buffer. I first issued a 1G command to move the cursor to the first byte of the buffer. Then I issued the search shown in the figure for the character string nothing more!. Obviously, this is another of those composite screen captures, because you can't have two cursors at the same time. As soon as I touched the ENTER key, the cursor moved to the first byte of the first occurrence of the character string nothing more!. This result shows that you can have a search string longer than a single character. Exclamation points and the character string nothing more (without the exclamation point) occur before the character string nothing more!. Had the character string I was searching for occurred 30 or 40 lines down the buffer, vi would have moved the cursor to that string.

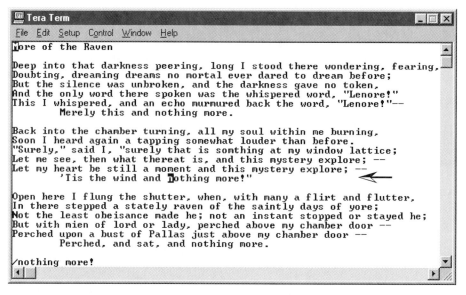

FIGURE 7.17

Searching forward into the buffer.

?

```
?[search string] (Both flavors)
[rep-count]?[search string] (Linux)
```

The question mark, **?**, works just like the forward slash except that it searches *backward* through the buffer. In the Linux version of vi, the command will accept a repeat count, just like the forward slash.

There are two more commands that are useful if you don't want to keep typing slashes or question marks.

n

---

n

The lowercase **n** command repeats the previous search. That's nice, but the slash or question-mark command, without any search string, also repeats the previous search. So why did Bill Joy include the lowercase n command? The difference between using the slash or the question mark and using the lowercase n is simply efficiency. If you use the lowercase n you don't have to touch the ENTER key! That's a little faster, and a little more efficient.

N

N

The uppercase **N** command repeats the previous search *in the opposite direction*. That's the same as typing a question mark after you have used a forward slash to search, or typing a forward slash after you have used a question mark to search. The significant difference, again, is that you don't have to use the ENTER key.

Okay, enough of this moving around stuff. Let's start hacking and slashing and having fun.

⊕ Deleting Data from Buffer

You have the choice in vi of efficiently deleting either individual characters or whole lines or parts of a line.

x

    [rep-count]x

It's extremely efficient to delete individual characters from the buffer in the vi editor. The lowercase **x** command deletes the character at or under the cursor. Figure 7.18 shows how this works. The top screen capture shows the first line of the file, with the cursor on the M of the sentence. I touched the x command and the M character was deleted. The second screen capture shows the result of the deletion.

If you wish to delete a series of characters, you can precede the x command with a repeat count and it will delete the number of characters specified.

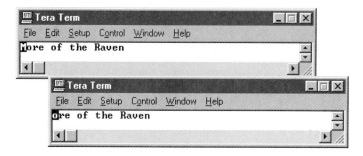

FIGURE 7.18

Using the x command to delete a character.

X

`[rep-count]X`

The difference between the lowercase x and the uppercase **X** command is exactly which character that is removed. The uppercase X command removes the character to the *immediate left* of the cursor, not the character *at* the cursor. Figure 7.19 shows how the uppercase X command functions.

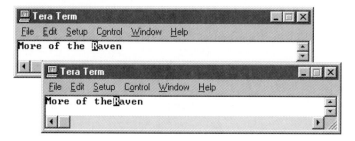

FIGURE 7.19

The uppercase X command at work.

In the top screen capture the cursor is on the R of the word Raven. I then typed an uppercase X, and the space to the left of the R was removed. You can include a re-peat count and remove more than one character to the left of the cursor. It may seem to be a trivial distinction now as to whether the deleted character is under or to the left of the cursor. As you become more experienced with vi, though, this type of small but distinct difference will become much more significant to you.

d

```
[rep-count]d[span of control]
```

The lowercase **d**, or *delete*, command is the first command we've seen that has a span of control as well as a repeat count. The span of control makes the d command extremely powerful. It also illustrates how Bill Joy's knowledge of Unix and concern with efficiency translated into a very useful command set. We can couple other commands we have learned with the delete command to perform specific deletions with wonderful ease.

Table 7.2 shows some of the more common delete combinations. As you can see, the delete command is very versatile. There are other, less often used combinations that you'll discover as you play with vi. Pay particular attention to the last example in Table 7.2. That d/stuff combination allows you to remove a large chunk of the buffer with one command. You can, of course, delete backwards using the question mark in place of the forward slash.

TABLE 7.2 Some Common Delete Combinations

Command	What It Does
dd	Delete current line.
dw	Delete current word.
db	Delete previous word (backward).
dG	Delete to end of buffer (usually a BIG delete!).
dM	Delete to middle of screen.
d0	Delete to left, to column zero.
d/stuff	Delete from cursor forward, to word stuff.

One delete command that seems to be missing from Table 7.2 is the d$, for deleting to the end of the line. The reason I didn't include that command is not because it wouldn't work—it would—but because there's another command available to do exactly the same thing more elegantly.

When delete removes data from the buffer, it temporarily stores the data in either the anonymous buffer or a named buffer. We will explore the use of these buffers when we talk about moving text and copying text. For now let's just think about getting rid of data.

D

D

The uppercase **D** command deletes forward or to the right from the cursor position to the end of the line. There is no repeat count on this command—you can include one and vi will politely ignore it. There's no span of control because D always deletes to the end of the current line. The D command also stores the deleted data either in the anonymous buffer or in one of the named buffers.

⊕ Combining Two (or More) Lines

There are times, as we saw when we learned about the ed editor, when it is convenient to be able to join two or more lines together. You can, of course, use the ex join command, but Bill Joy created an easier way to do it in vi.

J

```
[rep-count]J
```

The vi *join* command, **J**, is very intelligent. Figure 7.20 shows two different screen captures. The first displays the 10-line file, with one word on each line. There are no characters entered after the words. When I typed each word I touched ENTER immediately

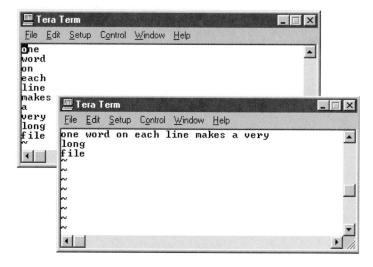

FIGURE 7.20

Combining lines using the J command.

afterward. The second screen shows the result of my typing 8J with the cursor on the first line.

Recall our discussion of the ed editor: when I joined the lines in the data file, I had to then go back and correct the buffer by inserting spaces between the enjoined lines. As you can see from Figure 7.20, the J command takes care of that for me.

⊕ Moving Data

When we talk about moving data around in the buffer—either parts of lines, whole lines, or even collections of lines—we're talking about removing those data from one part of the buffer and putting them into another part of the buffer. If you use a word processor you are no doubt familiar with the cut-and-paste operation. To do the same thing in the vi editor we need to combine a command you already know with a new command. To remove data from the buffer we use the delete (d or D) command. When the vi deletes data from the buffer, it stores those data in another buffer temporarily. Normally vi places deleted data into the unnamed, or **anonymous, buffer**. However, vi has 35 additional buffers that can be used to store data. As with the ex editor, these additional buffers are called the **named buffers**. However, unlike the ex editor, when Bill Joy wrote the vi editor, he added nine additional, numerically "named" buffers. So in addition to the alphabetic buffers named a through z, vi has numeric buffers named 1 through 9. These numeric buffers serve a special function: they hold the text of previous deletes.

You can think of the anonymous buffer as buffer 0. If you had a file with the following lines,

```
somewhere

    over

    the

rainbow
```

and you moved your cursor to line 1 (somewhere) and then typed dd, the first line (somewhere) would move into the anonymous buffer, buffer 0. If you then typed a second dd, your cursor would be on the new first line (over), and that line would move into buffer 0, the anonymous buffer, while the contents of the buffer 0 would move to buffer 1. If you then typed a third dd, you would send the new first line (the) to the anonymous buffer, buffer 0, and the previous contents of the anonymous buffer (over) would move to buffer 1, while the contents of buffer 1 (somewhere) would move to buffer 2. Whew! So at the end of three deletes the score would be snorbles 6 and blivits 2. Oops. What I meant to say was at the end of three deletes the numbered buffers would have the following contents:

Buffer 0—the
Buffer 1—over
Buffer 2—somewhere

You can use a put command to recover the contents of any of the named or numbered buffers. This is a pretty handy little trick!

The syntax for using named buffers is a little bit different than in ex. Rather than specifying the buffer name after the command, you need to precede the command and repeat count with a quotation mark followed by the buffer name. If I wanted to delete three lines and store them in the named buffer a, I would use the following command:

```
"a3dd
```

The starting quotation mark tells vi that I am using a named buffer. The single character following the quotation mark identifies the buffer I wish to use, and then I issue the actual delete command. Now that we understand buffers, let's update our actual description of the two delete commands.

d or D

```
["buffer][rep-count]d[span of control]
["buffer]D
```

Remember that the optional buffer name is a single character long. You'll find this very convenient if you're working with boilerplate and want to duplicate different chunks of the buffer in several locations.

One important note: the contents of the anonymous buffer remain only until you execute another vi command that places data in the anonymous buffer. The anonymous buffer is also flushed when you leave the current file you are editing, even if you are editing multiple files in one vi session. If you want to retain data from one file to the next, you need to place those data in a named buffer. Named buffers retain their data for the whole vi session (unless, of course, you deliberately replace the data in the buffer).

Having deleted the data from the editing buffer and stored them in either the anonymous buffer or a named buffer, we have completed half of the move process. Now we need to put those data somewhere else in the editing buffer.

p

```
["buffer]p
```

The lowercase **p**, or *put*, command takes the contents of the anonymous or named buffer and inserts it into the editing buffer *below or after* the position of the cursor. Exactly where put puts the data depends on what those data are. If you delete *part of a line*, then it will usually place those data after the cursor position *on the current line*. On the other hand, if you delete a *whole line* or group of lines, p will insert that line or group of lines *after the line* containing the cursor.

Figure 7.21 shows how p works with a partial line. Starting at the top of the figure, you can see that the first thing I did was move the cursor to the sixth byte of the first

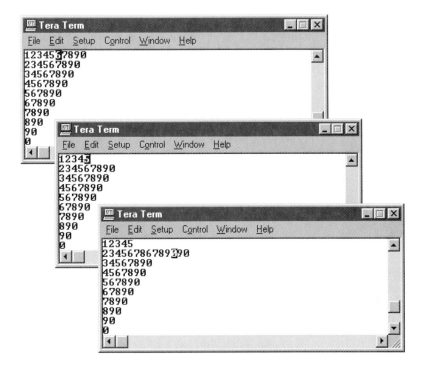

FIGURE 7.21
Deleting and replacing a partial line.

line. In the second screen I entered the uppercase D command to delete from the cursor to the end of the current line (a partial line.) In the third screen I moved my cursor down to the second line, at the seventh position (digit 8) and then entered the lowercase p command to put the contents of the anonymous buffer to the right of the cursor position. You can see that because the digits progress from 2 to 8, then from 6 to 0, and then from 9 to 0.

Now look at Figure 7.22, and we will see how p works when a full line is stored in the anonymous buffer. The progression here is very similar to that in Figure 7.21. The difference is that in the first screen I moved the cursor to the first byte of the second line. I then issued the dd command to delete the line that started with the digit 2. That left the cursor on the second line, which now started with the digit 3. Finally, I used the p command to put the deleted text back into the file. Since the p command puts the text back *after* the current line, I effectively reversed the line that started with 2 with the line that started with 3.

Remember that where the lowercase p command places the text depends on exactly what was deleted. If you deleted part of a line, p will place that text to the right of the cursor on the current line. However, if you delete a whole line, it will place the text on the line following the line containing the cursor.

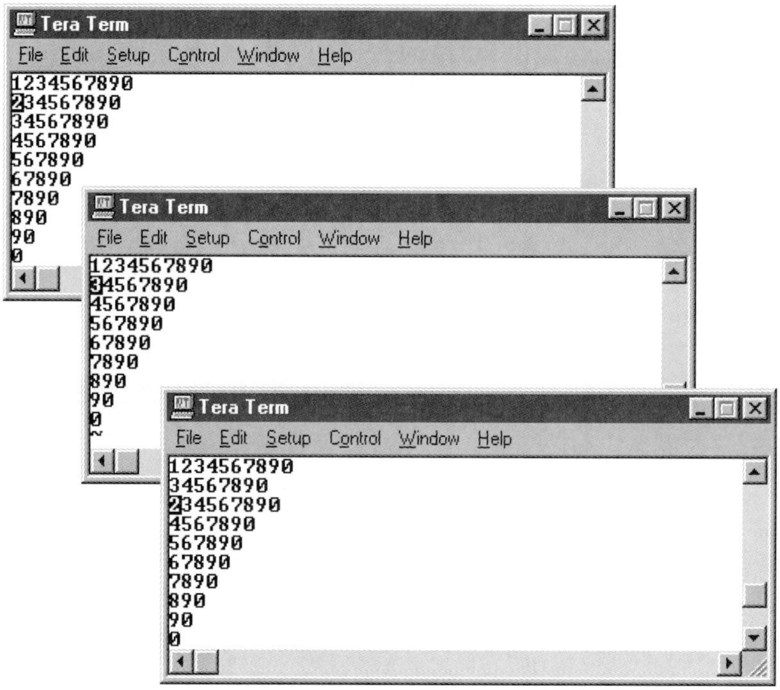

FIGURE 7.22

Deleting and replacing a complete line.

P

["buffer] P

The uppercase **P** command also puts text from either a named buffer or the anonymous buffer back into the editing buffer. The difference is that the uppercase P puts partial lines back to the *left* of the cursor and complete lines back into the editing buffer *above* the line containing the cursor. Of course, you don't need both the uppercase and lowercase versions of the put command—unless you wish to save yourself many keystrokes over time.

⊕ Copying Data

The other way to move data around in the buffer is to perform what a word-processing expert would call a copy-and-paste operation. Besides deleting text, the other way to move text into either a named buffer or the anonymous buffer is to yank it.

y

```
["buffer][rep-count]y[span of control]
```

The lowercase **y**, *yank*, command is very similar to the lowercase d command in terms of the span of control. Table 7.3 shows some of the common combinations of the yank command with different spans of control. You will notice that they look suspiciously similar to those for the lowercase d command. The one addition is the "yank to the end of the line" or y $, command.

TABLE 7.3 Some Common Yank Combinations

Command	What It Does
yy	Yank entire current line.
yw	Yank current word.
yb	Yank previous word (backward).
yG	Yank to end of buffer. (Usually a BIG yank!)
yM	Yank to middle of screen.
y$	Yank from cursor position to end of line.
y0	Yank to left, to column zero.
y/stuff	Yank from cursor forward, to word stuff.

It is sometimes a bit disconcerting for new vi users to use the yank command, because nothing changes after the command executes. Well, actually, either a named buffer or the anonymous buffer changes, but nothing on the screen changes except for a little annotation down on the status line (and that changes only if you yank several lines—exactly how many depending upon your implementation of vi).

Figure 7.23 shows an example where I yanked 10 lines into the anonymous buffer. Obviously, the arrow isn't part of the actual screen. I added it to point out the data on the status line that told me that it actually moved 10 lines to the buffer—in this case, the anonymous buffer. Yanking a set of lines and then putting them back into the buffer somewhere else is a fairly common practice. This is the same process as the copy-and-paste word-processing operation. While there are a number of different ways to use the lowercase y command, the up-shifted version is very specific.

Y

```
["buffer] [rep-count]Y
```

The uppercase **Y** command is used to yank *lines*. There is no span of control for the uppercase Y command because it always yanks the whole line. The repeat count determines

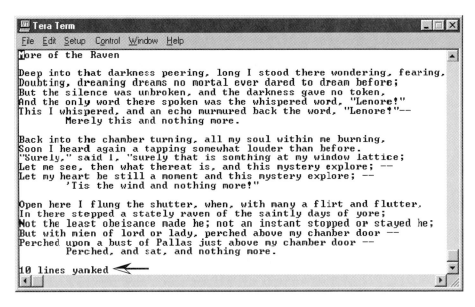

FIGURE 7.23

Yanking 10 lines into the anonymous buffer.

how many lines are actually yanked, and the buffer specifies which of the named buffers will contain the yanked lines. As with the lowercase y command, if you do not specify the buffer to use, the uppercase Y command will place the yanked line or lines into the anonymous buffer.

Changing Contents of Buffer

Up until now we have been working with and learning about commands that deal primarily with *lines*. The vi editor has several commands that alter one or more *characters* within one or more lines.

Changing within Line

You're already familiar with the commands that remove data at the character level from lines (x and X). Now it's time to learn about *changing* characters within the line.

r

    [rep-count]r

The **r**, *replace*, is one of the text-change commands I use almost every time I edit a file. The really handy thing about this command is that you don't need to worry about changing modes. The lowercase r command replaces the character under the cursor with the very next character you type. In other words, it performs a one-for-one substitution. You don't need to touch the ESC key to change back to command mode, because it puts you in text-entry mode only long enough to enter one character.

The repeat count allows you to substitute the *same character* for a series of characters on the current line. Figure 7.24 shows how this works. This simple Web page, written in HTML is representative of the most frequent places I use the repeat count on the `replace` command. The top screen capture shows the original page, with a text color of #660011, which is a sort of purple color. I wanted to change the text color to #333333 which is a lovely dark gray. To perform the change I first put my cursor on the first 6 of the text-color string, then typed

> 6r3

asking `vi` to replace the next six characters with the 3 character. You can see the result in the second screen capture in Figure 7.24.

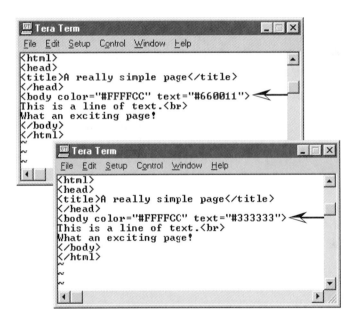

FIGURE 7.24

Replacing six characters with one command.

Although you cannot use `replace`, r, to replace a series of characters with another *series* of different characters, you can replace a series of characters with the same character. Thus, I can replace a series of eight characters with the x character by typing:

> 8rx

giving me xxxxxxxx as result. But if I wanted to replace the characters abcdef with the digits 123456, I would have to do six individual replaces, the R command (or use the substitute command).

R

```
[rep-count]R
```

The uppercase **R** differs from the lowercase r command in that it allows you to replace a series of characters. Using the uppercase replace command tells vi to replace each character as you type it. You must use the ESC key to exit from replace mode and go back to command mode. Another way of looking at this command is that it puts you in overstrike mode. You will replace all the characters you type over, leaving those you have not yet reached.

A word of warning: If you choose to use a repeat count with this command it will repeat all of the characters you typed after you touch the ESC key. I'm sure there's some wonderful use for this, but I can't think of one.

c

```
[rep-count]c span of control
```

The **c** command is the one I use most often when I want to change something on a page within a line. Notice that the span of control is required for this command. The c command by itself does nothing. This command is a good way to change unwanted words in a line.

Figure 7.25 shows how the two different versions of vi have slightly different displays when I ask them to change a single word using c. In both editors I moved the cursor to s in the word simple and then entered the command

```
cw
```

asking vi to change the word. In the Solaris version vi puts a $ in place of the last character of the word, showing me the word I am changing. In the Linux version, vim simply removes the entire word.

There's a special span of control used with the change command. If I enter the command

```
cc
```

in either editor, the entire current line will be deleted and I will be put into text-entry mode.

In either editor the lowercase c command puts you in change mode, and you must touch the ESC key to get back to command mode. By design, I can "change" one word into several words, so I need to tell vi when I'm finished entering text.

I can prepend a repeat count to the beginning of the command and change several words. All in all, c is a valuable command and one that I'm sure you'll use often.

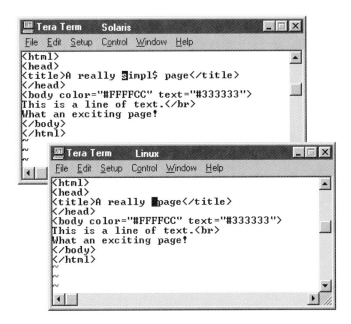

FIGURE 7.25

Changing the word simple in both Solaris vi and Linux vim.

C

[rep-count]C

The uppercase **C** command behaves like the uppercase R command in that it performs its task to the end of the line. Without a repeat count, the two editors differ just as they did with regard to the lowercase c command. The Linux editor deletes all the characters from the cursor to the end of the line and puts me in text-entry mode. The Solaris version of the **vi** editor puts the user in text-entry mode and places a $ at the end of the line.

Both editors behave similarly if you include a repeat count with the uppercase c command. They delete all the text from the cursor to the end of the nth line, where n is the repeat count. They both put the user into text entry-mode. As with the lowercase c command, you must touch the ESC key to leave text-entry mode and go back to command.

Now seems to be a good time for a little review. Remember that the lowercase u command will undo the most recent change made to the buffer—just what you need if you mistakenly change a line. Also remember that the uppercase U command will undo *all* of the changes made to a line *provided you have not left the line*. Since the change command is so powerful, it's sometimes very fortunate to be able to undo that which you have done.

~

`[rep-count]~`

While we're talking about changing things, I want to tell you about a special little command that you will find extremely useful from time to time. The tilde (~) command changes the case, upper to lower or lower to upper, of the letter at or under the cursor. It ignores punctuation, special characters, and numbers. By incorporating a repeat count you can use the ~ command to change the case of a block of text.

The tilde (~) key is located in the upper *left* corner of most PC keyboards and the upper *right* corner of most Sun Microsystems keyboards. We wouldn't want things to be too consistent, now would we? ☺

s

`[rep-count]s`

The lowercase version of the **s**, *substitute*, command allows you to delete a single character and remain in text-entry mode. Initially the substitute command looks a lot like the lowercase replace command except that it either puts a $ in place of the character you are substituting for (Solaris) or deletes the character that you are substituting for (Linux). Unlike the r command, substitute leaves you in text-entry mode, so you must touch the ESC key to get back to command mode.

S

`[rep-count]S`

Building on our pattern of consistency, the uppercase **S** command substitutes for the *whole line*. If I prepend a repeat count to the command, it will substitute the text I'm going to enter for several lines. In either case, the editor deletes the line or lines that are the target of the substitution.

That pretty much covers the commands that change the contents of a line or two. Now let's talk about making changes across the whole of the buffer.

Across the Buffer

You already know how to make large-scale substitutions across the buffer using the ex editor's substitute command. Since ex is vi, that means you already know how to perform large-scale substitutions in the vi editor! Boy, that sure was easy! That's right, when you want to apply changes across the buffer, the best tool you have is the ex mode substitute.

⊕ Switching from vi to ex and Back

You can invoke the ex editor and enter a single command by typing the colon (:) in command mode and entering the command. How about when you want to leave the visual mode and go back into the command line, or ex, mode? We have a command for doing just that.

Q

Q

When you enter the uppercase **Q** command in vi, the editor will switch to command-line, or ex, mode. You can enter a number of ex commands—for example, a series of substitutions—and switch back into the visual mode if you wish. Just enter the vi command at the colon prompt. Using these two different modes, you can share the commands to optimize the mode you use to interface with the editor.

Obviously, the Q command has no repeat count, nor does it recognize a span of control, it simply quits the visual mode.

⊕ The set Commands

Way back in the last chapter we learned about some of the **set** commands that could make life easier for you when using ex editor. We're going to expand on and review some of those commands now because many of those commands are specifically designed to make vi more efficient.

Remember that there are two types of options: those that require a value, which we referred to as *name-value pairs*, and those that are toggles, which are set either on (set option) or off (set nooption). The set command is an ex command, so I need to be at the ex prompt (:) when I use it.

To turn on a toggle, I use the set command with the toggle name or abbreviation. Therefore, if I want to turn on autoindent, I type

    set ai

and autoindent is turned on. If I want to turn *off* autoindent, I type

    set noai

which will turn the toggle off, and vi will no longer autoindent for me.

By the same token, if I want to set an option that has a value, I need to use the set command with the abbreviation (if there is one), an equal sign (=), and the desired value. For example, if I want to set the tab stops to four characters, I would enter this command:

    set ts=4

As a result, the TAB key would move the cursor to the right four characters instead of the default of eight characters. Notice there is no space around the equal sign. Most versions of vi will object if you try to put spaces there.

You can look back at Table 6.1 in Chapter 6 for review of the majority of the options. I will discuss only a handful that are very useful in vi here.

autoindent (ai)

The **autoindent** (**ai**) option is extremely valuable if you're writing in any type of coding language. It will remember the current tab stop and continue to insert text on subsequent lines at that tab stop. Use the Ctrl-D (^D) to move back to the left, one tab stop at a time.

errorbells (eb)

While the default for the **errorbells** (**eb**) command is usually off, on some systems it has been turned on, making your machine beep each time you make an error. That beep can be annoying, or embarrassing, so I always set errorbells off, as follows:

```
set noeb
```

exec

The **exec** is another command that varies widely among systems. If you're working with different programming languages, or with different types of data that have different formats, it's a good idea to have vi read the .exrc file in the local directory. We will discuss the .exrc file in a moment—it is the repository for a series of commands to be executed before the editor begins processing text. The exec option will direct vi to look for a .exrc file in the local directory instead of always using the .exrc file in the home directory. That way you can have a set of different .exrc files, one for each format of file you create. For example, the .exrc file in my HTML directory is set up differently than the one in my C programming directory.

number (nu)

You already know how to turn on line numbers, but **number** (**nu**) is such a handy option I want to review it here. Turning on line numbers is extremely useful if you deal with any kind of software that recognizes errors in your coding. (Okay, *you* won't make errors when you code, but I do, so I like having the line numbers automagically turned on for me.) I urge you to turn on line numbers anytime you are writing scripts or programs.

readonly

At times you may want to use the vi editor to read a file without the risk of accidentally altering the contents. If you set the read-only toggle, **readonly**, you won't be able to write to the file unless you force a write using the bang (w!). You already know another way to invoke the vi in read-only mode (view), but it's handy to be able to turn on that option at will.

showmode

We discussed the **showmode** option when we looked at the different modes of vi. I view this as an essential option simply because it tells me when I'm in text-entry mode.

tabstop (ts)

The **tabstop** (**ts**) option is one you'll need when you're writing computer code. For writing text, the default of an eight-character tab stop is just fine, but when you're writing computer code like HTML, you may have times when you're indenting four or five tab stops. Having the code shifted 30 to 40 characters to the right makes your page or program much more difficult to read. If you set your tab stop to just three or four characters, then your code still shows indention but without being spread all across the screen.

terse

Once you become more familiar with vi, you may not want to see all of those long, involved messages. You can shorten some of the messages by setting the **terse** option. With this option set, vi will give you abbreviated messages in some cases. Most of the time the only big change I have seen with terse is that instead of having vi tell me I'm in insert mode, it simply gives me an I message.

⊕ Other Useful vi Tools

There are a handful of additional commands I'd like to discuss but that seem to have no particular place in this chapter. I guess we could call these commands errata commands, or miscellaneous commands. I, however, prefer to call them simply useful vi tools. The first pair of such tools falls under the generic term of *macros*. For those of you who are technically astute, please pardon my simplified definition of a macro. I do know that a true macro needs to be expanded by a macro expander, and so on. However, for the sake of understanding, a **macro** is a single command that represents a series of other, often simple commands—sort of like a little program or function. There are two useful macros in vi.

⊕ Abbreviation (ab)

The first macro is the **abbreviation** (**ab**) tool. This macro allows you to define a set of one or more keystrokes (two or more are best) that will expand to a longer word or phrase. The purpose of the abbreviation macro is to save you typing. Figure 7.26 shows an example of its use. In the first screen I created the abbreviation nlc to stand for "North Lake College." In the second screen I entered in a new line on the page and used the abbreviation. Notice that the cursor is still next to the abbreviation. In the third screen you can see what happened after I touched the space bar. The abbreviation expanded from the three characters to the three words.

Abbreviations should be used when you have to type the same character string over and over again. As we'll see in a page or two, if you have a series of abbreviations you use day after day, you can set them up in a file so that they will always be available for you. (Okay, now for another little quiz: Looking at the last screen in the figure, can you figure out another set option that I have invoked?)

FIGURE 7.26
Using the abbreviation macro.

map

The second handy macro is also a form of abbreviation, but instead of abbreviating words, the **map** macro allows you to abbreviate commands. Now this gets a little bit beyond the basic vi concepts, and you may want to wait a bit to play with it, but it can provide some interesting shortcuts. I'm going to show you only one map macro, but it will give you the idea.

Figure 7.27 shows me defining a macro using the map command and then executing the macro. In the first screen capture I created a macro associated with an uppercase K (unused by vi). Let's dissect exactly what I did. First I entered ex mode, entered the map command, and then typed the character I wanted associated with the macro, in this case the uppercase K. I touched the space bar and typed the commands I wanted executed when I invoked the macro. Here it gets a little more complex. I first wanted vi to search for a line containing the character string snorble. Notice the Ctrl-M (^M)

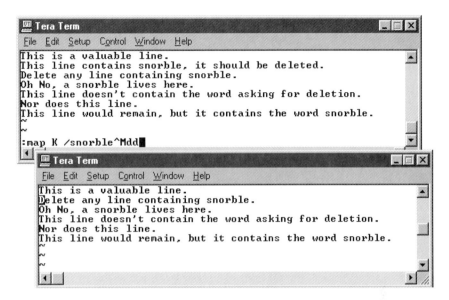

FIGURE 7.27

Creating and using a map macro.

after the search command. That ^M stands for the ENTER key (or the new line.) You create a control character in vi by first holding down the Ctrl key while you touch the v key, then typing the normal control character you wish, in this case control-M. The keystroke sequence to get the ^M into the vi editor, then, is

^V^M

After I inserted the ENTER command, I issued another command (dd), asking vi to delete the line. When I finished typing the macro definition, I touched the ESC key to end the macro definition. The net effect of all this typing is that when I type an uppercase K, I expect vi to search forward in the buffer for the first line containing the character string snorble and delete that line. The second screen capture in Figure 7.27 shows what happened when I type the uppercase K once. It worked!

As you learn shell programming, and later as you learn C programming, you'll be able to create extremely powerful macros in vi to do wonderful things. For now try to keep your macros simple, as they will be both easier to code and easier to understand.

(By the way, in Figure 7.26 I was using the Solaris flavor of Unix and had set the terse option in the editor. You should have known this because the A at the right end of line 24 told you I was in append mode and the single letter indicates the terse form of the commands.)

.exrc

Now that I've convinced you that the mapped macros and abbreviations will make your life simpler, as well as shown you some great options you can set, the natural question is, "Why do I need to type all this stuff every time I start vi?" Wonderful question! Answer is: "You don't!" I've mentioned the .exrc file in passing several times, now let's look at it in detail.

A number of files in Unix are used to initialize the environments for particular process. Those files are always dotted files, ending in the characters rc. The rc stands for "runnable commands." This collection of files is usually referred to as *dot rc* files. The letters before the rc identify the program that runs these particular commands. Some of the more common dot rc files are .cshrc, .pinerc, .bashrc, and .exrc. These four files all contain setup information for, respectively, the C shell, the pine mail program, the Bourn-again shell, and the ex/vi editor. If you have set the exrc option in the vi editor, you can have multiple .exrc files, one in each directory. So what do you put in your .exrc file? I would suggest that you include the following data, in the following order:

1. All your set options (note: it is better to spell out the option than use the abbreviation; in other words, set autoindent is better than set ai).
2. The abbreviations you wish to have available.
3. Any macros you wish defined for the editing session.

Your .exrc file is one of those things that you'll probably take with you whenever you move from Unix job to Unix job. It will grow and become more complex and interesting over time and is a very personal tool. You'll also find the time spent creating a useful and powerful .exrc file is time very well spent.

⊕ The Quickie vi Cheat Sheet (The requisite baker's dozen commands if you just can't wait.)

If you have conscientiously worked your way through this chapter to this point, you can go ahead and skip this section. On the other hand, if you've come here because you "just couldn't wait" to start playing with vi, then let's look at the requisite baker's dozen commands you need to be minimally—and I stress, *minimally*—functional. The commands listed in Table 7.4 are those that you need to know to hack and slash your way into a file using vi. To obtain the full effect of these commands, you'll need to go back into the chapter and read about them, I've just listed them with a brief description in the table.

These 13 commands will probably suffice for the first 12 or 14 minutes that you use the vi editor. After that you're going to realize that you are very limited in what you can do, and that the folks around you who have *read* the chapter are doing a lot of really cool things.

Now that you have played with the editor, go back and read how to use it effectively. Knowing what you are doing makes using vi a lot more fun!

TABLE 7.4 Requisite Baker's Dozen vi Commands

Command	What It Does
h	Move one character left (if you skipped the chapter, *no* arrow keys for you!)
j	Move one line down.
k	Move one line up.
l	Move one character right.
i	Insert text before the cursor position (touch ESC key to stop inserting).
dd	Delete the current line (tucks it into the anonymous buffer).
u	Undo the last change to the current line.
yy	Copy (yank) the current line into a safe place (the anonymous buffer).
p	Put what is in the anonymous buffer *after* the current line.
:s/old/new	Actually an ex command—substitute *new* for *old*.
:q!	Another ex command—bail out; exit the editor *without saving changes*.
ZZ	Save the changes to the buffer and exit the editor.
<ESC>	Exit from any type of text-entry mode and go back to command mode.

KEY TERMS

anonymous buffer
macro
named buffer
repeat count
span of control

NEW COMMANDS

view	/
vi	0
^B	:
^D	?
^E	{
^F	}
^U	^
^Y	~
space bar	a
$	A
(	b
)	B

NEW COMMANDS continued

c	P
C	Q
d or D	r
e	R
E	s
f	S
F	t
G	T
H	w
h, j, k, l	W
i	x
J	X
L	y
M	Y
n	ZZ
N	set
o	abbreviation (ab)
O	alias
p	map

REVIEW QUESTIONS

7.1 Define each of the key terms for this chapter.

7.2 Summarize the history of the vi editor. Who wrote it, and why?

7.3 Explain why the vi editor is the best choice for Unix folk to learn.

7.4 Describe the difference between the A, a, I, i, O, and o commands.

7.5 Discuss the advantages of typing h, j, k, l rather than using the arrow keys.

7.6 Explain the difference between the ^ and 0 (zero) commands.

7.7 List the three keys used to move to the top, middle, and bottom of the current screen, and explain how they work.

7.8 List the commands used to scroll through the buffer forward and backward.

7.9 What would happen if you typed the following command at the colon (:) prompt?
       /rutabagas

7.10 Then what would happen if you typed an n? An N?

7.11 What command would you use to delete

    a. An entire line?

    b. Three consecutive words?

    c. All the way down the buffer to the word rabid?

7.12 Explain how to do the word-processing cut-and-paste operation in vi.

7.13 Now how do you do (very well, thank you—oops!), a copy-and-paste?

7.14 How does the R command differ, if at all, from the r command?

7.15 What does the Q command do? How do you undo what it did?

EXERCISES

Okay, I know some of these look like the ed and ex exercises, but now you get to do them with yet another, different, exciting editor!

7.1   Start the vi editor without an associated file.

7.2   Turn on showmode so you know what mode you are in.

7.3   Enter this text:
Royal Rhonda's repulsive, roaring rabbits ruined Randy's rutabagas
Note: There is no final punctuation yet.

ZAP rattle snap crackle pop. Your arrow keys just disappeared! You may NOT use the arrow keys from this point onward in the exercises for this chapter.

7.4   Exit from the editor without saving your work.

7.5   Redo Exercises 1–3. Now save your work to the file rabbits.vi.

7.6   Use the append command to insert the word rancid after Randy's.

7.7   Use the insert command to insert the word really before repulsive.

7.8   With one keystroke, go to the first character of the line.

7.9   Move across the line by words, from left to right.

7.10 Move back across the line by words, from right to left.

7.11 Now move across the line *skipping the punctuation* (left to right.)

7.12 Skip back across the line while still ignoring punctuation (right to left.)

7.13 With one keystroke, move to the last character of the line.

7.14 Efficiently delete the word Royal.

7.15 Add an exclamation point to the sentence.

7.16 Now add the word Ruthless to the beginning of the sentence.

7.17 Duplicate the line in the file five times, you should end up with six identical lines in the file. (Use a differently named buffer for each of the third through sixth lines.)

7.18 Add numbers to each line (not with the set command; instead, actually change the contents of the file so that the file looks like the following:

```
1Ruthless Rhonda's really repulsive, roaring rabbits ruined Randy's rancid rutabagas!
2Ruthless Rhonda's really repulsive, roaring rabbits ruined Randy's rancid rutabagas!
3Ruthless Rhonda's really repulsive, roaring rabbits ruined Randy's rancid rutabagas!
4Ruthless Rhonda's really repulsive, roaring rabbits ruined Randy's rancid rutabagas!
5Ruthless Rhonda's really repulsive, roaring rabbits ruined Randy's rancid rutabagas!
6Ruthless Rhonda's really repulsive, roaring rabbits ruined Randy's rancid rutabagas!
```

7.19 Make the following changes to the file:

a.   In line 2 change Rhonda to Ruth.

b.   In line 4 change rancid rutabagas to round, red, radishes.

c.   In line 6 change the word roaring to rabid.

d.   In line 3, capitalize all the letters in the word rutabagas.

e.   In line 5, delete everything after the word really, then put it back.

f.   Duplicate lines 3–6 after line 6.

g.   Change the numbers on the new lines 7–10 to 7, 8, 9, and 0, respectively.

7.20 Make line 1 your current line and then find the first occurrence of the word radishes.

7.21 Duplicate line 8 after line 10.

7.22 Delete line 10.

7.23 Correct the number on line 10, changing it from 8 to 0.

7.24 Insert a line between lines 9 and 10 that says `Ridiculous`.

7.25 Starting with your cursor on the `R` of `Ruthless` in line 11, efficiently delete the words `repulsive` and `rancid`. (You should use only eight keystrokes.)

7.26 Restore line 11 to its original beauty and fullness with one keystroke combination.

7.27 Switch to the ex editor mode, look at the file using all three display tools, then switch back to `vi`.

7.28 Delete line 4.

7.29 Replace line 4 from the named buffer.

7.30 Join lines 10 and 11.

7.31 Move line 10 to line 1.

7.32 While in `vi`, check your mail.

7.33 Read the contents of `/etc/passwd` into your buffer after line 4.

7.34 Go to line 1.

7.35 Scroll down through the file one-half screen at a time, to the bottom.

7.36 Scroll upward to the top of the file, full screens at a time.

7.37 Go to the last line in the file.

7.38 Delete all the lines you added *except your entry*.

7.39 Save the contents of this buffer as the file `besteditoris.vi`.

7.40 Create two abbreviations and use them.

7.41 Build and test a simple `.exrc` file.

7.42 Experiment with any command we haven't played with as yet that piques your interest.

Interesting Commands

CHAPTER OBJECTIVES

After reading this chapter, you should be able to:

- Print files on the system printer in both Linux and Solaris type flavors of Unix.
- Check the status of jobs in the print queue.
- Identify the three types of standard queues.
- Remove jobs from the print queue.
- Determine the type of specific files using the file command.
- Use **chmod** to change the protection mask on files using both symbolic and absolute methods.
- Change the ownership of a file, (if permitted).
- Change the group of a file, (if permitted).
- Use common commands including `uptime`, `df`, `du`, `vmstat`, `top`, and `free` to determine information about the system.

Some interesting Unix commands give you information on the status of your system as you work. Others allow you to send your data to a printer or control what is happening when your files are queued to print. Let's look at the commands that relate to printing first.

lp/lpr

```
lp [options] [file]    (Solaris)
lpr [options] [file]   (Linux)
```

The **lp** or **lpr**, *line print*, command, in its simplest form, sends the contents of the optional file to the current system printer—that is, the default printer. The vast majority of time you will use the lp command in Solaris or the lpr command in Linux to create a hard-copy version of a file on your system.

Printer services can be very complex to set up, but we won't worry about that here, that's a concern for your system administrator. I will assume that you have a working set of print services to play with.

Certain options for the print command can make your life easier if you are aware of them. Before we delve into those options, though let's consider how the lp command works. I'm going to combine both the Solaris and Linux print commands in the overview, and then I will discuss the differences when we talk about specific options.

First let's consider queues. By general definition *queuing* refers to lining things up in some sort of sequential order. You could queue up for a movie, or in the cafeteria, and often during rush hour your car is stuck in a queue. Therefore, a **queue** is a collection of elements, arranged in a particular order, that will be processed in some fashion.

Another term for the print queue is the **print buffer**. The system maintains one or more print queues because users don't want to wait for the printer to become free before they can submit jobs to be printed. If your system didn't support print queues, you would first have to wait until the printer was free before you could start a print job, and then you would have to sit there waiting until your file finished printing. Some early versions of the DOS operating system worked this way. Fortunately, Unix is much more efficient than that old system.

The elements in a queue can be processed in at least three different ways. The printer services use two of these methods, but you will hear all three discussed, so I'd like to explore all three of them here.

The most common way to process the queue is called **FIFO**, which stands for *First In First Out*. This is the way most queues are processed in the real world as well. The first person in the line at the movie theater gets to buy his ticket first. The first person going into the queue is the first person out of the queue. Another way to look at this is to think of a train going through a tunnel. The first element of the train, the engine, is the first to go into the tunnel (queue) and is the first to come out of the tunnel. Most print queues process individual print jobs in a FIFO fashion. The process the system goes through to put jobs into a queue and the way the print services remove jobs from the queue is called **spooling**, or *print spooling*.

The second way elements can be removed from a queue is called **FILO**, which stands for *First In Last Out*. This is sometimes referred to as a *push-down stack* or a *push-down queue*. One way to look at FILO is to visualize a stack of coins. Let's say you placed eight individual coins in a stack, one atop the next. The first coin you placed in the stack would be at the bottom of the stack. As you take coins off the top of the stack, one at a time, the first coin in the stack, or the bottom one, is the last coin you would remove. The first into the stack is the last out of the stack. This queuing method is used for other queues in Unix, but usually not in print spooling.

A third way that print jobs can be selected from the queue is slightly more complex and was very common with older, slower printers. It involves assigning each job a priority in the queue and then removing the jobs in order of their priority. Sometimes queues are set up so that small jobs print first and other times so that jobs are given priority based on their relative importance. For example, your boss's memo would be printed before your daily emails. (Sometimes, for some strange reason, the system administrator's friend's jobs print quickly, too. It's always wise to be nice to your system administrator!)

One of the things that makes this method more complex is that the queue is constantly reshuffled as different jobs are assigned different priorities. If you were to look at the queue at, say, 10 A.M., and saw that your job was third to be printed, you could look again at 10:10 A.M. and find a dozen jobs, with higher priorities, in front of yours. Priority-based queuing is most often found in environments where printers are a scarce resource. Such queuing is unlikely to be used in most companies.

In some, usually larger Unix shops, several different print queues are associated with different printers that are used for different types of output. For example, in one company where I worked there was an "overnight" queue designated for printing very large jobs, usually program listings, another queue specifically for printing spreadsheets, and a third used only for printing classified documents.

One seemingly seldom utilized feature of the print command is to use it without specifying a filename. In this case, the print command (lp or lpr) reads from standard input and sends what you type on the keyboard to the printer. In other words, by specifying the print command without specifying a target file you can turn your Unix computer into a very expensive typewriter!

Figure 8.1 shows how I used this feature—using lpr without a filename.

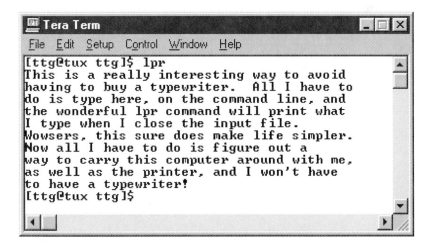

FIGURE 8.1

Using lpr to output text directly from keyboard.

Unfortunately, I can't show you the output from the printer. You will have to trust me that exactly what I typed showed up on paper on my local printer. I use this feature of the print command to create quick notes to myself. Obviously, if I were writing the great American memo, I would use one of the editors to write it, spell-check it (!), and then save it on disk for posterity. However, for short, little notes to myself this is a great feature. Remember that even though you can't see it in Figure 8.1, I needed to enter a ^D (Ctrl-D) to mark the end of the input file before the print services queued my data to be printed.

While it's sometimes useful to be able to use the printer like a typewriter, most of the time you will simply use the 1p or 1pr command to create a hard copy of a file. Figure 8.2 shows how you can submit a file to be printed. In some operating systems, in this instance Solaris, the print command gives me the print queue or print job number of the file. In Figure 8.2 the 1p command told us that we were printing job number 109 on queue 144_1, and that we were printing one file. On the other hand, when I submitted a print job in the Linux environment it simply was queued to be printed with no job number given. This shows one significant difference between a server flavor of Unix (Solaris) and a personal flavor of Unix (Linux). There will be some other instances when we will run across this type of difference. The Solaris version of Unix is designed primarily for large server environments, and Linux, at least the versions prior to the 2.4 kernel, are designed more as desktop or workstation tools.

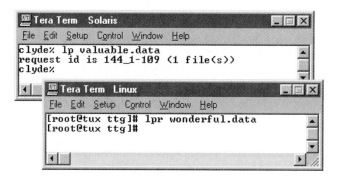

FIGURE 8.2

Submitting file to be printed.

A number of options on the 1p or 1pr commands control specifically how the printing process takes place. A few of these options are common across both operating systems, but there are many flavor differences as well. When we look at these actions I will differentiate between the 1p (Solaris) options and the 1pr (Linux) options.

Normally the print command sends its output to the default printer, which is set by the system administrator. However, if you work in a company where there are several different printers for specialized uses you can specify a particular printer using the -d option (Solaris) or the -P option (Linux) to force the output to a specified printer. To give you a practical application of this option, at my school there are three different classrooms of SunRay terminals. Each room (T-252, T-253, and T-254) has its own printer. All the SunRays run off the same E450 server. When a student in room T-252 wants to print a file, she can use this command to print her file on her local printer:

```
lp -d 252 myfile
```

Another useful option on the print command is to specify the number of copies you wish printed. In the Solaris environment you would use the −n 3 option to print three copies of the current document. In the Linux environment you would use the -#3 option to print three copies of the file. There can be no space between the octothorp and the digit. If you were to type

```
lpr -# 3 print.me
```

Linux would think you're trying to print one copy, the default number, of two files—the file 3 and the file print.me. There *is* a space between the −n option and the integer number of copies in the Solaris environment.

Lest you think there are no similarities, both flavors of the print command support the -m option, which instructs the print command to send a mail message to the user who requested the file be printed when the print job completes. You'll want to use this command when you are working with a remote printer. That way, when the print job completes you will see a message similar to the one shown in Figure 8.3. The email message here comes from a computer running the Solaris operating system. As you can probably guess, the file I printed was very small, the system is fairly fast, and the printer is also fast. It took all of 17 seconds to print the file and send me an email about it.

There is a very significant difference between the way Solaris spools print jobs and the way Linux spools them. In the Solaris environment, partly to accommodate printing very large files, a file sent to the print queue is *symbolically linked* rather than copied to the queue. That means in the Solaris environment, if you modify a file

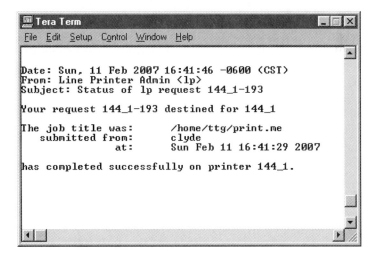

FIGURE 8.3

Email notification of completion of a print job.

between the time you submit it to be printed and the time it is actually printed, the modifications *will appear on the printed copy*. By the same token, if you delete a file that you have requested to be printed before it actually is printed, the print job will fail.

If you want Solaris to copy the file to the print queue rather than to symbolically link it you can use the -c (copy) option. On the other hand, the Linux operating system *copies* files to the print queue rather than linking to them. Consequently, any changes you make to a file between the time you submit the printer request and the time the file is actually printed will *not* be reflected in the printed copy. If you want Linux to act like Solaris, you can use the -s (symbolically link) option and have Linux symbolically link the file to the print queue rather than copying it.

Other options are available on both versions of the print command, and you can study the man page if you want to become an absolute print wizard. I think you'll find that the majority the time you will use the print command simply to create hard-copy versions of a file.

lpq

```
lpq [options] [print job #] [user]
```

Sometimes you want to see what jobs are in the print queue. The **lpq** command, *line printer queue*, will give you information about the status of all the jobs in the queue. The general format of the command is the same in Linux and Solaris; the flavor differences are very small. In most cases you will simply issue the command and look at the output.

Figure 8.4 shows the output of the command in both the Linux and Solaris environments. The top screen capture is from Solaris, and the bottom screen capture is from Linux. If you look closely at the Solaris screen capture you'll see three different users have entries in the print queue. Also notice that I can see only the names of files I am printing; the other files are hidden because I didn't submit them to the print queue.

Both screen captures contain the message Warning: [queue name] is down:. That's because I stopped each queue before I submitted the print jobs so I could show you what the queue looks like with jobs in it. If I hadn't stopped the queues, the jobs wouldn't have stayed there long enough from me to capture the data. (This is another of those things we do in an academic environment but not in the real world.)

Suppose you want to look at a particular print job. Refer again to Figure 8.2: when I submitted a file to be printed, Solaris told me the job number of the print job was 109. If at some later time I want to know the status of that print job, I can use the lpq command with the print job number. Figure 8.5 shows how this works. First I submitted a print job, and Solaris dutifully told me it was print job number 215. Then I used the lpq command to see the status of job number 215. Solaris told me that it was in first the queue (yay!) and that I was the owner. It also displays the job number and the name of the file.

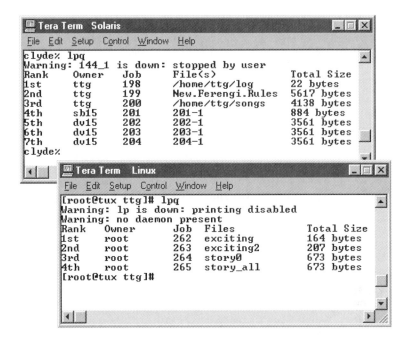

FIGURE 8.4

Output from the lpq command.

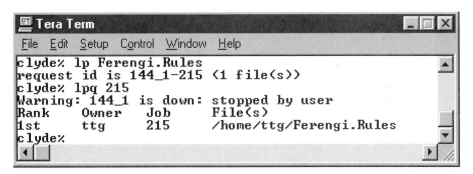

FIGURE 8.5

Using a print job number with lpq.

Sometimes it's very useful to be able to see the status of a print job—for example, to see whether you should walk down to the printer and get your output or if you should wait because your job hasn't printed yet. (Of course, if you remember our discussion of the lp and lpr commands, you could have had the system send you an email when your job printed and so not have to keep looking.)

You can also specify a user's login I.D. in the lpq command and see all the print jobs in the queue for a particular user. This particular option is more useful for system administrators, but there may be times when you wish to use it as well.

lprm

```
lprm [options] [print job #(s)] [user(s)]
```

What if you change your mind about printing something after you submit a file to be printed. Perhaps you submitted a print job to the wrong queue or mistyped the file you wished to print. In either of those cases, if the print job has not yet been given to the printer, you can cancel the print job by removing it from the queue using the **lprm** command.

Figure 8.6 shows how I canceled a print job in the Solaris environment. First I issued a lpq command to see which jobs I had in the print queue. I decided that I didn't really want to print the log file since it was so large, so I used the lprm command to remove that particular entry from the queue. Solaris dutifully informed me that it had canceled that print job, and when I issued a subsequent lpq command, I could see the canceled job had disappeared from the queue.

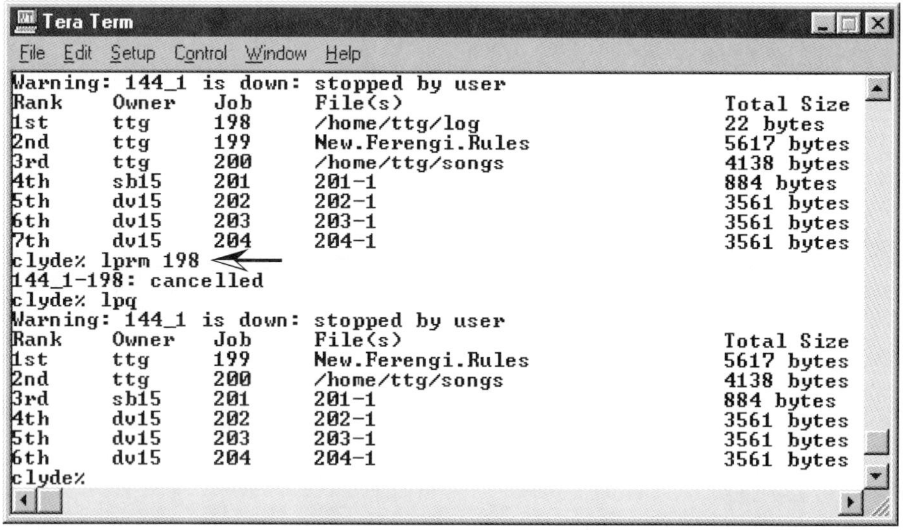

```
┌──────────────────────────────────────────────────────────────────┐
│ ▥ Tera Term                                            _ ▣ ✕      │
├──────────────────────────────────────────────────────────────────┤
│ File  Edit  Setup  Control  Window  Help                          │
│ Warning: 144_1 is down: stopped by user                      ▲    │
│ Rank      Owner    Job     File(s)                Total Size      │
│ 1st       ttg      198     /home/ttg/log          22 bytes        │
│ 2nd       ttg      199     New.Ferengi.Rules      5617 bytes      │
│ 3rd       ttg      200     /home/ttg/songs        4138 bytes      │
│ 4th       sb15     201     201-1                  884 bytes       │
│ 5th       dv15     202     202-1                  3561 bytes      │
│ 6th       dv15     203     203-1                  3561 bytes      │
│ 7th       dv15     204     204-1                  3561 bytes      │
│ clyde% lprm 198  ◄────                                            │
│ 144_1-198: cancelled                                             │
│ clyde% lpq                                                        │
│ Warning: 144_1 is down: stopped by user                          │
│ Rank      Owner    Job     File(s)                Total Size      │
│ 1st       ttg      199     New.Ferengi.Rules      5617 bytes      │
│ 2nd       ttg      200     /home/ttg/songs        4138 bytes      │
│ 3rd       sb15     201     201-1                  884 bytes       │
│ 4th       dv15     202     202-1                  3561 bytes      │
│ 5th       dv15     203     203-1                  3561 bytes      │
│ 6th       dv15     204     204-1                  3561 bytes      │
│ clyde%                                                       ▼    │
│ ◄ ▯                                                        ► ▮   │
└──────────────────────────────────────────────────────────────────┘
```

FIGURE 8.6

Removing a file from the print queue.

In addition to removing a particular print job by using its entry number, I can remove all of my print jobs from the queue with one command, as shown in Figure 8.7. Take a look at the center of this figure, and notice that I used only one lprm command, with my login I.D. as the argument. Solaris dutifully notified me that I had requested the cancellation of three print jobs. This was an efficient way to remove all the files I had queued for printing with one command.

Generally it's a good idea to print only those files you absolutely must have in hard copy. Many Unix users find that they need hardcopy only when they're going off-site or if they need to snail-mail something. Remember that in most cases the Unix environment provides such a useful command-line environment so that you can reduce your printing, and save trees.

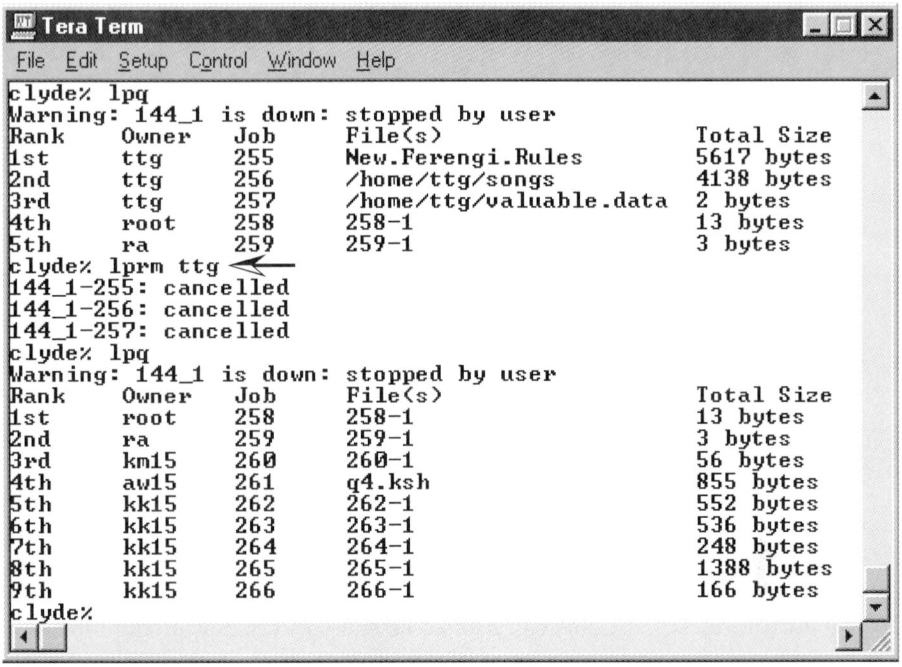

FIGURE 8.7

Removing all print jobs with one command.

file

```
file[options] file(s)
```

At times it's helpful to be able to determine, or at least try to determine, what a file contains before you cat it or more it. If you pass the file to the **file** command, the shell will give you its best guess as to what the file contains. It doesn't always guess correctly, but it does try.

Figure 8.8 shows the output of the file command in a small directory I created. The format of the output lists the filename followed by what the file command *thinks* the file contains. Some of the time it's very accurate. For example, in the case of the files CheckThisOut, Ferengi.Rules, boring, case.scr, loop3.scr, and stuff, the file command guessed correctly. However, in the case of the file patact.awk, the file command thinks it's a C-language program whereas in reality it's an awk script.

Occasionally, knowing the format of a file can save you from an unpleasant experience. Look at what the file command says the file CheckThisOut contains: Identifying a file as a Sun demand paged SPARC executable dynamically linked file is the fancy way of saying it's an executable program, a binary file. In this case it happens to be the "Hello World" program. The unpleasant experience that I was referring to would

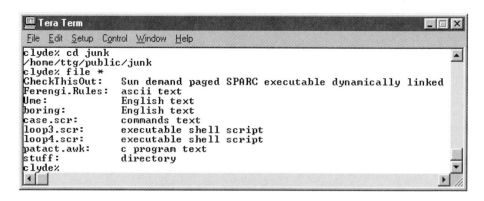

FIGURE 8.8

Output of the `file` command.

occur if you attempted to `cat` the file. In that case, the terminal control program would try to interpret this binary file as if it were ASCII text and in so doing would probably corrupt your terminal settings.

Figure 8.9 shows what happened when I issued a `cat` of that file. Gadzooks! What a horrible mess! Not only can I make no sense of the output, but look what happened to my command-line prompt. And the problem isn't limited to just the output of this one command. Figure 8.10 shows what happened after I cleared the screen and entered a couple of additional commands.

Figure 8.10 shows the output of the `ls -l` command, and a regular `ls` command. Obviously the terminal's ability to display lowercase letters has been damaged, but uppercase letters and numbers display correctly. You can temporarily damage your terminal's ability to display data if you aren't careful. Using the `cat` command to display a binary file is a great way to do that. As you can see from the figures, I have damaged my terminal's ability to display data. The easiest way to solve this problem is log off and log back on and let the system reset your terminal. However, if I were also working in `vi` and had not saved the file, it could be "interesting" to try to save the file before I log out. A good rule of thumb is to always use the `file` command on a file before you `cat` it if you don't know what it contains.

Let's explore the way the file command decides what a file contains. When Unix creates a binary file, at least in theory, the first 16 bits (2 bytes) of the file are information used by other applications programs, like the linker, to identify the file and decide what to do with it. These 2 bytes are called a **magic number**. In the first couple of versions of Unix these 2 bytes of data were usually branch instructions that jumped over the header data to the beginning of the actual executable code. Since then many additional magic numbers have been added for different file types—lots of different file types. You can see all of the magic numbers that your particular flavor of Unix recognizes by looking at the file /etc/magic. Fair warning: /etc/magic is a fairly long file and documents some amazing file types. I don't think that most of you will encounter files of the magic number 0407, which stands for a "pdp 11/pre System V vax executable," but it is nice to know that if you have one of those on your system, the `file` command will correctly identify it.

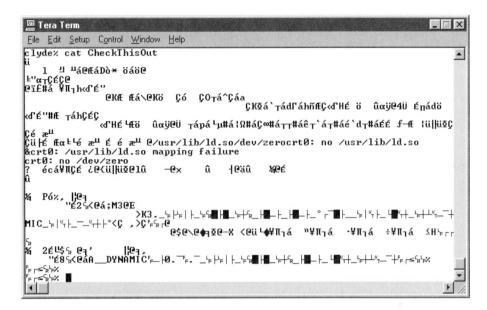

FIGURE 8.9

cating an executable.

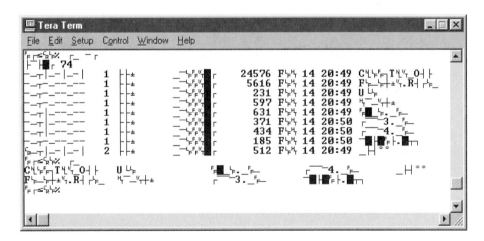

FIGURE 8.10

More problems caused by cating an executable.

But suppose there is no magic number in the file. For example, suppose it is a regular text file. In that case the `file` command will examine the first 512 bytes of the file in an attempt to determine what language it is written in. Note, by "language" I mean C, Pascal, FORTRAN, or English! This is where the file command can make a mistake, calling an awk script a C program and the like.

We will use magic numbers again when we come to shell scripting, because we will add a special code to the beginning of each one of our shell scripts to tell the shell exactly how to handle the contents. That particular magic number is #!, which tells the shell to read the rest of the line and consider it a command to run against the contents of the file. In other words, if the first line of the script is #!/bin/sh, it tells the shell, "Invoke the Bourne shell, and treat the rest of this file as Bourne shell commands." For now, though, just remember that the file command will try to determine the contents of file either by using the magic number or by examining what it finds in the file.

chmod

```
chmod [options] symbolic-coding file
chmod [options] absolute-permissions-mask file
```

There will be times you will need to change the permission on a file, a set of files, or even a directory. As you remember from our discussion of the ls command, three different levels of permission (user, group, and other) exist, with three different permissions at each level, (read, write, and execute.) If you are the owner of the file, you can modify the permissions for any level. If you don't own the file, you can't modify the permissions for any level (unless, of course, you're root.)

You can change the permissions on a file two different ways: symbolically or absolutely. *Symbolic* coding changes one or two permissions and leaves the rest alone. *Absolute* coding changes the entire **permissions mask**, the collection of all the permissions that control file access.

Symbolic permissions coding

In most cases, using symbolic coding to change one or two permissions on a file *will leave all the other permissions unchanged*. Most of the time users find that using symbolic permissions are sufficient; system administrators more often use absolute permissions, discussed later, which change all the permissions.

The format of the symbolic permissions coding when used with the chmod command is

```
[level] operator permission(s)
```

There are four different values for the *level* option:

1. u for user (the person who actually owns the file).
2. g for group (anyone in the same group as the user).
3. o for other (those who are neither the user nor a member of the user's group).
4. a for all [of the above] (use this to set the same permission for all levels).

If you don't code the level part of the permissions, **chmod** uses a level value of a. I strongly recommend always coding a level value for this command. Failing to do so can cause problems by setting permissions you don't wish set. The level option determines the **level of access** (user, group, or other).

Three different operators are available in this version of the chmod command:

1. + for adding the permission specified without changing the rest of the permissions mask.
2. - for removing the permission specified without changing the rest of the permissions mask.
3. = for setting only these permissions (works like the absolute permissions mask mode).

Normally, you will use the + (plus) to add and the - (minus) to remove particular permissions. If you're going to use the equal sign = operator, it would probably be better to use the absolute permissions mode rather than a symbolic permissions mode.

Table 8.1 shows the different individual permissions you can set using symbolic mode. Linux and Solaris share most of the permissions, but each has a unique permission. The unique permissions are designated by an L for Linux, or an S for Solaris, following their descriptions.

TABLE 8.1 Permissions Available for Each Level of Access

Permission	What It Allows
r	Reading the file, that is, taking the file as input.
w	Modifying the file's contents. In the case of a directory file, this allows modification of the directory contents, *adding or deleting* files. This permission is how you control who can delete a file.
x	Executing (running) a regular file. In the case of a directory, it allows file-matching metacharacter searches within the directory. To search in a directory you must have both read and execute permissions.
X	Executing permission only if some other level of access has execute permission already set (L).
l	Locking. If this permission is set, when one process has access to the file, other processes are prohibited from accessing it. This permission is always set at the group level (S). (See text discussion.)
s	Allowing anyone who runs the file to take on the ID of the owner of that file for the duration of the execution.
t	Setting the sticky bit. This was very important historically, when computers were slow and memory was expensive and scarce. It directed the system to keep the code in memory rather than swapping it out when the process completed. This saved I/O. It is seldom used for that purpose any more. (See text discussion.)
u	Setting the permissions for level to the permissions for user. (For example, chmod o+u myfile would set the permissions for other on myfile exactly the same as the permissions for the user.)
g	Setting the permissions for level to the permissions for group.
o	Setting the permissons for level to the permission mask for other.

Setting permissions is one of those places where you can cause yourself a great deal of trouble. Remember that the shell considers you to be cognizant, intelligent, and all-knowing (well, mostly knowing, at least). If you want to set the permissions on one of your files so that you can't access it, the shell will dutifully perform that operation for you. Consider what I did in Figure 8.11. I first began to display a file called shirt.txt with the more command. (I displayed only part of the file, then entered the q command to quit more.) Next I used the symbolic mode of chmod to remove read permission from the user level (u-r). After changing the permission I again tried to display the file but was unable to because I couldn't read it. Finally, I used the long version of the ls command to examine the permissions mask on the file, showing that although I (user) had write permission, I didn't have read permission. Without read permission I couldn't see the contents of the file.

In Figure 8.11 I used the chmod command to change one permission at one level. That is the most common way to use chmod but, you can also use it to change multiple permissions at one time. Figure 8.12 shows how that can be accomplished. The first step shows you the long file listing of all the files and directory. Notice the permission mask on file1. Next I used the chmod command to make the following permission changes:

1. Remove read permission from user.
2. Remove read permission for group.
3. Add both write and execute permission for other.

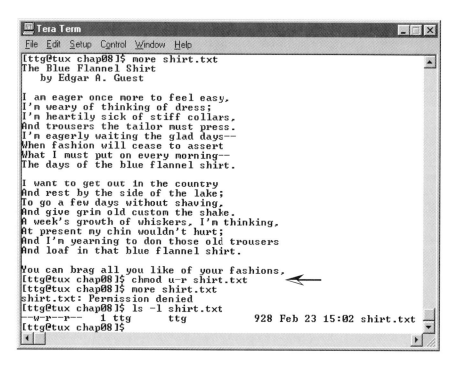

FIGURE 8.11

Making your own file inaccessible.

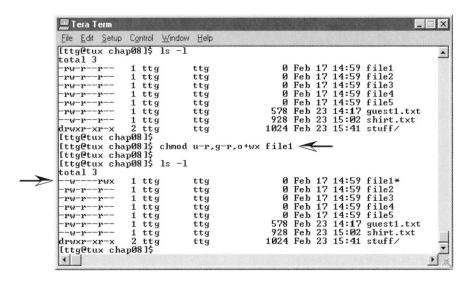

FIGURE 8.12

Changing multiple permissions at one time.

The second ls command shows the new permission mask for file1, reflecting the changes made. While it is possible to use the symbolic mode to set multiple permissions, as you have seen in Figure 8.12, it's usually much more efficient to use the absolute mode, as we will shortly see.

Using the all (a) level is a very efficient way to modify the permissions for user, group, and other in one quick command. Suppose, for example, I wanted to remove read permission for all levels for file2. Figure 8.13 shows how I can accomplish that using chmod and the a level. Look at the initial permission mask for file2—that's pretty much a standard default permissions mask. I used the chmod command with a level of a, to remove read permission from file2. The second long listing shows that user has write permission, and no one else has any permission to access file2. I could have accomplished the same thing by typing:

```
chmod u-r,g-r,o-r file2
```

Using the a level saved me eight keystrokes. That's pretty cool.

Interesting Permissions

A couple of permissions are more complex, and less intuitive, than good old read, write, and execute.

Set User/Group I.D. on Execution

The first of these complex permissions is the s, or *set* (either group or user) I.D. permission. It may seem odd at first that you might want the person running a particular

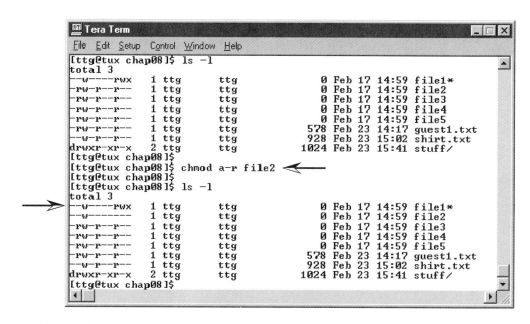

FIGURE 8.13

Efficiently setting one permission for all levels.

command or script to appear to be the owner of the script or command. However, from the systems point of view this is very handy. Consider the files /etc/passwd and /etc/shadow; root owns them, and no one but root should be able to modify them because they control access to the whole Unix machine. Yet any user must be able to change his password, and to change a password requires that the user modify either /etc/password or /etc/shadow. Seems like a conundrum. Setting the user I.D., setuid, enables a program like passwd, owned by root, to change the user's password. When the user runs the passwd process, she runs it as root (the all-powerful owner of /etc/passwd and /etc/shadow). For the life of that command the user *is* root. Obviously, you must have execute permission for either user or group set before someone else can execute a program as if he was the user, or a member of any user's group.

Figure 8.14 is a composite of two different login sessions, showing how setting the user I.D. can be used to access a file even though the user has no permissions on the file. In the upper window of the screen capture you can see my account, showing the permissions on two different files. The first file is the secret file. Notice that only the user has read and write permissions; there are no other accesses allowed. The second file shown in the ls listing is the script that others can use to read the secret file. Notice the lowercase s in place of the execute permission. The s indicates that the setuid permission and the execute permission are both set for that particular file as is required for setting user I.D. Sometimes you will see an uppercase S in place of the execute permission at the group level. That means that the setuid permission was set but the execute permission was *not* set at the group level.

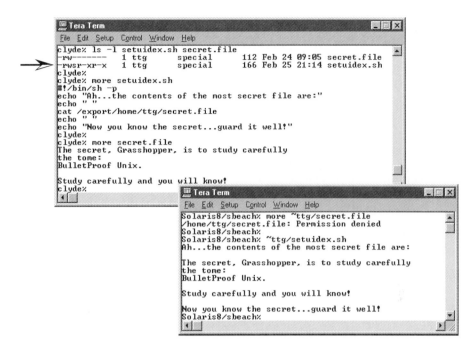

FIGURE 8.14

Setting the user I.D. permission (top), and the result of that permission (bottom).

Next I did a `more` on the script to show you the contents. Notice that all it really does is a `cat` of the `secret.file`. (The `echo` command is the verb used to send data to standard out. You will learn more about this when we talk about scripting.) Finally, I did a `more` of the `secret.file`—since I'm the only one who can read it—to show you its amazing contents.

In the second screen capture Sandi Beach first tried to look at my secret file using the `more` command. Since only the user can read or write the file, she was given the `permission denied` message. Next Sandi ran my setuid example script, and as you can see, it showed her the contents of the secret file. This proves that for the execution of that particular script, the shell considers Sandi to be me.

Most users will find very few applications where they need to set the user I.D. to the I.D. of the owner of a script or command. This is a procedure more likely to be useful for system administrators. I have included it here so you will understand the process and will know what that particular permission means if you should happen to see it.

It can take a lot of effort, and quite a bit of time to create a sample script to illustrate `setuid`. Some flavors of Unix make it very difficult to write scripts with this permission. Some file structures are created explicitly denying this permission, and you have to be very careful how you build commands in your scripts. Getting a script like this to work seems simple—at least it did to me, until I tried it. If you have difficulty, please check with your instructor or your system administrator. This permission is often misused and abused, so it may be difficult to create a script to demonstrate it.

This paragraph is included at the unspoken request of system administrators everywhere. Do not ever have a script in your directory with the setuid permission bit set unless you know *exactly* why you're doing it. Scripts or commands with the `setuid` permission are frequently compromised by cyber-terrorists. Your system administrator will not be pleased should he or she find that you have scripts that have the setuid permission. They could allow a nefarious individual to create a replacement for a particular command, in this instance the `cat` command, and use your account to run it. This is a major security breach. You must be very careful if you construct scripts that allow the setuid permission. Feel free to experiment, but when you're through, remove the `setuid` permission from your script. This is, of course, even more important if you are writing scripts as a more powerful user like root. However, by the time you ascend to root access, I'm sure you'll be much more conscientious about security and won't even need a reminder.

End of rant. <grin>

Setting the group I.D. is very similar to setting in the user I.D., except for adding the s to the group rather than the user. With the group I.D. set and execute for groups permitted, anyone who runs the script or program will be treated is if she were a member of the owner's group regardless of the group she belongs to. Therefore, access can be shared to files across multiple groups. For example, a database could be shared with engineering, research and development, and management personnel. But always remember that any time you give another person permission to be represented as you, or as a member of or your group, you are creating a security risk.

Since we are talking about security, there's another issue we should address. You may have noticed that in all the examples where you saw permissions listed, you never saw execute permission unless the file was a directory or shell script. It's dangerous to have execute permission on regular files, because if you, or another user who has execute permission, invokes that file as if it were a command, the shell will dutifully attempt to execute every line as if it were the command. The results can be catastrophic, as shown in Figure 8.15.

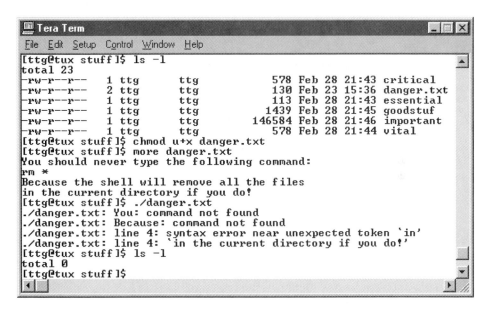

FIGURE 8.15

The problem with executing files that shouldn't be executed.

Figure 8.15 shows a series of steps where I made a terrible mistake. The first command shows a file listing of the files in this particular directory. Next I gave myself execute permission on the file danger.txt. Then I displayed the contents of the file, which looks like a portion of some notes on the rm command. Finally, just for fun, I executed the text file. The shell tried to interpret each line of the file as if it were a command, but it was unable to find the command You or the command Because. Line 4 contains the word in, which I think the shell is trying to interpret as part of a for looping command. If you look at what the shell complained about, it had problems with lines 1, 2, and 4. What about line 3? Unfortunately, the shell had no problem with line 3, as the final ls shows. It executed the remove command with no problem whatsoever.

Figure 8.15 illustrates the danger of a file that inadvertently has execute permission. Usually the only way a file can be given execute permission is if either you, the owner, or root explicitly grants it that permission. A good rule is never to give execute permission to any file that doesn't absolutely require it. After looking at Figure 8.15 you can see why.

Sticky Bit

Early on in the history of Unix, the sticky bit was used to speed up processing. If a commonly used executable had the sticky bit set, the program was not removed from memory when the current user finished with it. Instead, it was preserved in memory so it didn't have to be reloaded from disk for the next user. This meant a significant savings in time, at the expense of memory, and was common with many utility programs.

With the much faster machines we have today, this use of the sticky bit has become mostly arcane. But there's a very good use for the sticky bit when we set up special directories. At times we need a directory that all users can access but that no user can damage except by dealing with files that they own. One such directory is /tmp, the temporary storage directory for all programs on the system. Any user can write files to /tmp, and any user can delete or modify any file he owns in /tmp, yet traditionally /tpm is owned by root. No user can move, rename, or delete a file or a directory with the sticky bit set unless at least one of the following four conditions is true:

1. The user is the owner of the file.
2. The user is the owner of the directory itself.
3. The file is writable (has write permission) for that user.
4. The user is root.

Thus, the sticky bit is great to know about in cases where multiple groups of people need to have access to a common directory structure. Occasionally you will see instances in Unix where a file is used as a **semaphore**, meaning the existence of the file causes a particular action to happen. For example, at the beginning of the semester I have a script that runs every night and checks if the file add_users is present in a particular directory. If it is, the script adds the users from that file. If the file isn't there, the script waits till the next night. The add-users file is a semaphore. (The term *semaphore* goes back to the days when people, mostly sailors, communicated by waving a pair of red and yellow flags in particular patterns. The flags were known as semaphores. The signals on tall towers that direct trains are also called semaphores.) It's handy to have a directory in which many users can write such a file and yet they don't need to own the directory.

Although these three interesting permissions are seldom used by beginning Unix users, I have included them so you can understand the complete permissions mask when you see it presented. Please remember that scripts or programs with the setuid permission can cause serious problems—so be careful with them!

Now that we know about the different permissions and have seen the symbolic way to represent them, let's look at the more "professional" way of modifying the permissions mask.

Absolute (Octal) Permissions Coding

The symbolic method is both quick and fairly intuitive for changing one or two permissions, but when you wish to change more than two, you'll find the absolute, or octal, permissions coding method much more efficient.

One important difference between the absolute permissions method and the symbolic permissions method is that when you use the absolute method you must specify *all* the permissions, as the permissions you code will *replace, not modify*, the existing permissions. Thus, if you want to add execute permission to a file for the user, you must specify the complete permissions mask for user, group, and other. Fortunately, all the shells support a very efficient way to specify permission masks using the octal numbering system.

We need to speak briefly about numbering systems. The *octal* numbering system, also known as *base 8*, has the following unique digits: 0,1,2,3,4,5,6,7. Notice that the largest single digit in the octal numbering system is 7. (Now we get a bit technical.)

Each permission mask is represented by a single bit in the inode: the digit 1 grants the permission and 0 denies the permission. Since there are three different permissions at each level, there are three bits for each level—one each for read, write, and execute. And, as there are three different levels of permission, the inode has a total of nine regular permission bits. Actually, you know there's another bit, and we will talk about it in just a bit. (Sorry, couldn't resist.) ☺

If you remember the extensive work you've done in binary math, you know how to represent octal numbers and binary. Oh dear, you have forgotten that? Okay, let me remind you. In the binary numbering system, base 2, each bit position stands for a power of 2. Figure 8.16 shows the values for the low-order three bits, the bits that are most interesting to us. As you can see from the figure, the rightmost bit represents 2 raised to the zero power (2^0), the next bit to the left represents 2 to the first power (2^1), and the leftmost bit represents 2 to the second power, 2 squared (2^2). Think back to the layout of the permissions mask. It was arranged this way:

rwx rwx rwx

1	0	1	
4	2	1	- positional value

FIGURE 8.16

The positional values for the low-order three bits.

The first three permissions were for the *user*, the next three for the *group*, and the last three for *other*. Each level of permissions corresponds to 3 bits, and each 3 bits can be represented by a single octal number. That means we can represent the whole permissions mask as three (or four) octal digits.

Table 8.2 shows the eight possible arrangements of 3 bits, their octal value, and what permissions they allow. As you can see, there are actually eight different possible permission masks that can be set at each level. If you're going to use the absolute mode, you need to remember the octal value for each of the permission masks so that you can

TABLE 8.2 Permission Mask as Represented in Binary and Octal

Bit string	Octal value	Permissions Allowed
000	0	None; no access.
001	1	Execute only.
010	2	Write only.
011	3	Write and execute.
100	4	Read only.
101	5	Read and execute.
110	6	Read and write.
111	7	All permissions: read, write, execute.

set the complete mask, all three levels, for the file. Remember that you must set the *entire permission mask* for all three levels if you choose to use the absolute mode.

Figure 8.17 shows how I used the absolute mode to set some permissions. I used the absolute mode of chmod to set permissions on file2 twice. It seems the first time I made a small mistake: in the first chmod I specified a single octal digit. The chmod command interpreted that single digit as if I had typed 007 and set the permissions accordingly. You can see the results in the second ls output. Finally, in the second chmod, I entered the permissions mask correctly. I wanted to be able to read and write to file2 myself but allow those in my group and others to read only.

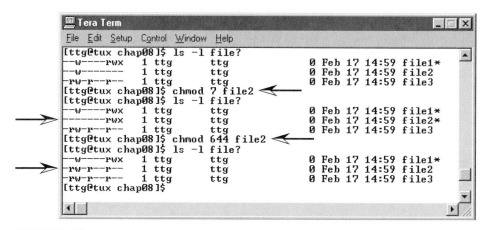

FIGURE 8.17
Using absolute mode to set permissions.

Using the absolute format is much quicker than the symbolic method if you're changing more than just a couple of permissions, and it is the method that most system administrators use. Most people, as they began to use chmod, prefer to use the symbolic method, but with a little practice, I know you'll find the absolute method equally useful and oftentimes much more efficient.

A few paragraphs ago I told you there was a fourth bit that you could use in the absolute method. That bit is used to apply those other "interesting" permissions like the setuid bit, the setgid bit, and the sticky bit. Table 8.3 shows you those additional bit patterns. Remember that you must specify all *four* digits if you're going to use these

TABLE 8.3 Permissions Set by Fourth Digit

Permission	Result
0xxx	Nothing; no extra bits set.
1xxx	Sticky bit is set.
2xxx	Setgid bit is set.
3xxx	Sticky bit and setgid bit set.
4xxx	Setuid bit set.
5xxx	Setuid and sticky bits set.
6xxx	Setuid and setgid bits set.
7xxx	Setuid, setgid, and sticky bits set.

specialized forms. You can't just set the setuid bit; you must specify the entire mask, including a `setuid` bit.

In Table 8.3 the character string xxx stands for the permission mask you saw in Table 8.2. Remember that the sticky bit is always set for *other*.

chown

```
chown [option] owner[:group] file
```

Just as there are times when you need to change permissions, they'll be times when you'll need to change the ownership of a file. For example, if you copy a file to another user, Refrigerator Rule No. 3 tells us, "The one who makes the copy owns the file." If you want the person *to whom* you copied the file to own the file, you will have to change the ownership of the file to that user. The **chown** (*change the owner*) option is provided for that purpose.

On many systems, the ability to change the ownership of the file is restricted to the super-user (root) by default. This is a security issue. For example, in the newer versions of the Solaris operating system, only the super-user is allowed to change the ownership of a file. This is an option that the administrator can change but the default prevents users from changing the ownership of files. The important thing for you to remember now is that it is possible to change the ownership of a file.

You can also use the chown command to change the group associated with the file. The command form is as follows:

```
chown user:group file
```

Suppose you use it this way:

```
chown ttg:admins myscript.sh
```

The file `myscript.sh` would be owned by `ttg` and have a group of `admins`—that is, provided that the current owner was a member of group `admins`. You're not permitted to change the group associated with a file to a group of which you're not a member. If you simply want to change the group associated with a file, you can use chown without a user I.D., but with a colon followed by a group name and one number. For example:

```
chown :acct beancount.sh
```

This code would change the group associated with the script `beancount.sh` to `acct` without changing the user who owned the file.

Using chown in this fashion is similar to using the chgrp (*change the group*) command. Remember that the use of this command is often very restricted. You might not be able to experiment with it on your system unless your system administrator makes a special provision.

chgrp

```
chgrp [options] group file
```

Changing the group identifier on a file, with **chgrp**, is less commonly necessary than changing either the permissions or the ownership. A few times, as a system administrator,

I needed to change the group associated with a file to allow additional members of a working team access to the file, but you are not likely to need this option as a user. Nevertheless you should know of its existence. Unix gives you the wonderful flexibility of being able to change all of the ownership attributes (levels of permission) of a file, as well as all of the permissions at each level.

⊕ Information about System and Resources

Various commands give you information about the state of the system. As a user, you'll find many of these commands merely informational rather than critical. When you become a system administrator, however, these commands will be essential tools to help you monitor and maintain the system. Moreover, I have found that informed users are much more likely to respect the resources on the system if they know about the state of the system. A wise user will stay at least peripherally aware of the state of the system. It's the right thing to do, and it will make your job easier in the long run. Besides, it's amazing how much a Unix system can really do. We will see even more of these kinds of data when we look at process control in Chapter 10. Now, let's look at some of the really interesting data Unix gives us about what is going on with its resources.

uptime

---

    uptime

One of the things that separates the Unix operating system from others is that as a general rule, the only time you'll reboot a Unix system is after you change its hardware (as in adding more memory or rebuilding the kernel) or if you have some sort of catastrophic failure or power outage. The only significant drawback I've ever seen in using a Unix machine is that they just don't seem to work well without electricity. Other than that, once you bring a Unix machine up, it just stays up! Sun Microsystems advertises "zero-reboot Solaris," and they mean it.

Figure 8.18 shows the output of the **uptime** command on my Solaris box in my office at school. You can see from this display that the computer has been up for 138 days, 8 hours, and 41 minutes. That's not long for a Unix system to be up, but 138 days

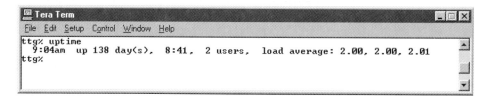

FIGURE 8.18

How long has the system been up?

ago the facility folks had to power down our building for two days to install new transformers. Since that's a little longer than my UPS can hold the system, I had to shut my machine down. Before that it had been up for over 250 days. One of the Web servers for Sun Microsystems had been up for over 400 days last time I checked. Unix machines just stay up.

If you think back to the output of the w command, you'll notice that the output from the uptime command is a very similar to the first line of that output. Besides current time and the number of days and minutes the system has been up, uptime tells the number of users on the system and the average load on the system for the last 1, 5, and 15 minutes.

Load figures can be very important depending on how much you need done on the system. Normally, administrators like the load figures to be somewhere around 1.0. A load number of 1.0 is a maximally efficient system load. Numbers greater than 1.0 indicate a system that is working with a greater than optimal load. As you can see from Figure 8.18, my office computer is a little busy. That's because I'm running a couple of sessions of seti@home on the weekends just keeping it busy—a bored computer is a sad thing.

Figure 8.19 shows the uptime output from a couple of other Solaris machines, both of them with more reasonable load numbers. The load factor on the clyde machine is pretty much optimal, whereas the machine at the top of the figure is rather underutilized.

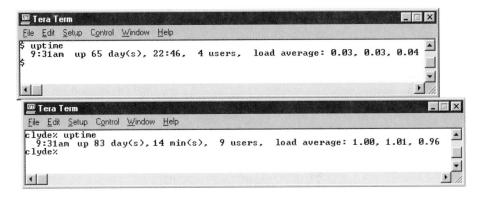

FIGURE 8.19

Output of uptime on different computers.

The uptime command can tell you a whole lot about what's going on your computer and can give you a pretty good idea about how busy your machine is. I would caution you, however, about displaying the output from this command where users of those "other" operating systems might see them. It's not kind to let folks who live in a "reboot one or more times a day" world see that our machines stay up for months or even years at a time.

df

---

df [options] [device]

The **df**, *disk free*, command tells us how disk space is currently being used in the file systems. There are a number of options for this command, many of which are of value only to system administrators. The most useful option for most users is -k, which directs the command to show the amount of disk space both used and available in kilobytes. You can also specify a file or directory and the command will dutifully report on the file system that contains that file or that directory.

Figure 8.20 shows examples of the df command on three different systems. On the first system, Linux with two hard drives and two file systems, the output is quite simple. The second is a Solaris system with one hard drive, a floppy disk drive (/dev/fd), and six file systems. The third is a larger system, an E450 with a floppy drive and four hard drives.

The column called either Use or capacity shows how much of the drive has been used. Subtract this number from 100 to determine the percentage of the drive that is

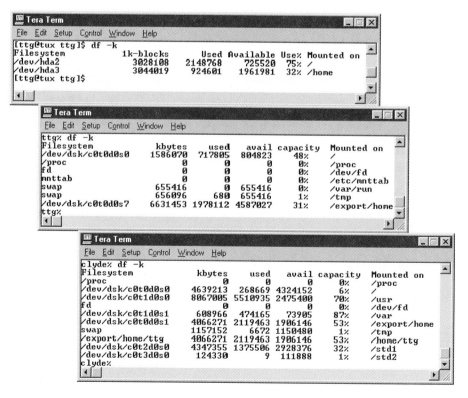

FIGURE 8.20

Output of the df command on three systems.

still available. Remember, the df command tells you about the status of the *system*, not about your own directory structure. (That is, of course, unless you're doing a df on your own personal computer.)

You'll likely notice that your system administrator becomes concerned when the percentage of available file space on a given file structure falls below about 10 percent. If you notice that one of the file structures where you have files is getting full, you might consider looking for large files that may have accumulated in your directory and cleaning them up. One file that sometimes appears in your directory is the *core file*, which is an image of the memory when a particular program failed. These files are often very large, and you may not even know the program you are running created a core file. Another large file the shows up less frequently than core is a *dump file*, an image of all the memory on the system. For example, the E450 at school has 4 gigabytes of RAM, so a dump file is a 4-gigabyte file! It wouldn't take many of those to chew up a significant part of a file structure. "But how," you ask, "do I know how much file space I'm using?" Excellent question!

du

---

du [options] [directory]

You know about file systems, and you may be very conscientious about how much disk space you're using, especially if you are living under an imposed quota. There are commands that will help you manage this resource. Obviously, to determine the size of and individual file you can use the ls command. Figure 8.21 shows how the ls command is used to show the size of a particular file. However, the ls command won't tell me how many bites are being used in the whole directory. For that, I would have to grab my handy pocket calculator and add up all file sizes to determine that there are about 654,350 bytes used in this directory. Using my calculator is a marginally

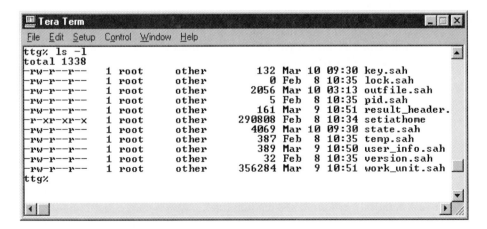

FIGURE 8.21

Using ls to see how much file space is being used.

workable proposition if there are only a dozen or so files, but if I'm trying to do the same sort of thing on a directory with 306 files, the procedure might get little tedious. Fortunately, both shells support the command that will tell me how much space is being used by each directory, the **du**, *disk utilization,* command.

Figure 8.22 shows the output of the du command run against the setiathome2 directory on my school machine. The figure shows that I ran the du command twice. The first time I ran it without any options and gave as the argument the directory I was curious about. It reported to me how many blocks, in this case 512 byte blocks, were used in the setiathome2 directory. The second time I ran the command I gave it the -k option, which asked it to report in kilobytes rather than in blocks. Not surprisingly, there were almost exactly half as many kilobytes as there were blocks.

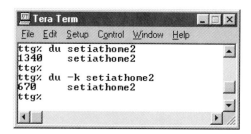

FIGURE 8.22

Using du to see how much disk space is
being used.

"But wait," you ask, "when we ran the numbers, there were only 654,350 bytes used." Ah yes, but each file in Unix is built of blocks, in this case 512 byte blocks. That means the file pid.sah, which used only 5 bytes, actually took up 512 bytes, with 507 bytes reserved but not used. If we go back and look at the size of the files in Figure 8.21 and round them *up* to the nearest 512-byte block, we will see that approximately 1338 blocks are used. The du command tells us that 1340 blocks were used because it takes into account some additional overhead. You must be careful using the ls command to determine file size unless you take into account that files are always composed of disk blocks and that block size can vary.

Another very useful option on the du command is the -s, or *summary*, option. If you're interested only in how much disk space you're consuming and don't really care about the disbursement of files to directories, the summary option is just what you want. Figure 8.23 shows part of the output of the regular du command and then the output of the du -ks command. (Yes, I know—the *ducks* command! ☺) The output from the du -k command shows how much space each directory under my home directory takes. The last line shows the total number of bytes (in kilobytes) taken up by the whole of my directory structure. If I don't want to sit through the scrolling of all of those directory names, I can use the -s, or summary, option to see just the total. As you can see from Figure 8.23, the second time I ran the du command, with both the k and s options, all I saw was the total for my directory structure. There are other options on the du command that you might find useful when you become a system administrator. Feel free to experiment with this command.

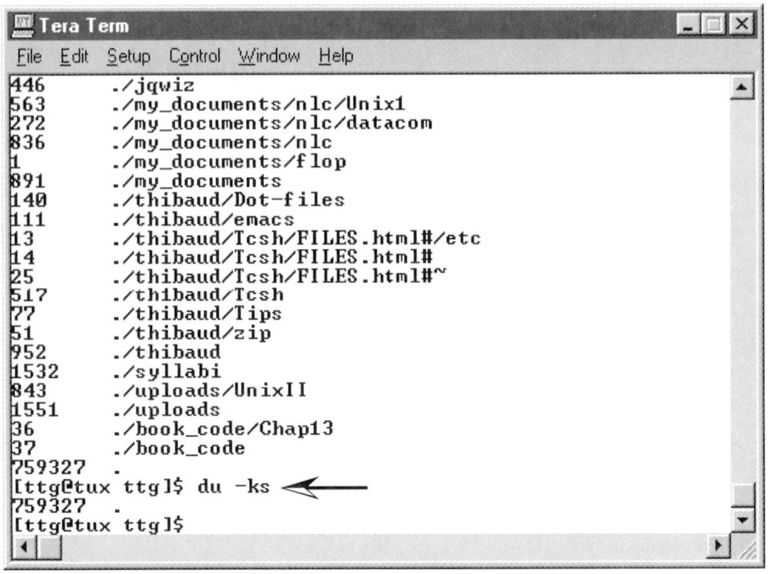

FIGURE 8.23

Output from du -k.

vmstat

```
vmstat [options] [interval [[count]]
```

This is another command gives you all kinds of information about what's actually going on the system. You may find it interesting to see what the state of the memory and such is inside the system. You most likely won't apply much of this information until you are a system administrator, but it's neat stuff to know. Figure 8.24 shows the output from the **vmstat** command on both Solaris and Linux.

There's a lot of data in the output from vmstat. Some of it is significant and some of it's of interest only to those who are consumed with the subject of system performance. The first line of data lists the average values since the last time the system was rebooted. Each line after the first line shows the state of the system in the *interval*, in this case 10 seconds, and is a much better measure of what's happening in the system. You may also specify a *count*, which tells vmstat the number of intervals to process. The things that I typically look at are

1. r, b, and w are the counters of, respectively, jobs that are ready to run, those that are blocked by resource waits, and those that are ready to run but are waiting, swapped on disk.
2. swpd is the amount of swap space available on the system—having a large number here is good.

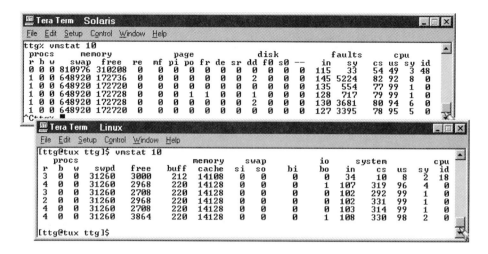

FIGURE 8.24

Using vmstat in both Solaris and Linux.

3. free is the amount of free memory—having a large number here is also good.

4. us, sy, id are, respectively, the percentages of CPU being used by the users, being used by the system, and not being used but staying idle.

Other information, like the number of page faults or number of bytes paged in or out, aren't of particular interest at the user level, so I generally ignore them.

top (Linux)

```
top [options]
```

The **top** command is part of the Linux distribution. It is also available in some other flavors of Unix, like HP-UX. It isn't part of the standard Solaris distribution, but it is available from the GNU site, so it might be on your system. Although there are a number of options to the top command, from the user's point of view, top is often best run without any options. Personally, I very seldom use any options with top, because I just want to see what's going on in the system.

Figure 8.25 shows an example of top running on my Linux box at home. The first line looks suspiciously similar to the output of the uptime command. That's because it *is* the output of the uptime command! The next line lists all of the currently active processes on system, followed by line that shows CPU states and the percentage of processes that have been niced. The last two lines of the heading provide information about the memory utilization.

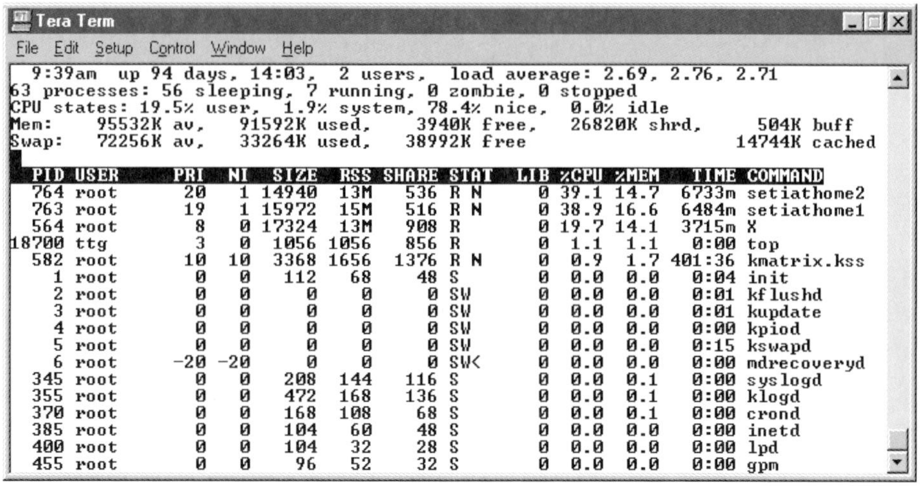

```
Tera Term
File Edit Setup Control Window Help
  9:39am  up 94 days, 14:03,  2 users,  load average: 2.69, 2.76, 2.71
63 processes: 56 sleeping, 7 running, 0 zombie, 0 stopped
CPU states: 19.5% user,  1.9% system, 78.4% nice,  0.0% idle
Mem:    95532K av,  91592K used,   3940K free,  26820K shrd,    504K buff
Swap:   72256K av,  33264K used,  38992K free                  14744K cached

  PID USER     PRI  NI  SIZE  RSS SHARE STAT  LIB %CPU %MEM   TIME COMMAND
  764 root      20   1 14940  13M   536 R N     0 39.1 14.7  6733m setiathome2
  763 root      19   1 15972  15M   516 R N     0 38.9 16.6  6484m setiathome1
  564 root       8   0 17324  13M   908 R       0 19.7 14.1  3715m X
18700 ttg        3   0  1056 1056   856 R       0  1.1  1.1   0:00 top
  582 root      10  10  3368 1656  1376 R N     0  0.9  1.7 401:36 kmatrix.kss
    1 root       0   0   112   68    48 S       0  0.0  0.0   0:04 init
    2 root       0   0     0    0     0 SW      0  0.0  0.0   0:01 kflushd
    3 root       0   0     0    0     0 SW      0  0.0  0.0   0:01 kupdate
    4 root       0   0     0    0     0 SW      0  0.0  0.0   0:00 kpiod
    5 root       0   0     0    0     0 SW      0  0.0  0.0   0:15 kswapd
    6 root     -20 -20     0    0     0 SW<     0  0.0  0.0   0:00 mdrecoveryd
  345 root       0   0   208  144   116 S       0  0.0  0.1   0:00 syslogd
  355 root       0   0   472  168   136 S       0  0.0  0.1   0:00 klogd
  370 root       0   0   168  108    68 S       0  0.0  0.1   0:00 crond
  385 root       0   0   104   60    48 S       0  0.0  0.0   0:00 inetd
  400 root       0   0   104   32    28 S       0  0.0  0.0   0:00 lpd
  455 root       0   0    96   52    32 S       0  0.0  0.0   0:00 gpm
```

FIGURE 8.25

Output of `top`.

The real interesting part of the `top` command is the display of what's actually consuming the majority of the resources. Processes are ranked by their CPU utilization and memory utilization. On my machine the top two processes currently running are both processing `setiathome` data. The next most intensive process is Xwindows, and then the `top` command itself, consuming all of 1.1 percent of the CPU and a whopping 1.1 percent of the memory. Notice that for purposes of the `top` command, there are many running processes (an `R` in the `STAT` column) and those that have an `N` after the `R` have had some `nice` value set. The `nice` modifier is shown in the `NI` column, four columns to the left of the `STAT` column.

If your system seems to be running slowly, it's often useful to run the `top` command and see what processes are consuming the resources. Besides, it's pretty interesting to see what processes are consuming the most resources. Often you'll find that the `top` process itself is the top process.

free (Linux)

```
free [options]
```

The last of the system status commands that we'll address in this chapter looks at the state of the system's memory. It's also part of the `top` command display but if you are just interested in memory, it gives you a focused output. Figure 8.26 shows the output of the **`free`** command on a Linux box that I use as the Web server for my HTML class, and for comparison the `free` command on my Linux box here at home.

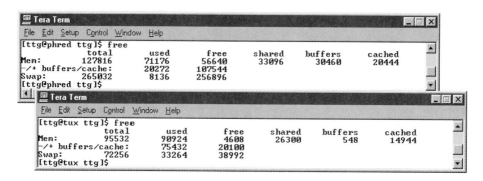

FIGURE 8.26

Output from the free command.

As you can see from the figure, phred, the top machine, has 128 Meg memory, of which only 71 Meg are currently being used. My machine here at home, tux, has 96 Meg of memory, of which 91 Meg are being used.

The free command gives you some interesting information about the utilization of memory. It's another place to look if your machine is running slowly.

Now it's your turn to play with these commands. In the next chapter we will look at some ways to help you be more efficient and find out about other ways to play with files.

KEY TERMS

FIFO
FILO
level of access
magic number
permissions mask
print buffer
semaphore
spooling
queue

NEW COMMANDS

chgrp
chmod
chown
df
du
file
free (L)

```
lp
lpq
lpr
lprm
top (L)
uptime
vmstat
```

REVIEW QUESTIONS

8.1 Define all of the key terms.

8.2 Explain the concept of a queue, and give three (noncomputer) examples.

8.3 Describe how a queue might be used other than with print jobs.

8.4 What does the lp command do?

8.5 How does the lp command differ from the lpr command?

8.6 Which command would you use to find out about the contents of the print queue?

8.7 Which command would you use to remove entries from the print queue?

8.8 Can you remove *any* job from the print queue?

8.9 How can you determine (or at least guess) the contents of a file before you cat it?

8.10 Which command format would you use to set the user's execute bit without changing any other permissions?

8.11 What is the permissions mask to give the following permissions: (a) user: read, write; (b) other: read; (c) group: read, write.

8.12 Explain the relationship between the binary number 110110100 and the octal number 664.

8.13 Explain what setuid will do for a file.

8.14 Discuss the security concerns about files with setuid.

8.15 Why would it be a bad idea to execute the following command on your home directory: chmod u+x * ?

8.16 Which command would you use to change the ownership of a file (besides cp!)?

8.17 Which commands can be used to change the group associated with a file?

8.18 What does the uptime command tell you?

8.19 Why wouldn't a second-class operating system want an uptime command?

8.20 How does df differ from du?

8.21 What does vmstat tell you?

8.22 When would you use the top command?

8.23 What does the free command tell you?

EXERCISES

The following exercises assume you have a printer available.

8.1 Print one of the files you created with one of the editors.

8.2 Print a second file, and try to remove it from the print queue before it prints.

8.3 Determine the status of the default print queue.

No printer? Start here!

8.4 Ask your instructor or system administrator if you have multiple print queues.

8.5 Change the permissions on one of your files so that someone else in your class may read it but you can't.

8.6 Modify all of the permissions on one of your files to prevent any access by anyone.

8.7 Attempt to read and write the file you "fixed" in Exercise 6.

8.8 Create a list of the nine possible permissions for a normal file. (You will need to memorize this table; it is essential to remember these permissions.)

8.9 Set the sticky bit (if possible) on one of your files.

8.10 Set the `setuid` bit on one of your files. Once you have verified that you have set that bit, unset it.

8.11 Set the permissions so group and other have no access to a file in your directory. Then change the ownership of the file to someone else in your class (if you are allowed to). Can you read the file? Can you change the permissions so you *can* read it? Experiment!

8.12 Determine how long it's been since your system was rebooted.

8.13 Determine how much free space exists on the file system you normally use.

8.14 See how much space your files are taking up individually.

8.15 Now just get the total for *all* your files.

8.16 See which processes are using the most resources on your system.

8.17 Determine the amount of memory that is free, right now, on your system.

8.18 Examine the output of the `vmstat` command.

9

Tools and Concepts

A number of Unix commands have been created to make your life easier, help you do the things you wish to do, and basically bring a great deal of fun to your life. (Well maybe I'm stretching things with the fun bit, but I do kinda like some of this stuff.) First let's discuss one that you will need only occasionally as a user but will find to be infinitely valuable as a system administrator.

find

```
find path [condition]
```

The **find** command is used to find files. While that sounds simple, the procedure can be enormously complex if you wish to push find to its limits. Yet, the command can be very straightforward to use. We will start out with a straightforward use and move toward more complex uses as we build on our experience with find.

The find command works **recursively**. Thus, as the command begins running in a particular directory it will work its way down through all of the directories underneath that directory looking for the file or files you've asked it to find. (By classic definition, a *recursive program* is one that can call itself. In this case, find is calling itself for each directory.) The first thing you have to tell find is where to start looking.

In most cases you also tell find what to look for. If you don't specify a condition, find matches all the files and directories, pretty much as a recursive ls command operates. You need to use one of find's many descriptive conditions to describe exactly what you wish to find. Almost any of the characteristics of a *file* can be described by a **find** expression. (The find command finds information *about the file itself*; we will learn other commands, like grep, to discover information about the *contents* of files.)

Table 9.1 shows some sample find conditions and how find interprets them. The first condition, atime, illustrates the way you code numbers with many different find conditions. If you code -atime and a number without a sign, let's say 5, you will find files that have been accessed *exactly* five days ago, no more, no less. Suppose you want to find files that have been accessed any time in the last five days, you would then code

TABLE 9.1   Some find Conditions and Their Meanings

Find Condition	What It Really Means
-atime +3	Find files that have been accessed more than (+) three days ago. If you code 3, you will find files accessed exactly three days ago. If you code -3, you will find files accessed less than three days ago.
-name pattern	Find files with names that match the pattern. You can use file-matching metacharacters in the pattern, but you must protect them from the shell by quoting or escaping them. (It is a good idea to *always* protect the pattern!)
-user user	Finds files owned by user.
-perm OOO	Find files with a permission mask that matches the octal three-digit string specified by OOO. (You can use this to search for files with the setuid bit set!)
-size n[c]	Find files containing *n* blocks (or *n* characters if c is specified).
-print	Required if you want to see the output in some instances of find; the default in other instances.
-exec command {}\; -ok command {}\;	If you find files that match, perform the command upon them. The {} takes the place of the filename. The protected semicolon, \;, is required to mark the end of the command, the ok version asks for confirmation.

an `atime` value of -6. That would direct `find` to report any files with an access time less than 6. By the same token, if you wish to find all the files that were accessed more than five days ago you would code an `atime` value of +5, which would direct `find` to report any files whose access time was greater than 5.

The second condition, `-name pattern`, shows you how to find files with names that match any one of many different possible patterns. This is a very important command for system administrators because there are many files like a file called `core` that an administrator wants to find and remove. *Core files* are created when a program encounters an abnormal condition and aborts execution. They are usually fairly large and of little value, because most folks don't even know how to read a binary core file.

You can use any of the file-matching metacharacters you have learned as part of the pattern, but if you use file-matching metacharacters, you must enclose the pattern in tick marks to protect it from interpretation by the shell. It's *never* wrong to enclose the pattern in tick marks, and if you use metacharacters you must, so my recommendation is to develop the habit of always enclosing your patterns in tick marks. To recap, it's never wrong, sometimes required, and always a good idea.

The fourth condition in the table, `perm`, is another one that's of great value to system administrators. In the previous chapter we talked about permissions on scripts that allow the user to take on the identity of the owner, setuid, and about how dangerous those scripts were. We also discussed the dangers involved with files that were executable but weren't scripts or programs. You or the system administrator can use the permissions option `perm` to find all files in the directory that have execute permission. Figure 9.1 shows how I used the `find` command to look at all the files in my directory that had execute permission.

Most of files that `find` found in my directory with execute permission were directories. I expected that. However, notice that there are some files in Chapter 8 that

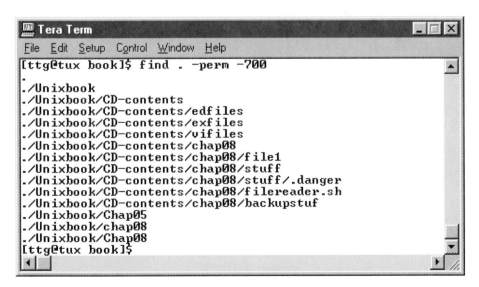

FIGURE 9.1

Looking for files with execute permission.

have an execute permission set. Another interesting thing is that find finds *hidden*, or dotted, files (.danger), because find doesn't always use file-matching metacharacters. The ability of find to discover hidden files was useful to me when I was tracking down a cracker who had broken into one of my systems. Even though he had very carefully hidden his files, find found them and dutifully reported them to me. And I dutifully cleaned them up and closed the door he had used to trespass inside the computer.

Notice that the way I coded the permission, preceding it with a minus (-), told find to find a file with 7 at any level—user, group, or other. Had I coded the permissions mask as 700, without a minus, find would have looked for files with exactly that permission mask (rwx--).

The next condition in the table, -size, specifies files of a particular size. As with other numeric values, I can specify a number and find will look for files exactly that size. I can put a plus sign before the number and find will look for files larger than the size specified, and I can put a minus before the number and find will find files smaller than the size specified.

The -print condition may be of more historical interest than practical application at this point since both the operating systems under consideration include it as the default for most conditions. If, however, you're using an older version of Unix, and if you run a find command and see nothing output at the command line, try adding a -print condition.

The last pair of conditions in the table, -exec and -ok, are considered to be the most useful options by many system administrators. They allow you to "automatically" execute a command or command set on each file that matches the conditions you specified. For example, I have a shell script that runs daily on my production machines and looks for core files, those large files created when a program abnormally terminates. When the script finds a core file in any users account it automatically deletes it, recovering the space in the file system. That script is shown in Figure 9.2.

This is a simple, little find script in Figure 9.2. The first line directs the script to run the Bourne shell (you will learn all about that in Chapter 14.) The lines that start with octothorps, #, are comments telling me what the script does. The find line finds all files named core and then executes the remove command to remove them from the system. I run the script every night to keep core files off my system.

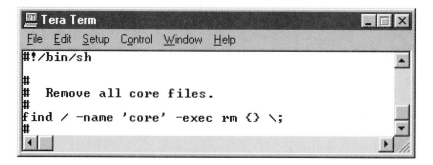

FIGURE 9.2

A script that finds and deletes core files.

Notice the format of the -exec option:

```
-exec rm {} \;
```

When the find command finds a file that matches the condition in the command, in this case a file with the name core, it executes the command specified. It replaces the curly brace pair with the path and name of the file it found. The protected semicolon marks the end of the command string that exec(ute) performs. Notice that there is no protection here—the remove command doesn't inquire whether it should remove the file or not; it just does its job. This is a very powerful tool. Use it carefully.

If you'd like to be a little safer, you can use the -ok version of execute, which works exactly like -exec but always prompts you for confirmation. This is a wonderful option if you're running a find command in the foreground and interacting with it. I really don't want to have to go up to school at midnight, when my core search find runs, to confirm that I want to delete the files. Which option you use really depends on your implementation.

Pipes

```
Command1 | command2
```

The idea of pipes (|) has been a part of Unix since the 1972, version 2, system. Indeed, pipes are one of the fundamental, founding ideas that makes Unix what it is today. According to Dennis Ritchie in *The Evolution of the Unix Time-sharing System* (http://cm.bell-labs.com/cm/cs/who/dmr/hist.html),

> Pipes appeared in Unix in 1972, well after the PDP-11 version of the system was in operation at the suggestion, (or perhaps insistence), of M. D. McIlroy, a longtime advocate of the non-hierarchical control flow that characterizes coroutines. Some years before pipes were implemented, he suggested that commands should be thought of as binary operators, whose right and left operand specify the input output files .... The idea, explained one afternoon on a blackboard, intrigued us but failed to ignite any immediate action .... Sometime later, thanks to McIlroy's persistence, pipes were finally installed in the operating system (a relatively simple job), and iteration was introduced.

As you can see from Ritchie's quotation, the concept of pipes has been part and parcel of Unix since the very early days. This relatively simple concept has some profound nuances.

As you learned earlier, each process is given three files at process-creation time: standard input, standard output, and standard error. You will also recall, I hope, that all files are nothing but streams of ASCII bytes. Streams of ASCII bytes provide a consistent and common interface between commands.

The early Unix developers created commands that were independent programs—taking input from standard in and writing output to standard out, with errors sent to a separate file (standard error)—so that they would work together as building blocks for complex functions. This idea of programs that work together is often called the *filter program concept*.

Filter Program Concept

A **filter** is a program that reads its input from standard in and writes its output to standard out. Simple and yet, as we shall see, profound. Most properly designed Unix commands, scripts, and programs are filters.

In other words, a process expects a stream of ASCII bytes as input, and generates a stream of ASCII bytes as output. That means you can take the output from one Unix command and pass it as input to a second Unix command. In the same vein, you can have the output from one Unix command passed as input to a second and the output of the second passed as input to a third and on and on. Various Unix systems have different maximum numbers of commands you can build into a pipe, but I've never exceeded that limit in any Unix system I have ever used.

Figure 9.3 shows two different pipes that I created to see how many people were currently working on my production machine. The first part of the figure is the end of the output from a who command. Since a number of users scrawled off the top of my screen, I couldn't very well count them, so I decided to let Unix do it for me.

The first time I ran the who command and piped (|) its output to the wc command, asking it to count the number of lines. In theory I should have one line for each user. However, notice the lines for ttg, krf, and nt15 near the end of the listing. In each

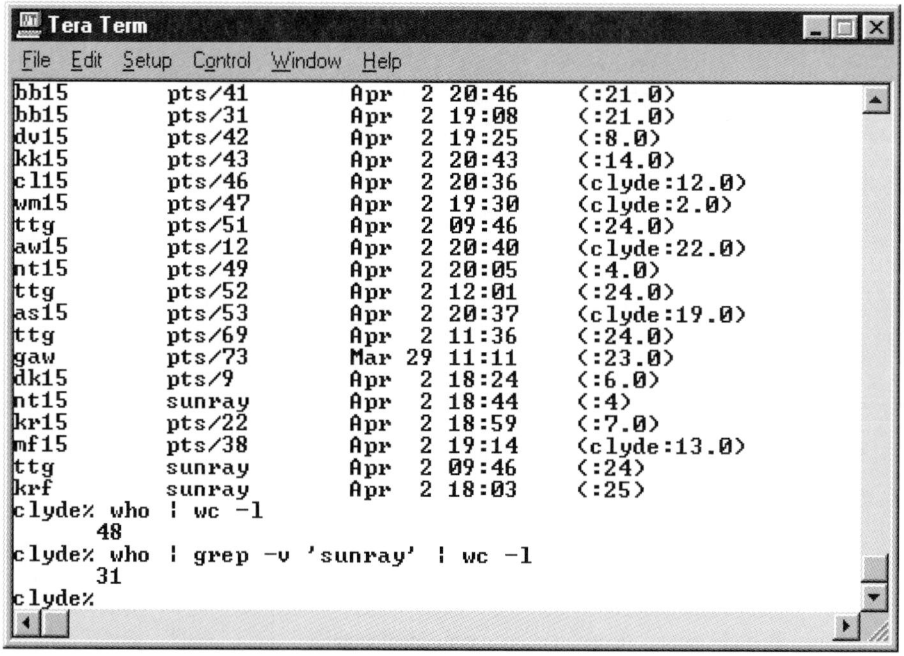

```
 Tera Term                                                    _ □ ×
 File  Edit  Setup  Control  Window  Help
bb15         pts/41        Apr  2 20:46      (:21.0)
bb15         pts/31        Apr  2 19:08      (:21.0)
dv15         pts/42        Apr  2 19:25      (:8.0)
kk15         pts/43        Apr  2 20:43      (:14.0)
cl15         pts/46        Apr  2 20:36      (clyde:12.0)
wm15         pts/47        Apr  2 19:30      (clyde:2.0)
ttg          pts/51        Apr  2 09:46      (:24.0)
aw15         pts/12        Apr  2 20:40      (clyde:22.0)
nt15         pts/49        Apr  2 20:05      (:4.0)
ttg          pts/52        Apr  2 12:01      (:24.0)
as15         pts/53        Apr  2 20:37      (clyde:19.0)
ttg          pts/69        Apr  2 11:36      (:24.0)
gaw          pts/73        Mar 29 11:11      (:23.0)
dk15         pts/9         Apr  2 18:24      (:6.0)
nt15         sunray        Apr  2 18:44      (:4)
kr15         pts/22        Apr  2 18:59      (:7.0)
mf15         pts/38        Apr  2 19:14      (clyde:13.0)
ttg          sunray        Apr  2 09:46      (:24)
krf          sunray        Apr  2 18:03      (:25)
clyde% who | wc -1
      48
clyde% who | grep -v 'sunray' | wc -1
      31
clyde%
```

FIGURE 9.3

Using pipes to count users.

case the input device is listed as sunray, which refers to the sunrays in the lab. Each user logged into a sunray causes the system to record a separate login. That means each user using a sunray has an extra entry, and that makes my count invalid.

In the second pipe I sent the output from the who command to the grep command, asking it to find all lines that did not have the word sunray in them. (Don't worry about the grep command—you will meet the three grep sisters in Chapter 11.) I sent the output from that command to the wc and asked it to count the lines passed to it. That told me that there were 17 people logged in to sunrays, working from the lab (48 − 31 equals 17, I hope!).

A second reason pipes are such a powerful and useful tool is that they speed up the execution of multiple processes because they allow pseudo-simultaneous execution of the commands in the pipe. Other operating systems have tried to imitate this feature of Unix using temporary files, but in those cases (for example in DOS), each command executes sequentially. If you have access to a machine running DOS you can prove this: copy a text file to a floppy disk, then write-protect that floppy, reinsert it, and change your default directory to the floppy. Finally, type this command:

```
type filename | more
```

You will find that the command fails because DOS can't create the necessary temporary file on the write-protected disk.

One of the easiest ways to see this phenomenon is to stop the man command and look at the commands it is running. (The man command invokes a pipe to handle its processing.) Figure 9.4 shows what I mean. This figure shows how the man command works on my Linux box. (We'll learn all about the ps, *process status*, command in the next chapter; for now, understand that it just tells us what processes we are running.)

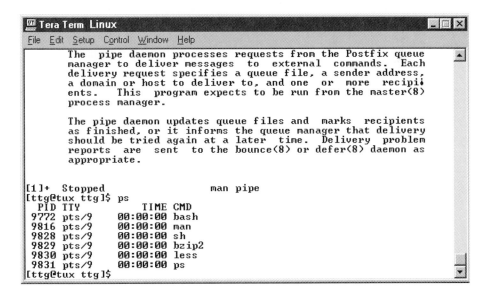

FIGURE 9.4

Processes involved in execution of the man command.

As you can see from the figure, the man process runs three concurrent processes (process I.D.s 9828, 9829, and 9830.) It passes information to the shell (`sh`), which passes it to the `bzip2` process to uncompress it. The uncompressed data are then passed to the `less` command for display.

The important thing to remember about the pipe is that each process in the pipe is running in pseudo-simultaneous execution. As the first few bytes of data move from the first process in the pipe to the second, the second process is initiated. As soon as the second process begins sending output to standard out, which is piped into standard in, of the third process, the third process initiates. Because of this pseudo-simultaneous execution, pipes speed up our processing; they allow us to do more than one thing at a time, or almost at the same time.

I hope you are beginning to see how significant these two features of Thompson and Ritchie's design are. Using ASCII text as a standard interface and creating most commands as filters allows us to build complex data-processing entities that pipe the output from one command into the next and so on. When you begin building scripts, in Chapter 14, you will find many of your scripts contain pipes. In addition, as you begin to work with more and more Unix commands at the command line, you will find pipes to be an invaluable tool. Later in your Unix career you will even find yourself building your own scripts and then using them in pipes!

Tees

Pipes are based on the concept of data flowing through a computer system like water through the pipes in a building. As with plumbing pipes, our pipes also can have a *tee* connection. The difference between a plumbing tee and a tee in a data pipe is that the latter are used to capture only intermediate results. You can save the contents of the pipe at a particular point by using a `tee` command. This is useful both to create files of data and, at least for me, to debug pipes.

Figure 9.5 shows an artist's rendering, (Okay, Okay, I drew it and I'm no artist, but only you and I have to know that) of a data pipe. Notice that the tee in the pipe divides

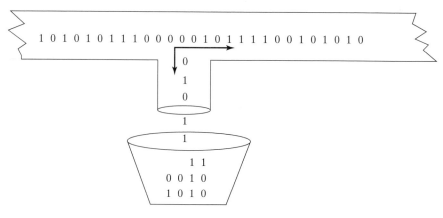

FIGURE 9.5
Rendering of a data pipe.

the data stream, creating a duplicate in the bucket that represents the file. It's important that you remember that *tees cannot be used to split a pipe into two parallel pipes.* That is a common misconception. Tees are used only to capture intermediate values in a pipe. As you can see in Figure 9.6 that can be advantageous.

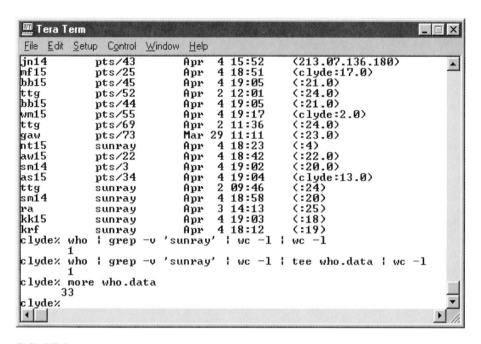

FIGURE 9.6

Using a tee to capture intermediate data.

Figure 9.6 (which looks a lot like Figure 9.3 except that the date is different) shows that the output of the first pipe isn't exactly what I expected. It certainly seems to me that there is more than one person logged on. I wonder what I did wrong. In the second pipe I added a tee to see what was happening (capturing intermediate results). Looking at the file who.data, which contains the result I expected, I see that I have inadvertently added an extra wc command. The last wc command saw only one line, the line containing the number 33. This is an example of using a tee to debug a pipe. You will have numerous opportunities to use tees; they'll become part of your stock in trade.

⊕ Redirection (<, >, >>)

Redirecting Standard Output (>)

Generally, standard input is connected to the keyboard, and standard output and standard error send their data to the monitor. However, as you just learned, you can use pipes to send standard out somewhere other than the monitor. The shells give us other tools to control *from where* a process takes its input, and *to where* a process sends its output. Telling a process to take input from somewhere other than standard input, and/or directing a process to send output or errors somewhere other than the monitor is called **redirection**.

Let's first look at output, because redirecting output or errors is more common than redirecting input. Figure 9.7 shows how easy it is to redirect standard output to file. The right angle bracket (>) tells the shell to send the contents of the data stream that is normally sent to standard output to the specified file instead, in this case today. So with this feature I can store the output of a command, or a pipe, in a file to preserve it.

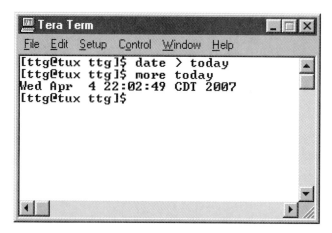

FIGURE 9.7

Using redirection (>) to store data in file.

One way I can use output redirection is to take roll call each day. Figure 9.8 shows how I'd go about doing this. As I mentioned before, we will soon discuss the grep command; for now please understand that we are using it as a selection tool. In the first case it selects lines that start with two characters and then a digit, because all student accounts are formed that way. The second grep should be familiar to you from previous examples. It selects all the lines that do not contain the word sunray. After finding the accounts of just the students who were logged on, I store those data in a file called whoson for later perusal.

If I'm going to use the whoson file for my class roll, I should add the date to the file so I will know the date of the roll. (Yes, since everyone logged an April 7th, I could guess this roll was from that day. I could also put the date in the name of the file. But just work with me here.) Figure 9.9 shows adding the date to the roll file, again using redirection. Oops, there seems to be a little problem with the "whoson" file. I used to have the whole list of who was logged on in that file, but when I redirected the date command into the

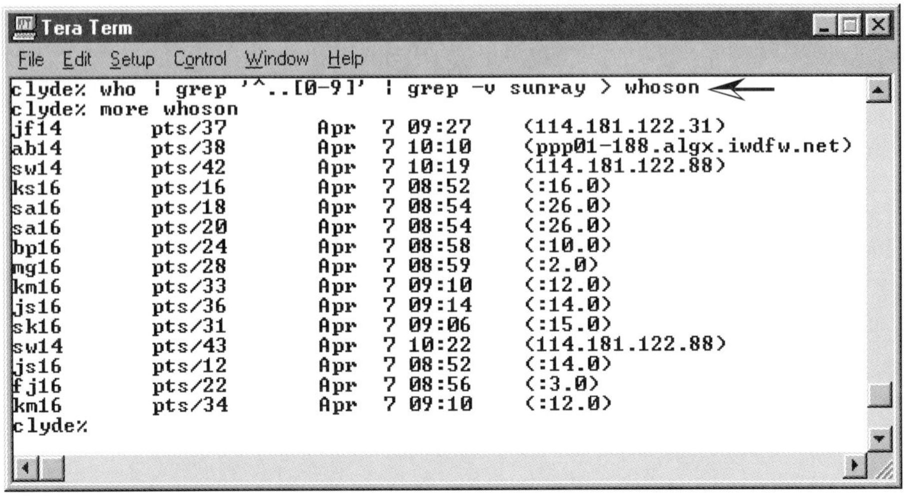

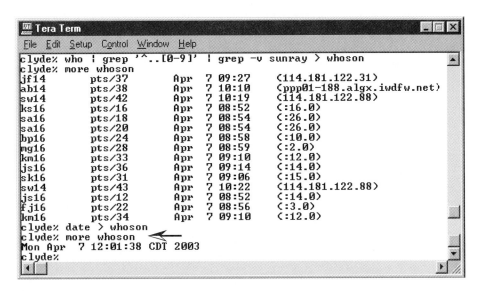

FIGURE 9.8

Redirecting standard output to take roll call.

FIGURE 9.9

Using redirection (>) to put the date into file.

same file I lost the login list. Figure 9.9 illustrates one of the easiest ways I know of to destroy the contents of a file. It also introduces us to Refrigerator Rule No. 4.

Refrigerator Rule No. 4:

When a file is the target of a redirection, the first thing that happens is the next byte pointer is set to byte zero.

Whew, what a long refrigerator rule! Even though it's long, you'll need to remember this refrigerator rule because it will save you a lot of lost files. To understand it, though, you need to understand a little bit more about how Unix writes files. Figure 9.10 is an, ahem, artist's rendition showing what happened the first time we used the whoson file. When I executed the who command and redirected the output to the file whoson, the system created the file and wrote the data to it. The **Next Byte Pointer (NBP)** was set to the next available byte in the file, in this case the byte after the 6 of km16. Had I continued to write to the same file, *without using redirection,* the data I wrote would have been written starting at the next byte pointer. (I realize I shortened the pipe and didn't write all of the data—but I think you get the picture.)

In Figure 9.11, another *artist's* rendering, you can see what happened when I redirected the date command into the existing file. The leftmost file, labeled "existing," shows the file as it looked at the end of the who command. When I executed the date command, redirecting that output to the existing whoson file, the first thing that happened was that the next byte pointer was set to byte zero, as per Refrigerator Rule

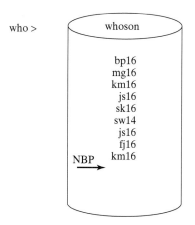

FIGURE 9.10

How data are written to file in Unix.

date > whoson

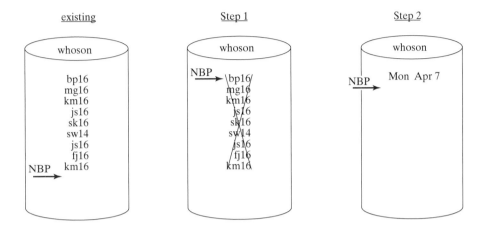

FIGURE 9.11

Redirecting data into an existing file.

No. 4. That action effectively deleted the contents of the entire file, because byte zero, the first byte of file, was now the current byte. In step 2 the shell executed the date command and redirected the output into the now functionally empty file whoson. The next byte pointer was then set to the byte immediately following the last byte of the date.

You may run into a problem playing with this type of redirection. If you, or more likely a kindly system administrator, have set the C shell variable noclobber, you'll be prohibited from overwriting existing files. If you try to redirect standard output more than once to the same file and encounter an error like the one shown in Figure 9.12, you'll need to execute the unset command, also shown in Figure 9.12. The first time I tried to redirect the date command in Figure 9.12, the system refused, telling me that the file whoson already existed. It did this because the shell variable noclobber (meaning don't override, or "clobber," the file) was set. To turn off that particular protection I used the unset command. If you need to unset noclobber to experiment with redirection, remember that the variable exists for your protection. I recommend that you set noclobber as soon as you finish experimenting with redirection.

Some shells (most notably the descendants of the Bourne shell) allow you to use the redirection operator as if it were a command to very efficiently empty a file without removing it. When you become a system administrator you'll use this trick to flush the contents files without having to remove them. Figure 9.13 shows this trick in both the Bourne shell on Solaris and the bash shell on Linux. You can see how the Bourne shell, and a descendent from the Bourne shell, implement redirection to quickly empty a file. Please remember as you experiment with this that *there is no undelete* in Unix. Nor, for that matter, is there an "un-redirect" for standard output.

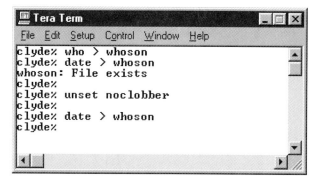

FIGURE 9.12

Handling the noclobber C shell variable.

FIGURE 9.13

Flushing the contents of a file using output redirection.

Appending (>>)

The problem I had with redirection was simply that I used the wrong tool. Rather than redirecting both the output from the date command and the output from the who command into a file, I should have used the append operator: >>. To **append** means to add on to the end of something, in this case to add on to the end of a file.

Figure 9.14 shows how I should have handled the who and date situation. The first thing I did was store the date, using redirection, in the file called whoson. Next I executed the who pipe, appending those data to the data ready in whoson. As you can see from the output of the more command, I now have both the date and a listing of those students who were logged on, in the same file. Being able to append data into a file is so useful—it's something you'll do quite often. However, I will caution you that if you use append with the wrong commands it can quickly create very large files. For the sake of your system administrator's sanity, you need to be careful about the size of files you create with append.

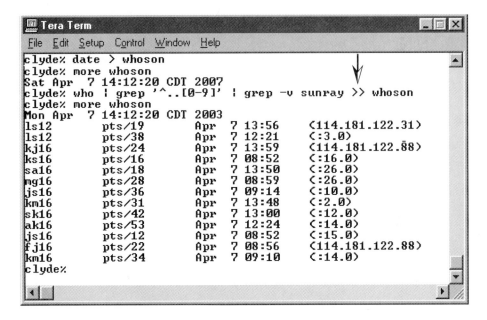

FIGURE 9.14

Creating the roll document with redirection and append.

Redirecting Standard Error

There are times when you may want to send error messages to a file instead of having them appear in the screen. A couple of examples will serve to illustrate this. First, if you're running a script in production, you may want to be able to review the error messages that the script generated but that scrolled off the screen before you could read them. Second, and very important, if you ever create a script that users will use, you need to ensure that they *never see error messages!* Showing the user error messages is like waving a red flag in front of a bull, or poking a stick into a hornet's nest—for some reason it seems to make them crazy. Whoever is handling the troubleshooting for your script, either you or the help desk, will certainly appreciate your users never seeing error messages. By the same token, it's important to save those error messages so you can determine what's going on with your script. The way to do that is to redirect the error messages to a file.

C Shell Family

Sending both standard output and standard error to the *same file* is relatively easy in the C shell. All you need do is add the ampersand (&) after the redirection operator. That will cause *both* standard out and standard error to go to the file specified. Take a look at Figure 9.15 to see an example. Here I first executed an ls command for two different file sets, looking for a file named z and any filename that started with a lower-case t. Since there was no file named z, the shell issued an error message about that, sent to standard error. Then the shell showed me the two filenames starting with t. Those data were sent to standard output. Next I ran the same ls command but redirected standard output to a file called ls_out. I still saw the error message at the command line, because standard error was still pointing to the monitor. However, I didn't see the names of the two files that started with t because those data were sent to standard out, which was redirected to ls_out. When I did a more of the file, I saw the expected output.

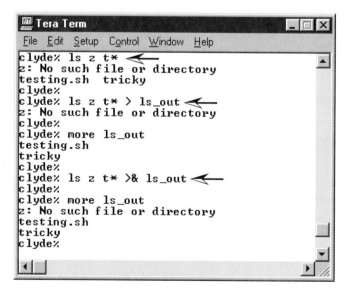

FIGURE 9.15

Sending errors and normal output to same file.

Finally, I executed the `ls` command the third time, redirecting both standard output and standard error to the same file, `ls_out`. The second time I did a `more` of `ls_out`, I saw both the error message and the normal output. By the way, each time I used the file `ls_out` as a target for the redirection I rewrote the file as expected because of what we've learned in Refrigerator Rule No. 4.

"But wait a minute," you ask, "suppose I want to send standard error to one file and standard output to a different file?" Excellent question! You can do it, but it's somewhat tricky in the C shell. Look at Figure 9.16 and I'll show you how it's done.

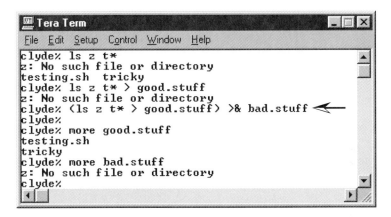

FIGURE 9.16

Sending standard out to one file and standard error to another.

As a bit of a refresher, the first thing I did in Figure 9.16 was just a simple `ls` for the two collections of files I looked for in Figure 9.15. Next, I redirected standard out but not standard error from the same `ls` command to see what was sent to standard error. Then I did the "tricky" thing:

```
(ls z t* > good.stuff) >& bad.stuff
```

This command contains a feature called **sub-shelling**. The part of the command in parentheses is said to be in a sub-shell and is executed first; then the part of the command outside the parentheses is executed. The command inside the parentheses is actually executed in a separate instance of the C shell. We can use this mechanism to fool the C shell. Inside the parentheses we executed the `ls` command and redirected the data that would go to standard out to the file `good.stuff`. Then, when we left the sub-shell, we redirected both the data stream for standard out and the data stream for standard error to the file named `bad.stuff`. Since we had already sent all of the data from standard out to another file (`good.stuff`), there was nothing left in the standard-out data stream, so the only data left in the combined data stream (out and error) were the error messages.

In just a moment we'll take a look at the Bourne shell and you will see that it is much easier to do this type of split-output redirection there, because we can address each file by its number. Remember this particular structure, however, because there will be times when you'll need to do this kind of redirection in the C shell.

Bourne Shell Family

Redirecting standard output and standard error to different files is much easier in the Bourne shell, because it allows you to address each file independently, by number. As you know, three files are given to all processes at process creation time. In the Bourne shell those files are

File 0 (standard input), opened first.

File 1 (standard output), opened second.

File 2 (standard error), opened third.

If you want merely to redirect standard out to file it doesn't matter which shell you are in—you just use the >, and the shell will redirect standard out to the file. If you want to be terribly proper, though, you can use the number in the Bourne shell to redirect standard out as shown in Figure 9.17.

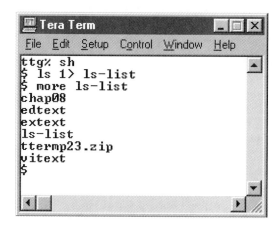

FIGURE 9.17

Oh so properly redirecting standard out in Bourne shell.

The first thing I did in Figure 9.17 was to start an instance of the Bourne shell. Then I redirected the output from the ls command using the Bourne-shell redirection, specifying a file number (1) in the redirection. Next I listed the contents of the file I created just so you could see that the redirection worked. Of course, I could have achieved the same results just using the redirection symbol without the file number, but that wouldn't have been quite so fancy.

In the Bourne shell file numbers simplify sending the data stream that would go to standard out to one file and the data stream that would go to standard error to another file. Figure 9.18 shows how this is done. First I showed the files in the directory. Then I executed an ls that will generate both good output and an error message. Next I ran the same ls command, redirecting standard out (1) to the file gooduns and standard error (2) to the file baduns. Finally, I showed you the contents of both files so you could see that it worked.

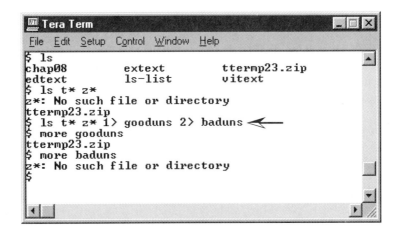

FIGURE 9.18

Sending standard error messages and standard output to different files.

As you remember, sending both standard out and standard error to the same file in the C shell was relatively simple, but it was more complex to send the two data streams to different files. Conversely, in the Bourne shell it's easy to send standard output to one file and standard error to another, but it's a little more, um, "interesting" to send both data streams to the same file. Consider what happened in Figure 9.19.

The first time I executed the ls command and redirected its output in Figure 9.19, I tried to send both standard out (1) and standard error (2) to the same file, output. When I looked at the contents of the file output, I noticed that the entire error

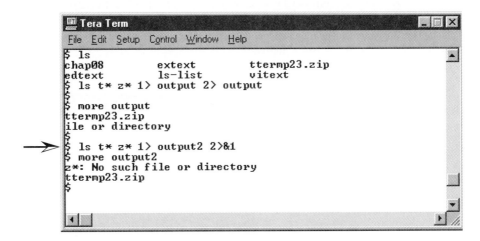

FIGURE 9.19

Sending both output and error data streams to the same file in Bourne shell.

message didn't show up. It seems that both data streams were competing for the same place in the file. Not nice. To solve that problem I used a slightly different syntax the second time I executed the ls command. What I told the shell was, "Send standard out (1) to the file called output2, and while you are at it, send standard error to the same place you are sending file number 1." Actually, as you can see from the second listing, the error message precedes the good output, just as it did in Figure 9.18 at the command line.

While we are talking about redirecting output, especially in the Bourne shell, I need to discuss a special place to send your output. Later on, as you build scripts, you may want to execute a particular command but not care about the output from the command. All you want to know is whether or not the command successfully executed. We will see this again in scripting, because each command in Unix sends a value back to the shell called the **return code** that tells the shell whether or not the command executed successfully. A return code of 0(zero) says, "Hey, everything worked just fine!" A non-zero return code indicates the command encountered some sort of error during its execution. Suppose, for example, we wondered whether the current directory contained any files starting with a lowercase t, but we didn't care what the names of the files were. (Okay, it's a contrived example, I know, but just stay with me because this principle will be important in scripting.) Figure 9.20 shows an example of how I would code this. The variable $? contains the return code of the previous command.

The part of Figure 9.20 that I want you to focus on is the *place* I redirected standard out and standard error. There is an almost magical black hole in every Unix system, the place where data goes and is never heard from again. It's under the device (/dev) file structure and is called the **null device**. Anything sent to /dev/null (this location is pronounced dev-null, you don't vocalize the slashes) disappears, without even a trace, forever.

All the output from the ls command I executed in Figure 9.20 went to the null device. When I echoed (output) the status of the previous command, I saw a zero, showing that the command was successful (it found at least one file that started with a lowercase t.) You'll also find that /dev/null is something of an inside joke in the Unix community. From time to time you hear someone say, "So-and-so came by my desk and was in babble mode, but I just redirected his output to /dev/null".

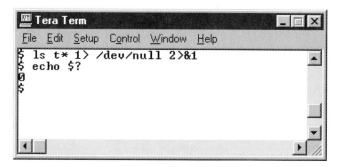

FIGURE 9.20

Sending all output to the bit bucket.

Now that you know about /dev/null, you can appreciate another one of these delightfully subtle elements of Unix humor.

Redirecting Standard Input (<)

It's much less common to redirect standard input than to redirect either standard output or, most commonly, standard error. However, in Chapter 12 will see that there is still one command, the `tr`, or *translate*, command, that requires input be redirected, or piped, into it. Other commands have evolved over time to anticipate the redirection of standard input. For example, when you type

```
cat myfile
```

you are, in effect, typing

```
cat < myfile
```

but since the `cat` command has evolved, you don't need to use the redirection of standard input into the command. Other than the translate command, the most frequent place you'll use redirection of standard input is in scripts. We'll get into that in detail in Chapter 14.

Here Document

Since we're already playing around with redirecting standard input, I'd like to introduce you to the *here document*, the last of the redirection-type operators. The term *here document* and the << command were added to Unix by Steve Bourne in the seventh edition of the research system. The reason he called it a here document was because the source of the input for the command was here, starting on the next line, right here.

This feature, while not unique to the Bourne shell, is significant in that it allows the scriptor to build the actual input stream for a command inside the script. It became necessary to do this in the seventh edition because machines were getting faster and commands were beginning to "read ahead," making the results of mixing data and commands unreliable. Dennis Ritchie shared the following pair of examples with me. In the sixth and earlier editions most interactive programs read only one character at a time, so it worked to have the following snippet of code in a program:

```
ed file
1,$s/X/Y/
w
q
echo "Done!"
```

The success of this code depended on the ed command reading only one character at a time and stopping when it read the q for quit. If the shell started reading ahead (buffering), then the echo statement could be included in the ed directives. Bourne tried to fix that. By adding notation that delimited the input stream for the command, he allowed the shell to buffer and still not overrun the end of the directives stream.

In the Bourne shell, the ed directives would look something like this:

```
ed file << !
1,$s/X/Y/
w
q
!
echo "Done!"
```

Allowing the shell to identify both the beginning and end of the data stream (standard input) for a specific command allowed programmers to enhance scripts with this sort of construct. Notice the bang serving as the delimiter in Dennis' example. That is another common practice, especially when the here document contains a series of directives for a command.

Here documents are often found in scripts, most often used to present "preformatted" output to the user. They are sometimes also used to direct a series of data into a command. Figure 9.21 shows a small shell script that demonstrates a simple here document. The top two-thirds of the figure show the actual code for the script. The first menu I created using an echo command, the common output command in scripts that sends the data following it to standard output. In the second half of the script I used a here document that starts with this line:

```
cat << EOF
```

and ends with this line:

```
EOF
```

Everything after the first line of the here document up to but *not* including the last line marker will be sent to the cat command, which in turn sends it to standard output. While the use of the three-character string EOF is a common "end of here document" marker, it is not required, nor is a magical bang (!). I could equally well use the character string blivit or KAZAM or any other character string I like as the delimiter for the here document. (Well, that's not exactly true. The character string I choose needs to contain no white space. It also shouldn't be a Unix command. But other than that there's room to be a bit creative!)

One absolutely critical thing to know about the "end of here document" marker is that it must be the *only data* on that line. No leading or trailing spaces are allowed. Figure 9.22 shows an example of this. I have seen students spend hours trying to debug

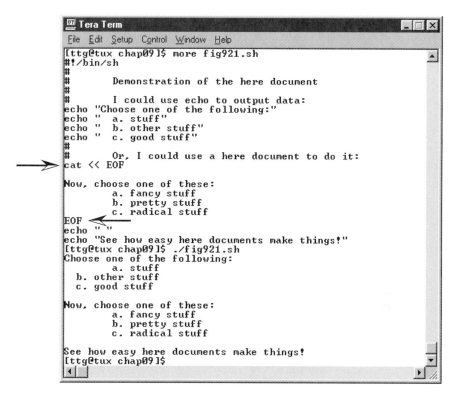

FIGURE 9.21

Using a here document to output a menu.

a here document that doesn't work because of a problem like the one I created in this figure. Let's look at that problem.

You'll notice in Figure 9.22 I first ran the script and then showed you the contents. The here document didn't stop with the EOF string. Rather, it continued and displayed the rest of the script. You could spend a long time looking at the code without seeing what was wrong (I know, I've done it!). That's because the problem is invisible. It so happens that there's a space after the F of EOF. Because the delimiter must be the *only thing* on the line for the here document to terminate, a delimiter plus a space doesn't work. This is a very subtle error but one that can drive you absolutely crazy if you don't remember to avoid it.

Here documents will be much more important to you as you develop shell scripts, but I discussed them in this section because they are fairly closely related to the other types of redirection.

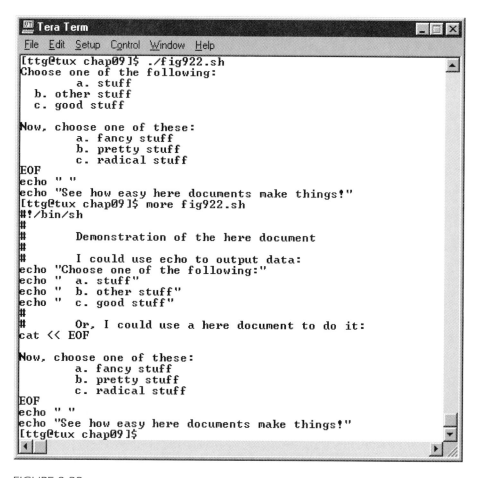

FIGURE 9.22

A here document with a problem.

alias

```
alias [options] [newname "command string"]
```

In day-to-day conversation, an alias is usually another name for a person. In the C shell and its descendants, an **alias** is much more—it is a way to create a wholly new command, or to create a special instance of an existing command. If you have a conservative system administrator, like me, you may already have some aliases set for you. For example, I created aliases for the dangerous commands like rm, cp, and mv so that in each case the command acted as if the -i option had been included.

Figure 9.23 shows an example of the three aliases that I set by default for my students (and for that matter, for myself.) With these three aliases set, each time one of my

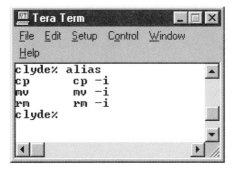

FIGURE 9.23

Three valuable aliases.

students (or I) types the rm command, the C shell uses the alias for the rm command and acts as if the student (or I) typed rm -i. Having these commands aliased provides an extra level of protection.

You can create aliases for commands, pipes, or even to execute a shell script. Figure 9.24 shows how you can use **alias** to create a new command. Here I used it to create the new command called load. I can use this new command to tell me how many people are currently logged into the computer. In other words, I can use it to find out the load on the system. In the first line I typed in the load command so you could see that it didn't exist before I used alias to create it.

Folks new to Unix sometimes get carried away creating aliases. It seems to be a very seductive tool. As handy as aliases are, becoming dependent on them is fraught with danger, for several reasons.

First, they aren't always there. I have heard horrible alias stories from a couple of my Unix students who were given practical tests while being interviewed for Unix jobs. In one instance, before I knew I should forbid them, one of my students had created a series of DOS aliases for Unix. He aliased dir to ls, type to cat, and things like that.

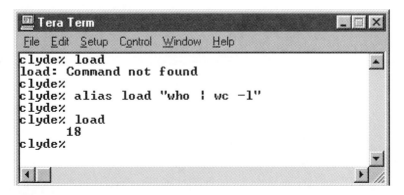

FIGURE 9.24

Using alias to create new command.

Then, during his practical test, rather than typing `ls`, he typed `dir`; and when he wanted to look at a file, rather than typing `cat`, he typed `type`! Needless to say, the folks he was interviewing with were not amused. He didn't get the job.

By the same token, many of my students run into problems when they move into the Bourne shell (the Bourne shell does not support aliasing), because they become too comfortable with the aliases they built and those I created for them. For example, one student was a little lazy and typed `rm -r` at the Bourne shell prompt because she wanted to remove four files, with different names, from the dozens in her directory. She expected the remove command to prompt her for the removal of each file and was a little puzzled when all she saw was the command prompt. When she did an `ls` and realized that all of her files had been removed, she said some of the most unprintable things!

Another danger is that if you always use aliases you can forget the actual commands. This is a special problem when you move into a shell like the Bourne shell that doesn't support aliasing. If the only way you know how to perform a particular operation is to use the alias for it, and the alias doesn't exist, you're in trouble. I see this problem most often when students move from the C shell, which supports aliasing, to the Bourne shell. A very rude awakening awaits some students.

One more reason to avoid becoming dependent on aliases is that you create an alias to an existing command that you seldom use, you might forget you've done so. Obviously, the result could be frustrating. It's best to confine aliasing to frequently used commands like copy and remove.

All in all, while aliases are very useful, you need to be careful with them. If you're in an older version of Unix, you also need to be careful about creating the infinite, or recursive, alias. Figure 9.25 shows an example of this. Please don't do it on your system! Fortunately for me, Solaris can recognize a recursive, or looping, alias. As you can see the command up was aliased to down, and down was aliased to up. Had the shell tried to execute the down command, it would have looked to the alias table and executed the up command, which was aliased to the down command, which was aliased to the up command ... I think you see the picture, and it isn't pretty. Recursive aliasing can cause serious problems in systems that don't intercept it.

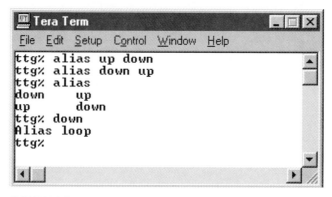

FIGURE 9.25
Creating a recursive alias—a Bad Thing!

Rules for Creating Aliases

If you're going to create aliases here are a few rules that will help you create meaningful, useful, yet safe aliases.

1. If you create an alias to an existing command, make sure you know the ramifications of that alias. For example, creating the alias `rm -r` for the remove command might have serious implications depending on where you use it.

2. Don't use one-character aliases. I realize it's very tempting to alias a single letter to a command, but it is very bad practice. Aliases can be combined with command-line parameters. If you create the alias with the trailing space after the definition, then the shell will try to interpret anything following the alias to see if it is also an alias. It's very easy to get in trouble if you have single character aliases that could be interpreted when used as command-line parameters.

3. Don't create aliases that look like commands in other operating systems. While it may be "cute" to do so in some very limited instances, if you get used to those aliases, you can look like a blooming idiot on the machine of someone who doesn't share your humor.

4. Don't create aliases that use questionable language. You may think it's most amusing to be able to type profanity on the command line and have Unix perform tasks for you. Be advised that many people could be offended, and one of them could be your boss!

5. Don't build an alias for a command until you *completely* understand that command. Remember that an `alias` is shorthand to help you be more efficient. Until you understand the command and can use it without the alias, you will not increase your efficiency, just your vulnerability. You always need to be able to run commands without using aliases, because they won't always be there.

If you follow these rules, and are very judicious when you create aliases, I think you'll be able to use them to create useful tools.

As you may have seen in Figure 9.23 (duplicated in Figure 9.26 so you don't have to page back), if you issue the alias command without any parameters it will show you

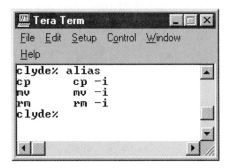

FIGURE 9.26

Duplicate of Figure 9.23.

a list of the aliases currently available to you. It's always wise to know what aliases you're working with. Your system administrator may have created aliases for you, as I do for my students, and you need to know that. You may have created aliases yesterday and forgotten what they were. One of the things I habitually do when I log on to a new system is check the aliases. Then I know what I am working with.

unalias

```
unalias [-a] [alias]
```

So, you have an alias you don't like. Let's make it go away. The **unalias** command removes the alias from the alias table. You can remove a *single* alias using the unalias command followed by the alias you wish to remove, or you can remove *all* the aliases for that particular session by using the -a, or *all*, option.

Since aliases are a feature of the shell, they exist only for the life of that particular shell. If you unalias some aliases in your current instance of the shell, they may well reappear when you invoke another instance of the same shell. (We will talk about automagically creating aliases each time you invoke the shell in a few pages.) Consider the situation in Figure 9.27. The first time I executed the alias command here, it showed the four aliases normally set for the C shell on my system. Next I created the alias load to see how many people were on the system. I ran the alias command again to show that my new alias was now in the alias table. Then I started a new instance of the C shell (see the arrow.) Finally, I executed the alias command a third time, now in the new instance of the shell, to prove that the alias I created in the previous shell was not here. This example proves that aliases are one of the many shell-dependent entities we will encounter.

I need to warn you about a phenomenon that happens to many new Unix users. As they develop their Unix skills they suddenly decide that "safe" aliases like those shown in Figure 9.27 are restrictive and boring. They think they are too good to need that kind of safety net, so they unalias all of the aliases set for them. Then they blithely go about their day-to-day business proud of the fact that they don't need their "training wheels" anymore. All's right with the world until suddenly they make a small mistake. For example, they forget they are in their home directory and think they're in a temporary subdirectory they created. They remove all files. Since there is no rm -i alias, the shell politely and quickly removes every file in their home directory. That's when they come to me and ask about some sort of undelete command. Most of the time, after one experience like that, the "training wheels" go back on, and the student is more than happy to have a little safety net. Now I'm sure you will never do anything like that, but just in case, I thought I'd share my students' experiences with you.

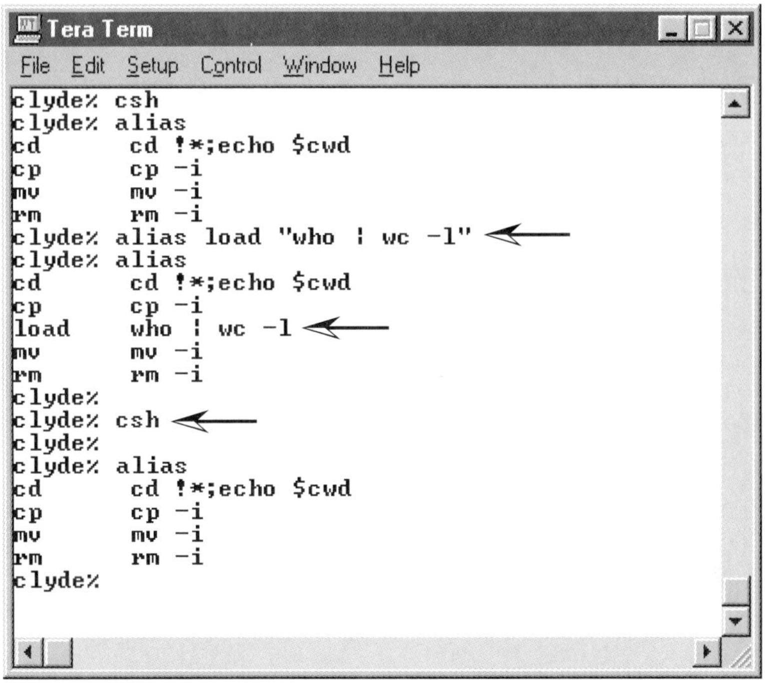

FIGURE 9.27

An example showing that aliases exist only for the instance of the shell in which they were created.

diff

```
diff [options] file1 file2
```

The **diff** command is one of those special-purpose commands that don't seem to be of much value when you first learn them, but in retrospect are very useful. This command has several options that enable you to do some very powerful things, but for now I'd like to focus on the common uses. The vast majority of the time when I use the diff command I use it to see what changes have been made in a particular file. For example, Figure 9.28 shows two different instances of an employee file, emp1.dat and emp2.dat.

The first, emp1.dat, is the original version of the file. The second, emp2.dat, is the updated version. By just looking at the two files, it's difficult to see what changes were made, but if we use the diff tool, the differences are obvious, as you can see in Figure 9.29.

Did you find all three differences just by looking at the files in Figure 9.28? Let's examine the output from the diff command, shown in Figure 9.29. It looks a little

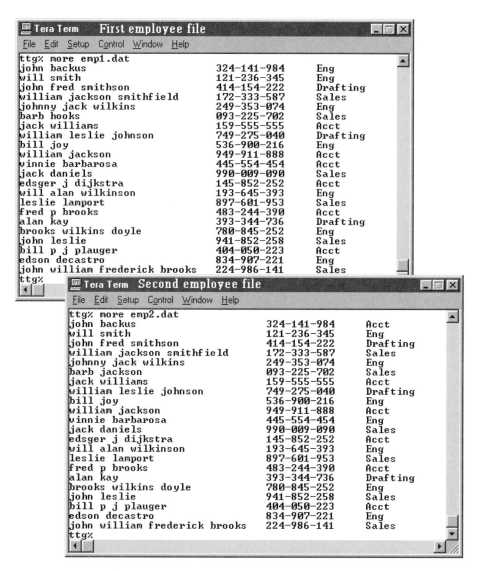

FIGURE 9.28

Two instances of an employee file.

strange, hmmm, perhaps similar to something we have seen before. What it tells us is that John Backus changed from the engineering department to the accounting department, Barb Hooks became Barb Jackson, and Vinnie Barbarosa moved from accounting to engineering. The output almost looks like a series of ed editor commands.

Using one of the options to diff, the -e (ed commands) option, generates output that is a series of ed commands necessary to make the first file look like the second file. Figure 9.30 shows what that output looks like. And I have a question for you about that output: why are the changes in reverse order?

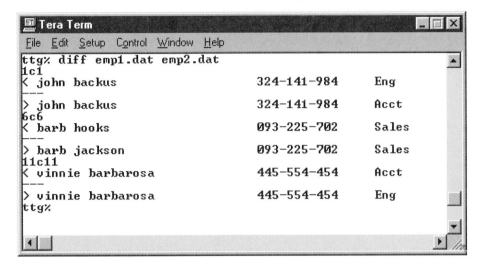

FIGURE 9.29

Using diff to find differences between two files.

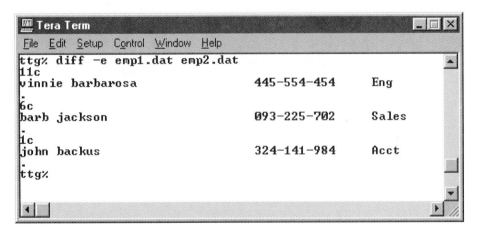

FIGURE 9.30

Generating a set of ed commands from diff.

The problem with the ed command output format is that it doesn't tell me what the differences are between the two files, but only that those three lines need to be changed. The first format we saw in Figure 9.29 is more useful in determining what's happened to the file. Since I maintain a Web server at the school, I often use diff to see what changes my users made to their pages over the course of a week or two. That makes it easy for me keep track of things that my users are changing.

The diff command tells you differences between two files, but what about finding different lines in a file?

uniq

```
uniq [options] file1
```

Sometimes you will have a process that writes a log file, indicating either normal execution or some small problem (or if you're having a really bad day, indicating really horrible problems). In this case, you might appreciate being able to compress duplicate lines into a single line, which makes reading a file a lot easier. Unix had such tool; it's called **uniq**.

You can use the uniq command to remove duplicate, concurrent lines. Figure 9.31 shows part of a very long, ugly log file called, not surprisingly, uglylog. This file is on the Web site if you really want to spend the time to peruse the whole thing. As you can see from Figure 9.31, most of the lines of the file contain the words All OK, but once in a while there's an error message. Obviously you don't want to spend hours, or even minutes, scrolling through line after line after line of the same thing looking for the occasional error message. That would be boring, and what's more, you could inadvertently miss a critical error. To be efficient, let's use the uniq command to compress all of the concurrent, duplicate lines into a single line. That's what I've done in Figure 9.32, and wow, it certainly is easy to look at compared to Figure 9.31. In addition, using wc, I can see the five error messages that were imbedded in the 1157 lines of the uglylog file.

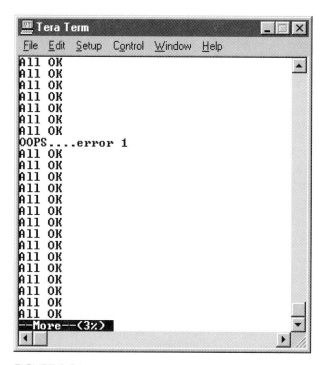

FIGURE 9.31
Part of the uglylog file.

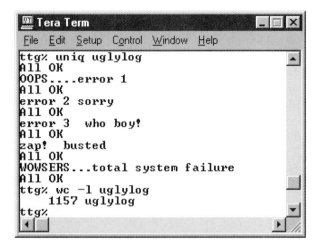

FIGURE 9.32

Output from the uniq command.

The most interesting option to the uniq command, in my opinion, is the *counting* option, -c. Figure 9.33 is the same uniq I ran in Figure 9.32, with the addition of this option. This result is a lot of information. The number of lines between error lines could possibly tell us how long the system ran between errors. Let's say, for example, that the

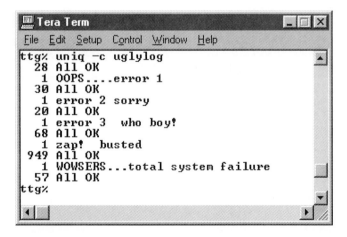

FIGURE 9.33

Using the -c option with uniq.

process output a message every 30 minutes. If so, it ran for 14 hours before the first error, 15 hours before the second error, and so on.

One small potential problem when you use the `uniq` command is that if you confuse the `diff` command with the `uniq` command, you can destroy the contents of a file without any warning. Consider the situation depicted in Figure 9.34. Look closely at the information presented. The first command in the figure, the `ls`, shows that I have two `uglylogs` that are about the same size. The next thing that I did was a `uniq` of `uglylog1` and `uglylog2`. There seems to have been no output! That's a little strange. On the second `ls`, did you notice that `uglylog2` suddenly became much smaller? Let's have a look at that second log file, in Figure 9.35.

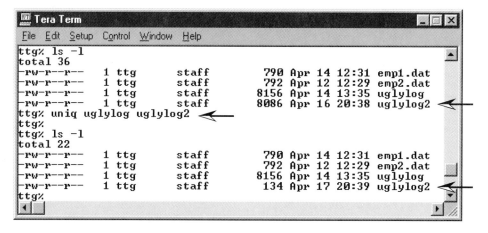

FIGURE 9.34

Misuse of the `uniq` command.

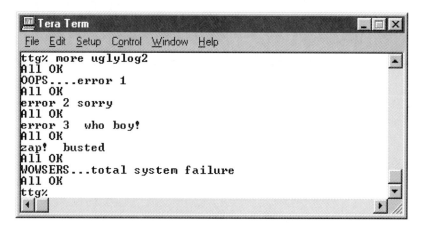

FIGURE 9.35

The result of misusing `uniq`.

Uh oh, it seems that my second log file has been replaced by the *output* from the uniq command in Figure 9.35. That's the danger I mentioned to you earlier: if you confuse diff and uniq and code uniq with two files instead of one, uniq will dutifully act as if you had redirected the output from the command into the second file. Most of the time that's a Bad Thing.

Oh, yes, right after presenting Figure 9.30 I asked you a question about the order of the file. The answer is, "Because, working from the bottom up, anything that changes the number of lines in the file won't affect subsequent edits, and all the line numbers are still good." But you figured that out yourself, didn't you!

Now that we investigated a couple of file-processing commands, let's look at some concepts and tools that can make your computer life a little easier.

⊕ Filename Completion

Many times we find ourselves burdened with long, albeit meaningful filenames that are a bugger to type. This is especially true if you suffer from fat-finger disease, the disease that causes your fingers to leap to different keys than you intended as you type, especially when you near the end of a long and complex command. What you are probably wishing for is some automagical way to have the shell type the filename for you. Enter filename completion!

Most of the shells, except the Bourne shell, support some form of filename completion. The differences among the shells are primarily which keys invoke this handy operation. Figure 9.36 shows some long filenames that are no fun to type, and the start

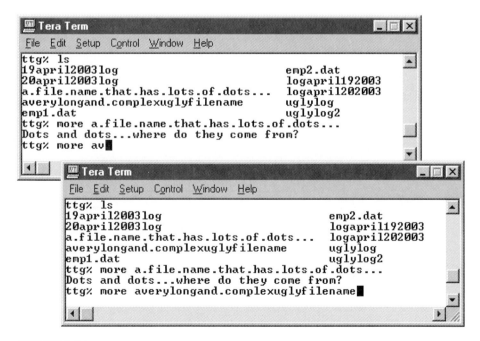

FIGURE 9.36

Using filename completion.

of an additional filename on the command line. Rather than typing that long filename, I simply touched the ESC key (or the TAB key in the bash shell). The second screen capture in Figure 9.36 shows what happened.

That's what I call efficiency! I touched a single key, ESC, and the system completed the filename for me, adding 30 characters. In the Solaris C shell, the ESC key activates filename completion once it's been turned on. In the bash shell, the TAB key does the same.

Filename completion is an example of a particular kind of shell variable called a *switch* or *toggle*. You turn on, or turn off filename completion much like you turn on or off a light switch. (And, yes, it is like the toggle noclobber.) In the C shell you turn on filename completion using a set command:

```
set filec
```

Once you type that, you can use the ESC key after typing a partial filename and the shell will complete it for you—that is, as long as what you have typed is unique, so the shell knows which filename you want.

Look at the top screen capture in Figure 9.37, I've tried to use filename completion, but the partial filename I typed isn't unique. I tried to use filename completion after typing

```
more log<ESC>
```

but since there was more than one filename that started with log, the shell didn't know which one I wanted to see. It completed the filename as far as it could, "logapril," and then rang the terminal bell and waited for me to give more indication of the filename I wanted to see.

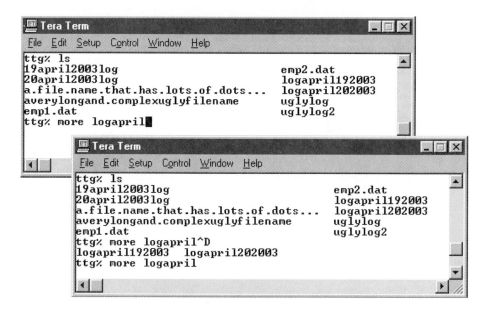

FIGURE 9.37

Using filename completion without a unique filename.

The second screen capture in Figure 9.37 shows another feature of filename completion in the shell. I know the file names are on the top of the screen, but let's pretend I didn't remember the names of the files that started with logapril. I ask the shell to show me the filenames that could be potential matches by entering a Ctrl-D (^D). It lists the two files that match the search string, then goes back to the command I originally entered and waits for more information. Using Ctrl-D this way can save a lot of time if you don't remember the exact filenames you are looking for.

Take another look at the files listed in Figure 9.37. Notice that there are two pairs of April log files shown. The first pair start with the date and the second pair with the character string logapril. Now that you know about filename completion, which pair of file names would be more efficient to use? Obviously, filenames that are unique as close as possible to the beginning of the name allow us to use filename completion most efficiently. To identify the second filename of the first pair, all I need to enter is the command

```
more 2<ESC>
```

and I have identified a unique filename that the shell can complete for me. On the other hand, to identify the second filename of the second pair, I must enter

```
more logapril2<ESC>
```

before I have created a unique string that the shell can complete for me.

Creating useful, easily completed filenames is very important if you wish to use filename completion efficiently. I urge you to keep filename completion in mind as you create your filenames. When I visit my students working at commercial sites, I can tell which system administrators and users appreciate filename completion simply by glancing at the filenames in their directories.

Filename completion works slightly differently in the Linux bash shell, as you can see in Figure 9.38. Here I typed the following:

```
more s<TAB>
```

The Linux bash shell immediately presented me with all the possible filenames that were potential matches. I didn't need to use Ctrl-D <^D>. This is a small difference, but it is useful.

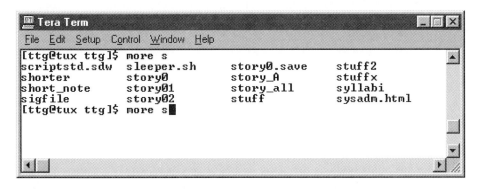

FIGURE 9.38

Using filename completion in Linux bash shell.

To reiterate, if you create filenames that are unique toward the beginning of the name, rather than toward the end, you will find that filename completion makes you very efficient. (And no, story0, story01, story02, story_A, and story_all aren't efficient names, but I *like* them ☺)

⊕ Shell Variables

The shell is both the user interface and a very complex programming environment. You will learn how to program in the shell in Chapter 14. At this juncture I would like to look at a small portion of the programming environment provided by the shell: variables. Each shell has its own unique, predefined variables, and we will explore both Bourne and C shell variables in just a bit. Before we look at the specific variables unique to each shell, though, we need to take a moment to talk about what variables really are.

Variables and Variable Names

In the common vernacular, a variable is something that, well varies, or changes. From a programmer's point of view, that isn't exactly the right definition. A variable isn't so much a "what" as much as it is a "where." Let's define it this way: A **variable** is the general term we use to describe a mnemonic representation for place in memory and the data stored at that location. In other words, a variable is a memory location where some particular data are stored. The **variable name** is the human-meaningful—at least to the creator it's meaningful—mnemonic we use to represent a particular memory location in our code. For some reason people find it easier to remember a programming statement like

```
total_pay = base_sal + otime
```

than something like

```
DB6FFD = FDB774 + EB7448
```

although for the life of me I can't see why.

Variable names, then, refer to places in memory where we store data. By that same process of logic, a **variable value** is that datum we store at the variable name.

Now that we know what variables are, let's see how to create C shell variables.

set

```
set [var [= value]]
```

The **set** command has two uses: first, it can show us which C shell variables have been set; and second, it can create new variables or change the value of existing shell variables. Figure 9.39 shows you the shell variables that have been set in a simple C shell on a Solaris 8 box. You have seen some of these variables, like filec, before. Now look at

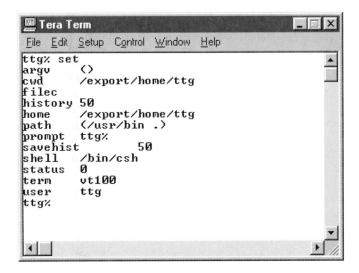

FIGURE 9.39

Values displayed by set command in C shell.

some of the others. You'll see some interesting things. For example, the variables used here show us the current working directory, the fact that I have enabled history and am storing 50 commands, my home directory, my prompt, and even who I am. Actually, that's a staggering amount of information.

In addition to showing us what variables are already set, we can use the set command to assign values to variable names. Take a look at Figure 9.40. I created a variable, best, and assigned the value Unix to the location specified by that variable name. Notice the syntax. When you declare shell variables it is a good idea, and sometimes required, to have no white space surrounding the equal sign (=). Nevertheless, as you can see from Figure 9.41, the Solaris C shell is quite forgiving if you fail to heed this guideline.

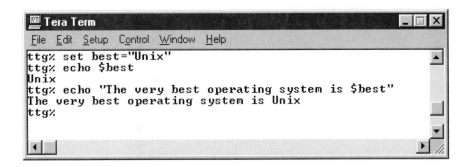

FIGURE 9.40

Setting a value for a shell variable and then displaying that value.

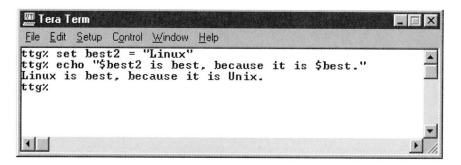

FIGURE 9.41

Using set command in C shell with spaces.

In both Figure 9.40 and Figure 9.41 I used the echo command to display the contents of the shell variables. Notice that in each case, when I wanted to display the *contents* of the shell variable I preceded the variable name with a dollar sign ($). Both the Bourne and C shells use this same syntax to display the contents of a variable.

Figure 9.42 shows what happens when I forget to put the dollar sign in front of a variable name. As you can see, the shell doesn't know that a particular string is a variable name without the dollar sign. Therefore, it doesn't interpret it as an address but instead considers it a string and displays it that way.

Creating shell variables in the C shell requires the use of the set command. The Bourne shell is more straightforward. In Figure 9.43 I performed the same variable value assignments and displays that I did in Figures 9.40 through 9.42. The difference is that Figure 9.43 shows us the Bourne, actually the bash, shell. In the bash shell all I need to do is specify the variable name and then set it equal to (assign it) the value I wish stored at that location. I created the best and best2 variables and displayed them using the echo command. I also included incorrect white space in the third assignment statement, and the shell gave me an error because it tried to interpret the variable name as a command.

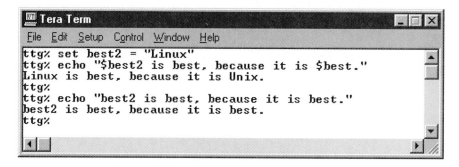

FIGURE 9.42

Trying to display contents of variable without the leading $.

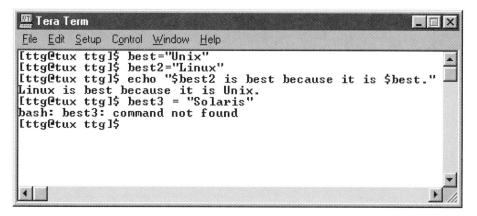

FIGURE 9.43

Setting variable values in Bourne (bash) shell.

One of the drawbacks of shell variables is that they are, well, *shell* variables. That means the variable name and its associated value exist only for the life of and in a particular instance of a shell. Figure 9.44 shows how this can be a small problem. I created two shell variable names, best and best2 and assigned them values. Next I displayed the values using the echo command. Then I forked a new instance of the C shell and tried to display the two variable values again. No such luck! Suddenly, the variable I had just created was undefined. Why? Because the variables I created are local to a particular instance of the shell, and the new C shell doesn't know about them.

There are two ways to solve this problem. First, I could let all the subsequent instances of the C shell know about the variables by including them in the C shell environment. Second, I could tell the shell to create the variables when it, the shell, started. We will explore that possibility in a few pages.

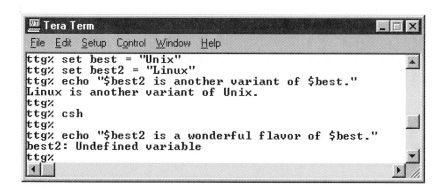

FIGURE 9.44

The problem with the scope of a shell variable.

setenv

```
setenv [var [value]]
```

The first way we can let other instances of the C shell know about a particular variable is to cause that variable to become an environmental variable rather than a variable known only to the local instance of the shell. I can use the **setenv** command to make a particular variable part of the current C shell environmental variable set for any C shell process created by this process. Figure 9.45 shows how I can make bests an environmental variable in the C shell.

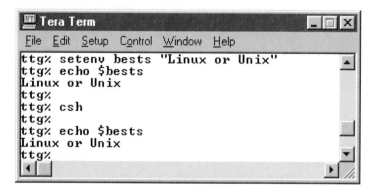

FIGURE 9.45

Using setenv to make a variable an environmental variable.

In the first part of the figure I used the setenv command to create the environmental variable "bests" with a value of "Linux or Unix". I then echoed the contents of that variable to show that the value had indeed been set. Next I forked a new shell and immediately echoed the same variable, showing that the variable and its value carry over from shell instance to shell instance. (For those of you who are purists, environmental variables are normally created in all uppercase letters. I chose not to do so here so that the variable name would be similar to those in the previous figures.) Finally, I used the echo command to display the contents of the bests variable in the new instance of the shell, proving that the new shell also knew the value of a particular variable.

unsetenv

```
unsetenv var
```

To remove a variable from the environment, you simply need to **unsetenv** the variable and it will be removed from the list of environmental variables for that shell and all subsequent shells you fork from that shell.

This can get little confusing. Look carefully at Figure 9.46 and notice what I have done. (I realize it is a long and complex figure, but we will puzzle it out together.) There are a number of steps here, so I numbered them to make the procedure easier to follow.

1. I executed a ps command to show that there was only one process, the C shell, currently running.

2. Next I created an environmental variable called quote, gave it a value, and then displayed the value of that variable. (Notice: sentenv doesn't use an assignment operator(=).

3. In this step I forked a new C shell. (I am now in C shell no. 2.)

4. In the new shell I displayed the value of the environmental variable to prove that it was indeed an environmental variable.

5. At this point I issued the unsetenv command for the environmental variable quote, so in C shell no. 2 the variable no longer exists.

6. I forked another new C shell. (I am now in C shell no. 3.)

7. I attempted to display the contents of the variable quote and found that it did not exist. (This is what I expected, since I had removed it.)

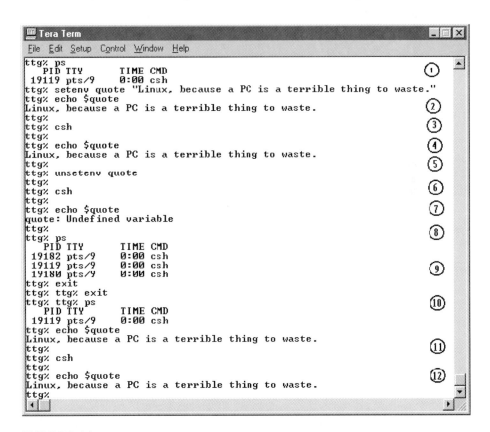

FIGURE 9.46

Following the trail of an environmental variable across shells.

8. This ps command shows that I have indeed three C shells.

9. I exit twice, bringing me back to the original shell (the question now is, "Does the variable quote still have a value?)

10. Echoing the value for the variable quote, I find that, indeed, it still has a value!

11. Once more I forked a C shell.

12. Now, in a new C shell no. 2, the environmental variable quote still has a value.

Okay, so what does all this prove? Well, it proves that environmental variables can be set by a shell and passed on to every shell forked from that original shell. It also shows that if we unsetenv an environmental variable, none of the shells forked *from that shell* will have access to the variable. This is a very important concept, and will be even more important later. If you're at all confused at this point, please go back and study the example in Figure 9.46 again.

In Figure 9.39 you saw variables that are set by default in the C shell. It is only fair that you see some bash shell variables as well. Figure 9.47 shows some of the variables that are set in the bash shell on my system. The screen capture shows a subset of all these values. Linux creates many more shell variables, for several reasons, the most significant being that it's running the X-windows system for me. The obvious

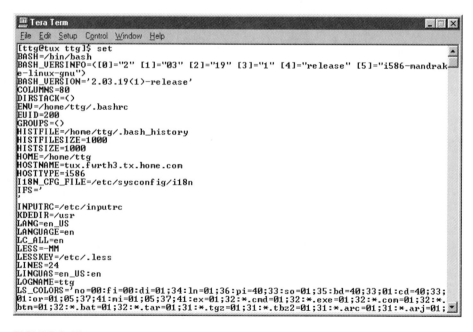

FIGURE 9.47

Some bash shell variables.

difference between the C shell variables and bash shell variables, besides that there are a lot more bash shell variables, is that the bash shell variables are all in uppercase. If you're running the bash shell, you can explore the variables created in your instance of the shell.

To complete our study, Figure 9.48 shows a subset of the variables created in the Bourne shell. Each shell has some unique variables associated with it, and some that are common across all the shells. The variables in the Bourne shell look similar to those in the bash shell (oh, big surprise, since the bash shell is descended from the Bourne shell), but each shell also maintains some unique variables. Like the bash shell, the Bourne shell variables are coded in uppercase.

As you begin programming in the Bourne shell, shell variables will become even more important to you. For now, it's enough to know that each shell has a set of variables it uses to control its environment and interact with you, the user. Now let's see how to pass the value of variable from one instance of the Bourne, or bash, shell to the next.

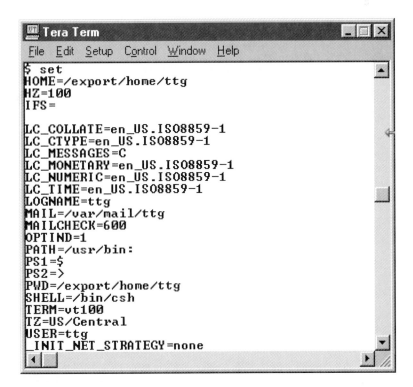

FIGURE 9.48

Some Bourne shell variables.

export

```
export var [= value]
```

As you as you saw, the Bourne, or bash, shell handles variables a little bit differently. By the same token, it uses different commands to make shell variables available to subsequent instances of the shell. Figure 9.49 shows an example of this process. Okay, one more time by the numbers:

1. I set the shell variable super to the value "Solaris".
2. Next I forked a new instance of the bash shell.
3. Using echo, I attempted to examine the value associated with the variable name super, and the shell demonstrated that the variable was empty. (Note: this is another difference between the Bourne shell and the C shell; the Bourne shell shows you what's there, or what's not there, whereas the C shell reports an error.)
4. I exited from the second shell, which dropped me back to my original shell.

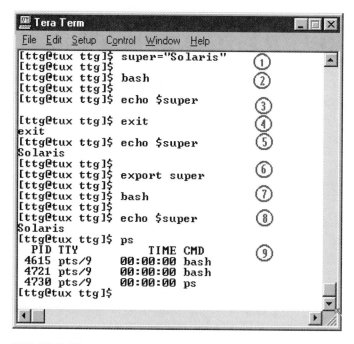

FIGURE 9.49

Setting a variable to be available to other bash shells.

5. To verify that I was in the original shell, I displayed the value associated with the variable name super.

6. Next I issued the **export** command which made the variable super known to any subsequent shell.

7. I forked another new instance of the bash shell.

8. Again I attempted to display the value associated with the variable name super and was successful.

9. To verify that I was indeed in a new shell, I used the ps command to display the currently running processes.

If you need to pass variable names and their associated values to subsequent shells, you can use the setenv command in the C shell or the export command in the Bourne (and bash) shells. As we will learn when we discuss process control, it is possible for the parent process to modify the environment of the child process, but the child process cannot modify the parent. Figure 9.50 shows an example of this. Most of what I did here should be familiar to you, so I will just discuss it briefly.

First, in the bash shell I created a new variable, displayed its contents, and exported it. I then forked a new bash shell and again displayed the contents of the variable to prove that it had been successfully exported. Here's where it gets interesting. I changed the value associated with the variable and displayed the value, proving it had changed. I next exited from that child process (in this instance the shell). In the original shell I displayed the value associated with the variable again, and saw that it had *not been altered* in the original shell. Using a data file is the only way I know of for child process to pass data back to the parent process.

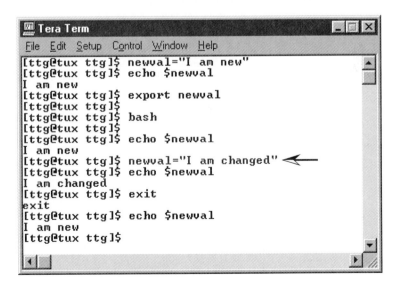

FIGURE 9.50

Trying to change the value of an exported variable in the parent shell.

⊕ .login

A few pages ago I told you there were two ways to have the shell know the value associated with particular shell variable names without having to enter it each time you invoke an instance of the shell. Now we will explore how to cause the shell to create variables, and modify its environment, each time it forks a new instance of the shell.

A set of initialization files are executed when you begin a session with a Unix system. While I don't want to get into the whole process of user initialization, I think it's important that you know that when you log in to a Unix system, a dotted file named **.login** is executed.

Figure 9.51 shows my .login file from a production Solaris box. The majority of the file shown in the figure deals with whether or not the shell should start an X-windows session. The last line of this file is also important; it sets the default backspace key to the erase key. You learned how to do that a long time ago. This makes it happen automatically each time I log in. That's extremely handy! An important thing to remember about the .login file is it will be executed only once, at login. You should set things at login that are *not* shell-dependent, since this file is executed before shell is forked.

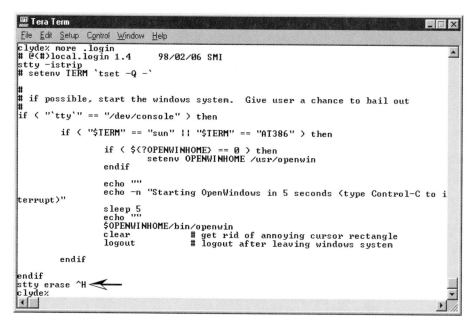

FIGURE 9.51

An example of a .login file.

⊕ .cshrc

As I am sure you remember from our discussion of .exrc in Chapter 7, there are a number of dotted files that end in the two-character sequence rc. These files are used as initialization or setup files for particular programs. The rc at the end of the name stands for *runnable commands*.

Figure 9.52 shows the four rc files I have on my Linux system. Three of the four files are used when a particular shell starts: .bashrc, **.cshrc**, and .tcshrc are the startup files for the bash, C, and T shells, respectively. The .pinerc file is the initialization file for the pine program.

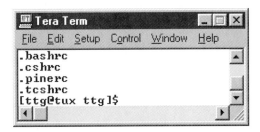

FIGURE 9.52

Some .rc files.

When a particular process has a file of runnable commands, those commands are executed *each time* an instance of the process is started. So each time I start the bash shell, the system looks to see if there is a .bashrc file in my home directory. If the file exists, the system will execute all the commands in that file, preparing the environment for the bash shell. If the file doesn't exist, then no setup processing will be done. Remember, the setup file is run *each time* the process is forked. That means that if I define variables in my .cshrc file, they will be defined for each instance of the C shell.

Let's look at an example of an extensive .cshrc file in Figure 9.53. Wow, what a huge and involved file! Each time I start a new instance of the C shell, I set my history to keep the last 50 commands, and I set up history to save the last 50 commands when I log out, plus I turn on filename completion.

I could also set up other variables in my .cshrc file. Look at Figure 9.54. For purposes of illustration I've created two additional variables in my .cshrc file, as you can

FIGURE 9.53

A long and involved .cshrc file.

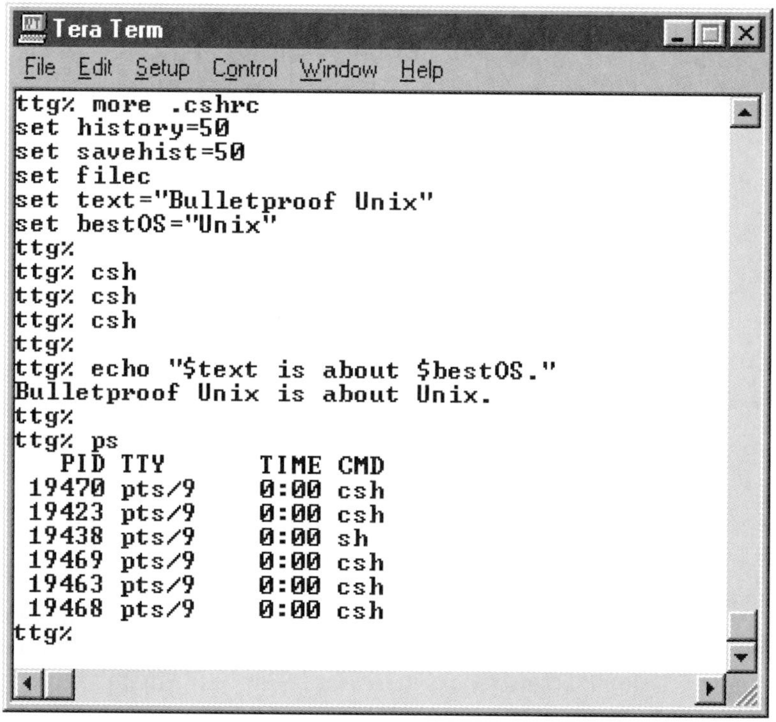

```
Tera Term                                          _ □ ×
File  Edit  Setup  Control  Window  Help
ttg% more .cshrc                                        ▲
set history=50
set savehist=50
set filec
set text="Bulletproof Unix"
set bestOS="Unix"
ttg%
ttg% csh
ttg% csh
ttg% csh
ttg%
ttg% echo "$text is about $bestOS."
Bulletproof Unix is about Unix.
ttg%
ttg% ps
    PID TTY         TIME CMD
  19470 pts/9       0:00 csh
  19423 pts/9       0:00 csh
  19438 pts/9       0:00 sh
  19469 pts/9       0:00 csh
  19463 pts/9       0:00 csh
  19468 pts/9       0:00 csh
ttg%                                                    ▼
◄                                                      ►
```

FIGURE 9.54

Setting variables in .cshrc and using them in subsequent shells.

see from the beginning of the figure. Please take note that there is no setenv command in the figure. I forked three instances of the C shell, then used the two variables I had initialized in the .cshrc file. Notice that the variables were defined and the echo command executed exactly as expected.

If you're going to use a series of variables over and over, or if you'd like to have features like filename completion turned on for you automatically, setting up files like .cshrc will make your work simpler and much more efficient. Another use for the .cshrc file is to define aliases. But a word of caution is necessary. Just as with aliases, you can't expect the same .cshrc file to be there on all machines. If you're using a new machine, you need to examine the .cshrc file to see what it does, and modify it to suit your purposes.

⊕ .bashrc

Just as the .cshrc file initialized the environment for the C shell, the **.bashrc** sets things up for the bash shell. Figure 9.55 shows the .bashrc file for my Linux box. The first thing that's very noticeable is that the bash shell supports aliases, and I have set the three "keep me from doing something stupid" aliases. The if block at the end of

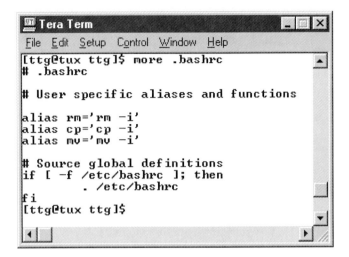

FIGURE 9.55

A sample .bashrc file.

the file looks for some machine-wide definitions stored in a file called .bashrc in the /etc directory. Your .bashrc file can be as complex as you want it to be, or it can be simple like mine is. That's one of the beauties of Unix—you're in control.

.profile

The last of the setup files we'll discuss is also the oldest. It even predates the idea of runnable commands, so it doesn't end with the rc suffix. The **.profile** file is read by the Bourne shell as its setup file. Figure 9.56 shows a pretty much default .profile file on a Solaris machine. The majority of the code involves starting X-windows, but you should recognize the export command from earlier in this chapter. Like all the other startup files, you can customize your .profile file to include the things you wish to have in your Bourne shell session.

One of the important techniques available to you in the Unix environment is the ability to modify the setup files for the utilities and shells that you run. But be aware that if you make mistakes in a setup file, you may not like the results. This is another time when Refrigerator Rule No. 2 becomes important. A wise Unix user will always keep a copy of the original file, so that should something untoward happen, you can always drop back to the way it "used to be." Now let's give you a chance to play.

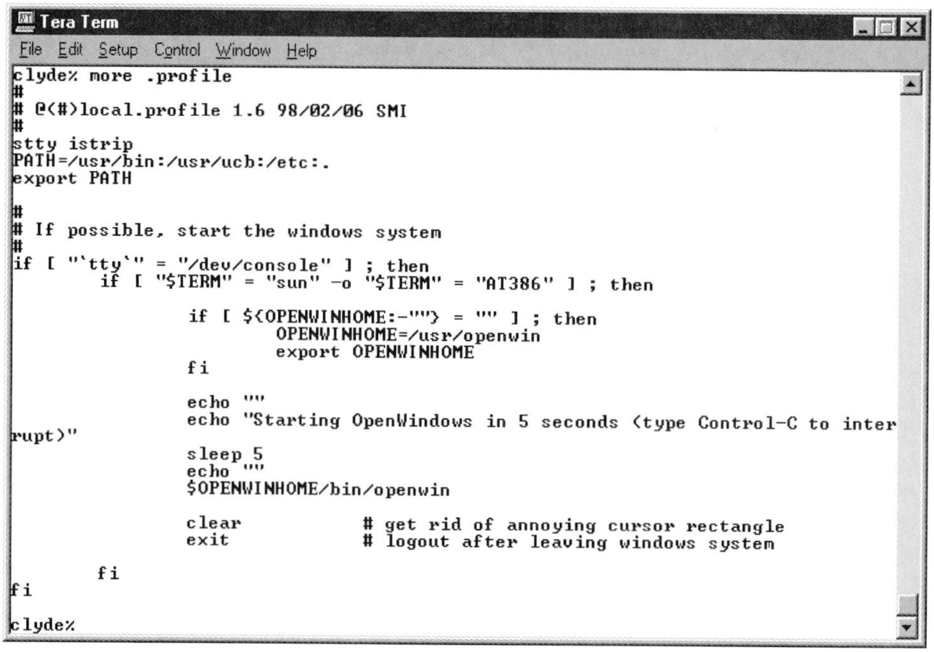


```
clyde% more .profile
#
# @(#)local.profile 1.6 98/02/06 SMI
#
stty istrip
PATH=/usr/bin:/usr/ucb:/etc:.
export PATH

#
# If possible, start the windows system
#
if [ "`tty`" = "/dev/console" ] ; then
        if [ "$TERM" = "sun" -o "$TERM" = "AT386" ] ; then

                if [ ${OPENWINHOME:-""} = "" ] ; then
                        OPENWINHOME=/usr/openwin
                        export OPENWINHOME
                fi

                echo ""
                echo "Starting OpenWindows in 5 seconds (type Control-C to inter
rupt)"
                sleep 5
                echo ""
                $OPENWINHOME/bin/openwin

                clear           # get rid of annoying cursor rectangle
                exit            # logout after leaving windows system

        fi
fi
clyde%
```

FIGURE 9.56

A standard `.profile` file on Solaris

KEY TERMS

append
filter
Next Byte Pointer
null device
recursive
redirection
return code
sub-shell
variable
variable name
variable value

NEW COMMANDS

```
alias
diff
export
find
```

```
pipe
set
setenv
tee
unalias
uniq
unset
unsetenv
```

REVIEW QUESTIONS

9.1   Define all of the key terms.

9.2   Explain the purpose of the find command.

9.3   Describe the difference in coding the find command in order to look for a file that was accessed five days ago versus one that was accessed anytime in the last five days. (The option is -atime.)

9.4   Explain the concept of a pipe in Unix.

9.5   What is a filter program in Unix?

9.6   How can you capture the output of the who command in the following pipe?
      who | wc -1

9.7   What tool do you use to capture the normal output of a command in a file?

9.8   How can you collect both the data sent to standard error and standard out in a single file?

9.9   What tool would you use to place both the date and the output of the ls command in a single file?

9.10 What is Refrigerator Rule No. 4? Now explain its significance.

9.11 Is it possible to send the data normally directed to standard out to one file, and the data normally directed to standard error to a different file in the C shell? In the Bourne shell?

9.12 How would you redirect standard input into the more command?

9.13 What is a here document?

9.14 What is an *alias* in Unix? How do you create one? Is it common to all shells?

9.15 List three problems with creating and using aliases.

9.16 List three rules for creating good aliases.

9.17 How do you remove an alias from the shell?

9.18 What command would you use to see the differences between two files?

9.19 What command would you use to compress identical, concurrent lines into a single line in a file?

9.20 How do you use filename completion? How do you enable it? What shells support it?

9.21 What is a variable? What is a variable name? What is a variable value?

9.22 How do you assign the value "wonderful" to the variable unixis in the Bourne shell? In the C shell?

9.23 How do you make the contents of the variable unixis available to any shell forked from the shell in which it was defined, in the C shell? In the Bourne shell?

9.24 What is a dot rc file?

9.25 How does .login differ from .profile?

EXERCISES

9.1 Start in your home directory. Find all the files that have any of your initials in their name. (This is a test of both your ability to use find and your ability to create a good file-matching metacharacter string!)

9.2 In your home directory, find any file that has been modified in the last three days.

9.3 Create a pipe to show how many people are logged onto the system right now.

9.4 Create a pipe to show how many files you have in your home directory.

9.5 Modify the pipe you created in Exercise 3 (okay, so do it over, then), and capture the actual users in a file called actual.users.

9.6 Take the output from the pipe you just built, and store the output in a file called how.many.

9.7 Add today's date to the file how.many.

9.8 Redirect the contents of how.many into the cat command.

9.9 Prove Refrigerator Rule No. 4.

9.10 Run the find command, starting at the root directory and looking for any files on the system that have any two of your initials in their name. Store the filenames that match in a file called files.that.match and any error messages in a file called error.messages. Examine both files to ensure that your redirections worked.

9.11 Now switch shells. (If you did what was asked in Question 10 in the Bourne shell, do it in the C shell this time, or vice versa.)

9.12 Create a here document on the command line. Make it work. (Yes, you *can* do it!)

9.13 Create three new commands using aliases. Test them. Remove them.

9.14 Now, if you really liked the aliases you built in response to Question 13, put them in your .cshrc file.

9.15 Copy the /etc/passwd file from your system to your home directory. Copy it to passwd2. Now delete at least 5 of the lines, and add several new lines to passwd2. Finally, use the diff command to see the differences.

9.16 Use uniq to clean up the output from the uglylog file (it's on the web site.)

9.17 Turn on filename completion. Play with it. Be amazed!

9.18 Create three shell variables in the C shell. Echo them to make sure you created them.

9.19 Now create the same three shell variables in the Bourne shell. Echo them again to make sure your creation worked.

9.20 Make subsequent instances of each of the shells in Questions 18 and 19, being aware of the variables you created.

9.21 Examine your .login file. Add the erase command if it isn't there.

9.22 Examine your .profile file.

9.23 Examine your .cshrc file.

9.24 Examine your .bashrc file (assuming you have a Linux box handy).

10

Process Control

Understanding processes—and the control of processes—is central to your appreciation and use of the Unix operating system. Before we start talking about the actual control of processes it's important to understand what a process is, and the different states in which a process exists.

Back in Chapter 2 you learned about the idea of a process and a simple definition: a process is a program and the environment necessary for that program to run. You also learned that a process, at process creation time, is normally given three files: standard input, standard output, and standard error.

Now it's time to explore process creation in a little more depth and actually look at the different states a process moves through during its lifetime. This part of the chapter is based on my study of the "Bach" book—*Design of the Unix Operating System*, by Maurice Bach. Considered the seminal work on the way the Unix operating system works, this complex and delightfully detailed text was published by Prentice Hall in 1986. I realize that this is an old book, but if you are serious about understanding Unix, I urge you to buy a copy of it and study it carefully. Be prepared, however, for the fact that the architecture described in the Bach text doesn't exactly match the newer, optimized Linux implementations.

Some authors choose to describe a different number of process states, others combine several of Bach's states into one state—for example, "swapped out" rather than identifying the two different states a process can be in while swapped out. Since Bach is considered to be *the* authority, I have based the following discussion on his nine states.

⊕ Process Creation

Every process in Unix except for the first process (process 0—init or sched depending on which flavor of Unix you are running) is created by the combined efforts of the fork and exec commands. Process 0 must be "hand-built" when the operating system initializes. Since this isn't a text on the internals of the Unix operating system it's enough for you to know that process 0 is created in a different way than any other process. All other processes are created using the procedure shown in Figure 10.1.

Actually, process creation in Unix is a little bit like cloning. When an existing process executes a command that requires the creation of a new process, the system runs the fork command, which exactly duplicates the current process. Then control is given to the exec command, which first removes the original command from the process environment and then inserts the new command into the process environment. This is similar to the process of cloning, wherein the original nucleus is removed from a cell and a new nucleus is inserted into the cell.

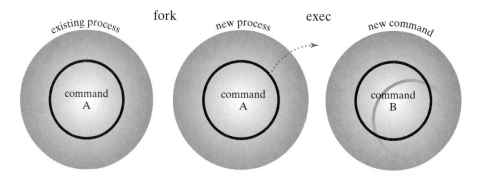

FIGURE 10.1
The steps in process creation.

Built-in vs. External Commands

Unix commands are either part of the shell (**internal commands**), or they are stored on disk and must be brought into memory before they can be executed (**external commands**.) Internal commands, sometimes also called *kernel space functions*, run within the environment of the current shell process. External commands, on the other hand, require that a new process be created for them to run in. Both the fork and exec commands are internal commands. (Actually, they would have to be internal commands; otherwise you would have a recursive nightmare. For example, the fork command would have to fork a process to run the fork command, but to fork that process the fork command would have to fork a process to fork the process to fork the process .... err, I think you see what I mean.)

⊕ Process States

Once the new process has been created, it begins a complex journey through nine different states. Figure 10.2 shows an artist's rendering (yes, a *real* artist this time), of these nine states. This figure shows one explanation of the nine possible states that a process can achieve. All processes do not pass through all nine states. The figure starts where Figure 10.1 left off, with the newly created process presented to the system. I have laid out the nine different states in an order that seems to make sense, at least to me. Let's look at the states in numeric order.

State 1—Created

After the fork and exec commands have done their work, a new process is created and is presented to the operating system. Depending on the load on the system at that particular time, the new process will either be built and left in memory or immediately placed on disk. If the system has room in memory, the memory-management tools will assign some pages of memory for the new process and the scheduler will schedule some CPU cycles for it. In that case the process will move to state 2 (ready to run in memory). On the other hand, if the system is busy and all of the memory is currently in use, the process will be moved to state 7 (ready to run on disk), and the scheduler will be notified of its existence. Before the process can begin executing, though, it must be moved back into memory. Moving an entire process from memory to disk or from disk to memory is called **swapping**. We will discuss both moving a whole process, swapping, and moving a part of the process—*paging*—in just a bit. For now let's focus on the process states.

State 2—Ready to Run in Memory

If the system is lightly loaded, or if you have a large amount of memory, the newly created process will be moved directly into memory. The process will stay in memory, in a ready-to-run state, until the scheduler gives it control of the CPU, for example when the running process goes to sleep. Usually a process will go to sleep when it is awaiting an I/O event from a file or a device such as the keyboard, a scanner, or a network connection.

When the scheduler gives the process access to the CPU, the process state changes to state 3 (running in kernel mode). But there are two other options for the

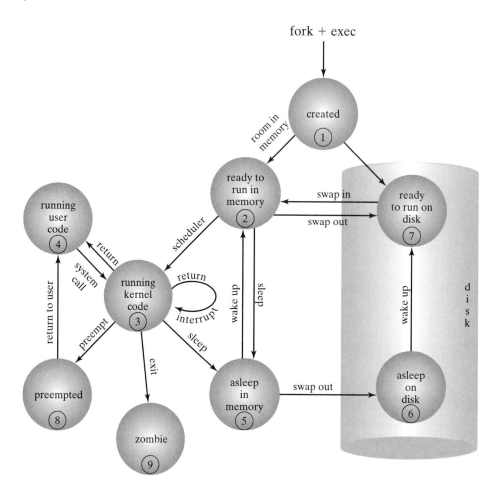

FIGURE 10.2

Process states.

process at this time: If the process is awaiting an I/O event or some other condition that causes it to wait, it could go to sleep, changing to state 5 (asleep in memory). On the other hand, if the system is heavily loaded and another, higher-priority process needs to execute, the new process could be swapped out to disk, changing to state 7 (ready to run on disk).

State 3—Running in Kernel Mode

When a process is executing code that is part of the system, like a system call, it is said to be running in kernel, or protected, mode. Most of the commands you run are system commands and so will be running in kernel mode.

Let's assume for purposes of this discussion that the scheduler gives our new process some CPU cycles to play with. In a normally loaded system, each process in turn is given an opportunity to use the CPU; this is called a **time slice**. The scheduler schedules each process, one after the other, giving each a turn at the CPU. The number of cycles or the length of processor time given to each process is called a **quantum**. When a process's quantum expires, the next process gets its turn. The technical term for this resource-sharing algorithm is **round robin**. And no, it has nothing to do with the shape of Batman's cohort. Rather, each of the processes that are eligible to execute is placed in a circular queue. The scheduler moves around the queue, giving each process its quantum of CPU time. "One for you, now one for you, and now it's your turn." If a process is still executing when its quantum expires, it is preempted by the scheduler and moved into state 8 (preempted by the scheduler).

If the process finishes execution before its quantum expires, it will voluntarily relinquish control of CPU, and the scheduler then gives control to the next process in the queue. This type of CPU-sharing depends on each process having the same priority. Obviously, if a higher-priority process needs the system, the scheduler will accommodate it.

Using a scheduling algorithm like the round robin ensures that no process monopolizes the CPU. In addition, it prevents the possible catastrophic condition in which a process begins executing an infinite loop. Were there no way to interrupt the process, this type of condition would result in a machine freezing or hanging.

State 4—Running in User Mode

An intelligent operating system like Unix realizes that there are two general classes of commands it can execute. Suppose you've written your own C-language program. When you run your program it will be stored in a particular place in memory reserved for user code. This memory, not surprisingly, is called the *user space*. While your program is executing these commands it is not using any system code and so is executing in what is referred to as **user mode**. When your program makes a system call and begins executing system code its then in **kernel mode**. As your program runs it will move to state 3, (kernel mode) when it makes a system call and then switch back to state 4 (user mode) when the system returns control to your program.

State 5—Asleep in Memory

When a Unix process isn't active it goes to sleep (perchance to dream of electric sheep?). A process that is asleep does not consume as many system resources as a process that is awake. There are two different states that a process can be in when it decides to go to sleep, either running in memory (state 2) or running in kernel mode (state 3). In either case, when the s1eep command is issued, the process goes to sleep, changing to state 5. Once asleep a process has two possible choices: it can wake up and go back to state 2 (running in kernel mode), or it can be swapped out to disk. If there's any load on a Unix system at all, sleeping processes will usually be quickly swapped to disk to save space in memory.

Often a process goes to sleep because it's waiting for an I/O event, either reading from the keyboard or a disk, or writing to the screen or disk. Because I/O events are so slow compared to the speed of CPU, it doesn't make sense to have an active process wait, consuming system resources, while the I/O event completes. When the condition that caused the process to go to sleep is resolved—for example, when the I/O event completes—the process can wake up and be switched back to state 2. Later in this chapter we will learn how to put processes to sleep and wake them back up.

State 6—Asleep on Disk (Swapped Out)

Most of the time when a process goes to sleep the system will recognize that it is idle and very quickly reclaim the space it was using in memory by moving the process from memory to disk. After a process has been swapped out, only a small collection of data about the process and a pointer to its location on disk are kept in memory. The rest of the memory is freed up for other processes to use. Many times a Unix system will swap a process out to disk while it's waiting for an I/O event to complete. Other times, if you put a process to sleep, the system will recognize that it is sleeping in memory and reclaim the space by swapping it to disk.

State 7—Ready to Run, but on Disk

Unlike waking up in memory (changing from state 5 to state 2), when a process that has been swapped out wakes up, it finds itself still swapped to disk. The system recognizes that the process is awake and moves the process from state 6 (asleep on disk) to state 7 (ready to run on disk). The system will not swap a process back into memory until it's ready to run, state 7. When resources become available, or when that process's turn at execution comes up again (round robin), the system will move the process from disk back into memory. Moving a process from disk back into memory is called *swapping in*. When the process is swapped in, it changes from state 7 to state 2 (ready to run in memory). The next two states don't fit in the cyclical flow as well as the others. Both are somewhat specialized states.

State 8—Preempted by Scheduler

When we learned about state 3 (running in the kernel), we also looked at the concept of a quantum. A process is **preempted** when it is still executing at the time its quantum expires. Another way a process can be preempted is when a different process with a higher priority is ready to run. In either case the execution of the current process is suspended and another process is given control. Most of the time a preempted process returns to user level when its quantum comes up.

State 9—Zombie, the Living Dead

When a process finishes executing, or when it is killed, it (briefly, we hope) enters what is called the *zombie state*, state 9. In the zombie state, the process is no longer active but still exists—in other words, it's dead but yet lives. (And you thought the folks that built Unix didn't have a sense of humor!) While the process is in the zombie state, the system recovers resources owned by the process and generally does the housekeeping necessary to clean up after the process. Then the process ceases to exist.

In some rare instances a process can stay in the zombie state. Most often this happens when the process is killed in such a way as to prevent the housekeeping that normally follows process termination. If a process remains in the zombie state, the only way to remove it from the system is to reboot! The most frequent cause of the zombie processes on my systems are bad modem connections that drop carrier while my students are logged in. Another way that I can create zombies is if I kill a login session without allowing it to clean up after itself (kill -9). Fortunately, zombie processes are fairly rare, and they occupy only one process slot and usually don't consume a significant amount of other system resources.

Understanding the relationship of the nine process states will be very helpful as we discuss the different aspects of process control in the rest of the chapter. Please refer to Figure 10.2 and make sure that you understand the different states and the transitions among them before we go on.

ps

---

ps [options]

To see what's happening with processes on the system, we can use the **ps** (*process status*) command. This command has a wealth of options! Subtle differences exist in the way the ps command is handled by the flavors of Unix. To make things even more interesting, even within a given flavor of Unix—for example Linux—the ps command will display its output differently depending on how you set the parameters, options, and switches. For purposes of this text we will most often use the ps command to explore the relationship among processes and to look at interesting things like process states. We need to also examine the relationship among processes before we look at the actual ps command.

Process Relationships

As you know, every process except process 0 (which is hand-built when Unix is loaded), is created by a combination of the exec and fork commands. Unix folks speak of this relationship as a **parent-child relationship**, in which the parent is the original process and the child is the newly created process. Two rules govern this relationship:

1. Under normal circumstances a child process cannot survive the termination of its parent process. (The exception to this is if the child process is "adopted" by another process, usually process 1 or 0.)
2. A child process *cannot* influence the environment of the parent process, nor can it pass data back to the parent process in the form of environmental variables. We saw this in the last chapter when we looked at changing environmental variables in the child process.

Each process keeps the process I.D. of its parent as part of the environment of the process. Using the *PPID (parent process identification)* you can create a family tree for any given process. When we look at the long output of the ps command, this is one of the things we will be looking for.

Figure 10.3 shows the normal (no options used) output from the ps command on both the Solaris and Linux machines. As you can see, the generic, or plain vanilla, version of the ps command is not terribly exciting. The four things it tells us are (1) the process I.D., (2) the I/O devices attached to the process, (3) how long it has been running, and (4) the command that is the heart of that process.

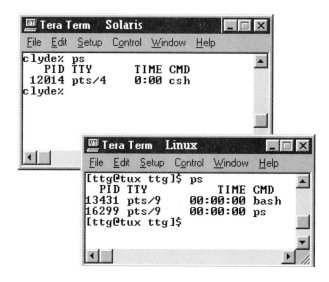

FIGURE 10.3

Default output of the ps command.

Remember that the output from the ps command is a snapshot in time and may not reflect the exact state of the system. Actually, it seems just the luck of the draw whether the ps command itself will appear in the output. Figure 10.4 shows output from a ps command with some options that display certain more interesting things. The first thing to notice is that I used an e option and an o option. The e option tells ps to show me all of the processes. The o option specifies that the ps command should use the output format I supply in the next argument. The argument for the formatting, o option, must be a single string with the format specifiers either separated by spaces or commas. I prefer to enclose my formatting options inside tick marks and separate them by spaces. In this example the data I've asked the ps command to supply are:

- user—the login I.D. of the user that owns the process.
- PID—the process I.D. for the process.
- PPID—the *parent* process I.D.
- s—the state of the process.

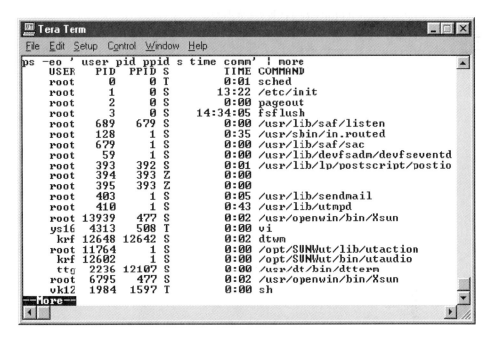

FIGURE 10.4

A more interesting ps report.

- time—how long the process has been running.
- comm—the command that forms the heart of the process.

(Please note, I cut and pasted lines from a much longer display to create what you see in Figure 10.4.)

There are some very interesting processes in Figure 10.4. For example, notice that on this Solaris machine process 0 is the scheduler and is the parent process for the first three other processes created (process I.D.s 1, 2, and 3). Also, the init process, process 1, is the parent process for several other processes. (Moreover, it is the process that usually adopts processes who become orphans.)

Looking down the stat column, you will quickly realize that I have a small problem. See PIDs 394 and 395? Zombies! Perhaps if I kill their parent process they'll go away. If not, they'll be there until I reboot the system. (It's really no fun to be a system administrator around Halloween!) Most of the processes shown in Figure 10.4 are sleeping, but notice that a couple of them have a status of T. Those processes have been stopped for some reason.

The default ps command on Solaris and Linux no longer shows whether or not a particular process is been swapped out to disk. On older and slower machines, like the one shown in Figure 10.5, the system not only reports sleeping or stopped processes but also adds a second character, W, to report that the process was swapped out to disk. In many versions of Linux, a swapped-out process is shown with square brackets surrounding the command.

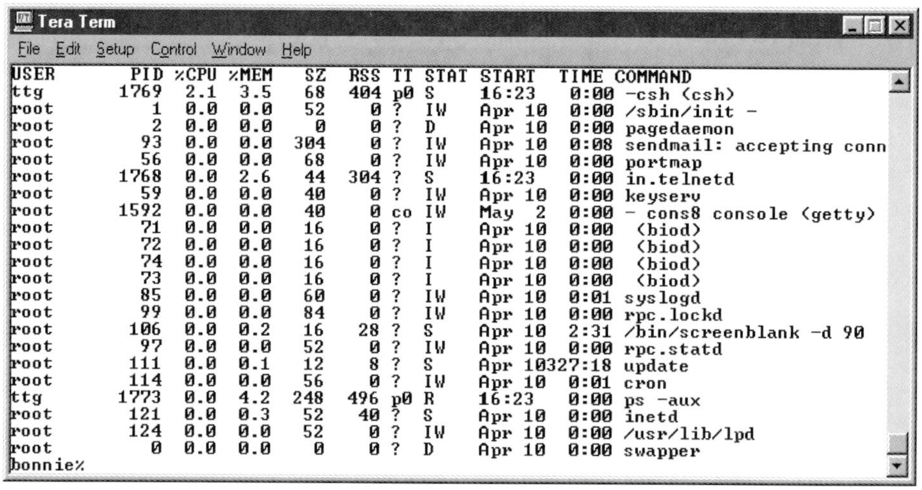

```
┌────────────────────────────────────────────────────────────────────────────────┐
│ ▥ Tera Term                                                          ▬ ▢ ✕        │
├────────────────────────────────────────────────────────────────────────────────┤
│ File  Edit  Setup  Control  Window  Help                                         │
├────────────────────────────────────────────────────────────────────────────────┤
│USER       PID %CPU %MEM   SZ  RSS TT STAT START   TIME COMMAND               ▲    │
│ttg       1769  2.1  3.5   68  404 p0 S    16:23   0:00 -csh (csh)                 │
│root         1  0.0  0.0   52    0  ? IW   Apr 10  0:00 /sbin/init -               │
│root         2  0.0  0.0    0    0  ? D    Apr 10  0:00 pagedaemon                 │
│root        93  0.0  0.0  304    0  ? IW   Apr 10  0:08 sendmail: accepting conn   │
│root        56  0.0  0.0   68    0  ? IW   Apr 10  0:00 portmap                    │
│root      1768  0.0  2.6   44  304  ? S    16:23   0:00 in.telnetd                 │
│root        59  0.0  0.0   40    0  ? IW   Apr 10  0:00 keyserv                    │
│root      1592  0.0  0.0   40    0 co IW   May  2  0:00 - cons8 console (getty)    │
│root        71  0.0  0.0   16    0  ? I    Apr 10  0:00 (biod)                     │
│root        72  0.0  0.0   16    0  ? I    Apr 10  0:00 (biod)                     │
│root        74  0.0  0.0   16    0  ? I    Apr 10  0:00 (biod)                     │
│root        73  0.0  0.0   16    0  ? I    Apr 10  0:00 (biod)                     │
│root        85  0.0  0.0   60    0  ? IW   Apr 10  0:01 syslogd                    │
│root        99  0.0  0.0   84    0  ? IW   Apr 10  0:00 rpc.lockd                  │
│root       106  0.0  0.2   16   28  ? S    Apr 10  2:31 /bin/screenblank -d 90     │
│root        97  0.0  0.0   52    0  ? IW   Apr 10  0:00 rpc.statd                  │
│root       111  0.0  0.1   12    8  ? S    Apr 10327:18 update                     │
│root       114  0.0  0.0   56    0  ? IW   Apr 10  0:01 cron                       │
│ttg       1773  0.0  4.2  248  496 p0 R    16:23   0:00 ps -aux                    │
│root       121  0.0  0.3   52   40  ? S    Apr 10  0:00 inetd                      │
│root       124  0.0  0.0   52    0  ? IW   Apr 10  0:00 /usr/lib/lpd               │
│root         0  0.0  0.0    0    0  ? D    Apr 10  0:00 swapper                    │
│bonnie%                                                                      ▼    │
└────────────────────────────────────────────────────────────────────────────────┘
```

FIGURE 10.5

A report from an older version of ps.

The system represented in Figure 10.5 is a Sun Microsystems SPARC classic running SunOS rather than Solaris. The STAT field shows the state of each process. This version of the ps command has some different states, as follows:

- S—sleeping for less than 20 seconds.
- I—idle, sleeping for 20 or more seconds.
- IW—idle and without any pages in memory (swapped out).
- R—runnable, in the round-robin queue to be executed.
- D—in an uninterruptible wait, usually looking for disk resources.

You can see from the output of the ps command that many of the idle processes have been swapped to disk. With newer systems like Solaris, especially on machines like clyde, with 4 gigabytes of RAM, swapping to disk isn't quite so common. However, it's important for you to understand all nine states that a process can be in even if you don't see them regularly.

Several other options are available that system administrators will appreciate, but for now all you need to know is to use ps to determine what's running on the system. As an interesting exercise you might consider creating a genealogy chart for the processes currently running on your system. Using the long ps output, you can determine which process is the parent process for each of the other processes. Then you can determine the "house and lineage" of each process in your system. Well, okay, that might not be the *most* exciting thing you've ever attempted, but it could be fun.

⊕ Virtual Memory

We've been talking about swapping, but I mentioned paging earlier and promised we would discuss that, too. To do that—and to delve deeper into the subject of swapping, I need to explain more about virtual memory. I don't intend to jump off the beaten track into the wild and woolly forests of computer science. Yet I think it's important that you have at least a general overview of how virtual memory works so you can understand why things like swap space are important in Unix. It's time for a definition of **virtual**.

> If I can see it and I can touch it, it's *real*.
> If I can't see it but I can touch it, it's *invisible*.
> If I can see it but I can't touch it, it's **virtual**.
> And if I can't see it and I can't touch it, it's, it's, it's … *gone!*

So by that definition **virtual memory** is memory that I can see but I can't touch; it looks like memory but it's not *real* memory. To create virtual memory, the system uses disk space as if it were memory. Consider for a moment the illustration in Figure 10.6. I am showing a system here with four pages of memory (a whopping 4 kilobytes) and four blocks of disk space. The size of a page of memory and the size of the disk block are equal but system-dependent. While most systems now run with larger pages and blocks, for our purposes the size of a page or block doesn't matter. What is important is that by some strange quirk of fate, a page of memory is *exactly* the same size as a disk block.

Before data or instructions can be loaded into memory they must be on disk. The designers of virtual memory took this into account and decided they could use disk space as if it were an extension of memory. In Figure 10.6 three of the four pages of our program need only to be read into memory from disk. (If the contents of a block or page doesn't change, there's no reason to move it back out to disk, since the copy on disk is still correct.) The fourth page, where the actual data are stored, is changed as the process runs, and so it must be written back out to disk if that page is removed before the process finishes.

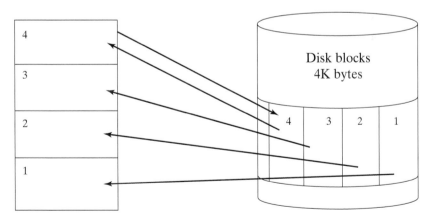

Memory pages
4K bytes

FIGURE 10.6
Illustration of virtual memory.

Two different operations are involved in virtual memory: swapping and paging. Swapping is the term used to describe moving an *entire process* from disk into memory, (*swapping in*) or from memory to disk (*swapping out*). Paging, on the other hand, is the process of moving one or usually a related cluster of pages from disk to memory (*paging in*) or from memory to disk (*paging out*). Although it's useful to think of paging as moving a single page, the actual paging algorithm is quite complex, and paging usually moves a cluster of pages at a time. If this were a computer-science text, I would now spend pages and pages waxing lyrical about the delights of the different virtual-memory algorithms. Fortunately or unfortunately, this is a Unix text, so we will skip all that.

Let's look at swapping first. When a new process is forked and is ready to run, or when it reaches the "ready to run, but on disk" state, the swapper is notified. If there is space in memory, the swapper copies the blocks of the process from disk onto pages in memory. The scheduler is then notified that that process I.D. should be added to the round-robin scheduling queue. If the system becomes more heavily loaded and memory becomes a scarce resource, then the swapper may move processes waiting in memory to disk—in this case moving from state 5 (asleep in memory) to state 6 (asleep on disk). When the process awakens, the swapper is notified to move the process back from disk to memory.

A note of clarification: when a process is swapped to disk, only those pages of memory *that have been changed* must be written to disk. Since disk I/O is very slow compared with moving data into memory, the system saves a lot of time by not writing superfluous pages to disk. The important thing to remember about swapping is that the entire process is moved. (Actually that's not true; a small part of the process and a pointer to its current location on disk are kept in memory. For purposes of our discussion, though, the whole process goes to disk.)

Paging is used to move a small collection of pages from disk to memory or from memory to disk. Suppose that the entire process and its associated data require 50 pages of 1K memory (a 50-kilobyte program). Now suppose that due to system load, only 10 pages of memory are available for that particular process to use. As the process works through the pages of instructions, new pages can be brought into memory—much like streaming audio on the Net.

The system keeps track of the pages that have been used and the pages that might next be needed. Then, the pager move those pages into memory just before the program requires them. Should the system not anticipate correctly, the running program will ask for code or data that are currently on disk. This situation is called **demand paging**. Obviously, it's more efficient for the system if processes don't need to demand pages, and then wait for them so a look-ahead paging algorithm usually satisfies the page requests before they're demanded.

The more heavily loaded the system and the smaller the actual memory, the more paging is necessary. On the production Solaris box, clyde, we have 4 gigabytes of RAM, which is enough for most of the processes so we don't often have a paging situation. On the other hand, on the old production system, the SPARC Classic bonnie, which has only 16 megabytes memory, paging was a way of life.

⊕ Perspectives in Foreground and Background

In addition to being in one of nine possible states, processes can execute either in the foreground or the background. A process running in the **foreground** takes its input from standard in (nominally the keyboard) and sends its output to standard out (usually the screen.) Error messages generated by a foreground process are also sent to the standard error (again usually the screen.) This is the normal state for the processes you run at the command line.

A process running in the **background** takes input through standard in *but in most cases cannot see the keyboard!* Therefore, a process running in the background cannot query the user or require keyboard intervention. If a background process asks for input from the keyboard, it will usually fail and terminate. If the programmer has been especially clever, the process may intercept the error and wait, but usually the processes fail. A background process will, however, send both its output and its errors to the usual standard out and standard error—that is, the screen.

The ability to run processes in the background is extremely useful. For example, to create accounts at the beginning of each semester I run a large script that does most of the work for me. It reports as each account is created; and, of course, should it encounter errors it sends out error messages. When I run the script I have two choices:

1. I can sit quietly, twiddling my thumbs, watching the monitor intently as it scrolls the neatly created accounts one after another (going slowly crazy in the process).

2. I can run the add-user process in the background and perform other useful tasks while the script takes care of adding the users for me. I will still see each user account as it is created, because the background process will write to the monitor, but I can do other things as well.

(Of course, I could bring up another terminal session, but let's pretend I am working from home, connecting through telnet or secure shell.) Hmmm, let me see, to be bored or to be productive? That's not a difficult decision to make! So let's see how we can run a process in the background.

I hope you know how to run processes in the foreground! Running a process in the background is just a little different. Figure 10.7 shows an example of me running a process, the sleeper script, in the background. The script `sleeper.sh` is available from the Web site. All `sleeper.sh` does is sleep for a given number of seconds, sending a message at regular intervals. I wrote it simply to give us a reliable process to control, and it is of no production use.

When we get to shell scripting, in Chapter 14, you will be able to dissect the sleeper.sh script and discover all its delights. For now, the way we use the script is to give sleeper.sh the command-line option of q and the number of seconds we want it to sleep, in this example 50. (The q option directs the script to run in *quiet* mode; otherwise it will tell us each second and be very annoying. We will see it running in that mode in a few pages.)

The last character on the command line, the ampersand (&), tells the shell to run the command or script in the background. It then gives us a process I.D. (PID) for the newly created process and gives us back control at the command line. In Figure 10.7 I

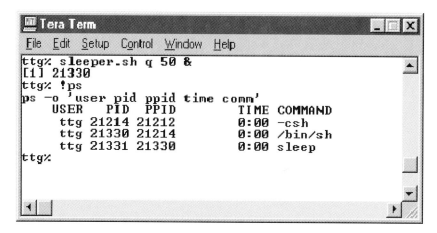

FIGURE 10.7

Running a process in background.

also reran the ps command I had used earlier to look at the current running processes. Remember that PID is the process I.D. and PPID is the *parent* process I.D. As you can see from the output, I have three processes currently running:

- **21214** is the current C shell.
- **21330** is the sleeper script (it starts by invoking the Borne shell). Notice that the parent process for this script is the C shell (21214).
- **21331** is the process running the sleep command. Its parent is the script, 21330.

Our first process-control command, the ampersand, as the last character on the command line, causes the process to be run in the background. (Gee, that's not the first process-control command you have learned—you know how to kill processes using the Ctrl-C.)

kill

```
kill [option] identifier
```

Now that you know how to start a process in the background, let's see how to control that process from the command line. As I mentioned in the last paragraph, to kill a process running in the foreground, you use the ^C (Ctrl-C) command. However, you can't kill a background process using the Ctrl-C because a background process *can't read from the keyboard.* You must use a different command. The command we are about to discuss is another example of one of those extremely obtuse Unix command names: to kill a process you have to use the **kill** command.

Figure 10.8 shows how I started the sleeper script and then killed it, first in the foreground (on the command line) and then in the background. Let's dissect what I did here. First I ran a sleeper script on the command line and killed it with a Ctrl-C. Notice that the control character actually shows in the figure. Then I ran the script again, in the background. Next I attempted to use the kill command to kill the script, and found no confirmation. Then I executed the ps command to see what was going on. The script lived! Some processes are considered *persistent*, which means they are very resistant to being killed. (Actually, what this means is that the process—in this case the shell—can trap a kill command and choose to ignore it.)

Another really interesting phenomenon is shown in Figure 10.8. Back when we talked about process relationships, we learned that a child process cannot survive the demise of its parent unless it's *adopted*. Look what happened to process number **21379** when its parent process, number 21378, was killed. The child process, sleep, was adopted by the process number 1 and thus continued to live. It lived long enough for the system to allow it to exit gracefully.

Among the options for the kill command is the -9 option. "Why the number 9?" You ask. You have to remember that people who write software may have been awake for a long, long time. This seems to be an example of one of those instances. Historically, cats are said to be very difficult to kill because they have nine lives. In other words, cats are very persistent. So, if you have a persistent process (one that acts like a

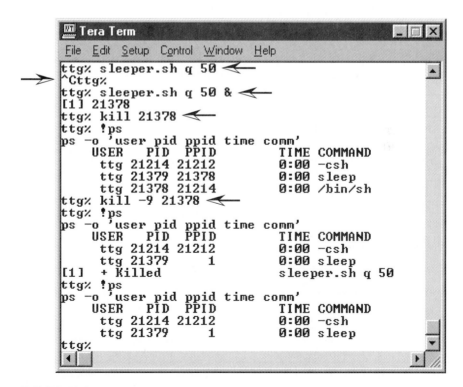

FIGURE 10.8

Killing a process.

cat), perhaps it too has nine lives, and so you have to kill all nine of them. (It really doesn't do nine kills; it is just an "untrappable" signal.)

signals

The options on the `kill` command are actually different *signals* in the Unix environment. In other words, the `kill` command sends signals to the specified process. In the Unix environment, a **signal** is a software interrupt used at the process level to control a process or send the process information. More than 30 different signals are defined in most Unix environments although only a few are actually used for process control. Many are specialized signals that report errors like an illegal instruction or some other very particular condition.

Even the common signals display differences across the flavors of Unix. For this text, I have chosen to discuss a dozen commonly used signals that can be sent to a process using the `kill` command (Table 10.1). These signals are the ones given the same signal numbers by Linux and Solaris. In Linux, the signal name is prefixed with `SIG`.

As you can see from the table, some of the signals are fairly straightforward, like TERM and KILL, while others, like FPE, are more obscure. It is important to note that using `kill -KILL (-9)` can cause problems, because it may not allow the process to clean up after itself. When we began using the Sun Microsystems SunRay stateless devices in our labs, I suddenly began seeing zombie processes. After some careful observation I

TABLE 10.1 Some Common Signals

Number	Name	Description
1	HUP	*Hangup.* Sent when a modem hangs up, or if you wish to emulate hanging up on terminals that can't, like PCs.
2	INT	*Interrupt.* This is like CTRL-C from the keyboard.
3	QUIT	*Quit.* Similar to INT, but represents the CTRL- key.
4	ILL	*Illegal instruction.* Sent when the hardware detects an illegal instruction.
5	TRAP	Sent after each instruction if the trace trap was set.
6	ABRT	*Abort.* Usually sent when the process calls the `abort()` system call.
8	FPE	*Floating-point exception.* Sent when the hardware detects a floating-point error, usually a program bug like dividing by zero.
9	KILL	*Kill.* The one way to absolutely kill a process; often prevents the process from going through normal housekeeping. To be used in emergencies only.
11	SEGV	*Segmentation violation.* Usually an addressing problem in a program.
13	PIPE	*Writing to a pipe not opened for reading.* Problem with named pipes; often indicates that the reading process has terminated.
14	ALRM	*Alarm Clock.* Sent when the process's alarm clock goes off. (The alarm is set with the `alarm()` system call.)
15	TERM	*Terminate.* This is the normal, and preferred, way to end a process. It is the default signal sent by `kill` and is also used during system shutdown to terminate all active processes. This signal allows the process to clean up after itself before exiting.

realized that when I killed student processes with large idle times, say two or three days, using the kill -9 command, I sometimes created a zombie. I believe this is because the Sun Ray process didn't have time to clean up after itself. As it says in the table, use the -KILL option only emergencies, or when -TERM won't work. Unless you're root, you can kill only those processes that you own.

In most cases the process I.D. is the process identifier you will use with the kill command. But when you're dealing with background processes or jobs, you can also use the job number to control the process. We will discuss job numbers when we discuss the jobs command in a few pages.

You can stop the current foreground process by using the ^Z (Ctrl-Z) command. Remember that stopping a process is different from killing a process, because a stopped process can be restarted while a killed process ceases to exist. Because a background process isn't reading from the keyboard, you cannot use ^Z to stop a background process for the same reason that you can't kill it with ^C.

stop

```
stop identifier
```

To stop a background process you use the **stop** command. (In some systems this is also called the suspend command.) Stopping a process is something like putting it into suspended animation. The process retains all of its resources, and the system treats it as if it were asleep. That means it can be swapped if the system becomes more heavily loaded.

Normally you use the process I.D. as the identifier when you stop a process. As with the kill command, you can also use the relative job number that you will learn about in a while.

You may have encountered stopped processes when you tried to exit. Figure 10.9 shows an example of this. As you might be able to guess, I was working in the vi editor on the file named sleeper.sh, and I used the Ctrl-Z to stop the editing process. The system dutifully told me that I had stopped the editing process. I then typed the exit

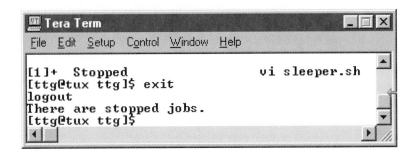

FIGURE 10.9

Trying to exit while there are stopped jobs.

command to log out of the system. Since I had stopped the vi job, rather than logging me out, the shell informed me that I had stopped jobs.

This is a service provided by most shells. If I were to log out, it would kill the shell process, which is the parent of the stopped job. Following the relationship rule, the child process would have to terminate before the parent. If that happened, it could cause me to lose data. Therefore, as a courtesy the shell tells me that I have stopped jobs rather than just logging me out.

If I enter the exit command again, the shell will log me out and kill all the stopped jobs. Generally speaking, it's best to individually terminate processes rather than just exiting and letting the system clean up after you. In other words, please finish what you start.

jobs

```
jobs [options] [identifier]
```

As promised earlier, there is a way to identify processes you own besides using the process I.D.: you use the job number command instead. The definition of **job** is somewhat vague. Some sources define it as every job or pipeline that the user enters at the terminal. Other sources described a job as a stopped or background process. For purposes of our discussion we will define a job as any process running in the background, or any stopped process that can be controlled without using control keys.

To see how many jobs we own, we use the jobs command. Figure 10.10 shows an example of the output of the jobs command where I have stopped one process and run another in the background.

There are a lot of data in this figure. The jobs command provides us with a wealth of information if we know how to interpret it. Let's take a close look at the information at hand:

1. The leftmost field, a number enclosed within square brackets, tells us the relative job number. This is the number we will use is an identification for the job instead than using the process I.D.

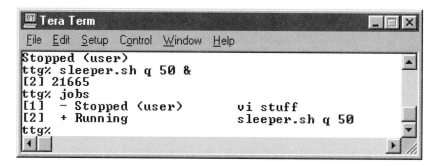

FIGURE 10.10

Output of the jobs command.

2. The next field, which will be either a plus sign $(+)$, a minus sign $(-)$, or blank, tells us the relative order of the job. The job that is prefixed with a plus sign is the most recently stopped or most recently started job. This is also known as the current job. If we don't specify a job number, it is the job that will be controlled by default.

3. The third field tells us the status of each job. If the job is stopped, it usually tells us who stopped it.

4. The last field tells us the command that composes the job. Notice that it also gives us the command-line options with the command.

Figure 10.11 shows us the difference between the output of the ps command and the output of the jobs command. As you can see, the ps command tells us about more processes—for example, sleep, which is called by the sleeper.sh script. In comparison, the jobs command tells us the status of the jobs. Many users will have the same job number (everyone running a background job will have a job 1 at some point), but each PID will be unique. "Remember, all jobs are processes, but not all processes are jobs": a famous quote by my good friend, Bob Nelson. Both commands are very useful, and both will become part of your tool kit as you explore further into Unix. Now let's use the job number to control some processes!

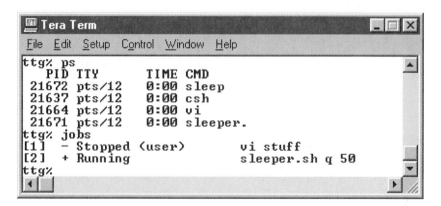

FIGURE 10.11

Comparison of the outputs from ps and jobs commands.

fg

```
fg [%job number]
```

Finally, you have your chance to play traffic police officer, or air traffic controller, in the sense that you can control where a process will execute. The fg and bg commands specify the foreground and background, respectively. The **fg** command causes the job specified to begin executing in the foreground, and it doesn't matter if the job is sleeping or running in the background. In either case the specified job will begin running in the foreground. Figure 10.12 shows how to control three different jobs, starting each one in the background and then stopping each job. As before, the scripts in this figure were created simply as demonstration scripts for this chapter. They are available on the Web site.

In the first part of Figure 10.12 I started the three demonstration scripts: one.sh, two.sh, and three.sh. Each script displays a message and then sleeps for 10 seconds. Each script will loop, displaying a message each time it loops. The number passed to the script on the command line tells the script how many times to loop. In this case each

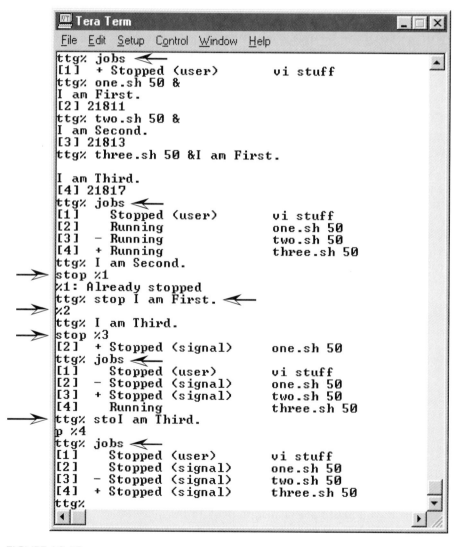

FIGURE 10.12

The beginnings of job control.

script will display 50 messages. Notice that I executed each of the scripts in the background so that I could continue to work at the command line. After starting all three scripts I entered the jobs command, to show what was going on, and was then interrupted by the script two.sh. At that time there were three scripts running in the background and one stopped the first job, the vi session.

Having determined their job numbers, I next stopped each of the three jobs using the stop command. When I tried to stop job [1] the vi session, the shell told me I couldn't because it was already stopped. Notice that while I was stopping the second job (%2), I was interrupted by the output from that job.

Once I had stopped all the jobs, I began orchestrating their execution using the fg (foreground) command. Take a look at Figure 10.13. Remember, the fg

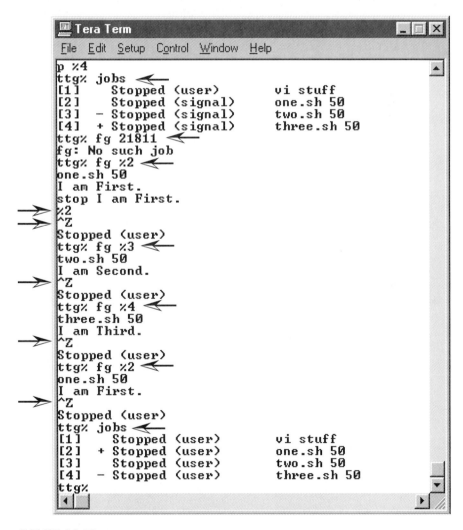

FIGURE 10.13

Controlling the processes.

command requires me to use the job number, not the process I.D., as I tried to do the first time. Working our way through this figure, we can see that the first thing I did was issue a `jobs` command to see the different jobs and get their job numbers. Then I attempted to bring the job `one.sh` to the foreground using the `fg` command and its process I.D. instead of its job number. No such luck. The shell looked for a job numbered 21811, but only the jobs numbered 1 through 4 were currently active.

Next I used `fg` correctly, giving it the job number, preceded by a percent sign (%), of the job I wanted to move to the foreground. In this instance I wanted the first script to run in the foreground. You can see what happened when I entered the `fg %2` command. The job, script `one.sh`, began executing.

And then I made another mistake. I tried to use the `stop` command to stop that particular job, which didn't work. Since I had brought the script to foreground execution, the script owned the keyboard! I couldn't enter a command because the script was interpreting my keystrokes. Before I could use the keyboard again I had to stop the script using Ctrl-Z. Once the script had relinquished control of the keyboard I was back in charge.

Now I started each of the other two scripts running in the foreground and then stopped them. Finally, I started the first script again, since it would become the "most recently run" job. You can see this in the output of the second `jobs` command.

Remember that the job preceded by the plus sign is the most recently run job. It is also the job that is used by default if you don't supply a job number to the `fg` command. Look at Figure 10.14 to see what I mean. You can see that job 2 is the most recently active job because it has a plus sign (+) in the second field. If I enter the `fg` command with no job number, the shell will use the most recently stopped job by default.

Being able to control a series of jobs is very handy, but suppose I want to run a job in the background, not the foreground. Let's see how we start jobs running in the background.

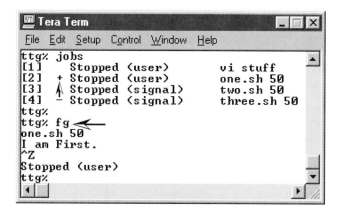

FIGURE 10.14

Using `fg` command without a job number.

bg

---

bg [%job number]

The fg command moved stopped processes to the foreground, and that's half the battle. The other half of the battle is using the **bg** command to move stopped processes to the background. Like the fg command, the bg command uses a job number (seen in the output of the jobs command) to control the process. Also, just like the fg command, if you don't give the bg command a job number, it will take the most recently run job by default.

Figure 10.15 shows an example of the bg command. At the beginning of the figure you see the output of the jobs command. By the way, when jobs tells you a job was stopped by a signal, that means it was stopped by the stop command. When it says the user stopped the job, the Ctrl-Z command was probably used.

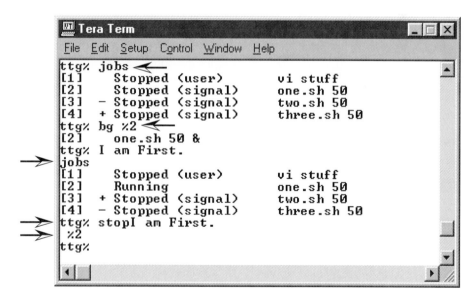

FIGURE 10.15

Using the bg command.

After seeing which jobs were available, I restarted the second job in the background. Since the process was running in the background, I still had control of the keyboard, so I could run the jobs command to see what was going on. (Remember, jobs shows both stopped and background processes.) Notice that it showed job 2 was running. While stopping the second job, I was interrupted by its output, proving that the job was still running.

You now have a complete collection of job control commands. You can stop jobs, kill them, move them to the background or the foreground. Figure 10.16 shows a combination of job-control commands. Initially, you see the jobs that I am running. I started job 2 running in the background and viewed its output. Notice that when the shell started the job it supplied the trailing & on the command line.

The next command may look little strange. Notice that *without stopping the job* I moved job 2 from the background to the foreground with the fg command. Since I had relinquished control of the keyboard to job 2, I had to stop that job before I could do anything else.

Next I decided to thin out the jobs a little, so I killed job 3. Yes, you can use job numbers with the kill command rather than process I.D.s. Actually, you can use job numbers with all the process-control commands. Finally, I started job 4 in the foreground, then stopped it.

Even though there were only three jobs left, the shell did not renumber them. It is important to remember that the shell won't renumber jobs, so the job number

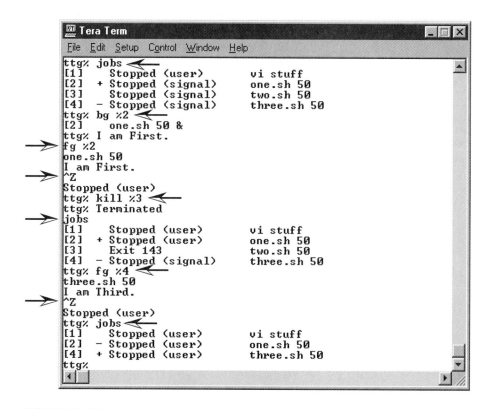

FIGURE 10.16

Job control at its finest (well, at least a busy example).

assigned will remain with the job throughout its life. Table 10.2 shows the relationship between process/job control in the foreground and the background.

When we get to the Chapter 14, and you start writing shell scripts, you'll learn another important reason to be able to control processes. Your scripts can create processes, stop them, and start them again depending on conditions with the system.

TABLE 10.2 Relationship between Foreground and Background Controls

Foreground	Background
^Z	Stop
^C	Kill

nice

```
nice [-increment | -n increment] command [argument(s)]
```

The **nice** command isn't exactly process control, but it does change the priority of process execution. Since it affects process execution, I have included it in this section. Usually nice is used to cause a process to run at a lower priority than normal. That means that a process that has been niced is being "nice" to the other processes on the system by giving them a relatively higher priority with the scheduler.

Most often the nice command is used with computationally intensive jobs, those that use a lot of CPU time. If you're running a process that is computationally intense, it will slow down the system for all the other users. Most users need very few CPU resources when doing things like editing text. To lessen the impact of your job on those users you should nice your job. If the system is lightly loaded, or if there are no other jobs on a system, let your job run normally. If there are other users on the system running processes like editors, give their work priority over your job.

Usually nice values range from 0 to 39, with 20 as the default value. Raising the nice value make your process "nicer." Figure 10.17 shows an example of running one of the processes using nice. I performed the following operations here:

1. I ran the nice command with a nice option of –10, which added 10 to the script's nice value and changed it from the default of 20 to 30. (The larger the number is, the lower the priority.)
2. I stopped the process, using the stop command.
3. I executed the ps command, specifying my own options in order to show the nice values of all the processes I own. As you can see from the figure, two of the processes, the shell and one sleep command, are running with nice values of 30. Looking at the process I.D.s for those two processes, you can see that the sleep command is the child process of the shell. This shows us that, along with other features of its environment, the child process inherits the nice value of the parent process.

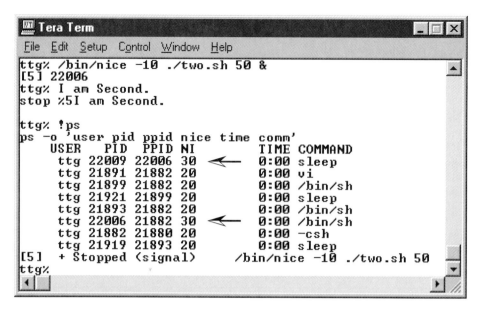

FIGURE 10.17

Using nice to change the priority of process.

The system response to the stop command occurs after the output of the ps command simply because I was very quick to type the ps command after the stop command.

You may have noticed that rather than using the C shell's built-in nice command, I chose to use the nice command in /bin. That's because the built-in command uses a different syntax, expecting the user to specify a sign for the nice value. Now, a normal user can't lower his nice value below the default of 20 (in other words, you can't give your process a higher priority); only root can do that. Had I done what I did in Figure 10.17, the C shell would have simply ignored my attempt to set my nice value lower, possibly muttering under its breath. Okay, don't believe me—then take a look at Figure 10.18.

As you can see from the figure, I attempted to set my nice value down by 10, which should have set it at 10. However, the ps command shows that the nice value for the process is 20, which means the C shell politely ignored me.

Even though the C shell has a built-in nice command, I recommend that you always use the version stored in /bin to avoid confusion. This is one example of an inconsistency among the shells. You'll probably encounter others as your experience with Unix increases, but for the most part they are not significant.

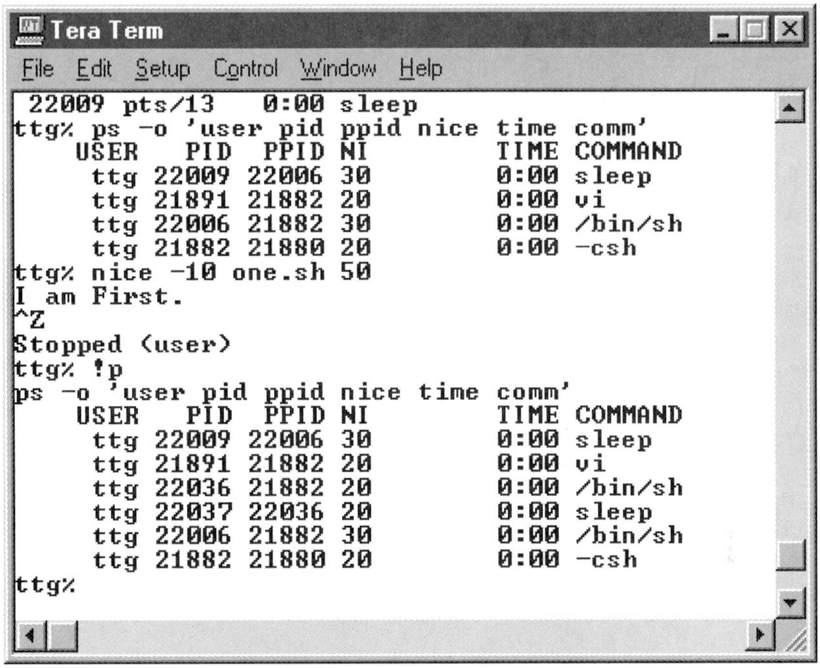

```
 22009 pts/13    0:00 sleep
ttg% ps -o 'user pid ppid nice time comm'
    USER    PID  PPID NI       TIME COMMAND
    ttg 22009 22006 30        0:00 sleep
    ttg 21891 21882 20        0:00 vi
    ttg 22006 21882 30        0:00 /bin/sh
    ttg 21882 21880 20        0:00 -csh
ttg% nice -10 one.sh 50
I am First.
^Z
Stopped (user)
ttg% !p
ps -o 'user pid ppid nice time comm'
    USER    PID  PPID NI       TIME COMMAND
    ttg 22009 22006 30        0:00 sleep
    ttg 21891 21882 20        0:00 vi
    ttg 22036 21882 20        0:00 /bin/sh
    ttg 22037 22036 20        0:00 sleep
    ttg 22006 21882 30        0:00 /bin/sh
    ttg 21882 21880 20        0:00 -csh
ttg%
```

FIGURE 10.18

Trying to change a nice value using the csh builtin.

⊕ Terminal Control (^S ^Q)

This last topic, terminal control, has absolutely *nothing* to do with process control. I
have included it here because some students think that the two commands of ^S and ^Q
are actually process-control commands when in fact they're *terminal-control commands*. It's important that you don't confuse process-control with terminal control. The
Ctrl-S command suspends terminal output and the Ctrl-Q command resumes output at
the terminal. When the output at the terminal is suspended, it seems as if the process
has stopped, and when the terminal output is restored, it seems as if the process has
restarted. This is an example of how observation without understanding can mislead us.
These commands date back to the days when there was no more command and process
output often scrolled by too quickly to read. Ctrl-S and Ctrl-Q are implemented at the
terminal, which is why they are called terminal-control commands. While they are useful, remember that they have nothing to do with process control.

Now it's your turn: work the exercises, and practice process control.

KEY TERMS

background
demand paging
external command
foreground
internal command
job
kernel mode
paging
parent-child relationship
preempted
quantum
round robin
signal
swapping
time slice
user mode
virtual
virtual memory

NEW COMMANDS

bg
fg
jobs
kill
nice
ps
stop

REVIEW QUESTIONS

10.1 Define all of the key terms.
10.2 Explain the difference between a built-in command and an external command.
10.3 List the nine process states. (Triple-space this list.)
10.4 On the list you created in Question 3, list each of the states that a process can move to from the numbered state. (For example, a process in state 1 can move either to state 2 or state 7.)
10.5 Describe the uses of the ps command.
10.6 Explain the rules that govern the parent-child relationship.
10.7 Explain what virtual memory is and why it is important in the Unix environment.
10.8 Describe the difference between a process running in the foreground and one running in the background.
10.9 Explain how killing a foreground process differs from killing a background process.

10.10 Explain how stopping a foreground process differs from killing a background process.

10.11 Explain how the jobs command differs from the ps command.

10.12 Describe the use of the nice command.

10.13 Why is the top command useful to a user? To a system administrator?

EXERCISES

10.1 Create a genealogy chart for 20 processes on your system. (You knew this was coming, didn't you!)

10.2 Using the ps command, examine all of the available processes on your system, and identify as many process states as possible.

10.3 Fork a second shell from your current shell, and use the ps command to examine the parent-child relationship.

10.4 Experiment with foreground and background processes. Use the scripts from the Web site or run other processes.

10.5 Fork a process and then kill it with the kill command. (First try to kill it politely, but if it won't die for you, you may use the "serious" kill command.)

10.6 Try to kill a process owned by another user. (Don't try this if you are running as root!)

10.7 Fork a process and then stop it with the stop command.

10.8 Try to stop a process owned by another user. (Again, don't try this if you are running as root!)

10.9 Once you have played with background and foreground, and with stop and the like, fork two or three processes, stop them, and then use the jobs command to see them.

10.10 Practice moving the sto pped processes from #9 to the foreground, stopping them there, and moving them to the background. Use first the job numbers and then the commands without the job numbers so you can see how the default works.

10.11 Experiment with using the nice command. I recommend you use /bin/nice rather than the default command in the shell.

10.12 If the top command is available on your system, use it to see which processes are consuming the most resources. Check this several times to see if it changes.

10.13 See how much memory your system is using. If it is using too much, suggest to your instructor that they purchase more, so your top output will look more reasonable. (Just kidding—don't make this sort of recommendation to your instructor!)

10.14 Explore the ^S and ^Q commands. For example, use them when listing a long file with the cat command, or with the command vmstat 1, which produces output once per second.

11

Regular Expressions and the grep Sisters

CHAPTER OBJECTIVES

After reading this chapter, you should be able to:

- Use fixed patterns to select lines from a file.
- Use regular expressions to select lines from a file.
- Employ the `grep` command to find particular lines in a file.
- Utilize the `egrep` command to find selected lines in a file.
- Properly use the extended regular expressions available in egrep.
- Use `fgrep` to find selected lines in a file without the use of regular expressions.

Up until now, with the exception of the editor tools, we haven't discussed any way to search for information based on the *contents* of a file. Oh sure, we could use the `cat` or `more` commands and manually search through a file looking for a particular word, but we had no tools to help speed up that process. And if you want to manually search for a particular line or two in a file of 3 million lines, more power to you. After studying this chapter I think you'll find yourself using `grep`, or her sisters, every day. They are so useful that you will probably marvel that you've gotten along without them this long.

⊕ **The History of** grep

The **grep** command has an interesting history. It seems that in the early days of Unix Doug McElroy was working with a hardware-software combination that would allow the computer to speak. (Well, at least it would make voicelike sounds—very mechanical but extremely advanced for the time, the early 1970s.) Those primitive voice-output units divided words up into *phonemes*, letter combinations that resulted in particular sounds. To build a file that this mechanical speaker needed, McIlroy had to find, pick out, and count the phonemes in many files. He was using the ed editor for this, and found it rather clumsy. The command he was using was: g/re/p. The g, of course, stood for global, the /re/ stood for the expression (or pattern) he was searching for, and the p caused the ed editor to print the lines that matched.

Enter Ken Thompson. Either he saw Doug using ed in a clumsy way, or Doug ran into Ken and explained his problem—the exact details are lost in the mist of human memory—but the next morning, when McIlroy came into his office there was a note from Ken that said "Try grep." Then, according to Ken, several more people heard about grep and linked to it. Soon afterwards Ken included grep on the distribution tape.

Going back to the origin of the name of the command, grep stands for *Global Regular Expression Print* (as Ken Thompson says, "Right out of the ed manual"). In some books you may see other explanations of grep's name. One of the more interesting is *General Regular Expression Parser*—sounds wonderfully complex, but alas, it is incorrect. I have even seen one text say that grep stands for *Global REPlace* (that one is terrible).

The grep command is a tool for *finding particular patterns* within a file. It is not an editor. It does not change the file; all it does is find things and then report what it has found. It's a very simple, yet elegant tool that I know you will use regularly. If I were comparing my collection of Unix commands to a toolbox, grep would be my trusty screwdriver. One very important rule you must remember about grep is that it returns *lines*. This fact leads us to part a of Refrigerator Rule No. 4.

Refrigerator Rule No. 4 (part a):

The grep command works line by line.

This is only the first part of Refrigerator Rule No. 4. We will learn another part in Chapter 12 and the third part in Chapter 13.

Something else you should know about grep is that she has two sisters: egrep and fgrep. They are younger and have different capabilities, which we'll discuss later in this chapter. For now, let's concentrate on grep and the patterns involved in her search efforts.

⊕ Searching within a File

The grep command searches within a file looking for particular patterns. There are many important options to the grep command that alter how it works; we'll discuss those later. For now it's enough to understand that all grep does is looks for patterns, either fixed patterns or regular expressions.

Fixed Patterns

Fixed patterns are just that, fixed. They don't change, they aren't magical, and they are very straightforward. Let's say, for example, I want to find out how many lines in a particular file contain the word *Street*. Look at Figure 11.1, and you can see how I used a fixed pattern with the grep command to do this in a file named buddy.song. The grep in this figure is a "plain vanilla" grep. It's also the most common grep you'll use. Notice that I enclosed the fixed pattern in tick marks (' ') to protect it from the shell. That protection is not necessary in this case. I would get exactly the same results if I typed

```
grep Street buddy.song
```

However, when we start talking about *regular expressions* a little later, you'll see there are some of those that you *must* protect from the shell. I have made it a habit therefore to *always* enclose the search pattern in tick marks. It is never incorrect to protect the

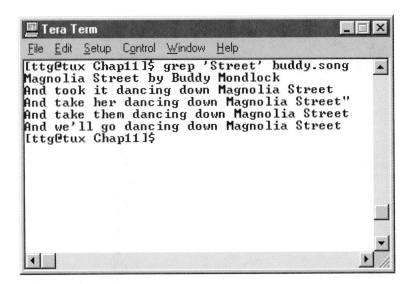

FIGURE 11.1
Using grep with a fixed pattern.

pattern, and if you, too, make it a habit, you won't run into problems when you start using patterns that must be protected.

By the way, the data file for the next set of examples contains the lyrics from Buddy Mondlock's song "Magnolia Street." He was kind enough to give me permission to use the lyrics as the data file. You can find out about his music at `http://buddymondlock.com`. Thanks, Buddy!

To create fixed patterns for which to search, it is important to make a distinction between the a *string* and a *word*. A **string** is a set of characters, not delimited by any particular characters. A string can be a part of a word, or it can be a whole word, or even several words. For example, the string *the* matches the word `the` but also matches `then`, `them`, `breathe`, `ethereal`, and even `thermodynamics`, because each of those patterns contains the three characters of `the`, in that order.

A **word** is a set of characters delimited by normal punctuation or white space. The word *the* would match only the string *the*, delimited by normal punctuation or white space. Look at the following two examples in Figure 11.2 to see the difference. The first `grep` in this figure looks for the *string* `the` in the file. It finds eight lines that contain the target string. The second `grep` looks for the *word* `the` in a file. To look for a word you need to use the `-w` option on the `grep` command. We'll discuss the options in a few pages but using that option now illustrates the difference between strings and words. The two lines marked with arrows do not contain the word `the` but rather have the string `the` embedded in the words `then` and `them`.

It's fairly easy to use fixed patterns with `grep`, and as you will find out later in the chapter, one of the grep sisters works very quickly because it accepts only fixed patterns. When you begin playing with `grep` you'll have lots of opportunities to use fixed patterns. But let's try a more sophisticated type of pattern now, shall we?

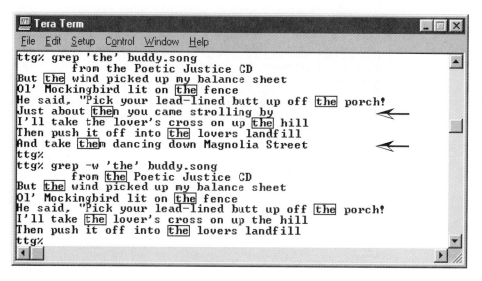

FIGURE 11.2

Illustrating the difference between a word and a string.

⊕ Regular Expressions

A **regular expression** is a shorthand, or abbreviated, way of creating a pattern. In geek-speak, a regular expression is called a *regex* and can be abbreviated as re or RE. You saw this in the name of the command we are studying, **g*re*p**.

Regular expressions can be created to describe text strings much like arithmetic expressions can be created to described surfaces or shapes. The key feature of a regular expression is that contains one or more metacharacters. You are familiar with the concept of metacharacters from our work with file-matching metacharacters. Some of the regular-expression metacharacters look suspiciously like file-matching metacharacters. Unfortunately, some of them don't have exactly the same meanings. One of the difficulties you may experience as a novice Unix user is confusing file-matching metacharacters with regular-expression metacharacters. It may help to remember the rule, "If it's a *filename* I use a file-matching metacharacter, but if I'm looking *inside* the file I use regular expressions."

Another thing to remember is that file-matching metacharacters are used only to match an entire filename, while regular expressions can match part of a word or line. It won't take long for you become comfortable with the difference. (By the way, one reason I suggested that you enclose regular expressions in tick marks was to prevent the shell from expanding them as if they were file-matching metacharacters. You wouldn't want to confuse the shell, now, would you?)

We will be learning about three different variants of grep. The oldest of these three sisters is grep. Any regular expression that grep recognizes egrep will also recognize, so we'll start with those regular expressions that are common to both of them. When we discuss egrep, we'll look at the extended set of regular expressions she supports. (The fgrep command doesn't recognize any regular expressions, and we will meet her last.)

The reason regular expressions are important to you as a Unix wizard is because they're used by so many different commands. For example ed, ex, vi, awk, and sed all use regular expressions to make your life easier. In addition, languages like Perl incorporate regular expressions as part of their command set. All in all, regular expressions are pretty much everywhere in Unix. After this chapter I know you won't understand how you have been able to live this long without a thorough understanding of them. Let's look at a handful of the most common regular expressions.

Period (.)
The period, as a regular-expression metacharacter, matches any single character *except the newline*. It matches exactly one character. For example, the regular expression

    '.wn'

would match the character string wn preceded by any single character. By the same token, the regular expression

    '.wn.'

would match any occurrence of the character string wn preceded *and* followed by another character, as long as that other character was not the newline. (Notice there are both leading *and* trailing periods in the .wn. expression.)

Look at Figure 11.3 to see an example of what I'm talking about. In the first `grep` I was looking for the character string wn preceded and followed by any other character—any character, that is, except the newline character. Notice that I found five lines that matched that particular pattern.

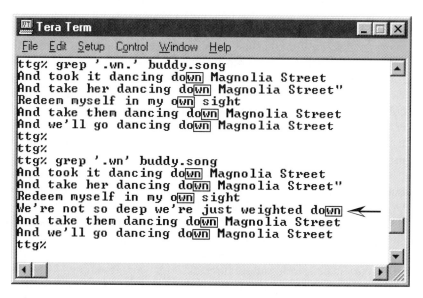

FIGURE 11.3

Using the period (.) regular expression.

In the second `grep` I was simply looking for the character string wn *preceded* by any other character. In that example I found six lines. The additional line is the fourth one of the lines grep found, the line that ends with the word down. The reason that the first grep didn't find the line that ends with down is because down is immediately followed by the newline character. And, as you know, the period type of regular expression matches any single character *except the newline*. This may seem a trivial distinction to you at this point, but, trust me, it can have grave implications if you forget it.

The true power of the period won't be seen until you begin combining it with other regular expressions. "Like what?" you ask. How about one of the more intriguing regular expressions, the asterisk?

Asterisk (*)

The trouble most people have with the asterisk is that they confuse it with the file-matching metacharacter that looks distressingly similar to it. As with prime real estate, the way you distinguish a file-matching metacharacter from a regular-expression metacharacter is simply by location, location, location.

As a regular expression, the asterisk matches *zero or more of the **preceding** character*. An asterisk metacharacter by itself is not a functional regular expression; it must be preceded by another character, and it matches any number of them.

Remember my recommendation that you always protect your regular expressions (enclose your regular expressions within tick marks)? The asterisk is one of the reasons why. It is the first regular expression you have learned that can cause you problems on the command line. When the shell interprets the command it first parses the command into individual pieces using white space. Next it attempts to expand any file-matching metacharacters. If the shell finds an unprotected asterisk, it will consider it a file-matching metacharacter.

Look at Figure 11.4 to see what I mean. Take a close look and notice the inconsistency. In the first grep I thought I was looking for the pattern tic* (the characters ti followed by zero or more cs). Since the title of the CD was *Poetic* Justice, I was pretty sure I'd find at least that line. Instead, I got some strange message about some files and lines that contained tictac1! What could be wrong? Aha, I forgot to protect my regular expression. Let's see how the shell interpreted the command I gave it.

The first thing the shell did was parse the command into three parts: the command, the pattern, and the file. Next it looked at the parts of the parsed command to see if there were any file-matching metacharacters it could expand. Since I had forgotten to protect the pattern, the shell saw the asterisk and dutifully expanded it. (I have included the output from the ls command, at the end of the figure so you can see what the shell expanded the file-matching metacharacter into (tictac1, tictac2, and tictac3).

After expanding the file-matching metacharacter, the shell passed control to the grep process. The grep command took the first string it found as the pattern, so it looked for the character string tictac1 in the files tictac2, tictac3, and buddy.song. The grep command reports both the name of the file and the line that contains the pattern if you tell it to search in multiple files. That is why grep showed us that it found the string tictac1 in the files tictac2 and tictac3.

In the second example in Figure 11.4, I protected the regular expression correctly and therefore grep worked as expected. If you make it a habit to always protect your regular expressions with tick marks, grep will work as expected for you, too.

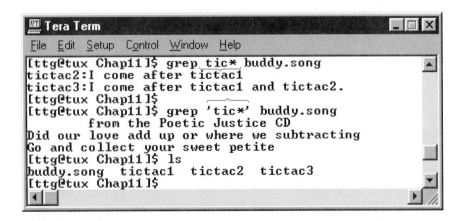

FIGURE 11.4

Illustrating the difference between a protected and an unprotected regular expression.

As I said the beginning of this section, the asterisk regular expression is never used by itself. It must always have another character preceding it. Now for a hard question: Can you think of a pair of regular expressions that you have already learned that will give the same results as the asterisk *file-matching* metacharacter? I'll give you a moment to think.

Right! The regular expression of period asterisk (.*) matches zero or more of any character. The period matches any character except the newline, and the asterisk matches zero of more of the *preceding* character. Don't be confused by the phrase *zero or more of any character*. It really means *any* character except, of course, the newline. Some of my students have been confused by thinking that if, for example, the period were to match the character a in the word `apple`, then the regular expression of .* (period asterisk) would match only a's. The asterisk as a duplicator multiplies the regular expression of the period, not the expansion of that regular expression.

Currency Symbol or dollar sign ($)

The next regular-expression metacharacter we will consider is sometimes referred to as an *anchor*. That's because it anchors the pattern to the end of the line or field. If you think back to learning about cursor movement in the `vi` editor, you'll remember that the dollar sign ($) moved the cursor to the last character of the line. At that time I mentioned that you should remember what the dollar sign did because it would be important to you later. Well, now is later.

In the case of a regular expression, a dollar sign causes the pattern to match only if it is at the end of the line. This statement is true for `grep`, but when we consider the awk command you will learn that the dollar-sign regular expression matches patterns at the end of fields as well as lines. So instead of remembering that the regular-expression metacharacter of the dollar sign matches patterns at the end of the line, I would rather you focused on the fact that the dollar sign matches patterns simply *at the end*. It doesn't matter whether it matches at the end of the line or the end of the field. As far `grep` is concerned, you could think of the dollar sign as matching the newline character, but that might lead to into trouble later when we get to awk.

Figure 11.5 shows an example of the use of this regular expression. Two different instances of the `grep` command are shown here. The first time I simply looked for the fixed pattern y anywhere in the file. The `grep` command found 17 such lines. In the second `grep` I looked for y at the end of lines. That `grep` found only two lines. The dollar-sign anchor is handy in `grep`, but it will be even more valuable when you start building awk scripts.

An, extremely important rule about using the dollar sign as a regular-expression metacharacter is that must be used as *the last character* of the regular expression. You cannot embed the dollar sign anywhere else in the pattern and have it work as anchor. You can see an example of this in Figure 11.6. Obviously, there are a lot of ys in this file—we saw that in Figure 11.5. Yet when I ran the `grep` for ys in Figure 11.6, I found nothing! I thought I had told `grep` to "go to the end of the line and find y," but what I actually told her was to "look for the fixed expression $y." Since there weren't any $ys in the file, `grep` has nothing to report. The placement of the anchor is absolutely essential.

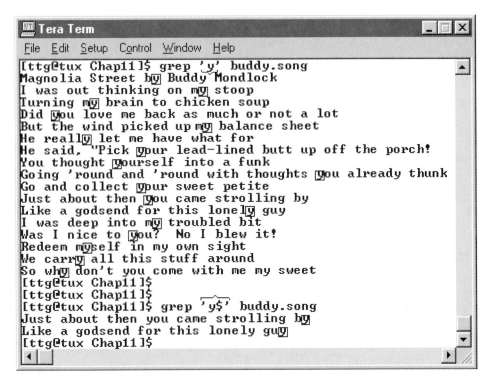

FIGURE 11.5

Using the $ regular expression.

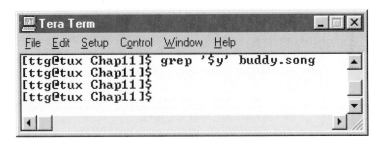

FIGURE 11.6

Results of a misplaced dollar sign.

Caret (^)

The caret (^) is the other regular-expression metacharacter that's referred to as an anchor. Again, thinking back to cursor movement in the vi editor, I'm sure you remember that the caret sent you to the beginning of the line. (Yes, you're right—it actually sent you to the "first nonblank character in the line." Good for you.) It should come as no surprise, then, that the caret regular expression anchors the pattern to the beginning of the line (or field).

Figure 11.7 shows an example of how this works. The regular expression I used here asked grep to find lines begining with an uppercase W. She reported back with five lines that began with W.

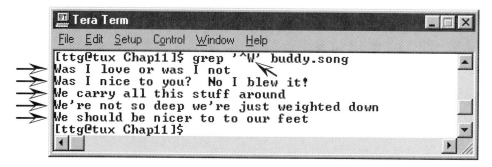

FIGURE 11.7

Using the ^ regular expression.

The beginning of the line anchor actually behaves very much like the ^ in vi. Take a look at Figure 11.8 to see what I mean. If you look closely at the poem in the figure, you'll notice that three lines start with Th, yet grep found only two of them. As far as grep is concerned, the line that starts with This starts with white space, followed by characters. Although the caret in vi looks at the first nonblank character in the line, the caret as a regular-expression metacharacter looks at the first character of the line. This is a small but important difference, as you can see from the figure.

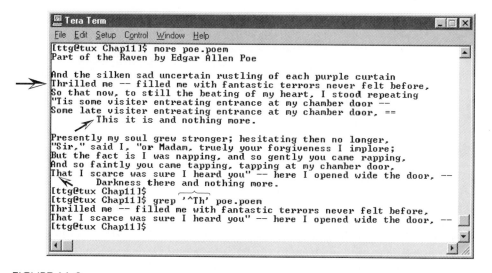

FIGURE 11.8

Investigating the behavior of the ^ regular expression.

The placement of the caret, like the placement of the dollar sign, is critical. The caret, if it is to serve as a regular-expression metacharacter, must be *the very first character* in the regular expression, just as the dollar sign must be the very last character.

As we have discussed before, the real power of regular expressions comes when you combine them. Here's another question for you: What does the following regular expression match? '^$' Let's little look a little more closely at this regular expression. It seems as though it is asking for something that starts and stops at the same place—a something that has nothing between its beginning and its end. What kind of line, pray tell, has nothing between its beginning and its end? (Sounds like one of those weird riddles your grandfather used to ask you, doesn't it?) Relax, it's really rather simple. The answer is, an empty line—not a blank line that has blanks, but an empty line that has nothing between its beginning and it's end. Another way to look at this is as an empty line that *starts* with the newline character. Wanna see it? Okay, look at Figure 11.9. Notice that the only lines grep found were empty. (I realize that just by looking at Figure 11.9 you can't tell those lines are empty and not blank; I fear you shall just have to trust me.)

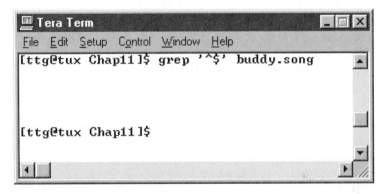

FIGURE 11.9

Playing with the '^$' regular expression.

How about taking a try at another one. What does the following regular expression match? '^.*$' That's not so tough, is it? In this instance the regular expression matches anything or nothing. Dissecting the regular expression, we see that it matches anything that starts with zero or more of any character and then ends. Go ahead, figure out what kind of line *won't* be matched by that particular regular expression. Let's see, what about an empty line? Well, an empty line starts, has zero characters, and then ends. That works.

What about a blank line? Hmmm, that starts, has a blank character or two or three, then ends. It works too. (Yes, blanks are characters; they are represented by the hexadecimal code 20 in the ASCII character set.) That last regular expression, using all of the regular-expression metacharacter bits we've learned so far, is exceedingly nice.

Now see Figure 11.10. Apparently, I managed to match every line in the file, both lines with text and lines that were empty. I realize that the cat, more, and less commands

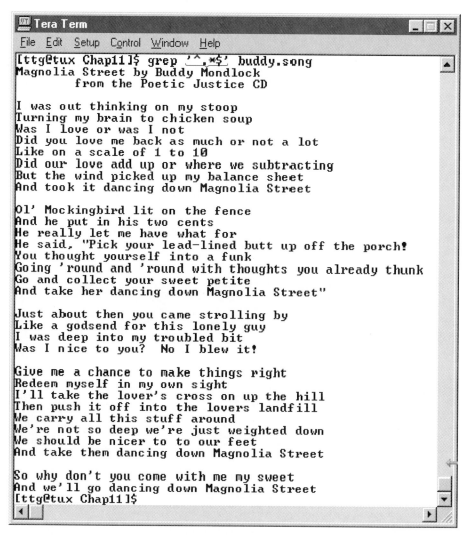

FIGURE 11.10

Using the '^.*$' regular expression.

are all shorter ways to display the contents of the file than this particular grep. I used grep instead to prove a point. Play a bit, as you did with file-matching metacharacters, and you'll get the hang of regular expressions, too. The next regular expression we'll consider works just like the file-matching metacharacter that resembles it.

Square Brackets ([ ])

Square brackets, [], allow you to choose *one* character entry from a range of entries, just as you did with file-matching metacharacters. You can use more than one set of square brackets in a given regular expression. Square brackets are probably the most misused regular expression, simply because people don't remember to use the power of the command but rather employ a hammer-and-tongs approach to achieve their ends. Once you've learned the options on the `grep` command, you'll realize, too, that using square brackets to handle all the upper/lowercase situations you encounter does not take advantage of the power of `grep`.

Take a look at Figures 11.11 and 11.12 and I'll show you a couple of ways to use square brackets. In the first command I simply displayed the contents of the file we are going to be playing with. Then I ran my first `grep` against the file. I used the square-brackets regular expression to select any lines that contained at least one of the four characters 1, 2, v, or x. Make sure you can explain why lines 6, 7, 10 and 11 showed up. The interesting thing about the regular expression in Figure 11.11 is it mixes numbers and letters in the same range expression.

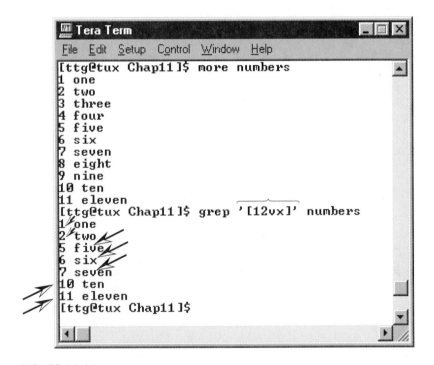

FIGURE 11.11

Using the [] regular expression to select lines from file.

Now take a look at Figure 11.12. It has a lot of information for you. The larger screen capture shows how `grep` in the Linux system processes the regular expressions. The smaller, inserted screen capture shows a difference in the way Solaris handles the same regular expression.

In the first command in Figure 11.12 I'm asking `grep` to show me any lines that contain one of a range of characters. That's pretty straightforward. The second `grep` is a little more creative. There I reversed the range of numbers to see what `grep` would do.

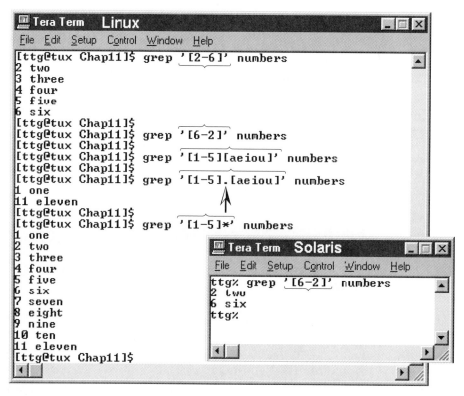

FIGURE 11.12

Interesting uses of the [] regular expression.

Remember our discussion of file-matching metacharacters. When we gave the bash shell in Linux a reverse range, it showed us every file except those at the ends of the range. When we did the same thing in the C shell on Solaris, it showed us just the two files that were at the ends of the range. The insert in Figure 11.12 shows what happens when we give grep a backward range in the C shell on Solaris. As with file-matching metacharacters, it gives us the two end points of the range and nothing in between. On the other hand, the bash shell in Linux shows us nothing. It finds no lines that match. This illustration reinforces what you learned way back in Chapter 4: don't use backward ranges.

The next grep in Figure 11.12 is looking for a number in the range of 1–5, followed by one of the vowels. Odd—it didn't find any. Taking a closer look at the data file, I realized that there were no lines that had a digit followed immediately by a letter. They all had a space between the last digit in the first letter. When I corrected my error in the next grep by adding an "I don't care" character between the two ranges, she found two lines that matched the pattern. Make sure you understand why grep found those two lines.

The last grep is really the most intriguing. Look at it carefully and see if you can figure out why it matched *all* the lines in the file.

Think about what the regular expression is actually saying. I find it helpful to say what I think is the interpretation of the regular expression out loud so as to evaluate my understanding of it. In this case I'm asking `grep` to display all the lines that contain zero or more numbers in the range of 1–5. That means that if a line contains one of the digits in the range of 1–5, it matches. If the line contains more than one of the digits in the range of 1–5, it matches. And if the line contains no digits in the range of 1–5, well, it matches, too.

As with the rest of the regular-expression metacharacters you have learned in this chapter, the square brackets become much more powerful when combined with other regular-expression metacharacters. You will have more than ample opportunity to experiment with this phenomenon as you work with the exercises at the end of the chapter and as you live in the Unix world.

Backslash (\)

The last character we are going to discuss in this section of regular-expression metacharacters, isn't a regular expression at all. I'm sure you have often used the back-slash (\) to prevent the shell from interpreting a file-matching metacharacter as a metacharacter. You can use the same character to prevent `grep` from interpreting the regular-expression metacharacter as a regular-expression metacharacter.

Suppose I wanted to find all the lines in the poem file that end in a period. Figure 11.13 shows what happened when I tried to match the period at the end of each line. It seems I matched *every* line. Something must be amiss. Remember that the period is the regular-expression metacharacter that matches any character except the newline character. I suppose every line in the poem that isn't empty has some character preceding the new line. That means I matched every non-empty line!

Time to bring out the backslash. Look at Figure 11.14. That looks decidedly better! This time I protected the regular expression. By preceding it with a backslash I told the `grep` to ignore the magical properties of the regular-expression period metacharacter. Because of the backslash, the period was treated like a regular character. Since

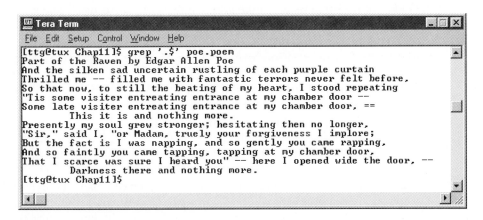

FIGURE 11.13

Trying to match the period at the end of a line.

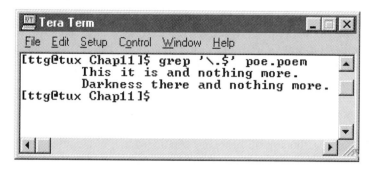

FIGURE 11.14

Successfully finding lines that end in a period.

the backslash protects only one character, the $ still functioned as an end-of-element marker, so all grep found were periods at the ends of lines.

Now that you have become a master of the regular expression, let's look at the three commands most often associated with regular expressions. By the way, if you feel the need to further research regular expressions, I recommend the book *Mastering Regular Expressions* by Jeffrey E. F. Friedl, published by O Reilly and Associates. This book delves deeply into regular expressions, and while it is mostly geared toward Perl programming, it will give you a much deeper understanding of regular expressions.

grep

```
grep [options] 'pattern' [file]
```

The oldest of the three sisters in the grep family is, of course, grep. She was created by Ken Thompson for his own use, and when others found out about her utility she became part of the standard distribution. The **grep** command has undergone numerous upgrades, changes, and revisions over time. Dr. Aho (the a in awk) created her two sisters, fgrep and egrep. We'll meet them in just a bit.

The version of grep that runs in many flavors of Linux, the GNU version, has many more options than the more traditional version that runs in Solaris. The GNU version even has options that allow you to emulate both fgrep and egrep, even though those tools are also available in the shells. We'll explore the more traditional version of grep, since all the options for that flavor will work with the newer versions as well.

Before we start looking at the options for the grep command, I'd like to share one of grep's special features with you that shows what a very smart command she is. If you ask her to search for a particular pattern in a *single* file, she will simply return the lines that match. But if you ask her search for that pattern in multiple files, she will not only return the lines that match but also precede those lines with the filename followed by a colon.

You see, grep has faith that if you ask her look in *one* particular file, then you know the file she's reporting on. On the other hand, if you ask her look in multiple files, you might not know which file a particular line comes from, so she will tell you.

Look at Figure 11.15 to see an example of this appealing grep feature. I asked grep to find all occurrences of the string all in three different files. Since I asked her look in more than one file, she preceded each line she found with the filename. Pretty smart for such an old command! As you'll see when we look at the options, you can ask grep to tell you only the filenames where she found the pattern, if that's all you're interested in, without displaying the lines found.

FIGURE 11.15

Using grep or multiple files.

grep options

Suppose you don't need to see the lines that contain a pattern but merely want to know how many times that particular pattern exists in a file. For example, maybe your boss wants you to change all the occurrences of a particular HTML pattern. Before you do it, she wants you to tell her how many times that pattern exists in a particular file. You could use grep with no options and count the lines yourself. Or you could use grep with no options and then pipe the output to the word count (wc -1) command. Or you could have grep count them for you. (This is a perfect example of letting the command to do the work.)

Figure 11.16 shows examples of all three approaches. Although Buddy's song isn't all that long, and eight lines aren't that many to count, consider this an educational example and pretend that the file is 26,804 lines long and that 13,292 of them matched. In the first example I must manually count the lines, that's the most labor-intensive for me. In the second example I am using commands to count the lines for me, but I must invoke two processes to do that, which is less efficient for the machine. In addition, I have to type more characters, which is less efficient for me. The last example is by far the most efficient—utilizing the power of grep and having her do exactly what I need done. Remember, always let the command do the work.

-c

The first option to the grep command, which you have already seen, is -c *(count)*. You're familiar with the way it works, having studied Figure 11.16 so carefully. The biggest problem most people have with this option is that it gives you only the count of

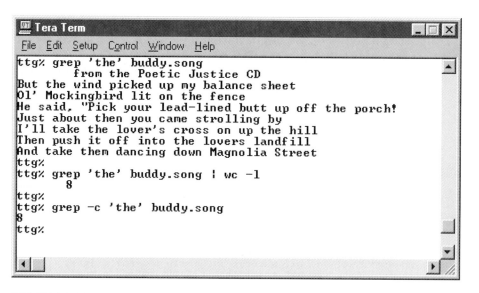

FIGURE 11.16

Letting the command do the work.

the lines, not the content. It is the option to use if you need to know how many times a particular string occurs in a file or a set of files. Actually, that's a little misleading: what the **-c** option will tell you is how many lines contain *at least one instance* of the particular string. Remember that grep finds lines that contain one or more instances of the pattern. If the pattern occurs three times in one line, grep will report that line just once, and will count it just once.

-h

The –h (*minus the head*) option allows you to suppress printing the filenames (the head of the lines) when you use grep to search for a pattern in multiple files. This lets you guess which file the lines came from, as a way to make your life much more interesting. But there may be times when you really don't care which file a particular line came from. In that situation, this is the option for you. Figure 11.17 shows -h coupled with its inverse, the -l option, discussed next.

-l

The -l (*minus the lines*) option is the inverse, or opposite, of the -h option. This option allows you see the filenames that contain the lines matching your pattern but not the lines themselves. It's often the case that you want to know which files contain a particular string without caring what else is on the lines that contain the target string. The -l option is frequently used.

Figure 11.17 shows both this option and the -h option. Notice that with the -l option, each file is listed only once. The first grep demonstrates the use of the -h option. Again, I looked for lines containing the character string all. Because I specified the -h option, grep showed me the lines without prepending their filenames.

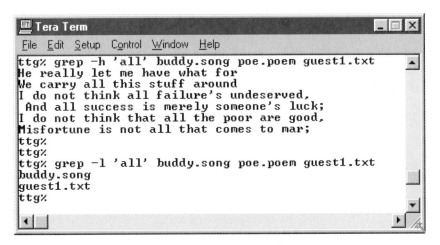

FIGURE 11.17

The –h and –l options.

The second grep in the figure demonstrates the use of the –l option. This time I looked for the same string, but with this option all grep told me were the names of the files that contained the string. In practice I find the –l option far more useful than the –h.

-i

I realize that the –i option is out of alphabetic sequence here. I chose to put the –h and –l options together because they are the inverse of each other. The –i (*ignore case*) option is one of those options that will save you the task of creating regular expressions if you simply let the command do the work. For example, suppose I wanted to find all the lines that contain the string the or The in a particular file. Figure 11.18 shows two different ways I could approach the problem.

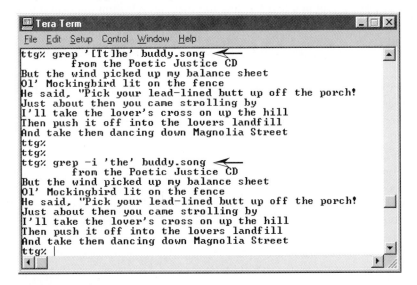

FIGURE 11.18

The nagging problem of case.

Obviously, the two `greps` gave the same results in this case. The difference is in how much work I had to do, and how much work I allowed the command to do. Creating a regular expression to handle the capitalization issue required me to type 50 percent more code in the first example. In addition, I didn't let the command do the work! What regular expression would I need to create if I wanted to a to have `grep` find any instance of the string `the` regardless of which letter or letters were capitalized? I think the regular expression would have to look like this:

[Tt][Hh][Ee]

Pretty ugly, isn't it? Well, I suppose, if you were a real aficionado of regular expressions you might think it's rather beautiful, but as far as I'm concerned, at least in this instance, it's very long and involved. Especially considering that the second `grep` in Figure 11.18 will find any occurrence of a string `the` regardless of which letter or letters are capitalized.

You do have to be a little bit careful with the ignore-case option. Certainly it is an ideal solution in many cases, yet it can give you unexpected results sometimes. If the file contains odd capitalizations of the word *the*, and all I want are instances where the *first character* is either upper or lowercase, then the `-i` option is definitely not my best choice. Most of the time, I need to let the command do the work. Nevertheless, I can't be unthinkingly tied to that particular directive. You need to let the command do the work when that is the most expedient solution. (As I stress to my students, I expect them—and you, dear reader—to create efficient, elegant, and exact solutions.)

-n

The `-n` (*line number*) option is probably most valuable to those of you are programmers or scriptors. As you can see in Figure 11.19, this option asks `grep` to include the line number from the target file with each line that it returns. When we're using `grep` to just poke about in a text file, line numbers aren't often important to us. If we are looking at a program, a script, or an HTML file, then line numbers can be extremely important. They can also tell us something about the size of a particular file, or the relative location of a particular string in a file.

The first `grep` in Figure 11.19 is the plain-vanilla version. It shows us that, indeed, a login I.D. of `ttg` exists. That's nice. The second `grep`, however, tells us something very significant. That ttg user is the fourteenth record in the file. Wow, he must be a really important person to be that far up in the password file! <Grin>

-v

For some reason that your humble author just can't figure out, this option is one of the most frequently forgotten, underutilized, and *amazingly useful* options for the three commands. The `-v` (*no cute memory trick*) tells `grep` to report every line that *doesn't* contain the pattern specified. (This is the direct descendent of the v command in *ex*.

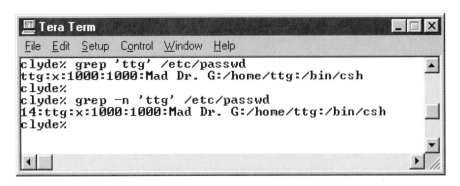

FIGURE 11.19

Finding a line's position within a file.

I am sure you remember that one!) Sometimes you will want to search through a large file, not knowing exactly what you're searching for yet knowing what you *don't* want to see. For example, suppose you have a process that runs continuously and reports its status every 30 seconds. Most of the time the process returns a "situation normal" message, but if there's a problem with the system it returns one of a dozen different error messages. After the processes run for 30 or 40 weeks, you probably won't want to manually scan through the file it created looking for any error messages it might have written. But since you know that the error message you are looking for won't contain the word "normal," you can ask grep, using the -v option, to show you all the lines that *don't* contain the string normal.

Even though you may not need this option very often, please remember it. There will be times, more of them that you might expect, when this option will make your life much easier. Besides, you'll impress people when you use it, and they'll be in awe of your amazing ability with grep.

-w

The last option were going to discuss, -w (*find words*), is a relatively recent addition to the family of grep options, and an extremely useful one. Figure 11.20 shows something of what you would have to go through if you didn't have the -w option and you were trying to find just the instances of the *word* all rather than the *string* all. To emphasis the difficulty that the -w option can save you, let me reveal that in truth, the first grep in the figure is actually my *eleventh attempt* at creating a set of punctuation and other word delimiters around the word the. (I know gack! isn't really a command, but sometimes . . .)

Anyway, the second grep in the figure shows how the -w option makes life much easier when you're looking for words. Remember, though, you use this only when you're looking for words. When you're looking for strings, this option can give you erroneous results.

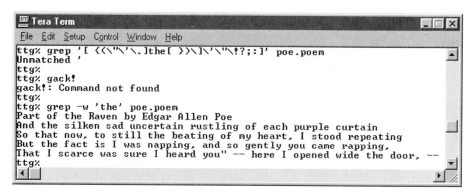

FIGURE 11.20

Trying to find words rather than strings.

Unhappily, the -w option may not be available for grep in every version of Unix. I know it's available in Linux and Solaris, but I can't speak for all the flavors of Unix. My best advice is to try it on your machine; then you'll know.

Let's look at a couple of more recent additions to the grep family.

egrep

```
egrep [options] 'pattern' [file]
```

As good as grep is, Alfred Aho decided it could be improved upon by making it recognize more regular expressions. But rather than simply rewriting grep using the same algorithm, to work as grep used to work, he incorporated new computer-science techniques that made egrep more efficient than grep. (On many systems **egrep** is the fastest grep, faster even than fgrep.) The e in egrep stands for *extended*, indicating that the set of regular expressions recognized by egrep is an extended set, beyond those that grep recognizes.

Another feature of egrep is that it can consume a very significant amount of memory when processing a complex regular expression. Since Aho had grep as a model, almost all of the grep options are supported by egrep, and he added a couple. We'll look at the new options in a moment, but first let's look at the new regular expressions that Aho built into egrep.

Expanded Set of Regular Expressions

+

The plus-sign (+) regular expression expands our capabilities, allowing us to match *one or more* contiguous instances of the character that immediately precedes it. The word "contiguous" is critical in this definition. Contiguous means without anything intervening between instances of the character. For example, if I were to use egrep to look for the regular expressions abb+cd, it would match lines that contain two or more bs in a row. It would not match a line that contained the string abacabacab, even though that string contains multiple bs. Why? Because they are not contiguous.

Figure 11.21 shows an example of the use of the plus sign. The first part of the figure shows you the numbers.file file. My task was to find all the lines that contained the digits 12 followed by one or more 3s, followed by the digit 4. Not a terribly daunting task, or is it? First I used grep to look for the string 1234 in the file. It showed me the three lines that contained a particular arrangement of digits. Not exactly what I wanted. "Fine," I said, "I'll have grep show me all the lines that have multiple threes, using the asterisk." Unfortunately for me, the asterisk also allows for *zero* instances of the preceding character, so two of the lines that grep showed me had no 3 at all! Then

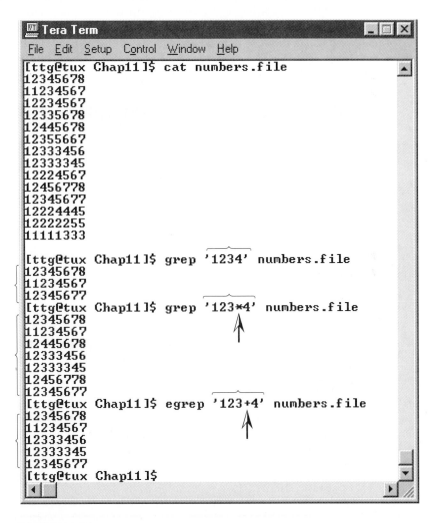

FIGURE 11.21

A somewhat contrived example of using the plus sign.

I remembered my good friend `egrep`, and the fact that extended `grep` allowed additional regular expressions.

The last command shown in Figure 11.21 shows how I used the regular-expression metacharacter of the plus sign to find all the lines that contained *one or more* threes. (Okay, it's a somewhat contrived example, but it does show how to use the + rather succinctly.)

?

There will be times when you don't want to find a one *or more* instances of a particular character. Instead you want to find those lines that contain either zero or exactly one instance of the character. In those cases the plus sign won't work, because it will find one *or more* contiguous instances. To accommodate this need, Aho chose to have `egrep` recognize the regular-expression metacharacter of the question mark.

The question mark will match *zero or one* instance of the character preceding it. Figure 11.22 shows another, again slightly contrived, example demonstrating this regular expression. As usual, the first thing I did here was to list the numbers.file again, for your viewing pleasure. As I was looking for lines with 12, followed by either no 3 or one 3, followed by a 4, I first tried our old friend the plus sign. Oops, the plus sign doesn't

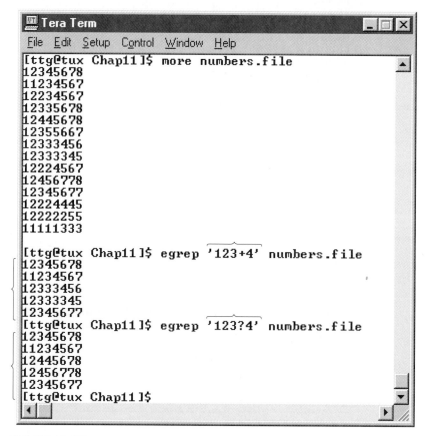

FIGURE 11.22

Using the ? regular expression.

support zero instances, and it also supports more than one instance. Since that didn't work, I tried our new friend the question mark. Success! The last egrep in the figure shows the lines that contain the digits 12 followed by either no 3s or one 3, followed by the digit 4.

It may seem that I am spending a great deal of time splitting hairs here. I assure you that as you began to create complex and sophisticated regular expressions you'll come to appreciate the power of the question mark and the plus sign and will be glad we spent the time to learn how to use them properly.

|

The vertical bar (which looks amazingly like the pipe symbol) is my favorite expanded regular-expression metacharacter. If you are a student of formal logic, you may recognize the vertical bar as the logical OR operator. This regular expression allows you to combine two *or more* regular expressions in a single egrep command and choose lines that contain *any* of them.

Look at Figure 11.23. As I hope you've come to expect, the first thing I did was show you the contents of the data file. Next I asked egrep to show me any line that

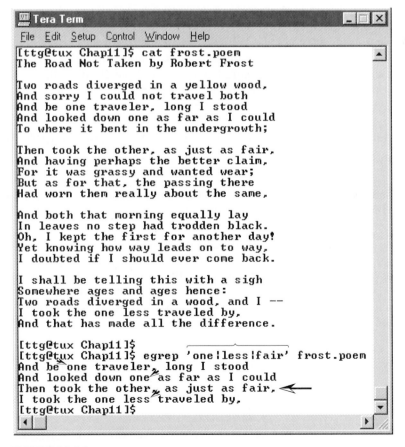

FIGURE 11.23

Using logical OR, |, regular expression.

contained the string one *or* the string less, *or* the string fair. This is a powerful pattern matching tool. Instead of fixed strings, I could have listed a series of regular expressions and found all lines that started with the words And, In, Two, or Somewhere. Being able to select one from multiple patterns in a single egrep gives this tool amazing flexibility.

( )

The parentheses enclose patterns or regular expressions that are treated as a single group. Assume that I want to match all the lines containing the words first, for, fair, and I want to be more efficient about it than creating a list with the vertical bar. Notice that all three of the strings I am searching for start with the letter f. Figure 11.24 shows how to use the parentheses, as well as the logical OR, to create a more efficient search. As you can see, I used the parentheses to group three possible ends to the words, so that egrep was looking for the three words I was interested in. There will be times when this regular expression can save you a great deal of coding, most often combined with the vertical bar (logical Or).

I was bemoaning the fact that I had only contrived egrep examples for my book to a good friend of mine. He said, "Well, let me tell you about how I used egrep to solve a problem at work." Following is my friend's real-life, right-out-of-industry example of using egrep in place of a very long and convoluted script:

My friend's company supplies software to radio stations. All the service notes for each broadcast client are stored in a plain-text file. It's done that way to allow the support staff to easily grep particular information from the files. The service notes from 1991 through 1994 have this format:

```
Technician: <Initials> Date: <YYYYMMDD> Time: <HH:MM>  Duration:
<MMM:SS> Calls: <Call_Letters>
```

Then in 1994 the company began taking some clients that weren't radio stations, so it changed the last field of the data record to

```
Client: <Call_Letters_or_Company>
```

In the volatile world of broadcasting, the owner of a station can change that station's call-letter identity at any time. One such case is KNJO in Thousand Oaks, California, which reimaged itself as K-Lite a few years ago and became KLIT. It added the "-FM" suffix a few months later.

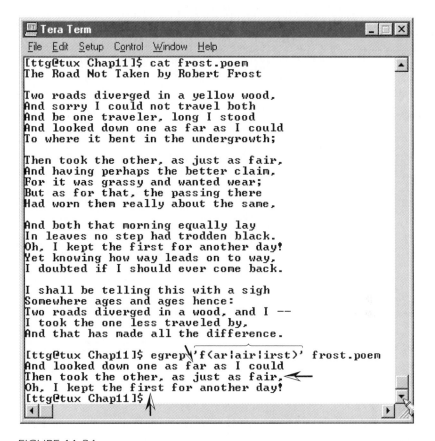

FIGURE 11.24

Using the () to group parts of a pattern.

In order to find all of the service records for this particular client, my friend needed to select records containing any of the following call letters: KNJO, KLIT, or KLIT-FM (but not KLIT-AM!). And remember, the call letters might be prefixed with either the string `Calls` or `Client`, followed by a colon and one or more spaces. Interesting problem! I have created a small sample database of these kinds of service records and incorporated my friend's egrep in Figure 11.25. Take a look: it's a very elegant egrep!

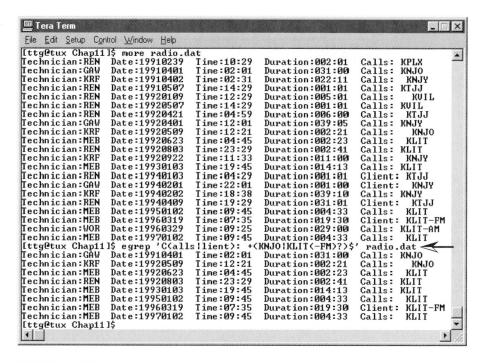

FIGURE 11.25

An elegant and powerful example of `egrep`.

Wow, Figure 11.25 certainly is busy! Buried in there, about three-quarters of the way down the screen, is the actual `egrep` I would like you to focus upon. It's an amazing example. It looks something like the following:

```
egrep 'C(alls|lient): +(KNJO|KLIT(-FM)?)$'
```

Have no fear, we will carefully dissect it. Remember that what he was trying to do was find all of the service records for a particular client based on that client's call letters. The first part of the regular expression identifies records that contain either the word `Calls` or the word `Client`. Using the parentheses is an efficient way to look for either of those two words. Notice how the vertical bar (logical Or) is used within the parentheses. It's a common construct to have two or more possible strings within a parenthetical phrase. Following the first word, my friend was looking for a colon followed by one or more spaces (remember that the plus sign says "one or more"). After the space(s), the regular expression looks for the patterns of the call letters for the particular station in question.

Notice that using the question mark immediately following the parenthetical (`-FM`) directs `egrep` to look for lines that contain *zero or one* instances of the phrase within the parentheses. That is an extremely elegant use of the question mark. Finally, just to make sure that this particular pattern doesn't occur somewhere else in the record, the dollar sign anchor ties the whole regular expression to the end of the line.

Spend a few more moments studying this regular expression, it's probably one of the prettiest ones you'll see for a long time. (Yes, a well-crafted regular expression can be pretty!) Although you won't be required to write one quite this sophisticated in the

TABLE 11.1   Some Extended Regular-Expression Characters

Character	What It Does
+	Matches one or more of the characters that precede it.
?	Matches zero or one of the characters that precede it.
|	Matches one of several patterns or regular expressions, the logical Or.
()	Groups patterns or regular expressions.

exercises, do remember when you get into the real world that regular expressions and egrep can give you this kind of elegance and power. If you make it a point to spend a little time thinking about the records you would like to find, you can craft elegant, efficient, dare I say it—"bulletproof"—solutions.

Table 11.1 shows all of these new regular-expression characters.

Additional Options

There are two additional options that are unavailable in grep but supported by egrep. The first is very specific and seldom used. The second is extremely useful if you're going to create a set of search patterns to use across multiple files.

-e

The -e option is used when you're looking for a pattern that begins with a hyphen. The -e option tells egrep that the data that follows is a regular expression or pattern, not an additional option, even though it begins with a hyphen. Figure 11.26 shows an example of

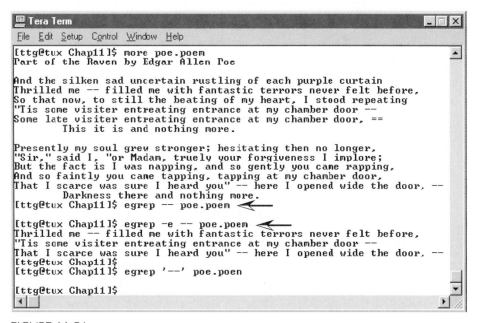

FIGURE 11.26

Using the -e option with egrep.

this, using the Poe poem. As you can see, several lines contain a pair of hyphens next to each other. If I want to find just those lines, I can't use the -- pattern by itself, because egrep thinks it's some sort of option and so waits for me to complete the command. (If you attempt this, you'll need to use either the ∧C or ∧D command to exit from egrep.) I tried this in the first egrep example in this figure. In the second example, I used the -e option followed by the -- pattern. In that instance I was successful! "But wait," you say, "you didn't enclose your pattern within tick marks. What if you had done that?" Excellent question. You are very astute! The third egrep in Figure 11.26 is the answer to your question. When I enclosed the -- pattern within tick marks, the egrep failed.

The -e option is not one you will use every day; you probably won't even use it every month. However, if you need to find patterns that begin with a hyphen, it will be invaluable.

-f

The -f option is extremely interesting. Many of the text-processing commands we will discuss in the next couple of chapters use an external file of directives. Using an external file is very efficient if you're going to search for regular expressions or patterns at different times across multiple files. It's also very useful if you're performing a complex task and might need to edit the directives for that task (something like using the history option on the command line to edit a command that has fallen victim to a fat-finger error). Aho added that functionality to egrep, and, as we'll see in the next section, he also added it to fgrep.

Figure 11.27 shows how to use this particular feature. Since I am sure you're familiar with the data files we've been using in this chapter, I didn't list them all again. Do notice, however, the contents of the file sample.egrep, which contains the egrep directive. It looks for patterns that begin with either an upper or lowercase b, followed by any other character, followed by a lowercase t.

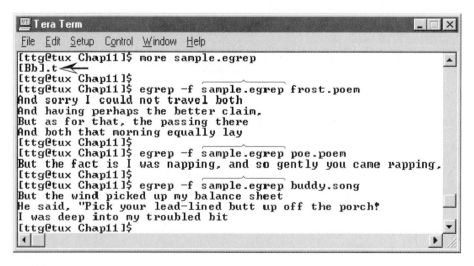

FIGURE 11.27

Using -f with egrep.

It's very handy to be able to create files that contain directives for commands. It's especially handy if you're creating a long command like the one in Figure 11.25. Remember that both egrep and her sister fgrep accept directives from a file if you use the -f option.

⊕ fgrep

Some folks think that the "f" in fgrep stands for "fixed." I have also read that it stands for "fast," because fgrep is supposed to be faster then either grep or egrep. (Research by an independent testing laboratory, (my fellow instructors, and myself), however, indicate that egrep is the fastest of the three grep sisters.) One book I read even went so far as to call **fgrep** "final grep," since it was supposed to be the last one Aho wrote. When I wrote to Dr. Aho, though, he told me that he chose the name fgrep because he had just written egrep, and, well, f follows e.

I will admit I have a problem with fgrep**'s** name. Remember that grep stands for Global *Regular Expression* Print. But fgrep *doesn't support regular expression metacharacters!* So fgrep really should be fgp, but that would be a little difficult to pronounce. To save our speech, and because Al named it fgrep, I guess we'll have to let it slide (nonetheless, it bothers me).

The fgrep command is wonderful if you're searching for patterns that might be considered to be regular expressions by the other two grep sisters. For example, if you're looking for asterisks or periods, or even a combination of asterisks and periods, the fgrep command is the one for you!

Take a look at Figure 11.28, and see how I used fgrep to find some lines that contain patterns both grep and egrep would've considered to be regular expressions.

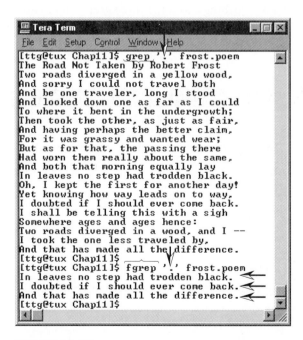

FIGURE 11.28

Using fgrep to find lines with a period in them.

Now I didn't really intend to output the whole poem in Figure 11.28, but since I used this particular regular expression, the result was the whole poem. What I asked grep to do was to show me all the lines that had at least one of any character in them, and it seems that every one of them had a character! What I actually wanted to do was find the lines that had periods in them. And if you look at that little fgrep way down near the bottom of the figure, that's exactly what she found for me.

This is an excellent example of using fgrep to search for something that would be interpreted as a regular expression by her two sisters. Of course, I could have protected the period, as you can see in Figure 11.29, but that would've cost an extra character in the regular expression. (Okay, go ahead and be picky—I know that fgrep is one character longer than grep and that I could've used grep instead of egrep. Sometimes you just have to work with me.)

As you can see in Figure 11.29, I could protect each individual regular-expression character and have the same effect as fgrep. But Aho didn't want us to have to protect all the regular expressions, so he gave us fgrep, which doesn't use them. Most of the time it's faster, at least for you, to use fgrep if you're looking for patterns that contain characters that might be interpreted as regular expressions rather than protecting them in either grep or egrep.

The fgrep command supports all of the options we learned in both grep and egrep, and it also supports one additional option that you will rarely use, yet will be invaluable when you need it. The option -x directs fgrep to match lines from the file only if the pattern provided *matches the entire line*. It's an important criteria, and it makes fgrep most helpful in an extremely specific application.

But that's enough reading about the three grep sisters. Now it's time for you to get personally acquainted with them.

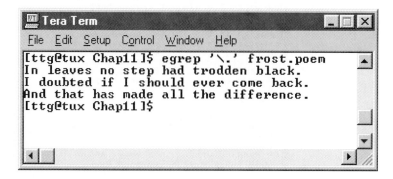

FIGURE 11.29

Protecting the regular expression in egrep to make it work like fgrep.

KEY TERMS

grep
regular expression
string
word

NEW COMMANDS

```
egrep
fgrep
grep
```

REVIEW QUESTIONS

11.1 Define each of the many key terms.
11.2 Explain how a regular expression can make searching in a file more efficient.
11.3 Who invented grep? egrep? fgrep?
11.4 List and describe each of the regular-expression metacharacters.
11.5 Differentiate among the three grep sisters, explaining their strengths and limitations.
11.6 Explain why it is always a good idea to enclose your patterns and regular expressions in tick marks.
11.7 Describe the use of the -f option in egrep or fgrep.
11.8 Explain the difference between a fixed pattern and a regular expression.
11.9 Describe what characters each of these regular-expression metacharacters matches:

    a. period
    b. asterisk
    c. currency symbol
    d. caret
    e. square bracket
    f. backslash

11.10 Explain the importance of the following grep/egrep/fgrep options:

    a. —c
    b. —i
    c. —v
    d. —w

EXERCISES

Use the file buddy.song **(on the website) for these exercises**:

11.1 Find all the lines that contain the string Mag.
11.2 Find all the lines that contain the *word* we.
11.3 Find all the lines that contain the character 1 preceded by any character, which in turn is preceded by the letter i. (For example, the word chitlin matches.)

11.4 Find all the lines that contain the string i t except those where i t are the last characters of a line.

11.5 Find all the lines that start with the character G.

11.6 Find all the lines that end with the character k.

11.7 How many lines are empty in the file? You don't need to see them, just count them.

11.8 Find all the lines that start with A, D, or W using a single grep.

Use the frost.poem **file for these exercises**:

11.9 Find all the lines that end with a period.

11.10 Find all the lines that don't contain any of the following characters: wxyz.

11.11 Which line number(s) contain the word as?

11.12 Find all the lines that contain the word For or for.

11.13 This one is a little more challenging. Find all the lines that contain at least one of the strings ff, tt, or 11, using a single command.

11.14 Find all the lines that contain one or more occurrences of the letter o, followed by the letter d.

11.15 Find the lines that contain any of these words: wear, worn, or wood.

11.16 Create a command file that contains your regular expression from Exercise 13, and execute that file in egrep.

Use the contrived.1 **file for these exercises**:

11.17 Find all the lines that contain an o, followed by zero or one r.

11.18 Find all the lines in the file that contain an asterisk.

11.19 Now find all the lines that contain a question mark or a backslash.

12

Types of Text Processing

CHAPTER OBJECTIVES

After reading this chapter, you should be able to:

- Use the translate command to replace characters in a text file.
- Successfully sort a file on one or more key fields.
- Employ the merge option of the sort command to combine two files.
- Modify the contents of a file using the sed editor.

As you no doubt remember from our discussion of the history of Unix, when Dennis, Ken, and the boys were caught working on the then embryonic Unix system they claimed it was a text-processing system. Since they were encouraged to build a text-processing system, and since a legal department was their first customer and used Unix solely as a text-processing system, there are still parts of Unix that look very much like text processing. In this chapter we will explore those text-processing roots and see how they are still of great value to us today.

Back when we learned about redirecting standard input, I told you that there was one command that still required standard input to be redirected into it. As I hope you remember, that command was translate (**tr**). Now it's time for us to look at tr in detail.

I must confess that when I began writing this chapter, and in all the years I've taught Unix, I've always looked at tr as a simple little command that was an interesting leftover from the days when Unix was a text-processing system. I knew it had some useful features and used it occasionally, most often in its simplest form. However, having done the research for this chapter, I find myself amazed at the power of tr and look at it with much greater respect. It's a very powerful tool and one I'm sure you'll find most useful as you take the time to study it.

tr

```
tr [options] [string1] [string2] [< target.file]
```

In its most basic form, the translate command simply replaces, on a positional basis, each character from string 1 with the corresponding character found in string 2. Translate reads only from standard input and writes only to standard output—it is a perfect filter. It's important that you understand that translate works *byte by byte*. In fact, it's so important that it will become part of one of our refrigerator rules.

Refrigerator Rule No. 4

(part a): grep works line by line.
(part b): tr works byte by byte.

So why am I expanding this a simple statement into a refrigerator rule? Because too many times I've watched students, and even professional Unix users, try to use tr to change words not bytes! For example, they try to change the to THE. And translate will do a fine job of that, with some slight side effects. Take a look at Figure 12.1.

As you can see from the first line of the second stanza in the poem, tr actually did translate the word the to the word THE. However, to accomplish that marvelous task, translate changed *every instance* of the lowercase t to T, *every instance* of h to H, and *every instance* of e to E. Not exactly what I had in mind. That just goes to remind us that translate works *byte by byte*, not with words or strings.

While I'm preaching a bit, I need to share two other observations with you. First observation: In other texts and even some reference manuals, you may see the following command sequence recommended with the translate command:

```
cat somefile | tr 'aeiou' 'AEIOU'
```

That's a perfectly fine tr, preceded by a perfectly fine cat, and I have a major problem with it. The problem is one of efficiency—not so much your efficiency as the system's efficiency. I don't see any reason to run two processes when one will do the job. Why waste the process space? Why load up the system with another whole process? The tr command is a perfect filter. It's designed to read from standard in or what's been redirected to it and

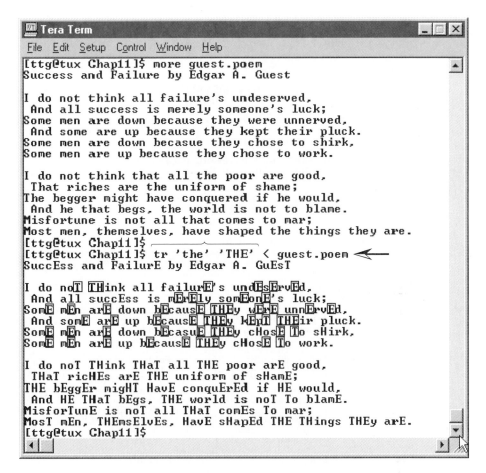

FIGURE 12.1

Using tr (translate) to change, ahem, words?

to write to standard out. It's true that the tr command will be often used in pipes. But why, oh why, create two processes when one will do the job? The following command will produce exactly the same output as the previous command. The difference is that it does it with one process!

```
tr 'aeiou' 'AEIOU' < somefile
```

Instead of piping the file into the tr command you can redirect the file into the command. Not only does it save you keystrokes, but it lightens the system's burden.

Second observation: When you're translating a series of letters to another series of letters, in most cases *you don't need to include either range of letters in square brackets*. Look at Figure 12.2 to see what I mean. Look carefully at the two translates. In the first, I surround the ranges of letters to be translated with square brackets. In the second, I just use the ranges of letters to be translated. The results are *exactly* the same. Because translate works positionally, the first tr translates [to [, a to A, b to B, . . .] to].

FIGURE 12.2

Brackets or no brackets, the results are sometimes the same.

Since there are no square brackets in the poem, that's sort of a waste of time. In addition, translating a square bracket to a square bracket doesn't make a whole lot of sense. In the second example I translated the range of letters abcdefghijklm to ABCDEFGHIJKLM. Since translate works byte by byte, I didn't need to tell it to choose one of the letters by using the square brackets.

As you known, Unix is an ever-evolving OS, and the latest version of Solaris requires the square brackets to enclose ranges like a-z. You don't need brackets around explicit series of letter like *abcdefg*, just around ranges like *a-g*. See, playing in Unix is never dull! This again brings us hard up against the hierarchy of truth, it's what a command does on your machine that truly counts. So test your tr to see how it works for you.

As I mentioned before, translate matches, based on position, each character in the first string with the corresponding character in the second string. It performs a simple one-for-one substitution. Take a look at Figure 12.3 to see how translate works in its simplest form. Here I translated the lowercase vowels to the digits 12345 in the poem. Notice that the A in the word HAD was not converted to a number. Neither were any of the instances of the I, O, or U, because tr, like the rest of Unix, is case-sensitive. As some of my more privacy-minded students have pointed out, you could use

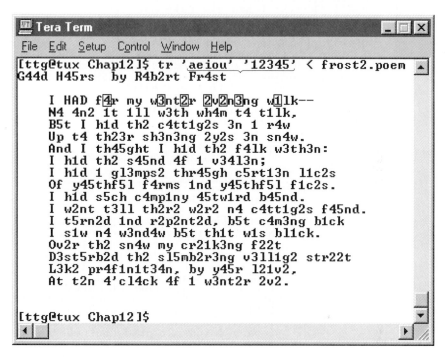

FIGURE 12.3

A simple translation.

tr to do a very simple encryption. I must warn you, however, that a simple substitution cipher is not secure. We will revisit tr and encryption in a few page.

Since translate replaces characters on a one-for-one basis, let's see what happens when string 1 is longer than string 2. Consider Figure 12.4, which shows a very significant difference between the way tr works in Solaris and Linux. In Linux, the top screen capture, all three letters, iou, are replaced by the digit 3, while in the lower screen capture, Solaris, the letters ou are not translated at all! It's almost as if in Linux tr says, "Well, if you don't give me enough bytes to translate to, I'll just reuse the last one you gave me," but in the Solaris version he says, "I'll translate bytes from the first string only if you give me a corresponding byte in the second string; otherwise I'll ignore bytes in the first string."

In either case, translate does its best to perform translation with more characters in the first string than the second.

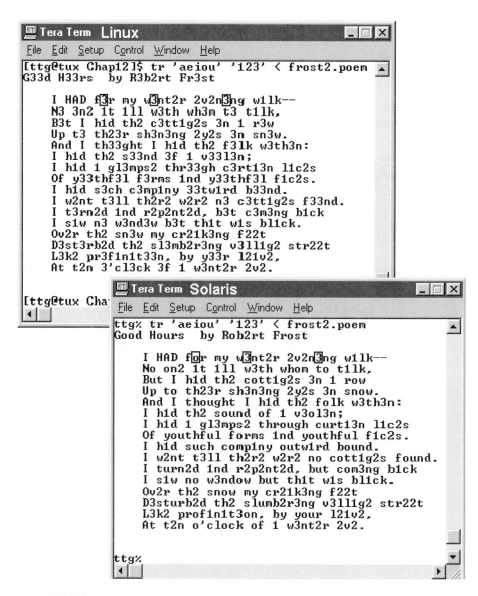

FIGURE 12.4

A difference in translate between Linux and Solaris.

Figure 12.5 shows what happens in the opposite case, when there are more characters in the "to" string than the "from" string. If you closely examine both screen captures, you'll see that there are no instances of the digit 6 in either version of `tr`. In this case translate in both versions ignores extra characters in string 2. This is as expected, since translate replaces on a one-to-one (byte-by-byte) basis. If there's nothing to cause `tr` to use the sixth character of the second string, we don't expect to see it, and we don't. In this instance both flavors of translate perform identically.

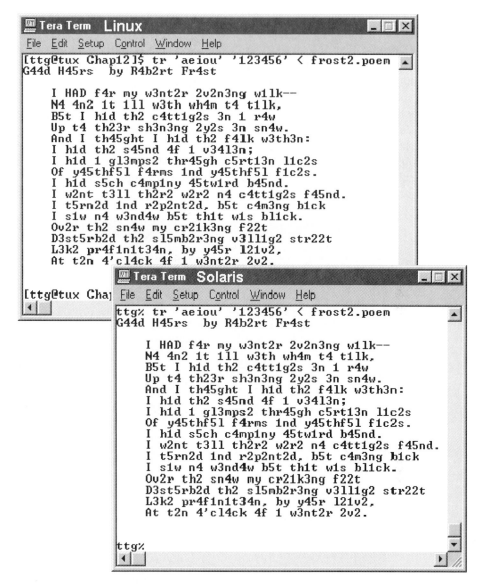

FIGURE 12.5

Translate with a shorter first string.

There are three standard options for the `tr` command. We will tackle them in order of use, not alphabetic order. Never fear, we will touch upon all three.

-d

The first option we will discuss for the translate command allows us to delete specific characters from the target file. You'll often encounter files with extraneous characters in them, either generated by some other operating system or by the hardware or software that produced the file. Cleaning up a file like this with the tr command is extremely easy using the **-d** (*delete*) option.

Look at Figure 12.6 to see an example of the -d option. Oops—well, that's not exactly what I wanted to have happen, but it is what I told tr to do, so I shouldn't be too surprised. The top of the figure shows you a text file that has some spurious colons and spaces embedded within it. In the lower half of the figure I have run a translate using the delete option to remove those spurious colons and spaces. It might look as if translate will be deleting the colon and space (:) pair, but of course we know that translate works byte by byte, so it will remove *all* the colons and *all* the spaces. That is a problem, as you can see, because we need some spaces to separate the words. Wouldn't it be nice if there was a tr option that squeezed out duplicate spaces?

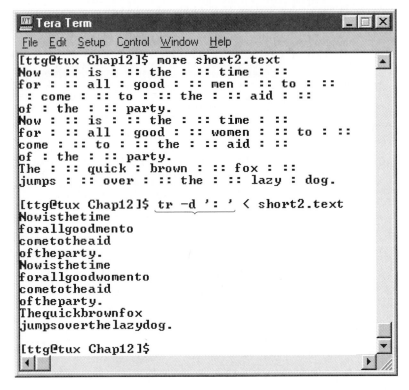

FIGURE 12.6

Using –d option with translate.

-s

The **-s** (*squeeze*) option will remove duplicate instances of the characters specified in string 2. It will compress duplicate, concurrent instances into one instance. Look at Figure 12.7 to see how I can use the –s option to clean up that ugly file. Notice that in this translate I am using two different options, the first, -d, tells translate to delete the

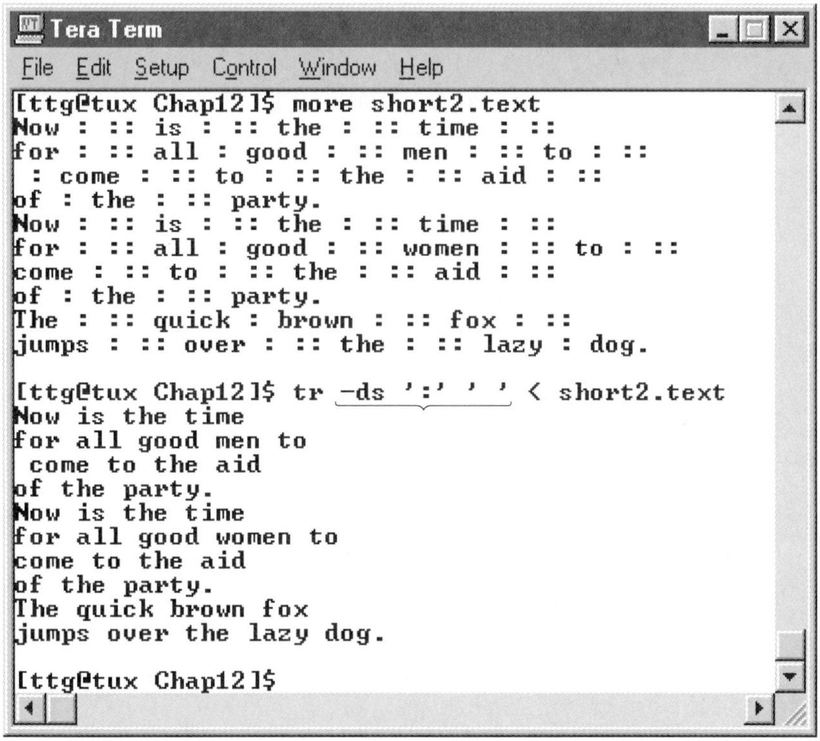

FIGURE 12.7

Combining options to clean up a file.

characters from string 1 (string 1 is the colon, :). The second option, -s, tells tr to "squeeze" all the characters from string 2 (string 2 is the quoted space after the colon). What that means is that tr will remove duplicate concurrent instances of the character or characters specified in string 2.

In the example in Figure 12.7 I first asked tr to delete all instances of :, and then directed him to squeeze all the spaces down to a single space. Most of the time you use multiple options to create powerful translates.

Let's look at those two options individually, shall we, just to see what tr's really doing. In the first step shown in Figure 12.8 I simply ask tr to remove all the colons from the file. Since tr is a perfect filter, I had to redirect the output to a file to store the intermediate result. I displayed the contents of that file so you could see what the first tr had done.

The second step in Figure 12.8 shows how I use the squeeze option to remove extra spaces from the file. Remember that the -s option squeezes out the characters found in the *second string*, but there is no second string in the example! This is an example of the precedence of truth. Remember way back in Chapter 1 when I told you that there were four levels of truth, the weakest being what you were told by someone else, and the best being what the command actually did? Well, here is an excellent

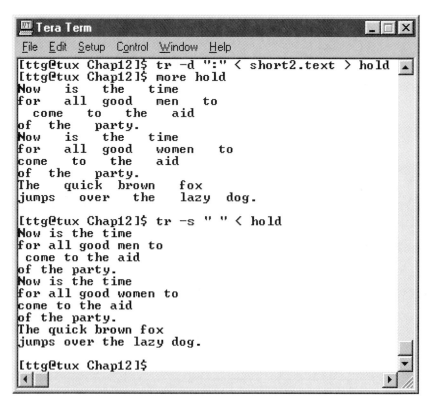

FIGURE 12.8

Separating the options for translate.

example of that. Most of the books and references you read will tell you that the squeeze option squeezes out the character or characters in the second string. I have even seen examples where the first string is null, so they could specify characters to be squeezed in the second string.

That is true as far as it goes. The problem with that description is that it assumes you are doing other things with tr, not just squeezing out some set of characters. If you use only the -s option, you don't need to have two strings; string 1 will specify the character(s) to be squeezed. Please remember to try commands to see what they really do on your system instead of taking anyone's word for what they do.

Combining the delete and squeeze options with the tr command gives you a very powerful text-processing tool. You will find it to be true with many Unix commands that combining options creates extra-powerful tools. Let's look at the third option for tr now.

-c

The -c option, most often called *complement*, is defined differently depending on the source you consult. One reference book I often use has the following description:

"complement characters in string 1 with ASCII 001-377." Now, I'm sure that makes wonderful sense to the person who wrote it, but it doesn't help me understand the command. After playing with the command, my explanation for the complement option is that it tells tr to replace all the characters in the input stream that don't match one of the characters in string 1 with the last character in string 2. I can hear you shaking your head and saying, "Great, so what does that do for me?" Well, suppose you wanted to create a glossary list of all of the words in a particular file. Let's see how we could use the complement option to accomplish that. Take a look at Figure 12.9.

I must admit that to save a tree or two or three, I didn't show you the complete output from the command. When you work the exercises, you'll have an opportunity

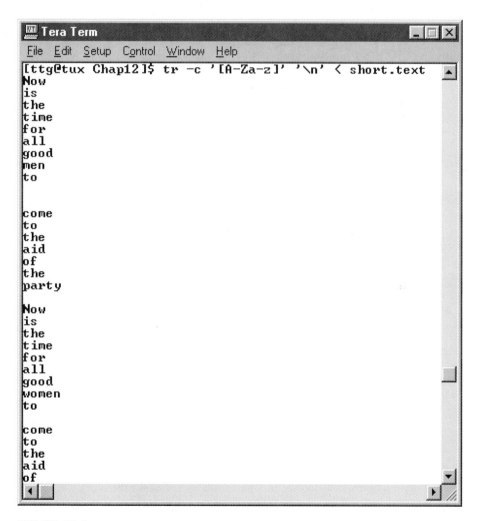

FIGURE 12.9

A nicely complemented file.

to see the output of this command in its grand and glorious fullness. What I did was tell tr to translate (complement) any character that wasn't an alphabetic character to a newline (**\n**) character. Translate changed all of the punctuation, and white space to newline characters (which is why there are some double spaces—tr complemented both the punctuation and the white space). That is a functional way to use the complement option.

The example in Figure 12.9 introduced another new feature, the *newline character sequence* (\n). There are a number of these special characters, often collectively referred to as the *backslash sequence characters*, because each is preceded by, of all things, a backslash. Table 12.1 lists the backslash sequence characters and their meanings.

TABLE 12.1 Backslash Sequence

Backslash Sequence	Meaning
\a	The alarm or bell character (^G). (Can be annoying!)
\b	The backspace character (^H).
\f	The form-feed character (^L).
\n	The newline character (^J).
\f	The carriage return character (^M).
\t	The tab character (^I).
\v	The vertical tab character (^V).
\###	Any octal character where ### is an octal number.
\\	The backslash character itself.

You may use these characters in either string 1 or string 2 of the translate command. It is often useful to be able to remove some of these special characters from a file. On the other hand, as you saw in Figure 12.9, it can also be useful to insert these characters into a document.

Now suppose I want to get rid of those silly extra blank lines in the output. I could make use of the squeeze option on the translate command to do that. Let's see how that works. As you can see from Figure 12.10, I again showed you only part of the output, but it looks much better. The duplicate newline characters have been removed, or squeezed out. In this case the second string is used twice. First it is used by −c, and then by −s. It is a very busy string! There are still duplicate words in the list, and we will deal with them when we talk about the next command, **sort**.

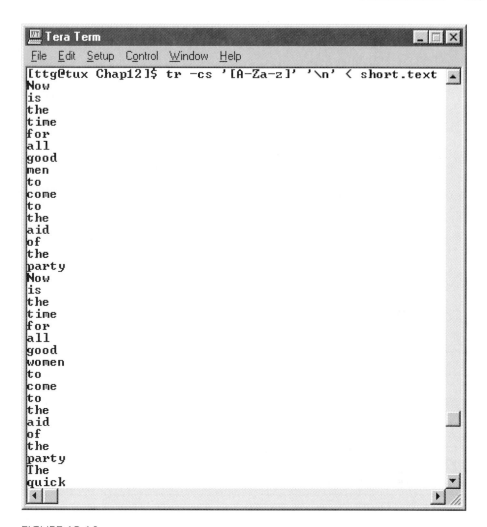

FIGURE 12.10
Cleaning up the list.

⊕ POSIX Extensions

One of the complaints about Unix is that there are too many versions, each with its own subtle variations. In response to these complaints, the Institute for Electrical and Electronics Engineering (IEEE) formed a group in 1984 tasked with developing a standard for Unix. The highest priority for this group now is to ensure that, where possible, existing applications continue to run and conform to the new set of implementations. A second goal was to improve the user interface for utilities, particularly at the command line, and the result was **POSIX**. It's this interface that interests us right now. POSIX is an acronym for **P**ortable **O**perating **S**ystem **I**nterface for Computer Environments. So why is the acronym POSIX instead of POSICE? Well, the folks at IEEE realized that every truly excellent computer environment ends with an X (Unix, Xenix, AIX, Ultrix, Linux). So instead of calling a standard POSICE, they abbreviated computer environment to an "X".

This standard was adopted as IEEE Standard 1003.1-1988. The Linux kernel has been POSIX-compliant from its inception. In the United States, the federal government adopted this standard and released a Federal Information Processing Standards (FIPS) publication regarding it: FIPS PUB 151-1.

The POSIX standard has provided a series of classes of characters that both Solaris and Linux recognize. While these new character classes are useful with several commands, `tr` can utilize them especially well. Table 12.2 lists them along with their meanings. If you spend a little time looking at the table, you'll see that some of these classes will save you keystrokes while others, like [:upper:], are actually longer than their equivalent pre-POSIX regular expression. Nevertheless, some of those longer classes are useful enough to make them worth the extra keystrokes.

TABLE 12.2 POSIX Character Classes

Class	Elements Contained
[:alnum:]	All the letters and digits. This is the same as [A-Za-z0-9].
[:alpha:]	All the letters. The same as [A-Za-z].
[:blank:]	All horizontal white space (blanks and tabs).
[:cntrl:]	All control characters—basically any character not part of any of the character classes.
[:digit:]	All the digits. This is the same as [0–9].
[:graph:]	All the printable characters *except those in the [:space:] class.*
[:lower:]	All lowercase letters. This is the same as [a-z].
[:print:]	All the printable characters *including those in the [:space:] class.*
[:punct:]	All punctuation characters: !@#$%^&*+=–_{}[]::|'"<>?/~'. You get the idea.
[:space:]	All horizontal or vertical white space. That includes newline, vertical tab, form feed, carriage return, and space.
[:upper:]	All uppercase letters. This is the same as [A-Z]
[:xdigit:]	All hexadecimal digits. This is the same as [0-9A-Fa-f].
[=CHAR=]	Local equivalence class. This is defined on your machine and is usually used to define a series of characters to be equal in non-English languages.

Take a close look at Figure 12.11; it's a very dense figure that shows us a lot of information. I tested some of the POSIX character classes here, and I urge you to do the same on your systems so you can see how these character classes actually perform. The file classes.text is available from the Web site. Feel free to modify it to suit your particular testing regime. I tested the digits, alpha, punctuation, alphanumeric, and control classes.

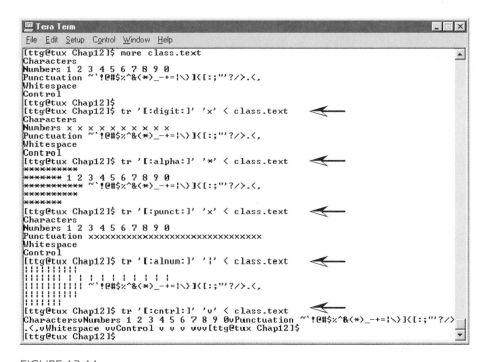

FIGURE 12.11

Using some POSIX character classes.

The class I was most interested in was the punctuation class [:punct:] because I wasn't sure exactly what it would match. As you can see, it matches every punctuation key on the standard keyboard.

With the addition of the character classes, translate has become even more flexible and powerful. I urge you to explore this tool and consider utilizing it to its fullest extent. In addition, try the POSIX classes with other tools like grep and egrep and see what happens. You may be amazed!

There's one final use of translate that I wish to share with you. It's not used much anymore, but you will still see it occasionally on newsgroups and in emails that contain questionable or off-color content. It is quite simple, used both to encode and to decode a message. This particular translation is called Rot-13, which stands for "Rotation about position 13," meaning that the letters of the message are rotated around the thirteenth position, the letter M. This technique goes all the way back to Julius Caesar who used a rotation cipher that moved each letter 3 positions, not 13.

Take a look at Figure 12.12, where I used Rot-13 to both encode and decode a simple message. First I wrote a secret message using vi. You can see where I saved it. No, I'm not going to tell you what it says—it's a secret message! Next I used the Rot-13 encryption pattern to create an encoded message. Then I showed you the message in encoded form, obviously nearly impossible to decipher. To decode the message I ran *exactly the same* tr, using exactly the same pattern. Finally, I showed you the decoded message. Oops, looks like I showed you what that secret message was, after all.

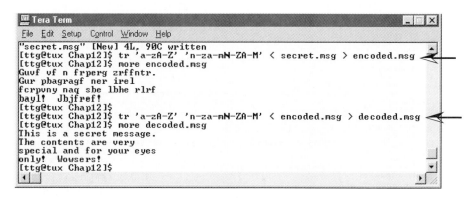

FIGURE 12.12

Using Rot-13 to encrypt message.

Note: If you try this example on a recent build of Solaris 8, you will need to enclose each range in square brackets. [a-z] [A-Z] ...

sort

```
sort [options] [file]
```

Back in the old days of computing, say the 1970s and 1980s, sorting was an extremely exciting and important process. File access was slow, and most of the business data processing evolved around updating master files, so finding efficient and elegant sorting algorithms was of utmost important. Enter the Unix **sort** command. It is fairly efficient, because it had its origins back in the days when processors were slow, memory was tiny, and sorts were thus very important.

Today, with the advent of extremely fast computers and relatively fast I/O devices with cheap memory, sorting is of less importance. Yet it remains an basic tool that an operating system is expected to provide, and, as you will see, sorting files can make your life much easier.

Before we begin looking at the specific options and uses for sort, though, we need to understand how it operates.

Key Fields

The simplest way to use sort is to just tell him to sort a particular file. If we do that he will begin looking at each line, starting with the leftmost character, and examine characters moving rightward until he finds a unique character combination that allows him to order the lines. In essence, he sorts each line using as many characters as he needs to. The whole line then becomes the *key field*.

Figure 12.13 shows an example of the sort command ordering the lines in a file based on the number of characters required to find a unique key field, starting with the leftmost character. In the case of apple strudel, sort had to look at only the first character, which was smaller than the first character in any other line. (By default sort uses the ASCII collating sequence, in which the letter *a* has a hexadecimal value of 61, the letter *b* has a value of 62, and so on.) On the other hand, when sort encountered the three chocolate desserts it had to look at the first 11 characters before it found unique differences. (No, I didn't misspell moose; if you can have chocolate bunnies and chocolate chickens, why can't you have chocolate mousse, er, moose?)

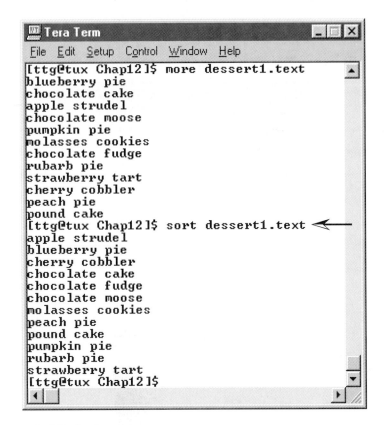

FIGURE 12.13
A very simple sort.

Obsolete +/-

At one time, if you wanted to specify a field other than the whole line for sort, you needed to code a starting and ending field position using the plus sign and minus sign. It was a little confusing to do this, because you needed to tell sort how many fields to skip before starting the key field and then how many fields to skip to the end of the key field.

Consider the sort in Figure 12.14. What I told sort to do here was to sort on the middle initial, or—to put it in sort's terms—to sort using the middle initial as the key. I told sort to skip one field, the first name, then start the key. Next I told him to end the key after skipping two fields. (Another way to think of this is to begin counting the fields with 0 instead of 1. Then you can just supply the field number to start and end the key. The first field would be +0, the second +1, and so on.) It worked, but that type of key specification can get very confusing when using multiple keys. For example, if I wanted to do a traditional name sort—last name, first name, middle initial—I would need to specify a sort that looked like this:

```
sort +2 -3 +0 -1 +1 -2 names1
```

Now that was pretty ugly. Using the -k option (discussed next) allows us to specify the key field in a much cleaner fashion.

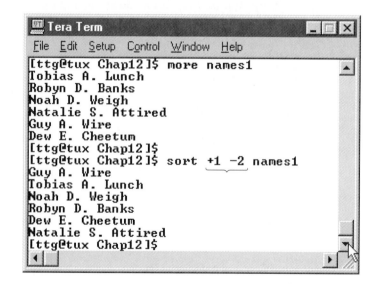

FIGURE 12.14

Specifying fields the obsolete way.

-k

The -k (key) option was used in Figure 12.15. Take a look, and compare it to Figure 12.14. I'm sure you'll agree that the keys specified for the sort shown in Figure 12.15 are easier to understand than they would have been if I used the +/- notation. Do notice, however, that I needed to specify three different key (-k) options to specify the three different keys.

In addition to specifying the entire field as the key, sort allows you to specify a subfield within a field as the key. Suppose, for example, I have a list of phone numbers, and I want to sort them using one of the digits in the area code as the key. Figure 12.16

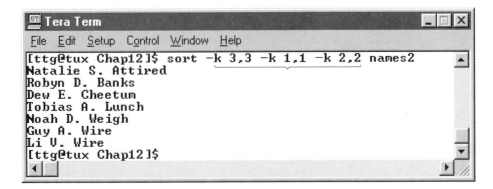

FIGURE 12.15

Using the newer, -k option to specify keys.

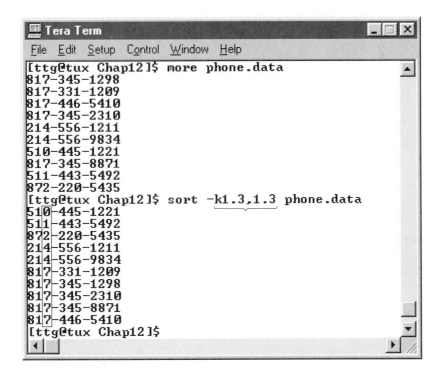

FIGURE 12.16

Specifying a subfield as a key.

shows how I accomplish this. As you can see, the list was sorted on the third digit of the first field. (Since sort uses white space as a field delimiter, there was only one field in each line. Oh, by the way, the phone numbers are all imaginary as far as I can tell, I made them up.) Being able to subdivide a field this way is extremely valuable; it gives you a great deal of control over exactly how your data will be ordered.

-c

Sorting a file of any size takes a lot of resources. Obviously, the files we use in the exercises for this text are tiny, but most of the time you will be sorting large files. It seems a shame to waste a large number of processor cycles attempting to sort a file that is already in order.

And therein lies the importance of the -c (*check the file*) option. If you include -c as one of your command-line options, sort will evaluate the file and indicate whether it is already in the order you specified. If the file already *is* sorted, a return status is set, and all you see is a command-line prompt. On the other hand, if the file is not sorted according to the criteria you specify in the sort command, sort will tell you that the file is not in the correct order. Figure 12.17 illustrates both of these cases.

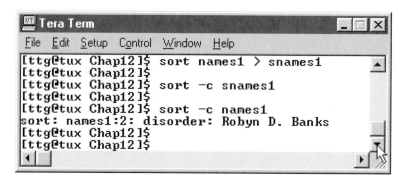

FIGURE 12.17

Using -c option on both a sorted and unsorted file.

The first thing I did in Figure 12.17 was to sort the names1 file and redirect the output to the snames1 file. Next I ran sort with the -c option on the sorted file. There was no response except a command-line prompt (which told me the file was in sorted order). Then I ran sort a third time, again with the -c option but this time against the unsorted file. As soon as sort found a line out of order, it quit checking and reported that the file was not in sorted order.

Before you ask the system to invest the time and energy necessary to sort a sizable file, it's a good idea to see if the file is already sorted. Make it a habit to use the -c option before you sort a large file that may already be in sorted order.

-b

Usually sort uses a single blank to divide the fields in a line, so extraneous blanks can cause problems with the way sort interprets data. That's why we need the **-b** (*ignore leading blanks*) command. For example, take a look at Figure 12.18. Linux (top screen capture) and Solaris (bottom screen capture) handle blanks somewhat differently. In Solaris the fields are divided by single blank, and extraneous blanks are prepended to the next field. This is the way sort normally behaves. As you can see in this screen capture, as far as the Solaris version of sort is concerned, D comes before B in the collating sequence. (That's exactly as it should be, because a space is hex 20, and the capital B is hex 42, and 20 is indeed smaller than 42.)

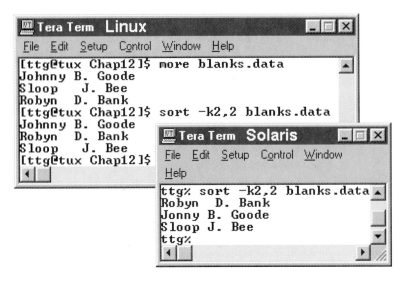

FIGURE 12.18

Sorting a field with leading blanks in Linux and Solaris.

In the Linux operating system the sort command seems to ignore leading blanks by default, which is rather handy. However, it does not follow the exact execution that we expect from the sort command. The bottom line is that you'll need to test the way sort responds on your particular system to see how it handles leading blanks. If you're running in the Solaris world, the -b option will tell sort to ignore leading blanks, as you can see demonstrated in Figure 12.19.

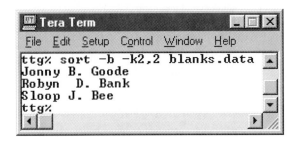

FIGURE 12.19

Ignoring leading blanks in Solaris.

Using the -b option on the command to tell sort to ignore leading blanks in the fields is useful in many cases. If you're sorting on the multiple keys, and want to direct sort to ignore blanks on particular keys, you can also code this option on the identifier for that particular field. Look at the example in Figure 12.20. The output here looks exactly the same as in Figure 12.19 except where I coded the b (*ignore leading blanks*), option. In Figure 12.20 the option is coded with the leading designator for the key field instead of on the command itself as was the case in Figure 12.19.

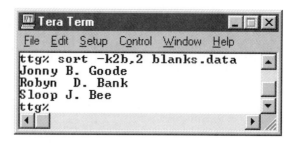

FIGURE 12.20

Ignoring blanks in a particular field.

Many times you can code an option either on the command itself or on one or more of the key designators. With the −b option, I urge you to code it only on the beginning key designator and *never on the ending designator*. If you put the ignore-blanks command as the designator on an end-of-field specifier you run the risk of confusing sort. Actually, I've never even tried it, because I was so strongly cautioned against it in my early Unix years.

-d

What if the key contains data that you don't particularly want to use in the sort? As an example, consider Figure 12.21. Notice the problem with the sorting because of the apostrophe in one of the names. The apostrophe is keeping the O'grady from sitting next to the Ogrady and so on. Let's see if we can use the **-d** (*dictionary* or *phone directory*) option to fix that.

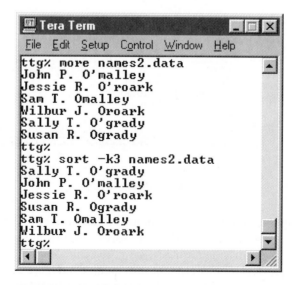

FIGURE 12.21

Problems with extraneous characters.

Look at Figure 12.22. That's nice—using Unix to bring together disparate families. It's amazing how powerful an operating system can be! What the dictionary (or phone directory) option does is direct sort to ignore any characters except blanks and alphanumerics. Accordingly, any apostrophes, periods, and such are ignored when sort attempts to order the lines or records. This can be an extremely handy option if you have fields that contain strange characters. On the other hand, you can lose some functionality if you sort in this manner. As always, the best approach is to try it and see what happens.

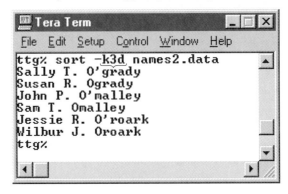

FIGURE 12.22

Using a dictionary type of sort.

-f

In some versions of sort, case sensitivity can cause problems for you. In the newer versions of sort that I have experimented with, it seems that case is no longer an issue. The -f option directs sort to *fold* both uppercase and lowercase alphabetic characters together—in essence, ignoring case. If you run into a problem where the lines or records are not sorting as you wish them to, consider the possibility that the case of the data is causing a problem with your version of sort and try this option.

-n

All the data out there that you may need to sort are not alphabetic. Sometimes—actually, fairly often—you may need to sort numeric data. But that's not hard to do, as you can see in Figure 12.23.

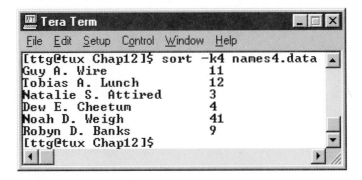

FIGURE 12.23

Sorting numeric data, or at least trying to.

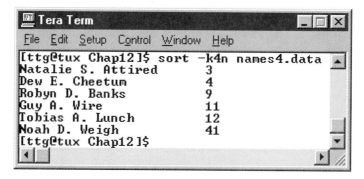

FIGURE 12.24
Sorting numeric data.

Well now, that looks like a perfectly fine sort to me, I always expect 11 and 12 to precede 3 and 4, and everyone knows that 41 always precedes 9. What? You don't think that's a good sort? Hmmm, perhaps you're right, perhaps sort is using an alphabetic sequence rather than a numeric ordering. Let's see if we can fix that using the -n (*numeric*) option on sort.

For those of you with a strong mathematical bent, the sort order in Figure 12.24 might look a little more reasonable. Notice that by adding the n option to the field specifier, I told sort to order the data from that field as if they were numeric rather than alphabetic. You can also code the numeric option on the sort command itself, and then sort will sort *all* the fields as if they contained numeric data. It's very important to tailor your sort to the type of data in each field. In the vast majority of cases you will specify the numeric option only on the particular field or fields that contain numeric data.

-o

Occasionally, you'll want to sort a file and then save the sorted version rather than the original. Your first inclination might be to simply redirect the output of the sort back into the original file. I tried that in Figure 12.25—and it's probably not a real good idea. I must admit, though, it's probably the fastest sort you could ever run. It's fast because there are *no data* in the file I'm trying to sort. Yes, that's right, Refrigerator Rule No. 4 came back to haunt me. Since the file names4a.data was the target of a redirection, the first thing that happened was that the next byte pointer was set to byte zero, emptying the file. Then, when sort took control, it read the empty file, politely dusted off its hands, realizing there were no data, smiled, and said, "I'm done." That's not exactly what I wanted to do.

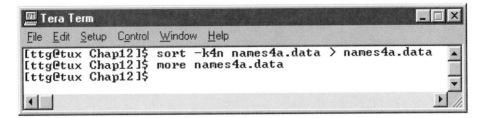

FIGURE 12.25

Trying to save output of sort using redirection.

Figure 12.26 shows another way I could go about saving the output of my sort back into the original file, eventually. As you can see from the final more command here, it is possible to end up with the sorted output replacing the original output using a two-step method. First I sorted the data, redirecting the output into a temporary file. Next I copied the contents of that temporary file to the original file, overwriting it. While this achieved the result I was seeking, there's got to be a better way.

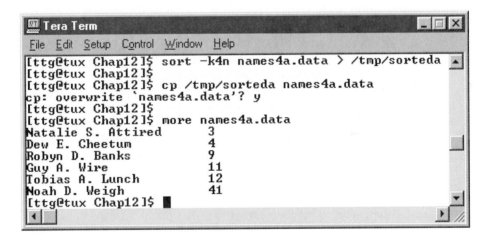

FIGURE 12.26

Using the multistep method of saving results of sort.

There is! Figure 12.27 finally shows the -o option (you knew it was coming). The first thing I did was to recreate the unsorted data file. Next I ran the sort with the -o option, directing it to put the sorted data (output) into the same file I was using for input. To prove to you that the sorted data replaced the unsorted data, I listed the contents of the file. Notice that sort did not ask if I wanted to overwrite the existing file. This is one of the dangers of this method of storing the output—you normally won't be asked before you overwrite a file. Although this method is much faster than the one shown in Figure 12.26, it does have that one inherent danger, so please use it carefully.

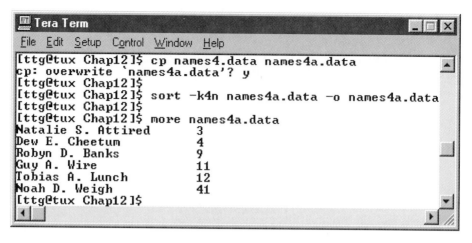

FIGURE 12.27

The best way to put the sorted version back in place of the original.

-r

Sometimes you might want to reverse the order in which sort presents its data. For example, suppose you want to look at the largest 10 files in a directory in order of largest to smallest. I address that problem in Figure 12.28. To find the 10 largest files in my directory, I first ran the ls command using the long listing option. I piped those data to the sort command, directing it to sort the fifth field numerically and to reverse the sort order so that the data would be sorted from largest to smallest. Finally, I piped those data to the head command, which gave me the first 10 lines from the pipe.

At this point, I hope none of the steps in the figure were a surprise to you. I would expect that you, too, could come up with the three commands necessary to solve that particular problem. As you can see our knowledge of Unix builds upon our earlier work.

-t

You may encounter data files in which the field delimiter is something other than white space. I think you've actually seen a file that could be considered colon-delimited,

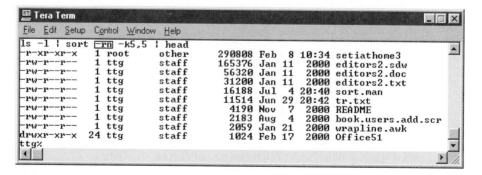

FIGURE 12.28

Reversing the sort order.

haven't you? Take a peek at Figure 12.29, and see if that particular data file looks at all familiar. You do recognize it, don't you? Of course you do. That's our old friend /etc/passwd. It's a fine example of a colon-delimited file. If I wanted to sort that file successfully I would need to tell sort that the field delimiter was a colon, not white space. You can see how I did that in Figure 12.30.

In Figure 12.30 I sorted /etc/passwd on the third field, which you remember is the user I.D. Since /etc/passwd is a colon-delimited file, I specified the delimiter using the -**t** option, I requested a numeric sort with the -n option, and, of course, I sorted on only the third field with the –k3,3 option. The figure shows you just the first 11 lines of the sorted output, but you can see the way it works from those lines.

-*u*
Remember back to Figure 12.10, where we used tr to create a list of words, one word per line, from a text file. When we left Figure 12.10 I promised you that later, in the discussion of sort, we would learn how to clean up that list by removing duplicate entries.

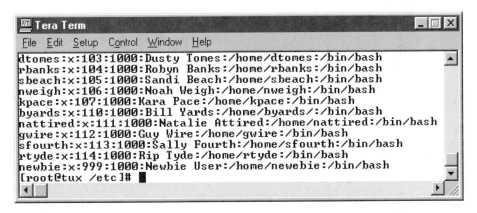

FIGURE 12.29

A colon-delimited data file.

FIGURE 12.30

Sorting /etc/passwd specifying an alternate delimiter.

That's right, now is later. Figure 12.31 shows one common way to do this kind of cleaning up, utilizing both the sort and uniq commands to remove duplicate lines.

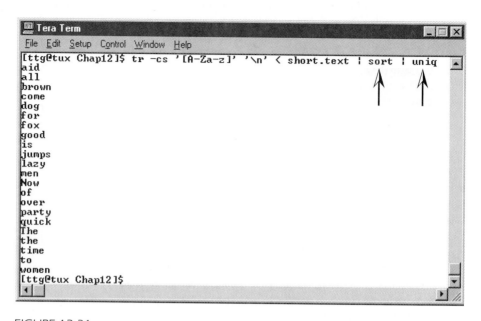

FIGURE 12.31

Removing duplicate lines the inefficient way.

The pipe shown in Figure 12.31 is fairly typical of those created by people who don't really understand the options available on the sort command. The sort in the pipe grouped all of the identical words on concurrent lines, then the uniq command suppressed the output of duplicate concurrent lines. The output from the pipe is absolutely wonderful—the problem is the inefficiency of running three processes when you need only two.

Consider Figure 12.32. The output in Figure 12.31 is identical to that in Figure 12.32. The difference is that instead of running a uniq process to remove duplicate current lines, I used the –u (*unique*) option on the sort command. This option saved an entire process—efficient indeed!

You do have to be careful, however, when you use the -u option and specify a particular field. Look at what happened to me in Figure 12.33. Even though each line in the file is unique, by sorting only on the first names and telling sort to give me only unique records, I effectively lost 70 percent of the data file (okay, 71.4 percent). This is an example of using the unique option on sort, specifying only one field, and badly damaging the data. As with many of the other powerful commands we have seen in the Unix world, you can create some undesirable situations. Of course, since sort is a filter and I didn't use the -o option, the original file, at least, was not damaged.

-m

The last sort option we'll discuss isn't really a sort option at all. The -m (*merge*) option directs the sort utility to merge two files. The files are assumed to have been sorted (in the same order) before they are merged. You can see example of the use of this merge

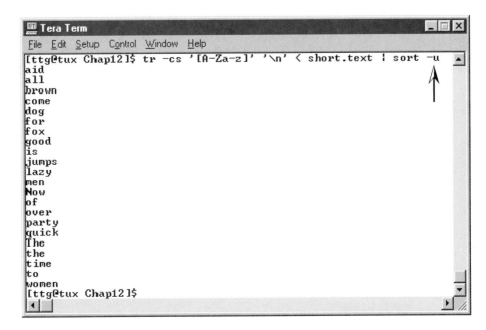

FIGURE 12.32

Efficiently removing duplicate lines from file with -u (unique) option.

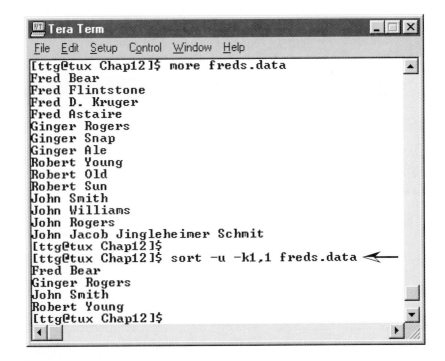

FIGURE 12.33

A small problem with sort -u.

option in Figure 12.34. As long as the two files are sorted in the same order, merge (sort within the -m option) will politely integrate them into a single, sorted file. However, as you can see from Figure 12.35, if one of the files is out of order, the results aren't quite so pretty. The sort command still combines the two files, but does not put them in order. Remember that to successfully merge two files they both must be sorted *in the same order*.

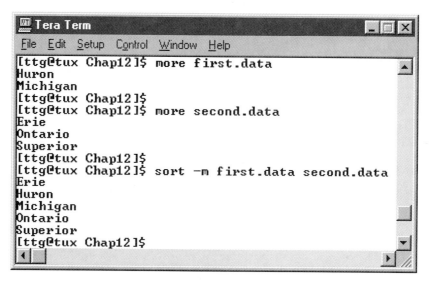

FIGURE 12.34

Merging two files with sort.

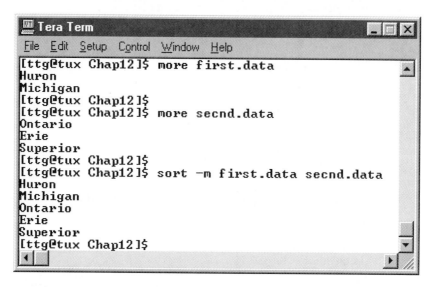

FIGURE 12.35

Trying to merge two unsorted files.

With its many options, sed is a command you'll use often. Experiment with it, especially with multiple key fields, and you'll find it to be quite versatile. Now let's consider one of the more underutilized commands in Unix.

sed

```
sed [options] [filename]
```

The sed command (**sed** stands for *stream ed*itor) is an outstanding tool for modifying the contents of files. Lee E. McMahon added the sed editor to Unix in the late 1970s for three purposes:

1. To edit files that are too large to comfortably edit interactively.
2. To edit files, regardless of their size, in which the editing commands are too complex to type in interactively. (You'll see this again a moment.)
3. To effectively perform a series of global editing changes, going through the file just once.

One difference between sed and the interactive editors is that sed loads only a few lines at a time from the target file into the buffer. That way it can handle very large files, files that would be far too large to load into the available memory on all but the very biggest systems. This capability of sed makes it the ideal choice for editing large files.

Another difference between sed and the other editors you've learned about (like ed and vi) is that sed is a batch-processing editor. Another way to say this is that the sed editor is noninteractive. You don't start the sed editor and issue a series of interactive commands to change the contents of the file. Rather, you can give sed an editing command on the command line, or, much more efficiently, you can direct sed to read a file of editing commands and he will apply them to the target file you specify. Therefore, you can create a file of editing commands and then apply those commands to a number of files—quite a time-saver, especially when the editing commands are too complex to easily type in an interactive mode.

This subject leads us to our next Refrigerator Rule.

Refrigerator Rule No. 5:

If you do it more than once, write a script!

At this point in your Unix career you might not be able to appreciate the importance and significance of Refrigerator Rule No. 5. However, after a couple of years of playing with Unix you will come to realize that this rule may well the most important, next to Refrigerator Rule No. 2. Refrigerator Rule No. 5 will follow us through the rest of this book, and provide the basis for your career as a system administrator.

Let me give you an example from real life. A few years ago I was the "scholar in residence" at our local public library. Part of what I was doing for the library was consulting with their staff about their newly acquired Unix system. The Unix server was being used as their Web server and also was going to serve as their firewall. When the representative of the firewall software company came to install the firewall code, he discovered a small problem. In every one of library's hundreds of Web pages the coders had specified the computer address by IP address not by domain name. Unfortunately, the IP address they had chosen for that computer was the IP address that *had to be* assigned to the firewall. The firewall software representative explained that each of the Web pages would have to be edited to replace the hard-coded IP address with a domain name. The task would take him a couple of weeks and cost the library a great deal money. Since the software rep had discovered this problem very close to lunchtime, he took his lunch break right after explaining the problem. While he was gone your humble author wrote a small shell script that drove a one-line `sed` script to edit each file, substituting the domain name for the IP address in all of the Web pages. When the rep returned from lunch, he was not terribly pleased to find that the entire problem had been resolved.

The reason I was able to fix all of the files was because I remembered Refrigerator Rule No. 5. Rather than going into each file and hand-editing IP addresses to domain names, I "wrote a script."

By the same token, each semester I have the privilege of creating accounts for several hundred Unix students. I could hand-build each account and spend an inordinate amount of time doing so. Since I am somewhat familiar with Refrigerator Rule No. 5, though, and since I have to do the "create student account" thing more than once, I have created a script. Instead of spending hours creating accounts, I simply spend a few minutes writing a file of student names, pass the file of names to my script, and all the accounts are created. Refrigerator Rule No. 5 will stand you in good stead if you simply remember it, and follow it.

Now it's time for a disclaimer. I'm going to introduce you to the `sed` editor, but I'm not going to teach you everything you can do with it. The `sed` editor is an amazingly powerful tool, so powerful that *whole books* have been written about it. Indeed, there are Web sites, newsgroups, and discussion groups devoted to the joy of `sed`. As you become more experienced with this marvelous tool you may wish to join them. Since Web sites and newsgroups sometimes change their names, I suggest that you simply search the World Wide Web using *sed* as a keyword, and you'll be rewarded with many pages.

We have neither the time nor the space to fully explore `sed`, but I'll give you a solid grounding and a place to start. After this, it's up to you to continue to develop your skill with `sed`. Each time you learn something new about `sed`, you'll increase the power and efficiency of your use of the tool. So let's begin.

You will remember that way back in Chapter 5, when you were studying the `ed` editor, I told you that the knowledge you were gaining would be of value later. And it was—for example, it was valuable to you when you were learning ex and vi. Now it will be of even more value as you apply what you learned to the sed editor. Since sed is, in the words of its author, "a lineal descendant of the Unix editor, ed," all that time and effort you spent learning ed will be repaid many times over as you work with sed. Be warned, however, that some differences arise between sed and ed because ed is interactive and sed is not.

I am going to assume for purposes of this discussion that you are already familiar with and comfortable using the ed commands. Most of the similar sed commands will be presented with examples and minimal discussion. The new and exciting features of sed will be explored in more detail.

sed from the Command Line

You can provide sed with directives by putting them on the command line or in a file. Now that you know Refrigerator Rule No. 5, the best place to put sed instructions would seem to be obvious: in a file. There are a couple of really good reasons for this.

First, it's much easier, much faster, and much more efficient to modify a file with an editor rather than to edit a command on the command line. (I know you know how to use history, but it's *still* simpler to use the vi editor to fix a file than to use editing on the command line.)

Second, once you have carefully crafted a set of editing commands for sed, if they're in a file you have them forever. If they're on the command line you may have them only as long as they live in the history buffer. Having to reinvent the steps of a complex task is a horrible waste of time. Take for example the case of Nicole, one of my students who got a job as a junior Unix system administrator at a local telecom. A couple of months after she started working at the company her boss came to her and said, "Nicole, make this series of edits to the monthly report file, please." Nicole used the vi editor, made the changes to the file, spending about four hours, and returned the results to her boss. A month later Nicole's boss came by her cube and said, "Nicole, remember those changes you made last month, we'd like you do that again, to this month's monthly report." Since Nicole was one of my better students, she remembered Refrigerator Rule No. 5 and thought, "Ah ha, I've done it more than once; I'll make a script." She spent just a little more than four hours carefully crafting a sed script to make the changes in the file. Then she ran the file against the monthly report and gave the results to her boss. True to form, a month later her boss again came in and said, "Nicole, do that monthly report thing again, please." This time Nicole simply had to run her sed script against the monthly report and within minutes provided her boss with the updated file. Her boss was so impressed that Nicole got a promotion and a raise. Now, I'm not going to tell you it was *all* because of Refrigerator Rule No. 5, but Nicole thinks it was certainly helpful.

For both of the reasons listened above I expect that for each exercise, and indeed for each use you discover for sed, you'll use a file for the directives rather than providing sed commands on the command line. (Actually, in Chapter 14 you'll be building files that are shell scripts, some of which will contain sed commands, and there you may use command-line directives—but only because the whole script is a file.)

If you do use sed with a command-line directive, be sure to enclose the directive in tick marks (apostrophes). That way, you will avoid any chance of confusing the shell. If, for example, you wanted to substitute all occurrences of the word "proper" with the word "inefficient" in the file myfile, you would use the following command:

```
sed 's/proper/inefficient/g' myfile
```

Notice the tick marks around the actual sed directive.

If you're going to have more than one sed directive on the command line, heaven forbid, you must precede each directive with the -e command-line option. Since you would never want to do that anyway, we don't need to talk about it any further.

sed with a Command File

In the vast majority of cases, you'll be providing sed with a file that contains the editing instructions. This is both the most efficient way, and the recommended way, to implement sed. Like other commands we have seen (consistency is a wonderful thing) sed uses the -f option to designate a file of commands. So if you wanted sed to take the instructions to modify myfile from the file goodandproper.sed, you would use the following command:

```
sed -f goodandproper.sed myfile
```

In this example you would have already created the directives file, goodandproper.sed, using an editor like vi. Notice that the directives file in the example ends with the suffix .sed. I strongly urge you to always put suffixes on directive files indicating which tool uses that particular file. Those suffixes will save you both frustration and possible embarrassment. Remember, very few Unix commands require a suffix (actually, the only one I can think of is the C compiler), but I encourage you to use them nevertheless to indicate the contents of particular files, as a wonderful way to help you organize your files.

You'll see a multitude of examples with sed using command files in this discussion. Emulate those examples!

The Other sed Option

Considering that sed is such a powerful tool, it has amazingly few command-line options. Along with the -e (shudder) and the -f options, the only other option is -n, which stands for *no print*. By default, since sed is a filter, each line that is read from the target file is echoed to standard out. If you direct sed to print a particular line, then that line will occur *twice* in the output. It occurs twice, that is, unless you specify the -n or no-print option. If you specify this option, sed will send only those lines you specifically request to standard out. We'll see where this is necessary when we look at the commands.

sed Command Syntax

The syntax of a sed command, not surprisingly, looks very much like the syntax of an ed command. The general form of a sed command is

```
[address1][,address2] command[argument/modifier]
```

where address 1 and address 2 can be any of the following:

1. Blank, in which case the command is *applied to every line.*
2. A single line number (in the case of address 1) or a range of line numbers (in the case of address 1 and address 2.)
3. A single regular expression or fixed pattern, (in the case of address 1) or a pair of regular expressions or fixed patterns designating a range.

Oh, yes, you can mix the two types. Look at Figure 12.36. I mixed two addressing types there.

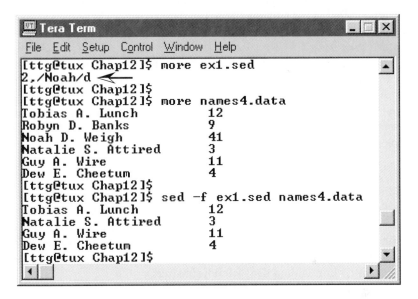

FIGURE 12.36

Mixing address types in sed.

The first thing I did in Figure 12.36 was show you the contents of the script I'm going to run. Obviously, anyone with an ounce of sense would never run sed from the command line. Next I showed you the contents of the data file I'm going to modify. Finally, I ran the script against the data file and showed you the result: lines 2 through (and including) the line containing the string Noah were deleted. Notice that in the first address I specified a line number and in the second address I specified a fixed pattern.

The last part of a sed command is the optional argument or modifier. As I'm sure you remember from ed, commands like append and insert take a text string as an argument; and you can specify which occurrence of a particular string to substitute with a number or the letter g. (What? You don't remember all about ed, and you haven't gone back and reviewed?)

How sed Works

When sed begins to execute, it takes all of the commands in the command file or (if the sed was written by someone who doesn't really understand) the commands from the command line, and loads them into memory. The place in memory used to store these commands is called the *command buffer*. Once all of the commands have been gathered together, they are compiled into a program. When this "sed program" has been compiled, the output is called *byte code*. This process is one reason sed runs so quickly.

Next, the first line from the target file, or the first line from standard input, is loaded into the **pattern space**—another buffer in memory, where all the changes are made to the input line. Then each command in the sed program is applied to the line in the pattern space. When all of the applicable commands from the sed program have been applied to the current line in the pattern space, that line is written to standard out. Then the next line is loaded from the target file into the pattern space, and the process starts over.

Two additional types of buffering are used by sed. The first is a specialized buffer called **hold space**, which is used something like the *anonymous buffer* in vi. You can put things into hold space and retrieve things from it. The second type of buffering is very specialized and used with regular expressions and protected parentheses. We will see how both of these are used near the end of the chapter. First let's look at some simple editing using sed.

Simple Editing with sed

Only a few commands are unique to sed. One is the set of commands involved in using hold space, as just explained. Most of the editing commands you supply to sed should be very familiar to you, because they look very much like ed or ex editing commands. Since most of sed will therefore be a review, I'm going to start with the most useful commands rather than going through the command series in alphabetical order. Let's start with our near and dear friend, substitute.

substitute

As we found with the other editors, *substitute* **(s)** can be used to alter existing text or to remove text from within a line. Substitute is probably the most commonly used command in sed. I'm sure you remember that with both ex and ed, substitute was your best friend. The same is true in sed.

Let's look at a simple example of substitution in Figure 12.37, where I am changing the name of one of the users in a data file. As before, I first show you the data file here, then the sed script I wrote, and finally the results. Initially things looked fine. Sally White became Susie White, which was the change I wanted. That was great, but look at Will Sallyson. He changed to Will Suzieson! That's not what I wanted.

The solution to my small quandary should be obvious. I can either anchor the pattern at the beginning of the line using the caret, or I can put a space after the name. Since I am trying to change first names, I prefer the caret method. I will leave it to you to correct the second example sed script so that it works correctly.

I'm sure you won't have any problems with simple substitutions, just like the ones you made in ed, but I would like to reinforce the idea of using a pattern as an address.

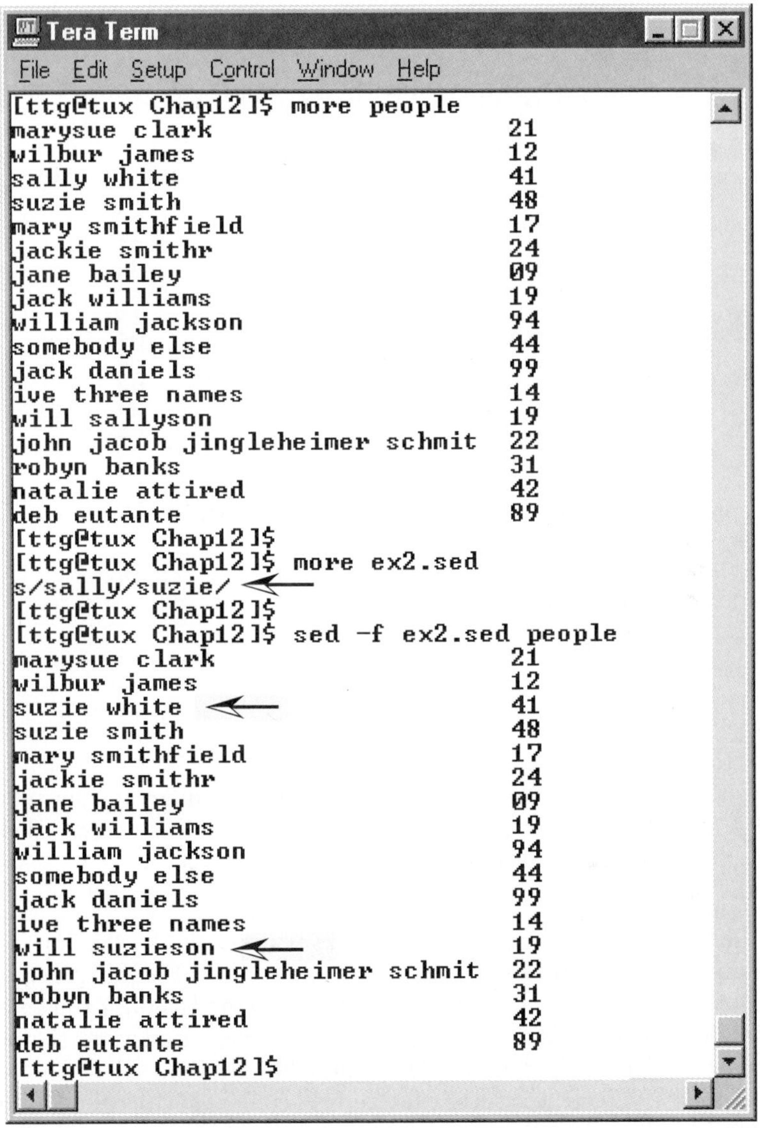

```
[ttg@tux Chap12]$ more people
marysue clark              21
wilbur james               12
sally white                41
suzie smith                48
mary smithfield            17
jackie smithr              24
jane bailey                09
jack williams              19
william jackson            94
somebody else              44
jack daniels               99
ive three names            14
will sallyson              19
john jacob jingleheimer schmit  22
robyn banks                31
natalie attired            42
deb eutante                89
[ttg@tux Chap12]$
[ttg@tux Chap12]$ more ex2.sed
s/sally/suzie/  <----
[ttg@tux Chap12]$
[ttg@tux Chap12]$ sed -f ex2.sed people
marysue clark              21
wilbur james               12
suzie white  <----         41
suzie smith                48
mary smithfield            17
jackie smithr              24
jane bailey                09
jack williams              19
william jackson            94
somebody else              44
jack daniels               99
ive three names            14
will suzieson  <----       19
john jacob jingleheimer schmit  22
robyn banks                31
natalie attired            42
deb eutante                89
[ttg@tux Chap12]$
```

FIGURE 12.37

Making a very simple substitution.

Please examine Figure 12.38. In the file ex3.sed I told sed to search for lines that started with the word jack and to replace that string with jacko. Notice that I did not need to specify jack a second time because substitute used the pattern from the search as the left-hand expression.

Of course, this method works only if I want to substitute for the pattern I am searching for. When we look at the more "interesting" examples toward the end of the chapter, you'll see other uses for substitute. However, with your vast experience with other editors, I'm sure you can easily pick up the method of using substitute in sed.

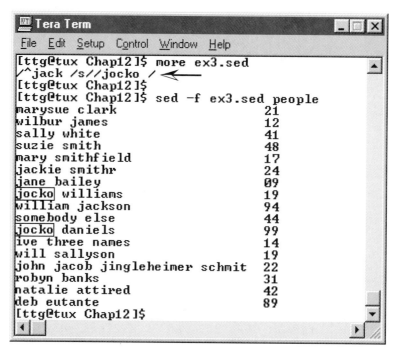

FIGURE 12.38

Using pattern as address.

By the way, why didn't I include the g modifier on the substitute command? Right, because there can only be one jack that starts a line. Asking sed to look for others would waste his time.

append

The *append* **(a)** command in sed works very much like the append command in ed. Both place the new line or lines *after* the target line. The difference is the way you indicate that you want to leave text-entry mode. In the ed editor you enter text-entry mode with the a command and exit from it by placing a period as the first, last, and only character on a line. In sed the syntax is a little bit different.

First, you need to specify the append command (a), ending with a protected newline (\) followed by the first line you wish to append to the file. Remember sed's addressing rules: if I don't specify an address, (the address is blank), then sed will perform the command on every line. If I specify a particular line number, sed will append the line *after* that line number. (Append appends *after*.) If I want to append a line at the end of the file, I can use the $, or end-of-file address designator. Normally that's the most often used append address, since most of the time we are adding something to the end of a file.

However, appending after every line can be extremely handy in certain situations. Suppose you are asked to double-space the lines of file. There are all kinds of gyrations you could go through, or you could write a very simple little sed script. As an example, I offer you Figure 12.39. The file shown here is a simple little text file. Also shown is my sed script, and it too is very simple. It consists of an a followed by a protected newline character (that's the required syntax), followed by a blank line.

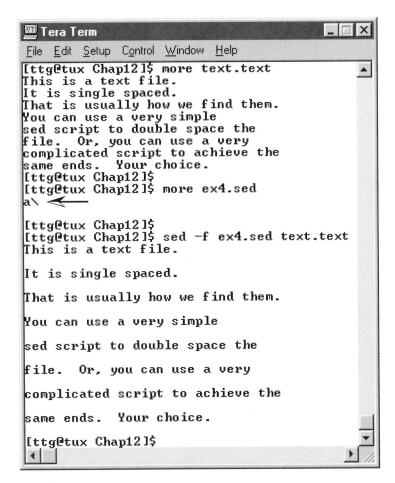

FIGURE 12.39

Using a (append) in sed to double-space a file.

The protected newline character is very important. You mark the end of the text to be appended by an *unprotected* newline character. (That character takes the place of the period in ed.) Yes, you're right, very good observation! That means you can append several lines, as long as you end each one except the last line with a protected newline.

Look at Figure 12.40, you see a four-line text file, a four-line sed script that appends three lines to the end of the file, and the result of using that script. Notice the three protected new lines; sed takes them and strips the protection off them so we see new lines in the output. All three of the text-entry mode commands—append, insert, and change—use the same syntax. They all use an unprotected new line to mark the end of the text-entry process. If you wish to insert more than one line, you must end each line except the last line with a protected new line. (Whew, that last sentence is almost a tongue-twister.)

insert

As you just read, *insert* (**i**) works just like append except that it adds the lines to be inserted *before* the specified line. (Insert inserts *before*.) Use the same syntax with insert

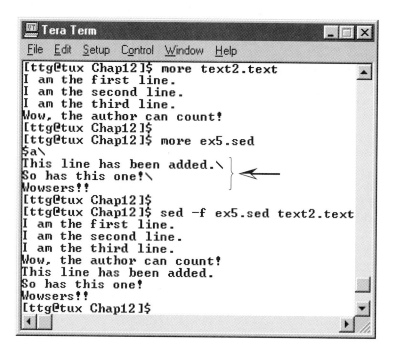

FIGURE 12.40

Appending more than one line with a.

that you do with append, ending the line or lines to be inserted with an unprotected newline character. Figure 12.41 shows you an example of this process. Notice the address in the example sed script. I am looking for lines that contain the word Wow and then inserting the two lines that follow the insert command *before* them. There's no real magic to insert, and since you're such a wizard with the ed editor, we can move on.

change

The *change* command (c) could really be considered a *replacement* command, because that's how it works. You specify a line, or range of lines, to change, and the sed editor takes the text following the change command and replaces the line or lines you specified with the new text. This is a very useful text-entry command, because it allows you to go into a file and substitute, oops, change particular lines throughout the whole file. Remember that, like append and insert, change is a *line*-altering command. You cannot use change to modify a word or two within a line—that's substitute's job.

Figure 12.42 shows you how change works. I first show you an extremely mundane file and then the sed script that will change this boring file into an exciting one. In the last part of the figure we see a marvelous transformation: the boring file becomes exciting.

As with append and insert, I can change a single line into multiple lines or multiple lines into a single line, depending upon how I write the script. You'll use the change command most often when you wish to replace a few lines of text. Of course, it is possible to use the change command to delete lines, but why do that when we have a special command just for that purpose?

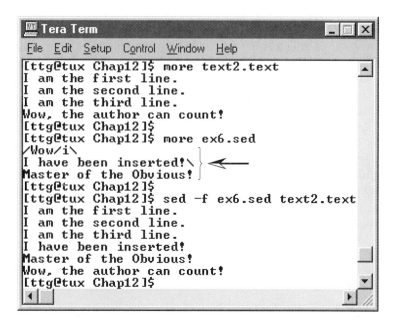

FIGURE 12.41

Inserting lines with i.

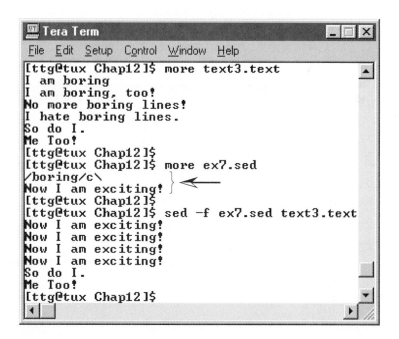

FIGURE 12.42

Using c (change) to replace a couple of lines.

delete

The *delete* (**d**) command in sed works exactly the same way as it does in the ed editor. You specify a line, or range of lines, or some other addressing mechanism, and delete will remove those lines. (Okay, delete doesn't actually delete the lines—rather, it simply doesn't write the lines specified to output. The effect is still deletion, but with d in sed, the original file is unchanged.) Again, this is a *line*-level command. If you want to delete an individual word from within a line, you'll use your old friend substitute.

When you're creating the address range for the delete command you must be very careful. Remember what happens in sed if we *don't specify an address!* You can see the example in Figure 12.43. Now, I must admit that is one way to deal with a boring file, but it's probably not what you normally want to do. (Well, maybe it *is* what you want to do but . . .) What I did was to specify the delete command without an address. Any command without an address is executed on every line. Therefore, the delete command deleted every line.

The delete command shown in Figure 12.44 is a little more "normal." I trust you remember the contents of text3.text, as you've seen it several times in the last few screen captures. The sed script illustrates another way of dealing with a boring file. In this case, I ask sed to delete each "boring" line—yet another way to handle boring text files. Isn't sed a marvelous tool!

One of the more common uses for sed, almost exactly the inverse of the append example, is to remove either blank or empty lines from a file. In other words, take a file that's double-spaced, or that contains spurious blank or empty lines, and single-space the file.

Figure 12.45 shows you how to do this. As you can see, the initial text file is loaded with empty or blank lines, and my sed script got rid of *most* of the problem lines, but there still a couple left. Looking closely at the sed script, and remembering our work

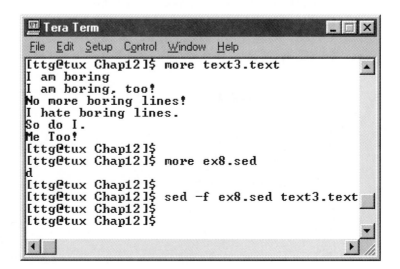

FIGURE 12.43

A rather comprehensive use of d (delete).

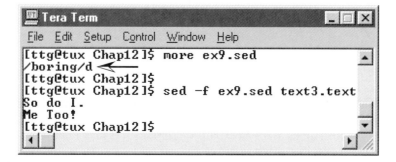

FIGURE 12.44

A more "regular" use of the delete command.

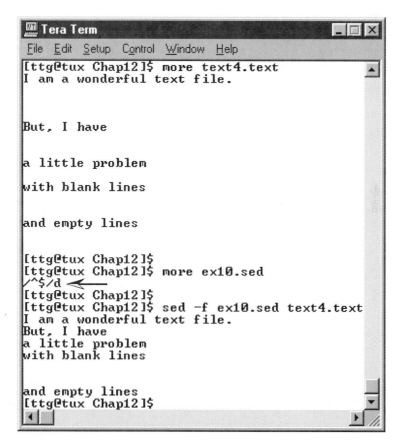

FIGURE 12.45

Removing extraneous lines from a file.

with regular expressions, what I'm removing are the *empty* lines but not the blank lines. I'll leave it to your exploration to modify the script to remove *all* the extraneous lines.

print

The *print* **(p)** command is designed to allow you to specifically request that certain lines be sent to standard out. This is the command to use if you want sed to select particular records from a file. In Figure 12.46 I chose all the records that started with a particular letter and asked sed to print them.

Well, it looks as it I have a little problem in Figure 12.46. For some reason, the two records I was interested in are displayed twice, and everything else is displayed once. Oh, that's right, sed always sends input lines to standard out, and this time I told him to send the line again. Let's see, wasn't there a command-line option that prevented sed from printing all the lines? Right you are! It's the -n option. I'll use that option in Figure 12.47 to see if it fixes the problem.

Yes, that looks much better. Now for a tough question: what command have I replicated with this sed? Did I hear you say grep? Yes indeed—instead of using a simple grep command, I can use a more complicated sed command that gives exactly the same results. Isn't Unix wonderful?

Seriously, one of the advantages that competent Unix users share is that they know more than one way to achieve a given result. As a Unix wizard, your task is to choose the most efficient tool in any particular situation.

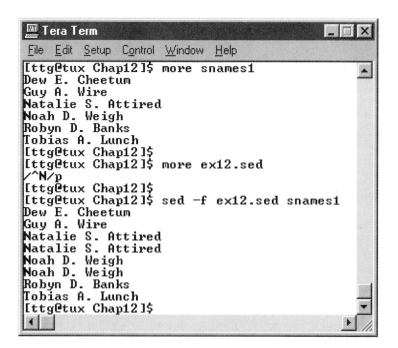

FIGURE 12.46

Selecting specific records for output with p (print).

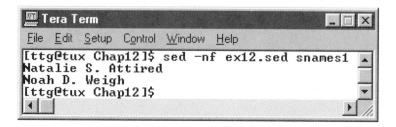

FIGURE 12.47

Using –n command-line option.

The script we used in both Figure 12.47 and Figure 12.46 works just fine as long as we remember to include the -n command-line option. Wouldn't it be nice if we could somehow embed that option within the script so we didn't have to remember to include the command-line option? Other Unix users have thought the same thing, and since Unix changes to meet the needs of the user, well, take a look at Figure 12.48. Notice the first line looks like a comment. This is a special case. If you have #n as the *first two characters* of the first line of a script, sed will interpret it exactly the same way as if you had coded -n as a command-line option. You may not think this is significant now, but when you get older like your humble author, you'll discover it's nice to have the script remember things that you might otherwise forget to do. Besides, it will save the time and effort of typing on the command line.

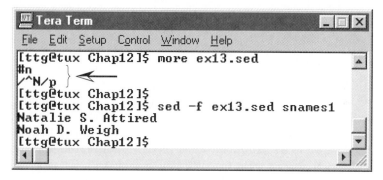

FIGURE 12.48

Embedding n command within a script.

write

The write **(w)** command is used to create a second file that contains all or part of the target file. You must be very careful when you specify the file to which you direct sed to write, because if the target file exists, it will be overwritten. The w command is great when you need to extract some particular lines from a file, or when you wish to create a file of the lines that you changed for documentation purposes. Suppose, for example, you want to remove some of the initials from the names in a file, and at the same time capture a copy of just those lines that you modified. That process is demonstrated for you in Figure 12.49.

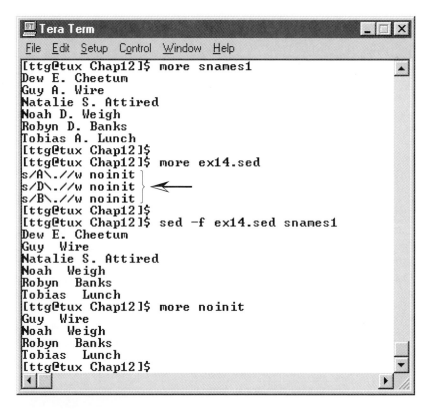

FIGURE 12.49

Using w (write) to create a file of changes.

All the names shown in the file in Figure 12.49 have middle initials. If for some reason we wished to excise the middle initials of BAD from the file, we could use the sed script shown. In addition to extracting bad middle initials, I could write the lines that were changed to a separate file. That file is also displayed in Figure 12.49. As you can see, the altered lines went to both standard out and the new file. You could prevent anything from going to standard out if you included the −n command-line parameter, or if you put #n as the first line of the script.

Writing a new file is a very handy thing to be able to do. You can even use sed to select specific lines and simply write them to a new file. Its just as if you were using a redirection with grep. Ah, the flexibility of Unix!

read

In addition to writing files, you can also *read* **(r)** the contents of a file into the current buffer, just as you did with ed. You will use the read command to insert text after a specified address. (No, you can't use the read command to insert text before the first line of the file.)

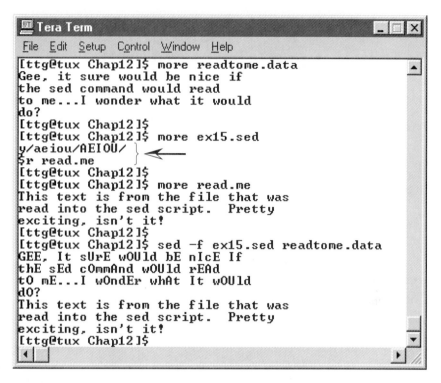

FIGURE 12.50

An example of the r (read) command.

One of the more common uses for the read command is to place footer information at the end of each of a series of files. Here's an example: suppose you are building a sed script to modify 7,349 HTML files, and you want to add a little JavaScript script to the end of each file containing code to update the date last modified. Instead of coding the append command inside the script, with all of the lines of the JavaScript included in that script, you could put the JavaScript in a file and then read that file after the last line of each of the HTML files.

A simple example of the read command is shown in Figure 12.50. First I show you the original data file, then the sed script that would modify the data file, the file the sed will read, and finally the results of running the sed script against the data file. As you can see, I translated all the vowels from lowercase to uppercase, then went to the last line of the data file and read the second file into the buffer. While this is, of course, a purely academic example, I'm sure you can see how the read command works from studying it.

One of the more noteworthy features of sed is the way it fails if the file you're attempting to read is either not available or you haven't permission to read it. I ran into that problem in Figure 12.51. Notice that the script contains a typo: instead of typing

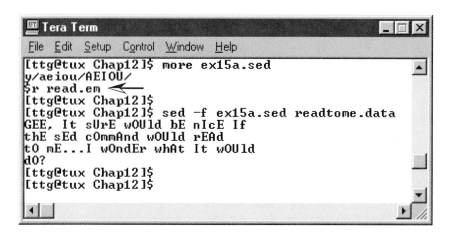

FIGURE 12.51

When the read command fails.

the filename read.me, I reversed two letters in the extension. Look closely at the error message sed generated. What? You can't find the error message? You can't find an error message because sed "fails silently" when there's any problem with the file it's supposed to read. This feature can be either a good thing, or a bad thing.

If you don't like to see error messages, and you're very conscientious about checking the output of the sed run, then sed's habit of failing silently is probably a good thing. On the other hand, if you're not inclined to carefully check the output of each execution of sed, it's probably not a good thing that sed doesn't tell you when the read fails. (For those of you who know about return statuses, the return status from the sed shown in Figure 12.51 was 0. If you don't know about return statuses, never fear; we will examine them in detail in the last chapter.)

translate

One of the more esoteric commands in sed is the translate (y) command. This command causes sed to act like tr, replacing each character in the first string with its positional equivalent from the second string. The biggest difference is that while tr is somewhat forgiving about length differences in the first and second strings, sed has no such flexibility. The target string and replacement string must contain exactly the same number of characters. The sed command will give you an error message if the two strings are not of identical length.

Figure 12.52 contains an example, albeit an academic example, of the use of the translate command. Here it simply translates the lowercase letters a-g to the numbers 1-7. The translation is applied to only the first three lines, as per the address in the command.

Generally you won't perform translation by itself, but it is useful to be able to translate certain characters as part of a larger editing process. One of the places translate is handiest is when you're replacing special characters. But remember that you must do a one-for-one replacement. If you're trying to *remove* special characters, then substitute is your best choice.

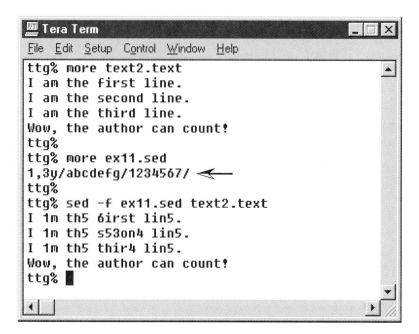

FIGURE 12.52

A simple translation using y command.

Using Hold Space

In addition to the pattern space buffer, sed also has another area in memory, called **hold space**. This memory area is similar to the anonymous buffer you're familiar with from your study of the vi editor. There are three important considerations to remember about using hold space.

First, you will put the whole contents of the pattern space, normally the current line, into hold space. Unless you edit the pattern space before you put in hold space, there's no way to get just part of a line into hold space.

Second, each time you put something into hold space, you overwrite the current contents of hold space (that is, unless you use the append-to-hold-space command, in which case you append the current pattern space to the end of the contents in hold space).

Third, when you move the contents of hold space into pattern space, you overwrite the current contents of pattern space (unless, of course, you use the append version of get to append the contents of hold space to the *end* of the current pattern space). This feature of hold space can be very significant, as you will see in Figure 12.53.

Five commands will move data to hold space from pattern space or to pattern space from hold space. All five are shown in Table 12.3, and the two most commonly used are shown in Figure 12.53. Note that the command h in the first line of the script asks sed to copy any line that contains the string First to the hold space. Since this is the first line of the script, it will move any line that contains the string First to hold space before applying any other edits. The second line of the script is our old friend

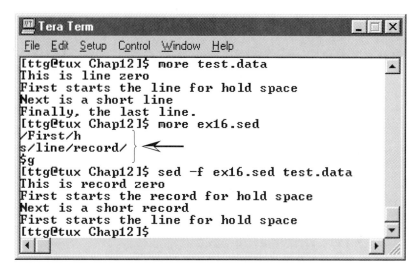

FIGURE 12.53

A first exploration of hold space.

TABLE 12.3 Hold-Space Commands

Hold-Space Command	What It Does
h (hold)	Copies the current pattern space to hold space, overwriting the current contents, if any, of hold space.
H (hold/append)	Copies the current contents about pattern space to hold space, *appending to the end of the current contents* of hold space.
g (get)	Copies the current contents of hold space to the pattern space, overwriting the current contents of the pattern space. If you're not careful, this has the effect of deleting the current contents of the pattern space, and data may be lost.
G (get/append)	This command works exactly like the lowercase g command except that it *appends the contents of hold space to the end of the current contents* of the pattern space.
x exchange	Copies the current contents of hold space to pattern space and copies the current contents of the pattern space to the hold space. This command exchanges the contents of hold space and pattern space. Note, no data are lost.

substitute, substituting the string record for the string line in each line. The last line of the script directs sed to move the contents of the hold space to the pattern space, *overwriting the contents of the pattern space.*

If you carefully examine the output from the execution of the sed in Figure 12.53, you'll see how hold space was used. The most obvious differences are that in all of the lines except the last line, the string line was replaced with the string record. The first

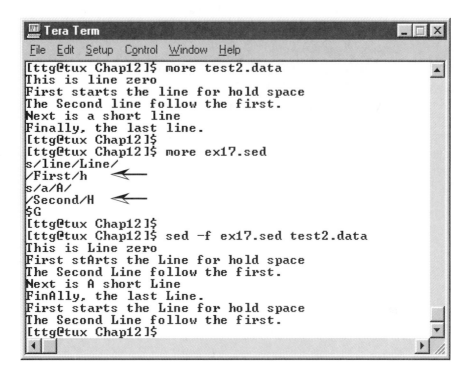

FIGURE 12.54

Using the append hold-space commands.

line of the target file replaced the last line of the target file, but the string substitution was not performed.

In terms of using hold space, the figure shows us two interesting features. First, copying pattern space to hold space does not alter the contents of the pattern space. And second, copying the contents of hold space to the pattern space overwrites the contents of the pattern space.

Now please look at the other commands we have available to manipulate hold space and pattern space (in Table 12.3). The lowercase hold-space commands overwrite and the uppercase hold-space commands append. Let's see the uppercase commands in action. In the sed script in Figure 12.54 I first copied the line that contained the character string First to hold space with h, then did a simple substitution, and next appended the line that contain the string Second to the data already in the hold space with H. Finally, I appended the contents of hold space to the end of the pattern buffer.

Notice that in Figure 12.54 the last line of the pattern buffer appears, whereas in Figure 12.53 the lowercase g command replaced the contents of the pattern space. Using the uppercase G command allows me to preserve all the lines in the original target file.

Now let's see how the exchange (x) command, the last one in Table 12.3, works.

The example shown in Figure 12.55 is pretty exciting. It very clearly demonstrates how the contents of hold space and the contents of pattern space are exchanged with

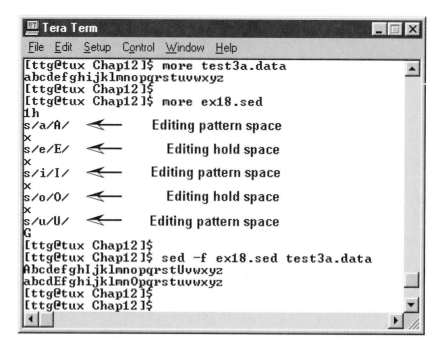

FIGURE 12.55

Using the exchange command.

the x command. The data file I built for this figure is simply all of the lowercase letters. Now let's examine the rest of the sed script.

The first thing I did was copy the pattern space, (the alphabet line), to hold space. Next I substituted uppercase "A" for lowercase "a" in the current pattern space. (The notes in Figure 12.55 identifying "pattern space" and "hold space" refer to the original positions of the two alphabet lines.)

Then I exchanged the contents of pattern space and hold space, so that the unmodified line which had been in hold space was now in pattern space. I substituted an uppercase "E" for the lowercase "e" in that line.

Next I exchanged the contents of pattern space and hold space so that the original line was back in the pattern space. I substituted an uppercase "I" for lowercase "i" in that line. Again I exchanged the contents of pattern space and hold space. Now the line that had been in hold space was in pattern space and available to be edited, so I substituted uppercase O for lowercase o in that line.

Finally (I can hear you sighing in relief), I exchanged the contents of hold space and pattern space one last time, and substituted an uppercase U for the lowercase u. In the last command in the script I directed sed to append the contents of hold space to the pattern space. That way you can see both the contents of hold space and the contents of pattern space.

If you look closely at Figure 12.55 you'll see that the first line of the output, the original contents of pattern space, has the letters A, I, U in uppercase. The second line of the output, the original contents of hold space has the two letters E, O in uppercase. This shows that sed was, indeed, exchanging the contents of hold space and pattern space each time it encountered the x command.

Using hold space can be very useful in certain editing situations. While I've not used it often, I've been glad of its availability at times.

Using Pseudo-Buffering with Substitute

Since you understand the idea of buffering, it's time to talk about how the substitute command can also support a type of pseudo-buffering. (I call it pseudo-buffering for lack of a better term.) Consider the example in Figure 12.56. I realize that the screen shown here is a tad long, but this is an excellent example of using the ampersand (&) pseudo-buffer. In a search pattern, the ampersand can replace the string that matches the "search for" part of the substitute command. In this example I used sed to create a backup script for all of the examples for this chapter. (When you get to Chapter 14, you'll learn how to use sed to create backup scripts.)

The sed script in Figure 12.56 may look a little strange. I used another feature of sed that allowed me to choose another character besides the forward slash as a command

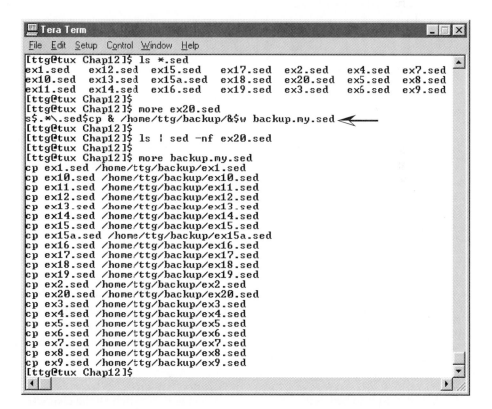

FIGURE 12.56

Using the ampersand (&) pseudo-buffer.

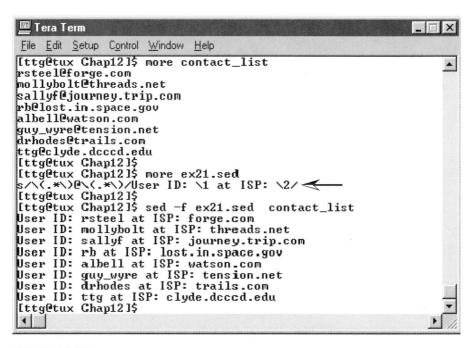

FIGURE 12.57

Parsing the input line and using the parts.

separator. In this instance I chose the currency sign ($) as the command separator because I needed to use the forward slash in the output string.

The rest of the script uses other features you have already learned about in sed. I looked at each line of the output of the ls command. If I found a line that contained some characters followed by .sed, I substituted the pattern that matched (in this case the filename) with the cp command to copy that file to a backup directory. Then I wrote the new line to a file, which, with very slight editing, will become my backup shell script. Notice that I used the ampersand pseudo-buffer twice, on both the "from" and "to" portions of the cp command.

You can use the ampersand in the replacement side of **substitute** as many times as you need. This is a very useful little tool.

Another, even more sophisticated, type of pseudo-buffering allows you to pick apart the pattern in the "from" portion of the **substitute** command and use just a portion of it. To do this operation you must enclose each part of the pattern you wish to address in a pair of protected parentheses. See Figure 12.57. And now take a deep breath; it's really not that bad—I promise. First, if we didn't have to protect the parentheses, the pattern would look like this:

    (.*)@(.*)

See, that isn't so bad, is it? All that code is saying is to match all the characters that occur before the at (@) sign, then match all the characters after the at sign. Since we are enclosing each match in parentheses, we can refer to them individually, by their relative position in the pattern. We refer to them using a protected digit for each individual pattern.

What the substitute command is saying is this: "In the input line, find all the characters that precede @, then find @, then find all the characters that follow @. For that complete string substitute the string User ID:, followed by the first set of characters, then the string at ISP:, followed by the second string."

Since the file contained a series of email addresses, the script worked regardless of how many parts each side of the @ had. This is an example of a very clean little sed script that is easy because of the way sed keeps track of parenthesized parts of the pattern. Without that feature, it would be a much more challenging script to write. We will see a more elegant example of this concept in the next section.

A "More Interesting" Example

Suppose you want to capitalize the first letter of each word in a file (initial caps). It is quite logical to use sed for that task. If your file had only one word per line, it would be easy to perform the task using a script like the one shown in Figure 12.58.

FIGURE 12.58

Initial-capping a simple file.

Yes, the script is long—26 lines long—but it works, and since it is a *script*, I need to code it only once and I can keep it forever. (I split the screen in the figure to save space; you can see that lines P and Q are in both halves of the screen capture.)

All the script does is identify the first character of the line, and if it is lowercase, substitute the uppercase letter. This is an example of a "hammer and tongs" approach to scripting. It isn't elegant. It isn't pretty. It isn't very much fun to write, or to read. But, hey, it works. Now that we have a working solution, let's try to improve upon it.

Suppose that we have a situation like that shown in Figure 12.59. If we were to use our existing uppercase script on the boring data file, it would capitalize the first names, but not the last names. We could modify the script, making it 52 lines long to handle both first names and last names, but that would be a bit excessive. You can see part of that long version in Figure 12.60. The script shown there started out as the same script shown in Figure 12.58. I added another 26 lines to take care of the last names. It search-es for a space preceding each lowercase letter and substitutes an uppercase letter, pre-ceded, of course, by a space. Still a hammer and tongs approach, but one that does solve the problem. Still, I'm sure we can do better.

Just to prove it works, I ran the script against the boring data file, Figure 12.59, and I show you the results in Figure 12.61. But now it's time to find a better way. Look at Figure 12.62 (on page 498).

Well, the script shown in Figure 12.62 is a lot shorter—infact, it's half as long as the one in Figure 12.60. In this instance we're using the regular expression, the protected less-than (\<) symbol, which says "a word that starts with." Using that particular regular expression frees us from worrying about the beginnings of lines, or words that are preceded by spaces. It simply recognizes any word that begins with one of the lowercase letters. (I know you are beginning to realize the value of regular expressions!)

The first two solutions presented for the "capitalize the names" were pretty straightforward and did not demonstrate the true power of sed. Our next solution, based on the work of Ken Fraser, one of the Unix faculty at North Lake College, is

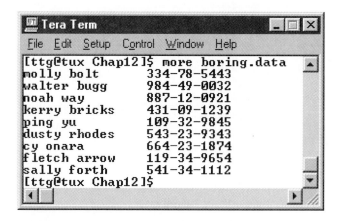

FIGURE 12.59

A typical, albeit boring, data file.

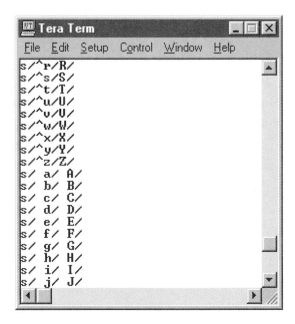

FIGURE 12.60

An excessively long uppercase script.

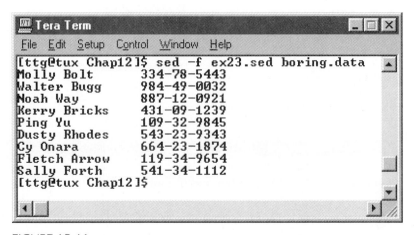

FIGURE 12.61

Running the excessive script against the boring data.

extremely well thought out and a great way to end the chapter because it uses many of the things we have discussed, including hold space. Before you read my explanation, look at the script in Figure 12.63 and see if you can figure it out. You may wish to log on to your system and build the sample sed script line by line, running it as you add each line to see what it does. It is truly wonderful.

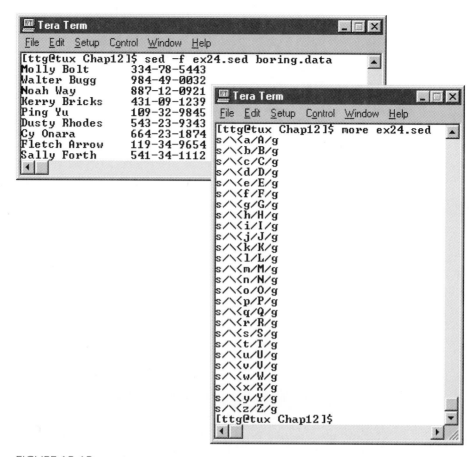

FIGURE 12.62

A more compact and elegant uppercase script.

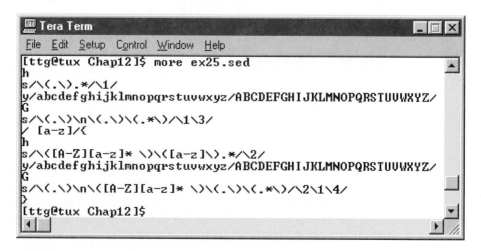

FIGURE 12.63

An extremely elegant sed script!

Did you try to figure it out on your own? Yes, I realize it looks quite confusing, but you really need to try to figure it out on your own first. You'll appreciate it more if you figure out how it works. I'm sure you can do it if you just take a little time.

Okay, here's how it works:

1. The line in pattern space is moved into hold space. This preserves the contents of the whole line while letting us play with particular characters.
2. Next we segregate the first character of the line and replace the whole line with just that first character. This isolates the first character of the line as the only character in the pattern space.
3. Then we translate that one lowercase character to uppercase using the y command. At this point the pattern space contains only a single uppercase letter corresponding to the first character of the line.
4. After translation, we append the hold space to the pattern space, in essence giving us two lines in pattern space, the first line containing a single uppercase letter and the second line containing the original, unmodified line.
5. This next bit is really interesting, because we are combining two lines into one pattern space. Look closely at the substitution. We first identify a single character (that's that uppercase character.) Next we identify the newline character that marks the end of the first line. Following the newline character, we identify another single character, which is the lowercase letter we are going to replace.
6. Finally, we select and identify the rest of the line. At this point the uppercase character is identified as the first field, the lowercase first letter of the first name is the second field, and the rest of the line is the third identified field.
7. For that two-line combination we substitute the first field (the uppercase letter), and the third field (the rest of the line.) Now we have capitalized the first name.
8. Next we search for a lowercase letter preceded by a space. (If a person has but one name, like Zeus, we would be finished processing that record.) If we find a lowercase letter preceded by a space, we then execute the next set of commands, which has the effect of capitalizing the second name.
9. To capitalize the first character of the second name, we first move the current pattern space to hold space to preserve the data.
10. Next we identify the first character of the second name. (To do that we identify the first name, because it starts with an uppercase letter followed by lowercase letters and a space.)
11. We then identify the first lowercase letter in the second name, and subsequently identify the rest of the line.
12. We substitute the second identified field (the first letter of the second name) for the whole line. This makes the first letter of the second name really a character in pattern space.
13. Then we run the good old translate that we've seen before, shifting that single character from lowercase to uppercase.

14. Next we append the contents of hold space to the contents of pattern space.
15. Finally, we identify the uppercase version of the first letter of the last name, the first name, the first character of the last name, and the rest of the line. We substitute the uppercase character for the lowercase character as the first character of the last name and we're done!

As you can see, this is an extremely elegant solution. Were we to have a data file that included names with middle initials, we would need to expand the script to account for that. Take the time to really understand the script shown in Figure 12.63. It will enable you to do wonderful things with sed.

The Road Not Taken

Since this is an introductory book about Unix, and because I can wait no longer to get into the wild, wonderful world of awk, there are a couple areas of sed scripting that I'll leave to your further exploration. The first is handling multiple-line records—not the simple stuff like Figure 12.63, using the three uppercase sed commands designed specifically to work with multiple-line records. If you need to process files with records that span multiple lines, acquaint yourself with the N, D, and P commands.

The other area I've chosen not to investigate is the flow-of-control command set. Once you spend some time with sed and have begun building long (60–200 lines) sed scripts, you will need to be able to create conditionally executing scripts where you branch from place to place. Since this is not a programming text, and because most new Unix users don't create terribly complex sed scripts, I am not going to discuss branching and gotos. Feel free to explore them at your leisure, as you discover the delights of sed scripting.

KEY TERMS

hold space
POSIX
pattern space

NEW COMMANDS

```
sed
sort
tr
```

REVIEW QUESTIONS

12.1 Why does Unix have elements of text processing as part of the operating system?
12.2 Which command would you use to change all the lowercase vowels in a file to uppercase?
12.3 List the first two parts of Refrigerator Rule No. 4.

12.4   Explain what, if anything, is wrong with the following command?

```
cat frost2.txt | tr 'unixrocks' 'UNIXROCKS'
```

12.5   Describe the use of the following translate options: -d and -s.

12.6   Explain the POSIX character classes, and list three of them.

12.7   What is a *key field* in terms of the sort command?

12.8   Describe six of the options for the sort command, including -o.

12.9   What does sed stand for?

12.10   Explain the differences between the sed editor and the ed editor.

12.11   Repeat, and then explain, Refrigerator Rule No. 5.

12.12   Is it better to use sed from the command line or with a script? Explain your answer.

12.13   Explain the general form of a sed command.

12.14   Differentiate between hold space and pattern space in sed.

12.15   How you mark the end of a multiple-line insert or append in sed?

12.16   If you want to output only specific lines from a sed script, what command-line option must you use?

12.17   If you don't want to use the command-line option, what must you include in your sed script?

EXERCISES

12.1   Convert all the lowercase vowels in the file frost2.txt to uppercase.

12.2   Use ROT-13 to encode a message to one of your classmates, e-mail the message, and have them decode it.

12.3   Create a list of all of the words in the file short.text.

12.4   Now modify the output from the previous exercise so that the list contains only one entry for each word (one the, one and, and so forth).

12.5   Demonstrate the use of each of the POSIX character classes. You don't have to be fancy; your output can look something like that shown in Figure 12.11.

12.6   Sort the file dessert1.txt by type of dessert, not flavor.

12.7   Sort the /etc/passwd file on your system by group numbers.

12.8   Repeat the sort you did in Exercise 7, but this time show only one entry for each group number.

12.9   Correct the second example sed script, ex2.sed, so that it changes only the first names of Sally to Suzie.

12.10   Create a sed script that will output only the lines of individuals with last names that start with the letter W.

12.11   Create a sed script that will capitalize each occurrence of the letters snorble in the file test.data.

12.12   Modify the script shown in Figure 12.45 to remove all the extraneous lines from the file text4.text.

12.13   Create a sed script that will demonstrate the use of both hold space and pattern space similar to the sample shown in Figure 12.55.

12.14   Modify the sed script shown in Figure 12.63 to handle names with middle initials.

awk

In this chapter you will learn about one of the most powerful tools in the Unix toolbox, **awk**. No, it isn't really the sound made by a large seabird, but it is fun to say aloud! A word of warning, however: one chapter, in one humble text, can't teach you all about awk. There have been whole books written about this incredible tool, so what we will do is get a taste of awk. I hope that it will whet your appetite, and you will decide to learn more on your own.

Overview

The awk tool started life as a simple concept. In fact, here is a description of its inception and early growth as written by the authors, Alfred V. Aho, Peter J. Weinberger, and Brian W. Kernighan in their book, *The AWK Programming Language*, copyright 1988.

Awk was originally designed and implemented by the authors in 1977, in part as an experiment to see how the Unix tools grep and sed could be generalized to deal with numbers as well as text. It was based on our interests in regular expressions and programmable editors. Although it was meant for writing very short programs, its combination of facilities soon attracted users who wrote significantly larger programs. These larger programs needed features that had not been part of the original implementation, so awk was enhanced in a new version made available in 1985.

What that tells us is that awk is a programming language that looks something like **sed** and **grep**, from whence it was created. Truth be known, you can probably create awk scripts, or programs, to perform almost all the functions of the other Unix tools, it wouldn't be efficient, but the capability exists. That is one reason awk is such a powerful tool—it is used to create all kinds of other tools.

There are four brothers in the awk family, something like the three grep sisters. The oldest brother, awk, was written in 1977. Then, in 1985, Aho, Weinberger, and Kerihigan updated awk, adding some new features and calling this version **nawk**, which stood for New awk. **Gawk** or **mawk** are some newer versions of the awk tool. You can download gawk from the GNU (GNU's Not Unix) free software project (www.gnu.org) if your system administrator allows users to install software on the system. It has the g in front of awk because it is part of the GNU project. It is the default version of awk seen in most releases of Linux and is gaining popularity across the wide Unix frontier.

A note on usage: In this chapter—indeed, in this text—I will refer to all of the awk brothers as awk. When we look at a particular command that is only supported by one of the brothers, I will tell you. Everything you can do in awk, you can do in nawk or gawk or mawk. However, the newer awk brothers support tools unavailable to awk.

⊕ Awk Syntax

The awk command has the following syntax:

```
awk [-F field_separator] 'program' target-file(s)
or
awk [-F field_separator] -f program.file target-file (s)
```

The program is one or more awk programming commands, and target-file(s) is one or more of the input files the command is to process. The second form is very much the preferred form unless you are doing a very simple task. (I bet you could have guessed that from the preceding chapter, couldn't you!)

In the second example, the -f option tells awk that the filename that follows contains the awk programming commands, or awk script. Awk then takes its instructions from that file rather than from the command line. This behaves like the -f option to the sed command with which you are already familiar. The difference is that in this case, of course, the file contains awk programming commands rather than sed scripting directives. Using the program.file option is preferred for three reasons:

First and foremost, it is far more efficient to create even very simple awk programs and store them in a file so you can easily debug, modify, and enhance them without having to retype the commands over and over.

Second, as you will learn with shell scripts, and as you have already seen with sed scripting, you will often find it necessary to repeat programming tasks. If you have your program stored in a file, all you need do is rerun the awk using that program file; you don't have to reinvent code to perform the same task.

Third, as you begin to work with awk, you will quickly find that some of your programs grow to substantial length. If they are in a file, it is easy to work with them, but if you try to write large programs on the command line, it quickly gets cumbersome. If you choose to enter awk commands on the command line, you should enclose the commands within tick marks to protect them from interpretation by the shell. If you put the commands into a program file, you will not use the tick marks.

The -F option allows you to change awk's field separator. Normally awk uses *white space* (one or more spaces or tabs) as the field separator. In most cases, this works just fine. However, if you are trying to *parse*, or divide into fields, a file that doesn't use white space as a field separator, it is handy to be able to specify another character. For example, if you wanted to parse /etc/passwd, you would need to specify the colon (:) as the field separator, or you would usually have only two fields (or three if the user had a middle initial) in each record. Here is an entry from /etc/passwd—notice that the only space is between the first and last names.

```
nattired:x:111:1000:Natalie Attired:/home/nattired:/bin/bash
```

Parsing this line from /etc/passwd with white space as the delimiter, the first field would be

```
nattired:x:111:1000:Natalie
```

and the second field would be

```
Attired:/home/nattired:/bin/bash
```

Obviously, /etc/passwd needs to be parsed using a colon as a field separator.

What this means is that awk is the first tool you have learned that will give you control of the data in files at the field level. With field-level addressability, you have the ability to create powerful programs that can take the place of higher-level language code. Although awk is no substitute for C when writing operating systems, it is complex and feature-rich enough to allow the development of simple interpreters, text processors, calculators, and even simple databases. Yes, awk is an amazing tool, sophisticated, powerful, and yet relatively easy to learn … well, compared with nuclear engineering or particle physics. No, really, it is easy to begin to use awk, and the language has enough features to enable you to write programs of almost any level of sophistication.

This brings us to the final part of Refrigerator Rule No. 4:

Refrigerator Rule No. 4

(part a): grep works line by line.
(part b): tr works byte by byte.
(part c): awk works field by field.

⊕ Awk Variables

When awk parses the data or target file, it assigns each field a unique name. However, awk is not very imaginative. Rather than using interesting names like Jon, Ling, Rebecca, Phred, or Michael, awk just counts the fields and names them in the order it finds them. (Actually, it's a rather boring way to name variables, but what do you expect from a programming language with such an odd name?) The first field awk parses out is called $1, the second is called $2, and so on through the whole input line or record. In addition, awk stores the whole input line in the variable $0 (zero). Therefore, to refer to the third field from the input record, you would use the variable $3. (That field is called dollar three, not three dollars!)

In addition to the variables awk parses from the data file, you have access to an additional set of very handy variables that awk creates. A discussion of the more common ones follows, and they are summarized in Table 13.1. Remember that Unix is case-sensitive, and note that all of these variables are written in uppercase. In addition, since we are talking about all of the awk brothers, some of these variables, notably the last two, are not available in awk, but only in nawk and gawk. There are several other nawk variables, but those discussed here are the ones you will use most often.

TABLE 13.1   Some Common awk Variables

Awk Variable	Contents
FS	Identifies the input field separator, usually white space.
OFS	Identifies the output field separator, usually a single blank space.
NR	Contains the count of lines or records, also is the number of the current line.
NF	Contains the number of fields, based on FS, in the current record.
$(n)	Serves as one of n positional variables corresponding to the relative position of the field in the record; $1 contains the first field, and $(NF) contains the last field.
$0	Contains the whole current line from the target file.
FILENAME	Gives the name of the current target file.
ARGV	Gives an array of the command-line arguments (not supported by awk).
ARGC	Gives the number of command-line arguments (not supported by awk).

ARGC is a count of the number of variables on the command line. It is sometimes helpful to know how many parameters the user has passed to nawk. This variable is not recognized by awk.

ARGV is an array, or list, that contains the command-line parameters that ARGC counted. You reference the elements of ARGV using the syntax ARGV[n], where n is the number of the variable you wish to use. This variable is recognized by nawk or gawk, but not awk.

FILENAME holds the name of the current data or target file.

FS stores the current field separator. It is possible to use this variable to change the field separator for an awk program. Rather than coding the -F option on the command line, a wise awk programmer can code a statement like

```
FS = ":"
```

to change the field separator from the default white space to a colon. Coding this within the awk program means that the user doesn't have to remember to code it on the command line. It is a very handy variable. Of course, you can change the field separator to any character or characters you need to use.

OFS stands for *output field separator.* It holds the character that is used to divide the fields in the *output line* or record. The default is a single space. This variable is important when you are using files that don't use the default FS. For example, if you were writing an awk script to parse and modify /etc/passwd, you wouldn't want the output fields to be divided by white space; they would need to be divided by colons. Using OFS=":" would solve that problem.

NF contains the number of fields in the current line or record, a useful thing to know. Just as ARGC keeps count of command-line arguments, NF keeps count of the number of fields in the current line. This variable also lets us address specific fields within the line. For example, if we know that every record contains the same number of fields, like /etc/passwd, then we can be sure that $5, for example, is the user's name in real life. But suppose that we know that the number of fields in a record varies. And we know that the second to last field is the one we always want. To reliably access it we can use the construct $(NF - 2), which says, "Address the field that is 2 less than the number of fields in the record."

NR holds the sequential number of the current line or record as it is read from the data file. This variable can also be used to determine how many lines have been processed from the current data file. Some awk programmers make the mistake of thinking that they can use this variable to count a subset of the records from a file. If you want to count only specific records, you will need to create and increment you own counter.

⊕ The Parts of a Program

As all Gaul could be divided into three parts, "vini, vidi, vici," so all programs can be divided into three basic structures. Any program you write in a procedural language will be composed of one, two, or all three of these structures. As you build awk scripts, since awk is a programming language, you will craft your scripts using these three constructs.

Sequence

Sequence, meaning that a series of commands are executed one after the other, is the basic building block of all programs. All the commands will be executed. Sometimes, as you will see, an awk program is a single line of code. That is the shortest example of a sequence. Other times you will construct dozens of lines that will be executed one after the other. Those are examples of longer sequences.

Selection

When the IF statement was introduced to programming, programs began to be able to make decisions. The first, tiny step toward artificial intelligence? When a program can decide which sequence of code to execute, the program is exhibiting conditional execution, or *selection*. In other words, how it executes is dependent upon one or more conditions. You can code selection into your awk scripts in two ways. First, you can use the pattern portion of the pattern/action pair to select specific lines upon which to work. You have seen this type of selection when you used patterns as addresses in sed, and when you selected lines with grep. The second way to select records is to use the more common IF-THEN-ELSE construct. Both methods will give your program/script the ability to make decisions. Selection is critical to modern program design.

Iteration

The third programming construct, and the most recently developed, is *iteration*—the ability of the program to repeat a sequence of instructions. Iteration was a great boon to programmers because it meant that they didn't have to retype the same lines of code five times in their program to have an operation execute five times. They just put those instructions in a loop and allowed the program to repeat them.

Looping, or iteration, allows you to write a fairly short script that will execute thousands of instructions, using the instructions coded in the loop many times. As you will see later, when we examine arrays, iteration and arrays allow you to create very small but very powerful scripts to process large amounts of data with very few instructions.

So there you have it: sequence, selection, and iteration, the building blocks of programs and scripts. Watch for them as we discuss the different parts of an awk program.

⊕ awk Program Format

When you think of awk programs, you must think of one or more *pattern/action pairs*. An awk program statement is composed of a pattern to be matched followed by the action to take when a line, or field, from the input file matches that pattern. This is the basic unit of an awk program. The actual format of an awk program statement is

```
pattern {action}
```

The curly braces (or French braces) are required syntax. *All* awk *actions must be enclosed within the curly braces*. An action in awk can be one or more verbs. In fact, some awk programs, composed of hundreds of verbs, are completely contained within one action (one set of curly braces).

To have awk do what you intend, you need to understand three important rules—rules that are so important, we made them into Refrigerator Rules (see next page).

These three rules are at the heart of how awk works. Wow, three new Refrigerator Rules!

(Look at them now.) I have a serious question for you: What other command that you have already mastered acts like Refrigerator Rule No. 6 part a? In what other command is the "action" applied to every line if you don't specify an address? Yes! The answer is sed. You did so well on that question let's try another: What other command that you have learned to love acts like Refrigerator rule No. 6 part b? That is, what command, or command family, displays lines that match a particular pattern? Did you say grep? That's what I thought—good for you! And which two commands did Aho,

---

Refrigerator Rule No. 6

(part a) An action, without a corresponding pattern, is performed for every line of the input or target file.

(part b) A pattern, without a corresponding action, performs the default action of printing each line that matches the pattern.

(part c) Each pattern/action pair is applied to every line in the input or target file, one at a time.

Weinberger, and Kernighan know and love that formed the basis for awk? Yes, indeedie, grep and sed! You will soon come to appreciate how knowing those two commands can make awk all the more useful and fun!

The combination of the first two parts of Refrigerator Rule No. 6 points out an important awk syntax issue. The action associated with a particular pattern must begin on the same line as that pattern. That means that the curly brace associated with an action must be on the same line as the pattern with which it is associated. For example, look at these two pattern/action pairs:

```
pattern {  ←————
      action verb 1
      action verb 2
      }
pattern   ←————
      {action verb 1
      action verb 2
      }
```

In the first example, the action (both verbs) would be performed only on lines that *match the pattern*. In the second example, each line that matches the pattern would be displayed and the action (both verbs) would be performed on every line. Quite a difference, and all dependent upon the placement of one little curly brace.

⊕ Patterns

The first part of an awk program statement is the pattern. It selects which of the lines from the file or files, if any, are acted upon. The pattern is a selection element and can be used like an IF statement (if the pattern matches, then perform the action). Let's look at the constructs used in a pattern.

Relational Expressions

A *relational expression* (also called a *logical expression*) specifies the relationship between two variables and uses one or more of the relational operators listed in Table 13.2.

Comparisons can be either string or numeric. (Remember that awk was developed to bring pattern-matching and the like to numeric data.)

TABLE 13.2 Relational Expressions in awk

Symbol	Meaning
<	Less than
<=	Less than or equal to
>	Greater than
>=	Greater than or equal to
!=	Not equal to
==	Equal to
~	Contains the regular expression
!~	Does not contain the regular expression
&&	Logical AND
||	Logical OR

Let's examine some example patterns using each of the relational operators in Table 13.2. Note: this is how they would appear in a program file, but if used on the command line (oh shame of shame), they would be enclosed in tick marks. Okay, here's our first example:

```
$1 < 4 {action}
```

If the value stored in the variable $1 (the first field from the input record) is less than 4, the action will be performed. Only lines in which the value of $1 is *less than* 4 will trigger the action portion of the program statement. Now for our second example:

```
$1 <= 4 {action}
```

If the value of the variable $1 is *less than or equal to* 4, then the specified action is performed.

```
$1 > 4 {action}
```

This is the reverse of the previous example. If the value of the variable $1 is *greater than* 4, then the action associated with this pattern is executed.

When two variables, A and B, are compared, there are always *three* possible relationships that must be taken into account:

1. A is greater than B.
2. A is less than B.
3. A is equal to B.

Many bugs in programs of all flavors happen because the programmer failed to take into account all three of the different potential relationships. Don't make that mistake in your awk programs. In the following case, the action is executed if the value of the variable $1 is *greater than or equal to* 4.

```
$1 >= 4 {action}
```

The next relationship specifies that the value in the variable $1 is *not* equal to 4.

```
$1 != 4 {action}
```

If the value in $1 is either less than or greater than 4, the action specified is executed. The bang (!) indicates the logical NOT of the action. In this case the NOT of the test for equality.

A brief note about logical NOT: In Boolean algebra, the result of a logical expression is a binary (1 or 0) value. When a relationship—like A is less than B (in awk parlance, A < B)—is tested, the result is a binary value, 1 or 0. A NOT operator, also called a *bit flipper*, simply reverses the resulting value, changing a 1 to a 0, or a 0 to a 1.

Therefore, in the preceding example awk first evaluates the relationship of $1 being equal to 4. Then the NOT (!) reverses the value of the result. If $1 actually contained the value 4, the equality test would return a result of 1, or true. And the NOT would flip that value to 0, or false.

When discussing NOT logic, our language can get us into trouble. Another way to describe the relationship $1 != 4, where $1 contains the value 6, would be, "Since $1 does not contain 4, the NOT of the equality causes the final value to be true." This description is cumbersome at best. The experts—meaning anyone with a briefcase who is more than fifty miles from home—usually recommend avoiding NOT logic whenever possible as it adds a level of confusion that should and could be avoided in most cases.

By the way, this is a wonderful illustration of why you need to protect the pattern from the C shell. What does the C shell use the ! for? Right you are—to recall commands from the history buffer.

Now let's look at the inverse relationship to the previous example:

```
$1 == 4 {action}
```

In this case the specified action will be taken only if the value stored in the variable $1 is exactly 4. Notice that the equality operator consists of *two* equal signs. One common error neophyte awk programmers make is to use only one equal sign ($1 = 4). That missing equal sign creates confusion, because awk will perform a value assignment rather than a check for equality, and the result will always be true. Consequently, the action will be taken, and the value of $1 will change.

The tilde (~) traditionally is used to indicate *matches the regular expression*, but the term *contains the regular expression* seems easier for students to understand. In the following case, the specified action is taken if the value stored at $1 starts with a lowercase t:

```
$1 ~ /^t/ {action}
```

Any regular expression can be used (and you thought you were done with regular expressions when we left the grep chapter, didn't you!). The regular expression *must be enclosed in forward or right slashes*.

A word of warning here: You can enclose only regular expressions in slashes. Some flavors of awk will balk if the expression in the slashes is not a regular expression.

The next relationship is the opposite of the previous one. In this case the action specified is executed if the value in the variable $1 does *not* start with a lowercase t:

```
$1 !~ /^t/ {action}
```

As with the test of equality, the bang (!) negates the relationship symbol that follows.

The next two relational operators—AND and OR—need to be used in combination with some of those discussed earlier. They provide a way for awk programmers (gosh, now you are an awk programmer; isn't that exciting?) to combine two or more relational expressions into one larger relational expression. Here's an example:

```
$1 > 4 && $2 < 3 {action}
```

The action in this case is performed if both relationships are true, $1 is greater than 4, *and* $2 is less than 3. The AND logical operator (coded as the double ampersand, &&) tests both the relationships, and then evaluates the Boolean result (true or false) based on the information in Table 13.3.

TABLE 13.3 Truth Table for the Logical AND

Condition A	Condition B	Result
True	False	False
False	True	False
False	False	False
True	True	True

As you can see, the only time that the AND operator will give us a result of true is when both condition A *and* condition B are true. Actually, some versions of awk test the first condition, and if it's false, they don't even bother to test the second condition, as they know the outcome must be false. If you want to make your awks just a tad more efficient, try to code the condition that is most likely to be false first.

```
$1 > 4 || $2 < 3 {action}
```

The next example shows the logical OR: Here the action is taken if either of the conditions is true. That is, if $1 is greater than 4 or if $2 is less than 3, the action is taken. Like AND, OR is a Boolean operator that evaluates the conditions surrounding it and then sets a resultant value in accordance with the truth table in Table 13.4. Thus, if either of the conditions is true, the logical OR sets True as the result. On most

TABLE 13.4 Truth Table for the Logical OR

Condition A	Condition B	Result
True	True	True
True	False	True
False	True	True
False	False	False

machines OR is as efficient as AND. It looks at the first condition, and if it is True, simply sets the result to True without ever looking at the second condition. (If one of the conditions is true, the OR of those conditions must be true.) OR is a very handy operator. Again for efficiency try to code the condition most likely to be true first. If it's true, so is the expression.

Complex Relational Expressions

It is possible to create some very complex patterns using multiple ANDs and ORs. Just for illustration purposes, look at the following pattern:

```
(($1 < $2 && $3 > $1) && $4 != "frog") || $6 > 0 {action}
```

Try to figure out the values for the variables that would allow the action to execute. Remember that grouping logical operations with parentheses causes them to be evaluated first, and evaluated as a unit. Otherwise, awk evaluates the expressions from left to right.

Got it figured out? Okay, let's look at it as awk does, from left to right, using parentheses to indicate groups. The first condition to check, because it is within two pair of parentheses, is

```
($1 < $2 && $3 > $1)
```

Breaking that down, we get

```
$1 < $2
```

If that is true, we can go on, but if it is false, we know that the whole first expression—everything up to the OR—is false. Why? Well, because looking at the truth table for AND, we see that if either of the expressions evaluates to False, the whole ANDed expression is then False. If the first condition is False, then the first ANDed pair must be False, and if that evaluates False, then the next ANDed pair also must be False. See? It is easy. Right, sure it is! Moving right along, assume that $1 < $2.

We then evaluate the other half of the first AND this way:

```
$3 > $1
```

If that is True, then the ANDed pair must also be True. See how simple it all is? ☺

If the whole first expression evaluates to True, then we look at the next level of parentheses, and evaluate that expression:

```
($1 < $2 && $3 > $1) && $4 != "frog"
```

Since the first ANDed pair is already true, all we need to evaluate is if the fourth field contains the string **frog**. As long as it doesn't, then the outer expression, as defined by the parentheses, is True, and we don't even need to evaluate the last expression, because the OR operator will return True if either of the expressions is True. However, if any of the relationships in the parenthetical relationships were False, then we would need to look at whether $6 is greater than 0. If it is, then the action is taken; if not, and if the left side of the OR evaluates to False, then the whole pattern is False, and the action is not taken.

Just for fun, here are some lines from an input file. Select the ones that would match the pattern.

```
(($1 < $2 && $3 > $1) && $4 != "frog") || $6 > 0
```

Data:

```
1 4 0 toad frog 0
3 7 9 frog salamander 0
3 7 9 fish salamander 0
0 0 1 cricket fish 9
5 1 3 toad spider -4
0 0 0 wasp bee 1
```

Which of these lines do you predict will match? When I ran an awk against this data file, it told me that the following lines matched:

```
3 7 9 fish salamander 0
0 0 1 cricket fish 9
0 0 0 wasp bee 1
```

The first line doesn't match because the third field is not greater than the first field and $6 is not greater than zero.

The second line doesn't match because the fourth field contains the word `frog` and $6 is not greater than zero.

The third line *matches*, because the first field (3) is less than the second (7), the third field (9) is greater than the first (3), and the fourth field does not contain the word `frog`.

The fourth line *matches*, because field 6 has a value greater than 0.

The fifth line doesn't match because the first field (5) is greater than the second field (2), and the value of the sixth field (-4), is not greater than 0.

The last line *matches*, just because the value of the sixth field is greater than 0. Now wasn't that just about the most fun you have had all week? It is important to build your logical expressions carefully, and evaluate them as awk would. If you aren't careful, you won't have the results you expect.

/Regular Expressions/

A third possible type of pattern is a *regular expression*. You can use a regular expression to match all or part of the entire input line; for example, the following set of regular expressions would match particular aspects of the line from the input file. Remember that a regular expression must be enclosed in slashes, but a simple pattern should not be enclosed in slashes. Here is an example of a regular expression as a pattern:

```
/40$/ {action}
```

In this case, awk performs the action specified on all of the lines that end in 40. Notice, in this case, as with all the cases using regular expressions as patterns rather than relational patterns, the regular expression will apply to the whole line, not just one specific field.

Let's look at this pattern when it is used in a real awk, running into a real data file. Figure 13.1 shows a little data file we will be using for examples, it is called `folks`.

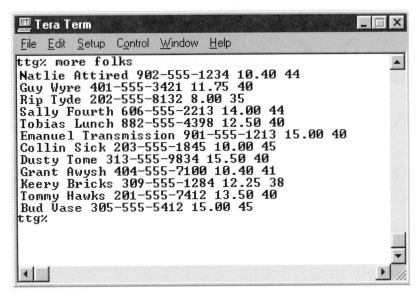

FIGURE 13.1

Output of the folks data file.

These data show the names (first and last), the telephone number, the hourly wage, and the hours worked for some of the folks that work at Grate Names Inc. One common use for awk is to generate reports. Let's see which elements of this data file would be selected by the regular expression pattern of /40$/: As you remember from our discussion of regular expressions, a regular expression that ends with a currency symbol means *matches at the end of the line*.

Okay, you asked for it: here is a real, live awk with a real, live action after the pattern. (Pedagogical note: I realize I have pretty much forbidden you to code awk pattern/action pairs on the command line. Yet here I am doing it right in front of you. The reason for that is twofold. First of all, it makes the examples shorter so they take up less space, reducing the number of pages in the book and so saving trees. Second, I want you to focus on pattern/action pairs, but I also want to show you how to use them in context, so I am "doing it on the command line" rather than more properly doing it in a script. Umm, how about, "Do as I say, not as I do?" <grin>)

```
awk '/40$/ {print $0}' folks
```

This awk will print the following records from the file:

```
Guy Wyre 401-555-3421 11.75 40
Tobias Lunch 882-555-4398 12.50 40
Emanuel Transmission 901-555-1213 15.00 40
Dusty Tome 313-555-9834 15.50 40
Tommy Hawks 201-555-7412 13.50 40
```

Each of these records (lines) ends in a 40, so each matches the regular expression in the awk. The action, {print $0}, is one of the more common ones in awk. From our discussion of awk variables, you will remember that the awk variable $0 stood for the whole line from the input file. That means that {print $0} simply sends the whole output line to standard out. (Remember the second rule of awk: a pattern without a corresponding action will take the default action of printing the input line. Now you can explain it properly: a pattern without a corresponding action will take the default action {print $0}. See how much nicer that looks?)

Besides looking at the end of the input line, you will remember that regular expressions can be used to find records that start with a particular set of characters as well.

```
awk '/^G/ {print $0}' folks
```

This regular expression would find all the lines that started with an uppercase G. These would be the lines reported:

```
Guy Wyre 401-555-3421 11.75 40
Grant Awysh 404-555-7100 10.40 41
```

Both of these lines start with G, so they match the pattern specified by the regular expression.

Likewise, regular expressions can match a particular string that occurs anywhere in the input line. For example,

```
awk '/10/ {print $0}' folks
```

would select the following lines from the folks file:

```
Natalie Attired 902-555-1234 10.40 44
Collin Sick 203-555-1845 10.00 45
Grant Awysh 404-555-7100 10.40 41
```

Each of these lines has at least one instance of the string 10 embedded within it. So using regular expressions as the pattern in an awk enables us to select any particular string from within the record. Remember back at the beginning of this section when I told you that you could use awk to recreate other Unix commands? How could you recreate the same output using a different Unix tool? How about grep '10' folks. That's right—we just used awk to recreate grep! Now wasn't that exciting? Actually, using regular expressions with awk is common, but they usually have a more interesting action associated with them.

I realize that I could have left the {print $0} action off from each of these examples and they would have worked just fine. However, I wanted you to see pattern action pairs, so I physically coded them.

Magic Patterns

The next pair of patterns are called *special* or *magic patterns*. There are only two of these—BEGIN and END—and they have absolutely no relationship to each other.

BEGIN
The first magic pattern is **BEGIN**.

```
BEGIN {action}
```

Here is a realistic BEGIN.

```
BEGIN {
      FS=":"
      count=0
      print ("This is a cool heading")
          }
```

Usually the BEGIN pattern is the first pattern in an awk script. Some variants of awk *require* it to be the first pattern if you choose to code it; others are not so fussy. The BEGIN pattern must be coded in all uppercase letters. Note: You must code the open curly brace on the same line as the BEGIN pattern. Some programmers put the first action on the same line as the BEGIN and the opening curly brace, but I have found that putting each verb of the action on a separate line makes the script more readable. Like all actions, the curly braces enclose the set of action verbs. The BEGIN pattern is special, because the associated action will be performed *before the target or data file is opened.* You can test this by creating an awk script file that contains a BEGIN pattern and another pattern/action pair. Invoke awk with that script file and use a nonexistent data or target file. The BEGIN actions will execute; then awk will discover that the target file doesn't exist and give an error message. Figure 13.2 shows a simple awk script that illustrates the use of the BEGIN. This is not a useful production script; it is more or less the awk version of the cat command. However, it does illustrate how the BEGIN magic pattern is evaluated. When this script is run into a nonexistent data file, awk sends the following stream-o-bytes to standard out. (Note: Applying an awk script to a particular data file is often referred to as *running the script into the data file.* Just one of those wonderful Unix expressions.)

Figure 13.3 shows what awk sends to the screen when the script is run. This example proves that the BEGIN pattern is executed before awk even checks to see if the target

```
BEGIN {
print "As the King of Hearts told the White Rabbit"
print " when he asked where to begin:"
print "\"Begin at the beginning\", the King said, very gravely,"
print "\"and go on till you come to the end: then stop.\""


        }
{ print $0}
```

FIGURE 13.2

A simple awk script showing the BEGIN magic pattern.

```
Tera Term                                                    _ □ X
[ttg@tux awk_files]$ awk -f fig1302 IDontExist
As the King of Hearts told the White Rabbit
 when he asked where to begin:
"Begin at the beginning", the King said, very gravely,
"and go on till you come to the end: then stop."
awk: fig1302:6: fatal: cannot open file `IDontExist' for reading (No such file
or directory)
[ttg@tux awk_files]$
```

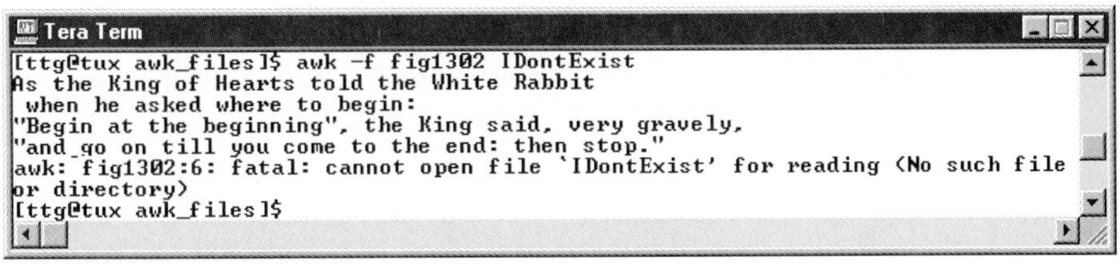

FIGURE 13.3

Output from the script in Figure 13.2.

file exists. That makes BEGIN a great place to print out headers, initialize counters, and set the field separator for the target file. Some novice awk programmers mistakenly try to manipulate the data in the target file from within the BEGIN. Remember, the BEGIN action is executed *before* the target file is even opened, so data from the target file cannot be processed in the BEGIN action. Note: if you are going to set the FS, you must set it in the BEGIN action.

END

The other magic pattern is **END**.

```
END {action}
```

Figure 13.4 shows is a pseudo-realistic script with an example of an END pattern/action pair. This script is almost as exciting as the last was. It echoes all the lines in the target file, then executes the action associated with the END pattern. In this case, it prints the number of records seen by the script. You do remember the NR awk variable, don't you? The action associated with the END pattern executes after the target file is *successfully* closed. That means that at the time the END action executes, the data file is already closed.

In Figure 13.5 we see an example of an awk running the script in Figure 13.4 into the folks data file. Notice that the correct number of records appears in that last line. The NR variable was incremented for each line as it was read in from the data file. The

```
{print $0}
END {
        print "This lovely script processed "NR" records"
      }
```

FIGURE 13.4

Simple awk script showing END magic pattern.

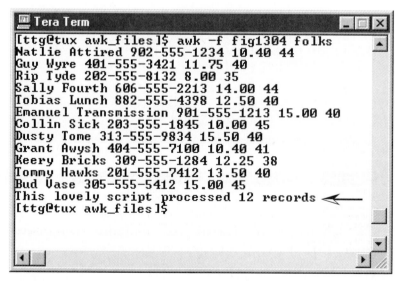

FIGURE 13.5

Output of the simple script in Figure 13.4.

END pattern/action pair is useful for putting trailers on files, summing up the data presented, and doing other end-of-file housekeeping tasks.

Unlike the BEGIN pattern, the action associated with the END pattern will execute only after the target file has *successfully* closed. In the next example, our script from Figure 13.4 is run into a file that doesn't exist. Notice the output shown in Figure 13.6. All that appears is the error message. Since the target file, IDontExist, was not successfully closed, the action associated END pattern did not execute.

```
Tera Term                                                    _ □ ×
[ttg@tux awk_files]$ awk -f fig1304 IDontExist
awk: fig1304:5: fatal: cannot open file `IDontExist' for reading (No such file
or directory)
[ttg@tux awk_files]$
```

FIGURE 13.6

Output of the END example with a nonexistent file.

So far, so good. Now let's put the BEGIN and END together to make a more interesting script. The only action verb we need is the print to make a super cat command. Figure 13.7 shows the script. It would be nice to be able to put the name of the file in the heading generated by the BEGIN action, but alas, BEGIN doesn't know the name of the input file as it hasn't been opened yet!

```
BEGIN {
        print "Here come the lines from the input file:"
        print " "
        }
{ print $0 }
END {
        print " "
        print "There were "NR" lines in the file "FILENAME"."
}
```

FIGURE 13.7

An awk script showing the BEGIN and END magic patterns.

Figure 13.8 shows the execution of the script in Figure 13.7. The output in Figure 13.8 shows exactly what we expect. The BEGIN action puts out the header, then the body of the script prints each line from the file, and finally the END action outputs the footer using two awk variables. Pretty amazing script! ☺

Remember that there is *no relationship* between the awk BEGIN and END. You can have a BEGIN with no END, an END with no BEGIN, or a script with neither of them. Usually if you choose to use BEGIN, it should be coded at the beginning of the script, and if you choose to use an END, it should be coded at the end of the script. This ordering is primarily for readability in most versions of awk. One of the rules of readability and programming in general is the "rule of the least astonishment." That means don't do things that astonish your reader.

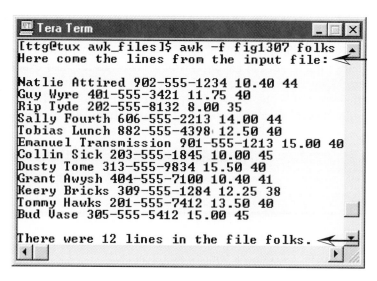

FIGURE 13.8

Output from awk running the script in Figure 13.7.

The version of awk I'm using doesn't seem to care where BEGIN and END are coded, and even works just fine if BEGIN follows END, but not all awks are so forgiving. There are a couple of other patterns available to awk, but the ones we have studied should give you plenty to work with.

⊕ Actions

Now that you are an expert on awk patterns, let's look at the other half of the pattern/action pair. An action is defined as one or more awk commands enclosed in a pair of curly braces. Awk is rich in commands. We will look at some of the more commonly used commands, but by no means all of them. For example, we won't consider most of the mathematical functions; you can look them up if you need them.

The first action we will examine might be one of the most important you will use. Good awk programmers *always* document their programs, so you will use this symbol often!

\#

```
# This is a comment
```

Actually, the octothorp, hash mark, pound symbol, tic-tac-toe board, or number sign (i.e., the #) isn't a command. However, it is one of the most important parts of an awk script. The octothorp signifies that anything that follows it—that is, the rest of the line—is a comment. Awk ignores comments; they are there for people not for awk, so the syntax is easy. Anytime you write a script, you should include a small block of comments at the beginning that tells the reader what the script does. If you perform some complex action, or if you test a condition that could be confusing, you should include a comment. Remember that you are commenting for yourself, not for somebody else. (If you do that, your comments will be good for anybody else who reads them as well.) Make sure that you are documenting the *why* of the code, not the what. By that I mean you need to explain why you are doing what you are doing, not what you are doing.

For example, if you code this conditional,

```
If (foo > bar)
```

a comment that says,

```
#Check to see if foo is greater than bar
```

is of little value other than to annoy the reader. On the other hand,

```
#Check if the rate of pay, foo, exceeds the maximum, bar.
```

is a much better comment, as it tells you the why of the conditional. (Don't worry if you don't understand the IF statement yet, we will examine it in detail later.) Make your comments meaningful to yourself, and they will be useful to others.

You've already seen the print command in action, in some of the figures so let's look at the input/output commands next. Besides, one of the more common uses for awk is to create pretty output.

print

```
print [arguments] [destination]
```

The **print** command is used to output one or more variables, fields, or strings (called *arguments*) to standard out. Output fields are printed in the order they are listed in the command. If you want to output a character string, it must be enclosed in quotation marks. If there are several arguments, forming an argument list, and the arguments are separated by spaces, they will appear concatenated on the output line. If the elements of the argument list are separated by commas, they will appear separated by the character referenced by OFS (output field separator) on the output line.

If you want to redirect the output of the script, you can use the redirection symbol and have print send the output to a file. You should enclose the target file name in quotation marks if it is a literal; otherwise awk gets confused and tries to use the name of the file as a variable. Do it this way:

```
print $1, $2, $4 > "myfile"
```

That code will send the contents of the first, second, and fourth field to the file called myfile. Redirection is not a frequently used option, but you might need it sometimes.

printf

```
printf ([format [, values]])
```

The **printf** (*print formatted*) command is the most powerful of the formatting tools. It gives you outstanding control over the format of the output, enabling you to make it more beautiful. It is also helpful for printing specific values like hex or octal numbers. In addition, it can let you see the actual contents of a variable, including the nonprinting characters. In this instance, again, it is best to print the variable's value in hex. It is also useful, at times, to be able to format the output of a print statement so you can create columnar output. Again, `printf` can meet this need.

You can code `printf` with or without parentheses, but I encourage you to always use parentheses since in some situations `printf` requires them. Therefore, if you get in the habit of always using them, you will not run into strange error messages, nor will you confuse those who read your awk scripts for fun or profit.

The format of a `printf` statement is

```
printf ( "format-specifier", variable1, variable2...variablen)
```

In this model, the format specifier is contained within a quoted string that may also contain literal text. For example, the following statement prints the decimal value of the variable count:

```
printf ("The variable count contains the value %d", count)
```

A series of format specifiers, shown in Table 13.5, provide particular capabilities for the printf command. Each format specifier starts with a percent (%) sign. Following any modifiers, the format type is specified using one of the characters listed in Table 13.6. Table 13.7 shows two commonly used special characters that control vertical and horizontal spacing: **\n** and **\t**.

TABLE 13.5 Formatting Modifiers for `printf`

Modifier	Function
–	Indicates that the value should be left-justified in the field Example: (`"%-4d"`,number) would print the value stored in number, left-justified in four spaces.
n	A number indicates the minimum width of the field (if it starts with a zero, it means pad with zero. Example: (`"%4d"`,number) would print the value stored in number in a decimal field four digits wide and blank-padded on the left. The zero prefix is specified as (`"%04d"`,number) to print a field a minimum of four digits wide, with zero padding, and zeros on the left of the value stored in the number if it was less than 1,000. For example, if the value stored in the number was 3, the output would be 0003. Note: If the value stored in number has five or more digits, all would show; 4 is the *minimum* field width. This also works for strings, which sometimes makes columnar lineup less complex.
.n	A decimal after the modifier number indicates maximum width, or the number of digits to the right of the decimal place. In the case of floating-point numbers, the number to the right of the decimal point shows how many digits will be shown to the right of the decimal point. It is rather self-explanatory. In the case of integers, it seems to be ignored. Example: (`"%5.2s"`,string) prints two characters of the string; only two characters, the first two, will be printed, but the field will be five characters wide.

TABLE 13.6 Formatting Characters for `printf`

Format	Meaning
c	A **single** ASCII character.*
d	A decimal (base 10) number *with no decimal point.*
e	A floating-point number in scientific notation (1.00000e+01): lowercase e.
E	A floating-point number in scientific notation (1.00000E+01): uppercase E.
f	A floating-point number (2498.337).
g	The awk command chooses between %e and %f, picking the one that generates the shortest string. Nonsignificant zeros are not printed.
G	The awk command chooses between %E and %f, picking the one that generates the shortest string. Nonsignificant zeros are not printed.
i	A decimal number (just as %d . . . i stands for integer).
o	An unsigned octal number.
s	A string (terminated with a null character).
x	An unsigned hexadecimal number (letters in lowercase).
X	An unsigned hexadecimal number (letters in UPPERCASE).

*Note: If the argument used for c is numeric, it is treated as a character and printed; otherwise the argument is thought to be a string, and *only the first character of the string is printed.*

TABLE 13.7 Spacing Characters for `printf`

Escape Character	What It Produces
\n	Newline character (note: this is a protected n).
\t	Tab.

Now here are some example `printf` statements that demonstrate a few of the features in the preceding tables. (Note: These are all designed to run within the context of an awk, but the awk script is not shown.)

This `printf` statement,

```
printf("Dec = %d Oct = %o Hex = %x Char = %c \n", 20, 20, 20, 20)
```

produces

```
Dec = 20 Oct = 24 Hex = 14 Char =
```

Note: Char 20 is not a printable character.
On the other hand, this `printf` statement,

```
printf("Dec = %d Oct = %o Hex = %x Char = %c \n", 60, 60, 60, 60)
```

produces

```
Dec = 60 Oct = 74 Hex = 3c Char = <
```

while this,

```
printf("Dec = %d Oct = %o Hex = %X Char = %c \n", 60, 60, 60, 60)
```

produces

```
Dec = 60 Oct = 74 Hex = 3C Char = <
```

Note: Use uppercase for X rather than lowercase, and usually, uppercase is the preferred for hex.

To align the text, this printf statement,

```
printf ("*%10c*\t%-5d\t%5d\n", "hello",10,10)
```

produces

```
*           h*   10          10
```

Note: There is no minus in the printf statement, and the c format tells printf to print a single character; that is why just the h shows up. Also note in the result the asterisks are at both ends of the field to show alignment.

Our next statement,

```
printf ("*%-10c*\t%-5d\t%5d\n", "hello",10,10)
```

produces

```
*h           *   10          10
```

Note: The minus sign tells printf to **left**-justify the data in the field.
This statement,

```
printf ("*%-10s*\t%-5d\t%5d\n", "hello",10,10)
```

produces

```
*hello       *   10          10
```

Note: The s format tells printf to print the *string*.
Finally, this statement,

```
printf ("*%-10.3s*\t%-5d\t%5d\n", "hello",10,10)
```

produces

```
*hel        *    10          10
```

Note: The decimal portion indicates the actual string length printed.

getline

```
getline [variable string] [< input file]
or
command | getline [variable string]
```
(Supported by nawk, etc., not by awk.)

So much for output—let's look at the other side of the I/O coin. The usual tool for moving data into nawk is the normal process of reading from a data file. However, it is sometimes necessary to read data from a different file, from the keyboard, or even from a command. The **getline** tool can supply all of these functions. Normally getline takes its input from the expected data stream, standard input. It is a very interesting command in that it seems to queue an input request that will be filled as soon as data are available.

Figure 13.9 is an example of a short script that reads in some data. Running this script with no data file gives the result in Figure 13.10. When you run this script (yes, of course, you should type it in and run it!), notice that you must touch the ENTER key before

```
{
        printf("Please enter two values > ")
        getline
        printf("$1 = %s\t$2 = %s\n",$1,$2)
}
```

FIGURE 13.9

A nawk script showing use of getline.

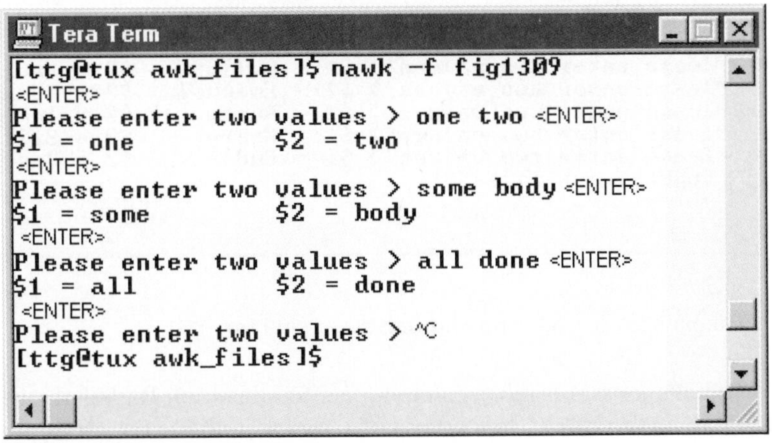

FIGURE 13.10

Sample execution of the nawk script in Figure 13.8 (Note: <ENTER> indicates a keystroke; it is *not* typed.)

the script starts working. That is because nawk reads a line from input (in this case the keyboard), then applies the pattern/action pair to those data. In this case, there is no pattern, so the action is applied to every line. Since the action involves a getline, the script then reads a line of input from the keyboard. After the user enters her input, she must enter another record or line to act as the stimulus, or trigger, for the next execution of the pattern, or the getline. The user needs to mark the end of the line or record by touching ENTER (which puts an EOL, end-of-line mark there). Then nawk will execute the action, prompting for input data.

The getline in this example has no variables associated with it, so it nawk proceeds like a normal nawk input, parsing the line based on the FS, loading the normal nawk variables $0, $1, $2, and so on. Next, the action calls for output of two of the variables, so they show up on standard out, and the script waits for the next line from input. When I touched the ENTER key, the action executed again. The procedure is not terribly efficient, but it does illustrate the simplest use for getline.

In most of the examples I have seen, either getline is used to gather additional information from the user or is used within the actions associated with the magic patterns of BEGIN or END. That way, the magic patterns act as the triggers for the action.

The process is even more interesting if we give the nawk a data file. In Figure 13.11, nawk is run into the good old folks data file. Very interesting! It seems as though our nawk is getting every other line. That makes sense in light of what we have already discovered. The nawk needs to read a line from the file to act as the stimulus for the action. Since the action has no associated pattern, it is performed on every line. In this case, however, it is performed on every *other* line because the getline is taking a line, then nawk takes one, and vice versa. You see, the nawk command and getline are playing nicely together, sharing the lines from the data file. Not exactly what we want them to do, but the action does illustrate how getline works.

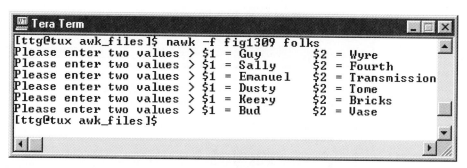

FIGURE 13.11

Output from an nawk script showing use of getline.

Let's look at a more common use for this tool. Rather than reading from the usual input file, getline is often used to pick up some data from the user before the target file is processed. In this case, getline is redirected to read from the keyboard. Figure 13.12 shows a more useful script, one that asks the user for a name, then uses that name to search the data file. Notice that the getline is coded in the BEGIN action,

```
BEGIN {
      printf ("Please enter the name I should search for: > ")
      getline name < "/dev/tty"
      }
$1 == name || $2 == name {
      printf("$1 = %s\t$2 = %s\n",$1,$2)
}
```

FIGURE 13.12

A more interesting awk script showing use of getline.

and that it is redirected to read from the keyboard /dev/tty. I know there are other ways to specify reading from the keyboard, but this solution seems to work on every flavor of Unix that I have had the good fortune to use.

In Figure 13.12, the getline takes input from the keyboard and stores the data in the variable name (such original naming conventions!). Then the nawk processes each record from the input file looking to match the pattern. Notice that this script works with either the first or the last name. If the script finds a match, it prints the first two fields from the line that matched. Not a very sophisticated script, but interesting nonetheless. Figure 13.13 shows a sample run of this script. Just to test, lets try using a last name. Figure 13.14 shows that the script works when it is supplied with either a first or last name, just as we expected.

Using getline with a command is much less common, and I leave it to your exploration.

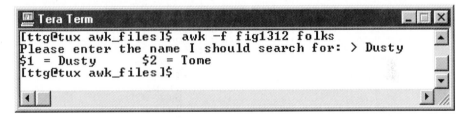

FIGURE 13.13

Sample run using a first name.

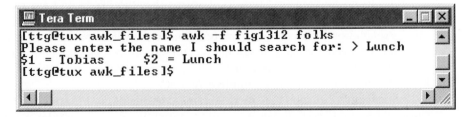

FIGURE 13.14

Sample run using a last name.

I would like to share one final, interesting observation about the getline command. In our earlier discussion of getline, we noted that getline seemed to queue up an input request. Notice how the script in Figure 13.15 works. Pay close attention to the prompt and getline in the BEGIN action. Remember that BEGIN actions are executed before the data file is opened. As you can see, the script looks fine. But Let's look at the output from this script in Figure 13.16, when we run it into the folks data file.

```
BEGIN {
        printf("Give me some data! > ")
        getline
        printf("\nThanks, you gave: %s\n\n",$0)
        }
{
        printf("More Data > ")
        getline
        printf("These are your data : %s\n",$0)
}
```

FIGURE 13.15

A puzzling awk script showing use of getline and BEGIN.

FIGURE 13.16

Output of the puzzling awk script in Figure 13.15.

Gadzooks! Look closely at the second line. It seems as if the BEGIN I/O events can read from the data file! Indeed, it seems that the BEGIN I/O events queue I/O events to happen, and once the data file is opened, those requests are satisfied. The other explanation is that the getline function actually goes out and opens the file it is to read from, even if it needs to get the filename from the command line. This is one of those fascinating areas of awk that beg for experimentation and exploration. Let me know if you come up with the definitive answer!

Some authors include the next statement as one of the I/O statements because it causes the script to go to the next line of the input file. We will consider it as part of the iteration process, because that is where it is most frequently used.

rand( )

```
rand ()
srand ()
```

The **rand()** and **srand()** functions are the only two mathematical functions in nawk that we will address. The rand() function generates a random number between 0 and 1. It isn't used all that often, but if you need to generate a set of random numbers, you will need this tool. The rand() function falls into the category of pseudo-random number generators. That means that rand() uses a mathematical formula to generate the values it supplies. Pseudo-random number generators need to have a seed to start the process. If you give the generator the same seed, it should always generate the same sequence of numbers, hence the appellation *pseudo*-random.

Figure 13.17 illustrates a little nawk script that will just keep generating random numbers as long as the user is willing to touch the ENTER key. I used nawk because my version of awk doesn't support the rand() function. (It will be lots more fun to play with this script once we learn how to do iteration, but this works fine for now.) Notice the arithmetic manipulation necessary to have the script return a value between 1 and 10.

```
BEGIN {
        printf("Here are some random numbers\n\n")
        printf("Touch Enter or ^D\n")
      }
{
        num = rand()
        printf("The generated number was: %f\n",num)
        goodnum = (num * 10 ) + 1
        printf("A useful number between 1 and 10 is: %d\n",goodnum)
        count = count + 1
        sum = sum + goodnum
        printf("Touch Enter or ^D\n")
}
END {
        mean = sum / count
        printf("The average of our random numbers was %d\n",mean)
    }
```

FIGURE 13.17

Script showing how to generate pseudo-random numbers.

In addition to generating and reporting all the pseudo-random numbers any user could ever want, this script also keeps track of the numbers and then calculates a rough average. We do need to multiply the number returned by rand() times 10 to give us a number between 0 and 9. To get the number in the range we want (1–10), we then need to add 1. Figure 13.18 shows a sample run of that script.

To get a better selection of pseudo-random numbers, you need to be able to specify a different seed each time you run the rand() function. The srand() function

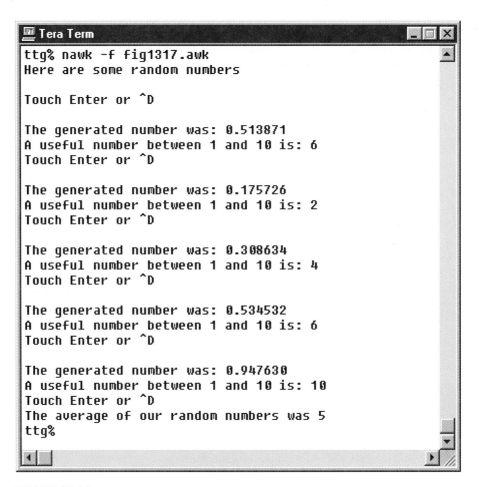

FIGURE 13.18

Sample run of the random-number generator in Figure 13.18.

allows you to pick a particular seed for the generator, or, if you code it without a value, the function uses the current time to seed the pseudo-random number generator. Generally the srand() function is coded as part of the BEGIN action.

A brief word about functions seems in order here. A *function* is a type of small program that returns a value. Actually, the call to the function is replaced by the value that the function generates or returns. There are a couple of rules about using functions that are important. First, you must always include the parentheses when you call a function, even if you don't have any values to pass to the function. Second, it is up to you, the user, to capture and save the value returned by the function. Generally those values are not stored unless the user makes provision to save them. That is why you will almost always see functions coded as an assignment statement: variable = function(). Of course, there are some exceptions; srand() is one of them.

system()

---

system (command)

(Supported by nawk, etc., not by awk.)

Sometimes it is handy to be able to call one of the regular system commands from within an nawk script. For this we use the **system()** function. The results of the execution of the command are *not* available to the script (use the command | getline structure if you need to capture the results of a command for later processing). One common use for this function is to clear the screen to make the output of the nawk appear on a blank screen.

Figure 13.19 shows a little script, very similar to one you have seen before, that prints out the lines in a file. The difference this time is that the script first clears the screen before it begins the output. The only difference between this script and the one in Figure 13.7 is the addition of the system() function in the BEGIN. Whereas the script shown in Figure 13.7 prints the lines from the input file wherever it happens to be on the screen, the script in Figure 13.19 first clears the screen, then presents the data from the top of the newly cleared screen. It is a little prettier output.

```
BEGIN {
     ─────▶ system("clear")
            print "Here come the lines from the input file:"
            print " "
            }
{ print $0 }
END {
            print " "
            print "There were "NR" lines in the file "FILENAME"."
    }
```

FIGURE 13.19

A script showing use of system() function.

Another way the system() function is commonly used is to check the results of some command. For example, let's say you want to perform a particular operation only if a particular file is in the directory you are working in. You could code the following system call within your script:

```
rstat = system("ls RedQueen")
```

If the file RedQueen is in the directory, the value of the rstat variable will be 0 (indicating True, or success.) If, on the other hand, RedQueen isn't in the directory, then rstat will have a value of 1 (indicating False, or failure.) It is easy to check the value of rstat and then proceed accordingly.

The system() function is very useful, although it's not one you will use every day. Note: The command must be enclosed in quotation marks; this is necessary syntax.

length()

---

length ([argument])

The **length()** function returns the length, in characters, of the argument passed to it. It is a simple function; all it does is count the number of characters in the argument. If the argument is a variable, then length() counts the number of characters stored at the location addressed by that variable. If you pass length() a number, it will return a count of the number of digits in the number. If you don't give length() an argument, it will use $0 as its default argument, so it is rather handy with or without arguments. This function illustrates, again, that the developers of the Unix tools tried to create default values that would make the tools as easy as possible to use.

Figure 13.20 contains a simple script to illustrate the use of the length() function. And Figure 13.21 shows us what happens when we run this script.

```
BEGIN {
string = "This is a string of 34 characters."
number=321
howlong = length(string)
howlong2 = length(number)
printf("String is %d characters long \n" \
" and num is %d long\n",howlong, howlong2)
}
```

FIGURE 13.20

Script showing the use of length() function.

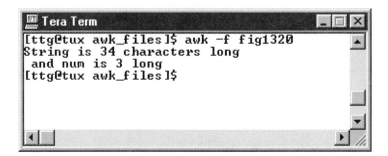

FIGURE 13.21

Output from the script in Figure 13.20.

index()

---

index (string, target)

The **index()** function returns the location, or byte position, of the first byte of the target string within the whole string. This is a tool for picking out specific parts of a record.

It can be used to set the beginning value for the substring function we shall examine next. Figure 13.22 contains a script showing how to use the index() function, and Figure 13.23 shows the output from an awk running this script against the folks data file.

You can look back and verify the locations of each of the first blanks and decimal points in each line. Notice that the index() function returns only the position of the *first* target in the string. You will need to be more creative if you wish to find the

```
BEGIN {
        printf("This script finds the decimal point in each line\n\n")
    }
{
        dpoint = index($0, ".")
        printf("The decimal point is located at position %d\n",dpoint)
        blankpoint = index($0, " ")
        printf("The first blank in the line is at %d\n",blankpoint)
}
```

FIGURE 13.22

A script showing the use of the index() function.

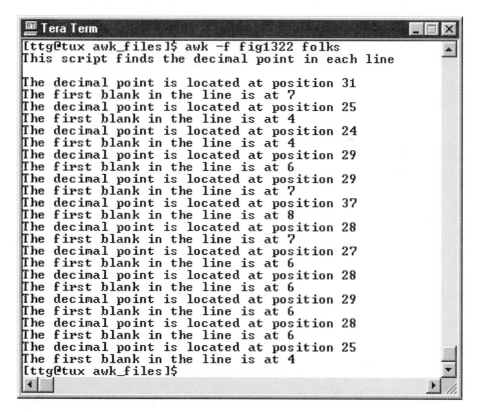

FIGURE 13.23

The output of a script using the index() function in Figure 13.23.

location of targets other than the first one. The function returns a value of 0 if the target is not located in the string.

Please note that in this instance, 0 is *not* the value we are seeking. In most cases, when a command returns a value of 0, it is an indication of success. However, in this case, the function is returning the actual position of the target, so if it returns 0, it means that the target is not within the string it searched.

substr()

```
substr(string, start [, length])
```

The substring function **substr()** enables you to pick out a part of the first argument passed to it (string); it returns to you just a portion of the string for processing. For example, suppose you want to be able to call your users by their first names. To do that, you need a report or list that shows each user I.D. and first name. You know their names are part of the user record in /etc/passwd. In fact, after careful research you find that the user names are in the fifth field. (Yes, if you haven't done so yet, you should learn the contents of the fields in /etc/passwd; it is a very handy thing to know.) To parse /etc/passwd you need to use a field separator of colon (:), but the name field uses a blank as a delimiter.

Figure 13.24 shows a sample of the /etc/passwd file for us to use in constructing an awk script to capture the first names. Figure 13.25 shows a little awk script to parse this file and create our report. In the BEGIN, I put out a standard heading and set the

```
tlunch:x:102:1000:Tobias Lunch:/home/tlunch:/bin/bash
dtomes:x:103:1000:Dusty Tomes:/home/dtomes:/bin/bash
rbanks:x:104:1000:Robyn Banks:/home/rbanks:/bin/bash
sbeach:x:105:1000:Sandi Beach:/home/sbeach:/bin/bash
nweigh:x:106:1000:Noah Weigh:/home/nweigh:/bin/bash
kpace:x:107:1000:Kara Pace:/home/kpace:/bin/bash
```

FIGURE 13.24

Snippet of /etc/passwd showing names.

```
BEGIN {
        print "Here are the user ID\'s and first names from /etc/passwd"
        FS=":"
        }
{
        blank = index($5, " ")
        first = substr($5, 1, blank)
        printf("User ID = %s first name = %s\n", $1, first)
}
```

FIGURE 13.25

An awk script to report user I.D. and first name using substr().

field separator to a colon, which is the field separator for /etc/passwd. In the body of the script I use the index() function to find the first blank in field $5, the user name, and store it in the variable blank. Then I parse out the first name by telling the substr() function to give me all the characters from the first byte to the location stored in blank. This is stored in the variable first. The rest is easy—all I have to do is print the user I.D. (first field, {$1}, of /etc/passwd) and the first name.

Figure 13.26 demonstrates a sample run of the script shown in Figure 13.25 run into the partial passwd file shown in Figure 13.24. This list gives me a great tool for talking to users on the telephone or sending them emails. In this example, I started at the beginning of the field and collected all the bytes up to the byte position that the index() function gave me. It is even more common to start with a point inside the field, and pick up the remainder of the field. To facilitate that procedure, the designers of the substr() function made that the default. If you specify just a starting point, substr() will pick up all the characters from that point to the end of the string passed to the function.

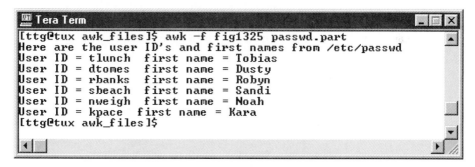

FIGURE 13.26

Running the script from Figure 13.25 against the file shown in Figure 13.24.

For example, if I want the last names of the users, all I would need to specify is

```
last = substr($5, blank+1)
```

This code would start at the first character of the last name and take the rest of the bytes in field 5. (Notice, I had to add 1 to the value stored in blank, because blank had the position of the white space, and I don't want the last name field to start with white space.)

split()

```
split (string, array [, separator])
```

The **split()** function is different from the substr() function in that it creates an array containing all the elements it parses out of the string. It is more suitable than substr() when you need to capture more than one part of the string. A brief word about arrays seems to be in order. An array is also called a **subscripted variable**. Subscripted variables are a way to store a set of related data in an easy-to-access method. From the shell's point of view, the difference between a set of unsubscripted variables and a subscripted variable is that the latter is stored in a contiguous block of memory. Unsubscripted variables can be stored anywhere in memory.

From our point of view, the difference between three unsubscripted variables—var1, var2, and var3—and three element subscripted variable—var[1], var[2], and var[3]—is the way they are coded. The other important difference will be more obvious when we learn iteration, as referencing data in arrays is very efficient if they are used with iteration. Actually, arrays and loops evolved together, and you will see how handy they can be when we code some loops later on.

Let's look at a situation in which I could use an array instead of a set of variables. Suppose I wanted to store the elements of the path to the user's home directory, with each element stored in a different variable. I could write the awk script shown in Figure 13.27. Remember, the sixth field in /etc/passwd is the path to the user's home directory. (Still haven't learned all those fields? It sure will help when you do.) This little awk script will report the path from root, /, to the user's home directory (provided there are no more than three steps), with an ellipsis between each step in the path.

```
BEGIN {
        FS=":"
    }
{
        first = index($6, "/")
        step1 = substr($6, 1, first)
        next1 = substr($6, first+1)
        second = index(next1, "/") - 1
        step2 = substr(next1, 1, second)
        next2 = substr(next1, second+1)
        step3 = substr(next2, 2)

        printf("Path to home directory = ")
        printf("%s...%s...%s\n",step1,step2, step3)
```

FIGURE 13.27

An awk script to report the path to the user's home directory.

Figure 13.28 shows an example of the output from the script in Figure 13.27. The script uses the two string-handling functions you just learned. Let's do a little analysis. The variable first picks up the byte address of the first / in the home directory path from the password file, $6. It so happens that the first slash is in the first position. The variable step1 holds the first step in the path, which is just the first slash. The variable next1 holds the remainder of the string, after the first slash in the path, first +1. The variable second holds the position of the first slash in the string next1. I must subtract 1 from this value to keep from picking up the actual slash in the next step.

The variable step2 holds the second element of the path, and the variable next2 holds the remainder of the path. In the last step, I parse out the actual directory

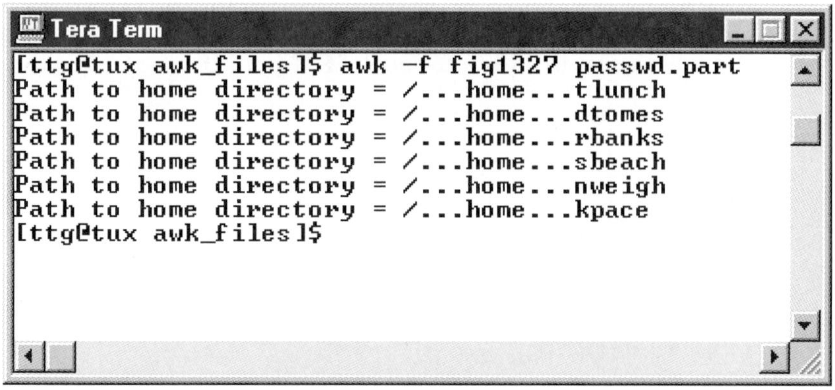

FIGURE 13.28

Output from the path awk script in Figure 13.28.

from the remaining path data and store it in step3. Finally, I print out the three-step variables.

Whew! That was a lot of work. There must be a better way. But before we look at that better way, let's think a minute about the variables I used to store the actual steps in the directory string. I used the variables step1, step2, and step3. I had to create each variable separately and then assign a value to it. I could have used a subscripted variable, but in this case subscripted variables would have been just as much work—in fact, more! If, place of step1, step2, and step3, I typed step[1], step[2], and step[3], I would be typing six more characters.

Remember that process as we look at a slightly more efficient way to find the path elements using the split() function. Figure 13.29 contains the equivalent script written using the split() function rather than substr(). Figure 13.30 shows the output from this script. Notice that it looks very similar to the output in Figure 13.28. The only difference is that the slashes are not shown, since the split command used the slash as a delimiter. That means that the first element of the path, the slash for root, isn't shown. That might pose a little problem, but I could simply code the slash into the printf format if I really wanted to see it.

```
BEGIN {
        FS = ":"
      }
{
        howmany = split($6, step, "/")
        printf("Path to home directory = ")
        printf("%s...%s...%s\n",step[1],step[2],step[3])
}
```

FIGURE 13.29

An awk script using split() instead of substr() to report the path to user's home directory.

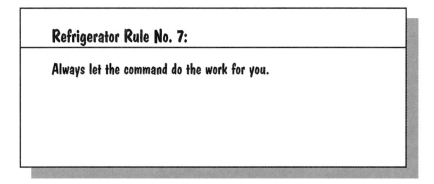

FIGURE 13.30

Output from awk running the script in Figure 13.29.

The script in Figure 13.28 is much shorter than the script in Figure 13.27, because in Figure 13.28 I am using a tool designed to do the job for me. This fact brings to mind another Refrigerator Rule:

Refrigerator Rule No. 7:

Always let the command do the work for you.

That is great advice, and you can see how much time and effort that little rule saved us in the previous example.

A final note on the split() function: If you don't code the separator, split will use whatever has been set as the field separator (FS). That field separator works in most cases, but it would not work in the preceding example, because FS was set to colon (:) and the data were separated by slashes.

if

```
if (condition)
     statement(s)
[else]
     [statement(s)]
```

Now that we have considered most of the sequential commands, let's try out the commands that regulate how the logic flows in an awk script. The first of these is **if**. The heart of the `if` command is the condition. This is an example of a *selection* programming construct. If the condition evaluates to True, then the statement or statements that follow the condition are executed, and any statement or statements following the `else` are ignored. If the condition evaluates to False, then the statement or statements that follow the `if` are ignored, and if an `else` has been coded, the statement or statements following the `else` are executed.

The `if` normally expects only one statement after the condition and only one statement after the `else`. If you need to have more than one statement, you must enclose each collection of statements in curly braces. Creating conditions should be old hat to you now; you created a bunch of them when we were exploring patterns!

Table 13.8 shows the relational operators that `if` understands. They look a lot like the relational expressions you learned when creating patterns, don't they? Now let's see how some simple `if`s work. Suppose you wanted to calculate the pay for the employees of the Grate Names, Inc. company. Remember that the `folks` data file contains each employee's wage rate and the hours worked. Figure 13.31 presents an awk script that does simple payroll calculations, including for overtime.

TABLE 13.8 Conditional Expressions Used with `if`

Operator	Means
A < B	A is less than B
A <= B	A is less than or equal to B
A == B	A is equal to B
A > B	A is greater than B
A >= B	A is greater than or equal to B
A != B	A is not equal to B
A ~ /re/	A contains the regular expression re

This is a very simple payroll script in Figure 13.31. It doesn't take into account social security taxes, income taxes, or the like, but it does illustrate a nice `if`/`else` structure. If the individual put in more than 40 hours, an overtime rate is calculated. If he didn't, the `else` code is executed, and he gets no overtime pay. (Notice the use of the French braces to enclose the commands after the `if` and `else`.)

Figure 13.32 shows the output from the script in the Figure 13.31. Okay, so it isn't the most wonderful report you have ever seen, but it does the job, and the output would work to write paychecks. Notice the formatting on the currency fields. The `%.2f` forces two places to the right of the decimal.

A good design feature is displayed in this code as well. Neophyte awk scriptors have a tendency to do everything in each **if block**, meaning the code between the condition and the `else`. The code that follows the `else` is called the **else block**. For example, in this script your inclination might be to calculate the total pay in the overtime code section, and calculate it in the no-overtime section as well. It is more efficient to calculate it in one place. In addition, variables should be reset to the correct values to

```
BEGIN {
        print "Payroll for Great Names corp."
        }
{
        if ($5 > 40)
                { pbase = 40 * $4
                othours = $5 - 40
                otpay = othours * ($4 * 1.5)
                }
        else
                {
                othours = 0
                otpay = 0
                pbase = $5 * $4
                }
pay = pbase + otpay
printf("%12s: Hrs: %d ot %d\n ",$2, $5,othours)
printf("\t Base: $%.2f OT pay: $%.2f Total: $%.2f\n",
        pbase, otpay, pay)
}
```

FIGURE 13.31

A simple payroll script.

```
awk -f fig1331 folks
Payroll for Great Names corp.
     Attired: Hrs: 44  Ot 4
         Base: $416.00 OT pay: $62.40  Total: $478.40
        Wyre: Hrs: 40  Ot 0
         Base: $470.00 OT pay: $0.00  Total: $470.00
        Tyde: Hrs: 35  Ot 0
         Base: $280.00 OT pay: $0.00  Total: $280.00
      Fourth: Hrs: 44  Ot 4
         Base: $560.00 OT pay: $84.00  Total: $644.00
       Lunch: Hrs: 40  Ot 0
         Base: $500.00 OT pay: $0.00  Total: $500.00
Transmission: Hrs: 40  Ot 0
         Base: $600.00 OT pay: $0.00  Total: $600.00
        Sick: Hrs: 45  Ot 5
         Base: $400.00 OT pay: $75.00  Total: $475.00
        Tome: Hrs: 40  Ot 0
         Base: $620.00 OT pay: $0.00  Total: $620.00
       Awysh: Hrs: 41  Ot 1
         Base: $416.00 OT pay: $15.60  Total: $431.60
      Bricks: Hrs: 38  Ot 0
         Base: $465.50 OT pay: $0.00  Total: $465.50
       Hawks: Hrs: 40  Ot 0
         Base: $540.00 OT pay: $0.00  Total: $540.00
        Vase: Hrs: 45  Ot 5
         Base: $600.00 OT pay: $112.50  Total: $712.50
[ttg@tux awk_files]$
```

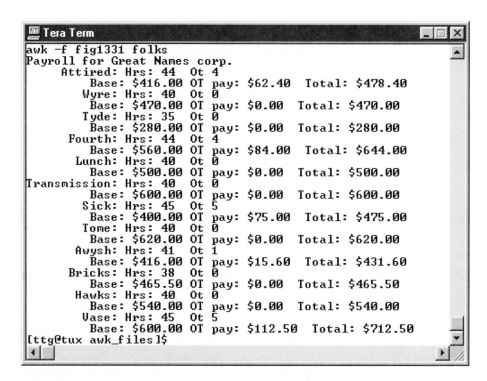

FIGURE 13.32

Output from the simple payroll script in Figure 13.31.

minimize mistakes, so in the no-overtime section, the otpay and othours are set to 0. While this code is not elegant, it does the job in a reasonably efficient manner. Heck, it's a good script—not a great script, but a good script!

Author's note: In reviewing this chapter I realized the script could be just a bit more efficient by leaving out the line that calculates pay altogether. It could simply add otpay and pbase right in the printf statement, like this:

```
printf("\t Base: $%.2f  OT pay: $%.2f   Total: $%.2f\n",pbase,
otpay, pbase + otpay)
```

Just goes to prove that you can most likely ***always*** improve your code or at least I can always improve my code.

Good programmers usually try to protect their users from making silly errors. One such error is to forget to code a target file on the command line, or to forget to pass data into the awk from the command line. In either case, you can use a couple of [ng]awk variables to check on your user. These two variables are available only in the newer forms of awk, nawk and gawk.

What if we need to see whether the user entered anything on the command line. Suppose you are building a data-mining script that your boss can run to collect and print the names of all the users in a particular department. Figure 13.33 shows the BEGIN part of such a script. I will leave the actual data retrieval for your later exploration.

```
BEGIN {
        if (ARGC > 1)
                {printf("ARGC = %d\n",ARGC)
                printf("ARGV[0] = %s\n",ARGV[0])
                printf("ARGV[1] = %s\n",ARGV[1])
                dept = ARGV[1]
                delete ARGV[1]
                }
        else
                { print "Sorry, you must tell me which dept. code to use."
                  print "Usage is: \n\t nawk -f fig1333 dept-code datafile"
                }

}
```

FIGURE 13.33

A BEGIN that looks for data from the command line.

Notice that there are no pattern/action pairs in the script in Figure 13.33 after the BEGIN magic pattern. That's because all I am interested in showing you is the way to get data from the command line. The rest of the script should be simple for you to code after you finish reading this chapter. What I am asking is whether there is a command-line variable or not. The way I determine that is by looking at the value of ARGC, which contains a count of the command-line arguments. If ARGC is greater than 1, then I assume that the second command-line argument, ARGV[1], contains the department code, and I display the contents of that variable. (In awk arrays start counting with element 0.) Notice that I deleted the contents of ARGV[1] after I stored it. That way, when the awk action runs, it won't try to open the "file" of the department code.

I have run this script a couple of times in Figure 13.34. The output shows you how you can use the ARGC and ARGV pair to collect data from the command line. But wait a minute! What's wrong with that first run? It shows me the error message, but I gave the script the data element of sales on the command line. Isn't that strange? No, not if you remember that awk doesn't recognize ARGC or ARGV. That is the only drawback to using them—they are not supported by awk, only by the newer brothers, nawk and gawk.

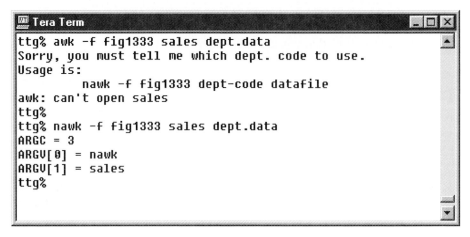

```
ttg% awk -f fig1333 sales dept.data
Sorry, you must tell me which dept. code to use.
Usage is:
          nawk -f fig1333 dept-code datafile
awk: can't open sales
ttg%
ttg% nawk -f fig1333 sales dept.data
ARGC = 3
ARGV[0] = nawk
ARGV[1] = sales
ttg%
```

FIGURE 13.34

Running the script from Figure 13.33, which collects data from the command line.

Another interesting thing you should notice in Figure 13.34 is the value ARGV[0]. It contains the value for the command. That is a significant bit of knowledge, indicating that you need to check to see if there is more than one command-line argument in order to see if the user passed you data!

The if conditional enables you to control the flow of the logic in your scripts, and you will use it often. The only thing that seems to cause students some problems with if is remembering to put groups of statements, following the conditional and else, within curly braces.

exit

_____

exit

One of the simplest flow of control commands is **exit**. When awk encounters the exit command, the target file is closed and control is sent directly to the END action, if one exists. If there is no END magic pattern, then the script simply exits. No new input is read; no other statements in the body of the awk script are read. Well-structured programming dictates only *one exit* from any routine. This command transfers control to the END action, so good structure is preserved. Generally, the exit command is used as a bailout when the script encounters an expected error that prevents further processing.

for

```
for (x = start; x <= maximum; x++) command(s)
or
for (element in array) command(s)
```

At long last, we have arrived at the third programming construct, iteration. Loops are a great time saver for programmers. They let us code one set of instructions that can be executed over and over and over and over—well, you get the idea. Looping is also called *iteration*, which is doing the same thing over and over—ah, yes. One of my favorite old dictionaries of computer terms has the following two definitions:

> **Iteration**: see loop.
> **Loop**: see iteration.

After you follow those instructions 10 or so times, you get the idea!

The **for** loop is used when you know how many times you want a loop to execute. The for loop is also called a **counted loop** because you set a counter to control the number of times it executes. The syntax of this loop allows the programmer to decide how many times it will execute, setting a starting value, ending value, and an increment (or decrement) value.

That's right, the loop can count either up or down. The default is to execute just one command; if you want to run multiple commands, those commands must be enclosed in curly braces, just as with the if.

Let's look at a simple awk script that has a loop in it. The script in Figure 13.35 will simply do a counting exercise to show how the for loop works. Looking at the code, you decide what the output will be. Obviously this script doesn't process any input, so I will run it without any input file and will just touch ENTER on the command line to cause the action to execute. Okay, write down what you expect to see as output from the loop. Got it? Great! Now look at Figure 13.36 and see if you were right.

```
{
        for (x = 1; x < 10; x++)
        printf("x = %d\n",x)
        prinf("\n That's all she wrote, folks\n")
}
```

FIGURE 13.35

A simple for loop.

Did you correctly predict the output? The loop ran nine times, and the value for x was printed out each time. (Yes, only nine times, because the ending condition was x < 10. If it had been coded x <= 10, then how often would the loop have run? That's right, 10 times. Remember when we talked about conditions, and I told you to account for all three conditions. This is another example of that idea/problem.)

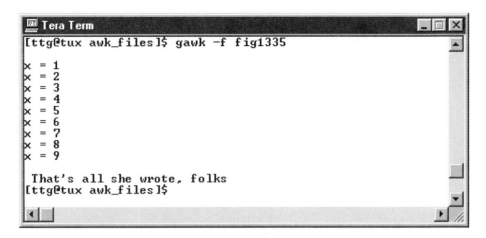

FIGURE 13.36

Output from the code counting for loop in Figure 13.35.

The That's all line showed up just once because the for structure expects a single command and iterated just the first command it found, printf. Had I wanted to have both lines iterated, I would have had to enclose them in curly braces.

Figure 13.37 demonstrates another version of the for loop, this time counting down from 10. Notice how the loop starts at 10 and counts down (x--) as long as the value of the counter is greater than 1.

The loop in Figure 13.39 is a little more substantial. Figure 13.38 shows a data file, folks2, that lists the employee name (first and last), social security number, hourly wage, and the number of hours worked this month, recorded by week, comma-delimited. Now let's build a script that will calculate how many hours each employee worked for the entire month. Gee, aren't these exciting examples!

```
{
        for (x = 10; x > 1; x--)
        printf("x = %d\n",x)
        prinf("\n That's all she wrote, folks\n")
}
```

FIGURE 13.37

Another simple for loop, showing a counter decrement.

```
Moly Bolt 419328776 12.00 40,41,39,40
Allen Rench 503569822 12.50 40,35,44,43
Lynn Gweenie 404345671 14.00 40,40,40,40
Vanna Tee 201445230 16.50 44,43,40,42
Ben Thare 887453294 12.00 40,41,41,40
Don Thatt 209115667 12.00 35,34,32
```

FIGURE 13.38

The folks2 data file.

Figure 13.39 contains a script that would sum up the three or four values in the hours-worked field. Notice how the `split` function both fills the array `hours` with the data and gives us the maximum value for the `for` loop. Figure 13.40 shows the output of this script.

```
BEGIN {
        printf("\nTotal hours worked this month:\n")
      }
{
        count = split($5,hours,",")
#               Collect the hours worked into an array
        total = 0
        for (x=1; x<=count; x++)
        total = total + hours[x]
        printf("%s %s worked %d hours this month.\n",$1,$2,total)
}
```

FIGURE 13.39

Script using the `for` loop to process data stored in an array.

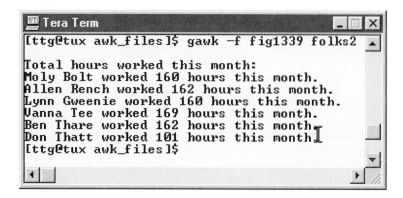

FIGURE 13.40

Output of the hours-worked `for` loop in Figure 13.39.

The loop shown in Figure 13.39 works just fine, but the code in Figure 13.39 doesn't make use of a special feature designed into awk. Because array processing is so closely connected with loops, there is a second form of the `for` loop designed to deal specifically with arrays. It has this form:

```
for (element in array)
    command(s)
```

In this code `element` is the value to be used in the loop counter, and `array` is the subscripted variable to be processed. Figure 13.41 demonstrates the hours calculator script rewritten using the second format. In this version of the `for` loop, the variable x acts like the loop counter. The difference is that I don't need to worry about starting and

```
BEGIN {
        printf("\nTotal hours worked this month:\n")
      }
{
        split($5,hours,",")
#               Collect the hours worked into an array
        total = 0
        for (x in hours) ←————
        total = total + hours[x]
        printf("%s %s worked %d hours this month.\n",$1,$2,total)
}
```

FIGURE 13.41

Script using the alternate form of the for loop to process data.

ending values, because the counter (x) starts at 1 each time, and it increments until it reaches the maximum number of elements in the array. Since I don't have to keep track of it, I don't even need to bother with storing it. That makes the split line shorter, and saves a little memory.

This is a very clean way to process data stored in a subscripted variable. Notice that the line that sums the hours is the same in either version of the loop. (Gadzooks, I would HOPE SO!) Using the optimized form of the for statement is another example of letting the command do the work.

If you know how many times you want some commands executed, use the for loop. However, in many cases you will want the code to iterate as long as some particular set of circumstances is true. In that case, the while loop is a better choice.

while

```
while (condition)
  command(s)
```

A **while** loop is one of a pair of conditional loops. A **conditional loop** is called that because, well, it is regulated by a condition. The while is usually considered the conditional loop of choice. It is the most structured of the loops, and it allows for the most flexibility. As we saw with the if and the for, if you want the while to execute more than one command, the collection of commands must be enclosed in curly braces. The condition specified can be any that are recognized by the if; you can return to that discussion to review the different conditional statements.

Figure 13.42 shows a handy little while that prompts the user for a name and won't let him continue until he provides one. If you were to use this code in production, you would probably want to add a command that would exit from the procedure if the user failed to supply a name after three times. The script in Figure 13.42 is a slight modification of the one we saw in Figure 13.12.

Running this script into the folks file gives us the output shown in Figure 13.43. The first two times he was prompted, the user just touched the ENTER key, and the script dutifully prompted him again for a name. This script will not leave the BEGIN

```
BEGIN {
        while (name == "")  <———
        {
        printf ("Give me a name please > ")
        getline name < "/dev/tty"
        }   #  End of the while loop
    }     #  End of the BEGIN action
$1 == name || $2 == name{
        printf("Here are the data you requested:\n\n")
        printf("\t%s\n\n",$0)
}
```

FIGURE 13.42

A very persistent while script.

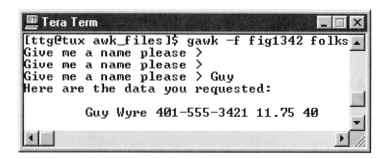

FIGURE 13.43

Running the persistent while script.

action until the user enters some string. Once the user enters a string, the BEGIN completes, and the body of the script executes. Although this is a fine example of the while loop, it is not a good production model, because it traps the user in the BEGIN action.

The while loop is the general-purpose loop for most occasions. There are times when you know exactly how many times you want the loop to cycle, and then you can use the for loop. The other time that the for loop is preferred is when you are using elements of an array. But for other situations you will probably use the while loop.

do/while

```
do
command(s)
while (condition)
```

The DO/WHILE looping structure (**do** and **while**) is just a little confusing, because it claims to be a WHILE loop, (notice the while hanging out down there), but in execution, it is an UNTIL construct. The difference is very important in some cases. An UNTIL loop always executes one time, and then the condition is evaluated to see if it should execute again. That is the classic definition of an UNTIL structure. Use this loop only when you can be absolutely certain that the loop will always, without question, need to be executed one time. If you detect a little cautionary note here, you are correct. The UNTIL construct has fallen out of favor with programmers because it is considered less structured. It is included here for completeness rather than as an encouragement for its use.

Use the do structure only if you are required to do so by forces beyond your control. Unlike the other loops, the do provides a beginning bound on the command or commands, and the while statement provides an ending bound, so the commands between do not need to be enclosed in curly braces.

break

---

break

The **break** command is used to exit from a while or for loop. When awk encounters the break command it passes control *to the statement following the last statement of the loop.* No variables are reset. This command is usually used to exit a loop when an error is detected. It is not a necessary part of either of the loops. Use it with care.

Figure 13.44 shows a script using the break command. This script is an expansion of the one in Figure 13.41. Here I have put back the count variable, and I use it to ensure that I have four data elements in the array. If some employee didn't have all four weekly totals, the script will not calculate that person's monthly total. To avoid having the script sum the values there, your faithful programmer has included a break command in the if statement at the beginning of the loop. If the value of the count variable is not equal to 4, then the script will print an error message and break out of the loop. If this happens, the value stored at the location pointed to by the variable total stays at 0, and the employee record is not printed. Figure 13.45 shows the output from this script.

```
BEGIN {
        printf("\nTotal hours worked this month:\n\n")
      }
{
        count = split($5,hours,",")
#               Collect the hours worked into an array
        total = 0
        for (x in hours) {
        if (count != 4)
                {
                printf("\tBad data. Only %d values for %s\n",count,$2)
                break
                }        # End of if block
        total = total + hours[x]
                }        # End of for loop
        if (total > 0)
                printf("%s %s worked %d hours this month.\n",$1,$2,total)
}
```

FIGURE 13.44

Code that includes a break command.

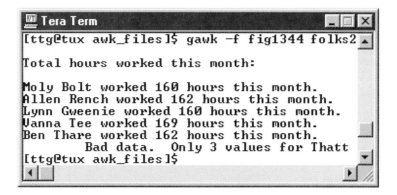

FIGURE 13.45

Output from the script in Figure 13.44.

continue

---

continue

The **continue** statement causes awk to skip the rest of the body of a for or while loop and transfer control to the condition, either the counter of the for or the condition associated with the while. This means that it continues the loop with the next iteration. This command is useful when processing variable-length records, some of which may only contain partial data. Unlike the break command, which ends execution of the loop, the continue simply ends processing of the current line or record.

Figure 13.46 shows a small script using the continue command. This script was written in response to the concern expressed by the owner of Grate Names, Inc. about

```
BEGIN {
        printf("\nTotal hours worked this month:\n\n")
      }
{
      count = split($5,hours,",")
#              Collect the hours worked into an array
      total = 0
      for (x in hours) {
      if (hours[x] >= 45)
           ———►   continue
      else
      total = total + hours[x]
                      }       # End of for loop
      if (total > 0)
              printf("%s %s worked %d hours this month.\n",$1,$2,total)
}
```

FIGURE 13.46

Script showing how to use the continue command.

the amount of overtime his people were working. He decided that if any employee sub-mitted more than 44 hours per week, it must be a data input error, and he wants the payroll program to skip that entry. Figure 13.47 shows the contents of the folks3 data file, and Figure 13.48 shows how the output of the script in Figure 13.46 when the folks3 data file is used as input.

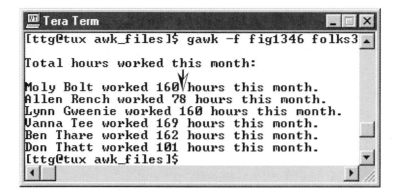

```
Moly Bolt 419328776 12.00 40,41,39,40
Allen Rench 503569822 12.50 46,35,47,43  ⟵
Lynn Gweenie 404345671 14.00 40,40,40,40
Vanna Tee 201445230 16.50 44,43,40,42
Ben Thare 887453294 12.00 40,41,41,40
Don Thatt 209115667 12.00 35,34,32
```

FIGURE 13.47

The folks3 data file.

```
🖳 Tera Term                                    _ □ ✕
[ttg@tux awk_files]$ gawk -f fig1346 folks3 ▲

Total hours worked this month:

Moly Bolt worked 160 hours this month.
Allen Rench worked 78 hours this month.
Lynn Gweenie worked 160 hours this month.
Vanna Tee worked 169 hours this month.
Ben Thare worked 162 hours this month.
Don Thatt worked 101 hours this month.
[ttg@tux awk_files]$                         ▼
◀                                          ▶
```

FIGURE 13.48

Output of the script in Figure 13.46 when used with the folks3 data file.

Notice Allen's record. He has worked, or so he says, 46 hours and 47 hours in two different weeks. Look at the output in Figure 13.48. If you add up his hours worked, you will see that only the 43-hour week and the 35-hour week were counted. Allen is probably pretty unhappy with his paycheck for this month!

next

next

As promised earlier, now that we have loops, it is time to discuss the **next** command, which causes the script to start over. It gets the next line from the input stream (the input file, or standard in) and sends control to the first pattern/action pair (after the BEGIN, if there happens to be one). Figure 13.49 presents a short script that uses the next command. It was written simply to illustrate next, so it probably makes little

```
BEGIN {
      printf("A script to illustrate the next command\n")
      }
{
      printf("Please give me a number > ")
      getline value < "/dev/tty"
      if (value > 11)
            next   ←
      printf("The number you entered was: %d\n",value)
      total = total + value
      printf("The  total of your numbers is: %d\n",total)
}
```

FIGURE 13.49

Script showing the next command.

sense outside the scope of the book. Reading the code, you can see that it will print a heading line, then ask the user to enter a number from the keyboard, requiring that the user touch the ENTER key to prompt the script to execute the action. The script then takes some number from input. If the value entered is greater than 11, the next command starts the action over, and the user must again touch ENTER to trigger the next action. If the number entered is less than 12 (not greater than 11), the script reports the number, adds it to a running total, and reports that total.

Figure 13.50 shows a sample run of the script in Figure 13.49. The <ENTER> notations in the figure were added to show where the user had to touch the ENTER key. Notice that when the user entered a number greater than 11 (in this case, 12), the script just ignored it and went back to a blank line waiting for the ENTER key again. The Next is useful occasionally, you'll be glad to know about it when you need it.

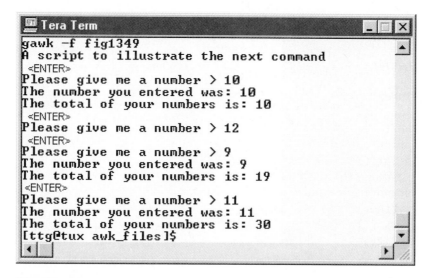

FIGURE 13.50

Sample run of the script in Figure 13.49.

⊕ A Very Handy Little vi Trick

One last thing before you leap into the wild, wacky, wonderful of awk scripting: there is a wonderful trick/feature of the vi editor that will help you debug your awk scripts. I didn't share it with you in Chapter 7 because you had no need for it then. Now, however, you can truly appreciate it.

Open an awk script, place your cursor on one of the French braces, and touch the percent key (%). Notice where the cursor automagically jumps! Yes, to the *corresponding* brace! This feature will help you discover where you have left out a necessary brace. It is a wonderful little trick that can save you *hours* of frustration debugging a long awk script. And, by the way, that same little feature works with parentheses and square brackets as well. Enjoy!

Now that you are an awk expert, here are some exercises, so you can practice what you have learned.

KEY TERMS

conditional loop
counted loop
else block
if block
subscripted variable

NEW COMMANDS/FUNCTIONS

```
break
continue
do/while
exit
for
getline
if
index()
length()
next
print
printf()
rand()
srand()
system()
substr()
split()
while
```

REVIEW QUESTIONS

13.1 List the names of the three awk brothers in chronological order.

13.2 What two other commands formed the logical basis for awk?

13.3 An awk program is composed of _____ pairs.

13.4 What is the difference between the -f command-line argument and the -F argument?

13.5 List two reasons why is it better to use a file for an awk script than to code it on the command line?

13.6 List at least five awk variables. Only two can contain numbers!

13.7 Which awk variable tells you the number of command-line variables?

13.8 List all three parts of Refrigerator Rule No. 6.

13.9 Since we are talking about Refrigerator Rules, what is No. 7?

13.10 Fill in the accompanying table of relational expressions:

Expression	Meaning
	Equal to
	Not equal to
	Less than
	Greater than
	Less than or equal to
	Greater than or equal to
	Contains the regular expression

13.11 Explain when you must and when you must not use slashes to enclose your pattern.

13.12 List the two magic patterns supported by awk, and explain when the action associated with each is performed.

13.13 Which is the most important awk action?

13.14 What does the f in printf stand for?

13.15 List and describe the two operators that allow you to build complex conditional expressions.

13.16 Explain what the following printf will produce if the data are read from /etc/passwd:

```
Printf("%-10s %d %d $10s",$7, $4, $3, $5)
```

13.17 List the printf formatting commands to produce the following types of data. If there is more than one way, list all of them:

    a. Strings
    b. Integers
    c. Floating-point numbers
    d. Uppercase hexadecimal numbers

13.18 What command is used to read from the keyboard?

13.19 Describe the purpose and use of each of the following functions:

```
rand()
srand()
system()
length()
index()
split()
substr()
```

13.20 Explain the difference between a counted loop and a conditional loop.

13.21 Why don't conscientious programmers use the DO/WHILE structure in awk?

13.22 If you want to code four verbs to be executed when a particular condition is True, what required syntax must you use?

13.23 Is it possible to have three exit commands in one awk script and not violate the rule of structured programming that requires a single exit? Why or why not?

13.24 Explain the difference in the way the break and continue commands affect the execution of a loop.

13.25 What does the next command do in an awk script?

EXERCISES

In all of the exercises, I expect you will create efficient, elegant awk scripts that will produce clean, neat, usable output. Remember Refrigerator Rule No. 7: "Let the commands do the work."

13.1 Build an awk script to print the words "Hello World" on the terminal screen. (This is the requsite first program <grin>. ☺)

13.2 Craft an awk script that reads /etc/passwd and lists the login I.D. for each user in the file. Also report whether that user is a privildeged user or not. (Consider any users with I.D.s of less than 10 to be privileged.) The output should look like this:

```
root      privileged
deamon    privileged
ttg       not privileged
etc.
```

13.3 Create an awk script that will list only the login I.D. and user name for each member of your class. (If you are working on your own machine, list *all* the users in /etc/passwd except root and nobody.)

13.4 Modify a copy of your script from the previous exercise (remembering Refrigerator Rule No. 2), to produce a list of all the members of your class, showing the following data:

Login ID   Name in Real Life   Home Directory   Login Shell

13.5 Now enhance the output from the previous exercise so that you don't show the path to the login shell, just the name of the shell itself. For example, if the login shell is /bin/csh, you would show just csh.

13.6 Alter the script you created in the previous exercise to use the opposite form of selection. If you used an if within an action to select the records from the target file, now use a pattern. If you used a pattern before, now use an if. Also have your report tell the reader how many users it found.

13.7 Build an awk script that will prompt you for a login I.D. and list the name in real life, the group, and the home directory for that user from /etc/passwd.

13.8 Modify a copy of the script for the previous exercise so that it will take the input data (login I.D.) from the command line. If the data are not on the command line, then prompt the user for the data.

13.9 Create an awk script that will generate 10 random numbers between 1 and 100, show you each number, the sum of the numbers, and the average of the numbers. Allow the user to provide the seed.

13.10 Build an awk script that will tell you the length of the first and last names of each member of your class.

13.11 Construct an awk script that will report the location of each colon in your entry from /etc/passwd. Now do it for root.

13.12 Modify your random number generation script so that it will continue to sum up the random numbers generated until either the total of random numbers exceeds 10,000 or a 1 or a 100 is generated. Have the script report which ending condition caused the script to stop.

13.13 Create two small awk scripts that use the same data file and that demonstrate the difference in processing between break and continue.

Shell Scripts

CHAPTER OBJECTIVES
After reading this chapter, you should be able to:

- Explain the logic of building shell scripts.
- Understand the reason for building Bourne shell scripts.
- Apply standards to shell scripts.
- Use shell variables to store and process data.
- Craft Bourne shell scripts to perform standard data processing activities.
- Employ the test process to evaluate different types of data.
- Create scripts that employ the three standard programming structures: sequence, selection, and iteration.
- Build well-documented, readable, efficient shell scripts.

You've already built scripts for both sed and awk, so now you're ready to put everything you've learned together, creating the epitome of Unix mastery, the shell script. You may not have realized it, but all this time you spent learning Unix, you really wanted to be a shell scriptor. I'm sure you remember Refrigerator Rule No. 5: "If you do it more than once, write a script." Now you can capture complex sets of actions in scripts. Mastering shell scripting will undoubtedly take you many years, but you can begin today!

⊕ The Concept of Scripts

A shell script is nothing more than a collection of shell commands. One of the rules of Unix is, "If you can do it on the command line, you can do it in a script." The only problem this rule causes us is when we are working on one shell's command line while running scripts in a different shell. For example, by now you're comfortable using the C shell in Solaris or the bash shell in Linux. If you write Bourne shell scripts while you're working in the C shell, you can't test what you wrote in the script at the command line. (Things that work in the C shell don't necessarily work in the Bourne shell, and vice versa.)

I urge you to use this model: write and run your scripts from the C or bash shells where you have the tools that you're used to, like history and filename completion. But always write your scripts to *run* in the Bourne shell.

⊕ Examination of Shells for Scripting

You can write shell scripts to run in any shell. Choosing which shell to use to write your scripts can take on the nuances of a "holy war." There are a number of these holy wars in Unix, and we've danced around most of them. For example, you'll find people, like those at IBM, who swear by the Korn shell, and you'll find people who swear *at* the Korn shell. Although it's possible to write wonderful Korn shell scripts or C shell scripts or tcsh shell scripts, the standard shell for scripting has always been the Bourne shell. And there are three really good reasons for that:

1. The Bourne shell is the standard shell for system administration. System administrators use the Bourne shell at the command line and write scripts in the Bourne shell. It is the standard shell for administration.

2. All flavors of Unix have a Bourne shell or Bourne-shell equivalent. Your system may not have a Korn shell, or a tcsh shell, or a zcsh shell, but I promise you it has a Bourne shell or Bourne-shell equivalent. If you build all of your scripts to run in the Bourne shell, they will always be usable. If you use another shell as your scripting language, your scripts may not work on a system without that particular shell.

3. The Bourne shell was the first shell. Running scripts in this shell keeps us in touch with our roots, and keeps us in touch with the historical aspects of Unix.

Now for one other reason to use the Bourne shell: because I want you to. From years and years of teaching experience I know that this scripting language is the best both for learning to script and for building production code. (Besides, it's my book and I can write about any shell I want. <grin>)

⊕ Command-Line Execution vs. Execution in a Script

I know you've heard this before—in fact it was Refrigerator Rule No. 5—but I feel compelled to again address the importance of crafting scripts to perform your day-to-day tasks. Smart Unix users write scripts. It's as simple as that. If you've done something more than once you really need to encode the process in a script. The time you spend writing scripts is paid back many times over by the convenience of having ready-made tools.

Scripts Are Tools

This is an extremely important concept: *scripts are tools*. If you build tools as you encounter situations, you will have those tools for next time you need them. You've heard the "E" words before, and now you'll hear them again: you need to build scripts that are Efficient, Elegant, and Exact. Those are the three measures of a good script, and you should spend at least as much time polishing your scripts as you do initially writing them. The measure of a Unix professional is often taken by the quality of his or her scripts.

As important as scripting is, don't fall into the trap of building scripts for *everything*. Remember that scripts are tools, and like tools you wouldn't spend a lot of time constructing one for a single use. Similarly, for simple, one-time operations you should use the tools available to you from the operating system. It's only when you find yourself doing that "something" a second time that you need to consider building a script, since a second time presages the likelihood of a third—and maybe tenth or more—time.

Forcing Execution in a Specific Shell

We've established the fact that the Bourne shell is the best shell for scripting. So how do we ensure that a script will always run in the Bourne shell? On many systems, unless you specify otherwise, the Bourne shell is the default shell for scripts. This is as it should be. However, you should *never trust defaults*. It's far better to force your scripts to run in a particular shell. To do that you need the use the **shebang**, a two-character construct, #!, that must appear as the first two characters on the first line of a script. The process you want to invoke is coded immediately following the shebang. Thus, if you want to run your scripts in the Bourne shell, the first line of each script should be

```
#!/bin/sh
```

Notice that there are no intervening spaces in this line. That's because space is the delimiter for the shell. If you put spaces in the line, the shell will parse the line on those spaces.

By the way, in *The Jargon Dictionary*, also called the *New Hackers Dictionary*, the term *shebang* has the following definition:

> **shebang** (/sh*-bang/ n). The character sequence "#!" that frequently begins executable shell scripts under Unix. Probably derived from "shell bang" under the influence of American slang "the whole shebang" (everything, the works).

If you're not familiar with *The Jargon Dictionary*, you need to become so. It's a very important resource for all Unix folks. I will warn you, however, that you well might lose hours of time perusing it. One of the places it's located, at least at the time of the writing this book, is

```
www.tuxedo.org/~esr/jargon/
```

I can't promise you it will still be there when you read this, but you can search the Web for "The Jargon Dictionary" and find other mirrors of it. Poke about in it, and enjoy!

If later in your career you decide to write scripts running other shells, you can use the shebang mechanism to force execution of those shells as well. The shebang causes the shell to fork the process specified in the shebang line, then uses the rest of the script file as input to that process. (Yes, you're absolutely right, that means you can use the shebang format to run processes *other than shells*, and pass input to them.) By the way, the octothorp by itself is the comment character.

To review: the Bourne shell is the best shell for scripting, and although it is the default in many systems, we should *never trust defaults*. Therefore, the first standard for our scripts is that they will always have the shebang on the first line, followed by the path to the Bourne shell. Speaking of standards, I have some others to suggest to you as well.

⊕ Scripting Standards (a Beginning)

In the real world, scripts and programs must adhere to a set of standards imposed by the organization you work for. Thus, standards will be imposed for the exercises in this text as well. Please make sure that all the scripts you create for the exercises in this chapter follow these standards:

I. Scripts must contain complete documentation.

    A. Each script must contain internal comments that document

        a. The name of the script.
        b. The purpose for the script.
        c. The normal usage of the script.
        d. The name of the author(s).
        e. The date the script was written.
        f. The date(s) the script was modified.

    B. The name of each script must reflect its use.
    C. Each script must have a suffix that describes the shell or program the script is designed to run under or with, for example `.sh` for Bourne shell scripts, `.awk` for awk scripts, `.cgi` for Common Gateway Interface scripts, etc.

II. Each script should be designed to do one thing, and to do that one thing well.

III. Interoperability is critical. Whenever possible scripts should read from standard input and write to standard output so they may be used successfully in pipes.

IV. Keep your scripts short, tight, and elegant. Readability is important!

        a. Indent to show subordination.
        b. Make sure your beginning and ending commands align.
        c. If you make more than three inter-related decisions, us a case structure rather than imbedded `if/elifs`.
        d. White space improves readability, use blank lines to enclose logical blocks of code.

V. Remember that awk is your friend.

These scripting standards are the ones that my students must comply with when they build scripts for me in school. They are loosely based on standards I learned in industry. Wherever you end up working, that shop will most likely have very well-defined scripting standards, for without standards it becomes very difficult to determine the purpose and functionality of a script.

The first couple of scripts I will show you are written to the standards. After that I will leave out some of the documentation to shorten the screen captures. Just because *I* don't have full documentation in each and every script doesn't give *you* license to do the same. (Well, I suppose you *can* do the same when you write *your* Unix textbook but until then . . .)

The purpose for the initial block of comments and its position at the beginning of the file is to allow someone to use the head command to see what your script does. If someone else can figure out what your script is to be used for, she may well use it too, and the fruits of your effort will be rewarded.

Shell Variables as They Apply to Scripting

As you remember from our discussion of awk, a *variable* is the name for a location in memory at which the shell stores data. There are two generic families of shell variables. *You* can create shell variables to store data, called **user variables**. In addition, *the shell* provides you with a series of extremely useful variables called **system variables**.

System, or *environment*, variables in the Bourne shell are by convention named with uppercase characters whereas user, or *local*, variables are lowercase. If you adhere to this convention you'll reduce the risk of changing an environmental variable.

Creating and using variables in the Bourne shell is a terribly complex task, as I have demonstrated in Figure 14.1. Yes, that's the complex task: you simply type the name of the variable and then use the assign symbol (=) to store value at the memory location identified by the variable name. It's important to notice that there are no spaces in the assignment statement. If you put spaces around the assignment symbol, it becomes a test for equality rather than assignment. (Remember, the shell normally parses on white space!)

FIGURE 14.1

Creating and accessing a Bourne shell variable.

Step by step, what I did in Figure 14.1 is this:

1. I forked an instance of the Bourne shell. (The % is pretty much a default C shell prompt, and the $ is the default Bourne shell prompt.)

2. I created a variable named `best` and assigned it a value of `"Unix"`. For those of you who are familiar with programming languages that require you to type and/or initialize your variables, you don't need to worry about those things in the Bourne shell. To define the variable, all you have to do is assign a value to it. The good thing about that is it makes it very easy to add variables to your script. The bad thing about it is that should you misspell a variable name, the system will consider it a new variable and it will have no value.

3. I then used the `echo` command to attempt to display the contents of the variable. The `echo` command is your "send this to standard output" command. We will examine it in detail in a few pages. What happened after the first `echo` command is another example of Unix considering the user to be a cognizant, fully functional adult. I told Unix to echo `"best"`, so it echoed "best" just like I asked it to. What I really wanted the shell to do was show me the contents stored at the variable named `"best"`. To do that I needed to precede the variable name with a $.

4. In the second example of the `echo` command, I remembered to precede the variable name with the $, and the shell politely displayed the contents (what was stored at that location in memory) of the variable for me.

In the normal state of affairs, shell variables are local to the shell in which they are created. If you leave the shell in which you created a shell variable, that variable no longer will be defined. In a few pages we will learn how to change that situation.

readonly

```
readonly [variable1 variable2...]
```

If just anyone can go around creating variables, don't you think it would be useful to be able to protect the values stored at certain variables from being changed? Consider the example in Figure 14.2. This screen capture is a continuation of the previous screen. Notice that I used the **readonly** command with the variable `"best"`. The `readonly` command permanently modifies the variable, making it as—you guessed it—read only. A variable that has been set to `readonly` *cannot be modified*. As you can see in Figure 14.2, I tried to change the value assigned to the location `"best"`, but the system knew better.

You cannot change the value assigned to a variable that has been declared read only. There is no *un*readonly command. Although this may seem odd, remember that these are shell variables, and a shell variable lives only as long as the shell that contains it. You don't have to worry about cluttering up the system with lots of extraneous shell variables, since they usually have a very short lifetime.

Now let's examine some of the variables that the shell provides for you in every script. Some of these variables are extremely important, and you'll have reason to use all

FIGURE 14.2

Protecting a variable.

of them at one time or another as you build scripts. Notice that the content of each of these variables, like all the shell variables, is accessed by the leading dollar sign. I'll list the variables for you in Table 14.1 and then show you some examples where I have used them.

The variables shown in Table 14.1 are called the **built-in shell variables** because they are built into the shell and set automatically when the shell takes control. Many other shell variables (also called *environmental* variables) can be set by .profile or other processes. For example, most systems support the shell variable $USER, which is a handy way to put the user's login I.D. in a script. The Bourne shell also supports $HOME, which points to the home directory of the current user ($USER). (Actually, some of these variables, like $HOME, are created at login and the Bourne shell simply uses them but working

TABLE 14.1 Some Shell Variables

Variable	Contents
$#	The count of command-line parameters or arguments.
$?	The return status of the most recently executed command.
$$	The process I.D. of the current process.
$!	The process I.D. of the last background command.
$*	All of the command-line parameters or arguments in one long string.
"$@"	All of the command-line parameters or arguments as individual strings. (You must enclose this variable in quotation marks.)
$0	The leftmost portion of the command line. In most cases this is the name of the script.
$n(1-9)	The first nine command-line arguments or parameters. In the Bourne shell, *only nine command-line arguments are addressable.*

with Unix at the user level their source doesn't really matter to you.) You will need to examine your system to see which shell variables are available to you in your local version of the Bourne shell. Usually I discourage the use of any but the most basic environmental shell variables, because they may not always be available to you. However, it is always good practice to use the built-in shell variables, and they are common across all of the Bourne shells that I have ever seen.)

Now let's look at how we can use some of these shell variables. Consider the script in Figure 14.3. Let's take a close look at what I did here. First I wrote a Bourne shell script and displayed that script for you. You will note that it is written to the standards listed earlier in this chapter. Next I tried to run the script, but alas, since I hadn't changed the permission mask, I had no execute permission and couldn't run it. (Remember our discussion of chmod, when we said that you should never set execute permission by default? That means that we must explicitly set execute permission on a script before we can run it.)

Then I set execute permission on the script, and ran it. The output from the script is shown as the last segment of the screen capture in Figure 14.3. As you can see, it worked perfectly—but of course! I passed the script zero variables on the command line. It showed me the process I.D., the contents of the first variable (it is null, *not* blank), who I am

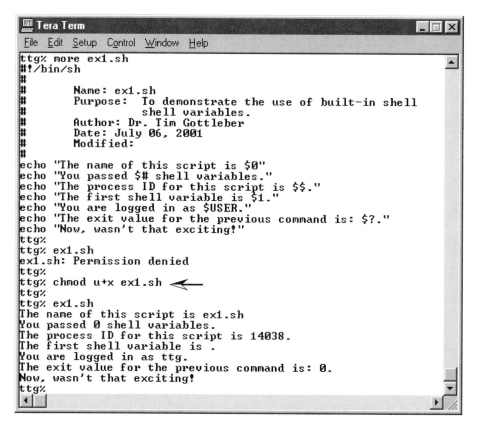

```
ttg% more ex1.sh
#!/bin/sh
#
#        Name: ex1.sh
#        Purpose:  To demonstrate the use of built-in shell
#                  shell variables.
#        Author: Dr. Tim Gottleber
#        Date: July 06, 2001
#        Modified:
#
echo "The name of this script is $0"
echo "You passed $# shell variables."
echo "The process ID for this script is $$."
echo "The first shell variable is $1."
echo "You are logged in as $USER."
echo "The exit value for the previous command is: $?."
echo "Now, wasn't that exciting!"
ttg%
ttg% ex1.sh
ex1.sh: Permission denied
ttg%
ttg% chmod u+x ex1.sh  ◄────
ttg%
ttg% ex1.sh
The name of this script is ex1.sh
You passed 0 shell variables.
The process ID for this script is 14038.
The first shell variable is .
You are logged in as ttg.
The exit value for the previous command is: 0.
Now, wasn't that exciting!
ttg%
```

FIGURE 14.3

Using shell variables.

logged in as, and the return status from the previous echo command. (Zero means success.) Takes your breath away, doesn't it? Let's run that script again with a couple of command-line variables and see what difference that makes.

This time the output, shown at the bottom of Figure 14.4, is more interesting. I showed the code again to exhibit my well-documented style! I ran the script with three command-line parameters. The script told me, rightly, that I had passed three shell variables; it gave me a different process I.D., as I expected; and it showed me that my first shell variable was "Wowsers". I am still the same user, and the previous echo command worked, so those two output lines didn't change.

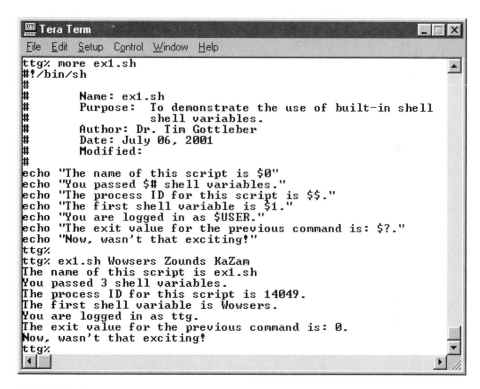

```
ttg% more ex1.sh
#!/bin/sh
#
#       Name: ex1.sh
#       Purpose:  To demonstrate the use of built-in shell
#                 shell variables.
#       Author: Dr. Tim Gottleber
#       Date: July 06, 2001
#       Modified:
#
echo "The name of this script is $0"
echo "You passed $# shell variables."
echo "The process ID for this script is $$."
echo "The first shell variable is $1."
echo "You are logged in as $USER."
echo "The exit value for the previous command is: $?."
echo "Now, wasn't that exciting!"
ttg%
ttg% ex1.sh Wowsers Zounds KaZam
The name of this script is ex1.sh
You passed 3 shell variables.
The process ID for this script is 14049.
The first shell variable is Wowsers.
You are logged in as ttg.
The exit value for the previous command is: 0.
Now, wasn't that exciting!
ttg%
```

FIGURE 14.4

Running the example script again, with command-line parameters.

Academically oriented scripts, like the one shown in Figure 14.4 and the one you will write for Exercise 2 are fine for demonstrating the contents in the variables, but they don't show how useful these variables can be. Suppose, for example, that you want to build a script that moves a file to a different directory. (Okay, sure, it is like the mv command, but building your own is good practice.) You would expect the user to enter two command-line variables, the first being the file to move, and the second the directory or file to which to move it. Your script could test the number of command-line variables and if there weren't exactly two, could send an error message to the user. Actually, you will see how to do that when we start talking about the conditionals.

In Table 14.1 I told you there were only nine addressable command-line variables. But, hey, remembering the precedence of truth, let's take a look at Figure 14.5. Gadzooks! Look at that—11 command-line parameters, and all of them are addressed! That's two more than I thought were available? Hmmmm . . . perhaps we should try a different set of input data before we jump to conclusions? Consider Figure 14.6.

All of a sudden, things look just a little different. Now, from Figure 14.6, you can see what is really happening. In Figure 14.5, we echoed the value of $1 followed by 0 and then the value of $1 followed by 1. There *are* indeed only nine addressable command-line variables in the Bourne shell.

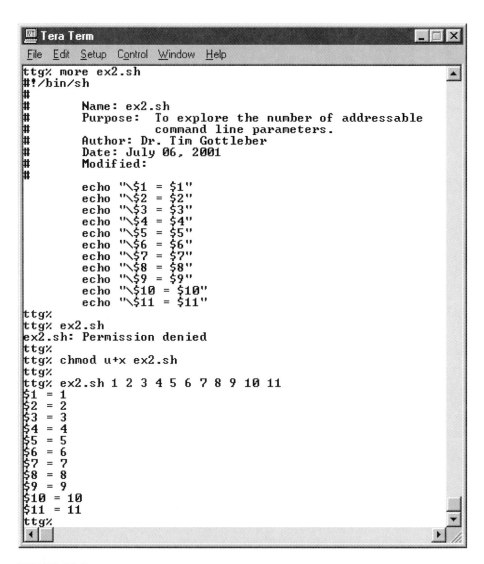

FIGURE 14.5

How many command-line variables can I address?

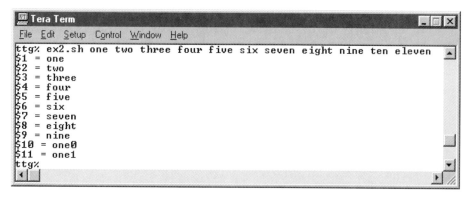

FIGURE 14.6

Another try, with different parameters.

The important lesson that I want you to learn from Figure 14.5 is that you can confuse yourself if you construct your test data carelessly. Anytime you are testing a script, you need to be very careful about the construction of the test data. Poorly constructed test data can give you results that may lead to erroneous conclusions, much like the conclusion we drew from the data shown in Figure 14.5. Paying careful attention to the construction of your test data is a critical part of building scripts.

I have a little test for you. Look back at Figures 14.3 and 14.5. What did I have to do in both of those figures before I could run the scripts I created? Look closely. Right you are! I needed to make the scripts executable by changing the permissions mask using the chmod command. Let's see, I used the chmod command to make a script executable in Figure 14.3 (that was once), and I did the same thing in Figure 14.5 (that was twice). As I remember, Refrigerator Rule No. 5 says, "If you do it more than once, write a script." I have "changed the permissions more than once," so I'd best write a script.

Take a look at Figure 14.7. The first thing I am sure you notice is that it doesn't follow our naming conventions. This is *one instance* where I created a tool, and use it so often that I wanted to save myself three keystrokes by not adding the extension .sh. You can create your own addx script, and name it that way, without an extension. But just this one time.

The addx script is an excellent example of creating a tool that saves time. I can save myself six keystrokes each time I add execute permission to a script. As I mentioned earlier, scripts are tools. You need to construct tools to help you do your job better. As you can see in Figure 14.7, I created a dummy file, then I did a long file listing of it to show its permissions mask. Next I ran the addx script against that dummy file and re-executed the ls command to show that the permissions mask had been modified.

set

---

set [option] [argument1 argument2 ...]

Now that you know how to assign values to be stored at the locations specified by user variables (variable=value), you should also know how to change the value of the

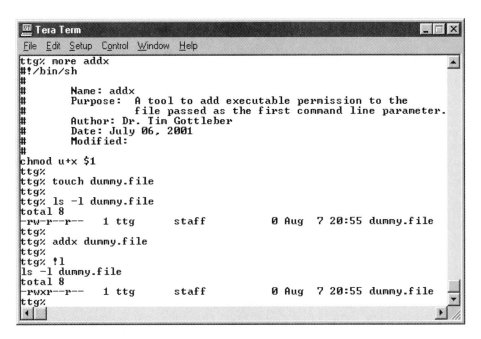

FIGURE 14.7

Our first real tool script.

command-line parameters. (You won't have call to do this very often, but there may be an instance or two where you need to change these values for testing purposes.) The **set** command is used to change the values of the positional variables that contain the command-line parameters. When used, the **set** command also changes the values of $#, $*, and "$@".

Figure 14.8 shows how the **set** command works. As you can see, it changed the values for the first three positional parameters. It also changed the number of command-line variables from four to three. Again, this is not a commonly used command, but you need to know that it is available.

FIGURE 14.8

Using set to alter the values assigned to positional variables.

env

---

env [option] [variable=value]

In addition to changing the values of the positional parameters, you can both display and change the values of the environmental variables in the Bourne shell with the **env** command. Figure 14.9 shows how I used the env command to display my current environmental variables.

Besides displaying environmental or system variables, you can use the env command to change their values. Notice how the value of the LOGNAME variable in Figure 14.10 is different from the one shown in Figure 14.9. This ability of the env command to change the value of an environmental or shell variable can be very useful when, for example, you need to modify the path for a particular script or in some other way change the environment.

FIGURE 14.9

Displaying environmental variables with the env command.

FIGURE 14.10

Changing the value of an environmental variable with the env command.

If you're going to create a child process from within a script, you can also alter the environment that child process inherits. As you remember from our discussion of process creation and control back in Chapter 10, the child process inherits the environment from the parent process. The environment the child process inherits by default is the normal shell environment, with the normal complement of shell variables. There will, of course, be some differences. For example, the process I.D. of the child process will be different from that of the parent process. However, normally any shell variable *you create* will not be passed to the child process as part of its environment. As I said a few pages earlier, shell variables are local for the shell in which they were created. Consequently, if you created a shell variable within a script, that shell variable will be local to the script in which it was created.

I could run the script that called another script and demonstrate this for you, but I can achieve the same results by simply forking another instance of the shell from the command line as I did in Figure 14.11. In the first shell shown here I declared a local shell variable goober and assigned it a value of "peas". After declaring it, I displayed it so you could see it. Then I forked a new instance of the shell and tried to display the contents of the variable there. As you can see, the variable has no value in the second shell, proving that it is indeed a *local* shell variable.

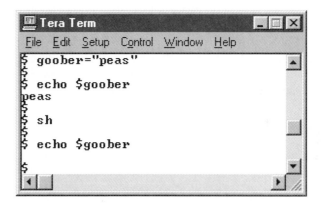

FIGURE 14.11

Showing how locally declared shell variables are not passed to a child process.

export

```
export [variable(s)]
```

"But," you ask, "suppose I *want* the child process to know a value for a variable I've declared?" Take a look at Figure 14.12. First I assigned the local shell variable goober again, then echoed it to show you that it had a value. Next I exported the variable.

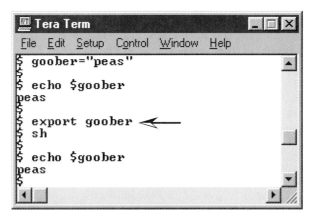

FIGURE 14.12

Adding a variable to the environment of a child process.

The **export** command causes the variable or variables specified to become part of the environment for any child process forked from this parent process (in this case, the shell). This command is designed to allow your child process to receive data from the parent process. The variables processed by the export command apply only to the child processes forked from this parent process. Processes forked from the child process (grandchild processes?) may or may not know the value of the variable but they always will if the child process also exports it.

⊕ Built-in Commands

Back in Chapter 10 we learned that each shell has both internal and external commands. The internal commands are **built-in commands**. They are part of the shell itself, so the shell need not fork a new process to execute them.

Some examples of the built-in commands in the Bourne shell, on a Solaris system, are shown in Table 14.2. To determine which commands are built into the Bourne shell on a Solaris system, all you have to do is ask

```
man shell_builtins
```

and **man** will list all the built-in commands for you. That option doesn't exist in the bash shell, but most if not all of the commands listed in Table 14.2 are probably are also built into the bash shell.

Several of the commands shown in Table 14.2 are old friends; many more will become near and dear to your heart as you become acquainted with them by developing shell scripts. Now let's explore some of these commands.

TABLE 14.2 Built-in Commands in Bourne Shell, on Solaris System

Bourne Shell Built-ins	
bg	newgrp
break	pwd
case	read
cd	readonly
chdir	return
continue	set
echo	shift
eval	stop
exec	suspend
exit	test
export	times
fg	trap
for	type
getopts	ulimit
hash	umask
if	unset
jobs	until
kill	wait
login	while
logout	

echo

---

echo [options] .[string]

The **echo** command is used to send data to standard output. (Remember that. It will be important later.) You're already familiar with the echo command, since it's been in almost every script we've examined so far. However, there's a little bit more I'd like you to know about it. Sometimes you might want to prompt the user to enter a value without having the cursor drop down to the next line. Figure 14.13 shows the usual ("plain") prompt, which does drop to the next line, and then a prompt that leaves the user in the same line. This screen capture is a combination of two different screen captures, one taken after each prompt. Notice the position of the cursor after each prompt. The protected c (\c) at the end of the second prompt directs the system to suppress the default of carriage return line feed.

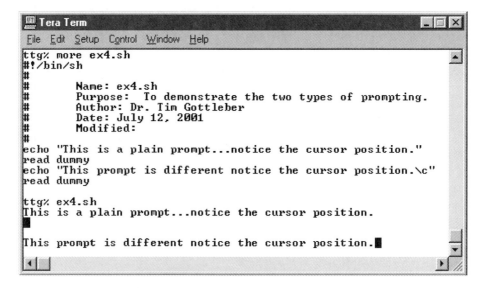

FIGURE 14.13

Two examples of the echo command.

The protected c at the end of the prompt is the mechanism you will use in the Bourne shell, on Solaris, to suppress carriage return line feed. In the C shell, though, you'd use the -n command-line option to suppress the new line. I have shown you both commands in Figure 14.14. There's no script to show here because I did all the testing on the command lines. Yes, command *lines*, because I show you both the C shell (%) in the top half of the screen capture and the Bourne shell ($) in the bottom half. The only way you can tell there was no newline is by the position of the prompt. For example, in the second echo, the -n command-line option worked because the ttg prompt appears at the end of the output line. Notice that I have tested both types of newline suppression in both shells.

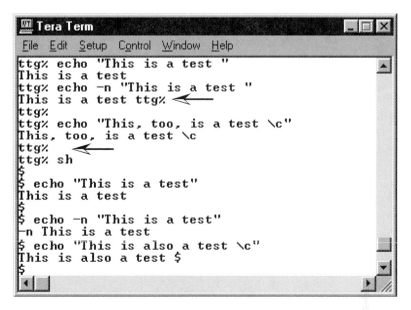

FIGURE 14.14

Suppressing newline in both Bourne and C shells.

The echo command supports a number of protected formatting options, shown in Table 14.3, some of which should be familiar to you from your work with awk. In Figure 14.15 I demonstrate a subset of these special characters. This script uses six of the special formatting options. Look carefully at the output. The three tabs in the first line are easy to see. In the second line, notice what happened to the word three. That's right, the backspaces took off the space and the last two es of the word three. The two new lines are obvious in the third line, the fourth line, and the fifth line. The backslash shows in the sixth line.

TABLE 14.3 Special Formatting Characters Used with echo

Option	Function
\a	The alert character
\b	Backspace
\c	Suppress newline
\f	Form feed
\n	Newline
\r	Carriage return
\t	Tab
\v	Vertical tab
\\	The backslash character itself

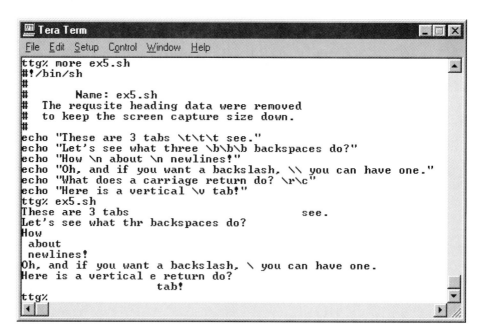

FIGURE 14.15

Some special characters.

The seventh line could be a little confusing. It should read, "What does a carriage return do?" The words "what does a carriage" are overwritten by the words Here is a vertical from the next command. That shows you what a carriage return does—it moves the cursor back to the beginning of the existing line. That action can be useful in some instances. The vertical tab in the last echo just drops the cursor to the next line at the same position.

You can see that the special characters in the echo command give you additional control over your output. Experiment with them.

sh

```
sh [options] [arguments]
```

Now that you can use the echo command to "see stuff," I want to talk to you about debugging your Bourne shell scripts. You can debug your scripts two different ways. First, you can use debug echo statements to help you follow what is happening. This method allows you to see the contents of various variables as your script executes. You will see debug echo statements in many production scripts when you get out into industry.

The other tool you have available to you is a tracing mechanism within the shell itself. Two options on the **sh** command will enable you to trace the steps the script is going through. This tool will be valuable when you are trying to figure out the exact execution steps in a script that has conditional execution. (The if or case statements cause only part of the script to execute; they are called **conditional execution** because only in specific conditions will some parts of the script execute.)

The first option for tracing is shown in Figure 14.16. This –v (*verbose*) option on the sh command directs the shell to show you each line in the script as it is processed. Notice that the output from the –v option looks the same whether there are more than three command-line arguments or not. This option does not tell you exactly what the shell did. You have to interpolate from the output. Used by itself, this option is not as helpful as the other one, shown in Figure 14.17.

The first thing I'm sure you'll notice about the output in Figure 14.17 is that it's much shorter than the output in Figure 14.16. The –x (*executed*) option directs sh to

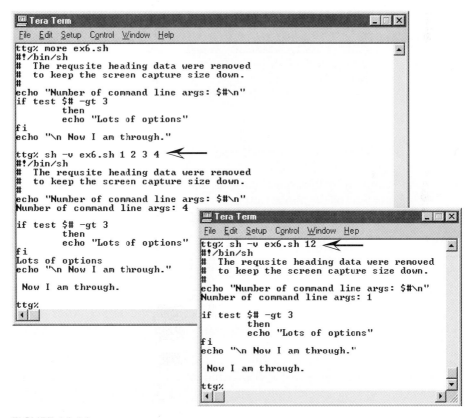

FIGURE 14.16

Using the –v option on the sh command.

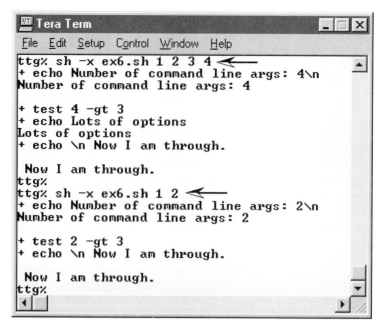

FIGURE 14.17

Using the –x option on the sh command.

display *each command it executed*, preceded by a plus sign (+). I find this type of output much more useful because I can track *exactly which commands are being executed*, and see the output from those commands. In addition, the leading plus signs make it easy to distinguish the code from the output.

The downside of the -x option is that I see only the commands that are executed, not the comments or the rest of the script. Figure 14.18 shows the best of all possible worlds. "And what," you ask, "is the best of all possible worlds?" Well, if you don't mind a little triple redundancy, I like using both options together. As you can see in Figure 14.18, I used both command-line options when I ran the script. That way I could see everything in the script, while also seeing exactly which of those commands were executed, as well as seeing the output. After testing the script with both options a couple of times, you can usually drop the -v option and just use the -x option.

Since this is Unix, and since Unix almost always gives as you more than one way to do something, you can also include the options to the Bourne shell on the she-bang line in your script. That's what I did in Figure 14.19. Since I used both the -v and the -x options here, I didn't even need to list the script for you because you can see each line as it is output. The only difference between the two scripts, ex6.sh and ex6a.sh, is the presence of the command-line options on the shebang line. As you can see, I simply ran the script, and the shell displayed the tracing output for me, just as I expected.

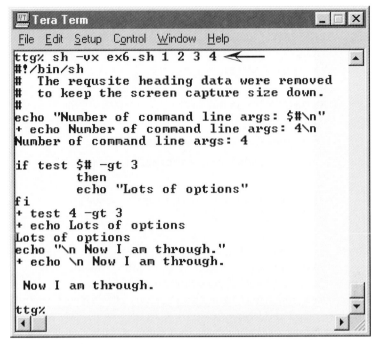

FIGURE 14.18

Combining –x and –v options.

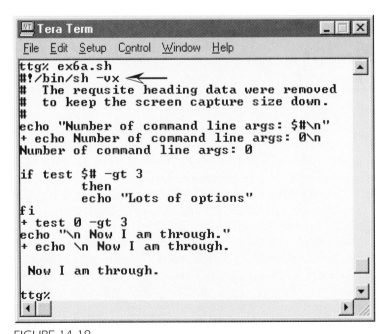

FIGURE 14.19

Including the tracing options within a shell script.

if

```
if condition1
    then
    commands if condition1 is true
    [elif condition2
        then
        commands if condition2 is true]
    [else
    commands when no condition is true]
fi
```

Since we mentioned conditional execution in the preceding section, and you've now seen an if statement in use, it's time to explore this tool. The **if** statement is an example of the second set of program constructs, selection. (You do remember the three program constructs from the previous chapter, don't you? Sure you do—sequence, selection, and iteration.)

In its simplest form, the if statement, or if block, determines whether one or more commands will be executed. The format of the if statement is very precise, and the shell demands that you follow this structure. The particular structure of a command and the order in which the parts of the command must be organized is called **syntax**. The proper syntax for a Bourne shell if statement is

```
if test condition
    then
        command1
        command2
fi
```

The indention isn't important, at least to the shell, but readability is extremely important to anyone who reads your scripts. Notice how the if statement lines up with the fi statement, which closes the if block. The reason we need to close the if block, or if structure, is to tell the shell which commands are to be executed if the condition specified is true. If we forgot the fi command, the shell would think that the rest of the script is to be executed only when the condition is true. In reality, if we forget the fi, the script will generate an error. In that case, the shell will run into the end of the script, or file, before it finds the end of the if block and will generate an error message telling us about it.

While we're talking about readability, I need to tell you about the use of the semicolon. Actually, that's not exactly true. I don't want to tell you about the *use* of the semicolon, but rather about the *problem* people create by misusing the semicolon. In the Bourne shell scripting language and, of course, on the Bourne shell command line, you can use the semicolon to separate commands. The semicolon is interpreted as if you had touched the Return key. So, for example, the if block shown previously could be coded like this:

```
if test condition
then
command1;command2;fi
```

By the same token, if you wanted to be obscure, you could code a series of echo statements like this:

```
echo "hi";echo "How are you?";echo "Fine, I hope."
```

But it would be better to build readable code like this:

```
echo "hi"
echo "How are you?"
echo "Fine, I hope."
```

Although I'm sure there may be, in some distant galaxy, some very strange circumstances under which you would need to use the semicolon form of scripting, I have never encountered any. Readability is critically important, both to you as you debug and modify your scripts, and to others as they study your scripts for insight. For that reason I urge you to *never use the semicolon* form. It's a bad practice and will only harm your readability. It may cause you to run with scissors in your hand, and some think it causes premature hair loss—all in all, it is simply a Bad Thing.

While I'm lecturing on do's and don't's, let me take on another sacred cow. There are actually two forms of the if statement, and you will encounter both of them as you peruse other folks' scripts. The first form and to my mind the preferred form, is to explicitly code the test command within the if. This is the form you have seen in each previous example and will continue to see in the rest of the sample if statements.

The other form of if uses square brackets to enclose the condition and does not explicitly show the test command. Thus, you *could* code an if this way:

```
if [ $# -gt 1 ]
    then
        echo "Multiple command line arguments..."
fi
```

And it would work! It is correct syntax. But it can be confusing, especially to folks who have just learned about scripting in awk, because it's easy to confuse parentheses with square brackets. In addition, the shell has to translate the square brackets to the test command, so you're just creating extra work. I urge you not to use this form of the if statement. If you're required to maintain scripts that use the square-brackets form, you should modify them to the test form.

To sum up, then, don't use semicolons, and don't use square brackets. You don't need either of them, and both will add confusion to your scripts.

The simple if statement can do a lot for us, but suppose we need to make a binary decision—that is, if the condition is true, do this, but if it's not, do that. Take a look at Figure 14.20. The if structure shown in this figure is known as the IF-THEN-ELSE structure. If the condition specified after the test command evaluates to *True*, then the first echo is executed. If the condition is the *False*, then the second echo is executed. In either

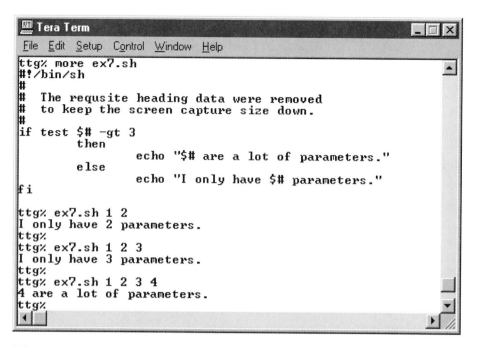

FIGURE 14.20

The famous IF-THEN-ELSE construct.

case one of the echo commands will be executed. As you can see from the sample runs at the bottom of Figure 14.20, either one or the other of the echo statements executes, depending on the number of command-line parameters.

There's only one fi command in this whole if block, because the else statement marks the end of the code associated with the then, so the fi is needed only to mark the end of the else code. Up until now, we have had only one command after either the then or the else. It is possible to include practically any number of commands in either of those locations. I've modified the script from Figure 14.20 to include multiple echo statements, and that modified script is presented for your viewing pleasure in Figure 14.21. Notice that three echo commands follow the then, and three different ones follow the else. Unlike C, awk, or other programming languages, with the Bourne shell version of if, you don't need to enclose multiple statements in curly braces, since the structure of the if block serves to delimit multiple statements.

Okay, now we know how to deal with one or two conditions, but suppose we have three? Let's say that you want to respond differently if the user enters a number less than 5, exactly equal to 5, or greater than 5 on the command line. I address that issue in Figure 14.22. The new command introduced there, elif, is a conjunction of the words "else" and "if." Make no mistake—an elif is not a small garden-dwelling creature with a pointy hat and curled-up toes on his shoes. No, it's just a form of if, and therefore you must use the test command and a condition with it. It also requires a then, just like a plain-vanilla if.

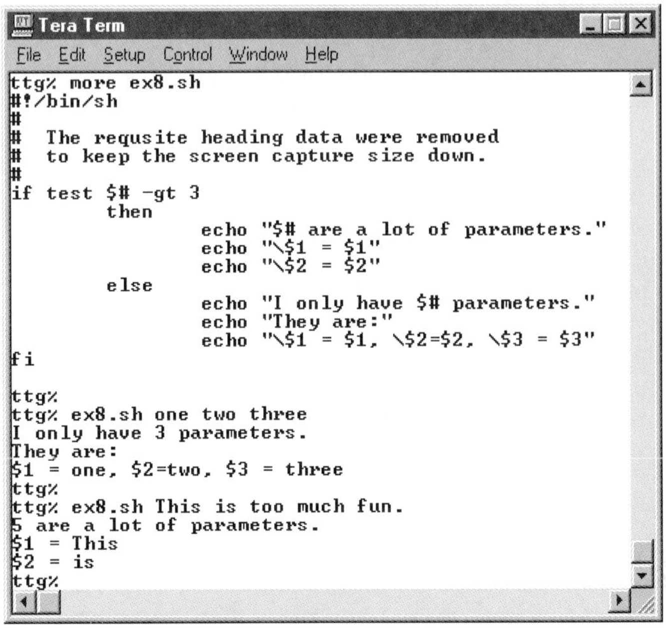

```
Tera Term
File  Edit  Setup  Control  Window  Help
ttg% more ex8.sh
#!/bin/sh
#
#   The requsite heading data were removed
#   to keep the screen capture size down.
#
if test $# -gt 3
        then
                    echo "$# are a lot of parameters."
                    echo "\$1 = $1"
                    echo "\$2 = $2"
        else
                    echo "I only have $# parameters."
                    echo "They are:"
                    echo "\$1 = $1, \$2=$2, \$3 = $3"
fi

ttg%
ttg% ex8.sh one two three
I only have 3 parameters.
They are:
$1 = one, $2=two, $3 = three
ttg%
ttg% ex8.sh This is too much fun.
5 are a lot of parameters.
$1 = This
$2 = is
ttg%
```

FIGURE 14.21

Multiple statements after then and else.

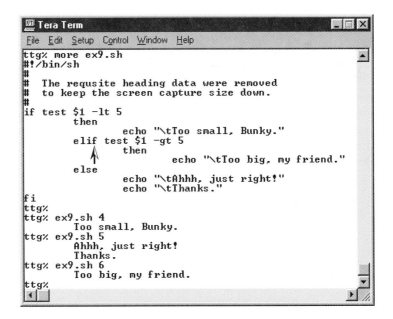

FIGURE 14.22

Using elif for three different conditions.

It is possible to use multiple elifs in one if block. See the contrived example in Figure 14.23. I set my tab stops down to four characters to try to keep the width of the screen capture reasonable. The top screen caption shows a five-level if -- then -- elif structure. The bottom of that screen capture shows where I ran the script six times testing it. I could have omitted the last elif and simply used an else statement in its place, but I chose the form shown so that each test would be a parallel structure. If you're going to use more than three conditions, you have to be Very Careful how you construct your code to preserve readability. In just a few pages we will discuss the case construct, which is designed for multiple conditions.

One of the more intriguing uses for the if statement is to help you in your debugging adventures. You can create a series of debug-if statements in your scripts that will make life easier for you as you add to and modify your code. I have presented a simple example in Figure 14.24 just to show you the idea. If you incorporate this structure into your longer scripts you will find it very useful, and at the same time simple to use.

The large screen capture in Figure 14.24 shows you the code from the simple script. The first of the two smaller windows shows you what happens when the script is run with the debug value equaling 1. With debug turned on, we see the value of the variables. That's the purpose for the debug-if statement in most cases. The second execution is smaller. In that case you see no debug print statements, and the script runs as it would in production. (The value of the debug variable was 0.)

Including debug-if statements in your scripts allows you to turn these debugging features on and off simply by changing the value of a single variable. This procedure may well save you hours of debugging time when you're working with a complex script. As soon as you begin seeing odd output from the script you are modifying, you can turn on the debugging variable and see exactly what's going on inside your script—provided, of course, that you have built your debugging statements to accurately reflect what's going on inside your script.

Any time I build a script that's going to be over 50 or 60 lines long, especially if I think I'm going to be modifying the script at a later date, I routinely build in debugging statements. Yes, it does make the script longer. Yes, it does make the script execute a tiny bit slower. And yes, this technique has saved me hours of debugging time. If you get into the habit of crafting debugging if statements into your scripts now, then when you get into the real world of production scripting you'll already have mastered a valuable technique.

Before you can do that, however, we need to look at the test command.

```
#!/bin/sh
#
#   The requsite heading data were removed
#   to keep the screen capture size down.
#
if test $1 -lt 5
    then echo "Too small."
    elif test $1 -eq 6
        then
        echo "Close, but not close enough."
        elif test $1 -eq 7
            then
            echo "Yes!  You got it!"
            elif test $1 -eq 8
                then
                echo "Ohhh, just a little too big."
                elif test $1 -gt 8
                    then
                    echo "Whoa there pardner, too big!"
fi
```

```
ttg% ex10.sh 1
Too small.
ttg%
ttg% ex10.sh 6
Close, but not close enough.
ttg% ex10.sh 7
Yes!  You got it!
ttg% ex10.sh 8
Ohhh, just a little too big.
ttg% ex10.sh 9
Whoa there pardner, too big!
ttg%
ttg% ex10.sh 5
ttg%
```

FIGURE 14.23

Multiple elifs.

```
ttg% more ex11.sh
#!/bin/sh
#
#   The requsite heading data were removed
#   to keep the screen capture size down.
#
debug=1
#debug=0
if test $debug -gt 0
        then
                echo "\t\tThe value for \$debug is $debug"
fi
if test $1 -eq 4
        then
                echo "For me? <grin>"
fi
if test $debug -gt 0
        then
                echo "\t\tdebug: \$1 = $1"
                echo "\t\tdebug: \$2 = $2"
fi
if test $2 -gt 100
        then
        echo "Why did you make \$2 so small?"
fi

ttg%
```

```
When debug=1
ttg% ex11.sh 4 99
                The value for $debug is 1
For me? <grin>
        debug: $1 = 4
        debug: $2 = 99
ttg%
```

```
When debug=0
ttg% ex11.sh 5 95
ttg%
```

FIGURE 14.24

Using debug-if statements.

test

```
test condition
```
or
`[ condition ]` (This is *not* a preferred form.)

The **test** command is used to evaluate three different general types of conditions:

1. File conditions.
2. String comparisons and conditions.
3. Integer comparisons.

We will consider the types of comparisons in that order.

File Conditions

The test command is extremely useful for determining information about files. Some common tests are shown in Table 14.4. You will find these tests valuable when you become a system administrator, but don't discount their importance to you now, either. Suppose, for example, you want to write to a file in your directory. What test would you use to see if you could write, or should write, to a particular file?

Figure 14.25 shows how to code this test condition. Notice that I'm not testing some sort of relationship, but rather I'm asking if a particular file status applies to the value, in this case stored in $1. Using test this way can give you a lot of useful data.

TABLE 14.4 Some Common Tests on Files

Condition	Meaning (If True)
-b file	File exists and is a block special file.
-c file	File exists and is a character special file.
-d file	File exists and is a directory.
-f file	File exists and is a regular file.
-g file	File exists and has the set-group-id bit set.
-k file	File exists and has the sticky bit set.
-p file	File exists and is named pipe (fifo).
-r file	File exists and is readable.
-s file	File exists and has a size greater than zero.
-u file	File exists and has the set-user-id bit set.
-w file	File exists and may be written to.
-x file	File exists and is executable.

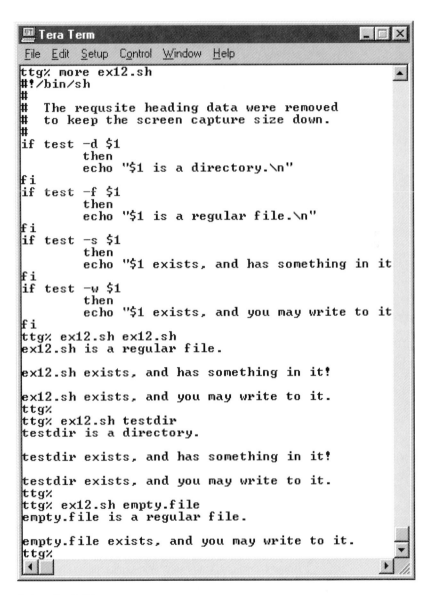

```
ttg% more ex12.sh
#!/bin/sh
#
#   The requsite heading data were removed
#   to keep the screen capture size down.
#
if test -d $1
        then
        echo "$1 is a directory.\n"
fi
if test -f $1
        then
        echo "$1 is a regular file.\n"
fi
if test -s $1
        then
        echo "$1 exists, and has something in it
fi
if test -w $1
        then
        echo "$1 exists, and you may write to it
fi
ttg% ex12.sh ex12.sh
ex12.sh is a regular file.

ex12.sh exists, and has something in it!

ex12.sh exists, and you may write to it.
ttg%
ttg% ex12.sh testdir
testdir is a directory.

testdir exists, and has something in it!

testdir exists, and you may write to it.
ttg%
ttg% ex12.sh empty.file
empty.file is a regular file.

empty.file exists, and you may write to it.
ttg%
```

FIGURE 14.25

Testing file conditions.

Earlier I talked about the alternate form of the `test` command. This is one place where that form looks totally ludicrous. For example, the preferred way of testing whether I have write permission to a file is by saying

```
if test -w $1
```

and that seems to make some sort of logical sense. I'm testing whether I have write permission on the first command-line parameter. However, using the square-brackets form looks very strange:

```
if [-w $1]
```

Now that will work, but I know it would be confusing to a new scriptor! I'm sure you can see the difference, and why the first form is preferred.

Another thing you'll notice about the scripting in Figure 14.25 is that I use a series of `if`s instead of a nested `if`,`elif` structure. I did not nest the `if`s because a file can be a regular file, and it can have some contents, and I can have write permission to it. If I had used the `if`,`elif` form, then I would have been able to select just *one* of those conditions to the exclusion of all the others. How you design your scripts is very important.

Back to the question asked before Figure 14.25: which `test` should I use to determine whether or not to write to file? The answer is hidden there in Figure 14.25. Can you see it? Yes, you're right, to determine whether or not I should write to file I will use the `-s` condition, because I don't want to write to a file that has something in it. The `-w` condition tells me only whether or not I can, or rather *may,* write to the file, but it doesn't tell me whether or not I *should*. Enough about file tests—let's move on.

String Comparisons

The `test` command distinguishes between testing strings and testing numbers. As I am sure you remember from our discussion of `sort`, numbers and characters are stored differently, sort differently, and now we learn that they are also compared differently. Table 14.5 lists the string comparisons or string tests you can make in the Bourne shell.

TABLE 14.5 String Tests

Condition	Meaning (If True)
`-n string1`	String1 has a length greater than 0.
`-z string1`	String1 is a length of 0 bytes.
`s1 = s2`	String1 is equal to `string2`. (Notice the spaces surrounding the equal sign. If you don't leave spaces, it is *assignment*, not a test of equality.)
`s1 != s2`	String1 is not equal to `string2`. (Remember, this is the Bourne shell, so ! means *not* instead of *history*.)
`string`	The string is not empty (null). This is not the same thing as the `-n` and `-z` tests. They assume that the variable for the test exists.

I know there aren't a lot of tests, but how much do you really need to know about strings? Well, you need to know if two strings are equal or not, or if a string has something in it. You don't need to know if one string is greater than the other unless you're doing a sort, and, well, we have the sort tool for that.

Figure 14.26 shows some of the string comparisons. The construction of this script is a little different than we have seen before. This is a true *nested if*. In this case, if there is something in the first command-line parameter ($1), then we test to see if that parameter equals the second command-line parameter ($2). We're assuming that both command-line parameters are strings, and that if the user has given us one command-line parameter, she has given us both of them. (In production it's probably not a good idea to make either of those assumptions, but we can get by with it here.)

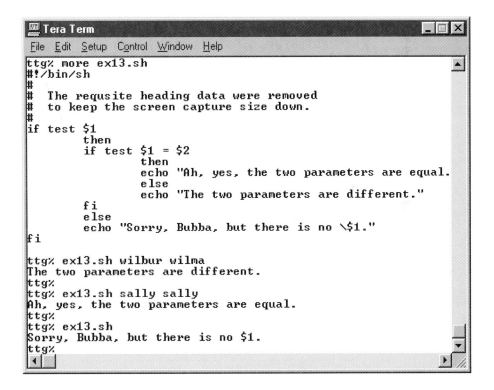

FIGURE 14.26

Some string comparisons.

As you can see from the figure, when I ran the script it worked as expected. Notice how I tested for the presence of $1. Had I tried to use -n, the test would have failed in the third example because the -n test assumes that the variable exists. That's an important difference among those three evaluation methods.

Just to prove to you that numbers and strings are indeed handled differently, look what happened when I used the string comparison script again in Figure 14.27. Gee, what a tiny little screen capture! But when you're making a big point, you don't necessarily need a big screen capture to do it. Back in the 1800s B.C., the Babylonians realized that 01 and 1 were the same number. Why doesn't the Bourne shell understand that? Ah, yes, because the Bourne shell is not looking at these two values as numbers but rather as character strings, and one of the strings has two bytes in it and the other string has only one byte. Obviously, says Bourne, they can't be equal. If we want Bourne to compare numbers, we need to use a different set of comparisons.

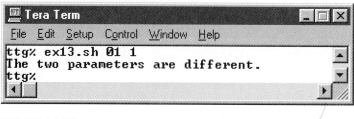

FIGURE 14.27

Trying to compare numbers as if they were strings.

Numeric Comparisons

In the Bourne shell all mathematical comparisons are integer comparisons. This is because the Bourne shell does not natively deal with floating-point numbers. It does integer math. We'll explore this concept further when we discuss the expr command in a few pages.

Table 14.6 lists the integer comparison tools available in the Bourne shell. Please notice that the leading hyphen is required syntax for each of the numeric conditions. Integer relationships are very straightforward; however, they also probably account for the number one logic error in most programs. The reason numeric tests

TABLE 14.6 Integer Comparisons

Condition	Meaning (If True)
n1 -eq n2	Number 1 is equal in value to number 2.
n1 -le n2	Number 1 is less than or equal to number 2.
n1 -lt n2	Number 1 is less than number 2.
n1 -ge n2	Number 1 is greater than or equal to number 2.
n1 -gt n2	Number 1 is greater than number 2.
n1 -ne n2	Number 1 is not equal to number 2.

frequently cause logic errors is that programmers forget the cardinal rule of numeric comparisons: There are *three* possible relationships between any two numbers.

The three relationships are

1. The first number is *less than* the second number.
2. The first number is *greater than* the second number.
3. The first number is *equal to* the second number.

That third relationship is the one that seems to cause the most problems. Whenever you're creating scripts that compare two integers, make sure, *absolutely sure*, that you account for all three conditions. I deliberately made this classic error in one of my earlier scripts and even ran the script with data that illustrated the error. Did you catch it? Look carefully at the Figure 14.28; it's a reprint of Figure 14.23 to save you from having to page back into the chapter.

FIGURE 14.28

Reprint of Figure 14.23, showing an error.

Notice what happened when I ran the script and passed it a value of 5. Yup, that's exactly right; my script *does not account* for the case where the user passes it a value *equal* to 5. And you can see from the last run in Figure 14.23 that when I pass the script a value of 5, it does nothing! Did you catch that error earlier? It's a very easy error to make, but if you follow the cardinal rule of comparisons you will never make it yourself. Since we've seen other examples, earlier in the chapter, using integer comparisons, I think you understand how to use them.

There's another problem with Figure 14.28, even after correcting the "equals five" problem, it's still an ugly script because it has too many conditions. As I mentioned earlier, readability is an important criterium for scripts. One of the things that contributes to good readability is good structure. The idea of structuring code has been around as long as there have been programmers, but back in 1975 Edward Yourdon wrote a classic text, *Techniques of Program Structure and Design,* that, for the first time, codified a series of rules for program structure. The book, published by Prentice Hall, is unfortunately out of print, but if you wish to learn about structured programming from the master, you should try to find it.

case

```
case value in
pattern1) commands for pattern 1;;
pattern2) commands associated with pattern 2;;

   .

   .

   .

esac
```

One of the tools added to Unix to make it a more structured programming environment was the **case** structure. The case construct takes the place of a multiple nested if – elif – elif... structure. Note, *only one of the patterns in the* case *structure can match the value passed to it.* If you want to be able to recognize multiple conditions, as we did when we were testing files in Figure 14.24, you would *not* use the case structure. However, if you find yourself creating a block that has three or more conditions, you should use the case structure instead.

Figure 14.29 is a little long, because I've created the same conditional tests using both a nested if and the case structure so you can see the difference. The case structure is much shorter, much more understandable, and contains far fewer lines that could house an error. Although this example has only one command after each pattern, I could have put a number of lines there. The double semicolon (; ;) marks the end of the block of commands for each pattern and is required syntax. In the example in Figure 14.29 the pattern is a single number, but it can be a regular expression or a fixed pattern. All in all, the case structure is extremely versatile.

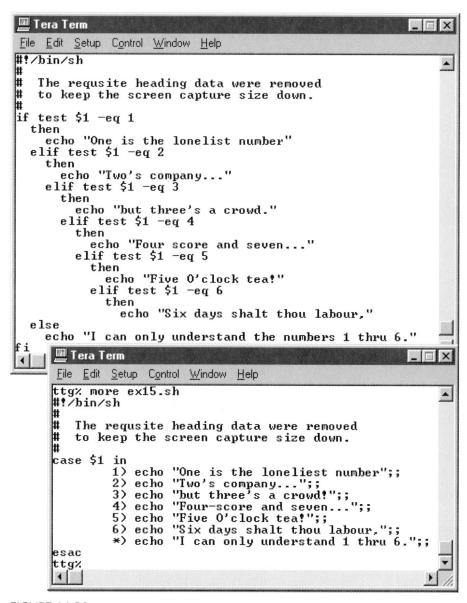

FIGURE 14.29

The nested if structure compared with the case structure.

Lest you think I'm trying to pull a fast one, Figure 14.30 shows the output from both scripts, the nested if and the case. The script labeled ex14.sh is the nested if script, and the script labeled ex15.sh is the case script. As you can see, both scripts produce the same output (well, each script produces its own output, but the results are similar). Now take another look at the case structure you first saw in Figure 14.29, reproduced for you in Figure 14.31.

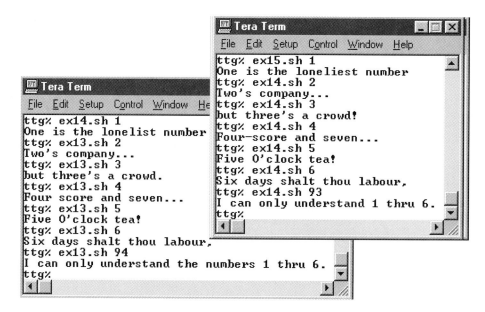

FIGURE 14.30

Output from both scripts.

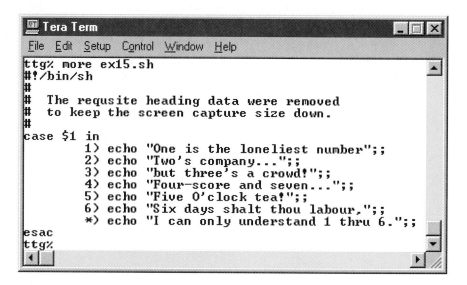

FIGURE 14.31

Another look at the case structure.

The syntax of the case structure shown in Figure 14.31 is very important. To introduce the `case`, you code a line that says

```
case variable in
```

where `variable` is the one you wish to compare to a series of patterns (possible values). Each pattern is terminated by a single close parenthesis. Following the close parenthesis, you can have one or more lines of code that will be executed in the event that the variable matches a particular pattern. Notice how indenting the patterns makes the code very readable. Patterns are always terminated by a double semicolon. If you forget to code the double semicolon at the end of each collection of statements, the `case` structure will continue to execute commands until it finds a double semicolon! (That can cause some very interesting errors).

The last pattern, the asterisk, *always* matches the variable. You don't have to use it—it is an optional pattern—but if you are expecting that one of your patterns will match, use the asterisk to catch any that don't. If you don't use the asterisk, and your variable doesn't match any pattern, the `case` structure will exit taking no action. It doesn't even set a non-zero return code. How you handle the situation where the variable doesn't match any of the patterns is up to you, but you do need to take it into account when you design your script, just as you need to account for all three cases when you build `if` structures.

The placement of the asterisk pattern is also very important. I had a student once who built an elegant `case` structure, but he put the asterisk *as the first pattern*. For some reason, his case would never recognize any of the other variables, and always gave him a "did not match" message. When he moved the asterisk, which *matches any input,* to the end of his case, things worked perfectly. You also need to consider placement when you add patterns to the `case`. Don't just add them to the end of the case, but be sure to add them *above* the asterisk!

The `case` structure should always be used if you are testing more than two independent values for the same variable. The `case` structure is also useful for fewer than three tests, if you anticipate a range of different possible values that all mean the same thing. Take a look at the script in Figure 14.32. The vertical stroke (|) that separates the different options corresponds to the logical **OR** command. What the script asks is, did the user enter any of the following: Y, y, Yes, yes, Yup? If so, clear the screen. Otherwise the script asks, did the user enter any of the following: N, n, No, no, Nope. If so, tell the user OK. Otherwise, tell the user his choices again.

Notice that the case structure is *not* an iterative, or looping, structure. The script asks the question and then processes one answer. In a few pages we'll see how to perform iterative operations in the Bourne shell.

In Figure 14.32 I also show you a couple of runs of the script so that you can see it does indeed work. Obviously, had I used one of the affirmative replies, all I would be able to show you is a blank screen, since the script would clear it. Play with this script to prove to yourself that it works.

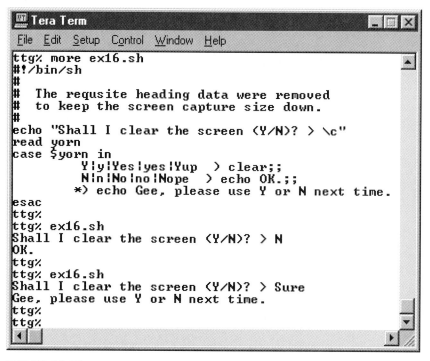

FIGURE 14.32

Using multiple options with the case structure.

By the way, notice the variable name I use to collect input from the read statement. It's one of the standard variables I use in many scripts, because it is very self-explanatory. The variable name yorn stands for Y or N. I also use torf when creating true/false questions.

You could construct the same sort of logical model shown in Figure 14.32 using the if structure, but it would be somewhat more awkward. Take a look at Figure 14.33. As you can see from the sample runs at the bottom, the script produces the same output as the script in Figure 14.32. The difference is it's much longer and more cumbersome. It does, however, somewhat elegantly show you how to use one of the combined forms of the test command. The -o operator is the logical OR for the test command in the Bourne shell. It specifies that if either of the conditions surrounding it is true, then the evaluation of the test command will indicate success. In the script shown in Figure 14.33 I sort of push the envelope on the logical OR by asking the test command to evaluate *five* different relationships and *if any of them are true*, indicate success. Feel free to experiment with the script that is shown in Figure 14.33; it can be found at the Web site.

The script shown in Figure 14.33 also uses a new I/O verb. Well, actually, it's a fairly old command, but we haven't learned it yet.

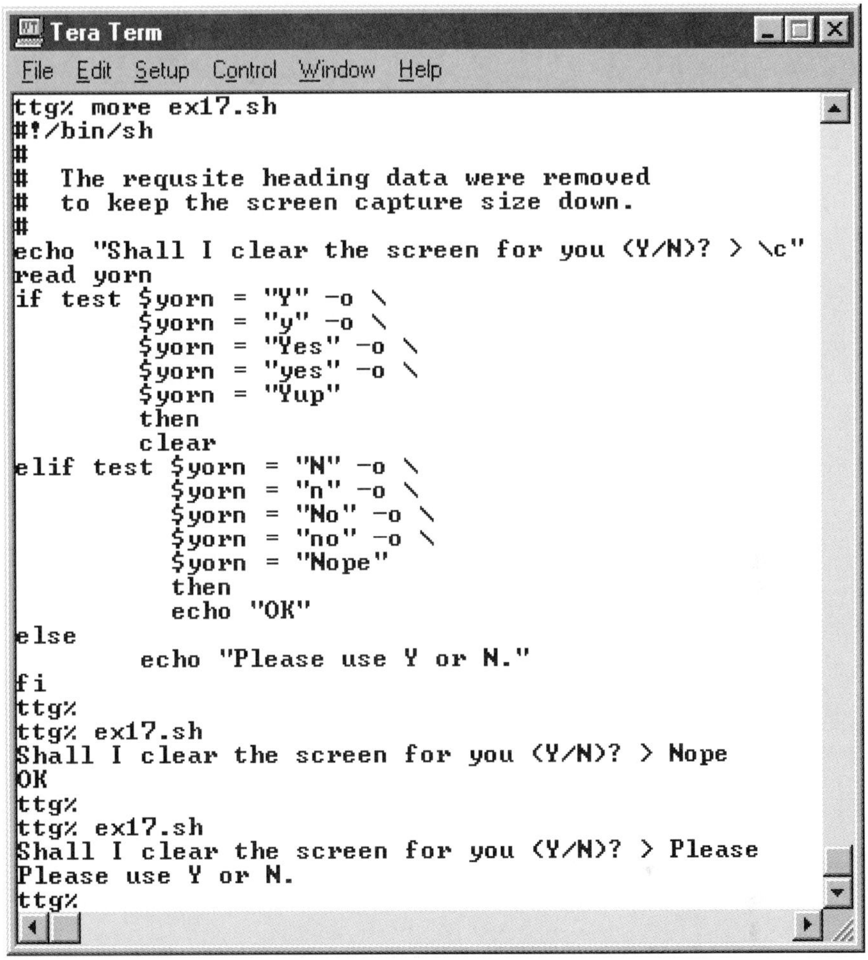

```
ttg% more ex17.sh
#!/bin/sh
#
#   The requsite heading data were removed
#   to keep the screen capture size down.
#
echo "Shall I clear the screen for you (Y/N)? > \c"
read yorn
if test $yorn = "Y" -o \
         $yorn = "y" -o \
         $yorn = "Yes" -o \
         $yorn = "yes" -o \
         $yorn = "Yup"
         then
         clear
elif test $yorn = "N" -o \
         $yorn = "n" -o \
         $yorn = "No" -o \
         $yorn = "no" -o \
         $yorn = "Nope"
         then
         echo "OK"
else
         echo "Please use Y or N."
fi
ttg%
ttg% ex17.sh
Shall I clear the screen for you (Y/N)? > Nope
OK
ttg%
ttg% ex17.sh
Shall I clear the screen for you (Y/N)? > Please
Please use Y or N.
ttg%
```

FIGURE 14.33

Creating a complex if structure.

read

```
read variable1 [variable2...]
```

The **read** command takes a text string from standard input and assigns it to one or more variables. The number of variables to which the string is assigned depends upon two things: the number of words in the input string and the number of variables associated with the read command. The shell parses the input line on its normal delimiter, usually white space, and assigns one "word" sequentially, to each variable listed in the read command. If there are fewer words than variables, any leftover variables contain a null value. On the other hand, if there are more words than variables, *the last variable contains all of the remaining words*. Take a look at Figure 14.34 and you'll see what I mean.

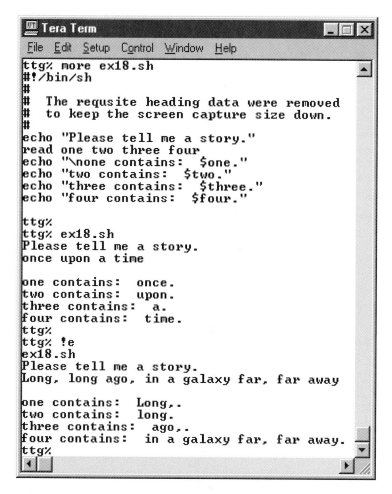

FIGURE 14.34

Using read on data from standard input.

As you can see from Figure 14.34, I prompted the user for a text stream and read those data into four variables. Then I output the values of the four variables so you could see what the script stored in each one. The first time I ran the script I gave it four words in the text string, and each variable had a single word in it. The second time I ran the script I gave it more words than there were variables. As you can see, the last variable contains all of the extra words from the string. This is a very important design consideration for your scripts.

"Suppose," you ask, "you had given it fewer words than there were variables?" Well, let's see. I'll try it for you in Figure 14.35. A careful analysis of that figure shows that if the read command receives fewer words and than there are variables, the variable or variables that don't match input words get nothing at all. They actually contain a null value. What that means to your script design is that if you are expecting a user to enter a particular number of words, you'll need to check each variable to see if it has a value. There is no shell variable like the $# awk variable that tells you how many of the variables were filled by the read command.

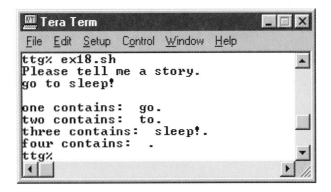

FIGURE 14.35

What happens when there are too few words?

I modified the script in Figure 14.34 to also output the number of variables that were filled. That script, and its execution, are both shown in Figure 14.36. The script in the larger of the two screen captures is the best I could come up with to count a number of variables actually read. Obviously, the script cannot read more than four variables as that's how many there are in the read statement. If none of the variables have a value, then the variable filled keeps its initial value of 0 and the script indicates that there is a problem.

There's one little trick in this script. Notice that in the test for the variable $four, the variable is enclosed in quotation marks. That allows us to test whether that variable contains a null value, one word, or a series of words separated by spaces. If I hadn't enclosed that variable in quotation marks and we had more than four words in the input string, test would have been confused. Suppose, for instance, that I entered the string "long, long ago in a galaxy far, far away" in response to the prompt. In that case the variable $four would have contained the string "in a galaxy far, far away" and the if command would have resolved to the following:

```
if test in a galaxy far, far away
```

Now, I don't know about you, but I don't know how test would resolve "in a galaxy far, far away" and neither does the shell! If you leave the quotation marks off that variable, and you enter more than four words in response to the prompt, the script will generate an error.

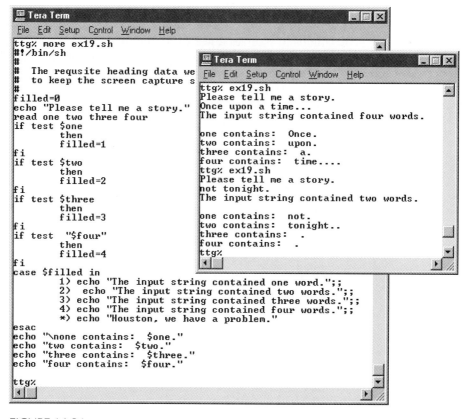

FIGURE 14.36

Counting the number of variables actually read.

A question: why don't I need to enclose the other three variables in quotation marks as well? That's right! I don't have to enclose them in quotation marks because they can, at most, contain only one word.

exit

---

exit [return status]

You may recall having used the **exit** command to leave a current login session. You can also use it to leave your script, setting a return status or return value that another script or program can evaluate. I have created a script that sets whatever number you passed to it on the command line as an exit value. Figure 14.37 shows the script and a couple of sample executions. I needed to drop into the Bourne shell to run the script because I wanted to look at the return status, and asking to see the value in $? confuses the C shell. As you can see from the script, I simply exit using the first command-line variable as the exit status.

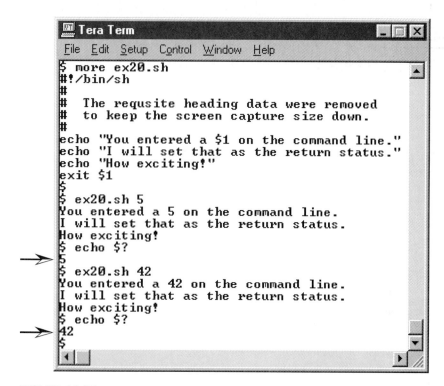

FIGURE 14.37

Setting and checking the return status.

This example shows you two things. First, I can use a variable for the exit status. Second, I can, if I want to, use a large number like 42 as an exit status even though the normal range of exit numbers is in the single digits.

The whole idea of the exit command raises another structured-coding issue. According to the rules of structured programming, any program or routine should have one entrance and *only one exit*. Following this rule requires some discipline on the part of the programmer. For example, at first blush, it seems very handy to build a program like the one shown in Figure 14.38. The script tests the number of command-line arguments, and, depending on the number (it's expecting exactly three), it generates a different message and different return status. Although this is a functional way to generate different return statuses depending upon the situation the script discovers, it absolutely and unequivocally violates the rule of structured programming we just mentioned.

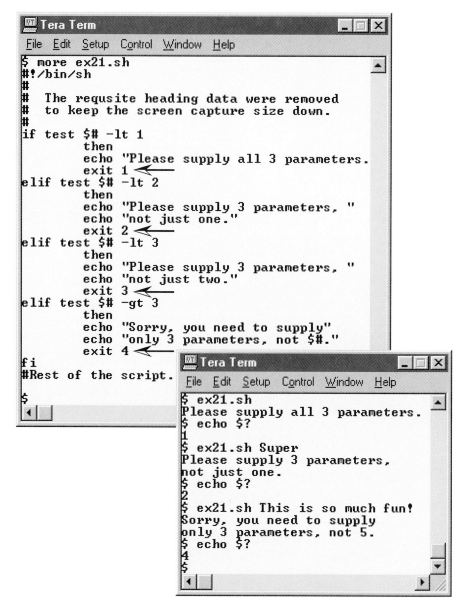

FIGURE 14.38

Script with multiple exits.

Figure 14.39 shows another way to accomplish the same thing in a structured fashion. Obviously, the code is somewhat longer, but building scripts that follow the rules of structure is an important consideration. Part of the reason the code in Figure 14.39 is longer is because I included some comments to help navigate through it. The way this code works is that first it checks for any error in the number of command-line parameters. You could check for other types of errors at that time as well. Then it checks to

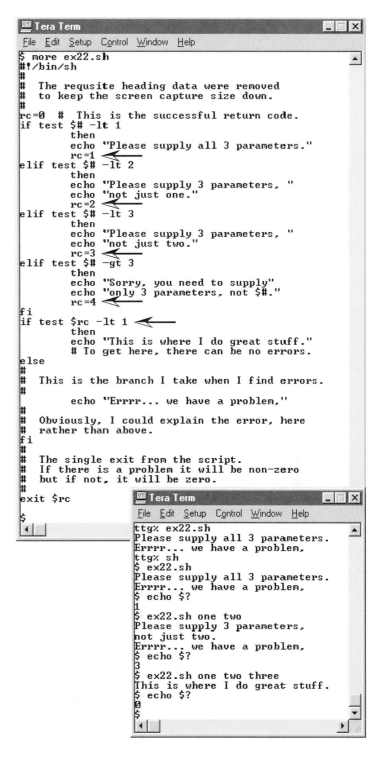

FIGURE 14.39

A script with a single exit.

see if it found any errors, indicated by non-zero value for the rc (return code) variable. If it found errors it reports that and exits, since it doesn't want to continue if there are an incorrect number of command-line parameters. If the return code remains 0, then the script found no errors and execution can continue.

Notice that there is only one exit from the script.

I realize that I should have incorporated a case structure into the script to capture and report the errors rather than building a long series of if/elif statements. Since you already know the case structure, I will leave it to you to correct that little structured programming omission when you rewrite the script. That will give you practice restructuring code, and give you a more readable example when you finish.

Remember that building scripts that play well with other scripts is a very important consideration. If other scripts are going to be able to determine whether or not your script was successful, it must set return code. You'll use the exit command to perform that particular communications operation.

sleep

---

    sleep duration

The **sleep** command allows you to suspend execution of the script for a particular number of seconds. This is useful if you want to have your script wait a certain number of seconds before it continues execution. For example, if your script waits for a particular user to sign on, or for a particular file to be created, you probably don't want your script checking on it every 30 or 40 nanoseconds. With the sleep command you can give your script some patience.

Take a look at Figure 14.40 to see how I use the sleep command to cause the script to pause for a bit. It's a terribly exciting command, especially while it's executing. It captures the time, echoes it, and then sleeps for 15 seconds. When it "wakes up" after its nap time, it again captures and displays the time. As you can see from the execution of the script, the process actually did sleep for 15 seconds.

You can't absolutely count on a sleeping process waking up after exactly the number of seconds specified, especially if you specified a large number of seconds. As we talked about in process control, if the system is busy, a sleeping process may be swapped out. Then, whenever the process wakes, it must be swapped in again before it can continue executing. The system will guarantee that your process will sleep for *at least* the number of seconds you specified, but not that it will sleep for *exactly* that number of seconds. Thus, you can use the sleep command for a very crude form of chronological process control. For example, if you want to run a particular script at about noon, and you come to school at 8:00 in the morning, you can tell your script to sleep for 14400 seconds, and it should run at about noon (4 hours times 60 minutes per hour times 60 seconds per minute). Now, remember, you can't log out for those four hours, or your child process will exit, too. There are two additional commands you can use to schedule processes on the system. You should discuss using them with your instructor or system administrator before you attempt to implement them.

The easiest scheduling command to use is the at command. You simply type at, followed by the time that which you wish the job or command to execute, and then the

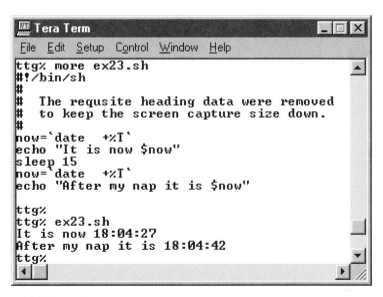

FIGURE 14.40
Using the sleep command.

command or job name. If you are allowed to use the at command, your command will be executed at approximately the time you specified.

The second way to schedule a task, usually used for a repetitive task like monitoring the system or performing maintenance, is to use the cron command (the name is derived from the word *chronological*). The cron command requires you to build a special entry in a table called crontab, which must be created using the crontab special editor. (Yes, the file and the editor both have the same name.) Building this file is a little tricky, as cron is very particular about the format of the entry in the crontab. I have several scripts that run daily or weekly on my systems to do maintenance and monitoring. Since they run on a regular schedule, I can use cron to run them.

In most systems, access to cron is even more tightly controlled than access to at. You will need to check with your system administrator or professor to see if you have access to these two commands. Since most Unix users don't schedule jobs or set up processes to run at regular intervals, we won't explore these commands any further.

Command Substitution

If you tried to duplicate the script shown in Figure 14.40, you might have run into a problem in using the date command and assigning the output to a variable. If you looked very closely, you might have noticed that a different form of punctuation surrounded the date command. Those marks are not apostrophes; rather, they are called *grave marks*. The grave mark is found under the tilde (∼), in the top left corner of the standard keyboard, and near the RETURN key on the Sun keyboard. The word *grave* is French, and pronounced like the word grave.

Using grave marks allows you to store the results of a command in a variable. That process is called **command substitution**. As you can see from the script in Figure 14.40, it is handy to be able to run a command and put the result in a variable. There are numerous uses for this particular functionality in your scripts, but you need to be careful about how you use it. For example, if you want to store a list of all the files in your directory in a variable, the output can get a trifle long. On the other hand, as you saw in Figure 14.40, storing some data in a variable makes it easy to format with your regular output tools.

You can use the grave marks to enclose an entire pipe so that you can process the data before you store them. For example, if I wanted to store those files from my directory that were scripts but not example scripts, I could build the script shown in Figure 14.41. You can see the difference between the grave mark and the tick mark, or apostrophe, very clearly in this figure since they are right next to each other. Notice that I store the output from the whole pipe in the variable `files` and then output those data.

Now let's look at doing math in the Bourne shell.

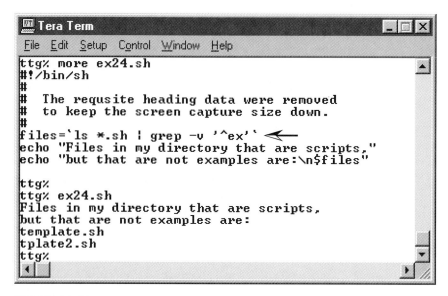

FIGURE 14.41
Using command substitution with a pipe.

expr

```
expr value1 operator value2 [operator value3...]
```

The most common use for the **expr** command is to perform arithmetic operations. However, as we shall soon see, it can perform both relational and logical tests, as well as arithmetic. It's important to understand that the Bourne shell does *integer* math. To badly paraphrase a Mel Brooks movie, "Decimal places, we don't need no stinking decimal places!" So if you want to divide 10 by 3, the answer is 3 in the Bourne shell, not 3.333. By the same token, if you want to divide 2 by 3, the answer is 0. We deal in whole numbers in the Bourne shell and leave fractional computing to programming languages and the like.

Suppose I want to divide 10 by 3. You can see how to do that in Figure 14.42. In this figure, I made all the `expr` errors I could think of. The best way to break `expr` is to

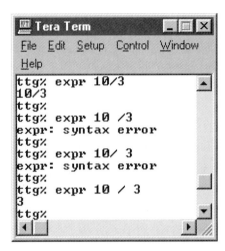

FIGURE 14.42

Using expr to perform arithmetic.

forget to put spaces between *each of the elements* on the command line. Notice that if I put no spaces in the mathematical expression at all, expr simply echos it back for me. If I forget one of the two spaces that surround the mathematical operator, expr generates a syntax error. And, finally, when I correctly space the operators, expr performs the integer division perfectly.

It's all well and good to be able to do simple math, but suppose I want to be able to use variables to store the results of certain mathematical operations and then use those variables in other mathematical operations. Let's see, do I know a way to store the output from a command in a variable? Gee, what about command substitution! You will often use command substitution to capture the results of an expr in a variable so you can use it later. Consider my mathematical expertise, as demonstrated in Figure 14.43.

The first thing to notice about Figure 14.43 is that I am running in the Bourne shell. The second thing to notice is that I have to protect the asterisk each time I use it.

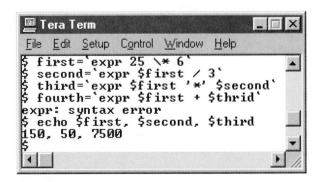

FIGURE 14.43

Using command substitution with expr.

The grave marks are no protection from the shell; they simply capture the output of the command and store it in a variable. In the first expr I used the backslash to protect the asterisk. In the third expr I used tick marks to protect the asterisk. Any of the protection tools (quotation marks, tick marks, or the backslash) work within grave marks. I use the backslash because it is one keystroke as opposed to two.

The error in the last expr is a little confusing. It tells me that I have made a syntax error, but I don't see what I did wrong. Ah, but looking a little more closely, I notice that I spelled third thrid. Since the Bourne shell creates a new variable each time I use a new name, it dutifully created the variable thrid and assigned it a null value. Then expr tried to perform an addition of the value stored at second with a null value. Since expr isn't comfortable working with null values, it calls it a syntax error. You must remember to initialize any variables in scripts that you will pass to expr. You can see what I mean by looking at the script in Figure 14.44.

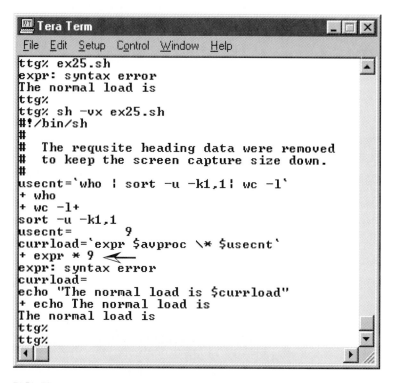

FIGURE 14.44

Results of failing to initialize a variable.

When I tried to run the script that tells me the average load on my system, I suddenly encountered syntax a error in expr. Since I couldn't figure out what the error was by looking at the code <ha ha>, I ran my friendly shell debugger and looked at the output. It's interesting to look at how the shell displays the parts of pipe. Since all three processes are in pseudo-simultaneous execution the shell sort of confuses them.

The important thing to notice is how the expr command is displayed. Notice that there's an operator but only a single value. That's because I forgot to initialize the value for the variable avproc.

In Figure 14.45 I set the average process count for each user to 4—that's the average on our system—and reran the script to see if it would work better. I then reran the script using the debugger just to see what was going on. (That's another useful implementation of sh with the -vx options.) As you can see from the output, the script calculates the value for the current load just as I expected it to.

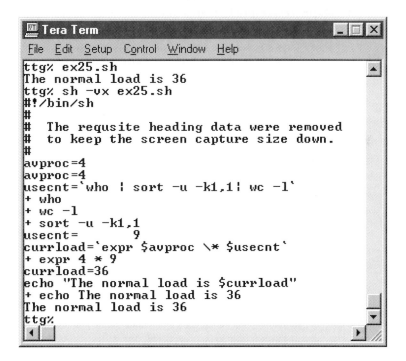

FIGURE 14.45

Running the repaired script from Figure 14.44.

I mentioned earlier that expr could be used with relational operators as well as arithmetic ones. Consider the example in Figure 14.46. Here the expr command did a fine job of testing a string against a known value. Notice that even using expr did not solve the problem of a null value when there was no first command-line parameter entered. It seems that expr returned a null value rather than a 1 or 0.

Table 14.7 lists the comparison operators you can use with expr. Remember, unlike test if the expr command evaluates True, the result value is set to 1, and if the command evaluates False, the result value is set to 0.

The third type of operation that expr can perform for you is called a *logical operation*. You can ask expr to perform a logical **OR** on argument 1 and argument 2. If argument 1 has a non-zero (or non-null) value, expr will return its contents. If the value of argument 1 is either 0 or null, expr will return the contents of argument 2.

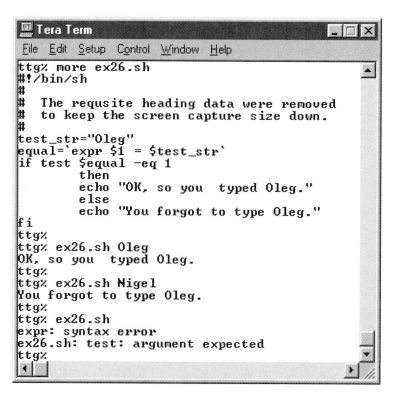

FIGURE 14.46

Using expr to evaluate a string.

TABLE 14.7 Relational Operators Available with expr

Operator	Meaning
=	The arguments are equal. The arguments can be strings or numbers. If they are strings, a < z and A < Z.
!=	The arguments are not equal.
>	The first argument is greater than the second.
<	The first argument is less than the second.
>=	The first argument is greater than or equal to the second.
<=	The first argument is less than or equal to the second.

You can also ask expr to perform the equivalent of a logical **AND** on argument 1 and argument 2. In this case, if argument 1 and argument 2 both contain non-zero (or non-null) values, expr will return the value of argument 1. If either argument 1 or argument 2 is zero or null, expr returns a value of 0. Note: zero does not indicate success here but rather that one of the two arguments has a 0 value.

The third type of logical operation that expr can perform is something like a grep in which argument 2 is the pattern you're going to search for *in argument 1*. If expr finds a match, it will return either the number of characters that match or the portion of the first argument that matches. If you want expr to return that part of the first argument that matches the second argument, you must enclose the second argument in protected parentheses.

Okay, lots of words, but let's see how it works. I've combined all three of the different types of logical operations in Figure 14.47. In the first test I used a logical **OR** (note that it must be protected) to see if argument 1 was either empty or not. Since argument 1 was not empty, expr returned the value of (arg1), which I stored in the variable first.

In the second test I asked expr whether arg1 and arg3 both had data in them. Since arg3 was null, expr returned a value of 0, indicating that one of the two variables contained no data. (But it didn't tell me which one.)

In the third test I used expr in its pseudo-grep mode, and asked whether arg1 contained the string stored in arg2. By enclosing arg2 in protected parentheses, I directed expr to return the part of the first argument that matched the second.

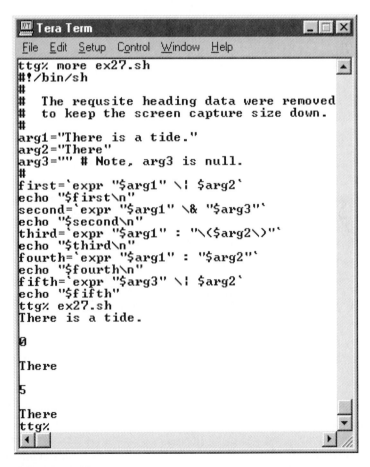

FIGURE 14.47

Using the logical forms of expr.

The fourth test was very nearly a duplicate of the third test, the difference being that I asked expr to simply return *the number* of characters that matched.

The fifth test was similar to the first test except that the first argument was null, so expr returned the value of the second argument.

You can do a number of useful things with the expr command, but in 95 percent of the code I've read and written, it's used to do math.

So far we've talked about two of the three building blocks we used to create programs. We've talked about sequence, with many commands, and we've considered selection using the if and case structures. All that's left to finish our triad of building blocks is to learn the tools for iteration. There are actually three different looping structures in Bourne shell scripting, but we'll discuss only two of them. As you learned back in awk, the logical UNTIL looping structure does not conform to structured methodology, so we won't consider it. There are two general forms of loops, a *counted* loop, used when you know the number of iterations you want, and the *logical* or *conditional* loop, used when you want the loop to execute only while a particular condition is true.

for

```
for variable [in list]
do
        commands to excute
done
```

The **for** loop, or **for** command, initializes a counted looping structure. The actual code to be executed is contained between the do statement and done statement. Everything between these two statements is executed once for each variable in the list (assuming, of course, that you don't have embedded iteration or selection statements). The variable, which must be specified after the for statement, takes on the value of each of the elements in the list one after the other. When the variable has taken on the value of each element in the list and executed all the commands in the body of the loop for each element, the looping structure exits passing control to the statement following the done.

The reason the for loop is called a counted loop is because you can count the number of times loop will iterate based on the number of elements in the list. Figure 14.48 shows an example of an amazingly simple little loop. In this for loop the variable word takes on the values of "all", "eve", "ages", and "wibbley". For each different value the variable takes, the loop runs a grep, searching for that string in the first command-line argument, which we assume is a file.

Look at the lower part of Figure 14.48 and you can see that I ran the script against one of the poems. The output isn't terribly useful, since I don't know which word the grep was looking for or which words it didn't find, but the idea here is to show you the simplest possible for loop you could create. Now let's make it a little more useful.

Figure 14.49 shows a for loop with a little longer output and a little longer script, but it does do a better job of both showing the output and, as I'm sure you've noticed, checking to make sure that the input file is actually a data file. You can see how we use commands to build scripts from this example.

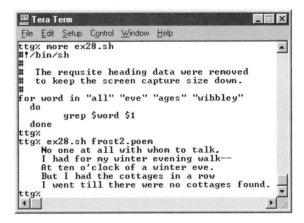

FIGURE 14.48

An extremely simple for loop.

FIGURE 14.49

A more useful for loop.

Now consider the loop shown in Figure 14.50. This script uses some of the options of the test command to check each file, passed as a command-line argument, to see whether it has contents and whether it's a directory. The script will process up to nine files, because only nine command-line variables are directly addressable without invoking one of the tricks of the Bourne shell. "What tricks?" you ask. Wait just a moment

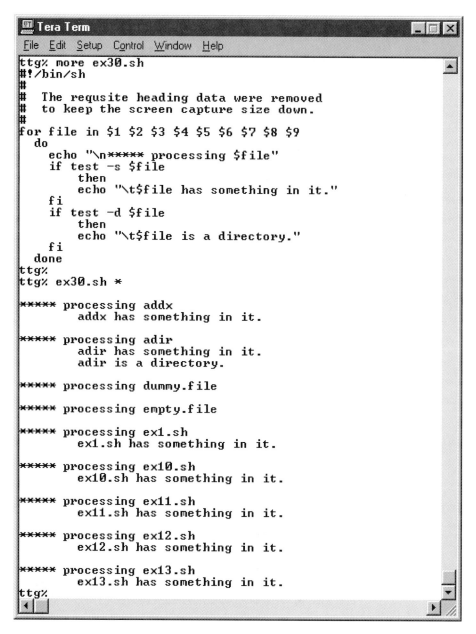

FIGURE 14.50

Using command-line arguments as input to a for loop.

and I'll show you. Notice that if the file passed to the script in Figure 14.50 is empty, all we see is the one line from the script that tells the name of the file.

It's very common to build scripts with for loops that read and process command-line arguments. It's so common, in fact, that the developers of the Unix operating system actually created a special version of the for loop that reads command-line variables automagically. Take a look at the script in Figure 14.51. This script is terribly short. I wrote it simply to show you the first trick, which allows you to access more than nine command-line arguments. Look at the format of the for command. Notice that the "in list" portion seems to be missing. If you code a for statement without the associated "in" portion, the for statement will use *all of the command-line arguments as its "list."*

Now take a look at the output from the script in Figure 14.51, and you'll notice that the script processed 23 files! That means the script read 23 command-line arguments!

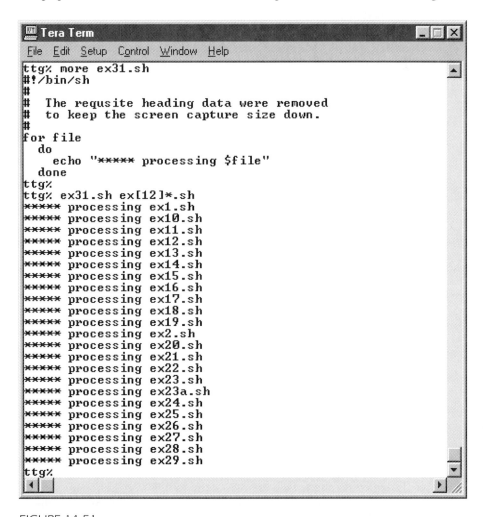

FIGURE 14.51

One "trick" to access more than nine command-line arguments.

No, it didn't address each one by name, but it did put each command-line argument into the variable file. That's one way to get around the limitation of nine addressable command-line variables. I'll show you another way when we look at the next looping structure.

continue

---

continue [count]

You can use the **continue** command to stop processing the current value of the variable in the body of a loop and go get the next value for the variable from the "list" (either implied or actual). I have built an example script to show that in Figure 14.52. This script reads all the command-line variables since there is no "in list" portion of the for command. It checks to see if the current value for the file variable is a directory. If so, the script executes the continue command and gets the next value for the variable file. If the value for the variable file is not a directory, it "processes" that file.

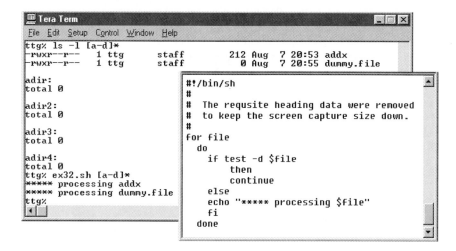

FIGURE 14.52

Using the continue command in a loop.

I did an ls in the figure to show you the names of the files that start with "a" through "d." Then I ran the script against that same range of files. As you can see, the script "processed" just those two files, those that were not directories.

Using continue to skip the rest of the loop is very handy in many data-processing situations. You can also specify a number after the continue, and the loop will skip that number of values for the variable. Skipping multiple input lines is useful when you are working with a file where, for example, each record encompasses multiple lines.

You could skip all the lines in a particular record by using the `continue` command followed by the number of lines that compose a record.

The `continue` command allows you to continue execution of the loop with the next record. But suppose you want to quit executing the loop altogether, yet not exit from the script?

break

`break [count]`

The **break** command allows you to exit from the loop, stopping the processing of the current value in the variable and continuing execution with the first command following the loop. As with the `continue` command, you can specify a count with the `break` command telling it how many levels of loops to exit from, assuming you are in a nested looping situation.

Figure 14.53 shows an example of how the simple `break` works. The script takes as input all the command-line variables, testing each one to ensure that it has actual contents. (Note how the ! works as a logical NOT instead of history, because we are playing in the

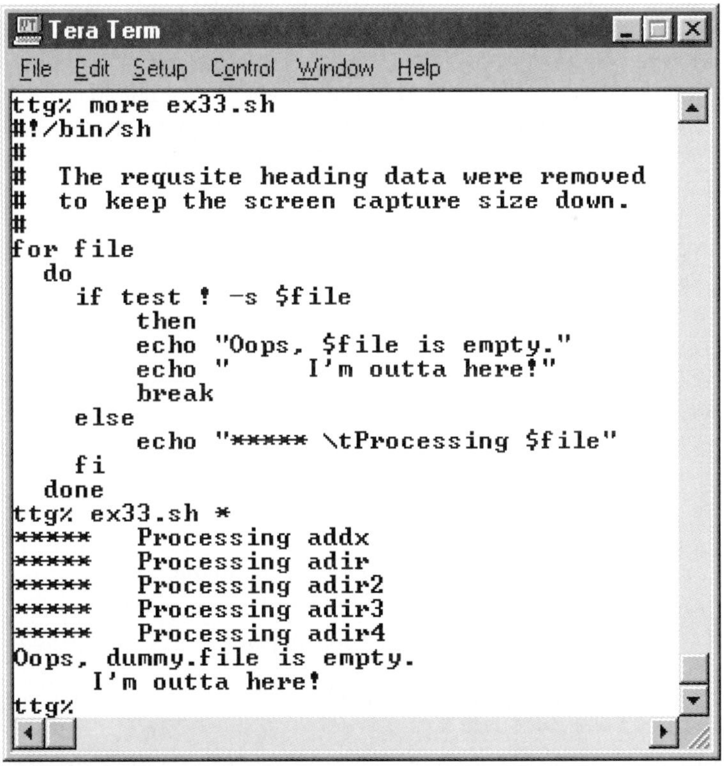

```
ttg% more ex33.sh
#!/bin/sh
#
#   The requsite heading data were removed
#   to keep the screen capture size down.
#
for file
  do
    if test ! -s $file
        then
        echo "Oops, $file is empty."
        echo "    I'm outta here!"
        break
    else
        echo "***** \tProcessing $file"
    fi
  done
ttg% ex33.sh *
*****    Processing addx
*****    Processing adir
*****    Processing adir2
*****    Processing adir3
*****    Processing adir4
Oops, dummy.file is empty.
    I'm outta here!
ttg%
```

FIGURE 14.53

Using the break command.

Bourne shell.) As soon as the script detects an empty file, it outputs the error message and then exits from the loop using the `break` command. Since there are no more commands after the loop, in this example the script exits right after the `break` command executes.

There's not a lot to say about the `break` command other than that its extremely useful if you need to get out of a loop without leaving the shell script. (The `exit` command would send you out of the whole script.) Depending on the logic of the particular situation you encounter `continue` or `break` will almost always serve you as the ideal tools to leave the loop so you won't need to use the `exit` command. Remember, you should have only one exit from your script.

Now that you are familiar with the counted loop, let's look at the conditional loop.

while

```
while condition
  do
    command(s)
  done
```

Many times the `for` loop will meet your needs perfectly, but not when you don't know exactly how many times you want the loop to execute but only *the conditions under which you want to loop to execute*. Then you need to use a conditional loop rather than a counted one. Two different types of conditional loops are available in the Bourne shell. We will discuss only one, the WHILE loop (`while` command), because the other loop, the UNTIL loop, is not considered good structure. If you encounter a script you must maintain that uses an `until` command, try to modify the logic to use a `while` command instead.

In every instance that I have ever seen in production, the condition specified in a `while` loop uses the `test` command. (You may encounter loops built with the `while 1` structure. They are infinite loops and will run forever. I am not taking those into account.) I suppose you could use the `expr` command, but I have never seen this done in production.

I have coded a sample `while` loop for you in Figure 14.54. Since there's no way of knowing how many times I need to cycle this loop, I can't use a counted loop but must use a conditional one. Each time I cycle through the loop I subtract 2 from the value the user supplied to the script as the first command-line argument. The loop continues processing as long as the value in the variable is greater than 0. When the subtraction in the `expr` command drops the value below 0, the test fails and control passes to the command following the loop. Since there is no command following the loop, the script exits.

The first two executions of the script work as we expect them to. Subtraction takes place, counting down the value in the variable, and when it reaches or drops below 0, the script exits.

It's the third execution script that is most exciting. When the script is passed a zero value, *the loop never executes*. That's the importance of the logical structure of a `while` loop. In a `while` loop the condition is tested ***before*** the body of the loop is executed. In essence, a `while` loop asks the question, "Shall I execute the commands?" In contrast, the `until` logical structure executes the commands once and then asks the

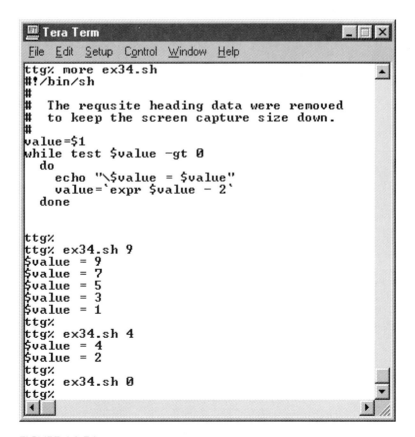

FIGURE 14.54

A sample while loop.

question, "Shall I execute the commands *again*?" From a structured point of view, it's always best to control any possible execution of the commands within a loop. That's why the while structure is preferred over the until structure.

---

shift [n]

A few pages ago I told you there were two ways to get around the limitation of nine addressable command line variables. The first way was the for loop without a list. Figure 14.55 shows you the second way, using the **shift** command. In addition, Figure 14.55 shows another use of the while loop. The script is rather long. Let's look at the output first. As you can see, I passed 16 command-line variables to the script. The script processed all 16 of them, *loading each one into the command-line variable* $1. That's right, the script addresses only command-line variable $1, and that variable takes on 16 different values. Reading the output from the script, we see that it reports that number of command-line variables, the current value of the command-line variable $1, and it also checks to see if the file represented by the variable $1 is empty or if it contains the word for. Okay, so it's a somewhat bizarre script, but it illustrates the concept in fairly straightforward fashion.

Tera Term

File Edit Setup Control Window Help

```
ttg% more ex35.sh
#!/bin/sh
#
#                Demonstrate the while and shift
#
while test $# -gt 0
do
  echo "Command line var count: $# \c"
  echo "current \$1: $1"
    if test ! -s $1
        then echo "$1 is an empty file!"
        else
          grep for $1 > /dev/null
          if test $? -eq 0
                then
                echo "** \c"
                echo ">>$1 \"for\" is in $1 \c"
                echo "** "
                fi
          fi
#
#  Here comes the magic!
#
        shift
done
ttg% !e
ex35.sh ex[2]*.sh ex3[135]*.sh
Command line var count: 16 current $1: ex2.sh
Command line var count: 15 current $1: ex20.sh
Command line var count: 14 current $1: ex21.sh
Command line var count: 13 current $1: ex22.sh
Command line var count: 12 current $1: ex222.sh
ex222.sh is an empty file!
Command line var count: 11 current $1: ex23.sh
Command line var count: 10 current $1: ex23a.sh
Command line var count: 9 current $1: ex24.sh
Command line var count: 8 current $1: ex25.sh
Command line var count: 7 current $1: ex26.sh
** >>ex26.sh "for" is in ex26.sh **
Command line var count: 6 current $1: ex27.sh
Command line var count: 5 current $1: ex28.sh
** >>ex28.sh "for" is in ex28.sh **
Command line var count: 4 current $1: ex29.sh
** >>ex29.sh "for" is in ex29.sh **
Command line var count: 3 current $1: ex31.sh
** >>ex31.sh "for" is in ex31.sh **
Command line var count: 2 current $1: ex33.sh
** >>ex33.sh "for" is in ex33.sh **
Command line var count: 1 current $1: ex35.sh
** >>ex35.sh "for" is in ex35.sh **
ttg%
```

FIGURE 14.55

Another magical way to bypass the limit of nine command-line arguments.

Now let's look at the code, which is duplicated in Figure 14.56. There's little here that should be new to you, but the figure illustrates how we can combine several commands into a more "interesting" script. Notice that the loop executes as long as we have at least one command-line argument. It also tests to see whether the first command-line argument, assumedly a file, has any contents. If it has contents, then it checks to see if it contains the word for. Look carefully at the grep command. It redirects its output to the null device, and the script tests whether the return status of the command is equal to 0, indicating success. If the grep was successful (the return code is 0), then I know that the file currently represented by $1 contains the word for. I don't care how many times the word occurs, and I don't want to see the lines that contain it; I just want to know if the word appears in the file. If the test fails, then the file doesn't contain the word for.

The line following the if block contains the magic. The shift command performs a *shift left logical* on the command-line arguments. What that means is that the current value of $1 is lost, and the current value of $2 shifts left, or numerically downward, and is stored in $1. The current value in $3 shifts left and is stored in $2. The current value in $4 shifts left and is stored in $3, and so on. Finally, the tenth command-line argument shifts into the variable $9.

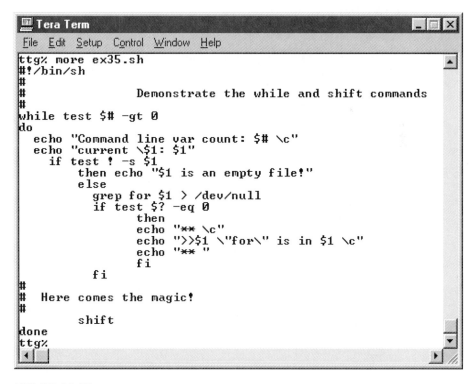

FIGURE 14.56

Another look at the shift y magical script.

Each time the shift command executes, all of the variable values move left one position. It's the Bourne shell's version of musical chairs. That's why the value of $1 changes each time we cycle through the loop. If you specify a number after the shift command, it will begin shifting with the command line parameter you specify. For example, if you were to code shift 3 the shift command would shift $3 to $1, $4 to $2, and so on. If you don't specify a number, shift will begin shifting with $2 to $1.

Now you know two different ways to get around the limit of nine addressable command-line arguments. In addition, you have seen a number of shell scripts, many quite simple, that illustrate different ways to perform activities in the Bourne shell. Reading about scripting, and looking at my scripts, are fine ways to begin to learn to write shell scripts. However, just like riding a bicycle, the only way you can learn to write shell scripts is to write them.

I would like to share one last technique with you before you set off to build your own scripts. This is a handy little trick that has been very useful to me. I realize that I could write a whole other book just on scripting with examples—maybe someday. For now, look at Figure 14.57 and notice the technique I used to send data from the command line to the

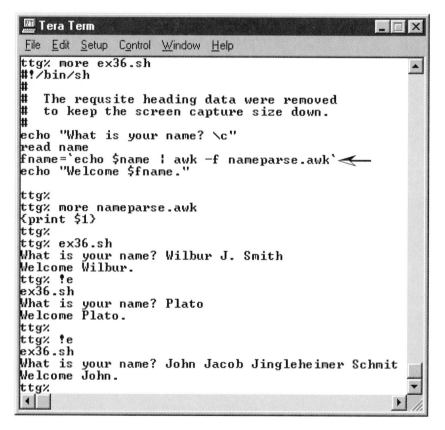

FIGURE 14.57

Sending data down a pipe.

awk process. This is the technique I want to share with you. It is in the third line of code. You already know how to prompt the user and read data, but how do you pass those data to another script or program? Well, if you want to pass data to a script called from your script, you can pass the data on the command line of the new script. But what of programs like awk? The trick is to remember that those programs, since wise Unix folks have built them, are filters. They read from standard input and write to standard output. That means you can pipe data to them!

In the script in Figure 14.57 I captured the user's name and wanted to parse it using an awk script. To pass the data to the awk, I echoed the value of the variable down a pipe. Very useful little technique, that. Use it wisely.

As I said before, there are dozens if not hundreds of cool scripts I could share and we could dissect, but now it's time for you to build your own scripts. Having come this far, you are potential Unix wizards. Welcome—and, oh yes, have fun!

KEY TERMS

built-in commands
built-in shell variables
command substitution
conditional execution
shebang
system variables
syntax
user variables

NEW COMMANDS

```
do
done
expr
env
sh
sleep
test
break
case
continue
exit
export
for
if
let
read
readonly
```

```
shift
until
while
```

REVIEW QUESTIONS

14.1 List the eight built-in shell variables.

14.2 How many command-line variables are directly addressable in scripts?

14.3 Explain the difference between $* and "$@".

14.4 Describe the purpose of the readonly command.

14.5 Explain how you can allow a child process have access to contents of user-created variables.

14.6 What is the purpose of the env command?

14.7 How can you change the values of the command-line variables within a script?

14.8 On your system, examine the other shell variables (not the built-in ones) available to you.

14.9 Explain what a built-in command is and how it differs from one that is not a built-in.

14.10 Describe the different ways to have the echo command not add a newline to the end of the output string.

14.11 List and describe five output formatting characters you can use with the echo command.

14.12 What are the parts of a complete if block?

14.13 What is the preferred form of the test command? Why is it preferred?

14.14 What is the difference in the outcome of the following two ifs?

```
a. if test -d $1
        then
        echo "$1 is a directory."
        elif test -w $1
             then
             echo "You have write access to $1."
    fi

b: if test -d $1
        then
        echo "$1 is a directory."
    fi
    if test -w $1
             then
             echo "You have write access to $1."
    fi
```

14.15 List three string-comparison tests.

14.16 Describe the "classic error" programmers make when comparing two numbers.

14.17 Explain the cases where you would use a case structure or a nested if structure.

14.18 State the rule of structured programming that talks about exits from a script.

EXERCISES

14.1 Look up the definition of the following terms in *The Jargon Dictionary*:
bogon
Unix
Kluge

14.2 Write a script that lists the contents of each of the built-in shell variables. Test your script.

14.3 Create your own version of the addx script, but make yours accept and change the permissions on any number of command-line parameters, not just one.

14.4 Prove that a child process can have access to the contents of a user-defined variable in the parent process but cannot modify those contents, *in the parent process*.

14.5 Change the value of an environmental variable.

14.6 Write a script to demonstrate that you can change the value of the command-line variables within the bounds of the script.

14.7 Demonstrate the various formatting options available with the echo command.

14.8 Create a script that details all the attributes of a file passed to it from the command line.

14.9 Create a script that tests all of the different string comparisons. Run your script and make sure you understand the difference between a zero-byte string and a null string.

14.10 Fix the script in Figure 14.23 to account for *all* the states $1 could assume.

14.11 Correct the script shown in Figure 14.39, replacing the if/elif series with a case structure. Test your solution!

14.12 Craft a script that uses the case structure to determine which of five different letters the user entered. If the user didn't enter one of your chosen letters, display an error. After you get your case script working, move the * pattern to the first matching pattern and see what happens.

14.13 Create a script that will read up to five variables after prompting the user for them. This script should have only one read statement. Then echo the values read into the variables. Try the script with 1, 2, 3, 4, 5, 6, and 7 input words to see what happens.

14.14 Build a script called nap.sh that sleeps for the number of seconds specified by the user when you prompt her for that number. (Note: When you test your script, remember that 10 seconds is a long time to wait for the script to come back!)

14.15 Construct a script that sets up to three different return codes based upon the input from the user. Test your script to ensure that it sets the return code correctly.

14.16 Build a script that stores the output of at least three commands in shell variables and then displays them.

14.17 Write a script that uses expr to perform a series of arithmetic operations, using the results of one operation in the next.

14.18 Now build another script that demonstrates the use of the expr command as a logical device and evaluates the relationship of a couple of strings. Display your results.

14.19 Craft a script that will use up to four command-line arguments as input to a script that will look for each of the arguments in a file. Make sure your script will take only four command-line arguments.

14.20 Modify the script you built in Exercise 19 to take any number of command-line arguments and use each as a search tool. Also have your script ensure that there is at least one command-line argument.

14.21 Now modify the script you built in Exercise 20 to take any number of command-line arguments that contain files, and look for the words for and Unix in them. If the user passes your script a directory or empty file, skip processing and go to the next argument.

14.22 Construct a script that will take as input any number of different words as command-line arguments. If the user enters the word "done," the script will exit. Otherwise, the script will check to see if the word is in a test file.

14.23 Write a script that will prompt the user for a number, add that number to a total, and continue prompting the user until the total exceeds 1,000.

14.24 Build a script that cycles through an unknown number of command-line arguments, always addressing the current argument as $1, and reporting whether the argument was greater than, equal to, or less than 42.

14.25 Modify the script shown in Figure 14.57 to parse the name and report the first and last names. Do take Mr. Schmit into account as well.

Playing with Numbering Systems

In order to understand and use some features of the Unix operating system, it is important to understand some features of numbering systems. First, some definitions:

1. A *numbering system* is a collection of rules and glyphs, or symbols, that describe the process of enumeration.
2. A *number* is a concept or idea that represents a particular quantity.
3. Each numbering system has *numerals* that stand for specific numbers. For example, 9, four, 00101010, DA4, and XIX are all composed of numerals.

Some Common Features of Numbering Systems

1. The largest single number (or digit) has a value that is 1 less than the base. (In the base-10 numbering system the largest numeral is 9; in the base-2 numbering system, the largest digit is 1.)
2. Each numbering system we will be discussing has the same number of unique digits as the base.

    a. Binary (base-2): **0, 1**.
    b. Octal (base-8): **0, 1, 2, 3, 4, 5, 6, 7**
    c. Decimal: **0, 1, 2, 3, 4, 5, 6, 7, 8, 9**
    d. Hexadecimal: **0, 1, 2, 3, 4, 5, 6, 7, 8, 9, A, B, C, D, E, F**

3. The position of a digit within the number represents a multiple of the base. (Note: This is true for all numbering systems that use a 0 to hold place. It is not, however, true for Roman numerals, so we shall not consider them in this discussion.)
4. Moving from right to left ($\leftarrow$) across the digits in a number, each digit position represents the base raised to the next higher power, starting at 0. In other words, that position -1 power. For example, in base-10, the third digit, the hundreds position, represents the base raised to a power of 2.

The accompanying chart shows the positional value for each of the first six digits in the decimal numbering system.

hundred thousands	ten thousands	thousands	hundreds	tens	ones
10^5	10^4	10^3	10^2	10^1	10^0

Using this methodology to calculate the value (by multiplication and addition) of a number like 34502, we have

$$
\begin{array}{rcr}
3 \times 10^4 &=& 30{,}000 \\
+4 \times 10^3 &=& 4{,}000 \\
+5 \times 10^2 &=& 500 \\
+0 \times 10^1 &=& 0 \\
+2 \times 10^0 &=& 2 \\
\hline
& & 34{,}502
\end{array}
$$

This same technique can be used to calculate the decimal value of a number in any other numbering system that uses positional notation. Here is an example using the binary numbering system:

Given the number 10111011, we can use positional notation to determine the value in decimal:

2^7	2^6	2^5	2^4	2^3	2^2	2^1	2^0
(128)	(64)	(32)	(16)	(8)	(4)	(2)	(1)

Using the multiply-and-add method, we find that the decimal value for the binary number is

$$
\begin{array}{rr}
1 * 2^7 & 128 \\
+0 * 2^6 & 0 \\
+1 * 2^5 & 32 \\
+1 * 2^4 & 16 \\
+1 * 2^3 & 8 \\
+0 * 2^2 & 0 \\
+1 * 2^1 & 2 \\
+1 * 2^0 & 1 \\
\hline
& 187 \text{ (decimal)}
\end{array}
$$

This method, while somewhat slow, will work for any base.

Inter-base Conversion Hints

Counting in Various Bases

A number is composed of one or more digits. Each base has *b* unique digits used to represent numbers. (For example, base-2 has two digits, 1 and 0; base-8 has eight unique digits 0, 1, 2, 3, 4, 5, 6, and 7, etc.) These digits are used in each position to form numbers. Let's count from 1 to 20 in each of the four bases so we can see how these digits are used.

Decimal	Binary	Octal	Hex
1	1	1	1
2	10	2	2
3	11	3	3
4	100	4	4
5	101	5	5
6	110	6	6
7	111	7	7
8	1000	10	8
9	1001	11	9
10	1010	12	A
11	1011	13	B
12	1100	14	C
13	1101	15	D
14	1110	16	E
15	1111	17	F
16	10000	20	10
17	10001	21	11
18	10010	22	12
19	10011	23	13
20	10100	24	14

Positional Notation

Positional notation is the term that explains why the relative value of a digit depends on the location of that digit within a series of numbers. The general formula for positional notation and place value is

$$B^n \ldots B^7\ B^6\ B^5\ B^4\ B^3\ B^2\ B^1\ B^0$$

where B is the base, and B^2 means squared, or raised to the power of 2.

This translates into the following place values:

Binary	2^8	2^7	2^6	2^5	2^4	2^3	2^2	2^1	2^0
Decimal value	**256**	**128**	**64**	**32**	**16**	**8**	**4**	**2**	**1**
This Number	**1**	**1**	**0**	**1**	**1**	**1**	**0**	**1**	**1**

Means $1*256\ +\ 1*128\ +\ 0*64\ +\ 1*32\ +\ 1*16\ +\ 1*8\ +\ 0*4\ +\ 1*2\ +\ 1*1$

Or   443 decimal.

A subset of the place values are:

Binary	2^{10}	2^9	2^8	2^7	2^6	2^5	2^4	2^3	2^2	2^1	2^0
	1024	**512**	**256**	**128**	**64**	**32**	**16**	**8**	**4**	**2**	**1**

Octal	8^7	8^6	8^5	8^4	8^3	8^2	8^1	8^0
	2097152	**262144**	**32768**	**4096**	**512**	**64**	**8**	**1**

Decimal	10^7	10^6	10^5	10^4	10^3	10^2	10^1	10^0
	10000000	**1000000**	**100000**	**10000**	**1000**	**100**	**10**	**1**

Hex	16^6	16^5	16^4	16^3	16^2	16^1	16^0
	16777216	**1048576**	**65536**	**4096**	**256**	**16**	**1**

Converting from Binary to Octal

Since each octal digit can be represented by exactly 3 bits, all you need do to convert from binary to octal is divide the binary number into groups of three digits, starting from the right. Then write the octal equivalent under each set of three numbers.

Following is an example using this simple binary number:

110101010101100010111110101010110

Binary	110	101	010	101	100	010	111	110	101	010	110
Octal	6	5	2	5	4	2	7	6	5	2	6

Converting from Binary to Hexadecimal

Hex works very much like octal, except each digit needs exactly 4 bits to represent it. That means that to convert from binary to hexadecimal, you will need to divide the binary number into groups of four digits, again starting from the right. Then write the hexadecimal equivalent under each set of four digits.

Following is an example using this binary number:

1111011101101011011101001001011010001001

(Notice that I had to add a leading zero to make 4 here.)

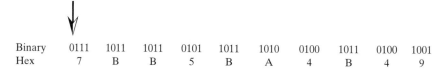

Binary	0111	1011	1011	0101	1011	1010	0100	1011	0100	1001
Hex	7	B	B	5	B	A	4	B	4	9

Converting from Octal to Binary

Converting from octal to binary is just the reverse of the conversion from binary to octal. Rewrite the octal number with some space between the digits, and then write the *three*-digit octal representation for each digit below it. Remember that you must always use three digits. The numbers 1 and 2 must be represented by 001 and 010, respectively.

Following is an example using this octal number:

2364700321

Rewritten:	2	3	6	7	0	0	3	2	1
In binary:	**010**	**011**	**110**	**111**	**000**	**000**	**011**	**010**	**001**

Converting from Hexadecimal to Binary

Converting from hexadecimal to binary is just the reverse of the binary-to-hexadecimal conversion process. Rewrite the hex number with some space between the digits, and then write the *four*-digit hex representation for each digit below it. Remember that you must always use four digits. The numbers 1 and 2 must be represented by 0001 and 0010, respectively.

Following is an example using this hexadecimal number:

AF3679DD002

Rewritten:	A	F	3	7	6	9	D	D	0	0	2
In binary:	**1010**	**1111**	**0011**	**0111**	**0101**	**1001**	**1101**	**1101**	**0000**	**0000**	**0010**

Converting from Hexadecimal to Octal, or Octal to Hexadecimal

Converting from hexadecimal to octal, or vice versa, is again a simple mechanical conversion. To convert from hexadecimal to octal, simply rewrite the hexadecimal number with more spaces, as we did previously, then write the four-digit binary representations. Divide the resulting binary number into groups of three binary digits, and write the corresponding octal number.

Following is an example using this hexadecimal number:

AF36D02

Rewritten:	A	F	3	6	D	0	2			
In binary 4s:	**1010**	**1111**	**0011**	**0101**	**1101**	**0000**	**0010**			

Regrouped in binary 3s:	**001**	**010**	**111**	**100**	**110**	**101**	**110**	**100**	**000**	**010**
In octal:	1	2	7	4	6	5	6	4	0	2

So we can see that AF36D02$_{16}$ is equal to 1274656402$_8$.

Going the other way, let's start with this octal number:

12773244

Rewritten:	1	2	7	7	3	2	4	4
In binary 3s:	**001**	**010**	**111**	**111**	**011**	**010**	**100**	**100**

Regrouped in binary 4s:	**0010**	**1011**	**1111**	**0110**	**1010**	**0100**
In hex:	2	B	F	6	A	4

So we can see that 12773244$_8$ is equal to 2BF6A4$_{16}$.

Converting from Hexadecimal to Decimal

Now we need to look at a couple of *mathematical* conversions. Unlike the three bases we have played with so far—binary, octal, and hexadecimal—the base-10 numbering system does not lend itself to clean, mechanical conversions. To convert hexadecimal to decimal, you need to begin by multiplying each of the hexadecimal numbers by their positional values as expressed in decimals. Then you must add the resulting values to calculate the value of the number. Let's look at a decimal example first:

1254 (one thousand, two hundred and fifty-four)
means

	Multiply		Add Up
	$1 * 10^3$	or	1000
+	$2 * 10^2$	+	200
+	$5 * 10^1$	+	50
+	$4 * 10^0$	+	4
			1254

The same is true of the other bases. (You might want to check back on page 636 for the positional translation table.)

For example, starting with the hexadecimal number,

A4D31

we look at the decimal value of each digit in relation to its place value:

		or		
	$A * 16^4$	or	$10 * 65536$	**655360**
+	$4 * 16^3$	+	$4 * 4096$	**16384**
+	$D * 16^2$	+	$13 * 256$	**3328**
+	$3 * 16^1$	+	$3 * 16$	**48**
+	$1 * 16^0$	+	$1 * 1$	**1**
				675121 in decimal

Converting from Octal to Decimal

You follow the same process converting from octal to decimal as you did in converting from hexadecimal to decimal. First you multiply the digits times their place values, then you add up the resulting numbers.

For example, starting with the octal number,

72435$_8$

We calculate the decimal value for each digit depending on its place value:

	or		
$7 * 8^4$	or	$7 * 4096$	**28762**
$2 * 8^3$	+	$2 * 512$	**1024**
$4 * 8^2$	+	$4 * 64$	**256**
$3 * 8^1$	+	$3 * 8$	**24**
$5 * 8^0$	+	$5 * 1$	**5**
			30071 in decimal

Converting from Decimal to Hexadecimal (Divide and Conquer)

All we have left is to convert from our favorite, decimal, to the other bases. This process is the reverse of the conversion to decimal, so rather than multiplying, we now divide. The first step is to determine the largest place-value number that will divide into the decimal number we are trying to convert. That will tell us how many digits we will have in our converted number.

One way to do this is to find the place value that is too big by 1 to divide into our decimal number. Then we take the next smallest place value as our initial number to divide by. For example, if we want to convert 52591 decimal into hexadecimal, we must first determine how many hexadecimal digits we will need: 16^4 (65536) is too big, but 16^3 (4096) will divide, so we know we have four digits in our number: $(16^3 \ldots 16^0)$. Once we have the starting value, we simply divide our target number by the place values, and record the results. Remember to always use the correct digits for the base you are converting into. Let's do one:

Starting with

52591

1. We look at the table on page 636, and see that 16^4 (65536) is too large to divide into our target, but 16^3 (4096) will work. Therefore, we know we will have four digits in our answer. I like to make a line for each digit.

   __ __ __ __

2. Now divide our target by the first positional value. This will give us our leftmost digit.

   52591/4096 = 12

   with 3439 left. That means our first digit is C.
   So now we know the leftmost, or highest order, digit:

   C __ __ __

3. Since we have 3439 left, and we have taken care of our leftmost positional value, we need to divide by the next position to see how many of those are in our number.

   3439/256 = 13

   with 111 left. That means our second digit is D.
   Now we know two digits:

   C D __ __

4. Next we need to divided the remaining number by our next positional value and see how many of them are in our number.

   111/16 = 6

   with 15 left. That means our third digit is 6:

   C D 6 __

5. Finally, since we have 15 left, we know our rightmost digit. The positional value is 1, and any number divided by 1 is itself, so all we need to do is plug in our final digit:

   C D 6 F

(Note: If you end up with more than the largest digit in the numbering system left, you have a small problem and probably need to review your division steps.)

6. Now our conversion is complete. The decimal number 52591 is equal to the hexa-decimal number **CD6F**. To test our answer and make sure we are correct, we can do the conversion from hexadecimal back to decimal.

$$
\begin{array}{llll}
C * 16^3 & \text{or} & 12 * 4096 = & 49152 \\
D * 16^2 & + & 13 * 256 = & 3328 \\
6 * 16^1 & + & 6 * 16 = & 96 \\
F * 16^0 & + & 15 * 1 = & 15 \\
\hline
& & & \mathbf{52591}
\end{array}
$$

So we can see that our conversion is correct.

A simple check is to count the number of digits you have in your answer. If you are converting from a smaller base, like decimal, to a larger base, like hexadecimal, you will always have *fewer* digits in your answer than in the number you are converting from. For example, converting from this five-digit decimal number, you end up with four hexadecimal digits. On the other hand, if you are converting from a larger base, like decimal, to a smaller base, like octal, you will end up with *more* digits in the conversion.

Converting from Decimal to Octal

The process for converting from decimal to octal is the same as we just saw with hexa-decimal, except we will be using powers of 8 rather than powers of 16. Let's convert 84543 decimal to octal.

1. First we need to determine the number of digits. From page 636 we see that 8^6 (262144) is too large, but that 8^5 (32768) will work. Therefore we have six digits in our answer:

   _ _ _ _ _ _

2. Divide 84543 by 8^5 to get our first digit:

   $84543 / 32768 = 2$

   with 19007 left. Therefore,

   2 _ _ _ _ _

3. Now divide our remainder, 19007, by 8^4 to get the next digit:

   $190007 / 4096 = 4$

   with 2623 left. Therefore,

   2 4 _ _ _ _

4. Divide 2623 by 8^3:

   $2623 / 512 = 5$

with 63 left. Therefore,

<u>2</u> <u>4</u> <u>5</u> __ __ __

5. Divide 63 by 8^2. Hmmm. We have a little problem here. We can't divide 63 by 8^2 because we can't divide 64 into 63. Since we can't divide, is seems we have zero 64s in that number. Put a 0 into our number to hold the place, and keep the 63 we have left for the next step.

<u>2</u> <u>4</u> <u>5</u> <u>0</u> __ __

6. Divide 63 by 8^1:

$63/8 = 7$

with 7 left. Therefore,

<u>2</u> <u>4</u> <u>5</u> <u>0</u> <u>7</u> __

7. Now we can just plug in the remainder as the last digit, and we have the conversion done:

<u>2</u> <u>4</u> <u>5</u> <u>0</u> <u>7</u> <u>7</u>

8. Let's check our answer to make sure we are correct by converting from octal back to decimal (Don't just skip this step!):

$$
\begin{array}{rllr}
 & 2*8^5 & \text{or} \quad 2*32768 = & 65536 \\
+ & 4*8^4 & + \quad 4*4096 = & 16384 \\
+ & 5*8^3 & + \quad 5*\ 512 = & 2560 \\
+ & 0*8^2 & + \quad 0*\ \ 64 = & 0 \\
+ & 7*8^1 & + \quad 7*\ \ \ 8 = & 56 \\
+ & 7*8^0 & + \quad 7*\ \ \ 1 = & 7 \\
\hline
 & & & \mathbf{84543}
\end{array}
$$

Woopie! We did two in a row correctly!!

Converting from Decimal to Binary
Converting from decimal to binary follows the same process as the conversions from decimal to hexadecimal or octal. The only differences are that you will have more digits in your answer than in the number you started with, and you must use the powers of two charts to determine your leftmost digit. Let's convert 863 decimal to binary:

1. Determine the leftmost digit: 2^{10} (1024) is too large, so our leftmost digit is 2^9 (512). That means we have 10 digits:

__ __ __ __ __ __ __ __ __ __

2. Divide 863 by 512:

$863/512 = 1$

with 351 left. Therefore,

$$\underline{1}$$

Note: Since we are building a binary number, we don't really need to divide. The largest digit we can have is 1, so all we need to do is subtract each place value from the number we start with. Don't forget to keep track of those zeros, though!

3. Subtract 256 from 351:

$$351 - 256 = 95$$
$$\underline{1\;\;1}$$

4. Subtract 128 from 95:

$$95 - 128 = 0$$
$$\underline{1\;\;1\;\;0}$$

5. Subtract 64 from 95:

$$95 - 64 = 31$$
$$\underline{1\;\;1\;\;0\;\;1}$$

6. Subtract 32 from 31:

$$31 - 32 = 0$$
$$\underline{1\;\;1\;\;0\;\;1\;\;0}$$

7. Subtract 16 from 31:

$$31 - 16 = 15$$
$$\underline{1\;\;1\;\;0\;\;1\;\;0\;\;1}$$

8. Subtract 8 from 15:

$$15 - 8 = 7$$
$$\underline{1\;\;1\;\;0\;\;1\;\;0\;\;1\;\;1}$$

9. Subtract 4 from 7:

$$7 - 4 = 3$$
$$\underline{1\;\;1\;\;0\;\;1\;\;0\;\;1\;\;1\;\;1}$$

10. Subtract 2 from 3:

$$3 - 2 = 1$$
$$\underline{1\;\;1\;\;0\;\;1\;\;0\;\;1\;\;1\;\;1\;\;1}$$

11. Place the final digit:

$$\underline{1\;\;1\;\;0\;\;1\;\;0\;\;1\;\;1\;\;1\;\;1\;\;1}$$

12. Convert from binary back to decimal to check our work:

$$
\begin{array}{rll}
 & 1 * 2^9 \ \ \text{or} \ \ 1 * 512 = 512 \\
+ & 1 * 2^8 & 1 * 256 = 256 \\
+ & 0 * 2^7 & 0 * 128 = 0 \\
+ & 1 * 2^6 & 1 * 64 = 64 \\
+ & 0 * 2^5 & 0 * 32 = 0 \\
+ & 1 * 2^4 & 1 * 16 = 16 \\
+ & 1 * 2^3 & 1 * 8 = 8 \\
+ & 1 * 2^2 & 1 * 4 = 4 \\
+ & 1 * 2^1 & 1 * 2 = 2 \\
+ & 1 * 2^0 & 1 * 1 = 1 \\
\hline
 & & 863
\end{array}
$$

Now you can convert any of the four common bases from one to another. I realize there are whiz-bang calculators that can do this for you, but it is important for you to be able to do this conversion by hand so you will understand the relationships among the bases.

B

GNU Free Software Directory Listing

31journal

    Web-based collaborative journal system

3DKit

    3D graphics and sound-rendering architecture

a2ps

    Any to-PostScript filter

abiword

    Word processor from the AbiSource Project desktop suite

abook

    Addressbook program

abuse

    Shoot-'em-up game

acct

    GNU system accounting utilities

acm

    Aerial combat simulation game

acon

    Displays Arabic text

acs
> C++ state engine and IVR components

adacom
> Toolset for Ada

adjtimex
> Displays or sets the kernel time variable

adns
> Resolver lib for C and C++ programs

aegis
> Software configuration management system

AFD
> Automatically distributes files

agnostos
> Web-based tool for managing to do lists

aide
> Free replacement for Tripwire (tm)

AllCommerce
> E-commerce/content application

alliance
> Cad tools

anteil
> Customer relationship management software

aolserver
> Web server

apache
> A patchy Web server

ape
> C++ framework for development of threaded servers and applications

aplus
> Programming language

APSEND
> TCP/IP packet sender to test firewalls and other network applications

aria
> Download tool with GUI that can pause, resume, and queue downloads

ASPSeek
> Search engine

asteroids3D
> Game of blowing up asteroids

astrocont
> Makes header files that define astrophysical constants

astyle
> Source code formatter

atchange
> Automation tool

atheism
> Perl script for XChat

atool
> Script for managing file archives

autochar
> Automates characterization of digital circuits

autoclass
> Automatic classification or clustering

autoconf
> Produces shell scripts that automatically configure source code

autodia
> Creates XML diagrams

autogen
> Automated program and text generation

automake
> Generates Makefile.in files

autoproject
> Creates a skeleton source package for a new program

AutoUpdate
> Automatically downloads and upgrades RPMs from different FTP sites

avdbtools
> Set of aviation database tools

AVFS
> Lets programs look at archived files without having to recompile them

awacs
> Monitors computer system(s)

AWStats
> Generates and displays Web server statistics graphically

babylon
> Lets groups chat and draw over TCP/IP connections

backgammon
> Plays and analyzes backgammon games and matches

BackupCopy
> Lets you keep a mirror of your data

balsa
> GNOME mail client

banner
> Displays a "banner" text

bannerkiller
> Page-filtering Web proxy

barcode
> Converts text strings to printed bars

bash
> Shell of the GNU operating system

battstat
> Applet that monitors the battery charge on a laptop

bayonne
> GNU telephony server

bc
> Interactive algebraic language

beest
> HTML viewer

BerkeleyDB
> Embedded database system

bigbrotherdatabase
> Contact management utility for Emacs

binkd
> FidoTech TCP/IP mailer

binutils
>   Collection of binary utilities

bison
>   Replacement for the parser generator 'yacc'

BitTorrent
>   Tool for copying files

blackarts
>   Organizes email automatically into a knowledge base

boa
>   Web server

bookland
>   Generates ISBN bar codes

Bool
>   Utility for finding files that match a Boolean expression.

botnet
>   Library for development of IRC bots

brl
>   Language for server-side Web applications

brltty
>   Gives blind users access to the GNU/Linux console

btl
>   Library for life sciences programming

BubblingLoad
>   Graphic display of CPU and memory load

bubload
>   Graphic display of CPU and memory load

buffer
>   Maintains a buffer of data collected from stdin and sends it to stdout

bugs
>   Private key encryption algorithm and applications

bugtrack
>   Bug-tracking system

burncenter
>   Text-based interface to the CD-burning tools for UNIX

busybox

> Tiny versions of many common Linux utilities

calamaris

> Generates statistics from log files from proxy cache servers

calc

> C-style arbitrary precision calculator

catdoc

> Changes Word files to ASCII text

cdcd

> Plays CDs

celestia

> Visual simulation of space

centerICQ

> Ncurses-based ICQ interface

cervisia

> Graphical frontend for CVS

cfengine

> Maintains configuration of a heterogenous UNIX network

cgi-util

> C library for developing Web programs

cgicc

> C++ class library for writing CGI applications

cgiutils

> C++ classes

cgiwet

> Themes GCIpm code for optimal page layout and site structure

cgoban

> Client program for the game of Go

changetrack

> Monitors changes to system files

chars

> Cron job to automatically visit the Web sites of various charities

checkal

> Reads and monitors a sendmail alias file

checker
>   Finds memory errors at runtime.

checkstyle
>   Java syntax checker

chemtool
>   Chemical structure editor

chess
>   Chess game

chupa
>   Administrative IRC bot

cilk
>   Algorithmic language for multithreaded parallel processing

cim
>   Compiler for the programming language of Simula

cish
>   Configuration shell for Linux routers

citadel
>   BBS program

class:date
>   Date/time datatype for Perl

clibrary
>   Library for use with GNU/Hurd and GNU/Linux

CLISP
>   ANSI Common Lisp compiler, debugger, and interpreter

CLN
>   C++ class library for numbers

clunixtools
>   Linux cluster management tools

cnocem
>   Applies NoCeM actions on the elocal mail spool

coas
>   GNU/Linux administration system

COBOLforgcc
>   Project to produce a free COBOL compiler

codecommander
>   Multi-language programming editor

coldstore
>   Persistent object store

commoncpp
>   Highly portable C++ class library

compare
>   Text analysis and comparison tool

cons
>   "Make" replacement

cook
>   Tool for constructing files

corkscrew
>   Small program for tunneling SSH through HTTP proxies

cosrc
>   Back end for cosource.com

cpio
>   Copies file archives

cpp2html
>   Converts C/C++ code to an HTML file

cpp2latex
>   Converts C++ into LaTeX

createusers
>   Adds or removes users in bulk

cscope
>   Browses through source code files for specific elements of code

CSSC
>   Free clone of SCCS

CTC
>   Daemon that prevents ads from downloading

cups
>   Portable printing layer

cURL
>   Gets files using URL syntax

cvs

Version control system

cvs2html

Translates cvs log output to HTML

cvsadmin

Tool to administer users of a CVS repository

cvsauth

Authentication daemon for the CVS pserver method

cvschk

Checks for new files and modifications to old files

cvsgraph

Generates graphical representations of CVS revisions and branches

CVSSearch

Searches code using CVS comments

cvsstat

Gives an overview of the CVS status of your files

cyberradio1

Live internet audio broadcast system

DBACompanion

GUI tool for Oracle databases

dcp

Chinese interface for Debian GNU/Linux systems

ddd

Graphical front end for command line debuggers

debfoster

Cleans up Debian packages

debrief

Analyses ship and submarine tracks in 2D and 3D

debris

Lightweight text-based HTML browser

dedoc

Translates JavaDoc into Java interface code

dejagnu

Framework to test programs

denemo
> Graphical music notation program

deroff
> Removes roff and preprocessor constructs

dforum
> Web site discussion forum

dgps
> Lets you get GPS corrections over IP

dia
> GTK-based diagram-drawing program

dia2code
> Makes code from a *dia* diagram

diction
> Checks text for readability and bad usage

dietlibc
> Library for creating small, statically linked binaries

diffutils
> Finds differences between and among files

dillo
> Small, fast Web browser

diogenes
> Scripts for searching classics texts

DirectoryAdministrator
> Manages UNIX users and groups in an LDAP directory

disccover
> Produces covers for audio CDs

djgpp
> GCC, G++, and GNU utilities for DOS

dld
> Loads files into a running binary

DMTools
> Data mining applications written in Python

doschk
> Utility to ensure that source names are distinguishable

DownloaderforX
> Downloads files from the Internet via both HTTP and FTP

doxygen
> Cross-platform documentation system

drall
> Allows remote access to files without telnet or FTP

DrGenius
> Interactive geometry program and calculator

drgeo
> Builds geometric figures

druid
> Tool to create graphical databases

dtemplate
> Template system

dumb
> Free engine for running doom worlds

e
> Automated theorem prover

easychains
> GUI for a console firewall script

easytag
> Views and edits the ID3 tags of your MP3 files

ecc
> Elliptical curve class library

ecgi
> C library to help create CGI-based Web applications

echoping
> Test tool for TCP servers

ed
> Line-oriented text editor

edma
> Modular development environment

efax
> Sends and receives faxes

eggdrop
> IRC bot

eject
> Puts removable media under software control

electric
> CAD electrical circuit design system

elegant
> Programming language

eli
> Compiler construction kit

elib
> Library of Emacs LISP functions

elog
> Electronic logbook with a Web interface

emacs
> Extensible, real-time editor

emacspeak
> Adds speech output to Emacs

emacspeakss
> Emacspeak speech server

emrem
> Email reminder scripts

enlightenment
> Window manager

enscript
> Replacement for Adobe's 'enscript' program

epeios
> A group of C++ libraries

esound
> Audio file player and sound daemon

etherboot
> Makes boot ROMS

evolution
> GNOME mailer and PIM

exim

   Message transfer agent for Unix systems

eXtrans

   Translates XML documents into other formats

fai

   Automatically installes Debian onto a PC cluster

FarsiTeX

   TeX typesetting program for Persian

fastDNAml

   Phylogenetic analysis software

fcron

   Schedules periodic commands

fdm

   Creates lines that run around your screen

ferm

   Tool to set up and maintain firewalls

fesi

   Implementation of the EcmaScript language

fetchmail

   Remote mail retrieval utility

ffcall

   Builds foreign function call interfaces in embedded interpreters

ffp

   Free Film Project

fftw

   Subroutine library for computing the Discrete Fourier Transform

filepp

   Provides C preprocessor functionality for any file type

fileutils

   Tools for file operations

filter

   Conversion routines from proprietary formats to XML-based formats

findutils

   Finds and then operates on files

finger
> Lets Unix users exchange information

fingerd
> A safer replacement for any 'fingerd'

firefly
> Professional help desk system

firestarter
> GNOME firewall tool for Linux

flowersol
> Games, card sets, and game pieces from all over the world

fltk
> C++ GUI toolkit

fontutils
> Converts between font formats and creates fonts

fplan
> Free flight plan software

freeamp
> An mp3 player

freeciv
> Civilization-like strategic game

freenet
> Filesharing program

freePascal
> Free implementation of the Pascal programming language

freeside
> Billing and account administration package for ISPs

freeSWAN
> IPSEC and IKE for GNU/Linux systems

freetype
> Font engine

freeVSD
> Web hosting platform

frontier

FRT
> Toolkit for 3D animations using low-end machines

g++

    C++ compiler

G-Kermit

    File transfer program

g-page

    Sends text messages to pagers or SMS enable PCS phones

g3data

    Extracts data from graphs

g95

    Project to create a free Fortran 95 compiler

gabber

    Jabber client for GNOME

gaby

    Small personal database manager

gag

    Graphical boot manager

gAIM

    GTK-based Instant Messenger

gale

    Instant messaging software

galway

    HTML editor

gatO

    Interface to the UNIX command 'at'

gawk

    Free version of 'awk'

gbiff

    Displays headers when new mail has arrived

gcal

    Prints calendars

gcc

    GNU Compiler Collection

GCL

    Compiler and interpreter for Common Lisp

gcompris

    Educational game for children age 3 to 10

gdb
> GNU Debugger

gdbm
> Replacement for the 'dbm' and 'ndbm' libraries

gdm
> GNOME version of xdm

gEDA-gaf
> Tools for electronic circuit design

gedit
> Lightweight text editor for GNOME

GenericColoriser
> Colorises files or output of commands

genericNQS
> Batch processing system

geneweb
> Genealogy software

gengetopt
> Generates a C function that parses and validates command line options

geomview
> Interactive 3D viewing program

getleft
> Downloads all links from a particular URL

getmail
> Simpler replacement for fetchmail

gettext
> Tools to produce multilingual messages

gfax
> Front-end fax manager for GNOME

gfe
> Graphical font editor

gforth
> Free implementation of the ANS Forth language

ggradebook
> Fully-featured GNU gradebook

ghostscript

Interpreter for the Postscript and PDF graphics languages

ghostview

Graphical front end to Ghostscript

GIFT

Content based image retrieval system

gimp

Free software replacement for Photoshop

gimpDynText

GIMP plug-in that modifies the text tool

gimpprint

Print plug-in for the GIMP and GhostScript driver for Epson printers

GiNaC

Open framework for symbolic computation within C++

ginac

Open framework for symbolic computation within C++

git

Tools for simple, daily file and system management tasks

gklog

Log analyzer and marker

glade

A user interface builder for GTK+ and Gnome

gleem

Library of 3D widgets

glibc

Library for use with GNU/Hurd and GNU/Linux.

glife

Evolutionary simulation game

global

Source code tag system for C, C++, Java, and Yacc

glpk

GNU Linear Programming Kit

glue

GNU Internet groupware project.

gmail
> SQL-based Vfolder email system

gman
> GUI for the man system

gmt
> Tools that manipulate datasets to produce Encapsulated Postcript (EPS) illustrations

gnat
> GNAT is a complete Ada95 compilation system

gnats
> Bug-tracking system

gnats2w
> Web interface to GNATS

gnatsweb
> Web interface to the GNU bug management system

gnet
> Network library

gno3dtet
> 3D Tetris

gnobog
> Bookmark organizer

gnochive
> GUI frontend for multiple archivers

gnofin
> GNOME checkbook program

gnome
> The GNU desktop

gnome-print
> GNOME printing architecture

gnomedb
> Framework for developing database applications

gnomedisplaymanager
> Implementation of xdm

gnomefind
> GUI version of the GNU 'find' utility

gnomeflow
>   Calculates and visualizes steady-state fluid flows

gnomepilot
>   Daemon for pilot synchronization

GnomerMind
>   MasterMind-type puzzle game for GNOME

gnometranscript
>   SQL database client

gnomeutils
>   Utilities/apps for use with GNOME

gnotepad
>   HTML and text editor

gnotes
>   Post-it notes for GNOME

gnu.free
>   Internet voting system

gnuBool
>   Utility for matching boolean queries in text

gnucash
>   Personal and small business money-management software

GNUComm
>   GNU telecommunications project

gnugo
>   Plays the game of Go

GNUHalifax
>   Client applications suite for fax applications

gnulightning
>   Generates assembly language code at run-time

gnum4
>   Macro processor

gnumed
>   Software for a paperless medical practice

gnumeric
>   Math program intended to replace commercial spreadsheets

gnump
> Library for arithmetic on arbitrary precision integers

gnuoctal
> Free digital sound workstation for Unix-like systems

gnuparted
> Manipulates disk partitions

gnuPG
> Complete implementation of the OpenPGP Internet standard

gnupg
> Complete implementation of the OpenPGP Internet standard

gnuplot
> Plots 2D and 3D graphs

gnurobots
> Real-Time Game

gnuscapenav
> Web browser that runs under GNU Emacs

gnushogi
> Japanese version of chess

GNUSkies
> Project to create a free version of the xephem program

GNUsl
> Routines for numerical computing

gnusql
> Database management system

GNUSQL
> Relational database management system

gnustep
> A graphical, object oriented programming environment

gnutls
> A library implementing TLS 1.0 and SSL 3.0 protocols

gnutrition
> Nutrition analysis software

gnuts
> GUI toolkit abstraction library

gnuVisualDebugger
>   Graphical front end for debuggers

goats
>   Post-It Notes applet for GNOME

gob
>   GTK+ object builder

goctave
>   Front end for the Octave language

goops
>   Object-oriented extension to *guile*

goose
>   Statistical computation library

gpa
>   The GNU Privacy Assistant

gpaint
>   GNOME paint program

gpc
>   GNU Pascal compiler

gperf
>   Generates a hash function

gperiodic
>   Periodic table application

GPGME
>   GnuPG Made Easy

gphoto
>   Retrieves, organizes, and publishes images

gps
>   Reports process staus

gpsimulator
>   Simulates particle behavior

Grace
>   2D plotting tool

grap
>   Language for typesetting graphs

grass
> Geographic information system

gravityd
> Graphical display of network testing tools

greg
> A framework for testing other programs

grep
> Finds lines that match entered patterns

grepmail
> Searches for emails in normal or compressed mailboxes

grg
> GNU Report Generator

groff
> Document formatting system

grub
> GNU GRand Unified Bootloader

gstat
> Geostatistical modelling, simulation, and prediction

gsysinfo
> System monitor for the GNOME panel

gtelnet
> GNOME frontend for telnet, rlogin, and ssh

gtk
> GNU toolkit for X windows development

gtkdiff
> Graphical diff tool

gtkeditor
> Source code editor widget for GTK+

gtkeyboard
> Graphical keyboard

gtkhtml
> HTML rendering/editing library

gtkstep
> Improves the look and feel of the GTK+ widget set

gtktalog
>   Organizes and browses a CD-ROM database

guarddog
>   Firewall generation/management utility for KDE 2

guile
>   GNU extensibility library

gup
>   Lets a remote site change its newsgroups subscription

GURGLE
>   Formerly the GNU Report Generator

gwenview
>   Image viewer for KDE

gwydiondylan
>   Dylan devlopment tools from the Gwydion Dylan Team

GYVE
>   Vector-based drawing program

gzip
>   Compresses and decompresses files

hackers
>   Lets you switch between various nethack characters

hanzim
>   Visual, interactive Chinese character and word dictionary

harbour
>   Cross-platform compiler for the xBase language

harmony
>   Free version of the QT toolkit

HebrewEditor
>   Lets users create and edit Hebrew/English LaTeX documents

heh
>   Opens files based on filename extension

hello
>   GNU version of "Hello, world!"

help2man
>   Generates manual pages from program files

HexCurse
>   Ncurses-based hex editor

hitchhiker2000
>   Astronomy simulation program

hldfilter
>   E-mail filter

hoard
>   Memory allocator for multiprocessors

hopla
>   Link between XML files and SQL databases

hp2xx
>   Reads and convert HP-GL filess to various formats

htdig
>   Internet search engine software

httptunnel
>   Creates a data path in HTTP requests

HTTrackWebsiteCopier
>   Offline browser utility

hurd
>   Project GNU's replacement for the Unix kernel

hyperbole
>   Information and text management program

hypermail
>   Converts mail into HTML pages

icecast
>   Streaming media server based on the MP3 audio code

icewm
>   Window manager designed for speed, usability, and consistency

idutils
>   Tools for indexing

ifmail
>   Fidonet transport and gateway

iGal
>   Generates and publishes online picture galleries

iGMT
>Visual tool for GMT script mapping

ImageMagick
>Image display and manipulation program

IMT
>Comprehensive system modelling toolkit

indent
>C source beautifier

indexpage
>Generates index pages and thumbnails for online image collections

inetutils
>Collection of common network programs

install-log
>Package management tool

installdb
>Records and stores info about installs on a system

integrit
>Intrusion detection system

Interchange
>Free e-commerce system

intlfonts
>Fonts for all characters Emacs 20 can handle

ipts
>Tracks off-site employees

ircgateway
>Builds a network of Web servers

IRCServices
>Administrative tools for IRC networks

irm
>Asset tracking system for IT depts. and helpdesks

ishmail
>Graphical mail reader for UNIX systems

IsoQlog
>Log analysis program

ispell

>   Spell checker

j

>   Programmer's editor written in java

jacal

>   Mathematics program

jaquemate

>   Turn-based Web chess system

java2html

>   Translates Java files to HTML

jaxml

>   Creates human readable XML documents

jboss

>   JavaBeans application server

jEdit

>   Text editor

jel

>   Compiler for simple expressions into Java byte code

JIGS

>   Lets Java programmers use the GNUStep libraries from Java

Jlint

>   Java debugger

jm

>   Distributed file sharing program

jMax

>   Programming environment for real-time audio

joyd

>   Executes commands via a joystick or joypad

junkbuster

>   Blocks unwanted banner ads and cookies

jwhois

>   Internet whois client

kagora

>   Web forum system

kaim
>   AOL-type instant messenger

kalcul
>   Interactive math game for ages 8-15

kalculator
>   GUI calculator for KDE

kannel
>   SMS and WAP gateway

kawa
>   Scheme and Emacs Lisp on a Java VM

kbabel
>   Tools for working with gettext PO files

kcd
>   Directory-change utility

kci
>   Simulates chemical reactions

KDE
>   Graphical desktop environment

KDevelop
>   C/C++ development environment for KDE

kinkatta
>   AOL instant messenger for KDE

kleandisk
>   Removes extraneous files from your hard disk

kmago
>   KDE-based download manager

kmplot
>   Plots mathematical functions

knetfilter
>   KDE frontend to iptables

knewmail
>   Checks incoming mail and displays headers

konqueror
>   Web browser

kperfmeter
> Performance statistics monitor for KDE

krusader
> KDE twin-panel file manager

kseg
> Euclidean geometry simulator

ksrc2html
> KDE front end for 'sourcehighlight'

ksymoops
> Kernel oops and error message decoder

Ktexmaker2
> LaTeX source editor and TeX shell for KDE2

KTouch
> Touch typing program for KDE

larbin
> Web crawler

less
> Display paginator

lesstif
> Free implementation of OSF/Motif

libavl
> Library for balanced binary trees

libbinio
> Portably stores and retrives binary data

libgaudio
> C/C++ library to incorporate sound and sound effects into games

libgcrypt
> Cryptographic library

libiconv
> Converts between character encodings

libping
> Makes ICMP_ECHO requests from a script or program

libpng
> Reference library for the PNG graphics format

librep
>   A shared library Lisp dialect interpreter

libsafe
>   Detect and handle buffer overflow attacks

libsmtp
>   Library for sending mail through SMTP

libtecla
>   Interactive command line editing faciltiies

libtool
>   Generic library support script

libungif
>   Operates on GIF files using uncompressed GIFs

libxmi
>   Library for rasterizing 2D vector graphics

licq
>   ICQ Clone

lightspeed
>   Simulates a geometric lattice

lilypond
>   Music typesetter

LinCity
>   City/country development simulation games

links
>   Text Web browser

linuxlab
>   Project to develop process control and data collection software

linuxvacation
>   Automatic mail-answering program

lout
>   Document formatting system similar to LaTeX

lpe
>   Small programminng editor

lynx
>   Text mode browser

magicfilter
>   Automatic printer filter

MagicStats
>   Web server log analysis tool

mahogany
>   GUI email and news client

mailman
>   Manages discussion lists

make
>   Generates executables and other non-source programs

maketool
>   GTK frontend for GNU make

man
>   Man page suite used to read GNU/Linux documentation

mandb
>   Reference manual page database and browser

ManhattanVirtualClassroom
>   Delivers courses via the Web

marst
>   Algol to C translator

maverik
>   Virtual reality micro kernel

maxima
>   Computer algebra system

mboxgrep
>   Small mailbox searching utility

mbuffer
>   Enhanced version of buffer

MC
>   Converts text documents into a vector space model

mcrypt
>   Encrypts files or streams

MeetingRoomBookingSystem
>   Meeting room booking system

melting
>   Nearest-neighbor compilation of nucleic acid hybridation

memwatch
>   Memory leak and corruption detection tool

mercury
>   Logic/functional programming language

mergelog
>   Merges and sorts HTTP log files

metahtml
>   Programming language for the Web

MHonArc
>   Converts email messages to HTML

midnightcommander
>   Unix file manager

miffmixr
>   Web-based MP3 jukebox

mifluz
>   Full text inverted index query library

MiG
>   Photo album/image gallery manager

mirodc1
>   Driver for the MIRO VIDEO DC1 (plus) mjpeg grabber/display ISA card

mirror
>   Turns your entire display black

miscfiles
>   Collection of various files

mll2html
>   Converts a mailing lists file to an HTML file

mnogosearch
>   Search engine

modutils
>   Kernel utilities

molasses
>   Sticky notes app

MondoRescue
> Disaster recovery suite

monit
> Utility that monitors daemons or similar programs

motion
> Motion-detecting device

motor
> Text mode IDE

motti
> Multiplayer, networked strategy game

mozilla
> Internet browser for the free software community

mp32ogg
> Coverts MP3 files to Ogg Vorbis format

mp3mover
> Renames audio files so they conform to a set scheme

mp3tools
> Tools to manage a collection of MPEG audio files

mpatrol
> Diagnoses runtime errors

mrbs
> Meeting room booking system

mrtg
> Monitors traffic load on network links

mtool
> GTK front end for GNU make

mtools
> Lets Unix systems work with DOS files

MToolsFM
> GUI front end for mtools

muddleftpd
> FTP server

mule
> Multilingual text editor for Emacs

multiCD
> Backs up a large number of files to multiple CDs

multignometerm
> Enhanced version of gnome terminal

multiscan
> Console portscanner

MultiuserAddressMS
> Web-based address system/book

mutt
> Text-based mail reader

mwForum
> Web based discussion forum system

mySiteMaker
> CGI tools to create Web interfaces to database tables

mysql
> Relational database management system

MySQLBackup
> Backs up databases

nabou
> Monitors file changes using MD5 checksums

naim
> Ncurses based AIM client

namazu
> A full-text retrieval search system

nana
> Library for assertion checking and logging in GNU C/C++

nano
> Pico clone for *NIX

nautilus
> File manager and graphical shell

ncocem
> Applies NoCeM actions on the local news spool

ncurses
> Displays and updates text on text-only terminals

NeDNS
> Multilingual domain system

nethack
> Adventure game

ninpaths
> Paths Survey reporting program

nonsense
> Random text generator

normalize
> Adjusts the volume of WAV files to a standard level

nosql
> a Relational Database Manegement System for UNIX

nsbd
> Automated software distribution system

nurbss++
> Hides the basic mathematics of NURBS

obst
> Object management system

octave
> High-level language for numerical computations

oggvorbis
> Free version of mp3

oleo
> Lightweight spreadsheet program

omniORB
> CORBA orb

openacs
> Advanced Web toolkit

openbios
> Project to develop a free IEEE 1275-1994 compliant firmware

OpenRealty
> Real estate listing manager

openWebmail
> Webmail system based on Neomail

oroborus
>   Small window manager

oroborusthemechanger
>   Changes the theme in an Oroborus window

p2c
>   Translates Pascal programs into C

pagecast
>   Submits lists of URLs to search engines

pan
>   Threaded newsreader for GNOME

panorama
>   Framework for 3D graphics production

paperclips
>   Webserver and dynamic content container

pasdoc
>   Documentation generator for pascal source code

patch
>   Applies a patch to a file

paxutils
>   Tool to manage file archives

pcb
>   Designs printed circuit board layouts

pdnsd
>   Proxy DNS server

perl
>   Scripting language

PerlBoard
>   Threaded messageboard system

perlfectsearch
>   Web site indexing and searching application

perlODS
>   IDE for developing Web applications in perl

pgmarket
>   Complete e-commerce solution

pgpenvelope
>   Interface to facilitate using Pine with GnuPG

phantomhome
>   Home automation system

phantomsecurity
>   Home security system

phorum
>   Web-based discussion software in PHP

photoArchive
>   Lets users place their photo archive on the Web

photonbands
>   Computes photonic band structures

photoseek
>   Image management system

photoshelf
>   Web based digital image archive and management system

php
>   Scripting language

phpCache
>   Lets you cache blocks of code on pages

phpcms
>   Web content management system

phpgroupware
>   Groupware suite writtten in PHP

PHPLetterIt
>   Newsletter script

phpLinkValidator
>   Validates links in HTML documents

phpmailer
>   PHP email client

phpMyAdmin
>   Handles MySQL administration over the Web

PHPMyEdit
>   Lets you display/edit MySQL tables in HTML

PhpMyExplorer
>   Lets you update your site online without ftp access

phpnuke
>   PHP interactive Web portal

phpsubmit
>   Automated search engine submission script

picbook
>   Automatically produces an HTML album of your images

picview
>   Image preview and viewing program for GNOME

pikt
>   System monitoring tool

ping
>   Library of functions that simplify software development

pingtools
>   Collection of UNIX utilities

pingutils
>   Library of functions that simplify software development

pips
>   Converts data between formats

pitchtune
>   Musical instrument tuning program

pizza
>   Software to run a pizza ordering and delivery system

pj
>   Toolkit for creating and manipulating PDF documents

playmidi
>   MIDI player for GUS, FM, and external MIDI devices

plex86
>   Free replacement for VMWare

pliant
>   Programming language framework

plotutils
>   Plotting and graphics utilities

pmc
> Perl/GNOME-based mail client

pngcrush
> Compression utility for PNG images

POPauthd
> Authorizes connecting hosts for SMTP relaying

popper
> Web-based POP3 mail client

postgresql
> A robust SQL Object-Relational Database

powerdaemon
> Monitors your UPS and shuts it down if needed

prcs
> Project Revision Control System

preps
> Bug-tracking System

procwatch
> Watches a /proc filesystem for new messages

profoil
> Wind tunnel data analyzer

prolog
> Prolog compiler

proto
> Tools to find function prototypes

protoize
> Creates or removes prototypes from C code

ProZilla
> Download accelerator

pspp
> Statistics package

pth
> GNU Portable Threads library

ptx
> Index generator

pwdgen

    Generates random passwords

pyb

    Manages bibliographic databases

pyFind

    Find File utility for GNOME

qDecoder

    C library for creating CGI software

qscheme

    Implementation of Scheme written in C

queue

    Batch processing and local rsh replacement system

quotatool

    Sets Linux filesystems quotas from the command line

R

    Statistical computation and graphics

ractive

    Front end for radio tuners

radius

    Remote authentication and accounting system

randomsig

    Produces random signatures

RazorBack

    Provides visual notification of possible intrusion attempts

rcs

    Version control and project management

reactOS

    Free clone of Windows NT

readline

    Lets users edit command lines as they are typed in

recode

    Translation program

Recruit

    Academic job application management system

reed
> Autoscroller

regex
> GNU regex library

RemembranceAgent
> Associative memory applications

remote_update
> Automates remote administration tasks

remstats
> Gathers, monitors, and maintains data from servers and routers

rep-gtk
> GTK+/libglade/GNOME language binding for librep

replace
> Replaces strings in files or from standard output

reveal
> Replaces tags in a file by text or file content

rhide
> IDE for DJGPP

rip
> Rips CD track to either MP3 or Ogg Vorbis files

ripMIME
> Extracts attachments from email

roseg
> MIDI sequencer and musical notation editor

roxen
> HTTP server

rpmlint
> RPM error checker

rpmstatus
> Shows which RPM packages are installed on machines

rpncalc
> RPN calculator emulating H-P 28S

rrdtool
> Stores and displays time-series data

rsync
>   FTP program to keep remote files in synch

rtf2htm
>   Converts from RTF to HTML

rtracker
>   Trouble ticketing system

ruby
>   Object-oriented programming language

rubyrss
>   Object oriented Ruby library for manipulations RSSs

rx
>   Replacement for the GNU regex library

safetynet
>   Keeps critical processes running

samba
>   File-sharing implementation

samhain
>   File system integrity checker

sane
>   API that provides access to raster image scanner hardware

sather
>   Object-oriented language

sauce
>   Anti-spam server

sawfish
>   Window manager

scheme
>   MIT Scheme programming language

scid
>   Chess database

scigraphica
>   Data analysis and technical graphics

scponly
>   Restricts remote shell access to ls and scp comands

screen

> Runs separate screens on a single terminal

sdcc

> ANSI-C compiler

sed

> A stream-oriented non-interactive text editor

sendmail

> Mail transport agent

sendpage

> Paging system

serveez

> Server framework

sharesecret

> Splits and recalculates secrets

sharutils

> Creates and helps unpack shell archives

shellutils

> Command line utilities

shtool

> The GNU portable shell tool

siege

> HTTP regression testing and benchmark utility

sig

> Automatic signature generator

sl

> Logs all executed commands

slang

> C-like programming language, designed to be embedded

slash

> News and message board

sloccount

> Counts lines of code in a program

smail

> Mail transport system

smalleiffel
>   Eiffel compiler

smalltalk
>   Implementation of the Smalltalk object oriented language

snacc
>   ASN.1 to C or C++ compiler

SNORT
>   Lightweight network intrusion detection system

solfege
>   Eartraining program for GNOME

source2html
>   Formats source code into hyperlinked Web pages

sourcehighlight
>   Turns source code into a file with syntax highlighting

spaminator
>   Web interface for sendmail's anti-spam functionality

speedx
>   Racing game

spell
>   Spell checker

spline
>   Akima spline interpolation

srm
>   Command line compatible rm

stat
>   Displays information about a file

statistX
>   GTK-based statistics program

SteelBlue
>   HTML-embedded Web application language

stow
>   Manages installation process

strace
>   Debugging tool

subterfugue
> System call tracing and rewriting utility

sugarplum
> Automated spam-poisoner

sunclock
> Clock for the X Window System

superopt
> Finds the shortest instruction sequence for a given function

sweater
> Generic database front end

sweep
> A sound wave editor

swiftsurf
> HTTP proxy

swish
> File indexer and searcher

swishe
> Web site indexing software

swm
> Window manager for computers with little memory and small screens

sxml
> Defines and implements a mark-up language

sympa
> List manager

taglog
> Time and activity tracking application

tar
> Creates tar archives

tau
> Utility to track student attendance and scheduling

tcl-tools
> Tools for TCL programmers

TCLink
> Runs credit card or electronic check transactions over TCP/IP

tclTk
> Tcl/Tk scripting language

tcob
> COBOL compiler

tcpspy
> Logs information about incoming and outgoing connections

tcpxd
> TCP/IP relay or proxy

tcup
> Helpdesk report management system

termutils
> Programs for controlling terminals

texinfo
> Manipultes and produces manuals, ASCII text, and on-line documentation

textutils
> Text utilities

threads
> Library designed to make treading under C++ easier

time
> Reports the user, system, and real time used by a process

tinyCOBOL
> COBOL compiler

tnt
> Emacs client for AIM

tochnog
> Mathematical modelling program

todolist.php
> Web-based to do list

toutdoux
> Project manager

traceroute
> NANOG traceroute

tradeclient
> E-mail client and PIM for X Window System

trueprint
: Prints source code to PostScript printers

tsbiff
: Mail notification tool

tulip
: Produces large graphs

tvset
: Displays TV images in X

TWIG
: Web-based groupware application

twiki
: Web-based collaboration and Intranet publishing tool

TwoFTPd
: FTP server

typist
: Typing tutor program

UDSCollection
: C++ development and debugging library

UNICON
: CJK (Chinese/Japanese/Korean) console input and display system

units
: Unit conversion and calculation

uri
: Library that analyses and transforms URIs

userv
: Security boundary tool

uucp
: File copying program

vcdi
: Lets you make video CD images from mpeg files

vfu
: Text-mode file manager

ViPEC
: Network analyser for electrical networks

vnc

  Lets you view and interact with a remote desktop

vocabumonkey

  Software focused on language and math skills

VorpalMail

  User-friendly sendmail replacement

vrweb

  Browser for 3D worlds and scenes

watchdog

  Software watchdog daemon

wboss

  Web-based spell checker

wcal

  Web-based calendar/planner

wdiff

  Front end to GNU 'diff'

webbase

  Web crawler

webwader

  Automatically browses a Web site

webwatcher

  Tool for tracking Web content

wget

  Retrieves files from the Web

wgetsg

  Script generator for wget

wgrab

  Automatically retrieves selected parts of Websites

whitespace

  Cleans up extraneous whitespace in source files

whois

  An advanced and intelligent whois client

willowstwin

  Cross-platform API

wims
> Hosts interactive mathematical activities

windowmaker
> Window manager for X Window System

wml
> HTML generation toolkit

wn
> HTTP server

word2x
> MS Word to HTML, LaTex, and ASCII converter

workon
> Sets up the environment to work on a CVS tree

WWWOFFLE
> Simplifies Web browsing from computers with dial-up connections

wxwindows
> Cross-platform toolkit in C++

xaos
> Real-time fractal zoomer

xbase
> Library for manipulating xBase files

xchat
> Graphical IRC client

xdb
> Library for manipulating xBase files

Xdialog
> Replacement for the dialog and cdialog programs

XDrawChem
> Program to draw chemical structures

xem
> Program to calculate Ph balance

xfce
> Lightweight desktop environment

xfig
> Drawing program for X Window system

xfs

  Journaling filesystem

xhippo

  Playlist manager

xine

  Video player for Unix-like systems

xinfo

  X window program for reading Info files

xlogmaster

  Monitors logfiles and devices

xmail

  Mail server

xmcd

  CD player utilities

XmHTML

  Motif widget set that displays HTML 3.2 documents

xmms

  GUI based mp3 player

xmmsctrl

  Controls xmms from the command line

xmorph

  Image morphing program

xosl

  Graphical boot loader

xpaint

  Image editor

xpenguins

  Lets penguins walk on top of your windows

XPM

  Format for storing/retrieving X pixmaps

xps

  Displays Unix processes as a tree under X

xshogi

  X window interface for GNU Shogi

xstroke

xtux

> Network shoot-'em-up game featuring free software mascots

yabasic

> Version of BASIC that includes only the commonest, simplest elements

YapBB

> Bulletin Board software written in PHP

YASE

> Text indexing and retrieving system

ygl

> 2D graphics library

ytalk

> Multi-user chat program

z

> Front end for compression utilities

zdisk

> Creates a boot/rescue floppy or CD

zebra

> Implementation of routing protocols

zlib

> Data compression library

zope

> Web application server

zthread

> Object-oriented threading and synchronization library

Copyright (C) 2001 Free Software Foundation, Inc.

C

ASCII Collating Sequence

Character	Decimal	Octal	Hex		Character	Decimal	Octal	Hex
{NUL}	0	000	00		{ETB}	23	027	17
{SOH}	1	001	01		{CAN}	24	030	18
{STX}	2	002	02		{EM}	25	031	19
{ETX}	3	003	03		{SUB}	26	032	1A
{EOT}	4	004	04		{ESC}	27	033	1B
{ENG}	5	005	05		{FS}	28	034	1C
{ACK}	6	006	06		{GS}	29	035	1D
{BEL}	7	007	07		{RS}	30	036	1E
{BS}	8	010	08		{US}	31	037	1F
{HT}	9	011	09		Space	32	040	20
{LF}	10	012	A		! (bang)	33	041	21
{VT}	11	013	B		" (double quote)	34	042	22
{NP}	12	014	C		# (octothorp)	35	043	23
{CR}	13	015	D		$ (dollar sign)	36	044	24
{SO}	14	016	E		% (percent)	37	045	25
{SI}	15	017	F		& (ampersand)	38	046	26
{DLE}	16	020	10		' (apostrophe)	39	047	27
{DC1}	17	021	11		((open paren)	40	050	28
{DC2}	18	022	12		) (close paren)	41	051	29
{DC3}	19	023	13		* (asterisk)	42	052	2A
{DC4}	20	024	14		+ (plus)	43	053	2B
{NAK}	21	025	15		, (comma)	44	054	2C
{SYN}	22	026	16		- (hyphen)	45	055	2D

Character	Decimal	Octal	Hex		Character	Decimal	Octal	Hex
. (period)	46	056	2E		S	83	123	53
/ (slash or virgule)	47	057	2F		T	84	124	54
0	48	060	30		U	85	125	55
1	49	061	31		V	86	126	56
2	50	062	32		W	87	127	57
3	51	063	33		X	88	130	58
4	52	064	34		Y	89	131	59
5	53	065	35		Z	90	132	5A
6	54	066	36		[(left sq. bracket)	91	133	5B
7	55	067	37		\ (backslash)	92	134	5C
8	56	070	38		] (right sq. bracket)	93	135	5D
9	57	071	39		^ (caret)	94	136	5E
: (colon)	58	072	3A		_ (underscore)	95	137	5F
; (semicolon)	59	073	3B		` (grave mark)	96	140	60
< (left angle bracket)	60	074	3C		a	97	141	61
= (equals)	61	075	3D		b	98	142	62
> (right angle bracket)	62	076	3E		c	99	143	63
? (question mark)	63	077	3F		d	100	144	64
@ (at sign)	64	100	40		e	101	145	65
A	65	101	41		f	102	146	66
B	66	102	42		g	103	147	67
C	67	103	43		h	104	150	68
D	68	104	44		i	105	151	69
E	69	105	45		j	106	152	6A
F	70	106	46		k	107	153	6B
G	71	107	47		l	108	154	6C
H	72	110	48		m	109	155	6D
I	73	111	49		n	110	156	6E
J	74	112	4A		o	111	157	6F
K	75	113	4B		p	112	160	70
L	76	114	4C		q	113	161	71
M	77	115	4D		r	114	162	72
N	78	116	4E		s	115	163	73
O	79	117	4F		t	116	164	74
P	80	120	50		u	117	165	75
Q	81	121	51		v	118	166	76
R	82	122	52		w	119	167	77

Character	Decimal	Octal	Hex		Character	Decimal	Octal	Hex
x	120	170	78		| (vertical stroke)	124	174	7C
y	212	171	79		} (close French br.)	125	175	7D
z	122	172	7A		~ tilde	126	176	7E
{ (open French br.)	123	173	7B		{DEL}	127	177	7F

* Characters enclosed in French braces { } are usually nonprinting.

What the nonprinting characters mean:

Hex	Character	Meaning
00	NUL	Null character.
01	SOH	Start of heading.
02	STX	Start of text.
03	ETX	End of text.
04	EOT	End of transmission.
05	ENG	Enquiry.
06	ACK	Acknowledgement.
07	BEL	Bell (or how to be really anoying.)
08	BS	Backspace.
09	HT	Horizontal tab.
A	LF	Line feed.
B	VT	Vertical tab.
C	NP	New page (also called FF or form feed.)
D	CR	Carriage Return.
E	SO	Shift out.
F	SI	Shift in.
10	DLE	Data link escape.
11	DC1	X-on.
12	DC2	
13	DC3	X-off.
14	DC4	
15	NAK	No acknowledgement.
16	SYN	Synchronous idle.
17	ETB	End transmission block.
18	CAN	Cancel.
19	EM	End of medium.
1A	SUB	Substitute.

Hex	Character	Meaning
1B	ESC	Escape.
1C	FS	File separator.
1D	GS	Group separator.
1E	RS	Record separator.
1F	US	Unit separator.
7F	DEL	Delete or rubout.

Useful ed Commands and Tools

Command format:

        [address[, address]] command [parameters]

Command	Action
!	Acts like a shell escape character and allows the subsequent keystrokes to be passed to the Unix shell and executed. In most cases control returns to ed after the execution of the command. Normally ed will output an exclamation mark to indicate the end of the generated output.
.(period)	End input mode and go to command mode.
'(tick)	Go to the line marked with the character following. 'r transfer control to the line marked with the letter r.
a	Allows you to leave command mode and append text *after* the current line.
c	Allows you to alter (change) a range of text. The generic format of the command is [#,#]c, where (#,#) is a range of lines you wish to replace with text you will type. This command first deletes the existing text over the range specified, then puts you into insert mode to type new text to replace that which has been deleted.
d	Allows you to delete one or more lines. The generic format of the command is [#,#]d, where (#,#) is a range of lines to be deleted. The line after the last line deleted becomes the current line.
e	Reads the previously saved version of the current file into the editing buffer. If a filename is specified, then ed loads the most recent version of that file into the editing buffer, *overwriting the current contents.*
f	By itself, displays the current filename. If you give f a filename, then you associate new file with the contents of the editing buffer. The syntax for this command is f or, f filename, to set a new filename.
g	The global option. If g *precedes* a command, then the entire buffer is searched for all first occurrences of the pattern in each line. If the g *follows* a command, then the whole line is searched, and ed does not stop with the first occurrence. It is possible to attach a command list to this command to be executed

Command	Action
	each time the pattern is matched. The normal syntax of this command is [#,#]g/RE/command-list. The commands in the command list must be separated by protected newlines (<enter>). If the g both precedes and follows a command, then the complete file is searched.
G	Same as the g command, except it can have only one command following it rather than a command list.
h	Displays the most recent error message.
H	Displays (or redisplays) the most recent error message and turns on the automatic verbose error message display for the current editing session. This command is a toggle. If you enter a second H, it will turn verbose error display off. The default for this option is off.
i	Allows you to **insert** text *before* the current line. If you precede the command with a number, the text will be opened for insertion *before* the line specified.
j	Allows you to remove the carriage return between any two lines, joining them into one line. The format is [#,#]j, where # and # are two contiguous lines to be joined. If you do not give j two line numbers, the command will fail, but no error message will be given.
k	Sets a marker in the text so you can find a particular line later. The format of this command is [#]kx, where x is one of the letters from the range [a–z]. If no line number (#) is supplied, the current line is marked. To transfer control back to a line so marked, use the 'x command (that is a tick mark followed by x.)
l	Lists either the entire contents of the buffer or, in the form [#,#]l, a range of lines specified. In the second form, the last line listed becomes the current line. (shows non-printing characters.)
m	Moves a specified range of text to a new location in the editing buffer. The correct form is [#,#]m#, where the #,# pair are the lines to be moved, and the # following the command shows where the lines will be moved. The line(s) will be moved to the line *following* the target line.
n	Generic form of the number command. It displays a line or lines ([#,#]n) on the screen, preceding each line with the line number and the tab character. At the end of the command, the last line displayed becomes the current line.
p	Prints either the current line or the lines specified by the number range that precedes the command ([#,#]p). Then the lines listed are printed (shown on the screen), and the last line printed becomes the current line.
P	Turns on or off the command-mode prompt. (The default for this toggle is off.)
q	Lets you quit an ed session. If you have not saved the contents of the editing buffer, ed will give you the ? error message. If you issue another q command, ed will exit and not save the contents of the editing buffer.
Q	Lets you quit an ed session without verifying that the contents of the editing buffer have been saved. This is a dangerous command.
r	Copies the contents of a file specified by filename into another file at the location following the line(s) specified. If no filename is specified, the current file is used, and if there is no current file, an error message is generated. The format is [#,#]r filename.
s	Searches the current line for the specified text (stext) and replaces it (substitutes) with the replacement text (rtext). The form of the command is [#,#]s/stext/rtext/n. If the line numbers are omitted, works on the first occurrence it finds. This command can take an n suffix. If used, the *n*th occurrence of the stext will be replaced. The global options are frequently used with this command.
t	Copies the line(s) of text specified and inserts them *after* the line number specified as the target. The format is [#,#]t# (to remember it, ask yourself if you are copying from a range *to* a line number).

Command	Action
u	Helps you recover from an error. You can undo the actions of the ***most recent*** a, c, d, i, j, m, r, s, t, u, v , G, or V command. You must use the undo command before you issue another command from the preceding list. If you leave ed and return, you cannot undo a change. You cannot undo a change that has been written to disk. Please note: You can undo the results of an undo command as well!
v	Opposite of the g command. Where g finds all occurrences of the pattern listed, v finds all lines that ***do not match*** the pattern. If a command list is supplied, that command line is executed for each line that does not match the specified pattern. The proper syntax is [#,#]v/RE/command-list.
V	Opposite of the G command. (See the discussion of v).
^V	Using this command allows you to enter non-displaying character ASCII code into the buffer. For example the string ^V^G imbeds the ASCII code for ^G (beep) into the text. Useful for some specialized ASCII (or "escape") sequences. (^ represents the CTRL or control key, so ^V means Control-V.)
w	If no file name is specified, this command writes the contents of the editing buffer to the disk file that was opened (or edited, or read) to initially load the editing buffer. This command will allow a subset of the editing buffer to be saved, that format is [#,#]w***filename***. If no line numbers are specified, the whole file is written. If a file name is specified as an argument, then that portion of the editing buffer specified is written to the disk and saved under the filename.
W	This command is similar to the w except that it ***appends*** to an existing file rather than writing over the contents.
/RE/	This is used to search ***forward*** through the file for the first occurrence of the pattern enclosed in slashes. In this case, that is the character string RE.
?RE?	This is used, like the slashes, but starts a search ***backward***. Please note, for purposes of these searches, the buffer is circular.

Useful Regular Expressions for ed

Regular Expression	Matches
/A/	The first upper case A in the line (Note: A does not have to be the first character in the line to match this RE.)
.	Matches any single character.
*	Matches zero or more consecutive occurrences of the single character preceding it.
$	Represents the end of the line.
^	Represents the beginning of the line: ^A matches only lines that start with A.
\	An escape, or protection, character that prevents the shell from seeing the very next character following the backslash.
[ ]	Delineates a set of zero or more characters as the search string, where in **any one** of the characters in the braces satisfies the match criteria.
&	Represents the value of the string to be matched. It is used in substitution commands.

Pseudo-Addresses for ed

Note: Do not confuse these with regular-expression metacharacters.

$	Represents the **last** line in the buffer.
.	Specifies the current line. Most often used to delimit the first or last line in a range.
,	Represents the range of lines 1 through $ (the first through the last lines in the buffer.)
;	Represents the range of lines . through $ (the current line through the last line in the buffer.)
24	Any number will make the line corresponding to that number the current line and print it. The command 24 (the number 24) is the same as 24p. It makes 24 the current line and prints that line. In many books line numbers are illustrated with the octothorp, #.

Command Overview for ex

Command format:

      [address[, address]] command [parameters]

' (tick mark)	Go to the mark specified by the ma[rk] command.
! (bang)	Execute a shell command from within the ex editor.
ab[brev]	Create an abbreviation for a string used in visual mode.
a[ppend]	Start text entry mode, adding text *after* the current line.
c[hange]	Replace the line or lines specified with the text.
chd[ir]	Change the current directory to the one supplied.
co[py]	Copy the current line or lines elsewhere in the file, after the target line.
d[elete]	Delete the line or lines specified.
e[dit]	Start editing another file.
f[ile]	Show the file associated with the buffer, or associate another file with the buffer.
g[lobal]	Apply a *search* across all the lines of a file.
i[nsert]	Begin text entry *before* the line specified.
j[oin]	Join one or more lines.
l[ist]	Display the contents of the buffer, showing nonprinting characters.
map	Create a macro associated with a particular key. Used only in visual mode.
ma[rk]	Set a marker in the file; return to it with the ' (tick) command.
m[ove]	Move one or more lines *after* the line specified.

n[ext]	Begin editing the next file in the list of files from the command line.
nu[mber]	Display lines preceded by their line numbers.
o[pen]	Allows you to edit one line of text as if you were in visual mode.
p[reserve]	Create a backup of the file as if your editing session had been interrupted. Recover the editing session with the rec[over] command.
p[rint]	Display the lines in the buffer with no special formatting.
pu[t]	Place a deleted line or one of the named buffers into the text *after* the line specified.
q[uit]	Exit from the ex editor.
r[ead]	Read the contents of the file specified, not the buffer after the currrent line or the line specified.
rec[over]	Attempt to recover from an aborted editing session.
rew[ind]	Reset the arguments on the command line (rarely used).
se[t]	Set one or more of the multitude of options that apply to the current editing session.
sh[ell]	Drop out to the command line. This allows you to perform one or more tasks on the command line, then return to the editing session with the exit command.
shift right [>] left [<]	Shift the text line eight (by default) characters right or left.
so[urce]	Execute a series of commands stored in a file. This is a neat way to redo a set of commands on several files.
st[op]	Stop execution of the editor and drop to the command line. The same as ^Z.
s[ubstitution]	Replace one character or character string with another (your best friend).
sus[pend]	Exactly the same as st[op].
ta[g]	Load the file associated with this tag form the tag list. (This is an advanced command.)
una[bbrev]	Remove the specified abbreviation used in visual mode.
u[ndo]	Undo the most recent change to the buffer.
unm[ap]	Remove the macro or command set mapped to the specified character.
vi[sual]	Begin visual mode.
w[rite]	Write the contents of the buffer to the associated file or the file specified in the command.
wq	Write and then quit the editing session.
x[it]	Write and then exit from the editing session. Serves the same function as wq, but will write the file *only if the buffer has been changed.*
y[ank]	Copy the text specified to the anonymous buffer or to a named buffer.
z	Display the contents of the editing buffer starting at the line specified.

Command Overview for vi

Command format:

> [repeat count] command [span of control]

Starting vi

view	Start vi in read-only mode.
vi -R	Start vi in read-only mode.

Exiting from vi

ZZ	Write the buffer to disk and exit the editor (:q, :q!, :wq also work, but they are ex commands).

The text entry

a	Add text after the current cursor position.
A	Add text at the end of the current line.
i	Add text before the current cursor position.
I	Add text at the beginning of the current line.
o	Add a new line of text below the current line.
O	Add a new line of text above the current line.

Moving about

> Cursor Control (letters instead of silly arrows)

h	Left one character.
j	Down one line.

k	Up one line.
l	Right one character.
space bar	Right one character.

Within the Line

w	Right one word.
W	Right one word, skipping punctuation.
b	Left one word.
B	Left one word, skipping punctuation.
e	Right, to the end of the word.
E	Right, to the end of the word, skipping punctuation.
^	To the first nonblank character at the beginning of the line.
0	To the first position on the line.
$	To the last position on the line.
f	Forward to the next occurrence of the character following the command.
F	Backward to the previous occurrence of the character following the command.
t	To the right or forward to the position just before the specified character.
T	To the left or backward to the position just after the specified character.

Within the Screen

H	The first line of the current screen (head).
M	The center line of the screen (middle).
L	The bottom line of the display (last).

Within the Buffer

G	Go to the last line of the buffer, or to the line specified.
^B	Scroll the buffer backward one complete screen.
^F	Scroll the buffer forward one complete screen.
^D	Scroll the buffer forward $\frac{1}{2}$ of the screen.
^U	Scroll the buffer backward $\frac{1}{2}$ of the screen.
^E	Scroll the buffer forward one line.
^Y	Scroll the buffer backward one line.

Other cursor movement commands

)	Forward, right, to the next sentence.
(	Backward, left, to the previous sentence.
}	Forward, right, to the next paragraph.
{	Backward, left, to the previous paragraph.
%	Jump to the other member of a pair of { }, ( ), or [ ].

Searching In the Buffer

/	Search forward for the string following the / or the previous search string.
?	Search backward for the string following the ? or the previous search string.
n	Repeat the previous search.
N	Repeat the previous search in the reverse direction.

Deleting Data From the Buffer

Deleting individual characters

x	Delete the character at the cursor.
X	Delete the character to the left of the cursor.

Deleting all or part of lines

d	Delete
dw	Deletes the word.
d	Deletes the line.
dG	Deletes to the end of the buffer.
D	Delete to the end of the current line.

Combining Two or More Lines

J	Join the current line to the next line.

Putting Data Back

After deleting or yanking the character, word, line, or lines,

p	Put the data in the anonymous (named) buffer *after* the current cursor position (if the buffer contains a line, then the insertion will be after the current line).
P	Put the data in the anonymous (named) buffer *before* the current cursor position (if the buffer contains a line, then the insertion will be after the current line).

Copying Data

y	Yank a word, line, or lines into the anonymous or (named) buffer.
Y	Yank the current line into the anonymous or (named) buffer.

Use one of the put commands to put the data back into the buffer.

Changing the contents of the buffer

Within the line

r	Replace the character under the cursor, and drop back to command mode after the replacement.
R	Go into overstrike mode, replacing characters to the right as they are typed over.

c	Enter change mode. For example,
cw	Changes the word.
cc	Changes the line, etc.
C	Change from the cursor position to the end of the line.
~	Change the case of the letter at the cursor position. Does not affect non-letters.
s	Substitute for the current character, and stay in text-entry mode.
S	Substitute for the current line, and stay in text-entry mode.

Across the buffer
Use the ex *commands you already know.*

Switching from vi to ex and back

Q	Quit visual mode, and drop into ex(line) mode.
vi	Quit line mode, and switch to visual mode.

Setting ex/vi options

set	Set one or more of the ex variables. I recommend you set the following:

showmode
autoindent (ai)
errorbells (eb)
exrc
number (nu)
tab stops to 4 (ts=4)
shift width to 4 (sw=4)

A Light Overview of Emacs

The Emacs editor is wildly popular in some Unix circles. It evolved as a lisp (LISt Processing) tool, and has migrated from that environment to become a general-purpose Unix editor. Actually, some Emacs users stay in the editor and use it as their desktop, since they can receive email, work with files, and even play games from within the Emacs process. It hasn't yet overtaken the old standards like vi, but it has made solid inroads into the editor camp.

Richard Stallman wrote Emacs back in 1975. At first it was part of the TECO system, a collection of macros. Now for the exciting part: some Unix historians say that the Emacs editor was named after an ice cream store called Emack & Bolio's. Alas, according to Mr. Stallman, he didn't even know of the place when he named his editor. Rather, Emacs was named in the standard TECO format, placing "mac" or "macs" at the end of a macro or program name. Emacs, therefore, stands for "Editing Macros." Not terribly exciting, but it is a really great editor, and a rose by any other name would still edit as sweetly.

This appendix is an overview of the Emacs editor, giving you some simple commands to allow you to get started editing. If you are going to commit to Emacs, plan to spend a while learning the complexities of this wonderful tool. Just as vi is more complex than ed, Emacs is far more complex than vi. Of course, anything that is powerful and useful usually takes a bit of effort to master. Should you begin using Emacs, I am sure you will come to love it and join the camp of Emacs-ers who sing its praises. Now, without further ado, here's Emacs!

Starting Emacs

When you start Emacs, you will probably see something like the screen in Figure G1. You might notice that this screen capture looks slightly different than those in the rest of the book. How very observant of you! Indeed, whilst writing this book—actually, just after I finished the main text and began the appendices—I experienced an attack on the systems I am responsible for at school by crackers using machines in France and

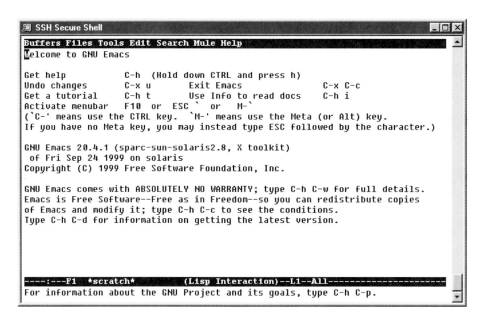

FIGURE G1

Emacs entry screen.

Germany. One of the attacks was a type of TCP/IP "sniffer" that read logins and passwords. Much to my chagrin, they managed to sniff my password and login I.D. since I was using plain old TeraTerm without any encryption. My student system administrators found it quite amusing that Dr. G. had been sniffed and that the crackers were using my account. I was less than amused! Anyway, that convinced me to stop using plain TCP/IP and start using a secure login. Secure Shell (ssh) encrypts everything sent to or from the server. It is pretty painless to use, but you *must* have ssh running on the Unix server before you can use it.

Help

Anyway, back to Emacs! One of the wonderful things about Emacs is that it contains a comprehensive Help system and even a tutorial on using the editor. To invoke Help, type ^H. Take a look at Figure G2. This is only one of the options for getting help in Emacs. You can also search through the help on your system and learn a great deal about this powerful editor. One of the best tools, in my humble opinion, is the tutorial within Help. That is shown in Figure G3. I urge you to work the tutorial. It will very efficiently teach you how to use Emacs. Actually, you probably could just use the tutorial and stop reading right now, but, hey, you're having fun, right?

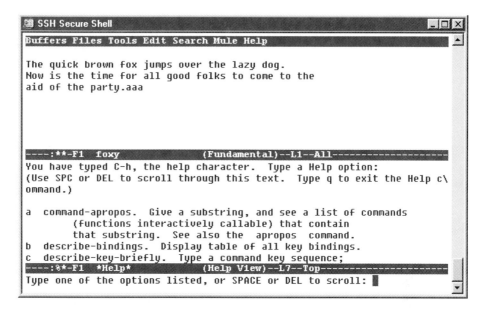

FIGURE G2

Emacs Help.

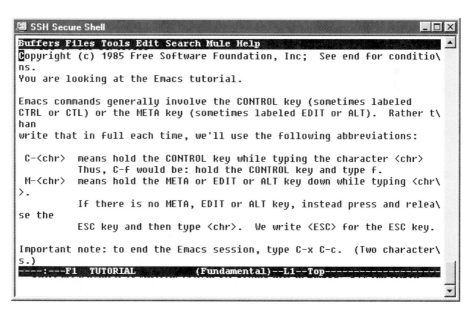

FIGURE G3

The Emacs tutorial.

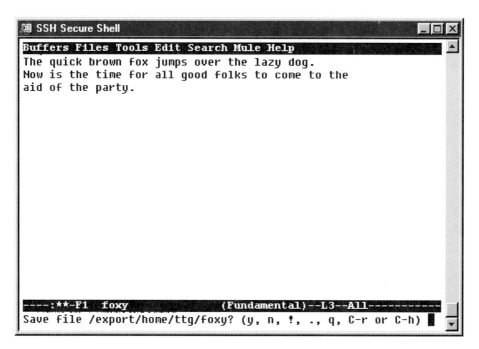

FIGURE G4

Simple text editing.

Text Entry

Simple file editing is pretty straight forward in Emacs. For example, in Figure G4 I have opened the editor and entered your favorite line from the earlier editing exercises. The commands I used to enter text-entry mode were none! I just started typing. Unlike the editors you have used up to now, Emacs starts you out in text-entry mode, and commands are all prefixed by the C or ^ (press and hold the Ctrl key) or M (press the Meta or ESC key once, then let it go) characters. Sometimes you will use a combination of a control sequences. For example, to exit from the Emacs editor and save your work, you enter ^X followed by ^C. Combining collections of keystrokes in this fashion gives Emacs a very large range of commands. That is one reason it takes a while to learn Emacs; it is very rich in commands.

Leaving Emacs

In Figure G4 I entered the keystroke combination ^X^C to exit the editor. Like the other editors you are familiar with, Emacs works in a buffer, and you must save the contents of the buffer to disk or you will lose your work. Fortunately, Emacs is somewhat careful and will ask you if you want to save the buffer to disk if you have made changes to it and try to exit without saving them.

On the other hand, Emacs will also save the contents of the buffer to disk automagically, if you just wait a bit. Take a look at Figure G5 and notice the status message in the echo area, or minibuffer, at the bottom of the screen. Emacs is telling me that it has saved the contents of the buffer to disk.

FIGURE G5

Automagically saving contents of buffer.

This is a good thing if I forget to save wonderful changes to the buffer, and a Bad Thing if I have made changes to the file I don't want to keep. Either way, you need to be aware that Emacs will automatically save the changes to the buffer if your buffer is associated with a file. The variable that controls the frequency of auto saving is called the auto-save-interval variable, and by default it is set to 300 keystrokes. You can modify that variable if you wish.

Mode Line

The informational line near the bottom of the screen is called the *mode line*. This line, seen in Figure G5, tells you a number of different things. If there are two asterisks, it means that the buffer has been changed and not saved. Next comes a code to tell you what Emacs thinks it is doing, then the name of the file associated with the buffer. After the filename, Emacs tells you where you are in the file, in this case at L8, Line 8, and then tells you where the current window you are editing lies in the file. It may be at the top of the file, at the bottom of the file, a percentage of the way through the file, or showing all of the file. That latter case is shown in Figure G5.

Cursor Movement

There are a series of commands that you can use to move around the screen. You can use the arrow keys instead, but real Emacs people wouldn't be caught dead using the arrow keys! Table G1 shows a set of useful movement commands. As you can see, there are a number cursor movement commands, and in keeping with Emacs premise that commands have a character prepended to them, all of these commands start with Ctrl (^) or ESC (ESC). Practice moving the point of action (the cursor) around a file, and

TABLE G1   Cursor (Point of Action) Controls

Key Sequence	What It Does
^F	Move **forward** one character.
^B	Move **backward** one character.
^N	Move **down** one line.
^P	Move **up** one line (You may need to repeat this in some cases.)
^A	Move to the **beginning** of the line.
^E	Move to the **end** of the line.
^L	Move to the **middle** of the editing window and refresh.
ESC F	Move **forward one word**.
ESC B	Move **backward one word**.
ESC <	Move to **top** of the buffer.
ESC >	Move to **bottom** of the buffer.
ESC X n	Type ESC X, then go to line RETURN. Emacs will prompt for the line number.
^V	Scroll **forward one page**.
ESC V	Scroll **backward one page**.

these commands will become second nature after a bit. Don't use the arrow keys; it's more fun to use the keyboard keys.

Removing Text

As with vi, there are a number of Emacs commands that remove text from the buffer. Table G2 shows a collection of different commands you can use to delete text.

When you learned the vi editor, we discussed the anonymous buffer. I am sure you remember how that works to hold deleted or copied text. The Emacs editor has a similar buffer, but it is called the *kill ring*. Any delete commands, except those that remove a single character, place the deleted text into the kill ring. To recover text from the kill ring, use the ^Y command. (Okay, you "yank" it from the kill ring to the editing

TABLE G2   Text Removal Commands

Key Combination	What It Does
Delete key	Delete the character before the cursor.
^D	Delete the character at the cursor.
ESC D	Remove the next word.
^K	Delete all text to the end of the line.
ESC K	Delete the sentence the cursor is within.
^X Delete key	Delete the previous sentence.

buffer. I know that is similar to, yet opposite from the vi command, but you *can* get used to it.)

Undoing What You Have Done

There are three critical undo commands in Emacs: one to abort the current command, one to undo the last edit, and one to undo everything.

Abort Current Command

To abort the current command, type ^G. This is just like typing ^C on the shell command line, and it will abort the current command. This is the "oops, changed my mind, forget what I was about to do" command.

Undo the Last Edit

To undo the last edit, type ^X u, which will undo the most recent change to the buffer. Unlike vi, Emacs lets you use several ^X u commands and back out change after change. This is really handy.

Undo Everything I Have Done!

Well, it isn't really possible to undo *everything*, but the command revert-buffer resets the contents of the buffer to the way it was the last time the file was saved (or the last time it was auto-saved.) Notice that there is no keystroke combination for this command. You will need to use the command name (revert-buffer) rather than a keystroke combination. For commands that have no key combination, type ESC x and then the command name. Figure G6 shows you how to do that.

The top screen in Figure G6 shows my hours and hours of work in the foxy buffer. Then I typed ESC x revert-buffer and touched ENTER. Emacs asked me if I wanted to revert to the state the buffer was in when I started editing (since I hadn't saved any of my changes). I said "yes." By the way, you must use the full word, "yes" or "no." Emacs is picky about that and will ask you to type the full word if you try a shortcut. I typed in "yes," and you can see the result in the lower screen of Figure G6. The "undo everything back to the last save" is wonderful to know about if you make a major mistake like deleting a whole range of lines, then adding stuff, then deleting more lines, and then realize you didn't want to do *any* of those changes.

Speaking of shortcuts, while Emacs seems somewhat pedantic about "yes" and "no," it is flexible about the command names. For example, in Figure G7 I again made massive changes to the buffer, then typed ESC x revert <RETURN>, and Emacs completed the command for me. Had I typed rever, Emacs would have asked me which of two different commands I wished to execute. That feature of Emacs is so helpful. If you don't remember all of the command, Emacs will help.

Searching

Another important task you need to know how to perform is to search through the buffer for a particular string. As with the other editors, you can search forward and backward with Emacs. The only difference is in the command string you use. Figure G8 shows how to search through a buffer for a particular string. When you type the key combination ^S, the search prompt appears. As you type characters, the cursor moves to the byte

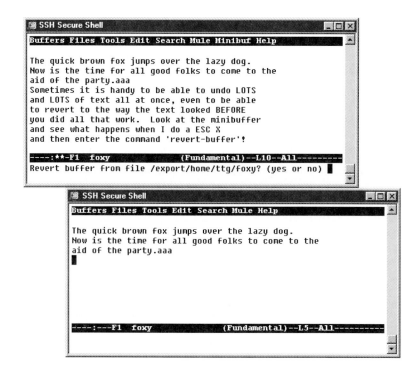

FIGURE G6

Reverting the buffer to the last saved state.

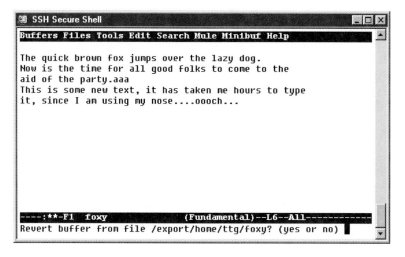

FIGURE G7

Allowing Emacs to complete a command for me.

following the last letter you typed. For example, when I typed f the cursor moved to the t of after. Then when I typed o, it moved to the x of fox. Like other the other editors you are familiar with, Emacs uses a circular buffer so you can search off the bottom of the buffer and end up at the top. The minibuffer will tell you when you have wrapped.

Note: Some terminal emulators will intercept ^S as a special key combination that is used to stop scrolling on the screen. If this is the case on your machine, you will need to use the ESC O R combination to search forward. Since my computer recognizes ^S, I can't test the ESC O R combination, but an online document said this would work. This is one of the very few times I haven't tested what I told you to do. (You could also customize Emacs to bind that key pair differently, but that is beyond the scope of this brief discussion.)

To search backward, you use the ^R for reverse search. By the way, the I- before the search stands for Incremental.

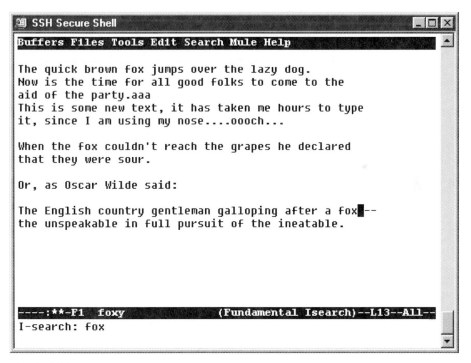

FIGURE G8

Searching through a buffer.

FIGURE G9
Replacing text.

Substitution

You can replace text in the file using the commands shown in Figure G9. Please note that this figure is a composite of four steps. First I started the replacement with the ESC X replace-string command shown in the first screen capture. After I touched ENTER, Emacs asked me for the string I wished to replace, and I told him fox and touched ENTER again. Then Emacs asked me what string I wanted to use to replace the string fox, and I entered wolf and touched ENTER a last time. Emacs replaced the next occurrence of the string fox with the string wolf.

In addition to substituting strings, you can use a regular expressions to identify the string to substitute. Figure G10 shows how I accomplished regular-expression substitution. The steps here are similar to those in the string replacement but with a different command, of course. Now look at Figure G11 to see the results of the replacement.

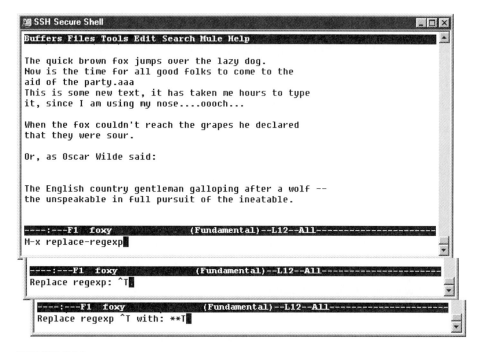

FIGURE G10

Replacement with regular expressions.

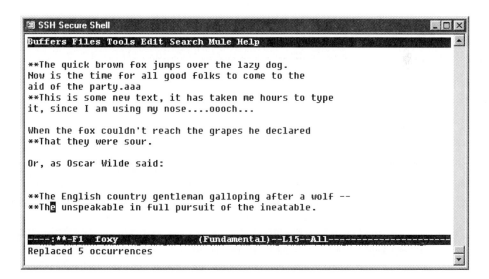

FIGURE G11

Results of the replacement shown in Figure G10.

Look carefully and see if you can find the difference in the way Emacs handles regular expressions. Notice how Emacs treats regular expressions just a little differently? In this case, lines that began with either an uppercase or a lowercase T were matched. The results were like those obtained from using grep with the -i option. I will leave it to your exploration to discover any other interesting differences.

Emacs also supports a query form of both replace-string and replace-regexp. Figure G12 shows how I could use that form to select which Ts I wanted to change. With the query option selected, Emacs will ask me if it should replace the initial T each time it encounters a line that starts with one. If I type y, Emacs will make the change, if I type n, Emacs will go to the next occurrence of the initial T and ask again.

One small word of warning: If you touch the RETURN key, Emacs takes that as a yes. Remember that you can use the query form of replacement with both regular expressions and fixed patterns/strings.

You now know enough Emacs to be dangerous to yourself and to files. Many other collections of commands are available, far more than I could cover in an appendix. If you want to explore Emacs, I strongly recommend you start with the built-in tutorial. Just to whet your appetite, here is a list of the collections of commands I have left to your careful investigation:

1. Editing in multiple buffers.
2. Building Macros.

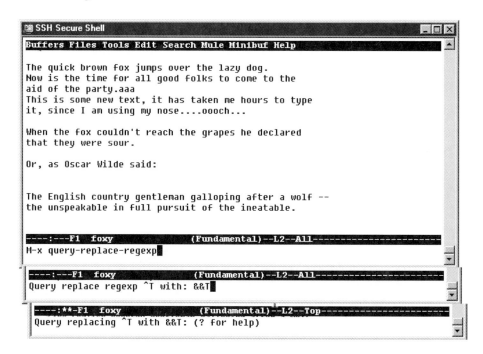

FIGURE G12

Selective regular-expression replacement.

3. Customizing Emacs.
4. Running mail and other commands from within Emacs.
5. Playing with different modes.
6. Playing with multiple windows.
7. Text formatting.

Quite a list! Enjoy playing with Emacs, you just might find that it becomes more than an editor for you. Indeed, it just might become your working desktop.

Glossary

(Note: This glossary contains other words besides those indicated as Key Words in the text. It is designed to be a bit more comprehensive than the run-of-the-mill glossary. Some of the entries are taken from the *New Hacker's Dictionary*, which you can access at

`http://www.tuxedo.org/~esr/jargon/jargon.HTML`

Take the time to check that dictionary out, it is an icon of the hacker universe.
If you have any words that you think should have been included, please send your suggested additions to ttg@clyde.dcccd.edu. I will consider any additions that will make this glossary more complete, and more fun! I look forward to your suggestions.)

A

absolute address—complete path or address of a data element. The absolute path starts with a slash, representing the root of the file system. An example is /etc/passwd. Compare with *relative address*.

absolute path name—*See* absolute address.

access—retrieve data from a storage medium like tape or disk. Also used to describe the process of establishing communication with a computer.

access time—the time it takes the read/write head to find requested data on a storage medium; or the time it takes you to log into a particular Unix box.

ACM—*See* Association for Computing Machinery (ACM).

active directory—directory or subdirectory that the operating system or application program uses as a default when accessing programs or data files from disk. Also called the *current directory*.

action—specialized term in awk that stands for the activity taken when a particular pattern is matched. An action can entail executing several verbs or commands.

address—unique number assigned to each memory location within a computer's processing hardware.

ADM-3a—an early monitor, important to us because it was the motivation for Bill Joy to move to the "full screen" and create the vi editor.

Aho, Albert—one of the early authors of parts of the Unix operating system. He is the "A" in awk, and also wrote egrep and fgrep.

algorithm—statement of a set of steps or procedures, of finite length, giving a known result. A program, a recipe, or script is an algorithm.

alias—generally a second name for a person; in the Unix sense an alias is a name you assign to a command, or a pipe. Using an alias is a way to create a new command, one that never existed before. The problem with creating and using aliases is that they are not always available, and some shells don't even support them.

alphabetic data—data composed of the characters of the alphabet and punctuation characters.

alphanumeric data—another name for textual data, data composed of numbers and/or letters and/or special characters. Contrast with *alphabetic* and *numeric data*.

American National Standards Institute (ANSI)—group that develops computer-related standards for use by industry and computer manufacturers—for example, standards for programming languages.

analog signals—signals representing data as patterns of frequencies, like sounds in which values flow from one frequency and or volume to another continuously. Contrast with *digital signals*

anonymous ftp—allows use of ftp without a password; user gives "anonymous" as name and e-mail address as a password. Often used to download code and scripts.

ANSI—*See* American National Standards Institute (ANSI).

appellation—the name of a thing. One of those words that just roll off the tongue. Try it!

append—to attach additional material to a data stream or file, usually data to the end of the file or data stream.

application program—a program that performs some specific task for the user, like the components of StarOffice, a game, or some other software the user runs.

application software—programs that solve specific user-oriented processing problems.

argument—(1) data passed to a script or command from the command line; not to be confused with command-line *options*. Also called command-line *parameter*. (2) A less than pleasant discussion between two people, often involving raised voices.

arithmetic operation—ability of a computer to do mathematical functions, like addition and subtraction, with numeric data.

array—contiguous area of memory used to hold several variable values. The advantage of an array is that the data are accessible via a subscript that specifies which of the several values is the one requested. Another name for an array is *subscripted variable*.

artificial intelligence (AI)—software application that simulates human thought and judgment by the use of heuristic problem-solving techniques.

American Standard Code for Information Interchange (ASCII)—code for storing data that uses 7 bits to a byte and is commonly used in microcomputers; an extended version of ASCII uses 8 bits per byte.

ASCII editor—produces an ASCII file; also called *text editor*. The common Unix editors are ASCII editors.

ASR-33—known to its many friends and admirers as a Teletype, the ASR-33 (Automatic Send and Receive) was the state-of-the-art hard-copy terminal in the late 1960s through the early 1980s.

Assembler—computer language slightly removed from the naked hexadecimal, in which mnemonics are used in place of the actual hexadecimal code. It is one of the favored languages of hackers and other wizards.

background—one of two ways a process can execute. Processes can run in the *foreground*, having access to the keyboard as well as the screen, or in the *background*, relinquishing control of the keyboard but still sending data to the screen.

backup—extra copy of data or programs on a disk or tape that is kept for use in case the original is destroyed or corrupted. As a verb, *back up* refers to the process of making such a copy. Smart users *always* back up their data!

Bad Thing—[very common; always pronounced as if capitalized. Orig. fr. the 1930 Sellar & Yeatman parody of British history *1066 And All That*, but well-established among hackers in the U.S. as well.] Something that can't possibly result in improvement of the subject. This term is always capitalized, as in "Replacing all of the 9600-baud modems with bicycle couriers would be a Bad Thing."

bang—common spoken name for! (ASCII 0100001), especially when used in pronouncing a *bang path* in spoken hackish. In elder days this was considered a CMUish usage, with MIT and Stanford hackers preferring excl or shriek; but the spread of Unix has carried *bang* with it (especially via the term *bang path*), and it is now certainly the most common spoken name for !. Note that it is used exclusively for nonemphatic written !; one would not say "Congratulations bang" (except possibly for humorous purposes), but if one wanted to specify the exact characters in "foo!" one would speak "Eff oh oh bang."

baud—measurement of the speed of a communications system. Up to 300 baud is the same as bits per second; after that baud represents the number of times the data stream changes state (1 to 0 or 0 to 1) in a second.

benchmark test—compares software and hardware performance against a minimum standard agreed upon by management and the application development team.

Berners-Lee, Tim—invented the World Wide Web in late 1990 while working at CERN, the European Particle Physics Laboratory in Geneva, Switzerland. He wrote the first WWW client and the first WWW server along with most of the communications software, defining URLs, HTTP and HTML. He is a graduate of Oxford University. Tim is now the overall director of the W^3C.

beta releases—experimental versions of software that test new features before they become part of the current release.

beta test—prerelease testing of commercial software by potential outside users.

bigot—[common] a person who is religiously attached to a particular computer language, operating system, editor, or other tool. Usually found with a specifier; thus, "Cray bigot," "ITS bigot," "APL bigot," "VMS bigot," "Berkeley bigot." Often bigots are the instigators of holy wars when poked or prodded, and there are few things more amusing than watching two bigots, with opposing views, "debate" issues like which editor is best.

binary—code pattern of on/off bits used to represent data or computer operations. This term is often used to mean a binary file, as in, "Just get the binary and install that."

binary digit—(also known as *bit*) the on or off state of a single computer circuit, represented as 1 and 0, respectively.

binary file—file of machine-readable code composed of 1s and 0s, as opposed to *source code*, which is human-readable.

bit—(also known as *binary digit*) the on or off state of a single computer circuit, represented as 1 and 0, respectively.

bits per second (bps)—measurement of data transmission speed by which the number of 0 and 1 digits per second is counted.

bleeding edge—just beyond the leading edge lies the bleeding edge, where it is very expensive to see if a new product or idea will work.

Boole, George (1815–1864)—developed two-state (true or false) logic theory for mathematical expressions during the nineteenth century. His theories later became the basis for binary code.

Bourne, Steve—wrote the Bourne shell, the first true Unix shell.

BSD—(abbreviation for Berkeley Software Distribution) a family of Unix versions for the DEC VAX and PDP-11 developed by Bill Joy and others at Berkeley starting around 1977, incorporating paged virtual memory, TCP/IP networking enhancements, and many other features. The BSD versions (4.1, 4.2, and 4.3) and the commercial versions derived from them (SunOS, ULTRIX, and Mt. Xinu) held the technical lead in the Unix world until AT&T's successful standardization efforts after about 1986; descendants including Free/Open/NetBSD, BSD/OS and MacOS X are still widely popular. Note that BSD versions going back to 2.9 are often referred to by their version numbers alone, without the BSD prefix. The most recent incantation of BSD is Macintosh OS X which is also a flavor of BSD.

buffer—region of memory used to either hold data, or in the case of editors, hold text being processed.

bug—error within a computer program. The first bug was a moth that was trapped in a relay in one of the first computers. Grace Hopper taped the moth in the log book and explained how they had de-bugged the computer. Actually the term *bug*, in entomology, refers to the family Hemiptera.

Computer bugs fall into two classes, syntax errors and logic errors. A *syntax error* is an error in the formation of the computer code. A *logic error* is correct syntactically, but produces an incorrect answer. For example, in the Bourne shell, a = 4 is a test for equality, not an assignment, because of the spaces around the equal sign. Confusing the two is a logical error.

built-in commands—commands that are part of the shell. These built-in commands don't require the process to fork a new process to run them, they run within the shell's process.

built-in shell variables—variables initialized by the shell. Different shells initialize different shell variables. Many times these variables are read-only.

Byron, Augusta Ada (Countess of Lovelace) (1815–1852)—the one who annotated and published Babbage's work in the 1840s. Her detailed instructions for operation are considered a precursor to modern programming. Actually Ada was really the first programmer. She was also the daughter of Lord Byron, the famous poet. The Ada language is named for her.

byte—group of bits representing a single character or digit of data, usually 8 bits (two nibbles).

C—high-level programming language written by Dennis Ritchie to rewrite Unix in a high-level language. It is used in system programming and graphics. It is portable and easy to structure but somewhat complex and not particularly easy to learn.

cache—to store data that may be needed again either on disk (in the case of caching pages) or in memory.

carriage-return line feed (CrLf)—new line of text, usually the result of touching the ENTER or RETURN key; also called a *newline* character.

case sensitivity—being smart enough to recognize the difference between uppercase and lowercase letters. Unlike substandard operating systems, Unix can tell the difference between an *A* and an *a*.

cathode ray tube (CRT)—(also known as monitor) an ancient output peripheral that used a cathode ray tube to project an electron beam onto the back of a phosphor-covered glass plate; replaced by LCD screens (don't we all wish!).

CD—*See* compact disk—no, not the music kind.

CD-ROM (*compact disk Read-Only Memory*)—(also known as *CD* or *compact disk*) removable disk that permanently stores data and cannot be changed.

central processing unit (CPU)—processing hardware of a computer, containing a processor and memory. This is where the real work happens.

CGI script—program, running on a server, written in any one of several popular languages, most often Perl or a Unix shell language, to process data sent from an HTML form.

character—smallest unit of text data; it is a single digit, letter, or symbol; also known as a *byte*.

chip—(1) a small silicon wafer holding integrated circuits and other processing circuitry. (2) One of the three basic food groups for Unix folks, along with chocolate and cola, known as the 3Cs.

circular buffer—arrangement of memory that functions as if the data were wrapped around a cylinder. Moving past the last line of the buffer takes you to the top of the buffer, and moving upward past the first line takes you to the last line of the buffer. The three common Unix editors use circular buffers.

client/server—network design in which the client, any end user's computer, takes on processing tasks traditionally handled by a network server.

clobber—to overwrite the contents of one file with another. This is usually an unintentional process, occurring when you run a command and direct its output to another file. In the C shell, the noclobber variable will prevent this from happening some of the time.

code—written program instruction. When you are writing instructions for a command like awk or sed, or when you are writing a shell script, the instructions are usually called a *script*.

coding—writing a computer program or script (also known as scripting). Scripting is often thought to be one of the highest callings for mortals.

colon delimited—term used to describe a file that uses colons rather than white space to identify the different fields; /etc/passwd is an excellent example of a colon-delimited file.

compact disk (CD)—(also known as **CD-ROM**) removable disk that permanently stores data by burning pits into the substrate of the medium; it cannot be changed.

compact disk–Read/Write (CD-RW)—high-capacity optical disk that has a surface that can be written and then erased and rewritten.

command—(1) the fundamental part of a Unix directive, or one of the components of a shell script. (2) Mode 1 of the two modes you can be in when using one of the standard editors. In command mode you supply directives to the editor; in the other mode, text-entry mode, you enter data into the buffer.

command line—the place where wise Unix wizards do their work. Folks who are burdened by living with substandard operating systems are stuck in a GUI, but real Unix folk know that the command line is much more efficient.

command mode—one of two modes the standard Unix editors can work in. In command mode, all keystrokes are interpreted as commands to the editor. The other mode is text-entry mode.

command substitution—term used to describe the process of storing the output of a command or pipe in a variable. Command substitution is accomplished by surrounding the command stream with grave marks (`) and assigning the result to a variable.

comments—documentation of choices made while writing a program or script with explanations of *why* particular choices were made. Arguably, comments are the most essential part of any program or script. The octothorp, or hash mark, #, precedes most Unix comments.

Common Gateway Interface (CGI)—program that processes the information sent in on a form.

compiler—high-level language translator that checks an entire program for errors while it is translating the code into machine language. If there are syntax errors, a list of errors is output by this program.

compiled language—language that is compiled. Most high-level languages, like C, are compiled. Compare with *interpreted language*.

computer architecture—physical characteristics of the computer, for example a 2 GhZ Pentium processor with a 64-million color a vector graphics card.

computer-assisted instruction (CAI)—using the computer to present material to students. A type of self-paced learning popular in the 1980s that is making a resurgence through the use of Web-based training.

concatenation—adding or extending to the end of an element or file.

conditional execution—term used to describe the execution of a sequence of code based upon a condition specified by either an IF or a case structure. Conditional execution is at the heart of the selection program element.

conditional loop—loop that is controlled by a condition rather than a count. The preferred form of conditional loop is theWHILE loop.

connectivity—the state of being connected to either a computer or a computer network and therefore being in communication with other computers.

cookie—small quantum of data stored by the browser that is associated with a particular HTML page on the Net. Usually cookies are used to store and retrieve information about the user. In most cases, cookies live only for the life of the browsing session and disappear when the browser is closed. The actual reason for the term *cookie* is lost in the mists of antiquity, but there are a couple of good possibilities. First, the term *magic cookie* was used to describe a small chunk of data that allowed access to some special functions of a computer program. These small data elements were used in the mainframe days. Another rendition of the cookie was the *cookie-monster program.* That was arguably one of the first computer virus programs. The user would be working along and all at once the computer would clear the terminal screen and say "Give me a cookie." If the user responded with any input, except the word "cookie," the program would continue to demand a cookie. The absolutely proper name for a cookie is a *persistent client state HTTP cookie,* but the term *magic cookie* is much more fun.

copy and paste—process of duplicating some element of data at another place in the buffer. The original data are not altered. At the end of this process the data are duplicated.

counted loop—loop that is controlled by a counter. This loop will execute the number of times as specified by the counter. The other form of loop is the *conditional loop.* Both conditional and counted loops are part of the iteration programming structure.

Ctrl-c—holding down the control key (Ctrl) and touching the c key to kill the current foreground process.

Ctrl-d—holding down the control key (Ctrl) and touching the D key sends an end of file signal to stop input when the command is reading from standard input.

Ctrl-z—holding down the control key (Ctrl) and touching the z key to suspend execution of the current foreground process and give you control at the command line.

CrLf—*See* carriage-return line feed (CrLf); the *newline* character.

CPU—*See* central processing unit (CPU).

crash—generically used to describe a spectacular computer failure but can also be used to describe the failure of any part of a computer system or a software failure. It initially referred to hard disks. When a hard disk crashed, the read/write head came into contact with the rapidly spinning platter. This caused a horrible screeching sound and much to-ing and fro-ing. It was, and remains, a Bad Thing.

CRT—*See* cathode ray tube (CRT).

cursor—blinking line or box that highlights where the computer is going to display the next keyboard entry.

cursor control—use of keys on keyboard to move the cursor up, down, left, or right through a document. Proper cursor control in the vi editor is achieved through the use of the h, j, k, and l keys rather than the arrow keys, unless you have an AMD-3a.

cut and paste—(sometimes called *move*) to change the location of data within a document or file.

data—facts, figures, and images—the stuff of data processing. Please note that *data* is a plural word. The singular form is *datum.*

data stream—term used to describe the movement of data from a device into a command, or from one command to another. Standard input, output, and error are all examples of data streams.

debug—to remove the moths from the machine, or, in more modern times, the errors from a script or program. *See also* bug

default value—the choice that the system or a script will make for you if you fail to specify a value. Usually this is not the best choice, unless an extremely wise scriptor has written the script. Never choose the default unless you *know* it is correct; and if you know the right value, just use that instead.

demand paging—one of the paging algorithms in which the CPU tries to resolve an address, discovers it is not on any page currently in memory, and issues a page request to the pager.

dereference—term used to describe accessing two files that have been soft-linked together.

/dev/null—null device, the ultimate bit bucket, an absolute black hole for data. Anything you send to /dev/null is instantly gone forever.

directory structure—term used to refer to the arrangement of files in some hierarchical fashion. The directory structure in Unix is an inverted tree.

DNS—*See* Domain Name Server (DNS).

domain name—handy substitute for the numeric IP address; an alphabetic name, such as foo.barr.com.

Domain Name Server (DNS)—program that translates domain names into IP addresses. Before a computer can access another computer by name, that domain name must be translated into the unique IP (Internet Protocol) address for that particular machine.

dotted file—file that has a dot (period) as its first character of the name. A dotted file is also called a *protected* or *hidden file* because it will not be found by file-matching metacharacter expansion. cshrc is a dotted file.

downloading—copying a file from another computer to your computer. This is the most common use for ftp.

echo—the aural reflection of a sound, sound, sound, sound. In the Unix world, this is the command used to display data, to standard out by default, or to some other file.

ELSE block—that sequence of commands within an IF statement that is executed if the condition is false. An ELSE block is normally terminated by a closing French brace or the fi statement, depending on the language used to create the IF.

encryption—storing something in the form of a code. There are a number of algorithms used to encrypt data. Some, like the one used to encrypt passwords, cannot be worked backwards, and so are called a *one-way* encryption algorithm.

end-user—person who can use computer technology to organize data, stimulate new ideas, solve problems, and communicate the results to others. This individual is also called a *user*. When you become a system administrator, you will discover that the world is divided into two groups; users for whom you work, and lusers who become the bane of your existence.

escape—(1) to beat a hasty retreat from the computer center in a vain attempt to escape from a Unix project or assignment. (They *will* follow you.) (2) To protect a character from interpretation by the shell. There are traditionally three ways of escaping a character: surrounding it with double quotation marks (''), rounding it with tic marks ('), or prepending a backslash (\) to the character.

execute—run, as in, "I executed the login process." It has no fatal connotations in the Unix world.

EOF (end of file)—marker that indicates the end of the input file or data stream. Each Unix file is terminated by an EOF marker, and you can terminate terminal input using the ^D (Ctrl-D key) to mark the EOF for the input stream.

EOL (end of line)—marker that indicates the end of the current line. Usually a newline character in Unix.

expunge—to mark for removal. It comes from the Latin *expungere*, meaning to mark for deletion by dots. This is an example of one of the wonderful words you can discover if you spend some quality time with your thesaurus. It is also exactly the correct word for the mail messages marked for deletion in pine.

external command—command that is not part of the shell and must be loaded from disk before it can be executed. Contrast with *internal command*.

field—related group of letters, numbers, and symbols—for example, a name, phone number, or street address.

FIFO (first in, first out)—one of the ways entries are removed from a queue. This is the most common method in many queues like the print queue. Envision a train passing through a tunnel. The first car (okay, the engine) into the tunnel is the first element (so there!) out of the tunnel. (Unless there is a Real Problem in the tunnel!)

file-matching metacharacter—one of the several metacharacters that the shell recognizes as being able to take on several different values. For example, the * (asterisk) can stand for any number of any character. Not to be confused with *wild cards*.

file transfer protocol (ftp)—process that allows you to move files across the Net.

filename—unique set of letters, numbers, and symbols that identifies a data file or program.

In the Unix environment, there are no required filename extensions, so the period, or dot (.) is just another character except for dotted files. See dotted file.

FILO (first in, last out)—somewhat uncommon method of handling entries in a queue. In this method, the first element into the queue is the last element removed from the queue. Think of a stack of plates. The first plate placed in the stack, on the bottom, would be the last plate removed from the stack.

filter—term used to refer to a process that reads from standard input and writes to standard output. Building scripts as filters allows them to play well with others and work in pipes. Always try to create filters when you write scripts.

firewall—program that protects one or more computers from attack from someone on the Net, outside the firewall.

floating-point number—number with a decimal point. Nonexistent in the native Bourne shell.

foreground—one of two ways a process may execute. Processes running in the foreground control the keyboard and the screen. Contrast with *background*.

freeware—software in the public domain. Most Unix tools fall in this category. The largest repository is the GNU software library, www.gnu.org. It is a wonderful collection.

ftp—*See* file transfer protocol (ftp).

function—predefined formula or code segment that performs common mathematical, text processing, or logical operations. By definition, a function name includes parentheses, ( ), and the call to the function is replaced by the value it generates.

gigabyte—one billion bytes of memory.

gigo (garbage in, garbage out)—meaning that errors in data produce useless information. Also used to describe sending data to programs that run on substandard operating systems.

global variable—value stored at a location known to more than one process or script. Due to memory protection schemes, few variables in Unix are global.

glob—to expand a metacharacter. The activity of expansion is called *globbing*.

globbing—process of expanding file-matching metacharacters. If you turn off globbing in the C shell, for example (set noglob), then the expansion of file-matching metacharacters will be disabled, and the command ls f* will list only the file f*, if that file exists in your directory.

GNU—recursive acronym that stands for GNUs Not Unix. This organization, ww.gnu.org, is the best place to find freeware for Unix systems.

Good Thing—[very common; always pronounced as if capitalized. Orig. fr. the 1930 Sellar & Yeatman parody of British history *1066 And All That*, but well-established among hackers in the U.S. as well.] (1) Self-evidently wonderful to anyone in a position to notice: "A language that manages dynamic memory automatically for you is a Good Thing." (2) Something that can't possibly have any ill side-effects and may save considerable grief later: "Removing the self-modifying code from that shared library would be a Good Thing." (3) When said of software tools or libraries, as in "YACC is a Good Thing," specifically connotes that the thing has drastically reduced a programmer's workload. Has *no* relationship to Martha Stewart; the terms significantly predate her. Compare to *Bad Thing*.

graphical user interface (GUI)—program, like a desktop, that uses images to facilitate users' selections of commands and a pointing device like a mouse. In most cases, the command line is much more efficient for day-to-day processing than a GUI.

grep—Unix tool for finding particular lines in one or more files. Stands for Global Regular Expression Print.

grok—[common; from the novel *Stranger in a Strange Land*, by Robert A. Heinlein, where it is a Martian word meaning literally "to drink" and metaphorically "to be one with"] The emphatic form is "grok in fullness." (1) To understand. Connotes intimate and exhaustive knowledge.

When you claim to "grok" some knowledge or technique, you are asserting that you have not merely learned it in a detached, instrumental way but that it has become part of you, part of your identity. For example, to say that you "know" Unix is simply to assert that you can code in it if necessary, but to say you "grok" Unix is to claim that you have deeply entered the worldview and spirit of that operating system and all its parts, with the implication that it has transformed your view of computational processing.

gonk—[probably back-formed from *gonkulator*] To prevaricate or to embellish the truth beyond any reasonable recognition. In German the term is (mythically) *gonken*; in Spanish the verb becomes *gonkar*. "You're gonking me. That story you just told me is a bunch of gonk." In German, for example, *Du gonkst mich* (You're pulling my leg). See also *gonkulator*.

gonkulator/gon'kyoo-lay-tr/—[common; from the 1960s *Hogan's Heroes* TV series] A pretentious piece of equipment that actually serves no useful purpose. Usually used to describe one's least favorite piece of computer hardware. See *gonk*.

grunt work—(also called *scutt-work*) the boringpart of any task—for example, creating user accounts as a system administrator. Wise Unix users build scripts to handle this part of their job.

GUI—*See* graphical user interface (GUI).

hacker—usually a self-taught computer expert who tends to try to find ways to access unauthorized computer systems. Hackers generally do no harm. Most Unix folk would be proud to be called a hacker. Not to be confused with *cracker* or *cyber-terrorist*. The term *hacker*, like *data*, is often horribly missused by the media.

hack mode—(1) what one is in when hacking, of course. (2) More specifically, a Zenlike state of total focus on The Problem that may be achieved when one is hacking (this is why every good hacker is part mystic.) Ability to enter such concentration at will correlates strongly with wizardliness; it is one of the most important skills learned during larval stage. Sometimes amplified as *deep hack mode*.

Being yanked out of hack mode may be experienced as a physical shock, and the sensation of being in hack mode is more than a little habituating. The intensity of this experience is probably by itself sufficient explanation for the existence of hackers, and explains why many resist being promoted out of positions where they can code. Some aspects of hacker etiquette will appear quite odd to an observer unaware of the high value placed on hack mode. For example, if someone appears at your door, it is perfectly okay to hold up a hand (without turning one's eyes away from the screen) to avoid being interrupted. One may read, type, and interact with the computer for quite some time before further acknowledging the other's presence (of course, he or she is reciprocally free to leave without a word.) The understanding is that you might be in hack mode with a lot of transient data in your head in your head, and you dare not swap that context out until you have reached a good point to pause. See also *juggling eggs*.

hard limit—actual, absolute maximum number of either bytes or inodes you are allowed to consume if you are subject to living under file quotas. You cannot exceed the hard limit.

hard link—link to a file created with the ln command. A link, or hard link, is simply another filename associated with a specific inode entry.

hard return—carriage return entered into the text when the user presses the RETURN or ENTER key.

hardware—computer and other associated equipment. Generally, if you were to kick the hardware with your bare foot, it would hurt.

hardware platform—another name for the hardware. Usually used when you want to specify the exact characteristics of your hardware, as in "My hardware platform has 1024 Meg of RAM, a 2000 Gig drive, and runs a Zoomeron 200 GhZ processor."

high-level language—programming language that resembles human language. Programs written in high-level languages, like C and Java, must be translated, often by a compiler, into the computer's machine language before being used.

history—(1) study of the past, either for its own merit or in an effort to understand the present and predict the future. (2) In most shells, the series of commands you have entered, which allows you to reuse them, saving yourself the task of typing them all over again. You can edit them if you wish.

hold space—special buffer available in the sed editor where you can store text and retrieve it.

holy war—a verbal/email duel that usually persists for weeks or even years and makes little or no sense to anyone except the participants. Some examples of holy wars are PC vs. Apple, DOS vs. Windows, emacs vs. vi, chocolate vs. vanilla, etc. It makes little or no sense to become embroiled in a holy war, yet they seem almost irresistible, especially to bigots (*see* bigot).

Horton, Mark—took over the ex editor from Bill Joy when Joy tired of it, and was a crucial part of the development of BSD Unix. Then built up the UUCP network as well as Usenet and guided their growth.

hoze—to completely mess up, break, or destroy. Often used to describe the results of a logic error. For example, one might say, "I coded the script name as an executable in the script, and it hozed the system." Someone who does this often (usually more than once is enough) can be called a *hozer*.

IEEE (Institute for Electrical and Electronics Engineering)—professional standards group.

IF...THEN—(scripting or programming) the basic element of the ***selection*** programming construct. If a particular condition is true, then the action specified is taken. If the condition is false, then the action is skipped.

IF block—sequence of commands that follow the THEN portion of an IF statement. Depending upon the language or shell, an IF block is normally terminated by a closing French brace, the ELSE statement, or the fi statement.

infinite loop—series of instructions within a computer program that are repeated continuously without exit. In rare instances you want this to happen, but most of the time infinite loops are an indication of a logic error.

information—knowledge derived by processing data, usually in the form of a printed report or screen display. We usually build scripts to create information.

inode—index node (inode), containing all the information about a file. Each file has exactly one inode associated with it. The inode is the repository for all the data about that particular file.

integer—whole number, without a decimal point. The kind of math the Bourne shell does.

interrupt key—key used to interrupt processing of a command. In the shells, the ^C (Ctrl-C) key is usually called the interrupt key. In the vi editor, the escape key (ESC) is called an interrupt key because it interrupts text entry and sends the user back to command mode.

intellectual property—material resulting from ideas, or mental processes; usually protected by a copyright, or copyleft in the case of GNU materials.

interactivity—exists when the user can input information to a page and receive a response. Java provides a degree of interactivity that allows users to play games, live, on the Net. The vi editor is interactive, the sed editor is not.

internal command—command built into the shell so it doesn't need to be loaded from disk before it can be executed. Contrast with *external command*.

Internet address—*See* Internet Protocol (IP) address.

Internet Protocol (IP) address—numeric address assigned to each machine on the Internet. Consists of four sets of one, two, or three octal digits separated by periods. Each computer attached to a network has a unique IP address.

Internet Service Provider (ISP)—company that specializes in providing World Wide Web access. Wise ISPs run Unix computers.

interpreter—translates source code into binary code, one line at a time, just before it is executed. Contrast this with a compiler that translates all of the source code into binary before execution.

interpreted language—language that is translated by an interpreter rather than a compiler.

interrupt—special datum sent to a process. An interrupt is generated by the hardware. Some computers are interrupt-driven; others, like Unix, are signal-driven.

intranet—computer network like the Internet except that it contains only the computers of a specific company.

IP address—*See* Internet Protocol (IP) address.

ISP—*See* Internet Service Provider (ISP).

iteration—basic structure of a computer program wherein a sequence of instructions is repeated until some processing condition is changed. *See* loop.

Jacquard, Joseph Marie (1752—1834)—developer in 1801 of mechanized looms using punched cards for patterns. He developed the idea of using cards to store and execute instructions.

Java—high-level programming language that uses object-oriented techniques, works across the Internet, is translated line by line, is safe and hard to crash, runs on many different computer platforms, and does powerful things quickly.

Java compiler—translates Java source code into bytecode; called *Javac*.

Java development kit (JDK)—includes a Java compiler (Javac), the Java bytecode interpreter to run stand-alone programs, a Java debugging tool, and an applet viewer.

Java Virtual Machine—Java interpreter.

Javac—Java compiler.

JDK—See Java development kit (JDK).

job—any process running in the background, or any stopped process that can be controlled without using control keys.

Joy, Bill—wrote the ex and vi editors.

juggling eggs—keeping a lot of intricate data and relationships among those data in your head while modifying a program. "Don't bother me now, I'm juggling eggs" means that an interrupt is likely to result in the program's being scrambled. In the classic 1975 first-contact SF novel *The Mote in God's Eye,* by Larry Niven and Jerry Pournelle, an alien describes a very difficult task by saying, "We juggle priceless eggs in variable gravity."

justification—alignment of text along the margins. Also used to explain why you need the latest and greatest computer hardware.

K—*See* kilobyte.

kernel—that part of the operating system that communicates directly with the hardware. The kernel in Unix is hardware-dependent. The shell, which is not hardware-dependent, talks with the kernel. The user talks with the shell.

kernel mode—when a command is running in kernel mode, it is executing kernel code. Contrast this with *user mode.*

Kernighan, Brian—was the "k" in awk, and also came up with the idea of building tools, and a collection of other graphical processes. He denies coming up with the name *Unix.*

key interrupt—using the facilities of the editor to associate commands with particular keys.

kHz—*See* kilohertz (Hz).

kilobyte (K)—approximately 1,000 bytes of memory. Actually, 1,024 bytes of memory, 2^{10} bytes.

kilohertz (kHz)—roughly 1,000 samples per second.

kill—to terminate a process. In its most severe form, *kill-9*, it means to kill with extreme prejudice (the hardest thing to kill, mythologically, is a cat, as it has nine lives.)

larval stage—period of monomaniacal concentration on coding apparently passed through by all fledgling hackers. Common symptoms include the perpetration of more than one 36-hour hacking run in a given week; neglect of all other activities including usual basics like food, sleep, and personal hygiene; and a chronic case of advanced bleary-eye. Can last from six months to two years, the apparent median being around 18 months. A few so afflicted never resume a more "normal" life, but the ordeal seems to be necessary to produce really wizardly (as opposed to merely competent) programmers. See also *wannabee*. A less protracted and intense version of larval stage (typically lasting about a month) may recur when one is learning a new OS or programming language.

LCD—see liquid crystal display.

levels of permission—in the Unix file system, levels for user, group, and other. The *user* is the one who created or owns the file, the *group* stands for anyone in the user's group as set by the system administrator. *Other* refers to anyone who is neither the user nor in the user's group.

levels of access—another way to describe the levels of permission.

line editor—an editor that is designed to work with one line of data at a time. The standard editors—ed, ex, and vi—are all line editors.

linear programming—type of programming wherein an optimum solution for a problem is found for a given set of requirements and constraints using a top-down method. Standard programming languages like C are linear languages. The contrast is object oriented programming.

link—in the Unix world, another name for a filename. Filenames, or links, are associated with an inode. You may have several links to the same inode. When all links to an inode are removed, the inode is freed for association to another file and the file space is reclaimed. In other words, when the link count drops to zero, the file is deleted.

Linux—the open source kernel, a Unix work-alike, created by Linus Torvalds and given to the Internet community in 1991. Linux is a major player in the Unix field.

liquid crystal display (LCD)—monitor in which an electric field causes configurations of molecules to align and light up, producing

characters. This is the new standard (I wish) instead of CRT displays.

literal—usually a member of the Democratic party—err, sorry, that is *liberal;* how about... a character that has no special meaning to the shell. By protecting a file-matching metacharacter, the shell interprets it as a literal.

local area network (LAN)—privately owned collection of interconnected computers within a confined service area.

local variable—value known only to the function or script in which it was created.

logic error—program error that is translatable but does not produce correct results.

logical operation—ability of a computer to compare two values to determine if they are equal or unequal, or which of the two is greater.

logical operator—symbol $(<, >, =)$ indicating which logical operation is to be used in a test statement.

loop—*See* iteration.

lynx—the most common text-only browser.

machine code—(also known as *machine language*) operating language unique to each computer that is made up of bits (0 or 1) representing electronic switches (off or on).

machine language—*See* machine code

macro—collection of commands, or keystrokes, that are associated with a particular key. Macros are a way to store and reuse collections of keystrokes.

magic number—a 16-bit number, sometimes represented by a character or characters that appear at the beginning of files to describe how to process the file. Initially the magic number told the kernel how many bytes of header data to skip to arrive at the actual executable code; #! is an example of coding a magic number created by the folks at Berkeley.

maintenance—process of fixing, updating, and revising an existing program or script.

maintenance programmer—person who modifies programs or scripts already in use in order to affect a change in content. This is the job in which most Unix scriptors begin their career.

McIlroy, Doug—wrote join, diff, look, dict, spell, and was the cause for the grep tool moving out of Ken Thompson's private toolbox into the normal Unix distribution.

McLuhan, Marshall (1911–1980)—author of books relating technology to society. His ideas have greatly influenced present-day data communications and multimedia.

megabyte (MB)—one million bytes of memory.

megahertz (MHz)—one million clock cycles per second; a measurement of processing hardware speed.

memory—computer circuitry that temporarily stores data and programs. Usually grouped by storage capacity of thousands (K) or millions (M) of characters; for example, a computer with 8M of memory can store up to 8 million letters, numbers, or symbols.

metacharacter—a character, like the * (asterisk) file-matching metacharacter, that can stand for or represent one or more other characters. These characters are special to the shell, and or to particular programs. Some metacharacters are file-matching metacharacters, like * and ?, and some are regular-expression metacharacters like . and *. Those who don't know better might call metacharacters *wild cards,* since they act like the wild cards in a poker game (able to become any other card), but wise Unix folk know better, and refer to them as *metacharacters.*

microfortnight—one millionth of the fundamental unit of time in the Furlong/Firkin/Fortnight system of measurement; 1.2096 sec. (A furlong is one-eighth of a mile; a firkin is one-fourth of a barrel; the mass unit of the system is taken to be a firkin of water). The VMS operating system has a lot of tuning parameters that you can set with the SYSGEN utility, and one of these is TIMEPROMPTWAIT, the time the system will wait for an operator to set the correct date and time at boot if it realizes that the current value is bogus. This time is specified in microfortnights!

microsecond—one millionth of a second; used to measure the speed of a computer's processing.

millisecond—one thousandth of a second; used to measure the access time of a computer's disk drive.

mips—millions of instructions per second; a measurement of a computer's processing speed.

monitor—output peripheral by which a visual display is shown on a screen; also called a *screen* or *CRT.*

multiprocessing—linking several computers together to work on a common problem, or having more than one processor in a single computer. For example, the Sun E450 can have up to four processors.

multitasking—one computer running two or more independent processes in pseudo-simultaneous execution. (If the computer has multiple CPUs, it can actually run more than one command simultaneously.)

multi-user—a computer system, like Unix, that can support multiple users at the same time.

MULTICS—acronym for MULTiplexed Information and Computing Service. The MULTICS project was intended to produce a general-purpose, multi-user, time-sharing system running on new hardware, supporting a new file system, and employing a new user interface. It never realized its potential. The important thing is that the MULTICS project brought together the major players in the development of the Unix operating system. For that, we need to thank MULTICS.

nanosecond—one billionth of a second; used to measure the speed of a computer's processor speed.

next-byte pointer—when you write data to a file, the system keeps track of where in the file the next byte of data is to be written. This is the next-byte pointer. If you redirect standard output into a file, the first thing that happens is the next-byte pointer is set to byte 0, effectively emptying the file.

newbie—[very common; orig. from British public-school and military slang variant of *new boy*] A Usenet neophyte. This term surfaced in the newsgroup talk.bizarre but is now in wide use (the combination, *clueless newbie,* is especially common). Criteria for being considered a newbie vary wildly; a person can be called a newbie in one newsgroup while remaining a respected regular in another. The label *newbie* is sometimes applied as a serious insult to a person who has been around Usenet for a long time but who carefully hides all evidence of having a clue.

newline—the character formed by a combination of the return and line feed characters. Usually accomplished by touching the <Enter> or <Return> key.

nibble—half a byte, 4 bits—really! Check it out in another dictionary.

not logic—using the inverse of the regular logical comparison as the correct, or true, condition. For example, to test if two string variables contain the same value in the Bourne shell, you could create this test: Test "string1" = "string2". The not version of that test would be Test "string1" != "string2". Usually, using positive logic is preferred to using not logic.

null—no value. Literally binary zeros in a field. Differentiate between null, which has nothing there, and *blank,* which is filled with blank characters. Null is also called *empty.*

null device—*See* /dev/null.

object—(programming) section of program code in object-oriented programming that contains both the processing code and descriptions of related data to perform a single task. Each object is an instance of a class; it has a state and a behavior.

object—refers to a programming element of an object-oriented language like Java. Objects make up the basis of such a language. They are composed of both the data and instructions that perform manipulations of those data. The data contained within the object are called the *properties,* and the instructions for manipulating the data or causing the object to interact with other objects are called *methods.*

object instance—a particular occurrence or use of a class (in object-oriented programming).

object-oriented programming (OOP)—programming methodology whereby a program is organized into objects, each containing both descriptions of the data and processing operations necessary to process the data described. (Contrast with linear programming.)

octothorp—symbol usually used to indicate comments in Unix code, also known as the sharp sign, pound sign, number sign, hash mark, tic-tac-toe board, or #.

offline—state of hardware when it is not communicating with the computer.

online—in direct communication with a computer, almost always the preferable way to exist.

open standard—standard that is still developing; anyone is free to use it and make suggestions about inclusions.

operating system—collection of system programs that oversee the execution of application programs, manage files, and control the computer system's resources—monitor, keyboard, disk drives, memory, etc. If the two words are capitalized (i.e. Operating System), then the individual is most likely referring to Unix.

option— the part of a command that is optional. Options affect the way the command works, or the way the output is formatted. Options almost always have a hyphen (-) prepended to them. Contrast with *argument.*

order of precedence—in mathematics, the order in which particular arithmetic operations will be performed, exponentiation is preformed before multiplication, etc. In Unix, we speak of the order of precedence of Truth: what a command actually does has the highest precedence, and what someone *says* it does has the lowest precedence.

paging—the process of moving one (or in reality a cluster) of pages from disk to memory or from memory out to disk. Paging moves only part of a process. *See* demand paging; contrast with *swapping.*

parameters—attributes that give the Web weaver some control over applets.

parent-child relationship—term is used to refer to the relationship between an existing process and a process that is forked from that process. The new process is called the child process and is bound by several rules in relationship to the parent process.

parse—to divide into component parts. We parse a sentence into words using white space and punctuation. So does the shell.

password—special combination of letters, numbers, or symbols hopefully known only to the user that allows access to protected computer systems and data.

passwd—one of the common Unix spellings, in this case both the file that contains the user information, including the password in non-shadowed systems, and the command that modifies the password in that file, or the shadow passwd file.

path— set of steps, through directory structures, that lead to a specific file. This term also refers to the set of directories and the order in which the shell will search for the commands specified on the command line. For example, the path to the passwd file is */etc/passwd*.

pattern—in awk, a specialized term that describes the string or regular expression to be matched which will trigger the execution of the action.

pattern space—buffer that sed uses to perform regular edits.

Perl—(Practical Extraction and Report Language) an elegant little programming language developed by Larry Wall, often used to write CGI scripts.

permissions mask—collection of permissions that control access to files in the Unix file system. Normally there are three permissions: read, write, and execute, for each level of permission, user, group, and other. There are some additional permissions, like the sticky bit, that can also be set using the chmod command.

personal digital assistant (PDA)—class of devices like the PalmPilot or the Avigo, or any of a series of small, usually palmtop, devices used to manage personal information. The quality PDAs run Linux.

picosecond—one trillionth of a second; used to measure processing speed within a computer's processor.

pipe—process of sending the output of one Unix command or script directly to the input of another Unix script or program. Piping is possible because of the design of the Unix process, which uses plain ASCII text as the interface and uses the three standard files.

platform—describes the specific type of computer and its operating system, browser, and so forth.

POSIX—an acronym for Portable Operating System Interface for computer systems. It is a creation of the group from the IEEE, begun in 1984, which was created to help standardize Unix.

prepend—to add data to the beginning of a file, variable name, or data stream. For example, accessing the data stored at a memory location in Unix is accomplished by prepending a dollar sign($) to the variable name.

preempted—occurs when a process with a higher priority interrupts a process with a lower priority and takes over the CPU before its quantum has expired. For example, when a process needs to have an additional page brought in from disk, that process must relinquish control of the CPU to the paging software. In that case the first process is preempted by the paging software.

preventive maintenance procedures—running diagnostic checks and verifying the correctness of scripts and programs before a crash occurs; or running diagnostic checks, link viability checks, and the like to ensure that a script is healthy.

primary storage—another name for a computer's internal memory.

print buffer—holds either the address of the file to be printed or a copy of the file to be printed. In order to streamline the print process, the Unix system has one or more print buffers. If it were not for the print buffer, you would have to maintain a connection to the printer until your file finished printing.

process—fundamental unit of processing in a Unix system. A process is a program in any state of execution, along with its associated resources. Each activity in a Unix system is run within the context of a process.

property—object-oriented term used to describe the data associated with an object. Some examples of properties are the colors of the text, links, and background of a document, or the current date and time. Properties are the data that an object's methods use or modify.

pseudocode—method of representing program logic by using English phrases in an outline form. You should pseudocode your scripts before you craft them.

public domain—not copyrighted; can be used for free, without obtaining permission. It is always a good idea to give credit to the source of public-domain material; that is just polite.

QED—text editor written by Butler Lampson and Peter Deutsch at Berkley in the early 1960s, then modified by Ken Thompson for the Multics project and by Dennis Ritchie for the GECOS system. This editor was the parent of the standard Unix editors.

quantum—in Unix, the length of time, or number of machine cycles, normally given to a process. Unless it is interrupted, a process will execute until its quantum expires; then the next process in the list is given a turn.

queue—(often spelled *que*) an ordering of elements to be processed. When you stand in line to buy something like lunch, you are participating in a queue. The most common thing that you will put in a queue in Unix are print jobs. The two common methods of removing elements from a queue are FIFO and FILO.

quota—generically, a minimum or limit, but in the Unix world, a system that can be invoked to control how much disk space any given user can consume. There are two different resources that quota can control; the number of bytes used or the number of inodes owned by the user. There are two limits to quota: the soft limit, which can be temporarily exceeded, and the hard limit, which is absolute.

readability—how easy a page is to read. Two factors that affect readability are (1) proper use of white space to separate logical elements and (2) starting new lines of code where appropriate. Readability of code is just as important as its correctness.

record—fundamental unit of a file. Records are usually composed of fields and are terminated by the EOR (end-of-record) mark, nominally the carriage return line feed, or newline, character.

recursion—*See* recursion.

recursive—property of being able to call or invoke itself. Unix supports recursion so you can write a process that invokes or calls itself. This is a useful tool in some instances, like the find command, which executes in all the directories below the one specified in the command. On the other hand, you can also consume many, many process slots if your script calls itself incorrectly. See recursion.

redirection—term used to associate standard input, standard output, or standard error with a different destination than the usual one. For example, you may redirect standard output to a file rather than having the data flow to the screen.

regular expressions—any one of several metacharacters that can stand for more than one character. They are similar to file-matching metacharacters but are used to match data within a file rather than matching filenames.

relative address—another way to say *relative path*. A relative address specifies where to go from the current point in the file structure, as opposed to an absolute address, which specifies the complete path from the root of the file system.

relative path name—as opposed to absolute path name, does not start with right slash. The shell or process supplies the current position in the file structure to the left of the information provided.

repeat count—in the vi editor, causes the editor to repeat the command that number of times. For example 5x would delete five characters (repeating the x command five times).

return code—numeric code set by a process that indicates whether the result of the execution of the process was successful or not. Historically a zero return code indicates success, and a nonzero return code means that the process encountered an error. You can set the return code for your process by using the exit command.

reverse video—setting the characteristics of the video terminal so that the text appears in the normal background color and the background is the normal foreground color. For example white text on a black background.

Ritchie, Dennis—one of the two major fathers of Unix, the other being Ken Thompson. He also wrote the C programming language, one of the early versions of the QED editor, and numerous tools.

root—(1) the almighty user/administrator on a Unix system. Root rules! Root has no restrictions on access. In some Unix systems, any member of the "wheel" group is a privileged user, and may be referred to as root. (2) The highest level of a file system, designated by the forward, or right, slash (/).

round robin—method of sharing the CPU among several active processes. Imagine all of the processes sitting in a circle and the scheduler walking around the circle giving each a turn to run. Each process is given an amount of time to run, called a *quantum,* and will run that long unless the process performs an activity like requesting I/O or is preempted.

scalar—one of two ways information can be accessed in a computer program. When the data are present in the command, without ever being stored in a specific location in memory, they are called **scalar** values. For example, the following print statement uses a scalar value:

```
print "Hello World"
```

The character data string Hello World is a scalar value. The other choice is to use

variables. A variable is handy name for a location in memory. In this example the data are stored in the variable string. Then the contents of that variable are printed. (Note: This is a Unix example, and the $ that preceeds the variable name is required. What it is saying is, "Print the contents of the variable string, not the word string.")

```
string = "Hello World"
print $string
```

screen pointer—icon, usually an arrow, on a screen that moves when the mouse or some other pointer device is moved. Program options are activated by using a mouse to move the screen pointer over the desired icon and clicking the mouse button.

script—program, usually written in a scripting language like Perl or JavaScript or one of the Unix shells. A script usually has one, well-defined function and is relatively small.

scripting language—language used to write scripts—for example, JavaScript, Perl, awk, or Unix shell languages.

scriptor—one who writes scripts, often revered as one of the chosen few. Not to be confused with scripture.

selection—basic structure in a computer program that allows execution of one of two different sets of code based on some condition. (Most often implemented by either an If block or a case structure).

semaphore—some unit of data, from a byte to a file, that is used to signal another process to perform some task. Semaphores were originally a pair of colored flags that folks used to communicate over distance. The position of the flags indicated numbers or letters.

sequence—basic structure of a computer program whereby instructions are executed in the order they appear in the program.

shareware—software that you can legally copy and use but that you should register and pay a registration fee for.

shebang—combination of two characters, #!, that form a particular magic number that directs the shell to execute the command that follows them and consider the rest of the file as input to that command. Most often used as the first two characters of a shell script to specify which shell to use to execute the remaining lines in the file.

shell—the hard outer layer of a mollusk, composed of a prismatic outer layer of calcareous material and an inner layer of thin, laminated plates of calcareous material, or, if you aren't a biologist, the shell is the user interface to the Unix system. The shell talks to the kernel; the kernel talks with the hardware. Shells are pretty much standard across all flavors of Unix, which is why Unix is said to be easily portable.

shell script—program, or script, written in one of the shells. The most common shell for scripting is the Bourne shell, but you can write a shell script in any Unix shell.

single thread—device that supported the sword of Damocles, representing the ever present danger inherent in rank and power, or in being a system administrator. Also the term used for a computer that processes a single program at a time. Older mainframes were single-thread machines. (Actually, the sword of Damocles was suspended by a single hair.)

signal—software interrupt sent to a process. You can send signals with keyboard combinations like ^C (Ctrl-C), ^Z, etc. You can also send signals with the kill command. Contrast with *interrupt*. (Unix is a signal-driven operating system.)

snail mail—regular postal service.

soft limit—when living under quota, one of the two limits imposed upon you. The first is the soft limit, which you may exceed for a short period of time. The other is the hard limit, which you may never exceed. If you do not lower your usage below the soft limit within a very few days, your hard limit will be reduced to your soft limit.

soft link—special form of link created with the ln–s command, which creates a pointer to a file, usually in another file structure. Soft links

are dangereous to create because they often try to link two different file structures and thus can cause problems.

source code—human-readable form of a program, usually written in a high-level language like Java or C. Contrast with *object code*.

span of control—in the vi editor, the varying number of characters, words, or lines that some commands can be applied to. For example, dw would delete a word (the span of control is the next word), while dG would delete from the current cursor position to the end of the document (the span of control is "to the end of the document").

spooling—another term for buffering, most often used with buffers like the print buffer; also called the *print spool*. Usually spools are FIFO queues, but some may use more complex algorithms to print small jobs first or some such.

standard input—one of three standard files given to all processes at process-creation time. Standard input is the data stream from which the process reads. It is given unit number 0 and is normally associated with the keyboard.

standard error—one of three standard files given to all processes at process-creation time. Standard error is the data stream to which the process writes error messages and prompts. It is assigned unit number 2 and is normally associated with the screen.

standard ouput—one of three standard files given to all processes at process-creation time. Standard output is the data stream through which the process sends normal output. It is assigned unit number 1 and is normally associated with the screen.

stream of bytes—the answer to the question, "What is a file?" Thompson and Ritchie made a brilliant decision when they decided that all files and devices would use a stream of ASCII bytes as the common interface. This made working with Unix, and creating device drivers for Unix, far easier. This term is sometimes written as "stream-o-bytes" by folks in the Deep South.

string—series of characters enclosed in either single or double quotation marks and displayed as ASCII text. Strings are processed differently than numeric data.

subscripted variable—another name for array. *See* array

subshell—technique, used most often in the C shell, to allow a command to execute within its own shell. You use subshelling to separate standard output from standard error.

swapping—moving a whole process from memory to disk or from disk to memory. (Actually, a small bit of the process remains in memory, pointing to the disk location of the rest of the process.) Contrast with *paging*.

switch—variable that can take one of two possible values. For example, in the C shell, turning globbing on or off is controlled by a switch.

syntax—word order, spacing, abbreviations, and special symbols used by a command-driven interface or programming language. This is not the price paid for doing something wrong.

System V—descendent of the original Bell Labs Unix, written by Thompson and Ritchie. This is one of the two major families of Unix; the other is the BSD side of the tree.

system variables—variables that are declared by the system, or the shell. Contrast with *user variables*.

telnet—allows you to work remotely on computers across the Net. The secure shell version is preferred.

terabyte—one trillion bytes of memory.

text—another name for textual data (also the short term for one of the highest forms of literature, the textbook).

text-entry mode—one of two modes that standard Unix editors work in. In text-entry mode, the editor takes all (or most) keyboard strokes as data to be entered into the buffer. The other mode is command mode.

text file—file consisting of just text, with no embedded word-processing codes; consists of only ASCII characters (also called a *plain ASCII file*).

Thompson, Ken—one of the Fathers of Unix, the other being Dennis Ritchie. Thompson also wrote grep, ed, uniq, sort, the B programming language, and numerous other Unix commands and tools.

tick (tic)—(1) single quote character (') (2) In simulations, the discrete unit of time that passes between iterations of the simulation mechanism. In AI applications, this amount of time is often left unspecified, since the only constraint of interest is the ordering of events. This sort of AI simulation is often pejoratively referred to as *tick-tick-tick simulation*, especially with the issue of simultaneity of events with long, independent chains of causes. (3) The annoying twitch seen on the faces of those poor doomed souls forced to use lesser operating systems that require regular, frequent rebooting.

time slice—length of time a process is given control of the CPU. *See* quantum.

time stamp—the time an event happened, most often used with files to determine when they were created or last accessed or updated.

toggle—type of variable or switch used to turn a preset feature on and off.

Torvalds, Linus—wrote the Linux kernel and gave it to the world. Likely the greatest computer operating system developer since Ritchie and Thompson.

tree structure—structure that looks like a tree, having a root, trunk, and branches. The Unix file system has been called the *inverted tree* structure because it looks like an upside-down tree.

Turing, Alan—(1912–1954)—developed the Turing test for artificial intelligence and provided a part of the basis for computer science theory.

upload—to send data or programs from your computer to another computer.

user friendly—an attribute of computers meaning easy to use. The term is horribly overused. It is included here to beg you not to use it when describing your scripts!

user mode—when a command is running in user mode, it is running code written by the user. This code is restricted in what it can do, what it can access, and what it is allowed to influence. Contrast with *kernel mode*.

user variables—variables declared by the user within the context of a script or at the command line. Contrast with *system variables*.

utility program—collection of programs that provide utility services to the user. This is one of three classes of programs, the other two being operating systems and applications programs.

vaporware—computer programs that have been promised but do not exist or that do not live up to expectations. This is a standard feature of the code produced by some operating system vendors.

variable—generic term used most often to refer to a variable name.

variable name—generic way of referring to a location in the computer's memory. For some reason people seem to find it easier to remember variable names like *salary* or *total* than the actual location addresses like FD7BB4 or 1CCDE8.

variable value—data stored at the location in memory specified by a variable name.

verb— term for a computer activity, like print, read, loop, etc.

virtual—opposite of physical. It looks like it is there, but it isn't. For example, *virtual reality* exists only within the confines of a computer; it isn't real. So *virtual* means you can see it, but it doesn't really exist.

virtual memory—complex set of algorithms that allows the computer to utilize disk space as an extension of memory. Data are stored on disk when they are not actively needed in memory. The amount of virtual memory for each process is unlimited.

virus—harmful software that destroys other software on the target machine and can reproduce itself and spread from machine to machine. Often confused with substandard operating systems.

wall time—as opposed to machine or computer time, wall time, or *clock time,* is the time you

normally live in. The computer lives in a universe with much smaller increments of time, like nanoseconds and microseconds.

wannabee—(also, more plausibly, spelled *wannabe*) [from a term recently used to describe Madonna fans who dress, talk, and act like their idol; prob. originally from biker slang] A would-be hacker. The connotations of this term differ sharply depending on the age and exposure of the subject. Used of a person who is in or might be entering larval stage, it is semi-approving; such wannabees can be annoying, but most hackers remember that they, too, were once such creatures. When used of any professional programmer, CS academic, writer, or suit, the term derogatory, implying that said person is trying to cuddle up to the hacker mystique but doesn't, fundamentally, have a prayer of understanding what it is all about. Overuse of terms from sources such as the *New Hacker's Dictionary* is often an indication of the wannabee nature. Compare *newbie*.

Weinberger, Peter—the "w" in awk, and also responsible for part of the FORTRAN 77 compiler and other tools.

What You See Is What You Get (WYSIWYG)—started as a tool for word processing and desktop publishing to show what the end result would look like. Now has come to refer to any application that shows the user what the output will look like as the code is being generated. Unix folks prefer text editors to WYSIWYG editors.

white space—one or more spaces or tabs. Most parts of Unix commands are delimited by white space.

wild card—a very imprecise term for file-matching metacharacters or regular expressions, used by those corrupted by substandard operating systems. Use the terms *file-matching metacharacter* or *regular expression* instead; they are more exact.

wizard—person who is a master of a particular discipline. You will often hear of awk wizards, sed wizards or vi wizards. One goal of most Unix professionals is to become a wizard with one or more commands. Or, according to the *Jargon Index,* a hacker is

1. Transitively, a person who knows how a complex piece of software or hardware works (that is, who groks it); esp. someone who can find and fix bugs quickly in an emergency. Someone is a hacker if he or she has general hacking ability, but is a wizard with respect to something only if he or she has specific detailed knowledge of that thing. A good hacker could become a wizard for something given the time to study it. 2. The term 'wizard' is also used intransitively of someone who has extremely high-level hacking or problem-solving ability. 3. A person who is permitted to do things forbidden to ordinary people; one who has wheel privileges on a system. 4. A Unix expert, esp. a Unix systems programmer. This usage is well enough established

that 'Unix Wizard' is a recognized job title at some corporations and to most headhunters.

word—unit of data bounded on both sides by some sort of recognized delimiter. Usually a word is bounded by white space or punctuation. Unix shells, and many of the Unix commands, use white space and punctuation to parse or divide the input stream into words for processing. By the way, so do you.

workaround—term used to describe an action or set of actions that take the place of some other, often broken, action. Usually a workaround is less than elegant but does provide the user with a way to accomplish the desired task. Sometimes called a *kluge.*

WYSIWYG—*See* What You See Is What You Get (WYSIWYG).

Zappa, Frank—one of the fathers of Rock and Roll. Why is he here? Why not!

Index

Symbols and signs are alphabetized as if spelled out. Hyphens are attached but not alphabatized. Carets are double posted under "caret" and attached but ignored in the scheme of alphabetizing. The main entry is case sensitive. The use of the control key is alphabetized under Ctrl.